# Handbook of FRENCH SEMANTICS

CSLI Lecture Notes No. 170

# Handbook of FRENCH SEMANTICS

edited by
**Francis Corblin**
**Henriëtte de Swart**

CSLI
PUBLICATIONS
STANFORD

Copyright © 2004
CSLI Publications
Center for the Study of Language and Information
Leland Stanford Junior University
Printed in the United States
08 07 06 05 04 1 2 3 4 5

*Library of Congress Cataloging-in-Publication Data*

Handbook of French semantics /
edited by Francis Corblin and Henriëtte de Swart.

p. cm. – (CSLI lecture notes ; no. 170)

Includes bibliographical references and index.

ISBN 1-57586-414-2 (pbk. : alk. paper)
ISBN 1-57586-413-4 (hardback : alk. paper)

1. French language—Semantics. I. Corblin, Francis.
II. Swart, Henriëtte de, 1961– III. Title. IV. Series.

PC2585.H36 2004
440.1′43–dc22 2004007002
CIP

∞ The acid-free paper used in this book meets the minimum requirements of the American National Standard for Information Sciences—Permanence of Paper for Printed Library Materials, ANSI Z39.48-1984.

CSLI was founded in 1983 by researchers from Stanford University, SRI International, and Xerox PARC to further the research and development of integrated theories of language, information, and computation. CSLI headquarters and CSLI Publications are located on the campus of Stanford University.

CSLI Publications reports new developments in the study of language, information, and computation. Please visit our web site at
http://cslipublications.stanford.edu/
for comments on this and other titles, as well as for changes and corrections by the author and publisher.

# Contents

# Preface

In the fall of 1998, Francis Corblin, Danièle Godard and Henriëtte de Swart started talking about the possibility of a joint research project on the formal semantics of French. These ideas took shape when we obtained funding from the French CNRS for a three-year (1999–2001) PICS project ('Projet international de collaboration scientifique') under the title *Sémantique formelle et données du français.* The Dutch organization for scientific research (NWO) provided matching funds for this collaboration project.

The aim of the project was to bring together a group of French linguists and linguists from the Netherlands, working on French, to discuss problems in the area of semantics, and the interface of semantics with other domains of linguistics (mainly syntax, phonology/phonetics, and pragmatics), with particular attention to French data. We chose to set up the collaboration in such a way that it would lead to a concrete result, namely the production of a Handbook of French Semantics. We contacted CSLI Publications and they supported this project from an early stage onwards.

We wanted to encourage interaction in small groups, so we split up the main project into five subprojects. The themes of the subprojects are motivated by the fact that they give rise to interesting observations and problems in French, and that, collectively, we had the expertise to treat them. Each group prepared one of the five parts of this Handbook. Every group had a French and a Dutch coordinator, who were responsible for the integration of the work of the group in the general project. Because the groups were relatively independent, and the questions addressed by the five groups were often quite different, the reader will find a certain amount of variation in terminology, tools and theoretical frameworks used from one part to the next. In such a complex project, this is unavoidable, and we hope the reader will agree with us that it reflects the rich nature of the field of semantics.

We are grateful for the comments we received from two external readers (sollicited by CSLI Publications and NWO), which were used to improve the first version of the manuscript. Of course, we are resposible for all remaining errors. Some caveats are in order. We are aware of the fact that many other interesting issues might have been addressed, but the research questions discussed here were chosen as the most pertinent ones by the participants in the groups. We assume that the reader has a working knowledge of semantic theory; this book is not an introduction to semantics per se. Because semantic questions are our central concern, the syntax of the French language is not fully elaborated in this book. Many analyses also merit a more indepth formalization, because we placed the emphasis on empirical data. But the book contains numerous references to the literature for further details and formal analysis.

We intend this book to be used as a handbook by anyone who has a (basic) background in semantic theory, and who is interested in the application of general semantic concepts and (formal) approaches to a particular language, in this case French. This book can be used as a text book for research seminars, or as a handbook for independent study. We welcome comments from the reader!

**Acknowledgments**

The editors would like to thank all the members of the PICS project for their enthusiasm, and their hard work over the last three years. We are grateful for the financial support from CNRS and from the Dutch Organization for Scientific Research NWO (dossier numbers: 240-70-010, 240-70-025, P32-179), and for the moral and editorial support of CSLI publications. We thank Jennifer Wong for correcting the Dutch and French quirks in our English, and Anne-Marie Mineur for her help in editing this book.

# Part I

# Determiners

1

# Generalized Quantifiers, Dynamic Semantics, and French Determiners *

Francis Corblin, Ileana Comorovski,
Brenda Laca, and Claire Beyssade

## 1 Introduction

In this introductory chapter, we briefly consider the interpretation of French expressions of quantity (e.g. *chaque, beaucoup, quelques*) that occur within the nominal domain. Syntactically, some of them are determiners (heading a DP), some of them are adjectives, and yet others have a categorial status that remains to be established. We will write about all these expressions using the term 'determiner'. As used here, the term does not designate a syntactic category, but a semantic class: in the theory of generalized quantifiers (Montague (1973), Barwise and Cooper (1981)), determiners constitute the class of expressions which combine with set expressions to form expressions that denote families of sets. For instance, the determiner *chaque* ('every', 'each') combines with the noun *reine* ('queen'), a set-denoting expression, to form the noun phrase *chaque reine*, an expression that denotes the family of sets which contain every queen. If sets are used to model properties of individuals extensionally, we can say that the noun phrase *chaque reine* denotes the set of properties that every queen has.

## 2 Some properties of determiners

Generalized Quantifier Theory makes possible several classifications of natural language determiners. One of them relies on the cardinal/propor-

*We wish to thank Petra Sleeman for her comments on the pre-final draft.

*Handbook of French Semantics.*
Francis Corblin and Henriëtte de Swart (eds.).
Copyright © 2004, CSLI Publications.

tional distinction. We briefly present it in section 2.1; in section 2.2, we compare it to the distinction between individual-denoting and quantifying noun phrases, brought to light by the theories of Kamp (1981) and Heim (1982).

Determiners can be viewed as denoting relations between two sets: the set denoted by the CN that immediately follows the determiner and the set denoted by the VP. This approach, equivalent to Barwise and Cooper's (1981), is taken by van Benthem (1984) and Zwarts (1981, 1983). The relational approach to determiner denotations makes it possible to consider some logical properties of natural language determiners in the light of conditions on binary relations; among the properties which van Benthem and Zwarts examine are monotonicity properties. We introduce them in section 2.3.

In section 2.4, we present a classification of French determiners in the form of a table which marks each determiner as having or not having the properties 'cardinal', 'monotone', and 'indefinite'.

## 2.1 The Cardinal / Proportional Distinction

The distinction between cardinal and proportional determiners is introduced by Keenan and Stavi (1986) and discussed in detail in Partee (1989).

Let us take a determiner denotation $D$ and two sets $A$, $B$, subsets of a universe $E$. If $D$ is the denotation of a cardinal determiner, the truth value of $D(A)(B)$ depends exclusively on the cardinality of $A \cap B$. Thus the semantic contribution of a cardinal determiner can be formulated as a cardinality condition imposed on the intersection of the CN denotation with the VP denotation. For instance, *Five (girl) (sing)* is true iff the intersection of the set denoted by *girl* and the set denoted by *sing* has five elements.

To determine the truth value of $D(A)(B)$, where $D$ is the denotation of a proportional determiner, it is not enough to know the cardinality of the set resulting from the intersection of $A$ and $B$; we also need information about the proportion between the cardinality of $A \cap B$ and the cardinality of $A$. For instance, to know whether the sentence *Most students are interested in astronomy* is true, it is not enough to know how many students are interested in astronomy; we also need to know how the number of students interested in astronomy compares to the number of students in general.

## 2.2 The indefinite / quantifying distinction

In light of the analysis of indefinites of Kamp (1981) and Heim (1982), it was observed by several linguists in the 1980's (Kadmon (1987),

Partee (1989), Roberts (1987:190ff), among others) that noun phrases containing cardinal determiners have the same type of denotation as indefinites: they denote an individual (singular or plural). In Kamp and Reyle's (1993) model, plural indefinites introduce plural discourse referents in the logical representation; Kamp and Reyle analyze cardinality expressions as modifiers, a view that had already been argued for on both syntactic and semantic grounds (e.g. Bowers (1975), Link (1987)).[1] In contrast to cardinal determiners, proportional determiners are analyzed as projecting quantifying noun phrases, which induce box-splitting in DRT or, correspondingly, a tripartite structure in Heim's (1982) model: proportional quantifiers require that a certain proportion of the set of individuals which satisfy the restrictor also satisfy the nuclear scope.

In order to reconcile the generalized quantifier approach to noun phrase interpretation, which uniformly assigns to all noun phrases the type $<< e, t >, t >$, with the theories of Kamp and Heim, who treat indefinites as expressions of type $e$, Partee (1987) proposes a number of type-shifting rules. She suggests that every noun phrase has a basic type, whose assignment depends on the form of the noun phrase and on the determiner it contains, should it contain one. The basic type of a noun phrase is shifted in certain syntactic positions, in compliance with type-matching requirements. For instance, the interpretation of definites, whose basic type is $e$, is lifted to type $<< e, t >, t >$ when they are coordinated with quantifying noun phrases, whose basic type is $<< e, t >, t >$, the type of generalized quantifiers; noun phrases introduced by cardinal determiners have their type shifted to $< e, t >$, the type of sets, when they appear in a predicative position, for instance as a complement of 'be'. Predicative noun phrases will be discussed in section 4.

### 2.3 Monotonicity

The monotonicity properties of a determiner denotation $D$ concern the change in the truth value of *D(A)(B)* when the denotation of one of the arguments is increased or decreased:

(1) D is *monotone increasing in its first argument* (or *left upward monotone*) iff $D(A)(B)$ and $A \subseteq A'$ implies $DA'B$.

(2) D is *monotone decreasing in its first argument* (or *left downward monotone*) iff $D(A)(B)$ and $A' \subseteq A$ implies $DA'B$. [2]

[1] Landman (2002) offers an excellent presentation of the so-called 'adjectival theory of indefinite determiners'.

(3) D is *monotone increasing in its second argument* (or *right upward monotone*) iff $D(A)(B)$ and $B \subseteq B'$ implies $D(A)(B')$.

(4) D is *monotone decreasing in its second argument* (or *right downward monotone*) iff $D(A)(B)$ and $B' \subseteq B$ implies $D(A)(B)'$.

Based on the definitions above, the following tests can be applied to find out the monotonicity properties of a determiner:

(i) Left upward monotonicity:
Some first year students are rich. → Some students are rich.

(ii) Left downward monotonicity
No students are rich. → No first year students are rich.

(iii) Right upward monotonicity:
Some students are rich and happy. → Some students are rich.

(iv) Right downward monotonicity:
No students are rich. → No students are rich and happy.

The monotonicity behavior of determiners has been shown to be linguistically relevant; thus monotonicity bears on the licensing of negative polarity items (Ladusaw (1979), Zwarts (1981)), a topic which is presented in Part IV of this volume.

## 2.4 Some properties of French determiners

In this section, we present some properties of French determiners in the form of a table. Table I shows that, in French, noun phrases containing a proportional determiner are quantifying and most, but not all, noun phrases containing a lexical cardinal determiner are indefinite. Some tests that help distinguish indefinite from quantifying noun phrases are presented in section 3.2.

A few comments on Table 1 are in order. Note that French does not have two different words for the singular indefinite article and the numeral 'one': the word *un* is used for both. We have included modified numerals in the table of determiners; we note, however, that expressions of the form 'at least *n*', 'at most *n*', 'exactly *n*' have been analyzed by Krifka (1999) as consisting of a particle that has a focused numeral in its scope. A detailed analysis of the determiner *certains* can be found in Corblin (2001b). The monotonicity properties of degree quantifiers (*beaucoup, peu*), which we have marked with a '?' in the table, are discussed by Doetjes (chapter 6, this volume). These determiners can have both a cardinal and a proportional interpretation (see Partee (1989) on

[2] Barwise and Cooper (1981) use the term 'persistence' for left upward monotonicity and the term 'anti-persistence' for left downward monotonicity.

| **Determiner** | Cardinal (as opposed to proportional) | Left monotonicity | Right monotonicity | Indefinite (as opposed to) quantifying) |
|---|---|---|---|---|
| *un*<br>('a', 'one') | yes | ? | ? | yes |
| *deux exactement*<br>*exactement deux*<br>('exactly two') | yes | no | no | no |
| *deux au moins*<br>*au moins deux*<br>('at least two') | yes | upward | upward | no |
| *des*<br>('of-the', 'some') | yes | upward | upward | yes |
| *plusieurs*<br>('several') | yes | upward | upward | yes |
| *quelques*<br>('a few') | yes | upward | upward | yes |
| *différents*<br>('different') | yes | upward | upward | yes |
| *divers*<br>('various') | yes | upward | upward | yes |
| *certains*<br>('certain-pl.')<br>(some-of-the') | ? | upward | upward | ? |
| *beaucoup*<br>('many','much') | yes | ? | ? | no |
| *peu*<br>('few', 'little') | yes | ? | ? | no |
| *la plupart*<br>('most') | no | no | upward | no |
| *tout, toute,*<br>*tous, toutes*<br>('all', 'any') | no | downward | upward | no |
| *chaque*<br>('every', 'each') | no | downward | upward | no |
| *aucun*<br>('no') | — | downward | downward | no |

TABLE 1 Some properties of French determiners

'many' and 'few'). We have chosen to represent the cardinal option in the table.

Two lexical items whose inclusion in the table deserves special mention are *différents* ('different') and *divers* ('various'). These lexical items can appear in both prenominal and postnominal position. It is only when occurring in prenominal position that they qualify as determiners semantically. Their syntactic category when in this position remains unclear. When occurring postnominally, they are uncontroversial adjectives and must be hosted by a DP projected by some D. Detailed analyses of *différents* and *divers* are given in Laca and Tasmowski (chapter 8, this volume) and Comorovski and Nicaise (chapter 9, idem).

The morphologically singular determiner *tout* can be immediately followed by a definite determiner ((5) below), but need not be. When not followed by a definite determiner (definite article, demonstrative or possessive), *tout* is a genuine free choice item, as shown by Jayez and Tovena (chapter 5 this volume). In contrast to *tout*, the morphologically plural form *tous* (fem. *toutes*) tends to occur immediately followed by a definite determiner; in this case, *tous* can float, as seen in (6) below:

(5) Il a mangé tout le gâteau.
'He ate all the cake.'

(6) Toutes les feuilles étaient mortes. / Les feuilles étaient toutes mortes.
'All the leaves were dead.' / 'The leaves were all dead.'

*Tous* can occur without a following definite determiner provided the DP it heads is not a subject. In this case, *tous*, just like *tout*, is interpreted as a free choice item:

(7) a. Pour toute / toutes question(s) concernant les conditions de vente, veuillez téléphoner au numéro ci-dessous.
'For any question(s) about the conditions of the sale, please call the number below.'
b. Nous effectuons tous travaux (à domicile).
'We do any kind of work (at the customer's home)'.

Finally, as Partee (1995: 561) notes, 'no' (Fr. *aucun, nul*) can be analyzed both as a cardinal and as a proportional determiner, since zero cardinality and a zero percent proportion coincide. Given that an analysis as a proportional determiner is available, the fact that 'no' projects quantifying noun phrases does not constitute a counterexample to the correlation between proportional quantifiers and quantifying DPs.

## 3 Dynamic semantics and the typology of French determiners

Kamp's DRT and Heim's File Change Semantics aim at doing more than (static) Generalized Quantifier Theory since they strive to account both for truth-conditional properties of noun phrases and for their dynamics (e.g. anaphoric properties). These theories induce a classification of noun phrases into two groups: individual-denoting and quantifying. The former class divides in turn into two subclasses: definites and indefinites.

Definite noun phrases introduce in the logical representation a variable which must be bound by a previously established discourse referent. Indefinite noun phrases introduce a variable that is bound by a local quantifier. In the absence of such a quantifier, an existential quantifier is inserted in order to obtain a representation without free variables; existential closure applies.

Quantifying noun phrases introduce a quantifier which binds a variable corresponding to the syntactic position of the noun phrase; the quantifier is also able to bind variables introduced in its restrictor by indefinites (the non-selective theory of quantification of Lewis (1975), developed by Kamp (1981) and Heim (1982)). As an example, take sentence (8a) below, which contains the noun phrase *la plupart des étudiants qui ont une voiture*. This noun phrase introduces in the logical representation (8b) the unselective quantifier *MOST*, which is applied to two arguments: a restrictive term and a nuclear scope. The indefinite *une voiture* introduces a free variable y in the restrictive term of the quantifier; the variable y is bound by *MOST*:

(8) a. La plupart des étudiants qui ont une voiture sont salariés.
'Most students who have a car are employed.'

b. $\text{MOST}_{x,y}$ [student(x) $\wedge$ car(y) $\wedge$ own(x, y)] [employed(x)]

In the following subsections, we will examine the DRT-induced typology of noun phrases in the light of French data.

## 3.1 Definite DPs

### 3.1.1 Specific properties of French definite DPs

The basic intuition for setting definite noun phrases apart from indefinites is that the interpretation of the former involves some shared information within which the referent of the noun phrase must be found; definite noun phrases cannot be used to introduce new referents in the discourse.[3]

The existence of the class of definites is supported by the presence of specific morphology in many languages, including French, and it is

[3]Note that definite noun phrases can be used to 'reactivate' old discourse referents; Heim (1982) calls such noun phrases 'novel definites'; as an example, take the two definite noun phrases in the sentence 'The President of France telephoned the Queen of Holland.' Novel definites reintroduce discourse referents that are already part of the knowledge shared by speaker and hearer, but which have not been used for a while.

also confirmed by the historical connection between its subclasses; for instance, both definite articles and third person pronouns developed in French from Latin demonstratives.

There are at least two constructions in French which allow definite noun phrases, while excluding indefinites and quantifying noun phrases: left dislocation and the verbless inverted sentence:[4]

(9) a. Le chien / ce chien / mon chien / Médor, il a aboyé
The / this / my dog / Médor he has barked.

b. * un chien, il a aboyé
a dog he has barked

c. ?? chaque chien, il a aboyé.
every/each dog he has barked

(10) a. Excellent, le devoir / ce devoir / ton devoir / Pierre.
excellent the / this / your homework / Peter
'The / this / your homework / Peter is excellent.'

b. * Excellent, un devoir
excellent a homework

c. * Excellent, chaque devoir
excellent every/each homework

Compare chapter 24, this volume, for more discussion of the definiteness effect in inversion contexts.

### 3.1.2 The analysis of definite DPs

Unlike Generalized Quantifier Theory, DRT contrasts definite DPs, which are analyzed as individual denoting, to universally quantified DPs. We will take a look here at the combination of plural definite DPs with non-adjacent quantifying expressions, a problem not limited to the often discussed floated quantifiers like *tous* ('all') (example (11)). For instance, in sentence (12), a definite subject co-occurs with a sentence-final quantifier:

(11) Les étudiants ont *tous* voté.
the students have all voted.

---

[4]An exception to this generalization are left dislocated sentences in which an indefinite interpreted generically is construed with the demonstrative pronoun *ça* ('this') occupying the subject position:

(i) Un enfant, ça pleure beaucoup.
a child this cries much
'A child cries a lot.'

Spoken French marginally allows left dislocation of specific indefinites construed with a subject resumptive pronoun.

(12) Les étudiants ont voté *à quarante pour cent.*
the students have voted at forty percent
'Forty percent of the students have voted.'

The licensing of non-adjacent quantifiers is a property of definite DPs only, as seen from the contrast between (11) and sentence (13) below, as well as from the contrast between examples (14) and (15):

(13) * Quelques étudiants ont *tous* voté.
a-few students have all voted.

(14) Les étudiants ont voté en majorité / à trente pour cent.
The students have voted in majority / at thirty percent.
'The majority / Thirty percent of the students have voted.'

(15) * Plusieurs / trois cents étudiants ont voté en majorité /
several / three hundred students have voted in majority /
à trente pour cent.
at thirty percent.

To explain how the two parts of the structure (definite subject and quantificational adjunct) combine to produce the resulting interpretation, Corblin (2001a) assumes an analysis of definite DPs as denoting context sets (Westerstahl (1984)). These sets are taken as the restrictor of a quantifier which can be implicit or explicit; if explicit, it can take the form of a floated quantifier (as in 11 above) or of a quantifying adjunct (as in 12 above)). Corblin's proposal is inspired by the analysis given by Lewis (1975) for conditionals. Lewis assumes that the structure *if P then Q* provides a restrictor *P* and a nuclear scope *Q*. If no explicit quantifier is present, the interpretation is by default universal, as in (16) below. If an explicit adverb of quantification appears, as in (17), it expresses the particular relation between cases satisfying the restrictor and cases satisfying both the restrictor and the nuclear scope:

(16) Si un enfant est blond, il a les yeux bleus.
'If a child is blond, he has blue eyes.'

(17) Si un enfant est blond, il a en général les yeux bleus.
'If a child is blond, he usually has blue eyes.'

In a parallel analysis of sentences with definite subjects *(les N VP)*, Corblin suggests that the definite subject denotes a familiar set and is part of a quantificational structure of the form *Q(NP)(VP)*, where *Q* is either implicit or it is provided by an explicit non-local quantifier, as in (11)–(12). As Link (1983) and Dowty (1987) observed, predicates do not necessarily distribute to all the members of the collection denoted by a plural definite; the number of members it distributes to is partly determined by the context. That the implicit $Q$ is not necessarily universal, but varies with the context, can be exemplified by the following sentence:

(18) Les étudiants ont tagué le hall d'entrée.
the students have covered-with-graffiti the hall of entrance
'The students covered the entrance hall with graffiti.'

Sentence (18) is true in a context in which the walls were covered with graffiti by a small group of students (say, three students) and not by all the students in the university. Thus the implicit $Q$ is not necessarily universal.

The dynamic side of the analysis of (11)-(12) (i.e. the identification of the context set) can be taken care of by theories like van der Sandt's (1992), while the truth conditions of these sentences are derived from the underlying quantificational structures. For instance, sentence (12) is an admissible update if one can identify the set of students under consideration; sentence (12) is true if, taking the identified set of students as a restrictor, (19) below is true:

(19) Quarante pour cent des étudiants ont voté.
'Forty percent of the students have voted.'

### 3.2 Indefinite versus quantifying DPs

Let us consider *un* and the numerals as typical examples of indefinite determiners and *tout*, *chaque*, and *40%*, as typical examples of quantifiers. The main contrastive properties of these determiners are:

**a) symmetry:** indefinite determiners are symmetric, quantifiers are not:

(20) Dans cette salle, deux Italiens sont mélomanes. ↔ Dans cette salle, deux mélomanes sont italiens.[5]
'In this room, two Italians are music lovers ↔ In this room, two music lovers are Italian'

(21) Tout Italien est mélomane. → Tout mélomane est italien.
'Every Italian is a music lover → Every music lover is Italian'

[5] The sentence-initial locative phrase *dans cette salle* ('in this room') is meant to introduce a given domain for the determiner *deux* ('two'). The presence of the locative phrase forces a partitive reading on the subject DPs *deux Italiens* ('two Italians') and *deux mélomanes* ('two music lovers'). The sentences in (16) are odd if the subject is not interpreted as a partitive, i.e. as dominating an NP which denotes a given, presupposed set; the oddity is due to the fact that individual-level predicates (as most common nouns are) require a strong DP as a subject, the strength being ensured either by the presence of a strong determiner or by the partitivity (hence presuppositionality) of the DP; on this issue, see Dahl (1974), Comorovski (1995),

**b) scope properties:** the scope of quantifiers is clause-bound, the scope of indefinites is free.

Quantifiers tend to get the scope that their syntactic position induces, whereas indefinites are able to outscope the clause which contains them (Farkas (1981), Fodor and Sag (1982), Abusch (1994)):

(22) Chaque enseignant récompense chaque élève qui a lu *40%*
every teacher rewards every pupil who has read *40%*
des livres.
of-the books

(23) Chaque enseignant récompense chaque élève qui a lu deux
every teacher rewards every pupil who has read two
livres.
books

Sentence (22) has only one interpretation: every student gets rewarded irrespective of the books (s)he read, as long as (s)he read forty percent of a given set of books. In contrast to (22), sentence (23) is three-way ambiguous. On one interpretation, every student is rewarded as long as (s)he read two books, no matter which. On the other two interpretations, only students having read two particular books are rewarded; these two books may or may not co-vary with the teachers, depending on whether *deux livres* takes widest scope, thus outscoping *chaque enseignant*, or whether it takes intermediate scope, thus outscoping only *chaque élève.*

To account for the scope of indefinites, Reinhart (1997) and Kratzer (1998) offer an elegant solution, consisting in the local interpretation of indefinite DPs by means of a choice function. They suggest that indefinites introduce in the logical representation a variable over choice functions. A function $f$ is a choice function ($CH(f)$) iff it applies to any non-empty set and returns a member of this set. Since Reinhart's and Kratzer's analyses use quantification over functions, they depart from the domain of first order logic. In Reinhart's analysis, the function variable is bound by an existential quantifier which can occur at any position in the formula, thus yielding a wide range of possible scopes for indefinites. We exemplify this result below. Consider first the representation of the wide scope reading of the indefinite in the simple sentence (24):

(24) Chaque étudiant a lu un livre.
'Every student has read a book.'

---

among others.

(25) a. $(\exists x)[\text{book}(x) \wedge (\forall y)(\text{student}(y) \rightarrow \text{read}(y, x))]$
b. $(\exists f)[\text{CH}(f) \wedge (\forall y)(\text{student}(y) \rightarrow \text{read}(y, f(\text{book})))]$

(25a), a formula of the first order predicate calculus, and the formula (25b) are truth-conditionally equivalent. In (25a), the argument of *read* is represented by the individual variable $x$; in (25b), the argument of *read* is represented by *f(book)*, that is, by a choice function applied to the set denoted by *book*.

Let us now take a more complex example. The sentence (26) below contains two quantifying DPs, namely the DP *la plupart des linguistes* and the DP *chaque analyse permettant de résoudre une question difficile.* The second DP contains the indefinite *une question difficile*, which can have narrow, intermediate, or wide scope. The intermediate scope reading of the indefinite will be represented as in (27):

(26) La plupart des linguistes ont étudié chaque analyse permettant de résoudre une question difficile.
'Most linguists have looked at every analysis that solves a difficult problem.'

(27) $\text{MOST}_x\ [\text{linguist}(x)]\ [\exists f)(\text{CH}(f) \wedge \text{ALL}_y[\text{analysis}(y) \wedge \text{solve}(y, f(\text{problem})]\ [\text{look-at}(x, y)]]$

Skolem functions are another type of function that has proved useful in the analysis of indefinites. Skolem functions are functions from individuals to individuals. Groenendijk and Stokhof (1984:196ff.) use them in the representation of indefinites that denote a dependency expressed elsewhere in the same sentence with the help of a pronoun. As an example, take the dependency between men and women expressed by the DP *sa mère* ('his mother') in sentence (28) below; Groenendijk and Stokhof translate the English version of this sentence as in (29):

(28) Il y a [une femme que tout homme aime], à savoir sa mère.
'There is [a woman that every man loves], namely his mother.'

(29) $(\exists f)[\text{mother}(f(x),x) \wedge (\forall x)[\text{woman}(f(x))] \wedge (\forall x)[\text{man}(x) \rightarrow \text{love}(x,f(x))]]$

Using Skolem functions in the representation of indefinites, Comorovski (1999) proposes a solution to the so-called 'proportion problem' raised by the asymmetric readings of donkey-sentences (Kadmon (1987, 1990)).

**c) distributivity:** quantifying DPs are inherently distributive, indefinites are not.

Since quantifiers are analyzed as variable binders, the basic interpretation of quantifying DPs is distributive. In contrast, plural indefinites denote a plural individual and consequently their basic interpretation is collective:

(30) Deux élèves m'ont fait un cadeau.
'Two students made me a gift.'

In (30), the interpretation 'collective present' is preferred. Note that the distributive interpretation is possible too. It can be obtained in the same way as the distributive interpretation of plural definite DPs, i.e. by postulating a covert distributivity operator (Link (1987), Roberts (1987), Schwarzschild (1996), among others).

In contrast, the interpretation 'collective present' is hardly, if at all accessible in (31) below:

(31) ?? Quarante pour cent des élèves m'ont fait un cadeau.
'Forty percent of the students made me a gift.'

Some other expected contrasts are more problematic. For instance, DRT predicts that indefinites offer an accessible antecedent for pronouns of subsequent sentences and that quantifiers do not. But the contrast is not always present, especially if the antecedent DP is morphologically plural. Thus the pronoun *ils* ('they') in the second sentence of (32) can be construed with the quantifying DP *quarante pour cent des électeurs* ('forty percent of the voters'), which occurs in the first sentence:

(32) Quarante pour cent des électeurs ont voté. Ils ont voté à droite.
'Forty percent of the voters voted. They voted for the right.'

Anaphora seem to be as easy in (32) as in (33) below, although the antecedent is quantificational in (32) and indefinite in (33):

(33) Deux millions d'électeurs ont voté. *Ils* ont voté à droite.
'Two million voters voted. *They* voted for the right.'

It is only with morphologically singular quantifying DPs that a contrast can be established:

(34) ?? Chaque électeur a voté. *Il* a voté à droite.[6]
'Every voter has voted. He voted for the right.'

(35) Un électeur a voté. *Il* a voté à droite.
'A voter voted. He voted for the right.'

To account for examples like (32), Kamp and Reyle (1993: 309) postulate a specific operation called 'abstraction' which forms the set of all DRs satisfying the conjunction of the conditions expressed in the

[6] The French determiner *chaque* corresponds to two English determiners: 'every' and 'each'.

restrictor and in the scope of a quantifier. In (32), *ils* ('they') denotes the set of voters. Abstraction achieves empirical adequacy, but at a high cost: it predicts that (32) and (33) provide accessible antecedents by means of completely different procedures, although it is difficult to find any empirical correlate of this difference.

Even for singular DPs, the absence of a contrast between (36) and (37) below is problematic for the DRT typology as long as the phenomenon called 'telescoping'[7] is not studied more in depth:

(36) Un homme entre. *Il* porte une torche à la main.
'A man comes in. He carries a torch in his hand.'

(37) Chaque soldat prend son arme. *Il la* met sur *son* épaule, puis *la* repose.
'Every soldier takes his gun. He puts it on his shoulder, then he puts it down again.'

## 4 Property-denoting noun phrases

In the Fregean tradition at the foundation of most current approaches to natural language semantics, predicates are unsaturated expressions that denote properties or relations, which can be conceived of extensionally as sets of individuals (respectively, of ordered n-tuples of individuals). Arguments combine with the predicate to obtain propositions, i.e. saturated expressions that can be conceived of extensionally as denoting a truth value. They can do this in two ways: either by providing the denotation of an individual that "fills" an open position of the predicate (as in (38a) below), or by providing an expression of restricted quantification that introduces a second predicate and specifies the relation between the two sets, as in (38b) below:

(38) a. Pierre est chauve.
Peter is bald

b. La plupart des présidents sont chauves.
the most of-the presidents are bald
'Most of the presidents are bald.'

Ideally, the semantic predicate-argument structure should coincide with the syntactic predicate-argument structure, and since syntactic predicates generally take noun phrases as syntactic arguments, it is assumed that noun phrases either contribute individuals or quantificational structures to the semantic representation. As we have seen

[7] The term 'telescoping' designates the extension of the scope of a quantifier beyond the sentence in which the quantifier occurs. For a study of telescoping, see Poesio and Zucchi (1992).

in section 2, the theory of Generalized Quantifiers treats all noun phrases as introducing quantificational structures (as expressions of type $<< e, t >, t >$), whereas DRT makes a distinction between expressions introducing a restricted variable (type $e$) and expressions introducing quantificational structures.

However, not all noun phrases occupy syntactic argument positions. According to most current analyses, the italicized noun phrases in the following examples function as predicates, constituting the main predication of the clause in (39a-c) and a secondary predication in (40a-c):

(39) a. Pierre est *étudiant.*
Peter is student
'Peter is a student.'

b. Bobby est *un chat.*
Bobby is a cat

c. Ces animaux sont *des girafes.*
these animals are *des* giraffes

(40) a. Il a été élu *président du Conseil.*
he has been elected president of-the council

b. Je le considère comme *un ami.*
I him consider as a friend
'I consider him a friend.'

c. Je les tiens pour *des personnes de confiance.*
I them keep for *des* persons of confidence
'I take them to be trustworthy people.'

(39a) and (40a) lack a determiner, so that they can easily be held not to be full-fledged DPs, but NPs. This is not the case of the predicative noun phrases in examples (39b,c) and (40b,c), which are introduced by determiners. In some syntactic positions, then, full-fledged DPs are expressions of type $< e, t >$, i.e. they denote a set.

As discussed in Partee (1987), only certain kinds of noun phrases can function as predicates, namely those whose type can be shifted to the type $< e, t >$; this is the case of indefinite and definite noun phrases, but not of quantifying noun phrases. Among French indefinites, we find in predicative position noun phrases introduced by the indefinite article *un(e)*, by the determiners *des/du*, or by a numeral; noun phrases introduced by other cardinal determiners can also function predicatively, provided the noun is modified.[8] The question arises

[8] An exception is the determiner *certains*, which is barred from noun phrases in predicative position.

whether other syntactic positions require noun phrases of type $< e, t >$. Possible candidates are noun phrases (determiner + noun sequences) which are themselves introduced by a determiner, as in:

(41) a. les trois soldats
the three soldiers

b. ces quelques remarques
these a-few remarks

In recent years, two other syntactic positions have been put forward as possible candidates for property-denoting noun phrases: (i) the argument position of existential constructions (McNally (1998)) and (ii) incorporated nominals in languages exhibiting a particular morpho-syntactic position for some arguments (van Geenhoven (1998)).

The data in (39)-(41) point to the necessity of positing property-denoting occurrences of noun phrases on combinatorial grounds: noun phrases that apparently combine with $e$ type expressions (as in the case of noun phrases in various predicative positions), or with $<< e, t >, << e, t >, t >>$ type expressions (as in the case of noun phrases introduced by a "second" determiner), or with $<< e, t >, t >$ type expressions (as in the case of nominal predicates with quantified subjects.

The question arises whether there are noun phrase types which should always be analyzed as property-denoting expressions, independently of the context in which they occur. Noun phrases lacking a determiner (bare noun phrases) are a case in point. In most languages which have articles, bare noun phrases show a restricted distribution and restricted interpretive possibilities. This defective behavior, which goes hand in hand with the absence of an overt determiner, can be explained if we assume that they introduce neither an individual nor quantificational structure. Interestingly, there is a determiner in French, namely *des/du* (the first form introduces plural, the latter, mass nouns), which heads DPs whose behavior parallels that of bare noun phrases on most relevant points, differing significantly from the behavior of staple indefinites. Attal (1976) concludes that *des/du* noun phrases neither introduce a new discourse referent nor quantify over some set. Dobrovie-Sorin and Laca (2003) suggest that *des/du* noun phrases denote properties.

The interpretation of noun phrases introduced by *des/du* is described by Bosveld-de Smet (chapter 3, this volume). To support the hypothesis that noun phrases introduced by *des/du* are best analyzed as denoting properties, we will consider here three of their characteristics.

First, noun phrases introduced by *des/du* do not show the same scopal properties as other indefinites. Indefinites are characterized by the variability of their scope. In contrast, *des/du* noun phrases take the narrowest possible scope, being as a rule dependent on other scoped elements, such as quantified expressions and intensional verbs:

(42) a. Tous les professeurs nous ont conseillé *des* / trois
all the teachers to-us have recommended *des* / three
*livres.*
books
'All the teachers recommended books / three books to us.'

b. Marie croit que Pierre connaît *des* / trois *politiciens.*
Mary thinks that Peter knows *des* / three politicians

Secondly, a collection-denoting DP co-occurring with a *des* noun phrase cannot have a distributive interpretation, as it can when co-occurring with an indefinite DP. Thus, in the interpretation of the sentence below, only one collection of experts can be involved:

(43) On a soumis deux dossiers à *des experts.*
one has submitted two files to *des* experts

Finally, noun phrases introduced by *des/du* do not delimit individual referents, as can be shown by the impossibility of their furnishing either the delimitation required for telic interpretations or the antecedent for a pronoun of disjoint reference:

(44) a. Il a mangé des gâteaux pendant / *en une heure.
he has eaten *des* cakes for / in an hour
'He ate cakes for / *in an hour.'

b. Il a mangé plusieurs gâteaux en / *pendant une heure.
'He ate several cakes in / *for an hour.'

(45) a. # Des étudiants sont arrivés en retard. Les *autres* étaient
*des* students are arrived late the others were
déjà là.
already there
#'Sm students arrived late. The others were already there.'

b. Trois étudiants sont arrivés en retard. Les *autres* étaient déjà là.
'Three students arrived late. The others were already there.'

The behavior of *des/du* noun phrases follows straightforwardly if they are analyzed as expressions of type $< e, t >$, a type which has been attributed to bare plural; see van Geenhoven's (1998) account of the interpretive properties of bare plural. Note, however, that the behavior of *des* noun phrases differs somewhat from that of bare plural. In some contexts, *des* noun phrases are able to acquire a partitive interpretation, denoting a part of an already given set. Moreover, when a noun phrase introduced by *des* has a partitive interpretation, it can be the subject of a negated predicate, as seen in (46) below:

(46) Des élèves ne m'ont pas rendu leurs devoirs.
'Some of the pupils have not turned in their homework.'

The following chapters will draw on recent theories in formal semantics in order to give an explicit analysis of French determiners.

## References

Abusch, D. 1994. The scope of indefinites. *Natural Language Semantics* 2:88–135.

Attal, P. 1976. A propos de l'indéfini *des*: problèmes de représentation sémantique. *Le Français Moderne* 2:126–142.

Bach, E., E. Jelinek, A. Kratzer, and B. Partee, eds. 1995. *Quantification in Natural Languages*, Dordrecht. Kluwer.

Barker, C. and D. Dowty, eds. 1992. *Proceedings of SALT*, vol. 2, Columbus, Ohio. Ohio State University.

Barwise, J. and R. Cooper. 1981. Generalized quantifiers and natural language. *Linguistics and Philosophy* 4:159–219.

Bäuerle, R., C. Schwarze, and A. von Stechow, eds. 1983. *Meaning, Use, and Interpretation of Language*. Berlin: Walter de Gruyter.

Bosveld-De Smet, L. 2004. Towards a uniform characterization of noun phrases with *des* or *du*. This volume.

Bowers, J. 1975. Adjectives and adverbs in English. *Foundations of Language* 13:529–562.

Coene, M. and Y. D'Hulst, eds. 2002. *From NP to DP*, vol. 1. Amsterdam: John Benjamins.

Comorovski, I. 1995. On quantifier strength and partitive noun phrases. In Bach et al. (1995).

Comorovski, I. 1999. Functional indefinites and the proportion problem. In Corblin et al. (1999).

Comorovski, I. and L. Nicaise. 2004. 'Divers'. This volume.

Corblin, F. 1997. Les indéfinis: variables et quantificateurs. *Langue française* 116:8–32.

Corblin, F. 2001a. Où situer *certains* dans une typologie sémantique des groupes nominaux? In Kleiber et al. (2001).

Corblin, F. 2001b. *Représentation du discours et sémantique formelle. Introduction et application au français*. Paris: Presses Universitaires de France.

Corblin, F., C. Dobrovie-Sorin, and J.-M. Marandin, eds. 1999. *Empirical Issues in Formal Syntax and Semantics*, vol. 2. The Hague: Holland Academic Graphics.

Dahl, O., ed. 1974a. *Topic and Comment, Contextual Boundedness and Focus*. Hamburg: Helmut Buske Verlag.

Dahl, Ö.. 1974b. Topic-comment structure revisited. In Dahl (1974a).

Dobrovie-Sorin, C. and B. Laca. 2003. Les noms sans déterminants dans les langues romanes. In Godard (2003).

Doetjes, J. 2004. Degree quantifiers. This volume.

Dowty, D. 1986. Collective predicates, distributive predicates, and *All.* In Marshall et al. (1986).

Farkas, D. 1981. Quantifier scope and syntactic island. *CLS* 17:59–66.

Fodor, J. D. and I. Sag. 1982. Referential and quantificational indefinites. *Linguistics and Philosophy* 5:355–398.

Gärdenfors, P., ed. 1987. *Generalized Quantifiers. Linguistic and Logical Approaches*. Dordrecht: Reidel.

Godard, D., ed. 2003. *Les langues romanes*. Paris: Editions du CNRS.

Groenendijk, J., D. de Jongh, and M. Stokhof, eds. 1987. *Studies in DRT and the Theory of Generalized Quantifiers*. Dordrecht: Foris.

Groenendijk, J., T. Jansen, and M. Stokhof, eds. 1981. *Formal Methods in the Study of Language*, vol. 135 of *Mathematical Centre Tracts*. Amsterdam.

Groenendijk, J. and M. Stokhof. 1984. *Studies on the Semantics of Questions and the Pragmatics of Answers*. Ph.D. thesis, University of Amsterdam.

Heim, I. 1982. *The Semantics of Definite and Indefinite Noun Phrases*. Ph.D. thesis, University of Massachusetts, Amherst.

Hintikka, J., J. Moravcsik, and P. Suppes, eds. 1973. *Approaches to Natural Language: Proceedings of the 1970 Stanford Workshop on Grammar and Semantics*. Dordrecht: Reidel.

Jayez, J. and L. Tovena. 2004. *Tout* as a genuine free choice item. This vol.

Kadmon, N. 1987. *On Unique and Non-Unique Reference and Asymmetric Quantification*. Ph.D. thesis, University of Massachusetts Amherst.

Kadmon, N. 1990. Uniqueness. *Linguistics and Philosophy* 13:273–324.

Kamp, H. 1981. A theory of truth and semantic representation. In Groenendijk et al. (1981), pages 277–322.

Kamp, H. and U. Reyle. 1993. *From Discourse to Logic*. Dordrecht: Kluwer.

Keenan, E., ed. 1975. *Formal Semantics of Natural Language*. CUP.

Keenan, E. and J. Stavi. 1986. A semantic characterization of natural language determiners. *Linguistics and Philosophy* 9:253–326.

Kleiber, G., B. Laca, and L. Tasmowski, eds. 2001. *Typologie des groupes nominaux*. Rennes: Presses Universitaires de Rennes.

Kratzer, A. 1998. Scope or pseudoscope? Are there wide scope indefinites? In Rothstein (1998).

Krifka, M. 1999. At least some determiners aren't determiners. In Turner (1999).

Laca, B. and L. Tasmowski. 2004. Différents. This volume.

Landman, F. 2002. Predicate-argument mismatches and the adjectival theory of indefinites. In Coene and D'Hulst (2002).

Lewis, D. 1975. Adverbs of quantification. In Keenan (1975).

Link, G. 1983. The logical analysis of plurals and mass terms: A lattice-theoretical approach. In Bäuerle et al. (1983).

Link, G. 1987. Generalized quantifiers and plurals. In Gärdenfors (1987).

Marshall, F., A. Miller, and Z. sheng Zhang, eds. 1986. *Proceedings of ESCOL '86*. University of Pittsburgh and Carnegie-Mellon University.

McNally, L. 1998. Existential sentences without existential quantification. *Linguistics and Philosophy* 21:353–392.

Montague, R. 1973. The proper treatment of quantification in ordinary English. In Hintikka et al. (1973).

Partee, B. 1987. Noun phrase interpretation and type-shifting principles. In Groenendijk et al. (1987).

Partee, B. 1988. Many quantifiers. In Powers and de Jong (1988).

Partee, B. 1995. Quantificational structures and compositionality. In Bach et al. (1995).

Poesio, M. and A. Zucchi. 1992. On telescoping. In Barker and Dowty (1992).

Powers, J. and K. de Jong, eds. 1988. *Proceedings of ESCOL '88*, University of Pennsylvania.

Reinhart, T. 1997. Quantifier scope: How labor is divided between QR and choice functions. *Linguistis and Philosophy* 20:335–397.

Roberts, C. 1987. *Modal Subordination, Anaphora, and Distributivity*. Ph.D. thesis, University of Massachusetts, Amherst.

Rothstein, S., ed. 1998. *Events and Grammar*. Dordrecht: Kluwer.

Schwarzschild, R. 1996. *Pluralities*. Dordrecht: Kluwer.

Ter Meulen, A., ed. 1983. *Studies in Model-theoretic Semantics*. Dordrecht: Foris.

Turner, K., ed. 1999. *The Semantics/Pragmatics Interface from Different Points of View*. Amsterdam: Elsevier Science.

Van Benthem, J. 1984. Questions about quantifiers. *Journal of Symbolic Logic* 49:443–466.

Van Benthem, J. and A. ter Meulen, eds. 1984. *Generalized Quantifiers in Natural Language*. Dordrecht: Foris.

Van der Sandt, R. 1992. Presupposition projection as anaphora resolution. *Journal of Semantics* 9:333–377.

Van Geenhoven, V. 1998. *Semantic Incorporation and Indefinite Descriptions*. Stanford: CSLI Publications.

Westerståhl, D. 1984. Determiners and context sets. In Van Benthem and ter Meulen (1984), pages 45–72.

Zwarts, F. 1981. Negatief polaire uitdrukkingen 1. *Glot* 4:35–132.

Zwarts, F. 1983. Determiners: A relational perspective. In Ter Meulen (1983).

2

# Nounless Determiners

FRANCIS CORBLIN, JEAN-MARIE MARANDIN, AND
PETRA SLEEMAN

## 1 Introduction

It has been observed that some expressions have the distribution of noun phrases even if they lack an overt noun. They are made up of one or more determiners, which we take here in a broad sense to also include adjectives:

(1) Marie a beaucoup de chiens. Certains aboient.
'Mary has many dogs. Some bark.'

(2) Marie a plusieurs chiens. Le plus jeune aboie toujours.
'Mary has several dogs. The youngest always barks.'

In this contribution, we discuss whether the absence of an overt noun also implies a syntactic absence of a nominal position and we discuss the ways in which a relation can be established with a noun in the context, so that the semantic lack of a noun can be undone.

## 2 Properties of determiners without a noun

Some expressions have the external distribution of noun phrases, they include a determiner, but they lack any overt noun. In order to be neutral about the analysis of such noun phrases we will call them DWNs (determiners without a noun). In their most typical uses, DWNs are context dependent: they rely on their context for finding which nominal content is associated by the speaker with the DWN.

Although most DWNs are classified as pronouns in most grammars

*Handbook of French Semantics.*
Francis Corblin and Henriëtte de Swart (eds.).
Copyright © 2004, CSLI Publications.

of French, together with third person clitic/tonic pronouns, it has been shown that they contrast sharply with those personal pronouns (Gross 1973, Milner 1978, Ronat 1977, Corblin 1990). The most salient specific properties of DWNs are the following:

**A. Dislocation**

DWNs allow a *de N* right dislocation[1], but not the dislocation of full noun phrases. For pronouns, the reverse is true (Milner 1978, Corblin 1990):

(3) Je déteste le petit, de crayon.
I hate the small one, of pencil

(4) *Je le déteste, de crayon.
I hate it, of pencil

(5) *Je déteste le tien, ton pull.
I hate yours, your sweater

(6) Je le déteste, ton pull rouge.
I hate it, your red sweater

**B. Anaphora and agreement**

DWNs must find an antecedent providing a noun that can be interpreted as their semantic head and must agree in gender with their antecedent, whereas pronouns must agree, in the unmarked case, in gender and number (Ronat 1977):

(7) Son chat est plus beau que les miens.
'Her cat is more beautiful than mine (m.pl.).'

(8) *Son chat est plus beau que les miennes.
her cat is more beautiful than mine (f.pl.)

**C. Licensing of preverbal *en quantitatif***

Non-definite direct postverbal DWNs trigger the occurrence of '*en* quantitatif' in French (Milner 1978):

(9) J'en veux un bleu / deux petits.
'(Of these), I want a blue one / two small ones.'

(10) *J'en veux un livre bleu / deux petits biscuits.
(of these), I want a blue book / two small cookies.

[1]Right *de N* dislocation in French was studied in Milner (1978). It is used mostly in spoken French. We use Milner's terminology which describes this construction in transformational terms and do not discuss its analysis in more recent syntactic formalism.

**D. Optional licensing of *en* when occurring as the complement of partitives**

If (and only if) the complement of a partitive noun phrase in the context described by (C) is a DWN, the occurrence of '*en* quantitatif' is optional (Corblin 1996):

(11) J'ai mangé trois des tiennes.
'I have eaten three of yours.'

(12) J'en ai mangé trois des tiennes.
of these, I have eaten three of yours

(13) J'ai mangé trois de tes pommes.
'I have eaten three of your apples.'

(14) *J'en ai mangé trois de tes pommes.
of these, I have eaten three of your apples

(15) *J'en ai mangé trois pommes.
of these, I have eaten three apples

(16) J'en ai mangé trois.
'Of these, I have eaten three.'

Considering the properties (A-D) as the set of defining conditions for the inclusion of an expression into the paradigm of DWNs, one must include in this paradigm the French noun phrases based on *celui-*, although it is not uncontroversial that these forms contain a determiner. The postulated natural class would then include:

1. noun phrases introduced by determiners which can also be found with a noun, e.g. *certains* 'some', *beaucoup* 'many', *une autre* 'another', *le seul* 'the only', *les deux petites* 'the two small', etc.
2. other noun phrases:
   (a) *celui* expressions:
      (17) J'ai lu l'article de Russell et celui de Strawson.
      'I have read the paper by Russell and the one by Strawson.'
      (18) *celui article de Strawson
      the one paper by Strawson
   (b) the possessive pronoun:
      (19) J'ai lu l'article de Russell et le tien.
      'I have read the paper by Russell and yours.'
      (20) *J'ai lu le tien article.
      I have read yours paper
   (c) forms ending in *un(s)*, such as *quelques-uns*:

(21) Quelques-uns coûtaient très cher.
'Some were very expensive.'

(22) *Quelques-uns livres coûtaient très cher.
some-ones books cost very expensive

Both *celui* and *le sien* were able to combine with an overt noun in old French. One can thus consider them as determiners of a special kind, so that the inclusion of these expressions in the paradigm of DWNs makes sense.

The conclusion arrived at is that DWNs form a natural class: all their specific properties are consequences of their very nature (i.e. the fact that they are noun phrases introduced by a determiner, but deprived of a lexical noun for their head). Corblin (1990) for instance assumes that the non-specification of the lexical nominal head in otherwise standard noun phrases triggers their anaphoric common properties: they look in the context for a nominal content, not for a referent. The lack of relevance of number agreement is explained by the fact that the anaphoric relation is not defined at the noun phrase-level, as a way of determining its referent, but only at the noun-level as a way of determining its content. The *de N* dislocation can also be related to the non-specification of the lexical head: the dislocated *N* is understood as a repetition of the intended nominal content which is not overt in the noun phrase itself. *En quantitatif* is analyzed in this perspective as a preverbal reflex of a nominal head that is missing from a direct indefinite noun phrase complement. The licensing of *en quantitatif* works, in fact, as a test for a sub-class of the postulated natural class, viz. indefinite DWNs. Corblin (1996) suggests in addition that *en* can also work as a test for another sub-class of DWNs, viz. definite plural DWNs. The argument goes as follows: *en quantitatif* is optional if and only if a direct complement noun phrase is partitive and has a DWN as a complement noun phrase. Consider for instance (23):

(23) Il (en) veut deux de celles-ci.
of these, he wants two of these

The preverbal *en* is optional and this remains true if one replaces *celles-ci* by another DWN, and only for such substitutions.

(24) Il (en) veut deux des miennes (des rouges, des plus mûres).
of these, he wants two of mine (of the red ones, of the ripest ones)

(25) *Il en veut deux de mes pommes (des pommes les plus mûres).
(of these), he wants two of my apples (of the ripest apples)

One reason might be that the head of the complement of a partitive *can* be treated as the head of the noun phrase as a whole, hence the licensing of *en* when this head is a non specified head in application of the rule illustrated by the (C) criterion.

Having provided evidence for the absence of a nominal content, which has to be borrowed from the context in order to interpret the DWN as a nominal expression, we now turn to the question of whether the semantic absence of a noun also implies the syntactic absence of the noun position. The answers that have been given to this question by several linguists, seem to be related to the linguistic framework these linguists make use of for their research. In the next section, we present some generative analyses in which the noun position is either syntactically absent or syntactically present but empty. In sections 4 and 5, we present an HPSG analysis in which the noun position is absent or is filled by the determiner.

## 3 Analyses in the framework of Generative Grammar

In the generative literature, DWNs have been analyzed either as noun phrases in which there is simply no noun position or as noun phrases dominating an empty category. In this section we discuss both approaches. We show that the analyses make crucial use of the idea that DWNs form a natural class to motivate an empty noun or the absence of a nominal head position.

Besides expressions of quantity, a small list of adjectives can be elided, i.e. can be used as DWNs in French. Barbaud (1976) calls them 'classifying adjectives'. They include superlatives, color adjectives and hierarchic adjectives (ordinals, *précédent* 'preceding', *suivant* 'following', *prochain* 'next', *même* 'same', *autre* 'other', *seul* 'only'). Furthermore, classifying adjectives include measure adjectives such as *grand* 'big' and *petit* 'small':

(26) De ses livres, je n'ai lu que le premier.
'Of his books, I have only read the first (one).'

(27) Je prends l'autre.
'I take the other (one).'

(28) De tous mes amis, ils sont les seuls à le savoir.
'Of all my friends, they are the only ones who know it.'

One of the first studies in the generative framework that tries to explain why only a limited class of adjectives in French can be used as DWNs, is Ronat's (1977). In Ronat's opinion, relational adjectives are generated as an adjunct to N°; quantifiers and adjectives that allow the ellipsis of the noun are dominated by N′; all the other intransitive adjectives, i.e. adjectives not followed by a complement, are dominated by

N″, and determiners and restrictive relative clauses (from which Ronat derives transitive adjectives, i.e. adjectives followed by a complement) are generated in [Spec, NP] (a kind of extraposition transformation within the NP moves the relative clause to a position to the right of the noun.[2]Structure (30) represents the noun phrase in (29):

(29) les seules vaches laitières blanches affreuses qui soient capables de me plaire
'the only awful white dairy cows that can (subj.) please me'

(30)

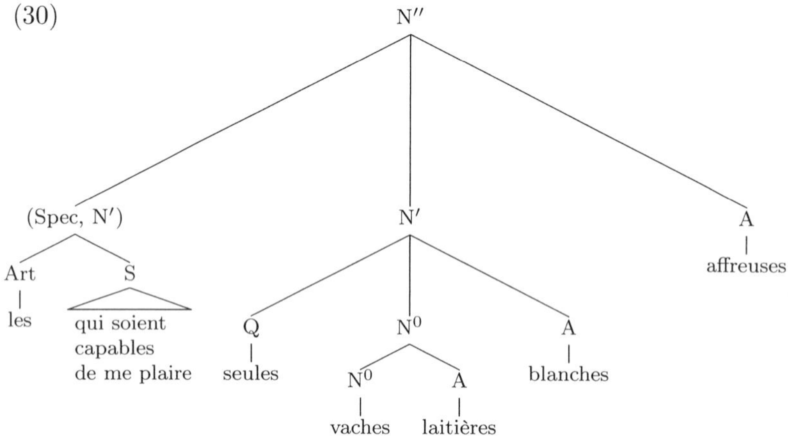


Ronat tries to explain why only quantifiers and a restricted class of adjectives allow the noun to be ellipted in French by means of the following claim:

(31) N′ has to dominate something at S-structure.

If this 'something' is not a noun then it has to be either a quantifier or an adjective such as a color adjective.[3] Since adjectives such as *affreux* are not dominated by N′, they do not license noun ellipsis.[4]

---

[2]Ronat mentions only three cases of noun ellipsis: with cardinal numbers, with *seul* and with color adjectives. Cardinal numbers and *seul* are quantifiers generated to the left of the noun, whereas color adjectives are adjectives generated to the right of the noun. In order to be able to account for the possibility of noun ellipsis with prenominal adjectives (the ordinals, *autre, même, précédent, suivant, prochain, grand, petit,* and the prenominal superlatives), Ronat would have to distinguish an adjective position to the left of the noun dominated by N′.

[3]Since relational adjectives are dominated by N', constraint (31) would predict that they allow noun ellipsis, but, in general, they do not:

(i) *De ces cartes, je préfère la postale. 'Of these cards, I prefer the postal ones.'

Ronat explains this by suggesting that adjunction to the empty N° is not possible.

[4]Adjectives that normally do not allow noun ellipsis do allow it if the adjective is explicitly used in a discriminating way:

Constraint (31) applies to the transformational rule called Eff(acement)-N, that deletes the noun position if there is already a referentially identical noun in the context.

There are several problems with Ronat's proposal. First, the treatment of the determiners that can be used as DWNs as a natural class that is generated under N′ is not motivated. Second, Ronat needs the ad hoc constraint (31) to account for the class of DWNs. Third, although N′ does dominate *deux* in (32) and *seul* in (33), the sentences are ungrammatical:

(32) *Je n'ai pas entendu les [$_{N'}$ deux] intéressantes.
I have not heard the two interesting ones

(33) *C'est le [$_{N'}$ seul] captivant que j'aie lu.
It is the only captivating one that I have (subj.) read

The adoption of a DP-analysis (Abney 1987) instead of an NP-analysis of noun phrases offered new possibilities to deal with the restriction on determiners in French noun ellipsis. Lobeck (1991, 1993, 1995) claims that noun ellipsis involves an empty category of the *pro* type, which, just like *pro* in null subject languages (Chomsky 1982), has to be licensed by morphological features such as *phi*-features (person, gender, and number features) of a proper governor in a functional projection of NP. Whereas morphology seems to play an important role in the licensing of noun ellipsis in most of the Germanic languages (see a.o. Olsen 1987 for German), in French morphological features such as *phi*-features do not seem to play any role, witness the ungrammaticality of (34) despite the presence of the feminine and plural inflection on the adjective:

(34) *Je n'ai pas entendu les intéressantes.
I have not heard the interesting ones

Since in French there is a natural class of adjectives that can license the ellipsis of the noun, Sleeman (1996) claims that at least in this language the semantics of the determiner play an important role. She argues that the determiners that can be used as DWNs have a partitive meaning, i.e. they take as an argument a subset of a larger set, which has already been introduced in the discourse. In this way, the nounless DP can be linked to a DP in the context, from which the interpretation

(i) Parmi les tableaux exposés dans ce musée, je distinguerai trois catégories: les magnifiques, les bizarres et les affreux.
'Among the paintings exhibited in this museum, I will distinguish three categories: the magnificent ones, the strange ones and the awful ones.'

The reason for this might be that the opposition with other adjectives makes the adjective 'classifying'.

of the empty noun can be recovered. These determiners include quantifiers, superlatives, hierarchical adjectives, and also pronouns such as *celui* 'that one', *quelques-uns* 'several', and *le mien* 'mine'. Color adjectives and measure adjectives are problematic for this analysis. Sleeman suggests that they can have a kind of partitive interpretation because of their clearly discriminating force.

Whereas in Ronat's analysis the noun position is deleted in the case of ellipsis, in Sleeman's analysis the noun position remains and dominates an empty category, *pro*, which has to be licensed by a proper governor with a partitive meaning. According to Sleeman, *pro* is the empty counterpart of the quantitative pronoun *en*, which is generated in the head position of the noun phrase and is moved to a verbal host. Sleeman shows that the determiners that license *en* as the head of the noun phrase are also proper governors with a partitive meaning. They form a subclass of the natural class of determiners that allow *pro* to be the head of the noun phrase, because they always have to be indefinite (see property C mentioned above). Sleeman argues that *en* is used to give the indefinite noun phrase a 'specific' interpretation, which is needed besides the partitive meaning of the determiner to relate it to a noun in the context. If the noun phrase already has a 'specific' interpretation by means of its syntactic position (subject position), or if it contains a strong determiner as defined by Barwise & Cooper (1981), the use of *en* is not necessary and *pro* can be used as the head of the noun phrase (see also López 2000):

(35) Il $\text{en}_i$ a vendu trois $t_i$.
'He has sold three of them.'

(36) Trois *pro* ont été achetés par Marc.
'Three have been bought by Mark.'

(37) *Il $\text{en}_i$ a vendu la plus belle $t_i$.
'He has sold the most beautiful one of them

(38) Il a vendu la plus belle *pro*.
'He has sold the most beautiful one.'

Sleeman argues that partitive constructions also contain a nominal head position. One of her arguments is the morphological form that the determiner *quelques* takes in the partitive construction. Since this form, *quelques-un(e)s*, is the form that *quelques* takes if *en* or *pro* is used as the head of the noun phrase instead of an overt noun, Sleeman concludes that partitives also contain a noun position that is filled by *pro* (see also Milner 1978):

(39) Il a vendu quelques livres.

'He has sold some books.'

(40) Il $en_i$ a vendu quelques-uns $t_i$
'He has sold some.'

(41) Quelques-uns *pro* sont très bons.
'Some are very good.'

(42) Il a vendu quelques-uns *pro* de ces livres.
'He has sold some of these books.'

In special cases the noun position in partitive constructions can also be filled by *en* (property D mentioned above), which is moved later in the derivation to a verbal host:

(43) Il ($en_i$) a vendu quelques-uns $t_i$ des siens.
'He has sold some of his.'

The idea that partitive constructions contain a nominal head position is not shared by all linguists. López (2000) argues against it. Kupferman (1999) claims that partitive constructions involve a DP, instead of an NP in non-partitive quantified noun phrases, selected by a quantificational head:

(44) beaucoup de $[_{NP}$ livres]
'a lot of books'

(45) beaucoup de $[_{DP}$ ces livres]
'a lot of these books'

However, in an analysis such as Kupferman's it is difficult to account for the morphological variation in (39)-(42).

The assumption that DWNs involve an empty category, the empty pronoun *pro*, is motivated not only by the (almost) complementary distribution with the overt pronoun en, but also by its position with respect to the determiner that, in Sleeman's view, licenses the nominal ellipsis. The sentences that are problematic for Ronat, sentences (32) and (33), repeated here as (46) and (47), are no longer problematic under an analysis in which there is an empty nominal head, which has to be licensed by an appropriate proper governor:

(46) *Je n'ai pas entendu les $[_{N'}$ deux] intéressantes.
I have not heard the two interesting ones

(47) *C'est le $[_{N'}$ seul] captivant que j'aie lu.
it is the only captivating one that I have (subj.) read

Following Lobeck, Sleeman assumes that the determiner that licenses the ellipsis is generated in a functional projection dominating NP. She assumes, following Valois (1991) and Cinque (1994), that even 'postnominal' adjectives such as color adjectives, but not relative clauses and adjectives followed by a complement, are generated in functional projections dominating NP, their postnominal position being the result of overt noun movement to a higher functional head, the head of NumP (Ritter 1990), see structure (52). In this way, she can account for the ungrammatical sentences (46)-(47), see (48)-(49), which were problematic for Ronat's analysis and which contrast with (50)-(51):

(48) *Je n'ai pas entendu les deux intéressantes *pro*.
I have not heard the two interesting ones

(49) *C'est le seul captivant *pro* que j'aie lu.
it is the only captivating one that I have (subj.) read

(50) C'est le seul *pro* que j'aie lu / capable de me plaire.
'It is the only one that I have (subj.) read / that can please me.'

(51) Je préfère la bleue *pro*.
'I prefer the blue one.'

(52)

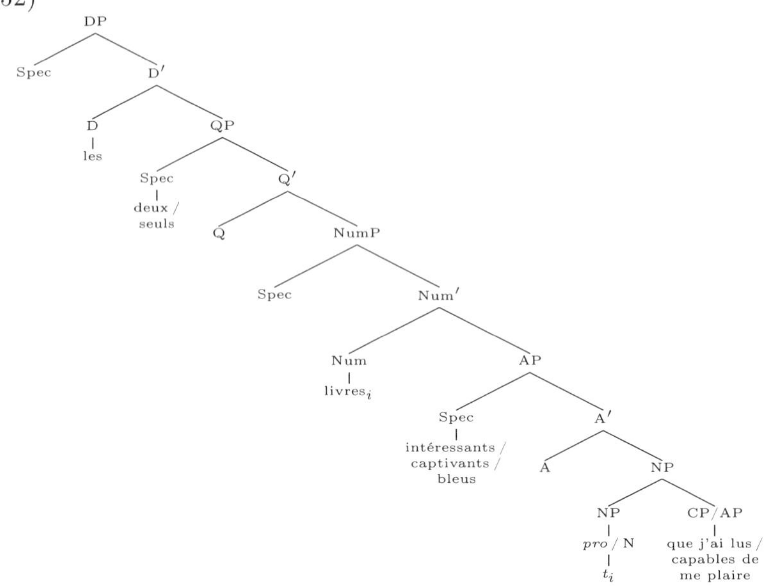


Since the proper governor of the empty noun in (48) and (49), the adjective, does not have the required partitive meaning, ellipsis is not allowed. Notice that in (48) and (49) the quantifier does not properly govern the empty pronoun, whereas it does in (50) and, with an extension of the notion 'partitivity', also in (51).

In Sleeman's analysis, the licensing of the (empty) pronoun plays a crucial role. The (empty) pronoun is licensed by a proper governor with a partitive interpretation. Sleeman has to assume, however, that color adjectives or adjectives such as *grand* 'big' or *petit* 'small' have a partitive meaning. According to Sleeman, they can have such a 'partitive' meaning because they denote salient properties. Because of this, they can easily create subsets out of larger sets. However, it remains true that these kinds of adjectives are problematic for the idea that partitivity is involved in the licensing of DWNs. In the next section, we present an analysis of DWNs in which color adjectives and adjectives such as *grand* and *petit* do not involve the presence of an empty noun.

## 4 Subclasses of DWNs

Marandin (1997) shows that color adjectives and *grand* and *petit* behave differently from other DWNs such as superlatives and adjectives that become classifying in a contrastive context (see footnote 4).

In their use as DWNs, color adjectives and *grand* and *petit* are possible in all otherwise canonical noun phrases, i.e. all kinds of determiners and modifiers are allowed. This is shown for the indefinite determiner *quelques* in (53), and for the possessive prepositional phrase and the restrictive relative in (54)-(55):

(53) J'ai acheté quelques vertes.
'I have bought some green ones.'

(Peter wears a red hat.)

(54) Marie porte le bleu de Paul.
'Mary wears Paul's blue one.'

(55) Marie porte le bleu que Paul a dessiné.
'Mary wears the blue one that Paul has designed.'

Other adjectives used contrastively can only be preceded by a definite determiner when they are DWNs, as exemplified by the oddness of (56), and cannot be combined with a possessive prepositional phrase (57) or a restrictive relative clause (58):

(56) (Have you only made syntactic remarks about this paper?)
?? Non, j'ai fait aussi quelques stylistiques.
'No, I have also made some stylistic ones.'

(The TLF and the Grand Robert include syntactic and stylistic remarks in their entries).

(57) ??Les syntaxiques du TLF sont très utiles pour les linguistes.
'The TLF's syntactic ones are very useful to linguists.'

(In an entry in a dictionary, the remarks do not have the same status).

(58) ??Les syntaxiques qui sont relatives à la construction du mot peuvent être utiles au linguiste, alors que les stylistiques sont normatives.
'The syntactic ones that concern the construction of the word can be useful to a linguist, whereas the stylistic ones are normative.'

Superlatives are always introduced by a definite determiner, even in a regular noun phrase with a noun. Superlatives as DWNs differ from superlatives in canonical noun phrases in that the combination with possessive prepositional phrases or restrictive relatives is not possible:

(Claire and Annie wear marvellous dresses.)

(59) ??Les plus belles de Claire ont été faites par de grands couturiers.
'Claire's most beautiful ones have been made by famous designers.'

(This library is organizing a book exhibition.)

(60) ??Les moins chers qui sont susceptibles de t'intéresser sont en anglais.
'The less expensive ones that might interest you are in English.'

On the basis of these differences between DWNs involving color adjectives and *grand* and *petit* on the one hand, and DWNs involving superlatives or adjectives such as *stylistique* on the other, Marandin (1997) proposes analyzing these two groups in a different way.

In their use as DWNs, color adjectives and *grand* and *petit* are analyzed as nouns that are the result of a morphological conversion rule in the lexicon, which forms deadjectival masculine and feminine nouns that serve to denote a referential category by means of one of its characteristics, which is expressed by the basic adjective. These nouns have a generalistic meaning and can serve to denote both animates and inanimates. That only these adjectives can be converted into nouns follows from the fact that they express only one dimension, color or height, which is furthermore a visual dimension. Since the adjectives are converted into nouns, they form the head of a canonical noun phrase and admit all kinds of determiners and modifiers:

(61)

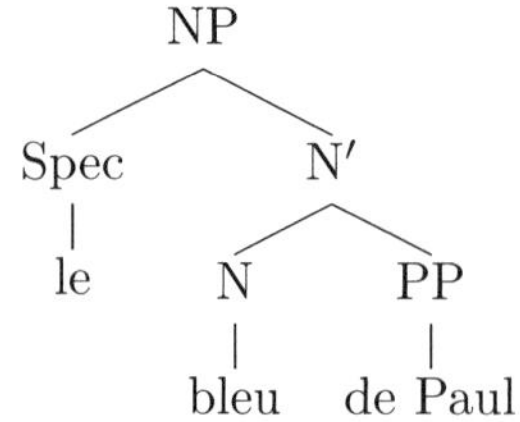

'Paul's blue one'

DWNs involving superlatives or adjectives such as *stylistique* are analyzed by Marandin in a heterocategorial way. A superlative is an N″ that immediately dominates an A″. Since there is no N′ projection, nominal modifiers are not possible. The superlative itself, which is analyzed as A″, permits internal modification:

(62) le plus apte à faire ce travail
'the most capable one to do this work'

(63)

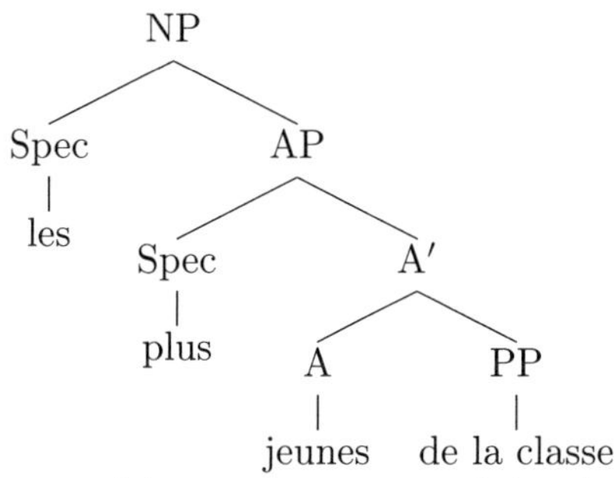


'the youngest ones of the class'

A relational adjective such as *stylistique* is analyzed as an N″ that dominates an A°. Neither nominal modifiers nor adjectival modifiers are possible:

(64)

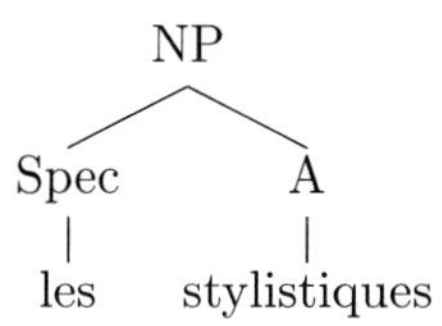


'the stylistic ones'

Whereas in Corblin's and Sleeman's analyses, the dependency relation is the consequence of the absence of a noun, in Marandin's analysis there is no empty noun, so that the relation has to be established in another way. We discuss the dependency relation in the next section.

## 5 Analysis of the contextual dependency

In all approaches presented here, contextual dependency is one of the characteristics of DWNs. They differ with respect to the analysis of the dependency relation. According to Corblin, the relation is the simple consequence of the absence of the noun. He assumes that the non-specification of the nominal head in an otherwise standard noun phrase triggers its anaphoric properties: it looks in the context for a nominal content, not for a referent. An exception is an example such as (65), in which *celui-ci* refers to the whole second noun phrase and not only to a lower N projection:

(65) Pierre a demandé à Jean de l'aider, mais celui-ci a refusé
'Peter asked John to help him, but the latter refused.'

Corblin (1999a,b) analyzes DWNs like *celui-ci*, or ordinals like *premier* 'first', *second* 'second' as members of a restricted set of NPs exemplifying a special kind of reference that he calls 'mentional reference'.

An inconvenience of Corblin's 'nominal anaphor' approach is that since the dependency relation only depends on the absence of the noun, it does not account for the restrictions on the type of determiner.

In Sleeman's analysis, the empty noun has to be identified, which is only possible if an inclusion relation can be established with an antecedent. This inclusion relation can be established because of the partitive meaning of the determiner. In Marandin's analysis, which is formulated in the HPSG framework, there is no empty noun position, but the DWN's context dependency also implies the inclusion of a subset in a previously established set. Marandin (1996, 1997) formulates this dependency as follows:

(66) $x \in Y$ where x is an element of the discourse referent X introduced by a DWN and where Y is a previously introduced discourse referent, the source

Marandin observes that the source is either an identified (plural) discourse referent or the denotation of a nominal predicate. In the first case, x has a restrictive reading (67), whereas in the second case x has a non-restrictive reading (68):

(67) Il y a des chapeaux dans la vitrine. Les rouges sont fripés.
'There are hats on display in the window. The red ones are crumpled.'

(68) Pierre a fait un chapeau bleu, mais Marie n'aime que les rouges que fait André.'
Peter has made a blue hat, but Mary only likes the red ones that Andrew makes.'

In the non-restrictive reading, the anaphoric DWN can be plural whereas the noun phrase in the context is singular (see Corblin's property B):

(69) Ce livre est plus intéressant que les autres.
'This book is more interesting than the other (ones).'

Determiners that necessarily form a subset, such as superlatives, have a restrictive reading, whereas *autre* can only have a non-restrictive reading. Color adjectives or measure adjectives such as *grand* 'big' or *petit* 'small' can have a restrictive or a non-restrictive reading.

Corblin's analysis of the dependency relation also allows for the restrictive and the non-restrictive reading.

In Sleeman's analysis, the superset that provides the interpretation of the missing noun is simply the whole set of N, e.g. a dislocated N (see property A mentioned above), and not necessarily a subset of this superset. This is the non-restrictive reading. Although the whole set provides the interpretation of the missing noun, the anaphoric DWN can also be a subset of a subset of N, which is the noun phrase in the context. This is the restrictive reading. In this case the subset is properly included in another subset. Sleeman observes that the subset can also be improperly included in another subset, i.e. be equal to another subset. This happens in the case of a numeral preceded by a definite determiner:

(70) Il y a deux garçons dans ce groupe. Les deux sont très grands.
'There are two boys in this group. Both are very tall.'

Since in all cases there is the inclusion of a set into another set, the dependency relation is always established by means of the partitive interpretation of the determiner. Sleeman's claim that the feature 'partitive' is involved in the licensing of DWNs has however been criticized by Giannakidou & Stavrou (1999). They reject Sleeman's extension of the meaning of partitivity to cover the non-restrictive reading. Since DWNs are possible in the non-restrictive reading, the notion of partitivity cannot be involved, in their view.

Whereas in Corblin's analysis the dependency relation is the result of the semantic absence of the noun from the DWN, in Sleeman's analysis, *pro* is licensed by the partitive meaning of the determiner, which provides the empty noun with an interpretation so that a relation with a superset can be established. In Marandin's (1996, 1997) analysis, the relation is established because the DWN does not contain a basic lexical noun. In the case of the color adjectives and *grand* and *petit*, the adjective has been converted into a noun in the lexicon, but this predicate is not sufficiently stable to furnish an individual belonging to a species. Therefore, the predicate has to be individualized by a noun in the context. In the case of superlatives and adjectives such as *stylistique*, there is no N, because N″ immediately dominates A″ or A°. In this case the DWN is also only possible if it is in a relation with an antecedent. In Marandin's analysis, the contextual dependency is thus a lexical property of the DWN involving color adjectives and *grand* and *petit*, whereas it is a configurational property of the superlatives and adjectives such as *stylistique* in their use as DWNs. The inconvenience of Marandin's analysis is that the DWNs are split up into two classes and hence do not form a natural class.

## 6 Conclusion

We have discussed several analyses that have been proposed for French DWNs, especially those by Corblin, Sleeman, and Marandin. We have shown that in all analyses a relation has to be established with an antecedent in the context, which can be a restrictive or a non-restrictive relation. The main differences between these approaches concern the analysis of the nominal position as being empty or filled by an adjective and the establishment of the relation with the antecedent: the simple interpretation of a missing noun, which is a nominal anaphor, or the inclusion of the DWN in a superset in the context. We leave the choice of one these options or an alternative for future research.

## References

Abney, S. 1987. *The English Noun Phrase in its Sentential Aspect*. Ph.D. thesis, MIT.

Barbaud, P. 1976. Constructions superlatives et structures apparentées. *Linguistic Analysis* 2(2):125–174.

Barwise, J. and R. Cooper. 1981. Generalized quantifiers and natural language. *Linguistics and Philosophy* 4:159–219.

Chomsky, N. 1982. *Some Concepts and Consequences of the Theory of Government and Binding*. Cambridge, MA: MIT Press.

Chuquet, J. and M. Fryd, eds. 1996. *Absences de marques et représentation de l'absence*, vol. 9 of *Travaux linguistiques du CERLICO*. Presses Universitaires de Rennes.

Cinque, G. 1994. On the evidence for partial N-movement in the Romance DP. In Cinque et al. (1994), pages 85–110.

Cinque, G., J. Koster, J.-Y. Pollock, L. Rizzi, and R. Zanuttini, eds. 1994. *Paths towards Universal Grammar. Studies in Honor of Richard S. Kayne*. Washington: Georgetown University Press.

Coene, M., W. De Mulder, P. Dendale, Y. D'Hulst, and C. Vetters, eds. 1999. *Hommages à Liliane Tasmowski*. Padova: Unipress.

Corblin, F. 1990. Les groupes nominaux sans nom du français. In Kleiber and Tyvaert (1990), pages 63–80.

Corblin, F. 1995. *Les Formes de Reprise dans le Discours. Anaphores et Chaînes de Référence*. Presses Universitaires de Rennes.

Corblin, F. 1996. Groupes nominaux sans nom et partitifs. In Chuquet and Fryd (1996), pages 47–68.

Corblin, F. 1999a. Les références mentionnelles: le premier, le dernier, celui-ci. In Mettouchi and Quintin (1999), pages 107–123.

Corblin, F. 1999b. Mentional references and familiarity break. In Coene et al. (1999), pages 535–544.

Fradin, B. and J.-M. Marandin, eds. 1997. *Mots et Grammaires*. Paris: Didier Erudition.

Giannakidou, A. and M. Stavrou. 1999. Nominalization and ellipsis in the Greek DP (nominal subdeletion, substantivization). *The Linguistic Review* 16(4):295–331.

Gross, M. 1973. On grammatical reference. In Kiefer and Ruwet (1973), pages 203–217.

Kiefer, F. and N. Ruwet, eds. 1973. *Generative Grammar in Europe*. Dordrecht: Reidel.

Kleiber, G. and J.-E. Tyvaert, eds. 1990. *L'anaphore et ses Domaines, Recherches linguistiques*. Université de Metz.

Kupferman, L. 1999. Reflections on partitives: partitive nominal phrases and relativization in French. *Langue Française* 122:30–51.

Lobeck, A. 1991. Phrase structure of ellipsis in English. In Rothstein (1991), pages 81–103.

Lobeck, A. 1993. Strong agreement and identification: evidence from ellipsis in English. *Linguistics* 31:777–811.

Lobeck, A. 1995. *Functional Heads: Licensing and Identification*. Oxford University Press.

López, L. 2000. Ellipsis and discourse-linking. *Lingua* 110:183–213.

Marandin, J.-M. 1996. Une autre perspective sur la dépendance contextuelle des GN sans nom du français. In Mulder et al. (1996), pages 135–157.

Marandin, J.-M. 1997. Pas d'entité sans identité: l'analyse des groupes nominaux Det + A. In Fradin and Marandin (1997), pages 129–164.

Mettouchi, A. and H. Quintin, eds. 1999. *La Référence (2). Statut et Processus*. Travaux linguistiques du CERLICO. Presses Universitaires de Rennes.

Milner, J.-C. 1978. *De la Syntaxe à l'Interprétation*. Paris: Seuil.

Mulder, W. D., L. Tasmowski-De Rijk, and C. Vetters, eds. 1996. *Relations anaphoriques et (in)cohérence*. Amsterdam: Rodopi.

Olsen, S. 1987. Zum 'substantivierten' Adjectiv im Deutschen: Deutsch als eine pro-Drop-Sprache. *Studium Linguistik* 21:1–35.

Postal, P. 1969. On so-called 'pronouns' in English. In Reibel and Schane (1969), pages 201–224.

Reibel, D. and S. Schane, eds. 1969. *Modern Studies in English*. Prentice Hall.

Ritter, E. 1991. Two functional categories in noun phrases: evidence from modern Hebrew. In Rothstein (1991), pages 37–62.

Ronat, M., ed. 1977a. *Langue*. Paris: Hermann.

Ronat, M. 1977b. Une contrainte sur l'effacement du nom. In Ronat (1977a), pages 153–169.

Rothstein, S., ed. 1991. *Perspectives on Phrase Structure: Heads and Licensing*, vol. 25 of *Syntax and Semantics*. San Diego: Academic Press.

Sleeman, P. 1996. *Licensing Empty Nouns in French*. The Hague: Holland Academic Graphics.

Valois, D. 1990. *The Internal Syntax of DP*. Ph.D. thesis, UCLA.

3

# Towards a Uniform Characterization of Noun Phrases with *Des* or *Du*

LEONIE BOSVELD-DE SMET

## 1 Introduction

*Des* and *du* can on their own form a noun phrase (NP) when followed by a plural or mass noun (N) respectively.[1] As such, they can be treated as determiners. Their historical origin and their distributional and interpretational characteristics however give rise to ambivalent attitudes among grammarians towards their analysis and characterization. Historically, the French articles *des* and *du* derive from the preposition *de* 'of' followed by the plural and singular form of the definite article respectively (Dubois et al. 1973). *Des* is the contracted form of *de* + *les*, *du* of *de* + *le*. But in contemporary French they are used in many contexts as if they were autonomous simple determiners. Not surprisingly there is no consensus about the grammatical categorization of *des* and *du* (see Kupferman 1979 for an overview of categorial proposals; see also Wilmet 1986). Are they partitive or indefinite articles? Most grammarians hesitate, some eventually deciding to consider *des* as the plural counterpart of the indefinite singular article *un(e)* 'a' and to label *du* as 'partitive article'. As for the meaning of *des* and *du*, there is

*We wish to thank Petra Sleeman for her comments on the pre-final draft.

[1]The determiner *du* is used with a masculine N beginning with a consonant or aspirated *-h* and has as variants *de la* (used when the N is feminine) and *de l'* (used when the initial letter of the N is a vowel or a mute *-h*). The variant of *des* is *de* in NPs with prenominal adjectives. In certain negative contexts *des* and *du* (and its variants) become *de*. It is however debatable whether *de* can still be treated as a determiner in these negative contexts.

*Handbook of French Semantics.*
Francis Corblin and Henriëtte de Swart (eds.).
Copyright © 2004, CSLI Publications.

more unanimity. Grammarians usually point out that *des* and *du* have a highly indeterminate sense as to the objects or substance referred to and as to the quantity of the entities referred to.

From a modern syntactic and semantic point of view, *des* and *du*, and the NPs formed with them (henceforth *des/du*-NPs) are still intriguing. Ambivalence is still present. The original contracted form gives rise to interesting syntactic constructions, which often suggest that they should be assigned a complex syntactic structure. In semantic studies, *des* and *du*, when discussed, are often treated separately, as *des*-NPs are generally treated as plural count NPs and *du*-NPs as singular mass NPs, and count and mass domains are usually considered apart from one another. As for their semantics, one observes that they are ambiguous between an existential and a partitive reading. The existential reading is the unmarked reading, the partitive, by far less natural, reading is clearly the marked reading.

A last aspect worth mentioning is the similarity between French *des/du*-NPs and English bare terms on their existential reading. This aspect will not be discussed here (but see Bosveld-de Smet 1994, 1998, 2000, and Dobrovie-Sorin 1998).

Despite all the ambivalence surrounding *des* and *du*, in this contribution I propose a uniform characterization for *des/du*-NPs (section 2) and provide linguistic evidence for it coming from a diverse range of phenomena (section 3). The proposed characterization applies to *des/du*-NPs in written French.[2]

## 2 Uniform characterization of des/du-NPs

*Des*-NPs and *du*-NPs can be classed among the indefinite NPs because of their felicitous use in linguistic environments exhibiting a definiteness restriction (Reuland and ter Meulen 1987) (1). In numerous contexts, they can be used interchangeably with indefinite NPs such as those containing numerals (*deux* 'two'), amount terms (*dix kilos de* 'ten kilos of'), or determiner expressions such as *quelques* 'a few', *plusieurs* 'several', *beaucoup de* 'many (much)', *un peu de* 'a little' (2):

(1) a Il arrive des trains.
there arrive of-the trains

[2]This contribution does not give a complete overview of properties of *des/du*-NPs or propose a syntactic or semantic analysis of *des/du*-NPs within a specific theoretical framework. It is meant to give an impressionistic view of properties characterizing *des/du*-NPs (see Bosveld-de Smet 2000 for a more detailed description of *des/du*-NPs, Bosveld-de Smet 1998 for their semantic model-theoretic analysis as Generalized Quantifiers (i.e. as sets of sets of entities), and Dobrovie-Sorin 1997 for a semantic account where *des/du*-NPs correspond to sets of entities).

b Il est tombé de la neige.
there has fallen of-the snow

(2) a On relève des / plusieurs / beaucoup d'inconséquences
one spots of-the / several / many of inconsistencies
dans sa théorie.
in his theory

b Il faut boire de l' / un peu d' / un litre d'eau.
one should drink of-the / a little of / one litre of water

Existentiality seems to be the main property shared by all these indefinite NPs. They introduce new referents into the universe of discourse. *Des*-NPs and *du*-NPs occupy a special position within the category of indefinites in that they have many properties in common which they do not share with the other indefinites. For instance, they are the only indefinite NPs that can occur in the attributive position of sentences expressing definitions and denoting an inclusion relation (3), and they give rise quite naturally to habitual readings (4):

(3) a Les chiens sont des / *quelques / *beaucoup d'animaux.
The dogs are of-the / a few / a lot of animals

b Cette poudre est du / *une boîte de / *trop de talc.
This powder is of-the / a box of / too much of talc

(4) a Son mari écrit des romans. (e.g. for a living)
Her husband writes of-the novels

b Ce paysan cultive du maïs. (idem)
This farmer grows of-the maize

The most conspicuous differences between *des*-NPs and *du*-NPs seem to be the following: *des* requires a plural N, and *du* a singular N, without the N being necessarily a count N or a mass N respectively (5); though reluctantly, *des*-NPs, but not *du*-NPs, can take on a distributive reading (6):

(5) a des oeufs / nuages / sels / vins / gens / épinards
of-the eggs / clouds / salts / wines / people / spinach

b du sucre / coton / bruit / poulet / fil
of-the sugar / cotton / noise / chicken / thread

(6) a Des plongeurs ont été mordus par un piranha.
Of-the divers have been bitten by a piranha
(More than one piranha can be involved.)

b Du gaz s'est échappé d'un tuyau.
Of-the gas has escaped from a pipe

(There is only one pipe involved.)

When the distribution and interpretation of *des/du*-NPs are examined more carefully, one finds that many observations can be explained by some more general property. I propose to characterize the core of *des/du*-NPs by the following informally formulated properties:

(i) *des* and *du* as determiner parts of NPs bear witness to their historical origin as complex constituents consisting of the preposition *de* 'of' followed by the definite article.

(ii) NPs construed with *des* and *du* have neither intrinsic quantitative nor intrinsic identificational force.

(iii) *des/du*-NPs pertain to something unbounded.

(iv) *des/du*-NPs have no intrinsic event or thing splitting force.

## 3 Linguistic evidence

### 3.1 Historical origin

*Des* and *du* originate in Old French as complex constituents. Although they are available in Old French as introductory elements of Ns, they occur rarely in this function. Old French prefers to use bare terms (*mangier pain* 'eat bread') instead of *des* and *du* (or one of its Old French variants *del, dou*) (*mangier del pain* 'eat of-the bread'). In Middle French *des* and *du* gain ground, as a result of the weakening of the original demonstrative force of the definite article, which takes place at about the same period. When used, they mostly occur in object position, with a restricted group of verbs, and with nouns referring to substances. In contemporary French, neither *des* nor *du* is restricted to substantial nouns, and one encounters *des/du*-NPs in any possible NP position. It should however be pointed out that for quite a long time there remained a close link with the object position. Englebert (1996) observes that *des*-NPs were the first to appear in subject position.

One of the traces left by this historical evolution is the ability of *des/du*-constituents to be interpreted as NPs and as prepositional phrases (PPs). As a result, ambiguities may arise in sentences such as (7), as the verbs used here allow for an indirect and a direct complementation (cf. Kupferman 1979):

(7) a Elle a mangé des cerises.
She has eaten of-the cherries

b Il a goûté du cognac.
He has tasted of-the brandy

In (7) the *des/du*-constituents may get a PP-reading and an NP-reading.

Containing originally a definite determiner (*le(s)*), neither *des* nor *du* can combine with another definite determiner, whatever the order. In contrast, the indefinite determiners that have a so-called pronominal or adjectival form can occur with definite determiners (see 8 and 9 below).

(8) a beaucoup / certaines / trois / *des + de + ces pommes
many / certain / three / of-the of these apples

b un peu / trop / *du + de + ce fromage
a little / too much / of-the of this cheese

(9) a les + quelques / dix / *des + pages
the many / ten / of-the pages

b ce + peu d' / *de l' + argent
this little of / of-the money

Although the most natural reading of *des/du*-NPs is not the partitive reading, this reading can be imposed in very specific contexts. Galmiche (1986) points out that a sentence such as (10a) is acceptable, but only on a partitive reading and in a context where it is pragmatically inferred that forks are clean. As a result, (10a) gets the interpretation of: 'among the forks, there are some that are dirty'. (10b) is an example of Kleiber (1988), who observes that 'du maïs' can get here a partitive reading, due to the fact that maize is considered as a heterogeneous rather than a homogeneous mass. As a consequence, (10b) is interpreted as: 'some part of the maize in this field is polluted'. The partitive reading imposed by these specific contexts is possible thanks to the fact that *des/du*-NPs originated as complex partitive NPs.

(10) a Des fourchettes sont sales.
Of-the forks are dirty
(Galmiche 1986)

b Dans ce champ, du maïs est pollué.
In this field, of-the maize is polluted
(Kleiber 1988)

### 3.2 Lack of quantitative and identificational force

There is a range of observations that supports the view that *des*-NPs and *du*-NPs lack any quantitative and identificational force. For instance, the kind of modifiers these indefinite NPs can be construed with is a clear indication to what extent they are able to quantify and identify referents involved in the N-denotation. They cannot occur with adverbials such as *par jour* 'a day', *à l'heure* 'per hour', *au mètre carré* 'per square metre', *par personne* 'per person', which imply some regular distribution of things or substance over a time span, over an area, or over individuals (11). On the other hand, they do allow modification by adverbials implying some quantity (e.g. *à la douzaine* 'by dozens', *à flots* 'in profusion') (12)

(11) a *Il habite ici des personnes au mètre carré.
There live here of-the persons per square metre

b *Paul boit de la bière par jour.
Paul drinks of-the beer a day

(12) a Ces pommiers donnent des fruits à profusion.
These apple trees have of-the fruits in abundance

b Luc gagne de l'argent en quantité.
Luc earns of-the money in profusion

*Des/du*-NPs do not only fail to specify any quantity, they also offer no clue as to the identity of objects or substance parts. Specific referents never seem to be involved. Hence their perfect combination with modifiers referring to physical characteristics of entities (13):

(13) a Ici, on fabrique des vases de diverses tailles, de
Here, one manufactures of-the vases of various sizes, of
divers styles.
various styles

b Ce magasin vend du papier de toutes épaisseurs, de
This shop sells of-the paper of all thicknesses, of
toutes couleurs
all colors

Evidence of this lack of quantitative and identificational force is also found, when one examines *des/du*-NPs in focalizing contexts. In general, when focus is put on an NP, either the determiner or the N becomes the focused element. However, in focused *des/du*-NPs, the focus nearly automatically shifts to the nominal part. Focus generally does not bear on *des* nor on *du*.[3] As an example, let us consider restriction and negation. These operations go along with the focusing of the expression they bear on. There exist restrictive contexts implying focus on the determiner part rather than on the nominal part of the NP. As expected, *des/du*-NPs are incompatible with these contexts (14). On

[3]As pointed out to me by Corblin (personal communication), focus can bear on *des* in a context such as (i), implying a quantitative contrast between a single object and a plurality of these objects.

(i)— Tu as écrit un livre?
— Non, j'ai écrit des livres.

the other hand, negative contexts contrasting two different Ns clearly prefer *des/du*-NPs (15):

(14) a *Ce long discours se résume en des mots.
This long talk is summarized in of-the words

b *Il ne lui reste que du temps pour finir ce
There remains only of-the time for him to finish this
travail
job

(15) a Marie n'écrit pas des romans, mais des poèmes.
Mary doesn't write of-the novels, but of-the poems

b On ne nous sert pas du champagne, mais du
One doesn't serve us of-the champagne, but of-the
vin pétillant.
sparkling wine

Another focalizing context, viz. the cleft construction with *c'est* 'it is', stresses the lexical content of the NP rather than any other aspect of it. Consequently, *des/du*-NPs are most easily accepted in these contexts, while other indefinite NPs are less felicitous (see Léard 1992) (16):

(16) a C'est des / ??trois enfants qui attendent devant la
It is of-the / three children that are waiting at the
porte.
door

b C'est de la / ??un peu de vraie neige qui tombe
It is of-the / a little of real snow that is falling
maintenant.
now

Interpretational properties of *des/du*-NPs do not run counter to but rather reinforce the picture just sketched. There is a general strong intuition that sentences such as (17a) should get paraphrases such as (17b) (see Attal 1976, Galmiche 1986). This intuition also pertains to the mass case (18). These paraphrases are possible, as no specific referents are involved.

(17) a Des étudiants ont manifesté.
Of-the students have demonstrated
(Attal 1976)

b Il y a eu une manifestation d'étudiants.
There has been a demonstration of students

(18) a De l'eau s'est évaporée.
Of-the water has evaporated

b Il y a eu une évaporation d'eau.
There has been an evaporation of water

The weak specifying force of *des/du*-NPs with respect to quantification and identification has other repercussions on the interpretational level. One of these shows up when interpretations of *des/du*-NPs are considered with respect to scope. One observes that *des/du*-NPs barely give rise to scope ambiguities. All NPs are often taken to correspond semantically to (logical) quantifiers. An argument in favor of this view is their scope behavior. Most NPs can indeed be shown to enter different scope relations with other scoped elements in sentences such as in (19):

(19) a Tous les Français lisent deux journaux.
All the Frenchmen read two newspapers
(Galmiche 1977)
(Either two specific newspapers are read by all Frenchmen, or all Frenchmen read two newspapers that are not necessarily the same.)

b Luc veut inviter plusieurs basketteurs.
Luc wants to invite several basketball players
(Either specific individuals, or a group of arbitrary basketball players are hinted at.)

With respect to scope, *des/du*-NPs do not exhibit a quantifier-like behavior. The preferred reading in sentences such as (20) is the narrow scope reading.

(20) a Des voyous ont volé deux bicyclettes.
Of-the naughty boys have stolen two bicycles
(No more than two bicycles are involved in the robbery)

b Il y avait de la visite tous les jours.
There were of-the people each day
(Each day there are visitors, but not necessarily the same visitors)

### 3.3 Unboundedness

In this subsection, I discuss three consequences of the inherently unbounded character of *des/du*-NPs. First, the distribution of these indefinite NPs in the subject position of various types of sentences shows that their felicitous occurrence as subjects is highly dependent on the availability of spatio-temporal boundaries. In Modern French, one encounters *des/du*-NPs in any possible NP position in a sentence. Yet, in certain positions, their use is limited due to contextual factors. The semantics of the predicate turns out to have an important constraining effect. This is especially true of the subject position. It is a well-known fact that individual-level predicates (i.e. predicates denoting permanent properties, see Carlson 1978) do not easily accept *des/du*-NPs as their subjects (21).[4] There are however also stage-level predicates (i.e. predicates denoting transitory properties) that constrain their acceptability as subjects. These are the stage-level predicates that denote a temporary state and moreover are non-specifying, that is, they do not provide any spatial and/or temporal anchoring (for the specifying/non-specifying contrast see Kleiber 1981). Although non-specifying stage-level predicates on their own do not accept *des/du*-subjects, the combination of the two becomes felicitous, when spatio-temporal information is added to the sentence. To see this compare the sentences in (22) with those in (23):

(21) a * Des enfants sont très observateurs.
Of-the children are very observant
(individual-level)

b * Du caoutchouc est élastique.
Of-the rubber is elastic
(idem)

(22) a * Des pas sont visibles.
Of-the steps are visible
(non-specifying stage-level)

b * Du linge séchait.
Of-the laundry was drying
(idem)

(23) a Des pas sont visibles sur la neige.
Of-the steps are visible in the snow
(specifying stage-level)

b Du linge séchait dans la salle de bains.
Of-the laundry was drying in the bathroom
(idem)

*Des/du*-NPs are most at ease as subjects of event-denoting predicates. Spatio-temporal boundaries are then constituted by the reported events (24). It comes as no surprise that *des/du*-NPs are not acceptable as existential subjects of sentences that negate an event (25) (cf. Attal

[4] According to some linguists, sentences such as (21a) are correct in French (see e.g. Corblin, 1987).

1976):[5]

(24) a Des bateaux entrent dans le port.
Of-the ships enter the harbour
(reported event)

b Du sang suintait de sa blessure.
Of-the blood seeped from his wound
(idem)

(25) a *Des ouvriers n'ont pas fait la grève.
Of-the workers didn't go on strike
(negated event)

b *Du vin ne s'est pas dispersé sur la nappe blanche.
Of-the wine wasn't spilt on the white tablecloth
(idem)

Spatio-temporal boundaries allow *des/du*-NPs, which, by themselves, refer to something unbounded, to become bounded and get an existential reading in (23) and (24) above.

Secondly, unboundedness allows *des/du*-NPs to get so-called dependent readings. A well-known example from Chomsky (see 26) illustrates what is meant by a dependent reading:

(26) Unicycles have wheels.

We know by the lexical meaning of *unicycle* that these vehicles have only one wheel. Yet, the object NP is plural, and this is so because the subject NP is plural. So the bare plural term *wheels* is to be taken as a dependent plural. It ranges over all wheels of all unicycles. Likewise *des*-NPs and *du*-NPs are most naturally interpreted as dependent NPs in sentences such as (27):

(27) a Ici, les hommes portent des bérets basques.
Here, the men wear of-the berets.

b Les hockeyeurs portent des jambières.
The hockey-players wear of-the pads

c Les épinards contiennent du fer.
The spinach contains of-the iron

d Les betteraves sucrières fournissent du sucre.
The sugar beets provide for of-the sugar.

[5](25a) is acceptable on a partitive reading. (25a) can indeed get the meaning of (i).

(i)Parmi les ouvriers, il y en a qui n'ont pas fait la grève.

Among the workers, there are some who didn't go on strike.

Finally, it is not only from a referential point of view, but also from an aspectual one, that *des/du*-NPs can be claimed to be unbounded. On the aspectual level, this is demonstrated by the fact that they cannot occur with *en*-adverbials, which require bounded NPs, while they are compatible with *pendant*-adverbials (28):

(28) a L'enfant a fait des dessins * en une heure /
The child has made of-the drawings in an hour /
pendant des heures.
for hours

b Du gaz s'est échappé du tuyau * en une heure /
Of-the gas has escaped from the pipe in an hour /
pendant des heures.
for hours

Adjunction of these two kinds of temporal adverbials constitutes the test for the discrimination between terminative and durative sentences (see Verkuyl 1993 among others). Obviously, sentences containing *des/du*-NPs have a durative aspect.

### 3.4 Inherent inability to split up events or things

When occurring in evenemential sentences, plural and mass NPs generally give rise to neutral readings, which means that these sentences are undetermined as to the exact involvement of the relevant referents in the predication (see Verkuyl and van der Does 1996). *Des/du*-NPs give rise to a similar indeterminacy. Consider for example (29):

(29) a Des amis sont venus me voir, lorsque j'étais malade.
Of-the friends came to visit me, when I was ill.

b Après l'explosion, de la vapeur s'est échappée de la
After the explosion, of-the steam has escaped from the
chaudière.
boiler

(29a) doesn't make clear whether friends came to see me individually, as a group, or in subgroups. Similarly (29b) leaves implicit how the whole steam substance involved is partitioned into steam parts such that these parts are just those that escaped from the boiler at certain time intervals. However, without any contextual or pragmatic clues being present, *des/du*-NPs do not easily bring about any event or thing splitting, and consequently total (one event), collective and cumulative readings, where subject and object remain outside each other's scope, are the preferred readings of sentences with *des/du*-NPs (see 30, 31, and 32 respectively):

(30) a Des soldats entraient.
Of-the soldiers came in
(one event)

b De la boue éclaboussait ses bottes.
Of-the mud spattered on his boots
(one event)

(31) a Des voyous ont cassé une vitre.
Of-the naughty boys have broken one window
(No more than one window has been broken)

b De l' acide a rongé une boîte en métal.
Of-the acid has corroded a metal box
(No more than one box has been corroded)

(32) a Des maraudeurs ont cueilli des fruits mûrs.
Of-the marauders have picked of-the ripe fruits
(There is a group of marauders picking fruits and there is a collection of fruits picked by marauders)

b De l' eau a dissout du savon.
Of-the water has dissolved of-the soap
(There is a portion of water dissolving soap and there is a portion of soap dissolved by water)

When there are no clear partitioning clues available in the sentence, *des/du*-NPs trigger a totalizing rather than a partitioning predication (for the concept of totalizing predication, see Verkuyl 1994).

Although by themselves *des/du*-NPs cannot bring about event or thing splitting, they allow contextual elements and pragmatic factors to do so. This is for instance the reason why distributive readings can be obtained for sentences such as (6a) above and (33) below:

(33) a Des enfants mangeaient une tartine.
Of-the children ate a bread
(each child ate his own bread; eating is considered an individual activity)

b Des filles se peignaient les cheveux devant la
Of-the girls combed their hairs in front of the
glace.
mirror
(both the reciprocal and the reflexive readings are possible)

## 4 Conclusion

Despite all the ambivalence contained in *des/du*-NPs (count-mass contrast; plural-singular contrast; indefinite existential-partitive contrast; NP-PP contrast), I have shown that a uniform characterization of *des*-NPs, which are plural NPs, and *du*-NPs, which are mass NPs, is possible and moreover validated by the numerous specific properties they have in common with each other on the distributional as well as on the interpretational level. I have proposed that the behavior of *des/du*-NPs is captured by four general properties. The uniform characterization proposed helps us get a better understanding of the functioning of *des* and *du* as determiners, and it helps us gain more insight into the elements playing a role in the functioning of determiners in general. It also gives rise to further questions. One of the questions raised by the characterization is the extent to which the proposed properties are related to each other. For instance, one could imagine that there is a link between the lack of quantitative and identificational force and the unbounded character of *des/du*-NPs.

## References

Attal, P. 1976. à propos de l'indéfini "des" : problèmes de représentation sémantique. *Le Français Moderne* 2:126–42.

Bosveld-de Smet, L. 1994. On objects in habitual sentences. In De Boer et al. (1994), pages 27–40.

Bosveld-de Smet, L. 1998. *On Mass and Plural Quantification. The case of French des/du-NPs*. Ph.D. thesis, University of Groningen.

Bosveld-de Smet, L. 2000. Les syntagmes nominaux en "des" et "du". In Bosveld-de Smet et al. (2000), pages 17–116.

Bosveld-de Smet, L., M. van Peteghem, and D. van de Velde, eds. 2000. *De l'indétermination à la qualification. Les indéfinis*. Arras: Artois Presses Université.

Carlson, G. 1978. *Reference to Kinds in English*. New York: Garland.

Corblin, F. 1987. *Indéfini, défini et démonstratif. Constructions linguistiques de la référence*. Genève: Droz.

David, J. and G. Kleiber, eds. 1986. *Déterminants: syntaxe et sémantique*. Paris: Klincksieck.

David, J. and G. Kleiber, eds. 1988. *Termes massifs et termes comptables*. Paris: Klincksieck.

De Boer, A., H. de Hoop, and H. de Swart, eds. 1994. *Language and Cognition*, vol. 4. Groningen: Repro Faculty of Arts, University of Groningen.

Dobrovie-Sorin, C. 1998. Types of predicates and the representation of existential readings. In Lawson (1998).

Dubois, J. e. a. 1973. *Dictionnaire de linguistique*. Paris: Librairie Larousse.

Englebert, A. 1996. L'article partitif: l'évolution des conditions d'emploi. *Langue Française* 109:9–28.

Galmiche, M. 1977. Quantificateurs, référence et théorie transformationnelle. *Langages* 48:3–49.

Galmiche, M. 1986. Référence indéfinie, événements, propriétés et pertinence. In David and Kleiber (1986), pages 41–71.

Kanazawa, M. and C. Piñón, eds. 1994. *Dynamics, Polarity and Quantification*. Stanford: CSLI Publications.

Kleiber, G. 1981. Relatives spécifiantes et relatives non-spécifiantes. *Le Français Moderne* 49:216–33.

Kleiber, G. 1988. L'opposition "massif / comptable" et les adjectifs. In David and Kleiber (1988), pages 267–92.

Kupferman, L. 1979. L'article partitif existe-t-il? *Le Français Moderne* 47, 1:1–16.

Lawson, A., ed. 1998. *Proceedings of SALT April 1997*, Stanford. Cornell University Press.

Léard, J.-M. 1992. *Les gallicismes: étude syntaxique et sémantique*. Paris / Louvain-la-Neuve: Éditions Duculot.

Milner, J.-C. 1978. *De la syntaxe à l'interprétation: quantités, insultes, exclamations*. Paris: Seuil.

Reuland, E. and A. ter Meulen, eds. 1987. *The Representation of (In)definiteness*, Cambridge / London. MIT Press.

Van der Does, J. and J. van Eijck, eds. 1996. *Quantifiers, Logic, and Language*. Stanford: CSLI Publications.

Verkuyl, H. 1993. *A Theory of Aspectuality*. Cambridge: Cambridge University Press.

Verkuyl, H. 1994. Distributivity and collectivity: a couple at odds. In Kanazawa and Piñón (1994), pages 49–80.

Verkuyl, H. and J. van der Does. 1996. The semantics of plural noun phrases. In Van der Does and van Eijck (1996), pages 337–74.

Wilmet, M. 1986. *La détermination nominale: quantification et caractérisation*. Paris: Presses Universitaires de France.

# 4

# Generic Plural Indefinites and (In)direct Binding*

CARMEN DOBROVIE-SORIN

Theoreticians of genericity agree that the generic reading of indefinite expressions is dependent on the genericity of the sentence: the indefinite contributes a variable (see DRT-type analyses) that gets bound by an overt or covert adverb of quantification (Q-adverb, henceforth). According to Lewis (1975), Kamp (1981), Heim (1982), adverbs of quantification are *unselective*: they bind all free variables in their domain. The unselective binding hypothesis is confronted with various empirical and conceptual problems, which have led to the view that Q-adverbs are to be analyzed uniformly as *selective* quantifiers over events or situations[1] (Rooth (1985, 1995), Schubert and Pelletier (1987, 1988), de Swart (1991, 1996), Krifka and alii (1995), Krifka (1995), etc.). Those configurations in which Q-adverbs seem to bind (one or more) individual variables would constitute a side-effect of quantification over events: quantifying over events induces quantifying over the tuple of participants to the event. Given this analysis of Q-adverbs, a generically-interpreted indefinite (generic indefinite, henceforth) is *indirectly bound* by a Q-adverb that quantifies over events.

In this contribution, I diverge from the above-mentioned authors in

*I would like to thank Claire Beyssade, Patricia Cabredo-Hofherr, Patrick Caudal, Francis Corblin and Benjamin Spector for their remarks on previous versions of this paper.

[1]Although event-based and situation-based accounts are technically different, in many particular cases they coincide in empirical coverage. In this paper I will use an event-based notation.

*Handbook of French Semantics.*
Francis Corblin and Henriëtte de Swart (eds.).
Copyright © 2004, CSLI Publications.

assuming that Q-adverbs may directly quantify not only over events, but also over individuals. The distinction between the two possibilities will prove to be crucial for the analysis of the generic readings of plural indefinites headed by *des* in French. I show that those *des*-indefinites that are *directly* bound by a Q-adverb can only express generalizations over groups of individuals. *Indirectly* bound plural indefinites, on the other hand, allow for number neutralization.

## 1 Generic indefinites: quantification over events and over individuals

According to the current view, stemming from Heim (1982), the generic reading of indefinites comes about when the variable supplied by an indefinite occurs in the restriction of a Q-adverb. For illustration, consider the example in (1). In line with the event-based approaches mentioned above, I will assume that this type of example relies on adverbial quantification over events. The variable supplied by the indefinite is not bound by the Q-adverb (the universal quantifier corresponds to *toujours* 'always'), but rather by an existential quantifier (de Swart (1996)):[2]

(1) a. Quand Jean invite une amie, il lui prépare toujours à dîner.
'When John invites a friend, he always cooks dinner for her.'

b. $\forall_e$ [[$\exists_x$ invite (e, John, x) $\wedge$ friend (x, John)] $\rightarrow$ [$\exists_x$ invite (e, John, x) $\wedge$ friend (x, John) cook-for (e, John, x)]]

The intuitive reading associated to this representation says that all events of John inviting some friend are events in which John cooks for that friend.[3]

Let us now consider an example such as (2a):

(2) a. Un chien est en général intelligent.
'A dog is usually intelligent.'

Quite clearly, the intuitive interpretation is that the Q-adverb quantifies over dogs. The most straightforward representation corresponding to this reading is the one in (2b):

(2) b. usually (dog (x)) [x is intelligent]

[2]De Swart (1996:176–178) uses dynamic existential quantifiers (Groenendijk and Stokhof (1991, 1992)) and dynamic generalized quantifiers (Chierchia (1995a)). Since this refinement is not needed here, I use the output of de Swart's derivations, which contains static existential quantifiers.

[3]This is a somewhat simplified analysis: the two sets of events should be treated as overlapping, rather than as identical events (see de Swart (1991)).

LFs such as (2b) rely on the hypothesis that Q-adverbs may quantify not only over events, as in (1), but also over individuals.[4] The difference between the two representations in (1b) and (2b) is due to a difference in the mapping rules between overt syntax and LF:[5]

(3) *If/when*-clauses go to the restriction of Q-adverbs (Lewis (1975), Heim (1982), etc.)

(4) Subjects of generic predicates (i.e., lexically i-level or habitual) that function as Topics go to the restriction of Q-adverbs.[6]

Which of these rules applies to a given example is entirely dependent on its overt syntax (including information structure). The domain of quantification of the Q-adverb is *read off* these representations: since propositions denote sets of events, the LF in (1b) corresponds to quantification over events; since nominal predicates denote sets of individuals, the LF in (2b) corresponds to quantification over individuals. Given this difference, it is possible to distinguish between two types of generic (readings for) indefinites.

(5) a. An indefinite takes a truly generic reading iff it is directly bound by a Q-adverb.
  b. An indefinite takes a pseudo-generic reading iff it is indirectly bound by a Q-adverb that quantifies over events.

## 2 Truly generic plural indefinites

It is a well-known fact that the generic reading of plural indefinites in French is subject to fairly strict constraints, which may vary slightly depending on the type of plural determiner. I will concentrate here on cardinal and *des*-indefinites,[7] leaving aside other plural determiners such as *plusieurs, certains*, 'several, some' etc. (for an insightful description of the basic data, see Corblin (1987), from whom I borrow most of the examples below).

[4]Event-based approaches assume instead that Q-adverbs can quantify *only* over events or situations (Rooth (1985, 1995), Schubert and Pelletier (1987, 1988), de Swart (1991, 1996), Krifka and alii (1995), Krifka (1995), etc.).

[5]Other mapping rules are needed for other types of sentences.

[6]This principle is inspired by, yet distinct from Diesing's (1992) Mapping Principle. Unlike Diesing, I do not think that the Mapping Principle is sensitive to a difference in syntactic positions (such as (Spec, IP) vs VP-internal subject position), but rather to (i) a lexical distinction between classes of predicates and (ii) information structure. Further refinement is needed, which can be ignored for our present purposes.

[7]Cardinal numerals and *des* can be grouped together insofar as they are "weak" determiners in the sense of Milsark (1977): in their unmarked use, they are not relational/proportional determiners, but rather intersective and symmetric.

## 2.1 Generic plural indefinites cannot express generalizations over atomic individuals

Corblin (1987:57–58) observes that generic *cardinal* indefinites cannot express generalizations over atomic individuals : “Il n’existe pas d’interprétation générique distributive stricte des indéfinis nombrés.” (There is no strictly distributive generic reading for cardinal indefinites). Corblin’s (1987: 57–58) explanation relies on a pragmatic principle that basically says that examples of the type in (6b) *can* be assigned (representations corresponding to) generic readings, but such readings are blocked (or neutralized, in Corblin’s terminology) because they can be expressed in a more direct way, by using the corresponding example constructed with a singular indefinite (see (6a):

(6) a. Une tortue vit longtemps.
‘A turtle has a long life-span’

b. *Deux/trois ... tortues vivent longtemps.
‘Two/three ... turtles have a long life-span’

The same principle would account for similar restrictions shown by *des*-indefinites.[8] Examples such as (7b) would be blocked by (7a), constructed with a singular indefinite:

(7) a. Un carré a quatre côtés.
‘A square has four sides’

b. *Des carrés ont quatre côtés.
‘**Des** squares have four sides’

Further examples of the same type are given below:

(8) *Overt Q-adverb*

a. *Des enfants marchent rarement avant 10 mois.
‘**des** children rarely walk before the age of 10 months.

b. *Des Indiens meurent en général jeunes.
‘**des** Indians usually die young.’

(9) *Default GEN operator*

a. *Des chats sont intelligents.
‘**des** cats are intelligent.’

b. Des Roumains parlent français.
‘**des** Rumanians speak French.’

[8]Corblin (1987) notes that strictly distributive readings (i.e., generalizations over atomic individuals) are marginally possible with *des*-indefinites. This issue is examined in Section 3.4. below. For the moment, I concentrate on those examples that are incompatible with strictly distributive readings.

## 2.2 Analysis

In what follows, I argue that the unacceptability of examples such as (6)b and (7)b is not due to pragmatic principles, but rather to formal constraints on LF representations. I develop Dobrovie-Sorin and Laca's (1998) proposal that the corresponding LF representations are ill-formed because of an incompatibility between the *plurality* of the indefinite and the selectional properties of the main predicates. Since the indefinites are plural, they supply group-variables, but this conflicts with the main predicates, which select atomic individuals. More precisely, the LFs in (7′) and (9′) are illegitimate (as indicated by $\neq$) because the variables in the restriction and in the nuclear scope range over different sorts of entities (groups and atomic individuals), and as such cannot be bound by the same operator:

(7) c $\neq$ GEN X (X is a group of squares) [x has four sides]

(9) c. $\neq$ GEN X (X is a group of cats) [x is intelligent]

d. $\neq$ GEN X (X is a group of Rumanians) [x speaks French][9]

Restated within the relational analysis of quantifiers, the problem is that the two sets that need to be related by GEN are not of the same sort: the set corresponding to the restriction is a set of groups, whereas the set corresponding to the nuclear scope is a set of atomic individuals.

## 2.3 Generic plural indefinites express generalizations over groups of individuals

The analysis proposed here correctly predicts that generic plural indefinites can combine with i-level predicates that select *groups* (denote sets of groups of individuals[10]

(10) a. Deux/des droites convergentes ont un point en commun.
'Two/**des** convergent lines have a point in common.'

b. Deux/des pays limitrophes ont souvent des rapports difficiles.
'Two/**des** neighboring countries frequently have difficult relations'.

[9]This LF can be obtained via the mapping rule in (4) if we assume that *speak English* is a habitual predicate obtained by applying a unary operator to the corresponding s-level predicate (Carlson (1977), Dobrovie-Sorin (2002)).

[10]The versions of (10a-c) constructed with *deux* are borrowed from Corblin (1987). I have added the examples with *des*-indefinites. For reasons that I will not examine here, the generic readings of *des*-indefinites are less acceptable than those of cardinal indefinites. The grammaticality judgments indicated for *des*-indefinites should be read as follows: starred examples are not acceptable for any French speaker, whereas non-starred examples are acceptable for at least some speakers.

c. Deux/de vrais jumeaux se ressemblent dans les plus petits détails.
'Two/**de** true twins look alike down to the smallest details'.

d. Deux/des amis intimes se critiquent toujours.
'Two/**des** intimate friends always criticize each other'

These examples are acceptable, because the variables in the restriction and in the nuclear scope both range over groups (or pairs, depending on whether the indefinite is headed by *des* or by *deux*):

(10) a′. $\text{GEN}_X$ (X is a pair/group of convergent lines) [X has a point in common][11]

b′. $\text{Most}_X$ (X is a pair/group of neighboring countries) [X have difficult relations]

c′. $\text{GEN}_X$ (X is a pair of true twins) [X look alike in the smallest details]

These LFs rely on quantification over groups of individuals, which corresponds to the intuitive interpretation (generalization over groups of individuals).

### 2.4 Generic *des*-indefinites versus English bare plural

The French data examined above shed serious doubt on the predominant analysis of English, according to which generic bare plurals are plural *indefinites* bound by the GEN operator. If English generic bare plurals were to be analyzed as plural indefinites of unspecified cardinality, they should behave on a par with French *des*-indefinites and the examples corresponding to (8) and (9) should be ungrammatical, contrary to fact:[12]

(11) *Overt Q-adverbs*

a. Children rarely walk before the age of 10 months.

b. Indians usually die young.

[11]Mathematically speaking, a group of convergent lines does not necessarily have one point in common. This problem can be solved by assuming that in the unmarked case, *des droites convergentes* denotes a set of groups of lines such that each line belonging to a group is convergent with all the other lines of the group.

[12]Because she endorses the current analysis of the English examples in (11)–(12), de Swart (1993, 1996) suggests that the limitations shown by French *des*-indefinites are due to supplementary restrictions linked to the fact that *des/du* goes back to a partitivity marker, which would be incompatible with the quasi-universal, generic interpretation. Partitivity is often invoked in connection with the generic reading of *des*. But insofar as this notion is indeed relevant, it holds in exactly the same way for *indefinite* bare plurals (see Longobardi (2002) on the generic reading of Italian bare plurals). In other words, *des*-indefinites are partitive compared to definite plural, but this is a general property of indefinites, not of *des* in particular.

(12) *Default GEN operator*
  a. Cats are intelligent.
  b. Rumanian students speak French.

Given the ungrammaticality of the plural indefinite subjects in the French examples in (8)–(9), the English bare plurals in (11)–(12) cannot be analyzed as plural indefinites. We may instead assume that they function as names of kinds (as first proposed by Carlson (1977a,b)). This means that the French counterparts of (11)–(12) are not the examples in (8)–(9), but rather those in (13)–(14), with definite plural subjects (see Dobrovie-Sorin and Laca (1996, 1998)

(13) a. Les enfants marchent rarement avant 10 mois.
  b. Les Indiens meurent en général jeunes.

(14) a. Les chats sont intelligents.
  b. Les étudiants roumains parlent français.

One may now wonder why these examples, unlike those constructed with plural indefinites (see (8)–(9)), *can* be interpreted distributively, as expressing generalizations that hold of atomic individuals. To answer this question, recall that plural definites are currently analyzed as supplying a constant term that denotes the maximal group of atomic individuals that have the property denoted by the corresponding singular noun. When occurring in the restriction of a Q-adverb, a constant denoting a group of individuals is shifted to denote the set of individuals belonging to that group:

(13) a′. FEW x ( x belongs to (the) children) [x walks before the age of 10 months].
  b′. GEN x (x belongs to (the) Indians)) [x dies young]

This type of LF representation cannot be assigned to plural *indefinites*, because such expressions supply a variable and a predicate that restricts the range of that variable; and since the nominal predicate is plural, the range of the variable must be a set of *plural* individuals (groups). As a consequence, generic plural indefinites can only express generalizations over groups.

## 3 Pseudo-generic plural indefinites

### 3.1 Plural indefinites that cannot be directly bound by a Q-adverb

Consider now the examples in (15):

(15) a. Deux/des hommes grands attirent toujours l'attention.
  'Two/**des** tall men always attract attention.'

b. Trois/des hommes forts peuvent soulever un piano.
'Three/**des** strong men can lift a piano.'

c. Deux/des pipelettes ne se supportent pas longtemps.
'Two/**des** chatterboxes won't stand each other for a long time.'

d. Deux/des enfants en bas âge donnent toujours beaucoup de travail'.
'Two/**des** small children are always a lot of work.'

e. Trois/des petites filles sont toujours en train de te préparer une surprise.
'Three/**des** small girls are always up to mischief.'

Examples of this type can be represented as relying on (direct) quantification over (groups of) individuals provided that the s-level predicate is analyzed as a habitual or dispositional predicate:

(15) a′. $\forall_X$ (tall men (X) $\wedge$ $|X| \geq$ two)) [$\mathbf{HAB}_i$ [X attract attention at $t_i$]]

These representations contain two distinct operators: the universal quantifier (corresponding to *toujours* 'always') and a silent *unary operator*[13], HAB, which functions as a frequency adverb (it applies to an episodic eventuality and returns a habitual eventuality). The reading associated with this representation can be paraphrased as follows: all groups of two tall men are such that they have the habit of attracting attention. This interpretation does not correspond to the intuitive reading: the example in (15)a does not say that all groups of tall men have a certain habit, or characteristic behavior, but rather that all events/situations in which (two) tall men happen to be together, are such that attention is attracted. We are thus led to conclude that the examples in (15) do not rely on direct quantification over (groups of) individuals.

### 3.2 Plural indefinites that are indirectly bound by a Q-adverb that quantifies over events

The examples in (15) can instead be represented as relying on quantification over events, combined with the indirect binding of the variable supplied by the indefinite. (The representations corresponding to the *des*-versions lack the restrictions concerning the cardinality of the group)

[13]For the idea that Q-adverbs can be either binary or unary, see de Swart (1991). Note, however, that according to de Swart, habitual predication does not rely on a unary frequency adverb, but rather on a binary operator that quantifies over events. My view is in line with Carlson (1977a,b) insofar as the operator that is responsible for the habitual use of s-level predicates is unary.

(15) a″. $\forall_e$ [[∃x be together (e, X,) ∧ tall men (X) ∧ |X| ≥2] →
[∃x be together (e,X) ∧ tall men (X) ∧ |X|≥2
∧ attract att (e, X)]]

b″. $\text{Gen}_e$[[∃x attempt to lift... (e,X) ∧ strong men (X) ∧ |X|≥ 3] →
[x attempt to lift... (e,X) ∧ strong men (X) ∧ |X| ≥ 3
∧ can lift a piano (e,X) ]

The interpretations that are read off the LFs in (15″) can be paraphrased as: 'all events of two-tall-men-being-together are events of attracting attention', 'in general, an attempt of lifting a piano by three strong men is successful'. These readings correspond to the intuitive interpretations.

The representation in (15″a), as well as those corresponding to (15c) and (15e) (which are not given here, for lack of space), can be obtained by assuming that cardinal and *des*-indefinites supply a predicate of events paraphrasable as 'be together'. In some other cases, the restriction of the Q-adverb is filled with the presupposition of the overall clause (Schubert and Pelletier (1987, 1988) *can lift a piano* presupposes *attempt to lift a piano* (see (15b)); *give a lot of work* presupposes *be taken care of* (see (15d)). There is yet another type of example that systematically gives rise to quantification over events:

(16) a. Des lions blessés sont vulnérables.
'**des** lions injured are vulnerable'

b. Des enfants malades sont grincheux.
'**des** children ill are irritable'

As observed by Heyd (2002), these examples are constructed with *des*-indefinites modified by predicates that can function as sentential predicates. Such predicates can provide the restriction of a quantifier over events:[14]

(16) a′. GEN e [[∃x injured (e,x) ∧ x is lions] →
[∃x injured (e,x) ∧ x is lions ∧ vulnerable (e,x)]

b′. GEN e [[∃x ill (e,x) ∧ x is children] →
[∃x ill (e,x) ∧ x is children ∧ irritable (e,x)]]

[14]The analysis sketched here and the one proposed by Heyd (2002) are alike insofar as nominal modifiers that can function as sentential predicates are analyzed as supplying the restrictive term of a generalization over events. The two proposals differ, however, regarding the existence of truly generic indefinites. Heyd (2002) follows the current view (see in particular Chierchia (1995a,b)) that Q-adverbs can only quantify over events, whereas I assume that Q-adverbs may also quantify over individuals, hence the existence of truly generic indefinites.

### 3.3 Comparing adverbial quantification over events and over groups of individuals

We may now wonder why quantification over (groups of) individuals is blocked in examples of the type in (15), but allowed in examples of the type in (10), repeated under (17):

(17) a. Deux/des droites convergentes ont un point en commun.
'Two/**des** convergent lines have a point in common.'

b. Deux/des pays limitrophes ont souvent des rapports difficiles.
'Two/**des** neighboring countries frequently have difficult relations.'

c. Deux/de vrais jumeaux se ressemblent dans les plus petits détails.
'Two/**de** true twins look alike down to the smallest details.'

d. Deux/des amis intimes se critiquent toujours.
'Two/**des** intimate friends always criticize each other.'

Since most of the predicates in (17) are i-level, while those in (15) are s-level, one possible hypothesis could be that quantification over individuals is allowed only if the main predicate is i-level. But this hypothesis cannot be correct, since most s-level predicates can be shifted to a corresponding habitual or dispositional predicate, and such predicates allow direct quantification over individuals. And indeed, among the examples in (17), we find an example, the one in (17)d, which shows that habitual sentences are compatible with direct generic quantification over (groups of) individuals.

(17) d′. $\text{GEN}_X$ (two intimate friends (X)) [X always$_i$ criticize each other at $t_i$]

There are two other differences between (17) and (15). First, the predicates in (17) necessarily select groups, whereas those in (15) can be saturated by either groups or atomic individuals. Secondly, the examples in (17) contain *relational* nouns, which denote sets of (stable) *pairs of individuals*: convergent lines, neighboring countries, twins, etc. Compare nouns such as *cook, strong man* or *chatterbox*, which denote sets of (stable) *individuals*: several cooks, strong men or chatterboxes can be defined as groups only because at some point in time they participate together in the same *episodic* event, occur in the same situation, or simply occupy the same space-time localization: in (15a), *three tall men* corresponds to "whenever three tall men are seen together", "in any situation in which three tall men are seen together"; in (15b), *three strong men* means something like "three strong men that attempt to lift a piano"; in (15c), *two chatterboxes* means two chatterboxes talking to each other. The impossibility of directly quantifying over groups of cooks, strong men, etc., can be analyzed as being due to the fact that such groups are not stable in time. Relational nouns, on the other hand, denote sets of stable pairs of individuals, and as such can be quantified over.

**Summary**

(i) In the unmarked case, plural indefinites are *indirectly* bound (they are "pseudo-generic" rather than "truly" generic): the default GEN operator (or an overt Q-adverb) quantifies over events or situations and indirectly over groups of individuals (the variable supplied by the indefinite is bound by existential closure). In other words, *two strong men* means "whenever two strong men are together" or "for any situation that contains two strong men".

(ii) Plural indefinites can be *directly* bound by a Q-adverb only if (i) the nominal predicate is a relational noun, which denotes a stable set of pairs of individuals (e.g., *twins* means "a pair of two people who are twins") and (ii) the main predicate selects a group-denoting subject.

### 3.4 Indirect binding and distributivity

Corblin (1987) observes that strictly distributive readings (i.e., generalizations over atomic individuals) are marginally possible with *des*-indefinites (although not with cardinals):[15]

(18) a. Des élèves ne peuvent pas travailler dans ce genre de salle.[16]
 '**Des**-students cannot work in this room.'

 b. Des jeunes filles doivent se montrer discrètes.
 '**Des** young women must behave discretely behavior.'

These examples are somewhat complex insofar as they contain modal verbs (see Section 3.5. below). Let us first concentrate on more neutral examples that illustrate the same observation:

[15] The difference between cardinals and *des*-indefinites is intuitively clear: because cardinals refer to a specific number, they cannot give rise to number neutralization.

[16] Corblin (1987: 73) also gives examples such as those in (i)–(iii):

(i) Des tortues vivent longtemps.
 '**des** turtles live a long time (turtles have a long life span)'

(ii) Des vaches ont un estomac énorme
 '**des** cows have an enormous stomach'

(iii) Des arbres ont besoin d'eau pour vivre
 '**des** trees need water in order to survive'

Most of my informants reject these examples; some informants marginally accept them only if *des* is interpreted as meaning 'some' or 'certain'.

(19) a. Méfie-toi, des guêpes énervées sont un danger terrible.
'Take care, excited wasps are a terrible danger.'

b. Des éléphants blancs se promenant dans la rue ont toujours/parfois suscité une très vive curiosité.
'White elephants strolling in the street have always/sometimes aroused intense curiosity.'

(Example (19b) is adapted from an Italian example due to Longobardi (2002).)[17]

The sentence in (19a) may be interpreted as a warning against groups of excited wasps, but also against a single wasp. In (19b), the curiosity may have been induced not only by groups of elephants strolling in the street, but also by a single elephant.

The existence of examples of this type immediately raises the following question: how can we distinguish between those generic sentences that allow strictly distributive readings for *des*-indefinites, and those that do not? Corblin (1987: 75–76) suggests that in the unmarked case, *des*-indefinites are number-neutral, and as such are compatible with strictly distributive readings. Number neutralization would be blocked in a fairly circumscribed environment: when the main verb denotes a property that "notoriously characterizes each member of a given class of individuals".[18] This characterization cannot help us understand the unacceptability of examples such as (8)–(9): they are constructed with predicates that cannot be viewed as defining properties of the individuals they are predicated of, and yet they block strictly distributive readings.

I have proposed above that truly generic *des*-indefinites, i.e., those *des*-indefinites that are directly quantified over, are not number-neutral: they can only express generalizations over groups. Below, I argue that number-neutralization is allowed in those examples that rely on quantification over events.

Given the results obtained in Section 3.3. above, examples of the type in (19) cannot be analyzed as relying on selective quantification over groups of individuals (because the nominal predicate of the indefinite is not relational), but may be assumed to rely on adverbial quantification

[17]Longobardi's (2002) analysis of generic indefinites is quite different from mine (for discussion see Dobrovie-Sorin and Laca (2003)).

[18]Corblin (1987) does not define the notion of 'property that notoriously characterizes each member of a class', but judging by examples of the type in (7), one may propose that the relevant properties are those that should be listed among the defining properties of the individuals of which they are predicated: having four (equal) sides can be viewed as an essential property of squares. This suggestion is due to Francis Corblin (personal communication (2002)).

over events:

(19) b′. $\text{ALL}_e$ [[∃x stroll in the street (e,x) ∧ white elephants (x)] →
[∃x stroll in the street (e,x) ∧ white eleph. (x)
∧ arouse curiosity (e,x)]]

We may then hypothesize that the strictly distributive readings observed by Corblin are allowed for pseudo-generic indefinites, i.e., for those indefinites that are existentially closed inside the scope of a Q-adverb that quantifies over events:

(20) Pseudo-generic *des*-indefinites are number-neutral.

Under the proposal made here, number-neutralization should be kept distinct from strictly distributive readings, which correspond to direct quantification over atomic individuals. It is number-neutralization, rather than strict distributivity, that characterizes indirectly bound *des*-indefinites. Truly generic indefinites on the other hand, supply a variable that gets directly bound by the Q-adverb. And when the indefinite is plural, the variable will range over groups, which will induce generalizations over groups.

### 3.5 Generic Plural Indefinites in Modalized Contexts

Carlier (1989) has observed that modalized contexts, in particular deontic/prescriptive generalizations, facilitate the generic reading of plural indefinites :

(21) a. Des agents de police ne se comportent pas ainsi dans une situation d'alarme.
'Police officers do not behave like that in an alarm situation.'

b. Des jeunes filles doivent se montrer discrètes.
'Young ladies must behave discretely.'

c. Des hommes forts peuvent soulever une voiture.
'Strong men can lift a car.'

Carlier's explanation is, however, a mere tentative suggestion: 'L'insertion d'un verbe modal à interprétation déontique virtualise le prédicat et peut faire apparaître ainsi la possibilité d'une lecture générique du SN sujet indéfini'. (The insertion of a modal verb with a deontic interpretation virtualizes the predicate and may thus make possible the generic reading of the indefinite subject).

Within the account proposed here, two LF analyses are in principle possible, relying (i) on quantification over atomic individuals or (ii) on quantification over events/situations combined with the indirect binding of the indefinite, as shown in (21′) and (21″), respectively:[19]

(21) a′ GENx (x is a police officer)
[not$\exists$e (x behaves like this in e $\wedge$ an alarm situation (e))]
b′. GENx (x is a young lady)
[ALL e (x shows discrete behavior in e)]

(21) a″. GENe,x (alarm situation (e,x) $\wedge$ police agents (x))
[not behave like this (e,x)]
b″. $\forall$ e,x (sit. adequate for being discrete (e, x) $\wedge$ young ladies (x)) [show discrete behavior (e,x)]

In the LF's in (21′), which correspond to selective quantification over individuals, the event-variables are bound by unary operators corresponding to the negation and to the modal verb *must*. In the LFs in (21″), the same overt markers translate as relational quantifiers over events.[20]

The LFs in (21a′-b′) are illegitimate: the direct binding of *des*-indefinites is incompatible with quantifying over atomic individuals. These LFs are independently ruled out by the constraint established above, according to which *des*-indefinites can be directly bound by a Q-adverb only if the head noun is relational. The only legitimate option is therefore (21″), in which the indefinite is *indirectly* bound by the Q-adverb that quantifies over events.[21]

## Conclusions

Summarizing, I have proposed that the type of distributivity allowed by generic *des*-indefinites depends on whether they are directly or indirectly bound by a Q-adverb. Because directly bound *des*-indefinites supply variables ranging over groups, they can only express generalizations over groups of individuals. Indirectly bound *des*-indefinites are number-neutral.

## References

Carlier, A. 1989. Généricité du syntagme nominal sujet et modalités. In Wilmet (1989), pages 33–56.

[19]The modal verb *must* that appears in (21b) is analyzed as a universal quantifier, which, depending on whether it is unary or relational/binary, translates as *always* or as *every* (see (21′b) and (21b)).

[20]When an event-variable is present, the time-variable becomes superfluous, since events are individualized by the time of their occurrence.

[21]Corblin (1987) observes a constraint on the use of examples of the type in (21a-b): they can be naturally used only if the speaker talks to a group of police officers or young ladies. Pragmatic constraints of this type are compatible with the formal constraints proposed here.

Carlson, G. N. 1977a. *Reference to kinds in English*. Ph.D. thesis, University of Massachusetts.

Carlson, G. N. 1977b. A unified analysis of the english bare plural. *Linguistics and Philosophy* 1:413–457.

Carlson, G. N. and F. J. Pelletier, eds. 1995. *The generic book*. Chicago: The University of Chicago Press.

Chierchia, G. 1995a. *Dynamics of Meaning. Anaphora, Presuppositions and the Theory of Grammar*. Chicago: University of Chicago Press.

Chierchia, G. 1995b. Individual-level predicates as inherent generics. In Carlson and Pelletier (1995), pages 176–223.

Corblin, F. 1987. *Indéfini, défini et démonstratif. Constructions linguistiques de la référence*. Genève: Droz.

De Swart, H. 1991. *Adverbs of Quantification: A Generalized Quantifiers Approach*. Ph.D. thesis, Groningen.

De Swart, H. 1993. Généricité, phrases conditionnelles et l´interprétation de *des* N. *Faits de Langues* 4.

De Swart, H. 1996. (in)definites and genericity. In Kanazawa et al. (1996), pages 171–194.

Dobrovie-Sorin, C. 2002. Adverbs of quantification and genericity, electronic version. In Falk (2002). Paper version in Proceedings of CSSP, Paris, 2001, Presses de la Sorbonne, On-line: Hebrew University of Jerusalem English Department; <http://atar.mscc.huji.ac.il/~english/IATL/17/.

Dobrovie-Sorin, C. and B. Laca. 1996. Generic bare NPs. University of Paris 7/Strasbourg 2.

Dobrovie-Sorin, C. and B. Laca. 1998. La génericité entre la référence à l'espèce et la quantification générique. *Actes de Langues et Grammaires* III:165–179.

Dobrovie-Sorin, C. and B. Laca. 2003. Les noms sans déterminant dans les langues romanes. In Godard (2003), pages 235–281.

Falk, Y. N., ed. 2002. *Proceedings of Israel Association of Theoretical Linguistics*, vol. 17, Jesuralem. Paper version in Proceedings of CSSP, Paris, 2001, Presses de la Sorbonne, On-line: Hebrew University of Jerusalem English Department; <http://atar.mscc.huji.ac.il/~english/IATL/17/.

Godard, D., ed. 2003. *Syntaxe des langues romanes*. Paris: Editions du CNRS.

Groenendijk, J., T. Janssen, and M. Stokhof, eds. 1981. *Formal Methods in the Study of Language*. Amsterdam: Mathematisch Centrum.

Groenendijk, J. and M. Stokhof. 1991. Dynamic predicate logic. *Linguistics and Philosophy* 14:39–100.

Groenendijk, J. and M. Stokhof. 1992. Dynamic montague grammar. In Kalman and Polos (1992).

Heim, I. 1982. *The semantics of definite and indefinite noun phrases*. Ph.D. thesis, University of Massachusetts.

Heyd, S. 2002. Prédication et interprétation générique des syntagmes nominaux en *des* en position sujet. Abstract. In *Colloque 'Indéfinis et prédications en français'*. Paris.

Kalman, L. and L. Polos, eds. 1992. *Papers from the Second Symposium on Logic and Language*, Budapest.

Kamp, H. 1981. A theory of truth and semantic representation. In Groenendijk et al. (1981), pages 277–322.

Kanazawa, M., C. J. Piñon, and H. De Swart, eds. 1996. *Quantifiers, Deduction and Context*. Stanford: CSLI.

Keenan, E., ed. 1975. *Formal Semantics of Natural Language*. Cambridge: CUP.

Krifka, M., ed. 1988. *Proceedings of the Tübingen Conference on Generics*.

Krifka, M. 1995. Focus and the interpretation of generic sentences. In Carlson and Pelletier (1995), pages 238–264.

Krifka, M., F. J. Pelletier, G. N. Carlson, A. ter Meulen, G. Chierchia, and G. Link. 1995. Genericity: an introduction. In Carlson and Pelletier (1995), chap. 1, pages 1–124.

LePore, E., ed. 1987. *New Directions in Semantics*. London: Academic Press.

Lewis, D. K. 1975. Adverbs of quantification. In Keenan (1975), pages 3–15.

Longobardi, G. 2002. How comparative is semantics? A unified theory of bare nouns and proper names. *Natural Language Semantics* 9(4):335–369.

Milsark, G. 1977. Toward an explanation of certain peculiarities in the existential construction in English. *Linguistic Analysis* 3:1–30.

Rooth, M. 1985. *Association with Focus*. Ph.D. thesis, University of Amherst, Massachusetts.

Rooth, M. 1995. Indefinites, adverbs of quantification, and focus semantics. In Carlson and Pelletier (1995), pages 265–299.

Schubert, L. K. and F. J. Pelletier. 1987. Problems in the representation of the logical form of generics, plurals, and mass nouns. In LePore (1987), pages 385–451.

Schubert, L. K. and F. J. Pelletier. 1988. An outlook on generic statements. In Krifka (1988), pages 357–372.

Van Geenhoven, V. 1996. *Semantic incorporation and indefinite descriptions: semantic and syntactic aspects of noun incorporation in West Greenlandic*. Ph.D. thesis, University of Tübingen.

Wilmet, M., ed. 1989. *Généricité, spécificité et aspect*, vol. 19 of *Travaux de linguistique*. Paris: Duculot.

5

# *Tout* as a Genuine Free Choice Item

JACQUES JAYEZ AND LUCIA M. TOVENA

## 1 Introduction

This chapter discusses the behavior of the French determiner *tout*.[1] Intuitively, its main contribution to the interpretation of a sentence seems to be that of stating that any element in the denotation of the restrictor is a suitable candidate for satisfying the nucleus—a contribution typical of Free Choice Items (FCIs). FCIs signal that the choice of an element from a given reference set is unconstrained. For instance, *Pick any card!* in English and *Prends n'importe quelle carte!* in French invite the addressee to choose the card she prefers, from some contextually salient set of cards. FCIs exhibit both existential and universal interpretations. For example, *Pick any card!* entails *Pick a card!* and *Any cat hunts mice* entails *(Absolutely) every cat hunts mice*. However, it is not clear whether universal quantification is always consistent with the idea of free *choice*. What choice is left once a universal quantifier signals that all the elements of a given set satisfy a certain property? For instance, in the cards example, the addressee must choose one card and may not pick every card. In this paper we show that *tout* is a genuine FCI, and that so-called 'free choiceness' is better conceived as a form of *Non Individuation* (Tovena 1996). Under this analysis, the distinction between existential and universal FCIs is no longer problematic, although it has certain effects. In section 2, we introduce the

[1] We do not consider here the complex expressions *tout le* ('the whole') or *tous les* ('all the'), which are semantically very different. They do not convey any idea of free choiceness; rather, they are closer to the traditional notion of universal quantification.

*Handbook of French Semantics.*
Francis Corblin and Henriëtte de Swart (eds.).
Copyright © 2004, CSLI Publications.

main observations concerning FCIs and in 3, we briefly review some recent proposals. In the last section we present our analysis of *tout*. For space reasons, we won't discuss the case of questions and adversative verbs (see Jayez and Tovena 2003). We will also ignore aspects of *tout* that do not pertain to its FC profile. We refer the reader to Kleiber and Martin (1977) and Paillard (2000) for more complete descriptions.

## 2 The distribution of FCIs

FCIs are not felicitous in affirmative episodic sentences when the FC phrase head noun is not modified. In addition, they are often not felicitous in negative and interrogative sentences, a distribution that distinguishes them from Negative Polarity Items. Haspelmath (1997) mentions permission possibility sentences, permission imperatives, generic sentences and protases of conditional sentences (or functional equivalents) as possible contexts for FCIs . Giannakidou (1998, 2001) extends this array of possibilities for Greek FCIs . Even if we restrict ourselves to the broad characterization given by Haspelmath, two problems emerge for *tout*. First, *tout* is not possible in certain imperatives when it specifies a bare noun. Second, it is banned from protases of conditionals.

(1) a. Prends *toute carte
'Pick any card'
[Intended interpretation: the cards belong to a particular pack]

b. Si tu as *tout problème, téléphone–moi
'If you have any problem, ring me up'

Analogous problems with conditional sentences are noted by Sæbø (1999, 2001) for the Norwegian/Swedish universal FCI *som helst*. *Any* FC behaves similarly, when the universal interpretation is forced on it. So, *Pick any card!* and *If you have any problem, ring me up* are very strange if *any* is roughly interpreted as *every*.[2]. If one is to retain the view that those items are FCIs , it is safer to reduce the set of discriminating environments for the class. We will assume, as a starting point, that FCIs satisfy the following criteria.

1. They are impossible in affirmative episodic sentences, at least when the NP head noun is not modified.
2. They are possible in generic and/or imperative and/or conditional sentences.
3. They clearly implicate that there is a free choice between the members of a set of entities in two possible senses:

[2]This reading emerges in some contexts, for example, in a sentence like *For all we know, the dope could be in any car in the garage; so, open* ??*any trunk*.

(a) The addressee is free to consider any member of a given set, which entails that she may consider every member of the set,
(b) the addressee must choose some member(s) of a given set and this choice is unconstrained.

Concerning *tout*, we note the following (im)possibilities. *Tout* is natural in generic sentences (2a), possibility/permission sentences (2b), with adversative verbs (2c), in habitual sentences (2d), and phrasal comparatives (2e). In general, *tout* is strange in other constructions, in particular in imperative sentences (28a), episodic affirmative or negative sentences (3a,b), episodic interrogative sentences (3c) and conditional sentences (28b). We will add some qualifications to this sketchy distributional picture in due time.

(2) a. Tout chat chasse les souris
'Any cat hunts mice'

b. Ici, tout dossier peut être consulté
'Here, any file may be accessed'

c. Il a refusé tout compromis
'He refused any compromise'

d. Tout arrivant était (habituellement) interrogé
'Any newcomer was (usually) questioned'

e. Je préfère Jean à tout autre membre de l'équipe
'I like John better than any other member of the team'

(3) a. Marie a lu *tout livre
'Mary read FCI book'

b. Marie n'a pas lu *tout livre
'Mary did not read FCI book'

c. Est-ce que Marie a lu *tout livre?
'Did Mary read FCI book?)

## 3 Recent proposals

It is impossible to review here all the proposals concerning free–choiceness, in particular because they often involve a discussion of polarity sensitivity and scalar phenomena (see in particular Lee & Horn 1994, Lee 1997, Tovena & Jayez 1999a). We will consider two types of contribution, those of Eisner (1994) and Dayal (1998), and of Giannakidou (1997b, 1998, 2001), which are directly relevant to the discussion of *tout*.

### 3.1 FC *Any* as a strongly modal quantifier

In the literature on *any*, there is a traditional distinction between Polarity Sensitive (PS) and FC *any*'s. The former is found in downward entailing contexts (negative and conditional sentences, typically), while the latter appears in generic sentences, imperatives and in some assertive episodic sentences where the NP head noun is suitably modified. Eisner and Dayal[3] consider FC *any* as a universal quantifier whose quantification domain is the set of possible worlds or situations. For example, Eisner accounts for the oddness of (4) by pointing out that it entails that every individual in every possible world stole (a part of) the tarts in the real world. But entities from outer worlds cannot intrude into the real world as causal agents.

(4) The tarts were stolen by *anyone

Similarly, Dayal sees *any* as a universal quantifier obeying the following constraint.

(5) In a sentence of the form $\phi$(*any* N), *any* is a universal quantifier which creates a tripartite structure: $\forall s, x$ [$x$ is a N in $s$] [$\phi(x)$ in $s$]

Again, this predicts that *any* is infelicitous in (4): according to (5), (4) means that, in every situation where there is a person, this person stole (some of) the tarts. This is absurd since there are situations where some individuals exist but where there are no tarts.

A well–known problem with *any* is that of *subtrigging*, a term coined by LeGrand (1975) to designate the fact that episodic sentences can be redeemed when the NP head noun is modified by an adjective or a postnominal modifier (a relative clause, for instance), see (6) and (7).

(6) a. Mary read *any book
b. Mary read any book which was on the reading list

(7) a. *Tout étudiant a été renvoyé
'Any student was excluded'
b. Tout étudiant qui avait triché a été renvoyé
'Any student who had cheated was excluded'

Eisner and Dayal account for subtrigging by assuming that the subtrigger introduces a spatio–temporal restriction which prevents the *any*–quantifier from ranging over the totality of possible worlds or situations. For example, in (6), Mary read the books in any situation contained in a limited situation, where the reading list exists.

[3]Although the two proposals are independent, it is clear that Dayal's (1998) paper echoes many themes and suggestions of Eisner (1994).

There are two major problems with this approach. First, the idea that *any* quantifies over possible worlds or situations is counter–intuitive. *Pick any card!* is not interpreted as 'Pick any card in any possible situation'. To account for such examples, Dayal assumes that, since the imperative is a permission, the addressee is entitled to pick no card at all. In this respect, the offending reading in which every possible card is picked is not satisfied. Astute as it is, this solution sounds extremely artificial. This reading simply does not exist.[4] It is more likely that FCIs give rise to certain vagueness effects because they emphasize the unlimited character of the choice (see Dayal's (1998) Contextual Vagueness). The second problem is that the role assigned to the subtrigger is too narrowly defined. There are cases in which the subtrigger does not bring in any spatio–temporal limitation. For instance, as noted in (Tovena & Jayez 1999a), in sentences like (8) the subtrigger does not introduce a spatio–temporal limitation since the mathematical dependence between two theorems is purely abstract.

(8) a. Marie a vérifié tout résultat dépendant du théorème de Craig
 b. Mary checked any result which depended on Craig's theorem

### 3.2 Giannakidou's approach

In (Giannakidou 1997a,b, 1998, 2001), it is proposed that FCIs are (i) nonveridical and (ii) subject to a variation requirement. By and large, an operator is nonveridical if its use in a sentence does not entail that the speaker believes the proposition to which it applies (Zwarts 1995). This definition captures cases like imperatives, which were not considered as downward entailing: in an imperative of the form $!\phi$ the speaker normally believes that $\phi$ is not realized. Variation means that there is a set of possible worlds in which the property described by the sentence applies to the members of the reference set individually. In the cards example, the different cards are picked in different possible continuations of the situation.

While Giannakidou's analysis is empirically more precise than many others, it also runs into problems. First, since Giannakidou claims that FCIs cannot be universal, the conditions she puts on variation do not extend to universal FCIs like *tout*. Second, nonveridicality and variation are not present in certain cases, for instance in subtrigged sentences like (9) which even lacks the iterative dimension which Giannakidou (2001) sees as a licensing condition for FCIs in subtrigged sentences. It is difficult to see in which alternative possible worlds (continuations,

[4]The same observation applies to the French equivalent *Prends n'importe quelle carte*, which does not necessarily refer to 'any possible card'.

epistemic alternatives, etc.) we would locate the fact that every theorem of a certain type is in the book referred to. Similar remarks hold for comparatives.

(9) Tout théorème indispensable à la maîtrise du sujet se trouve dans ce remarquable ouvrage
'Any theorem required for mastering the topic is in this outstanding treatise'

Third, nonveridicality does not account for examples based on *spaces*, in the sense of Fauconnier (1985) or *media*, in the sense of Ross (1988). (10) is nonveridical since the speaker does not believe that a knight killed dragons. The sentence is anomalous because it refers to a particular sequence of events (the killings). The fact that it is nonveridical and that the identity of the dragons might be unknown to the speaker are irrelevant. What counts is that the sentence *mimics* reference to a non–actual world.

(10) a. Dans cette légende, le chevalier a tué tous les / *tout dragon(s)
b. In this legend, the knight killed all the / *any dragon(s)

Fourth, the link between nonveridicality, which is an epistemic notion, and reference is unclear. For instance, belief sentences such as (11a,b) are out because John's belief targets an actual situation. However, John might not know which books Mary read. So, it is not technically possible to derive the impossibility of such sentences from a violation of variation, as proposed by Giannakidou (2001). In believing that Mary read all the books, John does not necessarily refer to specific books. He might entertain different epistemic alternatives in which different books are read. The fact that the sentence is veridical means that in every belief–accessible world, it is true that Mary read all the books, *not* that the books are the same in every belief–world.[5]

(11) a. Jean croit que Marie a lu *tout livre
b. John believes that Mary read *any book

## 4 Non Individuation

In her dissertation, Tovena (1996) proposes that *any* is not possible when the truth of the sentence where it occurs depends on the identity of the individuals which constitute the reference domain (Non Individuation, NI). In this section we reformulate this idea in a more precise form, to account for the FC distribution of *tout*.

[5]The reader is referred to (Jayez & Tovena 2003) for an extensive discussion.

### 4.1 Descriptiveness and referentiality

To deal with examples like (10), we use the notion of *descriptiveness*, defined intuitively in Definition 1. A sentence is descriptive whenever it sounds like a description of some part of a world. Veridical sentences (in the sense of Giannakidou) are descriptive but descriptive sentences may be nonveridical and exclude FCIs all the same, cf. (10).

**Definition 1** A sentence is descriptive when it refers to an actual situation/event or simulates such a reference in an imaginary world.

Providing a formal counterpart for descriptiveness is not trivial because of the general asymmetry between epistemicity and reference (see Dekker 1998). To see what is at stake, consider the *actually* operator studied by Gregory (2001) and redefined by Blackburn and Marx (2002) with the help of the 'at' operator @ from *hybrid logic* (Blackburn 2000). If $x$ is the name of a possible world, $g$ an assignment from (standard) variables to individuals and world–names to worlds, $w$ the current world and $\mathcal{M}$ a Kripke model, we have Definition 2.

**Definition 2** $\mathcal{M}, g, w \models @_x\phi$ iff $\mathcal{M}, g, g(x) \models \phi$.

For simplicity, let us treat worlds and their names as the same (so, $g(w) = w$). Let $w_0$ be the actual world and *actually* correspond to $@_{w_0}$ as proposed by Blackburn and Marx. Suppose now that we code sentences like (11a,b) as in (11').[6]

(11') $B_{John}(@_{w_0}($ Mary read a/every book$))$

(11') is true if and only if Mary read a/every book in the actual world, which is obviously not the intuitive interpretation of (11a,b). 'John believes that $\phi$' may be true even if $\phi$ is actually false. Yet, to capture descriptiveness, it is necessary to instill some form of reference to the actual world into the representation. What is required is a shift from a realistic operator like $@_w$ ('it is the case at $w$') to a *viewpoint* operator. Suppose we are at $w$ and that we express that $\phi$ is true at every world $M$–accessible from $w$, $M$ being a modal operator. What would make this modal situation descriptive? It is the fact that (i) $\phi$ is about what is the case at $w$ and that (ii), temporally, the $M$–accessible worlds are anterior to or simultaneous with $w$. In this case, the modal structure delineates an $M$–situation in which it is true that $\phi$ at $w$. $M$ is not necessarily epistemic, so the modal structure does not always describe what is already the case at $w$, but what is the case *if* $w$ is compatible with the information common to all the $M$–

[6]We ignore here the distinction between existential and universal FCIs because it is not relevant to the main point.

accessible worlds. This accounts for examples like (12a,b). Note that (12a) is nonveridical.

(12) a. Jean espère que Marie a consulté *tout dossier
'John hopes that Mary consulted any file'
b. Jean craint que Marie ait consulté *tout dossier
'John is afraid that Mary consulted any file'

Quite generally, if $M$ is an attitude of type $\Box$ (BELIEF, HOPE, etc.), we note $w^*_M$ the set of $\phi$ such that $M\phi$ is true at $w$ and $\phi$ is about what is the case at $w$. So, $w^*_M$ is the image that the $M$–accessible worlds give of $w$. Definition 3 says that a sentence is descriptive when the denotation of its restriction and scope are presented as determined in a unique world. In this case, although there can be epistemic variation, that is, the restriction and the scope can have different denotations in the different possible worlds, the sentence purports to refer to a particular situation in a particular word. For shortness, we use variable vectors: $\vec{x}$ refers to a sequence of variables. For an $n$–sequence $x_1 \ldots x_n$ $P(\wedge\vec{x})$ refers to $P(x_1)$ & ... & $P(x_n)$, etc.

**Definition 3** A sentence whose tripartite structure involves a restriction $[R]$ and a scope $[S]$, evaluated at $w$ with respect to a set of $M$–accessible worlds, is descriptive iff:
1. $@_{w^*_M} \exists\vec{x}(R(\wedge\vec{x})\ \&\ S(\wedge\vec{x}))$, or
2. $@_{w^*_M} \exists\vec{x}(R(\wedge\vec{x})\ \&\ \neg S(\wedge\vec{x}))$.

Descriptiveness is not sufficient since certain sentences, which are not descriptive, are nonetheless anomalous cf. (28a). This is because, although we do not refer to what is actually the case in a world, we refer to what will be necessarily the case and is already determined at speech time, namely the fact that the addressee will pick every card in the pack. So, the difference between the previous case and this one is small. Both cases illustrate the impossibility of making reference to particular individuals. Reference can be avoided through *domain shift*, that is to say through possible variation on the restriction of the *tout* phrase (Jayez & Tovena 2003), as in (13). In such examples, the denotation of the restriction may vary from world to world. Different continuations of the current situation may host different misdemeanors.

(13) Montre-toi extrêmement strict, punis tout délit
Be quite strict, punish any misdemeanor

In other cases where the restriction domain is rigid, *tout* may be licensed through standard variation, that is the set of individuals satisfying the restriction *and* the scope may vary, e.g. in (28b). We extend Definition 1 in a natural way by using the same localization operator @.

Definition 4 says that a sentence is referential whenever it is descriptive or determines at $w$ that certain individuals in the restriction do or do not satisfy the scope.

**Definition 4 Referentiality** A sentence whose tripartite structure involves a restriction $[R]$ and a scope $[S]$, evaluated at $w$ with respect to a set of $M$–accessible worlds, is referential iff:
1. it is descriptive or,
2a. $@_w \exists \vec{x}(\forall w'(w\mathcal{R}_M w' \Rightarrow (R(\wedge\vec{x}) \,\&\, S(\wedge\vec{x}))))$, or
2b. $@_w \exists \vec{x}(\forall w'(w\mathcal{R}_M w' \Rightarrow (R(\wedge\vec{x}) \,\&\, \neg S(\wedge\vec{x}))))$.

For simple examples, such as the cards example in (14), Definition 4 predicts exhaustive variation without stipulating it explicitly. The default interpretation is that the speaker must pick just one card. If no card is excluded and no card is imposed, this gives a one–card–picked–per–world interpretation.[7] When the modality is of the $\Box$ type and the restriction $R$ is rigid, *tout* is predicted to be anomalous as in (28a).

(14) Prends n'importe quelle carte
'Pick any card'

## 4.2 NI

It is tempting to hypothesize that FCIs are incompatible with referentiality, in the sense of Definition 4. However, subtrigged examples such as (7b) cannot be explained in this way since they refer to particular individuals. Following (Jayez & Tovena 2003), we propose that FCIs obey NI, as given in Definition 5.

**Definition 5** NI is the property that, in a given interpretation of a sentence S, the information concerning what makes S true or false cannot be reduced to the referential information associated with the interpretation. FCIs are not appropriate under interpretations that violate NI.

As noted by Dayal, subtrigged sentences exhibit a conceptual dependency between the restriction and the scope. This is why they cannot convey purely accidental relations, such as (15).

(15) Par un curieux hasard, *tout garçon que Jean a croisé hier après–midi portait une chemise bleue
('By a strange twist of fate, any boy John passed by yesterday afternoon wore a blue shirt')

Conceptual dependency means that two properties are related by virtue of causal or cultural rules/habits. Technically, one may ascribe

[7]However, the cards of the pack exist in all the possible worlds, in contrast to Giannakidou's condition. See (Jayez & Tovena 2003) on this point.

to these rules an implicative form $UNx(R(x) \rightarrow S(x))$, where $UN$ and $\rightarrow$ are suitable universal and implicative operators (classical, modal, nonmonotonic, etc.). The information that $R(a) \& S(a)$ for any $a$ is then derived from the referential information $R(a)$ and the non–referential information corresponding to the rule. This accounts for the fact that subtrigged sentences are not purely referential and can license FCIs . A similar analysis holds for certain comparative constructions in French, as shown in (Jayez & Tovena 2003).

## 5 Conclusion

In this chapter we have shown how to account for the free choice interpretation of the determiner *tout* and reconcile it with its nature of universal quantifier. The abstract constraint NI allows one to characterize free choiceness as a certain relation to reference. NI does not mention well–known distinctions such as indefinite vs. quantifier or existential vs. universal. The fact that items like *n'importe quel* and *tout*, which are distinct along these dimensions, can be described in a unified way under NI (Jayez & Tovena 2003) and suggests that such distinctions are not central for free–choiceness.

## References

Blackburn, P. 2000. Representation, reasoning and relational structures: A hybrid logic manifesto. *Journal of the IGPL* 8:339–365.

Blackburn, P. and M. Marx. 2002. Remarks on Gregory's "actually" operator. *Journal of Philosophical Logic* 31:281–288.

Blanco, X., P.-A. Buvet, and Z. Gavriilidou, eds. 2000. *Détermination et Formalisation*, vol. 23 of *Lingvisticæ Investigationes Supplementa*. Amsterdam: Benjamins.

Corblin, F., C. Dobrovie-Sorin, and J. Marandin, eds. 1999. *Empirical Issues in Formal Syntax and Semantics*, vol. 2. The Hague: Thesus.

Dayal, V. 1998. ANY as inherently modal. *Linguistics and Philosophy* 21:433–476.

Dekker, P. 1988. Speaker's reference, description and information structure. *Journal of Semantics* 15:305–334.

Dekker, P. and M. Stokhof, eds. 1997. *Proceedings of the eleventh Amsterdam Colloquium*. ILLC, University of Amsterdam.

Eisner, J. 1994. '∀'–less in wonderland? Revisiting *any*. In *ESCOL'94*, pages 92–103.

Fauconnier, G. 1994. *Mental Spaces: Aspects of Meaning Construction in Natural Language*. Cambridge: Cambridge University Press.

Giannakidou, A. 1997a. *The Landscape of Polarity Items*. Ph.D. thesis, University of Groningen.

Giannakidou, A. 1997b. Linking sensitivity to limited distribution. In Dekker and Stokhof (1997), pages 139–144.

Giannakidou, A. 1998. *Polarity Sensitivity as (Non) Veridical Dependency*. Amsterdam: John Benjamins.

Giannakidou, A. 1999. Affective dependencies. *Linguistics and Philosophy* 22:367–421.

Giannakidou, A. 2001. The meaning of free choice. *Linguistics and Philosophy* 34:659–735.

Gregory, D. 2001. Completeness and decidability results for some modal propositional logics containing the "actually" operator. *Journal of Philosophical Logic* 30:57–78.

Haspelmath, M. 1997. *Indefinite Pronouns*. Oxford: Clarendon Press.

Horn, L. R. 2000. Pick a theory, not just *any* theory. In Horn and Kato (2000), pages 147–192.

Horn, L. R. and Y. Kato, eds. 2000. *Negation and Polarity*. Oxford: Oxford University Press.

Jayez, J. and L. Tovena. 2003. Free choiceness and non individuation. To appear in *Linguistics and Philosophy*, or http://pweb.ens-lsh.fr/jjayez/LPjt-2up.pdf.

Kleiber, G. and R. Martin. 1977. La quantification universelle en français. *Semantikos* 2:19–36.

Lee, C. 1997. Negative polarity and free choice: where do they come from? In Dekker and Stokhof (1997), pages 217–222.

Lee, Y.-S. and L. Horn. 1994. *Any* as indefinite plus *Even*. Ms. Yale University.

LeGrand, J. E. 1975. Or *and* Any*: The Semantics and Syntax of Two Logical Operators*. Ph.D. thesis, University of Chicago.

Moeschler, J. and M.-J. Béguelin, eds. 1999. *Référence temporelle et nominale*. Berne: Peter Lang.

Paillard, D. 2000. *Tout* N en français versus *vsjakij* N en russe. In Blanco et al. (2000), pages 273–290.

Ross, J. 1988. *The Semantics of Media*. Dordrecht: Kluwer.

Sæbø, K. J. 1999. Free choice items in Scandinavian. Tech. rep., University of Oslo.

Sæbø, K. J. 2001. The semantics of Scandinavian free choice items. *Linguistics and Philosophy* 24:737–787.

Tovena, L. and J. Jayez. 1997. *Any* as a Finian quantifier. In Dekker and Stokhof (1997), pages 295–300.

Tovena, L. and J. Jayez. 1999a. Déterminants et irréférence. l'exemple de *tout*. In Moeschler and Béguelin (1999), pages 235–268.

Tovena, L. and J. Jayez. 1999b. *Any*: from scalarity to arbitrariness. In Corblin et al. (1999), pages 39–57.

Tovena, L. M. 1996. *Studies on polarity sensitivity*. Ph.D. thesis, University of Edinburgh. Published by Garland (1998).

Zwarts, F. 1995. Nonveridical contexts. *Linguistic Analysis* 25:286–312.

6

# Degree Quantifiers *

JENNY DOETJES

## 1 Introduction

Determiners are usually restricted to the nominal system. However, there is a class of quantifying expressions that, when used in the nominal system, function like determiners from a semantic point of view, but that can be used outside of the nominal system as well. Some examples are *beaucoup* 'a lot' (more than the norm), *davantage* 'more' and *trop* 'too much/many'. The contrast between these expressions and 'pure' determiners, such as *plusieurs* 'several' which are restricted to the nominal system, is illustrated in (1):

(1) a. Sylvie a lu beaucoup / trop de livres / plusieurs livres
Sylvie has read a-lot / too-many of books / several books

b. Pierre a beaucoup / trop / * plusieurs travaillé
Pierre has a-lot / too-much / several worked

Since expressions such as *beaucoup* and *trop* can be said to indicate a degree of quantity, we refer to them using the term Degree Quantifiers (DQs). In this chapter we will discuss a number of properties of DQs.

*This chapter, and especially section 2.3, has benefited greatly from fruitful discussion with Francis Corblin as well as from his detailed comments on a previous version of the text. I would also like to thank Johan Rooryck, Petra Sleeman, Henriëtte de Swart and Henk Verkuyl as well as the members of the PICS project group on determiners. Obviously all errors remain mine. The research for this chapter has been made possible by NWO, whose support is hereby gratefully acknowledged.

*Handbook of French Semantics.*
Francis Corblin and Henriëtte de Swart (eds.).
Copyright © 2004, CSLI Publications.

Section 2.1 discusses semantic properties of DQs. In general, the meaning of a DQ is defined in terms of comparison with a 'quantity of reference'. Section 2.2 discusses proportional readings of DQs such as *beaucoup* and *peu* in relation to the role of the quantity of reference. The context dependency of the quantity of reference explains a number of further properties of DQs, such as the difficulty of defining their monotonicity properties (section 2.3) and their compatibility with habituality (section 2.4). From a selectional point of view, DQs differ from 'pure' determiners as well (section 2.5). They are compatible with mass nouns and with plural, or, in some cases, with mass nouns only. This type of selection is extremely rare for 'pure' determiners.

The properties of adverbial DQs are discussed elsewhere in this book (see chapter 12, 'Adverbs and Quantification'). However, in section 3 we will discuss two constructions (quantification at a distance and a special type of quantifier float) in which the wide distribution of DQs plays an important role. In these constructions the DQ can be used precisely because it can function both as an adnominal and as an adverbial Q expression.

## 2 DQs in the nominal system

### 2.1 The meaning of adverbial determiners

Contrary to, for instance, cardinal numerals such as *three* and cardinal determiners such as *several*, DQs depend for their interpretation on a contextually given 'quantity of reference', where 'contextually' is taken in a broad sense as will be shown below. Consider the following intuitive descriptions of the meaning of a number of DQs:[1]

(2) *beaucoup*: more than $n$, where $n$ is a contextually given norm
*énormément/vachement* etc.: much more than $n$, where $n$ is a contextually given norm
*peu*: less than $n$, where $n$ is a contextually given norm
*moins*: less than $n$, where $n$ is contextually given, for instance in a *que*-clause (*than*-clause)
*plus/davantage*: more than $n$, where $n$ is contextually given, for instance in a *que*-clause (*than*-clause)
*trop*: more than $n$, where $n$ corresponds to the maximum quantity that is appropriate in the given context

[1] I will not discuss the interpretation of the different DQs in detail here. As many DQs also function as modifiers of APs, the literature on adjectival modification gives a great deal of information on the meaning of DQs. See for instance Von Stechow (1985), Bierwisch (1987) and Neeleman, Van de Koot & Doetjes (2004). Anaphoric reference to DPs containing the DQ peu is discussed in Corblin (1997), (1999), who argues against Moxey & Sandford (1993).

*assez/suffisamment*: at least $n$, where $n$ corresponds to the minimum quantity that is necessary in the given context
*tant/tellement*: at least $n$, where $n$ exceeds a contextually given norm; $n$ can be further specified as the minimal quantity resulting in what is described in a *que*-phrase (*than*-clause)

In all these descriptions, we find the quantity $n$ which has to be filled in by the context in one way or another. With *beaucoup*, it is usually knowledge of the world that plays a role (for the proportional reading of *beaucoup*, see section 2.2 below). In the case of comparative *davantage* it is either the preceding context that provides a value for $n$ or a satellite clause of the form *que...* 'than...'. The meaning of the DQ is defined as compared to this quantity $n$, which we call the 'quantity of reference'. Given that the quantity of reference is not (or not necessarily) defined by the meaning of the DQ, DQs are strongly context-dependent for their interpretation. They are not simply vague, and differ in that respect from expressions such as *plusieurs* 'several'. *Plusieurs* can be informally characterized as 'more than one', where the context-independent quantity 'one' functions as the quantity of reference (for a discussion of *plusieurs*, see Gondret 1976 and Gaatone 1991). The difference between *beaucoup* and *plusieurs* will be further illustrated in section 2.4 below.

There is a strong correlation between this type of interpretation and the distribution of Qs. On the one hand, the only DQs that cannot be defined with respect to a quantity of reference mean 'a bit' (*un peu, un tantinet*) (cf. Ducrot 1980, Doetjes 2001a). On the other hand, 'pure' determiners that are defined with respect to a quantity of reference are rare.[2] The only exception in French is *plein* 'a lot', which, unlike *beaucoup* and *énormément*, is restricted to the nominal system.

## 2.2 Proportional readings

According to Partee (1988), Qs such as *many* and *few* are ambiguous between a proportional and a cardinal reading. Her arguments could be extended to a number of French DQs including *beaucoup*, *énormément* and *peu*, which all can have proportional readings.[3] Let us first consider one of Partee's examples that illustrates the contrast between the proportional and the cardinal reading:

[2]Measure phrases, such as *un (plus) grand nombre de*, differ in this respect from ordinary determiners. They may have the same distribution as DQs within the nominal system, while they cannot be used outside of the nominal system. The distribution of these expressions will not be considered here, but see Doetjes (1997:99), (2001a).

[3]Westerståhl (1985) distinguishes several proportional readings of *many*.

(3) a. Many linguists in this room are women iff there are many women linguists in this room

b. Three linguists in this room are women iff there are three women linguists in this room

The implication in (3a) is odd, because we tend to interpret the first *many* as proportional (a large proportion of the linguists in this room) and the second one as cardinal (a relatively large number in general). In (3b), where a cardinal numeral is used, the implication holds, because *three* always has a cardinal reading.

If it is obviously true that the cardinal reading and the proportional reading exist, it is questionable whether this is a result of ambiguity. Rather, it seems to be the case that the strong, partitive reading of *many* is necessarily proportional, while the weak cardinal reading is not. This suggests that proportionality is a property of the strong reading, while cardinality is a property of the weak reading. In case of ambiguity, such a correlation is not expected. More specifically, we would expect to find cases where the strong reading is cardinal rather than proportional given the fact that cardinal determiners normally can have both a weak and a strong cardinal reading (e.g. *(moins de) cinq de ces étudiants* '(less than) five of these students'; see also De Hoop 1992). Now consider the following example, in which the strong reading is forced by an overt partitive:

(4) Peu de ces étudiants ont une télévision en couleurs
'Few of these students have a color television'

Consider now the following situation: *ces étudiants* refers to a group of five students. If four of them have a color television, the sentence is false, even though one could say that four is a small number. The (intuitive) reason is that it is not a small number in relation to the five students we are talking about. This shows that the strong cardinal reading is excluded.

This property of *peu* and *beaucoup* seems to be related to their meaning in terms of comparison with respect to a quantity of reference. Strong readings are anaphoric, and their restriction corresponds to a previously given set. The necessarily proportional reading of strong DPs containing *peu* and *beaucoup* suggests that the size of this set is a decisive factor in determining the quantity of reference. Instead of defining several separate meanings for an ambiguous *many/beaucoup* to account for different readings, it seems more fruitful to determine the different readings in terms of contextual conditions on the interpretation of the quantity of reference.

## 2.3 Entailments and monotonicity

From a semantic point of view, we can observe that the monotonicity properties of DQs can be hard to establish (cf. the discussion in Keenan & Stavi 1986 on intensional determiners and Corblin 1996, 1999). Consider for example (5):

(5) a. Beaucoup d'étudiants ont une télévision en couleurs
'Many students have a color television'

b. Beaucoup d'étudiants ont une télévision
'Many students have a television'

At first sight, (5a) entails (5b).[4] This would qualify *beaucoup* as a monotone increasing determiner for its second argument (mon $\uparrow$). If the number of students having a color TV is important, we can be quite sure that if we add those students having a black and white TV, the number is slightly more important, and definitely still qualifies as *beaucoup*. However, the entailment properties of *beaucoup* are far more complicated, which becomes clear when we consider the example in (6):

(6) a. Beaucoup de garçons anglais jouent au criquet
a-lot of boys English play to-the cricket

b. Beaucoup de garçons anglais font du sport
a-lot of boys English do of-the sport

If it is true that there are relatively many English boys who play cricket (as compared to boys from other countries), this does not imply that there are many English boys who play a sport. Similar problems arise for the monotonicity properties of *beaucoup* and other DQs with respect to their first argument, as we will see below.

Note also that we would like to say that expressions such as *peu* are monotone decreasing, as they license certain negative polarity items that are sensitive to the presence of a monotone decreasing context, such as *le/la moindre* (see chapter 18, 'Polarity Sensitive Items' (Negation) and Miller 1991):

(7) Peu de / * les journalistes ont émis la moindre critique
few of / the journalists have uttered the slightest criticism

At the same time, when we replace *beaucoup* by *peu* in (6), (6b) does not entail (6a), which suggests that it is not downward monotonic. This

[4]In order for the entailment to hold, it is important that there is no contrastive accent on *en couleurs* (see the discussion on the so-called C accent in chapter 21, Prosody and Information in French). If so the sentence is interpreted as: many of the students who have a television, have a color television. In this case the entailment is clearly excluded. For the influence of focus on the interpretation of the domain of quantification, see a.o. Partee (1991).

is not expected given its ability to license *la moindre* in (7).

We can explain the behavior of DQs given the role of the 'quantity of reference' in the interpretation of the DQ. Let us reconsider the case of *beaucoup*. As long as the quantity of reference is kept relatively constant from one example to the other, *beaucoup* behaves like a mon ↑ determiner. The proportion of students we expect to have a color television is not much lower than the number of students we expect to have a television, unless we expect many students to have black and white televisions. As a result the quantity of reference with respect to which *beaucoup* is interpreted in (5a) and (5b) is of the same order, and as a result the entailment between (5a) and (5b) seems to hold. However, in the examples in (6a) and (6b), the quantity of reference with respect to which we have to interpret *beaucoup* is clearly not the same, and as a result we immediately see that (6a) does not entail (6b). For the first sentence, the quantity of reference is determined by the percentage of cricket-playing boys we expect based on the average of cricket-playing boys in countries other than England. For the second sentence, it is based on our expectation with respect to the number of boys playing a sport in countries other than England.

In the case of *beaucoup*, it is very hard to keep the quantity of reference constant. Even for (5), we would like to say that we have the impression that the implication holds because of world knowledge. Our norm for having televisions and our norm for having color televisions are of the same order. (5b) is true whenever (5a) is true. For those who consider black and white televisions as the standard, (5) is similar to (6).[5]

In the context of *plus*, the quantity of reference can be really kept constant independently of our world knowledge. Consider first the example in (8). This example is similar to (6), in that the quantity of reference is clearly different in the two cases and as a result there is no entailment possible between the two examples:

(8) a. Jean a lu plus de livres linguistiques que Pierre
Jean has read more of linguistics books than Pierre
b. Jean a lu plus de livres que Pierre

[5]Francis Corblin has suggested to me the following alternative. According to him, *beaucoup* can have the reading 'more than 50%'. With this reading, the entailment in (5) holds. In (6), world knowledge blocks the 'more than 50%' reading and therefore the entailment is blocked. Note that this is in accordance with the generalization I make: *beaucoup* is defined as 'more than 50% of the students in the domain of discourse' in both (5a) and (5b), and thus the quantity of reference is kept constant. I am not sure whether we want to say that 'more than 50%' always would qualify as *beaucoup*, independently of contextual factors and our expectations based on these factors.

However, in (9) the quantity of reference is the same for both examples (namely the number of comics Pierre read). We can observe that (9a) entails (9b), on the basis of which we can conclude that, once the quantity of reference is kept constant *more* is monotone increasing for its first argument (↑ mon):

(9) a. Jean a lu plus de livres linguistiques que Pierre
Jean has read more of linguistics books than Pierre
n'a lu de bandes dessinées
NE has read of comics

b. Jean a lu plus de livres que Pierre n'a lu de bandes dessinées

We can conclude at this point that DQs do have monotonicity properties, but that these properties affect entailments only when the quantity of reference is kept constant over the different examples.

## 2.4 The use of DQs in habitual sentences

DQs can very well be used in habitual contexts. In this respect they differ from cardinal determiners such as *plusieurs* 'several'. Compare for instance the examples in (10). The example in (10a) is fine. On the other hand, (10b) is odd, unless we embed *plusieurs livres* under a quantificational modifier such as *par semaine* 'per week':[6]

(10) a. Jean lit beaucoup de livres
Jean reads a-lot of books

b. Jean lit plusieurs livres #(par semaine)
Jean reads several books per week

This property of DQs is directly related to their semantics. Habitual sentences characterize a time interval in a homogeneous way. In order for a habitual sentence to be true for a time interval X, it should be true for every subinterval of X as well (cf. a.o. Ducrot 1979. This explains why the use of *plusieurs*, 'more than one', is not felicitous. If it is true that Jean read several books in a certain period, we cannot say anything about the subintervals of this period. There will be subintervals in which he read several books, but there will also be subintervals in which he read only one book or even no book at all. If we add *par semaine*, the interpretation of *plusieurs livres* becomes dependent on the time interval. Depending on the number of weeks the interval contains, the number of books Jean read during this interval will vary. Note that in this case, we need minimally a time interval of a week. Similarly, if *lire*

[6]The same contrast is found between *souvent* and adverbial *beaucoup* on the one hand and *trois fois* on the other. See chapter 12 'Adverbs and Quantification' and references cited therein.

*beaucoup de livres* corresponds in a given context to reading more than one book per week, we need to look at subintervals of at least one week in order to judge whether the sentence is true.

In the context of DQs it is often possible to interpret $n$, the quantity of reference, in function of a time interval. Whenever this is possible, DPs of the form DQ NP are compatible with the homogeneous nature of the habitual reading.[7]

## 2.5 Selection within the nominal system

When looking at the selectional properties of adverbial determiners, we can observe that they are all compatible with plural and with mass nouns. They cannot combine with count nouns, unless the count noun has shifted towards a mass interpretation. This is illustrated for *beaucoup* in (11):

(11) beaucoup de théières, beaucoup de soupe, # beaucoup de théière
a-lot of teapots a-lot of soup a-lot of teapot

Since the noun *théière* is not easily used as a mass noun, its combination with *beaucoup* yields a strange result. This selectional pattern is typical for DQs as they select on the basis of semantic properties of their host. They select an expression which offers a scale with respect to which the DQ can be interpreted, and are insensitive to the categorial properties of this expression. 'Pure' determiners combine with either singular count nouns (*chacun* 'each'), plural (*plusieurs* 'several') or other combinations of types of nouns (*quelque(s)*) (cf. Doetjes 1997, 2001a, Tovena 2001, and chapter 7).

It has often been observed in the literature that mass nouns and plural have much in common from a semantic point of view (cf. a.o. Link 1983). Both can be said to introduce a quantitative scale: when using the plural *books* or the mass noun *soup*, the number of books or the amount of soup may vary on an ascending scale. The noun *books* can be used to refer to any number of books, while the noun *soup* can

[7] As in the case of (9), the quantity of reference may be absolute. This results, as expected, in the impossibility of the habitual reading:

(i) Jean lit plus de livres que Pierre (# en a lu pendant les vacances de Noël)
'Jean reads more books than Pierre did during the Christmas holidays'

As we said above, *un peu* 'a bit' is in this respect similar to *quelques* and *plusieurs* and not to the other DQs. As expected, it cannot be used in habitual contexts: *Il boit un peu de vin* 'He drinks a bit of wine' is not a habitual sentence.

be used to refer to any quantity of soup.[8] Typically, it is not possible to use DQs with a singular count noun, which does not introduce a quantitative scale: *beaucoup de théière* 'a lot of tea pot' is excluded.

## 3 Distribution outside of the DP

### 3.1 Preliminary remarks

As we already said, an important property of DQs is that their distribution is not limited to the nominal system. They can be used as adnominal modifiers (in which case they resemble determiners), but they can also be used outside of the nominal domain. They can function as adverbial modifiers, and usually also as degree modifiers of an adjectival projection:[9]

(12) a. Les étudiants ont beaucoup dansé
the students have a-lot danced

b. Pierre est peu allé au cinéma ces derniers temps
Pierre has little gone to-the movies these last times

c. Sylvie apprécie énormément ce film
Sylvie appreciates a-whole-lot this movie

d. Paul est trop fatigué pour aller à la fête
Paul is too tired to go to the party

The selectional properties of DQs can be accounted for if we assume that they do not select a specific syntactic category. The only thing they need in order to be used is a scale with respect to which they can be interpreted.

Let us first consider the case of (12a,b). It has been argued by Bach (1986) that the linkean approach to the nominal system and the domain of objects can be extended to the verbal system and the domain of events. Processes and events are structured as complete Boolean algebras. Within this approach we expect to find *beaucoup* type expressions as modifiers of mass and plural VPs, on a par with their use as modifiers of mass and plural noun phrases. The predicate *danser* can be seen as a mass predicate. Two eventualities that can be characterized

[8]Cf. Link 1983, Krifka 1992, who define this property in terms of cumulative reference in a lattice theoretic framework:

(i) $\forall$P (CUM(P) $\leftrightarrow$ $\forall$x,y[P(x) & P(y) $\rightarrow$ P(x $\vee$ y)])

A predicate $P$ has cumulative reference iff for every $x$ and for every $y$ that have the property $P$, the join of $x$ and $y$ ($x \vee y$) has the property $P$ as well, where the join of $x$ and $y$ corresponds, roughly speaking, to $x$ and $y$ put together. This property holds for plural and mass nouns, but not for count singulars.

[9]See Doetjes 1997, 2001b, where the incompatibility of *beaucoup* and adjectives is accounted for in terms of the Elsewhere Principle.

by *danser* taken together can again be characterized by the predicate *danser*. The predicate *aller au cinéma* can be seen as vague with respect to plurality. Any number of events that count as visits to the movies, can be referred to with the predicate *aller au cinéma*. In both cases the predicate has cumulative reference, which explains the possiblility of modification by a DQ.

The acceptability of (12c,d) shows that the use of these expressions is not restricted to cases where we find a quantitative scale, as in the examples discussed so far. Here, we are dealing with a scale of quality or intensity.

As we will see in the next two sections, there are two constructions in French in which the wide distribution of DQs is crucial. In both Quantification at a distance and DQ-float we find a DQ that has adverbial properties, but that is interpreted as (part of) a nominal expression.

### 3.2 Quantification at a distance

DQs can be used in the so-called 'quantification at a distance' construction (QAD) illustrated in (13) (see also chapter 12, Adverbs and Quantification). The DQ is located in an adverbial position preceding the past participle, and the direct object has the form *de NP*:

(13) Sylvie a beaucoup lu de livres
Sylvie has a lot read of books

'Sylvie read a lot of books'

In this example, *beaucoup* precedes the past participle, but as the translation shows, it is understood as the determiner of the direct object *de livres*. The form of the direct object is licensed by the presence of the DQ. In the absence of *beaucoup*, the direct object would have the form *des livres*. One way to approach the construction makes use of determiner raising: *beaucoup* is base generated in the DP and has been moved to a derived position. However, there are several indications that suggest that 'determiner raising' is, at least at the surface, not an option in French. All 'pure' determiners are disallowed in , including *plein* 'a lot', which only differs from *beaucoup* in its restriction to the nominal system.

The idea that the possibility of using DQs as adverbs is crucial for the acceptability of (13) was first defended by Obenauer (1983, 1984). Obenauer argues that, even though *beaucoup* seems to quantify over books in (13), must involve adverbial quantification in terms of *x-times*, where x stands for the Q. This implies that is impossible in contexts where *beaucoup* can only have an intensity reading as in (14):

(14) *Pierre a beaucoup apprécié de films
Pierre has a-lot appreciated of movies

As argued in Doetjes (1995, 1997), Obenauer's requirement is too strong. Even though always involves adverbial modification by the DQ, this can lead to both a mass reading and a count reading. The count reading corresponds to Obenauer's x-times reading. The mass reading is necessary in order to account for examples such as (15), which crucially does not have a *many*-times reading:

(15) La fontaine a beaucoup craché d'eau
the fountain has a-lot spouted of-water

Doetjes 1997 proposes a modified account of Obenauer's hypothesis: is only possible in contexts where the object 'measures out' the event, that is, the quantity of the object determines the type of quantity of the event. Unbounded events (corresponding to cumulative predicates; see note 8) typically combine with adverbial expressions of the type *pendant <time period>* 'for <time period>' while bounded events (corresponding to non-cumulative predicates) typically combine with expressions of the type *en <time period>* 'in <time period>'. As a result of measuring out, the event inherits the referential properties of the object. In (16a), the event of reading is unbounded, as is the amount of books, which makes it incompatible with the adverbial *en deux mois* 'in two months'. In (16b), the event of reading is bounded, as is *ce livre* 'this book' (cf. part III on Tense and Aspect).

(16) a. # Pierre a lu des livres en deux mois
Pierre has read DES books in two months

b. Pierre a lu ce livre en deux mois
Pierre has read this book in two months

The DQ in a sentence determines both the quantity of the event and the quantity of the object, as these are dependent on one another. This explains the interpretation of sentences such as (17):

(17) a. Jean a beaucoup porté de livres
Jean has a-lot carried of books

b. Pendant les dix minutes du concours, Jean a assez
during the ten minutes of the contest, Jean has enough
bu de bière pour désaltérer un peloton de
drank of beer to quench-the-thirst-of a troop of
soldats suisses
soldiers Swiss

In these sentences, the amount of books / beer is modified by the DQ through modification of the quantity of the event corresponding to the verb phrase: (17a) describes a 'big' event of book carrying and (17b) a drinking event that is comparable to a drinking event during which a troop of Swiss soldiers quenches their thirst. As such the construction is an example of a construction that makes use of the fact that VPs and NPs both define a scale of quantity that can be modified by a DQ.

### 3.3 DQ-float

A second phenomenon which seems to be dependent on the property of DQs having both an adnominal and an adverbial use is DQ-float, a special type of quantifier float (cf. Doetjes 1997). Consider the examples in (18):

(18) a. Elle a beaucoup fait pour eux
she has a-lot done for them
b. Elle a fait beaucoup pour eux
c. Elle a tout fait pour eux
she has everything done for them
d. *Elle a fait pour eux
e. Elle a fait quelque chose pour eux
f. *Elle a quelque chose fait pour eux

The verb *faire* needs a direct object (18d), which can be provided by bare *beaucoup* (18a,b). *Beaucoup* can occupy a position that is excluded for the normal direct object (cf. 18a vs. 18f). At first sight, we would like to say that in (18a) and (18b) we are dealing with determiner *beaucoup* used in a nounless DP. In (18a), this determiner occupies a 'floated' position, as does *tout* in (18c). However, there are reasons to believe that *beaucoup* in (18a) and also (18b) is in fact generated as an adverb (note that adverbial *beaucoup* can either precede or follow the past participle). A first argument in favor of this idea is that only adverbial determiners are allowed in this position. Even a determiner like *plein*, which shares all relevant properties with *beaucoup* when used as a determiner, but is exceptional because it cannot be used as an adverb, cannot float:

(19) * Elle a plein fait pour eux / fait plein pour eux
she has a-lot done for them / done a-lot for them

Moreover, if bare *beaucoup* could be a nounless DP, we would expect to find it in positions that we are sure are DP positions, contrary to the one it occupies in (18a), which is ambiguous between a DP position and an adverbial position. It turns out that bare *beaucoup* is excluded in all positions that we are sure are not adverbial, such as the object position of a preposition, and the subject position.[10] In this respect it differs from *tout*.

(20) a. *Il a pensé à beaucoup
he has thought at a-lot

b. Il a pensé à tout
he has thought at everything
'He thought about everything'

c. *Beaucoup a été arrangé
much has been arranged

d. Tout a été arrangé
everything has been arranged

Similarly, the sentence in (21) only has a meaning in which *beaucoup* is an intensity modifier on the verb; it cannot be interpreted as the direct object of the verb (which in the context of this verb can be covert, see Fónagy 1985):

(21) a. Il a beaucoup apprécié
he has a lot appreciated
'He appreciated it a lot'; not: 'He appreciated a lot of things'

b. Il a tout apprécié
he has everything appreciated
'He appreciated everything'

The data in (20) and (21) strongly suggest that there are two types of bare quantifier float in French. On the one hand, nominal Q expressions such as *tout* can occupy a position to the left of the verb, while being in essence nominal. On the other hand, adverbial expressions such as *beaucoup* can license the absence of a direct object when used as an

[10] *Beaucoup* can occupy the subject position, and in some rare cases even the object position of a preposition, but not with the same interpretation as the bare Q *beaucoup* in (18a,b). In subject position, *beaucoup* is usually plural and presuppositional, as in *Beaucoup sont venus* 'Many of them came' (cf. chapter 2, 'Nounless determiners' for cases). Singular *beaucoup* can be a subject as well in sentences such as *Beaucoup reste encore à faire* 'A lot still has to be done' (Petra Sleeman, p.c.). It turns out that these cases are restricted in an interesting way: they depend on the possibility of a partitioning of the domain, as introduced by the verb *rester* 'to remain' and in *Beaucoup a été fait, mais le plus important reste encore à faire* 'A lot has been done, but the most important thing still has to be done'. In the absence of such a partitioning, the use of singular *beaucoup* in subject position is odd (Johan Rooryck, p.c.). Such a restriction does not obtain for *beaucoup* in the examples in (18a,b). This is in accordance with the claim that in these cases we are dealing with a bare Q expression lacking DP structure.

adverbial on the VP. Again this property seems to be related to 'measuring out'. By acting as a measure on the quantity expressed by the verb, the adverbial DQ replaces the direct object and gives the impression of being a nominal expression, on a par with Qs such as *tout*, which measures out the event in the regular way. This also explains the impossiblity of the floating *beaucoup* reading in (21a).

## 4 Concluding remarks

DQs are not real determiners. However, they are found in the nominal system, where they are used as if they were determiners. They differ from 'pure' determiners in a number of ways. Their interpretation and their selectional properties within the nominal system correlate strongly with their large distributional possibilities outside of the nominal system. DQs are typically interpreted with respect to a 'quantity of reference'. This property is responsible for their properties with respect to entailments and habituality. They combine with mass nouns and plural because these allow us to define a scale of quantity with respect to which the DQ is interpreted. As we have seen, there are two phenomena in French in which DQs function as adverbs, but are interpreted as if they constitute (part of) a nominal expression.

## References

Bach, E. 1986. The algebra of events. *Linguistics & Philosophy* 9:5–16.

Baüerle, R., C. Schwarze, and A. von Stechow, eds. 1983. *Meaning, Use and Interpretation of Language*. Berlin: Walter de Gruyter.

Beckman, J., ed. 1995. *Proceedings of NELS (North Eastern Linguistic Society)*, vol. 25.

Bierwisch, M. 1987. The semantics of gradation. In Bierwisch and Lang (1987).

Bierwisch, M. and E. Lang, eds. 1987. *Dimensional Adjectives: Grammatical Structure and Conceptual Interpretation*. Berlin: Springer Verlag.

Bok-Bennema, R., R. de Jonge, B. Kampers-Manhe, and A. Molendijk, eds. 2001. *La modification adverbiale*. Amsterdam: Rodopi.

Corblin, F. 1997. Peut-on anaphoriser le complément d'un ensemble? In Moeschler and Béguelin (1997).

Corblin, F. 1999. Quantification et anaphore discursive: la référence aux complémentaires. *Langages* 123:51–74.

De Hoop, H. 1992. *Case Configuration and Noun Phrase interpretation*. Ph.D. thesis, University of Groningen.

Doetjes, J. 1995. Quantification at a distance and iteration. In Beckman (1995), pages 111–26.

Doetjes, J. 1997. *Quantifiers and Selection. On the distribution of quantifying expressions in French, Dutch and English*. Ph.D. thesis, Universiteit Leiden, Den Haag.

Doetjes, J. 2001a. Beaucoup est ailleurs. Expressions de degré et sous-spécification catégorielle. In Bok-Bennema et al. (2001), pages 125–138.

Doetjes, J. 2001b. La distribution des expressions quantificatrices et le statut des noms non comptables. In Kleiber et al. (2001), pages 119–142.

Ducrot, O. 1980. *Dire et ne pas dire*. Collection Savoir. Paris: Hermann.

Fónagy, I. 1985. J'aime □ je connais □. Verbes transitifs à objet latent. *Revue Romane* 20:3–35.

Gaatone, D. 1991. Les déterminants de la quantité peu élevé en francais. remarques sur les emplois de quelques et plusieurs. *Revue Romane* 26(1).

Gondret, P. 1976. "Quelques", "plusieurs", "certains", "divers". Etude semantique. *Le francais moderne* 44:143–152.

Keenan, E. and J. Stavi. 1986. A semantic characterisation of natural language determiners. *Linguistics and Philosophy* 9:254–326.

Kleiber, G., B. Laca, and L. Tasmowski, eds. 2001. *Typologie des groupes nominaux*. Rennes: Presses Universitaires de Rennes.

Krifka, M. 1992. Thematic relations as links between nominal reference and temporal constitution. In Sag and Szabolcsi (1992), pages 29–53.

Link, G. 1983. The logical analysis of plurals and mass terms: A lattice-theoretical approach. In Baüerle et al. (1983), pages 302–23.

Megerdoomian, K. and L. A. Bar-el, eds. 2001. *Proceedings of the 20th West Coast Conference on Formal Linguistics*. UCSC.

Moeschler, J. and M.-J. Béguelin, eds. 1997. *Référence temporelle et nominale*. Peter Lang.

Moore, S. and A. Winner, eds. 1991. *Proceedings from Semantics and Linguistic Theory 1 [= Cornell Working Papers in Linguistics 1]*.

Moxey and Sandford. 1993. *Communicating quantities. A psychological perspective*. Laurence Erlbaum Associates.

Muller, C. 1991. *La négation en français*. Genève: Droz.

Neeleman, A., H. van de Koot, and J. Doetjes. 2004. Degree expressions. *The Linguistic Review* 21:1–66.

Obenauer, H.-G. 1983. Une quantification non-canonique: la "quantification à distance". *Langue Française* 58:66–88.

Obenauer, H.-G. 1984. On the identification of empty categories. *The Linguistic Review* 4:153–202.

Obenauer, H.-G. 1994. *Aspects de la syntaxe A-barre. Effets d'intervention et mouvements des quantifieurs*. Ph.D. thesis, Université de Paris VIII.

Partee, B. 1988. Many quantifiers. In Powers and de Jong (1988), pages 383–402.

Partee, B. 1991. Topic, focus and quantification. In Moore and Winner (1991), pages 159–188.

Powers, J. and K. de Jong, eds. 1988. *Proceedings of the fifth Eastern States Conference on Linguistics*. The Ohio State University.

Sag, I. and A. Szabolcsi, eds. 1992. *Lexical Matters*. Stanford: CSLI.

Stechow, V. 1985. Comparing semantic theories of comparison. *Journal of Semantics* 3:1–77.

Tovena, L. 2001. Between mass and count. In Megerdoomian and Bar-el (2001), pages 565–578.

Westerståhl, D. 1985. Logical constants in quantifier languages. *Linguistics & Philosophy* 8:387–413.

# 7

# *Quelque*[*]

Francis Corblin

## 1 Quelque

As observed by van de Velde (2000:255–263), the singular *quelque N* ('some N') is less frequent in modern French than the other forms of the paradigm, namely *quelques Ns* ('some Ns') and *quelqu'un* ('someone'), *quelque chose* ('something'). *Quelque* can combine with count nouns and with mass nouns, but only abstract mass nouns:

(1) Il aura rencontré quelque camarade et se sera arrêté.
'He will have met some friend and will have stopped.'

(2) Pierre a montré quelque courage en la circonstance.
'Peter demonstrated some courage on this occasion.'
(Wilmet 1996)

(3) * Il aura renversé quelque eau.[1]
'He will have spilled some water.'

A peculiarity of *quelque N* noted in the litterature (cf. Culioli 1984, Dobrovie Sorin 1985, Wilmet 1996) is its association with epistemic/modal contexts. Although it does not extend to all uses of *quelque* (*quelqu'un/quelque chose* can be used in simple assertive sentences), it is a property which is particularly interesting for the theory of polarity-like phenomena.

*Thanks are due to the members of the PICS "Determiners" group for useful questions and comments after presentations of the initial material of this chapter. I am very grateful to Ileana Comorovski for her very helpful comments and suggestions on the last draft of this chapter.

[1] According to van de Velde (2000: 258), such sentences are odd in modern French.

*Handbook of French Semantics.*
Francis Corblin and Henriëtte de Swart (eds.).
Copyright © 2004, CSLI Publications.

A property common to all uses (extending to plural *quelques*), and not mentioned in the literature about French, at least to our knowledge, is the "anti-negative" nature of *quelque*, i.e. the fact that *quelque* is interpreted as a variable that cannot appear in the scope of negation.[2]

### 1.1 *Quelque N* and epistemic/modal contexts

*Quelque* (singular, followed by a count noun) is restricted to epistemic/modal contexts. As noted by Culioli (1984: 7), "*quelque N* est nécessairement lié à la présence d'un marqueur modal", "*quelque N* est incompatible avec l'assertion stricte".[3]

There are three kinds of licensing contexts:[4]
A) Sentences expressing a hypothesis (1) or a question (4).

(4) Avez vous rencontré quelque coquille, ou quelque faute d'orthographe dans ce devoir?
'Have you found any typo or any spelling error in this homework?'

B) Sentences involving a reiteration:

(5) Si quelque lièvre ou chevreuil traversait la route, il fallait s'arrêter.
'If some deer or some hare crossed the road, you had to stop.'

C) Sentences expressing some sort of ignorance:

(6) Il avait rencontré quelque voisin ou parent dans ce train.
'He had met some neighbor or relative on this train.'

(7) Quelque vague général qui se trouvait disponible, se vit confier les rênes de l'état. (Culioli (1984))
'Some general or other, who was available, was given the direction of the state.'

If *quelque* occurs in a past tense sentence, there is a strong tendency to interpret the sentence as expressing a supposition:

(8) Il a rencontré quelque camarade.
'He met some friend'

And this reading is very often reinforced by a disjunction, as in (6).

It is not clear whether this restriction to epistemic/modal contexts fully holds for *quelque* followed by an abstract noun, as can be seen from (2) above. The restriction to epistemic/modal contexts does not

[2] Since Jespersen (1922) and Baker (1970), who introduces the notion of "positive polarity item", this kind of prohibition has received less attention than negative polarity licensing. A notable exception is Szabolcsi (2001) on English and Hungaria.

[3] '*quelque N* requires the presence of a marker of modality', '*Quelque N* is incompatible with genuine assertion'.

[4] My presentation is very close to Culioli's taxonomy.

extend to *quelqu'un, quelque chose* and *quelques Ns*, which can be freely used in any context.

A natural assumption is that *quelque N* (singular) is an indefinite licensed by a special class of modal contexts. The common feature of the licensing contexts is that they play with the existence of an entity as a value for a variable, without giving any real importance to its nature, and even to its singularity; very often, *quelque* $N_i$ occurs as a member of disjunctions like: *quelque* $N_i$ *ou* $N_j$, *quelque* $N_i$ *ou plusieurs.* In other words, the precise identity of the individual does not seem to really matter. As compared to the standard indefinite *un N*, *quelque N* is not ambiguous, and can only be interpreted as a dependent variable, not as a wide scope (existential) indefinite. It could thus be compared to polarity items like *le moindre.* The main difference from true polarity items is that the sets of licensing contexts are not identical, and the most salient difference is that negation is *not* in the licensing set of *quelque* as shown by (9):

(9) * Je n'ai pas mangé quelque pomme.
I not-have neg. eaten some apple

If we see *quelque N* as a variable to be interpreted in the scope of a specific set of logical operators, negation is excluded from this set. It is thus clearly different from negative polarity items (NPI), but also from positive polarity items (PPI).

## 1.2 *Quelque* as an anti-negative item

### 1.2.1 *Quelque* N

Sentences like (9) above are ungrammatical, unless one reinterprets them as questions: *(N'aurais-je pas mangé quelque pomme?).* This indicates that if *quelque N* occurs in the C-command domain of negation, the sentence as a whole must be reinterpreted not as a true negation, but as a question. In the following example, it is the epistemic value of the *futur antérieur* ('future in the past') which is the licensor:

(10) Il n'aura pas prévenu quelque collègue de son départ et celui-ci aura été mécontent.[5]
'He will not have warned some colleague that he was leaving, and he would have been upset.'

We can find examples involving the interpretation of *quelque N* in the C-command domain of negation, provided that this negation is outscoped by another logical operator:

[5]It is worth noticing that in this case, *quelque* will have to take scope over negation. The sentence means: (it is likely that) there is one colleague that he did not inform. It cannot mean: (it is likely that) he did not inform any colleague.

(11) S'il n'a pas rencontré quelque collègue, ou ami, il sera là bientôt.
'If he has not met some colleague or friend, he will be here soon.'

More surprisingly, double negation can license *quelque N*:[6]

(12) Je ne dis pas qu'il n'a pas rencontré quelque collègue.
'I don't say that he has not met some colleague.'

But if we consider examples like (13) and (14), we might conclude that it is not the higher negation *per se* which is the licensor of the negated *quelque*:

(13) ?? Marie ne savait pas qu'il n'avait pas rencontré quelque collègue.
'Marie did not know that he had not met some colleague.'

(14) ?? Marie ne croyait pas qu'il n'avait pas rencontré quelque collègue
'Marie did not believe that he had not met some colleague.'

Although the syntactic configuration looks similar, *quelque N* is not licensed. We might suggest that the licensing context of (12) is the complex *I do not say that + negative*, which is interpreted, as a whole, as an epistemic-modal context: *it is possible that S*. On the contrary, the double negation of (13)–(14) would count as an assertion and would not provide the required epistemic context.

To sum up, the data shows that *quelque N* can only occur in the C-command domain of negation if this negation is not the highest operator of the representation, and if the highest operator can be interpreted as the epistemic/modal licensor of *quelque*.

## 2 Quelques Ns

### 2.1 The negative constraint

This fact points to another one concerning the two French indefinite pronouns *quelqu'un* and *quelque chose*: if these pronouns are in the syntactic scope of negation, the only way to accept the sentence is to interpret the indefinite as taking scope over the negation:

(15) Je n'ai pas mangé quelque chose / Je n'ai pas vu quelqu'un.
'I did not eat something / I did not see someone.'

These sentences can only be interpreted as: "there is something I did not eat, there is someone I did not see". Moreover, most speakers feel

[6] Such intervening contexts are mentioned in the literature on PPIs since Jespersen (1922), see Szabolcsi (2001). The interesting point about French data is that *quelque* (singular) is *not* a PPI: it is not licensed in simple assertive sentences (see above).

that (15) is not a natural way to express this meaning. The same is true for *quelques N*:

(16) Je n'ai pas salué quelques amis.
'I did not greet some friends.'

This sentence can only mean: "there are some friends I did not greet". It is important to state correctly the precise nature of the constraint. One cannot say that *quelques N* is not licensed by negation, or is ruled out by negation. In fact, *quelqu'un* is syntactically correct in the syntactic scope of negation. One cannot say either that *quelques N* is a wide scope ("existential") item. Although, and this is the main difference with *quelque N*, it *can* be interpreted as an existential (wide scope) indefinite, it is perfectly correct as well with any other subclass of NPI licensors (e.g. questions and conditionals).

(17) Si vous avez besoin de quelqu'un / de quelque chose, appelez-moi.
'If you need someone / something, call me'

The point is precisely that *quelques N* cannot be interpreted in the scope of widest scope negation; we will take this as a feature of the whole *quelque* paradigm.

(18) **Negative constraint:** a variable introduced by *quelque* cannot be interpreted in the scope of widest scope negation.[7]

This constraint makes nice predictions for more complicated sentences. Consider (19):

(19) Pierre ne mange pas quelque chose le matin.
'Pierre does not eat something in the morning.'

The sentence can only mean that there is something Pierre does not eat. But consider (20):

(20) Si je ne mange pas quelque chose le matin, j'ai faim à midi.
'If I do not eat something in the morning, I am hungry at noon.'

The negative constraint does not prevent the interpretation of *quelque chose* in the scope of the negation outscoped by the antecedent of the conditional, which is a nice consequence, since (20) can be used for saying: "if I eat nothing in the morning, I am hungry at midday."

[7]By 'widest scope negation' we mean a negation taking scope in the representation over any other operator like questions, conditionals, etc. We do not take the indefinite itself as a logical operator, but as a variable (as in DRT).

### 2.2 *Sans*

One could object that *sans* ('without') has licensing properties which are very close to negation (see chapter 19) and can nevertheless be used with *quelque*. But it is striking to observe that *quelque N* is licensed after *sans* mainly when *sans* is itself in the scope of a clause-mate negation. If *sans* is in an affirmative sentence, *quelque N* is not licensed:

(21) *Sa jovialité était sans quelque cynisme.
her joviality was without some cynicism

We have found empirical confirmation of this strong constraint in the data base FRANTEXT. We found 26 occurrences of *sans quelque N* in a given set of texts. In *all* examples, the main sentence contains some negative particle: *ne … pas* or *non*. Typical examples are:

(22) Le tout, je crois, ne sera pas sans quelque grandeur… (Hugo, Correspondance)
'The entire thing, I think, will not be without some greatness.'

(23) Arrivé, non sans quelque peine, au pied de la tour… (Hugo, Le Rhin)
'Once arrived, not without some pain, at the foot of the tower.'

This preference of *sans … quelque* for a clause-mate negative particle seems to hold for *quelqu'un/quelque chose*.

(24) ? Marie se promenait sans quelqu'un / Marie ne se promenait jamais sans quelqu'un.
'Mary was walking without someone / Mary would never walk without someone'

(25) ? Marie était toujours sans quelque chose à faire / Marie n'était jamais sans quelque chose à faire.
'Mary was always without something to do / Mary was never without something to do.'

Many examples in our corpus illustrate this:

(26) Je n'ai pu faire un pas sans rencontrer quelqu'un qui m'en parlât. (Zola)
'I was unable to make a step without meeting someone who told me about it.'

(27) … puis, comme elle ne voulait pas s' en aller sans dire quelque chose, (Zola)
'… then, as she did not want to go without saying something.'

Moreover, there is a strong collocation between negation and *sans quelques N*, as illustrated by the following examples:

(28) Gringoire monta sur l' escabeau, et parvint, non sans quelques oscillations de la tête et des bras, à y retrouver son centre de gravité. (Hugo)
'Grégoire climbed on the ladder, and succeeded, not without some oscillations, in finding his balance.'

(29) Il ne passait guère devant cet homme sans lui donner quelques sous. (Hugo)
'He rarely walked past this man without giving him some money.'

How can we explain these rather strange data involving *sans*? We will show that as strange as they are, they follow to some extent from our hypothesis.

Let us assume that *sans* has most properties of the negative, in particular the property of taking an indefinite in its scope.

*Quelque N* is a member of the *quelque* paradigm: as such, it cannot be interpreted in the scope of widest scope negation; see the negative constraint (18) above. But *quelque N* cannot be interpreted by existential closure, as asserting the existence of an individual. This is why (30) is not acceptable:

(30) * Pierre n'a pas appelé quelque camarade.
'Peter did not called some friend'

If *sans* shares with *ne ... pas* the property of introducing a negative operator in the representation, the following sentence should be ruled out for the same reason:

(31) *Pierre est parti sans quelque camarade.
'Peter is left without some companion

and I think that this prediction is borne out.

We have now to explain why the combination of the negative particles *(ne ... pas, non)* with *sans ... quelque* is fine, and, in fact, highly typical. Pursuing the parallelism between *sans* and the negative particles, we can try to generalize to *sans* the properties which hold of the negative particles, which would give: *sans quelque N* cannot be interpreted unless a higher operator is a licensor for *quelque*. We have found for instance, that a higher conditional can play this role (see (16) above). It can also license *sans quelque N*:

(32) Si Pierre est parti sans quelque camarade pour l'aider, il est stupide.
'If P. has gone without some companion to help him, he is stupid.'

In (32) the variable contributed by *quelque* is neither existential, nor bound by widest scope negation. In this very context, any member of the *quelque* paradigm is licensed and can be interpreted in the scope of the out-scoped negation.

How then should we analyze the context created by the negative particles, illustrated by (22)–(23)? It can be taken as satisfying the negative constraint: the variable contributed is in the scope of negation, but the negation does not have widest scope (there is another negation taking scope over it). This would predict that the whole *quelque* paradigm will be licensed, which is true.

Nevertheless, it is not enough to predict that *quelque* will be fine, since *quelque* requires, except with abstract nouns (cf. supra), a variable in the scope of an "epistemic" operator. Again, we can solve the problem, by making the assumption that double negation is an operator which does not give any real importance to the identity of the individual satisfying the predicate.

## 3 Conclusion

The *quelque* paradigm in French seems to illustrate a very specific constraint: it contributes a variable which cannot be interpreted in the scope of widest scope negation. Our formulation of the constraint exhibits three interesting features: it is a semantic constraint (it signals a scopal configuration in which the variable cannot be interpreted); it is a constraint which sets negation apart from any other logical operator; it is a constraint concerning widest scope negation. It might be the case that such items should be compared to the category of Positive Polarity Items, introduced for English in the literature in the 70's, but the data regarding *quelque N* (singular) shows that this category cannot apply to all uses of *quelque*, and we think that the members of the *quelque* paradigm are better characterized as anti-negative items.

As for singular *quelque*, we showed that it is governed by an additional licensing condition requiring the interpretation of the variable in some kind of epistemic-modal context. It should, in this respect, be compared with other dependent indefinites (e.g. *vreun* in Romanian (Comorovski 1984, Farkas 2002); reduplicated cardinals in Hungarian (Farkas 1997)).

Both constraints offer an interesting enrichment of the landscape of dependent indefinites in natural languages.

## References

Baker, C. 1970. Double negatives. *Linguistic Inquiry* 1:169–189.

Beyssade, C., R. Bok-Bennema, F. Drijkoningen, and P. Monachesi, eds. 2002. *Romance Languages and Linguistic Theory 2000*. John Benjamins.

Bosveld-de Smet, L., M. van Peteghem, and D. van de Velde, eds. 2000a. *De l'indétermination à la qualification. Les indéfinis*. Artois Presses Université.

Bosveld-de Smet, L., M. van Peteghem, and D. van de Velde, eds. 2000b. *De l'indétermination à la qualification. Les indéfinis*. Artois Presses Université.

Comorovski, I. 1984. A marker of intensionality in Romanian. Manuscript, University of Massachusetts, Amherst.

Corblin, F., D. Godard, and J.-M. Marandin, eds. 1997. *Empirical issues in Formal Syntax and Semantics*. Peter Lang.

Culioli, A. 1984. A propos de quelque. In Fisher and Franckel (1984), pages 21–29.

Dobrovie-Sorin, C. 1985. *Actes de langage et Théorie de l'énonciation*. Collection ERA 642. DRL – Laboratoire de linguistique formelle, Paris 7.

Farkas, D. 1997. Dependent indefinites. In Corblin et al. (1997), pages 243–269.

Farkas, D. 2002. Extreme non-specificity in Romanian. In Beyssade et al. (2002), pages 127–153.

Fisher, S. and J. Franckel, eds. 1984. *Linguistique, énonciation, aspects et détermination*. Paris: Editions EHESS.

Jespersen, O. 1917. *A Modern English Grammar*. George Allen and Unwin.

Kleiber, G., B. Laca, and L. Tasmowski. 2001. *Typologie des groupes nominaux*. Presses Universitaires de Rennes.

Szabolcsi, A. 2004. Positive polarity – negative polarity. *Natural Language and Linguistic theory* 22:409–452.

Van de Velde, D. 2000. Les indéfinis comme adjectifs. In Bosveld-de Smet et al. (2000b), pages 203–269.

Wilmet, M. 1996. *Grammaire critique du français*. Paris: Duclot.

# 8

# *Différents*

BRENDA LACA AND LILIANE TASMOWSKI

*Différent* is originally a predicate denoting a symmetric and irreflexive relation of non-identity (*pas le même* 'not the same') or non-similarity (*pas pareil, pas semblable* 'not similar, not alike'). Unlike its English counterpart, it exhibits quite distinct syntactic and semantic properties when it functions as an adjective and when it functions as a determiner, so that it is possible to distinguish between two items, Adj-*différent* and Det-*différents*. We briefly review the distributional properties of both items, then compare the properties of Det-*différents* to those of other indefinite plural determiners, and conclude by comparing the semantic properties of Adj-*différent* to those of Det-*différents*.

## 1 Adj-*différent* vs. Det-*différents*

Adj-*différent* appears in predicate or adnominal position (1a–b); it can be preceded by intensifying adverbs (1b), and it has a second argument position to be filled by a prepositional phrase introduced by *de* (1c):

(1) a. Je vous imaginais différente
I you imagined different
'I thought you were different'

b. Ce texte existe en deux versions entièrement différentes
This text exists in two versions entirely different
'This texts exists in two fully different versions'

c. Il souhaitait un avenir différent de celui de son frère
He desired a future different of that of his brother
'He wanted a different future than his brother's'

*Handbook of French Semantics.*
Francis Corblin and Henriëtte de Swart (eds.).
Copyright © 2004, CSLI Publications.

Det-*différents* can only appear in prenominal position and it is necessarily plural (2a). It is in complementary distribution with other indefinite determiners, in particular with *de(s)* (2b):

(2) a. Différents organismes / * Organismes différents ont
Different organizations / Organizations different have
demandé sa collaboration
requested his collaboration
'Various organizations requested his collaboration'

b. * Plusieurs différents / * De différents organismes ont
Several / *De* different organizations have
demandé sa collaboration
requested his collaboration

Furthermore, Det-*différents* cannot be preceded by intensifying adverbs and has no second argument position. Thus, adjectival syntax requires the introduction of *de* in the determiner position that cannot be occupied by *différents*:

(3) a. *(De) si différentes personnalités ne pourront jamais s'accorder
*(*De*) so different personalities not will-be-able never REFL-agree
'Such different personalities will never get to agree'

b. Il a *(de) bien différentes aspirations de ce que tu t'imagines
He has *(de) well different ambitions of that that you REFL-imagine
'He has very different ambitions than what you imagine'

Note that there is no perfect correlation between pre- vs. postnominal position and determiner vs. adjectival status, since Adj-*différent*, though most often found postnominally, can also appear in prenominal position. This is also the case in DPs introduced by a definite determiner (4a). The possibility of adverbial modification is evidence for the adjectival status of *différent* (4b):[1]

(4) a. Les / Ces différentes objections qui ont été soulevées
The / These different objections that have been put forward

b. Les / Ces si / bien différentes objections qui ont été
'The / These so / very different objections that have been
soulevées
put forward'

[1] Although more marginal, there are analogous occurrences of prenominal Adj-*différent* in DPs introduced by an indefinite determiner, such as *quatre différents services* 'four different wards'. This type of example was much more frequent in 17th and 18th century French, where sequences like *beaucoup de différents N* 'many different N', *plusieurs différents N* 'several different N' are attested. The prenominal position of indefinite nominal projections has become increasingly specialized for Det-*différents* in Contemporary French, so that some speakers might reject examples like (3a) above, preferring versions with postnominal Adj-*différent*.

## 2 Det-*différents* and other indefinite plural determiners

Det-*différents* does not exhibit the same syntactic distribution as the other indefinite determiners. It is either awkward or downright impossible in the absence of a lexical nominal head:

(5) a. Les films de ce régisseur sont très populaires.
The pictures of this director are very popular.
J'en ai vu certains / plusieurs / *différents et
I of-them have seen some / several / *different and
ils ne m'ont pas plu.
they not me have pleased.
'This director's pictures are very popular. I've seen some / several / *different of them and I haven't liked them'

b. Les étudiants étaient très fâchés. Certains / Plusieurs /
The students were very angry. Some / Several /
*Différents sont venus se plaindre
*Different are come REFL-complain
'The students were very angry. Some / Several / *Different of them came to complain'

As (6) shows, *différents* patterns like an adjective in the absence of a lexical nominal head:

(6) a. J'en ai vu *différentes / * belles
I of-them have seen different / pretty

b. J'en ai vu de bien différentes / de bien belles
I of-them have seen of well different / of well pretty
'I have seen very different ones / very pretty ones'

This seems to indicate that Det-*différents* has not acquired all the syntactic properties of full-fledged determiners.[2]

As to its semantic properties, Det-*différents* resists group interpretations, strongly favoring distributive readings. Thus (7a) necessarily involves more than one gift, which is not the case for (7b):

(7) a. Différents invités m'ont apporté un bouquet de fleurs
Different guests me have brought a bunch of flowers
'Different guests brought me a bunch of flowers'

---

[2]It is true that, at least in Standard French, *des* exhibits a similar behavior. Note, however, that in spoken, everyday language, one finds marginal instances of *des* without a lexical nominal head, as in *Des comme vous, il y en a pas des masses* 'People (lit. *des*) like you, there are not so many'. This is entirely impossible with *différents*.

b. Quelques invités m'ont apporté un bouquet de fleurs
Some guests me have brought a bunch of flowers
'Some guests brought me bunch of flowers'

Generic interpretations of plural indefinites, which rely on generic quantification over group variables, are also excluded by Det-*différents*:

(8) a. # Différentes personnes décidées peuvent entraîner une foule
Different people determined can lead a crowd
[* COLLECTIVE GENERIC]
'Different determined people can lead a crowd'

b. Plusieurs personnes décidées peuvent entraîner une foule
Several people determined can lead a crowd
[OK COLLECTIVE GENERIC]
'(A group of) some determined people can lead a crowd'

On the contrary, Det-*différents* favors taxonomic generic readings, in which the entities quantified over are subkinds of the kind N:

(9) Différents oiseaux font leurs nids dans ces falaises
Different birds make their nests on these cliffs
'Different birds nest on these cliffs'

These properties distinguish Det-*différents* from the determiners expressing vague cardinality (*quelques, plusieurs*) and resemble those of *certain.* Furthermore, like *certains*, *différents* is not compatible with distributive modifiers (Bosveld-de Smet 1997:21), that seem to require bona fide quantity expressions:

(10) a. Il lisait quelques / plusieurs articles par jour
He read some / several articles by day
'He read a few / several articles a day'

b. * Il lisait certains / ?différents articles par jour
He read certain / ?different articles by day
'He read certain / different articles a day'

And, like *certains*, Det-*différents* requires the possibility of some qualitative difference among the instantiations of the noun it introduces, which explains why both are impossible with measure nouns:

(11) a. * Il a parcouru certains / différents kilomètres
He has traveled certain / different kilometers

b. * Il a bu certains / différents litres de bière
He has drunk certain / different liters of beer

But Det-*différents* does not pattern like *certains* with regard to partitivity or D-linking, or in its scope properties. Whereas *certains* strongly suggests partitive readings, Det-*différents* does not carry any implicature as to the existence of a non-null complement set (N–N∩P). Thus, (12a) suggests that there are other editions of *Don Quixote* apart from those to be found in the catalog, a suggestion which is not conveyed by (12b):

(12) a. Ce catalogue ne contient que certaines éditions du Don Quichotte
This catalog not contains but certain editions of Don Quixote
'This catalog contains only some editions of Don Quixote'

b. Ce catalogue ne contient que différentes éditions du Don Quichotte
This catalog not contains but different editions of Don Quixote
'This catalog contains only various editions of Don Quixote'

Unlike *certains*, and like cardinal indefinites, Det-*différents* can have large (13a′) or narrow scope (13a″) with regard to negation:

(13) a. Je n'ai pas voulu évoquer différents avantages de cette proposition
I not have wanted mention different advantages of this proposal
'I didn't want to mention various advantages of this proposal'

a′. Il y a différents avantages de cette proposition que je n'ai pas voulu évoquer.
'There are different advantages of this proposal I didn't intend to mention'

a″. Je n'en avais qu'un seul en vue
'I only had a single one in mind'

In the narrow scope reading, negation affects the cardinality (>1) expressed by Det-*différents*. In fact, Det-*différents* (like *plusieurs* and unlike *certains*) needs to be verified by a plurality (Corblin 2001):

(14) a. – Est-ce que certaines personnes font obstacle? – Oui, Dupont
– Is-it that certain people make hindrance? – Yes, Dupont
'– Are some people opposed to this? – Yes, Dupont is'

b. – Est-ce que différentes / plusieurs personnes font obstacle? –
– Is-it that different / several people make hindrance?
#Oui, Dupont
– #Yes, Dupont
'– Are various/several people opposed to this? – #Yes, Dupont is'

As for scope interactions with other quantifiers, Det-*différents* favors narrow scope readings, and this even in inverse scope configurations. Thus, the NP in subject position can fall under the scope of the quantifier contained in the VP in (15):

(15) a. Différents rapporteurs examineront chaque article
'Different referees will examine every article'

On some accounts, then, Det-*différents* patterns nearly like *plusieurs* and on some others like *certains*. This particular behavior can be accounted for if we assume that Det-*différents* suggests the discriminability of the instantiations of the noun it introduces. It thus contains, like *certains*, a qualitative element, but whereas in the case of the latter this qualitative element introduces a contrast between the identifiable subset introduced by *certains N* and its complement, in the case of *différents* it discriminates among the members of the subset. Since discrimination at the level of identity is already implied by *plusieurs* (which entails a cardinality >1), *différents* will be normally taken to mean non-similarity with regard to some property. Thus, over and above the entailment of plurality in (16a), (16b) suggests that the collaborators differed in some respect (for instance, because of having different fields of specialization or because of having participated in different stages of the project):

(16) a. Il a accompli le projet avec plusieurs collaborateurs
'He carried out the project with several collaborators'

b. Il a accompli le projet avec différents collaborateurs
'He carried out the project with different collaborators'

## 3 The semantics of Adj-*différent* and Det-*différents*

Adj-*différent* has several distinct readings, only one of which is paralleled by Det-*différents*. The NP-internal reading of Adj-*différent* provides the link between both items.

First of all, Adj-*différents* has sentence external readings, in which one of the terms of the relation is provided by the context.[3] This reading is not available for Det-*différent*:

(17) a. Pierre se contenterait d'être instituteur, mais Marie a
Pierre REFL-content of be schoolteacher, but Marie has
des aspirations différentes.
*des* ambitions different

'Pierre would be happy to be a schoolteacher, but Marie has other ambitions'

b. #Pierre se contenterait d'être instituteur, mais Marie a
Pierre REFL-content of be schoolteacher, but Marie has
différentes aspirations.
different ambitions

In addition, *des N différents* has sentence-internal readings, which show important parallels to the phenomenon of dependent plurality (Carlson 1987, Moltmann 1992, Beck 2000, Laca/Tasmowski 2001). In

[3]It should be noted that external readings are more easily obtained with *d'autres N.*

such readings, a partition of a plurality denoted by some NP in the sentence (the licensor of the internal reading) contributes to create a cover[4] for the plurality introduced by the noun phrase hosting *différents*, and it is asserted of the members of this cover that they are not identical. Such a relationship is established between individual students and individual courses or sets of courses) in (18)[5]:

(18) Tous ces étudiants suivent des cours différents
All these students follow *des* courses different
'All these students are taking different courses'

Following Beck (2000), the truth conditions of such a reading can be captured by a reciprocal interpretation of *différent* which is relativized to a cover of the set of courses:

(19) a. $\exists$X [cours (X) & **suivent (tous ces étudiants, X) & $\forall$x [x$\leq$X & x $\in$ Cov $\rightarrow$ $\forall$y [y$\leq$X & y$\in$Cov & x$\neq$y $\rightarrow$ différent (x, y)]]]
b. Cov : {le ou les cours suivis par l'étudiant A, le ou les cours suivis par l'étudiant B, le ou les cours suivis par l'étudiant C...}

This sort of reading is not available for Det-*différents.* In (20), we only obtain a distributive reading in which pluralities of courses co-vary with individual students:

(20) Tous ces étudiants suivent différents cours
These students follow different courses
'All these students are taking various courses'

Whenever the conditions for dependent plural interpretations are not met, either because there is no licensing plural expression in the sentence (21a), or because the host NP is introduced by a determiner other than *des* (21b), or because a singular expression intervening between the licensor and the host NP blocks the relation (21c), sentence internal readings of Adj-*différents* are excluded. A second type of internal reading may arise in these cases, in which the arguments of the relation denoted by Adj-*différents* are determined NP-internally (they correspond to an atomic partition of the set of Ns):

(21) a. La reconstruction scientifique peut se faire avec des
The reconstruction scientific can REFL do with *des*

[4]A "cover" amounts to the break down of a group in subgroups extending over the group as a whole (for a discussion, see Landman 1996, 452 ff.).

[5]That the partition of the licensor is atomic in this case (pairing individual students with courses) is a consequence of the fact that *tous les N* favors strict distributive interpretations.

matériaux différents: formules mathématiques, images,
materials different: formulae mathematical, images,
modèles ...
models ...

'Scientific reconstruction can be carried out with different materials: mathematical formulae, images, models ...'

b. Tous les étudiants suivent plusieurs cours différents
All the students follow several courses different

'All these students are taking several different courses'

c. Les deux témoins ont aperçu une voiture de couleurs
The two witnesses have seen a car of colors
différentes
different

'The two witnesses saw a car of different colors'

The application of *différents* as a reciprocal predicate expressing non-identity in NP-internal readings is truth-conditionally vacuous, since non-identity is entailed by the cardinality > 1 of the plural expression. This does not mean, however, that *différents* is "a seemingly otiose adjective" (Carlson 1987, Beck 2000) in NP-internal readings. On the contrary, it is used to stress the cardinality >1, as in examples (21b–c) above, or to suggest qualitative differences, as in (22 a–b):

(22) a. Dans l'aquarium nageaient trois poissons différents
In the aquarium swam three fish different

'In the aquarium swam three different fish'

b. Il a planté trois arbres fruitiers différents
He has planted three trees of fruit different

'He planted three different fruit trees'

Interestingly enough, these overtones are also conveyed by prenominal Adj-*différents* when it is preceded by a definite determiner. Thus, (23a) stresses cardinality[6] and (23b) qualitative differences:

(23) a. Inutile de revenir sur ces différents points.
Useless of return upon these different points

'No need to return to these different points'

b. Ce tarif s'applique aux différents modes d'expédition
This rate REFL applies to the different modes of shipping

'Those rates apply to the different shipping modes'

[6]In such contexts, *différents* seems to function as a suppletive form for *plusieurs*, which cannot appear in this position, cf. *les trois / quelques / différentes / *plusieurs objections qu'il a soulevées* 'the three / few / different / *several objections he put forward'.

NP-internal readings of Adj-*différents* share with Det-*différents* (which, as shown in §1, stresses qualitative differences and plural cardinality) a further property: they favor narrow scope (24a). Note that NPs containing postnominal *différents* admit inverse scope readings which seem excluded in the versions without postnominal *différents* (24b vs. 24c) :

(24) a. Chaque professeur a recompensé chaque étudiant qui a
Every professor has rewarded every student who has
lu trois romans différents
read three novels different

b. Deux policiers sont intervenus dans la plupart des
Two policemen are intervened in the majority of the
interrogatoires
interrogations

'Two officers were involved in most cross-examinations'

c. Deux policiers différents sont intervenus dans la plupart
Two policemen different are intervened in the majority
des interrogatoires
of the interrogations

'Two different officers were involved in most cross-examinations'

The link between *différents* as a relational predicate and *différents* as a determiner is to be found in NP-internal readings. In fact, in contexts which only allow for the NP-internal reading, while excluding stress on non-similarity or on cardinality (because *des* expresses no cardinality whatsoever), *des N différents* is only marginal, and *différents N* is preferred instead:

(25) a. Pierre suit trois cours différents / ??des cours
Pierre follows three courses different / ??*des* courses
différents / différents cours
different / different courses

'Pierre is taking three different courses / different courses'

b. Ce rite a été combattu pour plusieurs motifs
This rite has been fought for several reasons
différents / ??des motifs différents / différents motifs
different / ??*des* reasons different / different reasons

'This practice was fought against for various reasons / different reasons'

## Conclusions

A number of distributional properties — such as obligatory plural number and prenominal position and, most importantly, the absence of any other determiner — make it possible to isolate a determiner *différents* from the corresponding adjectival item. As a plural determiner, *différents* shares (i) with *certains*, the property of distributivity and that of building on equivalence classes of Ns with regard to some property, (ii) with *plusieurs* and with cardinality determiners, an implication of cardinality greater than 1, and (iii) with *des*, the impossibility of heading DPs without a lexical N head and the absence of implicatures as to the existence of a non-null complement set. *Différents* can have either narrow or wide scope, but it favors narrow scope even in inverse scope configurations, a property it shares with DPs containing its adjectival counterpart. The link between determiner and adjective is to be found in the NP-internal (so called "redundant") readings of the adjective.

## References

Beck, S. 2000. The semantics of different: Comparison operator and relational adjective. *Linguistics & Philosophy* 23:101–139.

Bosveld-de Smet, L. 1998. *On Mass and Plural Quantification: The Case of French des/du-NPs*. Ph.D. thesis, University of Groningen.

Carlson, G. N. 1987. Same and different: Some consequences for syntax and semantics. *Linguistics & Philosophy* 10:531–565.

Corblin, F. 2001. Où situer *certains* dans une typologie sémantique des groupes nominaux? In Kleiber et al. (2001), pages 99–117.

Gondret, P. 1976. "Quelques", "plusieurs", "certains", "divers". Étude sémantique. *Le francais moderne* 44:143–152.

Kleiber, G., B. Laca, and L. Tasmowski, eds. 2001. *Typologie des groupes nominaux*. Rennes: Presses Universitaires de Rennes.

Laca, B. and L. Tasmowski. 2001. Distributivité et interprétations dépendantes des expressions d'identité. In Kleiber et al. (2001), pages 143–166.

Laca, B. and L. Tasmowski. 2003. From non-identity to plurality. French *différent* as an adjective and as a determiner. In Quer et al. (2003), pages 155–176.

Moltmann, F. 1992. Reciprocals and same/different. Towards a semantic analysis. *Linguistics & Philosophy* 15:411–462.

Quer, J., J. Schroten, M. Scorretti, P. Sleeman, and E. Verheugd, eds. 2003. *Romance Languages and Linguistic Theory 2001*. Amsterdam/Philadelphia: Benjamins.

9

# *Divers**

Ileana Comorovski and Laurence Nicaise

Dictionaries often compare *divers* and *différent*, which they find quite similar (see, for instance, *Le Petit Robert*, *Trésor de la langue française*); this intuition is shared by Gondret (1976), according to whom prenominal *différents* 'is a simple variant of *divers*'. In order to better analyze *divers*, we too will compare it with *différent*. We rely on the analysis of *différent* in Laca and Tasmowski (2001, 2003; chapter 8, this volume).

## 1 The distribution of *divers*

*Divers* can occur in both prenominal and postnominal position. *Divers* appears prenominally only in plural noun phrases. Prenominal *divers* ('various') can, but need not be preceded by a determiner. If it is, the determiner can be the definite article, a demonstrative or a possessive, but not the indefinite determiner *des*:

(1) Paul a visité (les) diverses régions de France.
Paul has visited (the) various regions of France.

(2) Marc a buté sur (ces) diverses questions.
Mark has tripped up on (these) various questions.

(3) (Vos) divers ouvrages sur ce sujet ont été inclus
'(Your) various works on this subject have been included
dans la bibliographie.
in the bibliography.'

(4) * Il a lu de(s) divers ouvrages sur ce sujet.
He has read of-the various works on this subject

*We thank Francis Corblin and Leonie Bosveld-de Smet for their comments.

*Handbook of French Semantics*.
Francis Corblin and Henriëtte de Swart (eds.).
Copyright © 2004, CSLI Publications.

Why should prenominal *divers* be analyzed semantically as a determiner? The main argument is a feature of its distribution illustrated in 1–3: noun phrases of the form *divers* N can occur in any canonical nominal position. In contrast, bare plurals, i.e. noun phrases which contain neither an uncontroversial syntactic determiner nor some other expression of quantity (e.g. a numeral) have an extremely limited distribution in French (see Anscombre (1991)).[1] The fact that the distribution of *divers* N is not restricted to the contexts that allow bare plurals indicates that prenominal *divers* must be analyzed as an expression of quantity; in section 2.2, we will analyze it as a vague cardinality indicator. Expressions of quantity that occur in the nominal domain are treated semantically as determiners. As was pointed out in Chapter 1, lexical items which are determiners semantically do not necessarily belong to the syntactic category Determiner. Prenominal *divers* is a case in point: since it can be preceded by a determiner, prenominal *divers* cannot be analyzed syntactically as a determiner.

The syntactic category of prenominal *divers* is not easy to establish. Could prenominal *divers* belong to the category Adjective? The following evidence suggests that it does not. First, unlike adjectives, prenominal *divers* can occur in the initial position of a noun phrase ((1–3) above). Second, unlike adjectives and unlike postnominal *divers* (see 17 below), prenominal *divers* cannot be modified by a degree word:

(5) ??Ses très diverses œuvres sont exposées dans une galerie d'art.
His very various works are exhibited in a gallery of art

Finally, prenominal *divers* cannot be preceded by *de(s)*, whereas prenominal adjectives can; compare 4 above with 6 below:

(6) Nous avons vu de(s) vieilles maisons.
We have seen of-the old houses
'We have seen some old houses.'

Note, however, that the acceptability contrast between 4 and 6 is quite likely due to semantic rather than to syntactic reasons. Semantically, *divers* is an existential determiner.[2] Hence, its co-occurrence with *des*, an existential determiner with no descriptive content, creates a redundancy — a plausible cause of the unacceptability of 4.

The distribution of prenominal *divers* is similar, but not identical, to that of numerals. It most resembles the distribution of *quelques* ('a few') and of prenominal *différents*. Numerals, *quelques* and *différents*

[1] French differs in this respect from English, since English allows bare plurals in all canonical noun phrase positions.

[2] See Keenan and Stavi (1986) and Keenan (1987) for a characterization of existential determiners.

all allow, but do not require, a preceding determiner; this determiner cannot be the indefinite determiner *des*:

(7) J'ai lu (les) trois / quelques / différents / divers livres que
I have read (the) three / a few / different / various books which
vous m'avez recommandés.
you to-me have recommended.
'I have read (the) three / few / different / various books which you recommended to me.'

(8) *J'ai emprunté de(s) trois / quelques / différents / divers livres.
I have borrowed of-the three / a few / different / various books

But, unlike numerals, and like *quelques* and *différents*, *divers* cannot be immediately followed by a partitive *de*-phrase ('of'-phrase): [3]

(9) Marc a invité trois / *quelques / *différents / *divers de ses
Mark has invited three / a few / different / various of his
amis.[4]
friends

Related to the contrasts in 9 is the fact that, if construed with an occurrence of partitive *en* ('of them'), bare numerals can occur in object position; in contrast, *quelques*, *différents*, and *divers* cannot so occur. This difference is illustrated in 10 below:

(10) – Marc t'a-t-il jamais présenté ses amis ?
'Has Mark ever introduced his friends to you?'

– Il m'en a présenté trois / *quelques /
he to-me of-them has introduced three / a few /
*différents / *divers – .
different / various

'He's introduced three / a few / *different / *various of them to me.'

The bare numerals in 10 are interpreted as partitive noun phrases.

A related contrast obtains between the numerals on the one hand, and *quelques*, *différents*, and *divers* on the other, when they are construed with an occurrence of '*en* quantitatif':[5]

---

[3]This is a relatively recent historical development — occurrences of *divers* followed by a partitive *de*-phrase are still attested at the beginning of the 20$^{th}$ century; and so are occurrences of bare *divers*.

[4]Sentences 9–11 become acceptable if *quelques* is replaced by the nominal form *quelques-uns*.

[5]As Milner (1978) observes, the clitic *en* can denote a set already introduced in the discourse, as in the answer in 10 ('*en* partitif'), or the set of Ns in the universe, as in the answer in 11('*en* quantitatif').

(11) – As-tu vu des étudiants hollandais sur le campus ?
'Have you seen any Dutch students on campus?'

– Oui, j'en ai vu trois / *quelques / *différents / *divers.
yes, I of-them have seen three / a few / different / various

'Yes, I have seen three / a few / *different / *various of them.'

From 9–11, we conclude that prenominal *divers*, *différents*, and *quelques* do not belong to the same syntactic category as the numerals.

Having seen that, syntactically, prenominal *divers* cannot be classed with determiners, adjectives or numerals, we suggest that in a French DP the elements that are semantically determiners fall into (at least) three syntactic classes: 1) determiners (*le(s)*, *ce(s)*, *des/du*); 2) *quelques*, *différents*, *divers*; 3) numerals.

Let us turn now to postnominal *divers*. *Divers* can appear in postnominal position in both singular and plural noun phrases. The noun phrase that hosts it can be introduced by a definite or an indefinite determiner. Postnominal *divers* ('diverse', 'varied'), just like postnominal *différent*, is an uncontroversial adjective: it can be modified by a degree word and it can be coordinated with other adjectives:

(12) 'L'île Bourbon, (...) habitée par une population *très diverse mais ardemment française*, n'entrait pas directement dans les plans des alliés.' (Charles de Gaulle: *Mémoires de guerre*, 1956)
'The Bourbon Island, (...) inhabited by a very diverse but ardently French population, was not part of the Allies' plans.'

(13) a. Il aime les paysages *divers et infinis.*
He likes the landscapes diverse and infinite

'He likes landscapes that are diverse and infinite.'

b. 'qui comporte des événements *multiples et divers*'
which involves of-the events multiple and diverse

'which involves numerous and diverse events'

(*Dictionnaire de l'Académie française*, 1992, entry for *accidenté*)

*Divers* can occur after the copula and function predicatively. Post-copular *divers*, just like postnominal *divers*, is an adjective: it allows degree modification and it can be coordinated with other adjectives:

(14) Les langues parlées en Inde sont *très diverses.*
the languages spoken in India are very diverse/varied

(15) Ses goûts en matière de musique restent *divers et variés.*
his tastes in matter of music remain diverse and varied

## 2 The interpretation of *divers*

### 2.1 Postcopular *divers* and collective predication

Let us first take a look at postcopular *divers*. Unlike postcopular *différent*, postcopular *divers* cannot be used to relate two arguments:

(16) Vénus est (très) différente / *diverse de Saturne.
Venus is (very) different / diverse of Saturne
'Venus is (very) different / *diverse from Saturn.'

*Différent* denotes a symmetric relation; one of its arguments can be syntactically realized as a noun phrase introduced by *de* ('of'), as in 16. In contrast, *divers* cannot take a complement. The intransitivity of *divers* is a syntactic reflex of its being semantically a one-place predicate.

A consultation of the FRANTEXT database reveals the fact that *divers* denoted a binary relation until the end of the $18^{th}$ century; the second argument of *divers*, if expressed overtly, was introduced by the preposition *de* or by the preposition *à*. Thus *divers* and *différent* used to be much more similar than they are in present-day French. The difference in interpretation between contemporary *divers* and *différent* is due to the fact that, over the centuries, *divers* lost its second argument. This change in valence has had consequences on the interpretive possibilities of *divers* not only in postcopular position, but also in DP-internal position. Thus *divers* lost several readings which it used to share with *différent* (see Comorovski (2003) for details). The interpretation of contemporary *divers* is similar, without being identical, to what Laca and Tasmowski (this volume) term "the NP-internal reading" of *différent*.

Given that *divers* does not denote a relation, how can we explain the intuition that the meaning of *divers* is very close to that of *différent*? To answer this question, we will first consider the interpretation of singular *divers* occurring in postcopular position:

(17) Cette assemblée est très diverse.
'This assembly is very diverse.'

(18) a. 'Le parc (...) n'était pas grand, mais si *divers* que je n'avais jamais fini de l'explorer.'
'The park (...) was not large, but (it was) so diverse that I had never finished exploring it.'
(Simone de Beauvoir: *Mémoires d'une jeune fille rangée*, 1958)

b. '– Mon idée, disait Simon, c'est que le monde est *très divers* et que rien n'est éternel et que tout passe très vite.'
'My idea', Simon would say, 'is that the world is very diverse and nothing is eternal and everything goes by very fast.'
(Jean d'Ormesson: *Le Bonheur à San Miniato*, 1987)

The choice of nouns in the subjects of 17 and 18 is significant. The collective noun *assemblée* denotes a set of collections of entities. The denotation of the nouns *parc* and *monde* in 18 is regarded as a set of collections of entities, even though in other contexts these nouns have the ordinary denotation of a count noun (i.e. they denote a set of individuals). Thus the speaker's perspective of the denotation of a noun phrase plays a role in determining whether singular *divers* can take a noun phrase as an argument. The unacceptability of 19 shows that singular *divers* cannot be predicated of a subject whose denotation is (perceived as) an atomic individual:

(19) * Cette feuille est très diverse.
This leaf is very diverse

Nor can singular *divers* be predicated of subjects whose head noun is a mass noun:

(20) * Ce riz / liquide est très divers.
This rice / liquid is very diverse

Significantly, there is a difference between the denotation domains of singular count nouns and of mass nouns. Whereas the denotation domain of singular count nouns has minimal elements (atoms), the denotation domain of mass nouns, while having parts, does not have minimal elements (see Link (1983)).

The generalization that emerges from the data in 17–20 is that singular *divers* can only be predicated of subjects whose head noun denotes a set of collections of entitites. Thus *divers* is one of the few purely collective predicates in the sense of Dowty (1987); these are predicates which, unlike 'gather', do not have distributive subentailments.[6]

The unary predicate *divers* indicates that the collections in the denotation of the noun phrase it applies to are constituted of elements that are not similar to each other. Thus, unlike *différent*, *divers* applies to the collections directly, and not to their members.

Like predicative *divers*, postnominal singular *divers* also has a denotation domain made of collections of entities. We find the same constraints on the choice of nouns as we saw in the case of postcopular *divers*:

(21) a. '... une *foule diverse* de marchands, d'artisans, de paysans, de gens de tous métiers.' (Edmond Faral: *La Vie quotidienne au temps de saint Louis*, 1942)

[6]Other examples of purely collective predicates are 'be a large group, 'be numerous', 'be plentiful'. It is of interest to note that the phrase *nombreux et divers* ('numerous and diverse'), a coordination of two purely collective predicates, appears in modern French with the frequency of a collocation.

'... a diverse crowd of merchants, artisans, peasants, people of all trades.'

b. '... le journal officiel (...) publie un *ensemble très divers* de matières officielles.' (D.W. Lidderdale: *Le parlement français*, 1954)
'... the Official Government Journal publishes a very diverse set of official matters.'

(22) * J'ai cueilli une feuille diverse.
I have picked a leaf diverse

(23) * Il aime cuisiner du riz divers.
he likes to-cook of-the rice diverse

22 and 23 are not acceptable because the nouns modified by *divers* do not have collections in their denotation.

Let us now extend our analysis to plural *divers*. The sentence below, which contains an occurrence of plural *divers*, is ambiguous:

(24) Les planètes du système solaire sont très diverses.
the planets of-the system solar are very diverse

24 can have a distributive or a collective interpretation. On the distributive interpretation, diversity is predicated of each of the planets; on this interpretation, the planets are seen as collections, for instance collections of landscapes. On the collective interpretation, diversity is predicated of the collection the planets form together. The sentence is disambiguated in favor of the collective interpretation if we insert the phrase *en tant que groupe* ('as a group'), as in 25 below. According to Landman (2000: 163), 'as a group' is an expression of the operation of group formation; we will not take a stand here on the nature of the collections in the denotation domain of plurals.

(25) Les planètes du système solaire, *en tant que groupe*, sont
the planets of-the system solar as group are
très diverses.
very diverse

*Divers* imposes a restriction on the form of the noun phrase which realizes its argument: this noun phrase must denote a collection without listing its members.[7] The role played by the form of the subject noun phrase can be illustrated as follows: suppose a miner uses a pick-axe, a shovel, a chisel, and a hammer. His tools are successfully described by the acceptable 26, which contrasts with the unacceptable 27:

[7]We owe this observation and the examples 26–27 to Francis Corblin.

(26) a. Les outils qu'il utilise sont (très) divers.
'The tools that he uses are (very) diverse.'

b. Sa panoplie (d'outils) est diverse.
'His set of tools is diverse.'

(27) * La pioche, la pelle, le burin et le marteau sont très divers.[8]
the pick-axe the shovel the chisel and the hammer are very diverse

Sentences 26–27 present an instance of predicate non-sharing: a predicate which applies to a plural definite or to a noun phrase containing a collective noun (*panoplie*) cannot apply to an apparently coextensional noun phrase constituted of a coordination of terms.

That some collective predicates do not take a coordination of terms as an argument was observed by Link (1991), who gives 'be numerous' as an example. We note that the predicates in this class are purely collective adjectival predicates; in contrast, purely collective nominal predicates can take a coordination of terms as an argument (e.g. 'John and Mary are a (happy) couple.'). We will not address here either the issue of the contrast between collective predicate nominals and collective adjectives, nor the question raised by predicate non-sharing.[9]

Like other purely collective predicates, *divers* cannot apply to quantified subjects. Dowty (1987) observed that 'all' cannot co-occur with purely collective predicates:

(28) * All the students are numerous.

Note that *divers* cannot co-occur with *tous* ('all'), whether *tous* is hosted by the subject noun phrases, as in 29a, or is floated, as in 29b:

(29) a. * *Tous* ses outils sont (très) divers.
all his tools are (very) diverse

b. * Ses outils sont *tous* (très) divers.
his tools are all (very) diverse

Nor can *divers* co-occur with other quantifying noun phrases, as seen from the unacceptability of 30 below, patterned on an example in Bosveld-de Smet (1998: 140), reproduced in 31:

[8]Some of the speakers we consulted judged 27 as marginal; they also found the strings in 28–30 and 33 to be marginally acceptable. These consultants are from the Anjou region. The entry for *divers* in the mental lexicon of these speakers appears to represent a phase of transition in the history of *divers*: while they do not allow *divers* to be followed by a PP complement (see 16 above), *divers* behaves for these speakers very much like it did in earlier stages of French, when *divers* and *différent* were little differentiated syntactically and semantically.

[9]For a discussion of predicate non-sharing, see Schwarzschild (1996:173ff.); for an analysis of collective predicative NPs, see Schwarzschild (1996:178ff.).

(30) * La plupart de ses outils sont (très) divers.
the majority of his tools are (very) diverse

(31) a. These apples are various in origin.
b. * Many (of these) apples are various in origin.

Collective predicates often select their arguments in terms of cardinality (Schwarzschild (1996: 153ff.)), and so does *divers*. For some predicates, the restriction on the cardinality of the collections they apply to is quite precise (e.g. 'be a (happy) couple', 'be five in number'), while for others it is looser. *Divers* belongs to the latter class: it applies to collections of a relatively large number of elements, just like, for instance, the predicate 'be a cohesive group'. As a consequence of the cardinality restriction imposed by *divers* on its argument, sentence 32 is not ambiguous, diversity being predicated of each park individually; 33 is unacceptable, since tools, unlike parks, are not easily perceived as collections of entities:

(32) Les deux parcs sont (très) divers.
'The two parks are (very) diverse.'

(33) * Les deux outils sont (très) divers.
the two tools are (very) diverse

## 2.2 Prenominal and postnominal *divers*

Prenominal *divers* is a determiner which indicates a cardinality that is vague, but is larger than two; consequently, prenominal *divers* does not occur in singular noun phrases. This is related to the fact that adjectival *divers* is a purely collective predicate. Just like adjectival *divers* denotes a set of collections of entities, the set which prenominal *divers* takes as an argument must be a set of collections of entities.

In Chapter 1, we have seen that most noun phrases containing a cardinal determiner are individual-denoting. Moreover, they introduce a discourse referent that is free. This is the case of *divers*-DPs, as evidenced by the fact that a *divers*-DP that is under the scope of a quantifier can be anaphorically related to a plural pronoun bound by the same quantifier. As an example, take the following donkey-sentence:

(34) En général, si Jacques demande des conseils à *diverses*
in general if Jacques asks of-the advice to various
*personnes*, il *les* en remercie après avoir pris sa décision.
people he them of-it thanks after have taken his decision
'In general, if Jacques asks for advice from various people, he thanks them for it after having made a decision.'

In 34, *diverses personnes* ('various people') is under the scope of the adverb of quantification *en général* ('in general') and is anaphorically related to the pronoun *les* ('them'). This relation is indicative of the fact that *divers*-DPs denote the same type of entity as plural pronouns.

Unlike prenominal *différents*, prenominal *divers* does not force distributive readings. This is evidenced by sentences with a *divers*-N subject and a mixed predicate, i.e. a predicate that allows both distributive and collective interpretations. Such sentences are ambiguous, unlike corresponding sentences with prenominal *différents*. For instance, 35 below can have both a distributive and a collective interpretation, whereas only a distributive interpretation is available for 36:

(35) Divers invités m'ont chanté "Joyeux anniversaire".
various guests to-me have sung happy birthday
'Various guests sang "Happy Birthday" to me.'

(36) Différents invités m'ont chanté "Joyeux anniversaire".
'Different guests sang "Happy Birthday" to me.'

Like prenominal *divers*, prenominal *différents* is a cardinal determiner, and the noun phrases which host it are individual-denoting. Generally, plural noun phrases which are individual-denoting allow both distributive and collective predication (see Chapter 1). In this respect, *divers*-DPs are "well-behaved", whereas the fact that prenominal *différents* forces distributive interpretations calls for an explanation; Laca and Tasmowski (2003) suggest that the explanation is to be found at the syntax/semantics interface.

Gondret (1976) noticed that, unlike *plusieurs* and *quelques*, prenominal *divers* cannot co-occur with measure nouns, resembling in this respect prenominal *différents*:

(37) Anne à marché plusieurs / quelques / *différents / *divers kilomètres.
'Anne has walked several / a few / *different / *various kilometers.'

The noun *kilomètre* denotes a measure function (see Krifka (1990: 494ff.)). In 37, the argument that the function denoted by *kilomètre* applies to is the stretch of land that Anne walked. As the acceptability judgments given in 37 indicate, the determiners *quelques* and *plusieurs* can denote the value of the function *kilomètre* for this argument, whereas prenominal *divers* and *différents* cannot. We suggest that *divers* and *différents* cannot be used to refer to the values of a measure function for the following two reasons: (i) their descriptive content is too rich, going beyond the pure indication of an amount, and (ii) the amount they indicate is quite vague. The second reason leads us to consider the interpretation of 38 below, which contains the equally vague determiner *des* co-occurring with the measure noun *kilomètres*:

(38) Anne a marché *des* kilomètres (avant de trouver une auberge).
Anne has walked of-the kilometers (before of find an inn)
'Anne walked many kilometers (before finding an inn).'

38 is acceptable, but notice that its interpretation is not compositional; the idiomatic meaning of 38 is brought out by the *avant*-phrase, whose omission would make the sentence sound less natural.

The difference between the descriptive content of prenominal and postnominal *divers* is fairly subtle; we illustrate it with the pair of sentences below:

(39) Marc a emprunté divers livres.
Mark has borrowed various books

(40) Marc a emprunté des livres divers.
Mark has borrowed of-the books diverse
'Mark bought a variety of books.'

Sentence 40 is true if the differences among the books Mark bought are (considered) major ones; for instance, the books belong to different fields of inquiry or to different literary genres. In contrast, the magnitude of the differences among the books Mark bought does not affect the truth value of sentence 39.

## Conclusions

*Divers* can occur both in prenominal and postnominal position. Syntactically, postnominal *divers* is an uncontroversial adjective; semantically, it is a purely collective predicate. The syntactic category of prenominal *divers* is not easy to determine; the distribution of prenominal *divers* closely resembles that of *quelques* and of prenominal *différents*. Semantically, prenominal *divers* is a determiner which indicates a cardinality larger than 2. The fact that prenominal *divers* can co-occur only with plural nouns is related to the fact that adjectival *divers* is a purely collective predicate.

## References

Anscombre, J.-C. 1991. La détermination zéro: quelques propriétés. *Langages* 102:103–124.

Bäuerle, R., C. Schwarze, and A. von Stechow, eds. 1983. *Meaning, Use, and Interpretation of Language*. Berlin: De Gruyter.

Bosveld-de Smet, L. 1998. *On Mass and Plural Quantification: The Case of French 'des'/'du'-NPs*. Ph.D. thesis, University of Groningen.

Comorovski, I. 2003. On the emergence of purely collective predication. In Dekker and van Rooy (2003).

Dekker, P. and R. van Rooy, eds. 2003. *Proceedings of the 14th Amsterdam Colloquium.*

Dowty, D. 1987. Collective predicates, distributive predicates, and *All.* In *Proceeedings of ESCOL '86*. Linguistics Department, OSU, Columbus.

Gondret, P. 1976. 'Quelques', 'plusieurs', 'certains', 'divers': Etude sémantique. *Le Français Moderne* 44:143–152.

Keenan, E. 1987. A semantic definition of 'indefinite NP'. In Ter Meulen and Reuland (1987).

Keenan, E. and J. Stavi. 1986. A semantic characterization of natural language determiners. *Linguistics and Philosophy* 9:253–326.

Kleiber, G., B. Laca, and L. Tasmowski, eds. 2001. *Typologie des groupes nominaux*. Rennes: Presses Universitaires de Rennes.

Krifka, M. 1990. Four thousand ships passed through the lock: object-induced measure functions on events. *Linguistics and Philosophy* 13:487–520.

Laca, B. and L. Tasmowski. 2001. Distributivité et interprétations dépendantes des expressions d'identité. In Kleiber et al. (2001).

Laca, B. and L. Tasmowski. 2003. From non-identity to plurality: French *différent* as an adjective and as a determiner. In Quer et al. (2003).

Laca, B. and L. Tasmowski. 2004. Différents. This volume.

Landman, F. 2000. *Events and Plurality*. Dordrecht: Kluwer.

Link, G. 1983. The logical analysis of plurals and mass terms: A lattice-theoretical approach. In Bäuerle et al. (1983).

Link, G. 1991. Plural. In Von Stechow and Wunderlich (1991).

Link, G. 1998. *Algebraic Semantics in Language and Philosophy*. Stanford: CSLI Publications.

Milner, J.-C. 1978. *De la syntaxe à l'interprétation*. Paris: Seuil.

Quer, J., J. Schroten, M. Scorretti, P. Sleeman, and E. Verheugd, eds. 2003. *Romance Languages and Linguistic Theory 2001*. Amsterdam: Benjamins.

Schwarzschild, R. 1996. *Pluralities*. Dordrecht: Kluwer.

Ter Meulen, A. and E. Reuland, eds. 1987. *The Representation of (In)definiteness*. Cambridge, MA: MIT Press.

Von Stechow, A. and D. Wunderlich, eds. 1991. *Semantik. Ein internationales Handbuch der zeitgenössischen Forschung*. Berlin: Walter de Gruyter.

# 10

# *Quel**

ILEANA COMOROVSKI

## 1 The interrogative determiner *quel*

*Le Petit Robert* defines interrogative *quel* ('what', 'what kind of', 'which', 'who') as a lexical item which serves to ask a question about the identity or the nature of a person or a thing. In question 1 below, *quel* ranges over a set of (ordinary) individuals, while in 2 it ranges over a set of kinds:

(1) Quels contes de fées a-t-elle lus ?
'What fairy tales has she read?'

(2) Quels oiseaux vivent dans ces forêts ?
'What kinds of birds live in these woods?'

*Quel* can range over a set already introduced in the discourse, in which case it is equivalent to *lequel* ('which (one)'), heading a discourse-linked interrogative phrase:[1]

(3) Quelle fille était la plus belle des trois ?
'Which girl was the prettiest of the three?'

*Thanks go to Francis Corblin and Brenda Laca for their insightful comments on an early draft of this chapter. For valuable discussion, I wish to thank Anne Abeillé, Gilles Boyé, Bernard Combettes, Danièle Godard, and especially Georges Rebuschi. Lastly, I am grateful to Petra Sleeman for her detailed comments on the pre-final draft.

[1]A more fine-grained characterization of this notion is presented in Comorovski (1996:11ff.). Note that *lequel* is a more recent lexical item than *quel*. *Quel* is a descendant of Latin 'qualis' ('what', 'which'), while the compound *lequel* is first attested in 11th century French (*La Chanson de Roland*).

*Handbook of French Semantics*.
Francis Corblin and Henriëtte de Swart (eds.).
Copyright © 2004, CSLI Publications.

It is tempting to relate the interpretation of the questions in 1–2 to a suggestion made by Carlson (1977:330ff.). According to Carlson, some common nouns are ambiguous: they can denote either a set of individuals or a set of kinds. A noun N can denote a set of subkinds of Ns if the existence of such subkinds is part of the encyclopedic knowledge of the speakers of the language. A determiner can therefore take as an argument either a set of individuals or a set of kinds (taxonomic reading). Carlson bases his observation on examples like the following:

(4) a. Two birds have just flown away.
    b. Two birds are extinct = Two kinds of birds are extinct.

The predicate *extinct* occurring in 4b is a kind-level predicate.

Just like non-interrogative determiners, *quel* can take as an argument a set of individuals or a set of kinds. Thus the sentence below is ambiguous:

(5) Dans quel restaurant irez-vous ce soir ?
    in what restaurant will-go you this night

5 can be translated into English as 6 or as 7:

(6) 'What/which restaurant will you go to tonight?'

(7) 'What kind of restaurant will you go to tonight?'

The rest of this chapter will focus on *quel* occurring without a following noun, hence 'bare *quel*'.

## 2 The distribution and interpretation of bare *quel*

### 2.1 Bare *quel* as a clitic

Bare *quel* occurs only as an argument of the verb *être* ('be'), as noticed by Ruwet (1972:73); the limited distribution of bare *quel* is illustrated by the contrast between the acceptable 8, on the one hand, and the unacceptable 9, on the other. In 8, *quel* is an argument of *être*, whereas in 9, *quel* is an argument of other verbs. (*Quel* is in subject position in 9a and it is related to an object gap in 9b):

(8) a. Quelle a été votre réaction ?
       'What has been your reaction?'
    b. Quels sont les écrivains qui t'ont influencé ?
       'Who are the writers who have influenced you?'

(9) a. * Quel a invité Georges ?
       who has invited George
    b. * Quel$_i$ as-tu vu $-_i$ ?
       what/who have you seen

As illustrated in 8, bare *quel* occurs in copular questions in which the verb *être* is followed by a noun phrase. Ruwet (1982: 223ff.) argues at length for the non-subject status of bare *quel* in such questions.

Bare *quel* shows some of the distributional characteristics observed by Bouchard and Hirschbühler (1986) and Poletto and Pollock (2002) for French *que* ('what'), which distinguish *que* from other French interrogative phrases. Since bare *quel* occurs only as a non-subject in copular clauses, only some of the characteristics observed for *que* can be tested for bare *quel.* The results are the following: just like *que*, bare *quel* requires subject clitic inversion, cannot occur in situ, and, as pointed out by Ruwet (1982), it cannot be separated from the rest of the sentence by a parenthetical. We illustrate these facts by contrasting bare *quel* to *qui* ('who'):

(10) a. * Quel il est ?
what he is

b. Qui il est ? (colloquial French)
who he is
'Who is he?'

(11) a. * La conclusion est quelle ?
the conclusion is what

b. Cet homme est qui ?
this man is who
'Who is this man?'

(12) a. * Quelle, à ton avis, est la conclusion ?
what at your opinion is the conclusion

b. Qui, à ton avis, est le coupable ?
who at your opinion is the culprit
'Who, in your opinion, is the culprit?'

Bouchard and Hirschbühler (1986) and Poletto and Pollock (2002) relate the properties they observe for *que* to its clitic status. Based on the data in 8–12, we suggest that bare *quel* too has the status of a clitic. Just like *que*, bare *quel* requires an immediately following verbal host: notice that in the unacceptable (10a–12a), bare *quel* is not immediately followed by a verb.

The hypothesis that bare *quel* is a clitic is supported by the placement of the word *diable* ('devil'), which can generally occur immediately after interrogative pronouns. As observed by Ruwet (1982), *diable* cannot occur immediately after bare *quel* (13a). But *diable* can occur immediately after *être*, as if *quel+être* together form an interrogative (13b):[2]

(13) a. * Quelle diable est la question ?
what devil is the question

b. Quelle est diable la question ?
what is devil the question
'What the hell is the question?'

In contrast, a question introduced by an interrogative word other than *quel* is unacceptable if *diable* occurs immediately after the verb:

(14) a. Qui diable est leur chef ?
who devil is their boss
'Who the hell is their boss?'

b. * Qui est diable leur chef ?[3]
who is devil their boss

The position of *diable* shows that *quel* is even more tightly linked to *être* than *que* is to its host; as observed by Ruwet (1982), *diable* can immediately follow *que*:

(15) a. Que diable fais-tu là ?
what devil do you there
'What the hell are you doing there?'

Bare *quel* cannot be related to a gap that is under the scope of a verb of propositional attitude, as seen from 16 below. Contrast the unacceptable 16 with the question in 17, in which *qui* is related to a gap in the complement clause of *penser* ('think'):

(16) a. * Quelle$_i$ penses-tu [ que la différence est / soit–$_i$ ] ?
what think you that the difference is / be-subj.3p.sg.

b. ?? Quelle$_i$ penses-tu [ que soit la différence -$_i$ ]?[4]
what think you that be-subj.3p.sg the difference

---

[2]I owe this observation to Anne Abeillé.

[3]14b becomes acceptable if *diable* is preceded and followed by a robust intonation break (*Qui est, diable, leur chef* ?).

[4]Some of the speakers I consulted found sentence 16b marginally acceptable, while judging it as archaic and literary. Note that bare *quel* was an independent word in Classical French, as can be seen from the following examples:

(i)– Avez-vous vu *quel il* est ?
– Je ne sais point *quel il* est. (Molière: *L'avare*, act III, scene 4, 1668)
'Have you seen who he is?'
'I don't know at all who he is.'

(ii)'... *quel pensez*-vous que fût le devoir d'un homme fait pour présider également aux uns et aux autres ?' (abbé Augustin Barruel : *Les Helviennes ou Lettres provinciales philosophiques, Lettre 37*, 1781).

(17) Qui$_i$ penses-tu [ que cet homme est $-_i$]?
who think you that this man is
'Who do you think this man is?'

However, bare *quel* can appear in the scope of expressions of propositional attitude which are not matrix verbs, as illustrated below:

(18) Selon toi / D'après Jacques / Selon ton opinion,
'According to you / According to Jacques / In your opinion,
quels sont les vrais coupables ?
who are the real culprits?'

Given the acceptability of 18, we conclude that the unacceptability of 16 is not due to semantic reasons, but to the fact that bare *quel* is morpho-syntactically dependent on a limited class of verbs.

Besides *être*, the host of bare *quel* can be an auxiliary cliticised on *être* or a raising verb (e.g. *sembler* 'seem', *devoir* 'must', *pouvoir* 'can'). Ruwet (1972) observes that if *quel* is hosted by a raising verb, the latter must embed a clause containing *être*:

(19) Quelle$_i$ pourrait / semble [ $-_i$ être la bonne réponse ] ?
what could / seems be the good answer
'What could / seems to be the right answer?'

In 19, bare *quel* occurs in the subject position of a matrix clause whose VP is headed by a raising verb that embeds a copular clause. Sentences with this type of structure led Ruwet (1972) to argue for the subjecthood of bare *quel* in copular clauses; on this view, bare *quel* would be raised in 19 from the embedded subject position to the matrix subject position. In later work, Ruwet presents compelling evidence against a subject analysis of bare *quel* in copular clauses (Ruwet (1982)); in this later work, the analysis of 19 is left as an open issue.

It should come as no surprise that it is not easy to identify the subject of questions of the form *Quel est DP?*. In clauses of the form *DP-copula-DP*, it is often the case that properties characteristic of subjects are displayed not only by the clause-initial DP, but also by the postcopular DP (see Partee (1998) for discussion). This cross-linguistic observation applies also to questions of the form *Quel est DP?*, whose postcopular

'... what do you think was the duty of a man made to chair the discussions of the opposing groups?'

As evidenced by 10a above, bare *quel* cannot immediately precede a subject pronoun in present-day French. The dialogue in (i) shows that bare *quel* could do so in Classical French. In (ii), we see that bare *quel* could attach to a verb other than *être*. From these observations on the diachrony of bare *quel*, we conclude that the speakers who found 16b marginal and archaic may have reflected in their judgments their contact with writings from the Classical French period.

DP is shown by Ruwet 1972 to display subject properties. Given the weight of Ruwet's (1982) arguments, we adopt here the view that bare *quel* is not a subject in copular questions.

## 2.2 Interpretive differences between bare *quel* and *quel N*

In copular questions introduced by *quel N*, where N is [+human], non-discourse-linked *quel* can be interpreted only as ranging over kinds, and not over ordinary individuals. Thus the sentences in 20 below cannot be used to ask for the identity of the subject, but only for its qualities. These sentences are felt by speakers of French to be obsolescent:

(20) a. Quel homme est ce médecin ?
 'What kind of man is this doctor?'

 b. Quel collègue est-il ?
 'What kind of colleague is he?'

In contrast, if the N is [–human], a copular question introduced by *quel N* can be interpreted either as a request for identity, or as asking for the qualities of the subject, as seen from the answer pattern below:

(21) Quelle voiture est cet amas de feraille ?
 what car is this heap of metal?
 A1: C'est la voiture de mon petit frère.
 'It's my younger brother's car.'
 A2: C'est une vieille Renault.
 'It's a(n old) Renault.'

(22) – Il a fait une faute grave. – Quelle faute est-ce ?
 'He made a serious mistake.' 'What mistake is it?
 A1 Il a volé.
 'He stole.'
 A2 C'est une faute passible d'emprisonnement.
 'It's an error liable to imprisonment.'

A question introduced by bare *quel* has two interpretations, irrespective of whether the subject DP is human or not. This fact is illustrated by the answer pattern in 23 and 24:

(23) – Quelle est cette voiture ?
 what is this car
 A1: C'est la voiture de ma soeur.
 'It's my sister's car.'
 A2: C'est une Renault.
 'It's a Renault.'

(24) – Quel est cet homme ?
'Who is this man?'
A1: (C'est) mon garagiste.
'(It's) my mechanic.'
A2: C'est un très bon médecin.
'It's a very good doctor.'

While we do not attempt here to explain the restrictions operating on *quel N* in copular questions, we note that the facts described here rule out an analysis of bare *quel* as an elliptical form of *quel N*: bare *quel* is not a noun phrase which contains an empty N. Had this been the case, we would not expect any interpretive differences between *quel N* and bare *quel*. We suggest that, like other determiners occurring without a noun, bare *quel* has acquired pronominal status.[5] We analyze bare *quel* as an interrogative clitic pronoun unspecified for [± human].[6]

## 2.3 Semantic restrictions on the distribution of bare *quel*

In addition to occurring only in copular questions, bare *quel* can only co-occur with subject noun phrases that meet certain semantic conditions: a) the subject cannot be indefinite (Barbaud (1974), Ruwet (1982));[7] b) a definite subject cannot be a rigid designator. The rigidity requirement is illustrated by the paradigm below:

(25) a. Quelle est *la température* ?
what is the temperature

b. Quelle est *l'adresse de Brigitte* ?
what is the address of Brigitte

c. 'Quel est *le véritable auteur de la Bible* ?'
who is the true author of the Bible
(Eric Orsenna: *Grand amour*, 1993)

d. Quelle est *ta meilleure amie* ?
who is your best friend

e. Quelle est *cette rue* ?
what is this street

---

[5]Examples of such determiners are the Latin and the English demonstratives. Note that part of the determiners without a noun discussed in Corblin et al. (this volume) are not pronominal.

[6]A consultation of the FRANTEXT database has revealed a tendency in contemporary French to use bare *quel* with [– human] subjects.

[7]Ruwet (1982: 237, n.22) notices that this generalization is not without exceptions. In Ruwet's example, the verb *être* is in the conditional mood:

(i)Quel serait, à ton avis, un bon directeur de banque ?
'In your opinion, what would be the qualities of a good bank director?'

'What street is this?'

f. (?) Quel est cet *homme* ?
who is this man

g. * Quel est-il ? (OK if *il* is anaphoric)
who is he

h. * Quel êtes-*vous* ?
who are you

i. * Quel est *ça* / *ceci* ?
what is this / this (one)

j. * Quel est *Jacques* ?
who is Jacques

An examination of the noun phrases in 25 reveals that their rigidity is crucial in determining the acceptability of a sentence containing bare *quel*. Sentences (25a–f) have non-rigid designators as subjects. The subject noun phrases of the ungrammatical (25g–j) are all rigid designators.

A few comments on some of the data in 25 are in order. The subjects of (25e-f) present a middle ground case: they are complex demonstratives, i.e. noun phrases formed by a demonstrative determiner and a common noun; the rigidity of complex demonstratives has been an issue of debate; see King (2001) for a recent discussion. Some of the speakers we consulted found that question 25f sounds archaic and literary unless the subject *cet homme* is anaphoric. Question 25g is unacceptable only if the pronoun *il* ('he') is used deictically. If used anaphorically, personal pronouns can co-occur with bare *quel*:

(26) – Il m'a posé une drôle de question et puis il m'a donné lui-même la réponse.
'He asked me a funny question and then he gave me the answer himself.'

– Ah oui ? Et quelle était-*elle* ?
oh yes and what was she

'Really? And what was it?'

Note that, in their anaphoric use, personal pronouns and demonstratives are not rigid designators.

Interestingly, some of the French demonstratives can also co-occur with bare *quel* if they are used anaphorically. Thus, 27 below is a possible reply to the first sentence in 26, but 28 is not, even if the pronoun *ce* is used anaphorically:

(27) Et quelle était *celle-ci* ?
and what was this-one
'And what was it/the latter?'

(28) * Et quelle était-ce ?
and what was this/it

The unacceptability of 28 is plausibly due to morpho-syntactic factors. Notice that if *c'est* is followed by a personal pronoun, the pronoun must occur in its strong form; clitics are barred from the position immediately following *c'est*:

(29) C'est toi / *te.
'It's you.'

We suggest that 28 is ruled out because of the clitic status of bare *quelle*.

In sum, a rigid designator cannot be the subject of a copular question introduced by bare *quel*. This restriction indicates that the subject of a copular *quel*-question cannot denote an individual, but must be of type $< s, e >$, the type of individual concepts.

A copular question introduced by bare *quel* asks for the value at a particular index of the individual concept denoted by the subject. Given that a copular *quel*-question has a subject of type $< s, e >$, it can be analyzed compositionally by: (i) assigning to bare *quel* the type $< s, e >$ and (ii) adopting for *être* Montague's (1973) treatment of 'be'; in Montague's approach, 'be' expresses the identity between the values of two individual concepts at a given index.

## Conclusions

This chapter has shown that the interrogative determiner *quel* can take as an argument a set of individuals or kinds, irrespective of the nature of the predicate occurring in the question (kind-level, individual-level, stage-level). Next, we have concentrated on the syntax and semantics of bare *quel*. Building on work by Ruwet (1972, 1982), we have analyzed bare *quel* as a pronominal clitic; the host of bare *quel* can be the verb *être* or a raising verb which takes a copular clause as a complement. We have shown that a copular question introduced by bare *quel* cannot have a rigid designator as a subject.

## References

Barbaud, P. 1974. *Constructions superlatives et structures apparentées*. Ph.D. thesis, Université de Paris-Vincennes.

Bouchard, D. and P. Hirschbühler. 1986. French *quoi* and its clitic allomorph *que*. In Neidle and Núñez Cedeño (1986).

Carlson, G. 1977. *Reference to Kinds in English*. Ph.D. thesis, UMass, Amherst. [published by Garland Press, New York, 1978].

Comorovski, I. 1996. *Interrogative Phrases and the Syntax-Semantics Interface*. Dordrecht: Kluwer.

Corblin, F., J.-M. Marandin, and P. Sleeman. 2004. Nounless determiners. This volume.

Herbert Coats, K. D., Cynthia Vakareliyska, ed. 1998. *Formal Approaches to Slavic Linguistics: The Seattle Meeting*, Ann Arbor. Michigan Slavic Publications.

Hintikka, J., J. Moravcsik, and P. Suppes, eds. 1973. *Approaches to Natural Language: Proceedings of the 1970 Stanford Workshop on Grammar and Semantics*. Dordrecht: Reidel.

King, J. 2001. *Complex demonstratives*. Cambridge: The MIT Press.

Montague, R. 1973. The proper treatment of quantification in ordinary English. In Hintikka et al. (1973).

Neidle, C. and R. Núñez Cedeño, eds. 1986. *Studies in Romance Languages*. Dordrecht: Foris.

Partee, B. 1998. Copula inversion puzzles in English and Russian. In Herbert Coats (1998). [also in UMOP 23: Issues in Semantics and its Interface, 2000, Department of Linguistics, UMass, Amherst. GLSA].

Poletto, C. and J.-Y. Pollock. 2002. On the left periphery of Romance interrogatives. In *GLOW newsletter*. Amsterdam.

Ruwet, N. 1972. *Théorie syntaxique et syntaxe du français*. Paris: Editions du Seuil.

Ruwet, N. 1982. *Grammaire des insultes et autres études*. Paris: Editions du Seuil.

# Part II

# Adverbs

# 11

# Adverb Classification *

OLIVIER BONAMI, DANIÈLE GODARD, AND
BRIGITTE KAMPERS-MANHE

## 1 Introduction

The syntactic category of adverbs is generally associated with the copresence of two properties. First, adverbs, which are typically used with the function of an adjunct, have a remarkable distributional freedom. Second, at least some adverbs are scopal elements, whose scope properties may have consequences on their position. Accordingly, adverbs pose a number of acute questions for the syntax-semantics interface. Moreover, since different (syntactic and/or semantic) classes of adverbs are associated with different behaviors at the syntax-semantics inter-

*Olivier Bonami and Danièle Godard are the primary authors for sections 2 to 5, while Brigitte Kampers-Manhe is the primary author for section 6. In addition, Elisabeth Delais-Roussarie and Jean-Marie Marandin made crucial contributions to the description of the phonetic data discussed in section 2.

We wish to thank Anne Abeillé and Jean-Marie Marandin for their comments and suggestions. We also thank Christian Molinier, who participated in the initial meetings this chapter grew out of, and whose work influenced much of what is presented here.

While we attempt throughout this paper to remain at a descriptive level and avoid specific theoretical assumptions, the discussion of the syntax-semantics interface in sections 2–5 is influenced by work on semantic underspecification in phrase structure grammars, such as that embodied in Minimal Recursion Semantics (Copestake et al. 2000). Since in such a framework, it is not expected that semantic scope follows from syntactic structure in a direct way, descriptive hypotheses are available which many researchers working in other frameworks would not even entertain.

*Handbook of French Semantics.*
Francis Corblin and Henriëtte de Swart (eds.).
Copyright © 2004, CSLI Publications.

face, these questions are at the heart of adverb classification itself.[2]

There are at least three different views in the literature. For Jackendoff (1972), there is a strict correlation between adverb positions and types of interpretations, and adverbs lexically specify which rule(s) of interpretation they can be associated with, so that no syntactic information need be specified on adverbs in addition to their interpretive type(s). This proposal has been amended in two opposite directions. In some proposals, the scope of adverbs as well as adverb classes themselves are defined in syntactic terms (Cinque, 1999; Alexiadou, 1997; Laezlinger, 1998; Tenny, 2000). These authors assume that there is a unique, universal hierarchy of abstract functional heads in every clause; Cinque explicitly argues that this hierarchy is not entirely predictable by semantics, although other authors take a more moderate approach (see Cinque, 1999: 134–136; Tenny 2000: 290). Each adverb occurs in the specifier position of a given head, which is determined by its semantic class. Apparent misfits are resolved by two means: either the adverb must be taken to be ambiguous, and thus occupy different specifier positions depending on its interpretation; or some constituent must have been moved across the adverb. On the other hand, recent proposals (e.g. Ernst 1998, Shaer 1998) adopt Jackendoff's basic claim, while giving a more precise semantic basis for the positional properties of adverbs. Adverbs specify the semantic type of their argument,[3] and can only combine with a syntactic object with the appropriate semantic type. There is a correlation between portions of the sentence and semantic types, that is rendered flexible by type-lifting mechanisms. In this way, a given adverb may occupy different positions, provided its semantic requirements are satisfied.

Our goal in this paper is threefold. First, we give a systematic description of the relevant French data. The presentation attempts to be neutral with respect to specific theoretical frameworks. Second, while a complete study of adverbs is outside the scope of the paper, we show that the data point towards a more complex view of the syntax-semantics interface than is usually proposed: the distribution of adverbs depends to a certain extent on semantic typing, but is not completely explained by it, even with a flexible view of the interface for

[2] The same questions must be raised for adjuncts in general. Starting with adverbs seems to be legitimate since, on the one hand, we lack even a basic descriptive classification of non-adverbial adjuncts; and on the other hand, adverbs are subject to specific distributional constraints that do not apply to adjuncts in general (as hinted at e.g. in Parsons 1990; Cinque 1999).

[3] See e.g. Bartsch 1976, Bellert 1977, Mc Connell-Ginet 1982, Parsons 1990, for classifications of adverbs based on their semantic type.

the sentence, and there remain some intriguing facts. Third, and most importantly, we point out a basic inadequacy of all existing classifications: while it is customary to exclude so-called 'parenthetical' adverbs from discussion, such a decision can only lead to a distorted view of the data. Having clarified the phenomenon in question, by distinguishing between the (syntactico-) prosodic property of certain occurrences (called here 'incidental' vs 'integrated' occurrences) and the semantic property of some adverb classes, we evaluate the consequences of including incidentals in adverb classification.

As a result of important overall studies of adverbs (Greenbaum 1969, Jackendoff 1972, for English; Bartsch 1976 for German; and Schlyter 1977, Molinier & Lévrier 2000 for French), there is a large consensus concerning the major semantic classes. We consider the following:[4] speech act adverbs (*franchement* 'frankly'), connectives (*donc, pourtant, premièrement* 'therefore, however, first'), evaluatives (*malheureusement, bizarrement* 'unfortunately, strangely'), modals (*probablement, peut-être, certainement* 'probably, perhaps, certainly'), agentives (*intelligemment, généreusement* 'intelligently, generously', cf. the 'subject-oriented' adverbs of Jackendoff, which we call agentives following Geuder 2000), frames (*légalement, théoriquement, syntaxiquement* 'legally, theoretically, syntactically'), frequency adverbs (*souvent, fréquemment, rarement* 'often, frequently, rarely'), duration adverbs (*longtemps* 'for a long time'), time adverbs (*immédiatement, bientôt* 'immediately, soon')[5], degrees (*beaucoup, complètement* 'a lot, completely'), and manners (*calmement, gentiment* 'calmly, kindly').

We examine in turn the positions of adverbs, the constraints on their

---

[4]We leave aside adverbs of focalization, and concentrate on adverbs in the verbal domain (some of the adverbs that we consider may occur in other domains, see chapter 12 of this book for adverbs of quantification). Note that negation adverbs do not form a homogeneous class: besides the sentential negation *pas/plus*, we find the quantifier *jamais* ('never'), and manner adverbs *aucunement, nullement* 'in no way' (see part IV for more details on negation). One class of adverbs which was not discussed explicitly in broad classificatory studies, but has received much attention in the formal semantics litterature, is that of intensional adverbs in the class of *intentionally*. We discuss this class explicitly in section 4.1 below.

[5]Notice that there do not seem to be spatial localization adverbs in French. Candidates such as *ici, là, ailleurs, où* ('here, there, elsewhere, where') are best analyzed as PPs: they do not occur between tense auxiliaries and participles (except possibly as incidentals, see section 2), whereas all French integrated adverbs occur in that position, even when subcategorized (Bonami 1999). Acceptability judgments concerning the time localization adverbs *hier, aujourd'hui* ('to-day, yesterday') are less clear-cut.

(i) * Jean avait ici posé les lettres 'Jean had here left the letters'

In addition, adverbs such as *localement, régionalement, nationalement* ('locally, regionally, nationally') seem to function like frames.

positions relative to one another, and their (main) lexical semantic properties, before evaluating the interpretations of such properties in terms of semantic types. Finally, we give an overview of the subclasses of manner adverbs, which are remarkable for their variety.

## 2 Adverb positions

In this section, we discuss the relation between the class of an adverb and the surface positions it can occur in. Attempting to remain theory-neutral, we describe the data in terms of order rather than structure.

We first discuss the notion of 'parentheticality', which is often introduced in adverb studies only to dismiss some of the data. We show that parentheticality as usually conceived is a cluster concept, blurring a distinction between a prosodic property (which we call *incidentality*) and a semantico-pragmatic one (which we call *parentheticality* in the strict sense, see chapter 13 of this book). Then in section 2.2, we review the surface positions of adverbs in French, taking into account the distinction between incidental and non-incidental occurrences. In section 2.3, we finally describe the possible positions for the different adverb classes, concluding that much of the known classification must be recast to take into account incidentality.

### 2.1 Incidentals and parentheticals

So-called 'parentheticals', which are known to have different pragmatic, semantic, prosodic, and/or positioning properties are usually mentioned only to be left aside (but see Marandin 1998, Molinier & Lévrier 2000, Schlyter 1977 for relevant observations in French). Once the question of what the difference between parentheticals and other uses of adverbs (or other adjuncts) is taken seriously, it appears that the term covers two distinct concepts. First, an adverb may have a special, 'parenthetical' interpretation, in that the semantic contribution of the adverb is not integrated into the proposition the sentence asserts; rather, it has the status of a 'comment' on that assertion. Second, in some positions, adverbs have a particular prosody which sets them apart from other constituents of the sentence — a prosody we attempt to characterize more precisely below. To avoid confusion, we use the term *incidental* to denote the prosodic property, and reserve the term *parenthetical* for the pragmatic property.

In principle, it might be the case that the two properties of parentheticity and incidentality coincide. As it happens, it is not the case at all. First, one and the same adverb may take either an incidental prosody or a non-incidental one; this is shown in 1, 2:[6]

(1) a. Mon frère, malheureusement, a raté son avion.
My brother, unfortunately, has missed his plane
b. Mon frère a malheureusement raté son avion.

(2) a. Marie, probablement, viendra à Paris.
Marie, probably, will come to Paris
b. Marie viendra probablement à Paris.

Second, the prosody does not correlate with the pragmatic status. For instance, the evaluative adverb *malheureusement* gets a parenthetical interpretation not only in 1a where it is incidental, but also in 1b, where it is not. On the other hand, the modal adverb *probablement* clearly makes a contribution to the asserted proposition, even when it gets an incidental prosody as in 2a. Finally, parentheticality appears to be a lexical property of adverbs, whereas incidentality is a property of particular occurrences (Espinal, 1991).

To clarify our intuitive idea of the two prosodies, we compare occurrences of adverbs in the VP, and in sentence-initial position.[7] This allows us to identify two prosodic patterns, which are independent of the position: both patterns are possible in the VP, as shown in 3, and in sentence-initial position, as shown in 4:

(3) a. Paul a (,) malheureusement (,) oublié ses rendez-vous.
Paul has (,) unfortunately (,) forgotten his appointments.

(4) a. Malheureusement, Paul a oublié tous ses rendez-vous.
Unfortunately, Paul has forgotten all his appointments.
b. Alors le gouvernement a cédé.
Then the government gave in.

The two patterns may be described as follows. The prosody of an integrated adverb is that of a normal constituent: first, it can itself constitute an Intonative Phrase, or form an Intonative Phrase with an adjacent word (preceding or following it if it occurs in the VP, following it if it is in S-initial position). Second, if it is initial, it can bear a sentence-initial stress (realized on the first rythmic group). On the other hand, incidentals do not seem to take part in the normal prosody of the sentence: the sentence has the same prosody as if there were no incident. The incidental constitutes an Intonative Phrase by

[6]Incidence is noted by commas (commas are not systematic in conventional orthographic usage). Throughout the paper, we provide glosses rather than translations.

[7]The definition of the relevant notions can be found in part V of this book.

itself, and its melody and intensity are contrasted with those of the rest of the sentence (they are lower if the incidental is within the sentence, and either higher or lower if it is initial). If the incidental adverb is not initial, its final contour is a copy of the final contour of the Intonative Phrase which precedes it.

## 2.2 Incidence and adverb positions

Let us now examine the correlation between the position of the adverb in the sentence and its prosodic status. To avoid the bias of particular syntactic frameworks, we do not characterize the position of adverbs with respect to a specific structural hypothesis. Rather, we define a number of surface 'zones', which may be mapped onto positions in a phrase-structure tree according to the reader's theoretical preferences.[8]

The delimitation of the zones is directly motivated by the distribution of adverb classes, and we make no more distinctions than seem necessary to account for this distribution.

In these terms, one can distinguish four adverbial zones in finite clauses, and three in infinitives (we leave aside participial clauses). In finite clauses, one must distinguish the zone before the subject (zone 1), the zone immediately before the finite verb (zone 2a), the zone after the finite verb (zone 3), and the zone among the complements (zone 4). In infinitival clauses, there is a unique preverbal zone (zone 2b), which happens to have very different properties from the corresponding zone in finite clauses, as we will see shortly.

| (5) | 1 | Subject | 2a | V | 3 | (V[past-part]) | 4 | (finite clauses) |
|---|---|---|---|---|---|---|---|---|
| | | | 2b | V | 3 | (V[past-part]) | 4 | (infinitives) |

Note that zone 3 is the zone between the auxiliary and the past participle in sentences with so-called 'compound tense'; in sentences with a simple tense, there is no overt boundary between zone 3 and zone 4, since there is no past participle.[9] Also note that we do not distinguish different zones after the (possible) past participle, since it is our observation that adverbs which are possible among or after complements are possible in all such positions, subject only to rythmic and information-

[8] Note that one pre-theoretic zone may correspond to a number of different positions in the tree, since a zone can contain two or more adverbs:

(i) Malheureusement, souvent, rapidement, Paul s'en va.
Unfortunately, often, quickly, Jean goes away

[9] Note that what we label V in 5 would presumably correspond to the Infl position in the GB framework — it is the position of finite verbs and auxiliaries in surface structure — and to the head position of the VP in a lexicalist phrase-structure grammar. It is not clear that the past participle itself marks the boundary between zones 3 and 4. In fact, Schlyter (1977) proposes that the negation *pas* or the floating quantifier *tous* constitutes this boundary.

structure constraints.[10] In the rest of this paragraph, we show that each of the four zones can host both incidental and integrated adverbs, but under different conditions.

**Initial zone (zone 1)** In the vast majority of cases, adverbs in zone 1 have an incidental prosody, as illustrated in 6:

(6) Franchement,/Malheureusement,/Donc,/Souvent, Paul est malheureux.
Frankly/Unfortunately/Therefore/Often, Paul is unhappy.

There are exceptions to this broad generalization. In a number of particular cases, well-documented in French grammars, small and highly idiosyncratic classes of adverbs are allowed with an integrated prosody. First, a few adverbs may occur in position 1 if the sentence is marked with the conjunction *que*, as illustrated in 7. The adverbs possible in this zone do not seem to form a coherent class; notice e.g. the contrast between *heureusement*, and its antonym *malheureusement* or the near synonyms *peut-être* and *possiblement*. Second, a few short modals and connectives are possible in zone 1 if the verb hosts an inverted subject clitic.[11] Finally, a few short connectives or temporal adverbs with a connective flavor (*alors, donc, aussi, aussitôt, vite*) and quantificational adverbs (*jamais, longtemps*) do occur in initial position with integrated prosody, without the presence of the adverb triggering any particular property in the sentence.

(7) a. Heureusement/*malheureusement que Paul est venu.
Fortunately/Unfortunately that Paul came

b. Peut-être/*possiblement que Paul viendra.
Perhaps/Possibly that Paul will come

(8) Aussi Paul a-t-il accepté immédiatement.
For this reason Paul has-CL accepted immediately

In addition to these well-known data, there is a construction which has escaped attention, where manner adverbs occur in zone 1 as non-incidentals.[12] In such cases, the initial occurrence is associated with a

[10] On the other hand, as Marandin (1998) shows, some non-adverbial incidentals are subject to further constraints; for instance, vocatives can occur only after all complements, not between the verb and one of its complements.

[11] The complete list is: *sans doute, peut-être, probablement, aussi, aussi bien, au moins, du moins, à peine, tout juste, tout au plus, encore, en vain* (see Grevisse 1969, Guimier 1996 for details). The class of adverbs which are possible before an inverted clitic overlaps with that of adverbs possible before *que*, but they are distinct. The latter are: *certainement, heureusement, même, non (pas), nul doute, sans doute, peut-être, probablement, sûrement.*

[12] In Laezlinger (1998: 108), the possibility that manner adverbs be 'moved' to ini-

very specific prosodic pattern (not yet identified in the literature, as far as we know): the adverb bears stress on (one of) the initial syllable(s) (while stress is normally final in French); and the stressed syllable is followed by a low tone. This pattern is most easily identified by contrasting initial manner adverbs with homophonous initial agentive adverbs, as in 9 (where capitalization indicates main stress):

(9) a. GENtiment, il m'a parlé, le prof!
Kindly he talked to me, the teacher
b. GentiMENT, il m'a parlé (le prof).
c. Il m'a parlé gentiment, le prof.

In 9a, the adverb has a manner reading; the sentence is synonymous to 9c, but 9a would only be used in a context where kindness is somehow unexpected or otherwise noticeable on the part of the teacher. 9b on the other hand only has an agentive reading.

This intonation pattern is thus associated with an affective flavor, whose exact nature we will not examine here.[13] The important points here are that subcategorized adverbs are found in position 1 with this intonation, and an adverb in sentence-initial position can modify an embedded clause:

(10) a. GENtiment, il s'est comporté, cet idiot!
Kindly, he behaved, the stupid guy
b. PRUDEmment, il m'avait promis qu'il parlerait!
Prudently, he had promised me that he would talk

These two facts indicate that we are dealing with an extraction construction. As adverb extraction is beyond the scope of this work, we leave this interesting construction aside in the following pages.

To sum up, the default situation is that non-extracted adverbs occurring in zone 1 are incidentals. Only particular, idiosyncratic subclasses are allowed with an integrated prosody, often with syntactic side effects.

**Pre-verbal zones (zones 2a and 2b)** As hinted at above, the preverbal zone has different properties in finite and infinitival clauses. In finite clauses, an adverb positioned between the subject and the finite verb always bears incidental prosody, and those adverbs which

---

tial position is recognized, but not distinguished from cases of S-initial adverbs with incidental prosody which are said to occur in a TopP (with multiple realizations).

[13]This pattern is similar to that of prosodically marked focal elements in French, although the interpretation is not exactly that of an ordinary informational focus. The structure is ruled out with normal stress on the final syllable and incidental prosody (Molinier & Lévrier 2000: 133):

(i) * Prudemment, il a agi dans cette affaire, je t'assure.
Prudently, he acted in that matter, I can asssure you

cannot be incidental are excluded. In infinitives we observe a different pattern. First, the prosody is always integrated; second, although there is a considerable amount of variation as to which adverbs can occur here (see § 2.3), some speakers clearly allow before the infinitive those adverbs which are excluded before the finite verb (compare 11b and 12b):[14]

(11) a. Mon frère, souvent, vient à Paris le lundi.
My brother, often, comes to Paris on Monday.

b. *Mon frère, bruyamment, a manifesté son mécontentement.
My brother, noisily, has shown his displeasure

(12) a. Paul a décidé de souvent venir à Paris.
Paul has decided to often come to Paris

b. % Paul a décidé de bruyamment manifester son mécontentement.
Paul has decided to noisily show his displeasure

**Post-verbal zones (zones 3 and 4)** The two remaining zones allow both intonation patterns: an adverb in one of these zones can be either integrated or incidental. They differ however in that some adverb classes are possible in zone 3 but not in zone 4, as we will see shortly.

(13) a. Paul a (souvent) dépassé les bornes (souvent).
Paul has (often) passed over the bounds (often)

b. Paul a (, franchement,) dépassé les bornes (,franchement).
Paul has (frankly) passed over the bounds (frankly)

c. Paul a (magnifiquement) parlé à ses enfants (magnifiquement).
Paul has (splendidly) spoken to his children (splendidly)

## 2.3 Incidence, positions, and adverb classes

What remains to be seen is how adverb classes correlate with positions and intonation. We consider first incidental occurrences, then integrated occurrences. Finally, we discuss in more detail the case of manner adverbs, which exhibit a particularly complex distribution.

**Incidental occurrences** Not all adverbs can be incidentals. If we look at zone 3, we observe that, among the traditional adverb classes, negative adverb, degree adverbs, and a subclass of manner adverbs cannot be incidentals.

[14]Adverbs which are always incidental (such as speech act adverbs) are also excluded before the nonfinite V, but this could be due to semantic/pragmatic factors. Here and throughout '%' notes speaker variation.

(14) a. *Jean n'a, pas/jamais, rencontré Marie.
Jean NE-has, not/never, met Marie

b. *Jean a, partiellement, lu ce livre.
Jean has, partially, read this book

c. *Jean est, bruyamment, sorti de la salle.
Jean has, noisily, gone out of the room

An interesting property of incidentality is that the precise linear position of the adverb does not seem to matter: adverbs are either possible with incidental prosody in every zone or in no zone at all.[15]

We illustrate this here by contrasting the degree adverb *partiellement* with the evaluative *heureusement.*[16]

(15) a. (Heureusement,) mon frère (,heureusement,) a (,heureusement,) envoyé (,heureusement,) son CV (,heureusement,) à d'autres boites que celle-là (,heureusement).
(Fortunately,) my brother (,fortunately,) has (,fortunately,) sent (,fortunately,) his CV (,fortunately,) to other firms besides that one (,fortunately).

b. (*Partiellement,) mon frère (*,partiellement,) a (*,partiellement,) lu (*,partiellement,) ce livre (*,partiellement).
(*Partiallly,) my brother (*,partially,) has (*,partially,) read (*,partially,) this book (*,partially).

**Integrated occurrences** Adverbs with an integrated intonation have a more complex distribution. The only adverb class which excludes any integrated use is that of speech act adverbs, as shown in 16:

(16) a. Jean s'est (*honnêtement) comporté (*honnêtement) comme un imbécile (*honnêtement).

[15]Adverbs which cannot be incidentals are found in final position, with a non-integrated intonation distinct from that of incidentals. They seem to be afterthoughts, and their syntactic status is not clear (see the co-occurrence of *pas* and *jamais*, impossible in the same VP):

(i) Il a chargé la barque, lourdement même.
He has loaded the boat, heavily even.

(ii) Il a aimé le film, énormément, je pense.
He loved the movie, enormously, I think.

(iii) Il n'a pas rencontré ce personnage, absolument jamais.
He has not met this person, absolutely never.

[16]This does not imply, of course, that incidentals are not constrained by the grammar. As Cori & Marandin (1995) and Marandin (1998) show, incidentals are not 'freely inserted' among constituents of the sentence, but are subject to the same kind of order constraints as other constituents. Rather, the observation is that the different incidental positions do not contrast with respect to their 'occupability' by adverbs.

Jean has (*honestly) behaved (*honestly) like a stupid man (*honestly)

b. *Jean était étonné d'honnêtement s'être fait avoir.
Jean was astonished to honestly have been taken in

For other adverb classes, a distinction must be made between the various zones compatible with integrated intonation.[17] Table 1 summarizes the distribution of the various adverb classes (manner adverbs are discussed in the next paragraph). The possibility for an adverb to occur in zone 2b (i.e., before an infinitive) is subject to a lot of variation, and a number of complex constraints, some of which are mysterious. Note first that evaluatives and connectives are possible only for some speakers. Frame adverbs are even less likely to occur in this position. Turning to postverbal zones, we observe a clear contrast between two types of adverbs: some adverb classes (connective, evaluative, modal, agentive adverbs) are only possible in zone 3 while others are possible in both postverbal zones (manner, quantification, negation, degree, time, frame).[18] It thus appears that zone 3 in French is the equivalent of the 'pre-auxiliary' zone in English, where all adverb classes are possible.

| zone 2b (pre-infinitive) | zone 3 (postverbal) | zone 4 (among complts) |
|---|---|---|
| %connective | connective | |
| %evaluative | evaluative | |
| modal | modal | |
| agentive | agentive | |
| frequency | frequency | frequency |
| negation | negation | negation (some) |
| %degree | degree | degree |
| time | time | time |
| | %frame | %frame |

TABLE 1 Integrated occurrences of adverb classes

[17] Remember that we leave out the few cases of integrated S-initial adverbs enumerated in paragraph 2.2. More generally, we focus on broad generalizations applying to classes of adverbs, rather than on individual behavior. For instance, whereas most connectives, such as *donc*, can be postverbal, the connective *alors* cannot when it has its consecutive meaning (**Ce triangle est alors rectangle*, this triangle is then right-angled).

[18] If the participle does not constitute the boundary (see note 9), those integrated adverbs which may occur among complements are always in zone 4 when they are postverbal, even when they precede the participle.

**The case of manner adverbs** As already hinted at above, there is no distributional pattern common to all manner adverbs.[19]Rather, it appears that four syntactic subclasses must be distinguished. Some manner adverbs have a rather free distribution, occurring both as incidentals and in all integrated zones (2b, 3 and 4). Following previous work (Abeillé et Godard, 1997) we call these adverbs 'S-manner adverbs.' Other classes are subject to various restrictions. Some adverbs ('VP manners', among which *bruyamment*, for some speakers at least) can occur in all integrated positions; others ('V manners') occur only in zones 3 and 4 (e.g. *verticalement*) or 2b and 3 (e.g. *bien*).

(17) **S manner adverbs**

a. Silencieusement, les enfants sortirent de la pièce.
Silently, the children went out of the room

b. Les enfants avaient essayé de silencieusement sortir de la pièce.
The children had tried to silently go out of the room

c. Les enfants sont (silencieusement) sortis de la pièce (silencieusement).
The children have (silently) gone out of the room (silently)

(18) **VP manner adverbs**[20]

a. *Bruyamment, Jean est sorti de la pièce.
Noisily, Jean has gone out of the room.

b. % Jean s'est décidé à bruyamment sortir de la pièce.
Jean (finally) decided to noisily go out of the room.

c. Jean est (bruyamment) sorti de la pièce (bruyamment).
Jean has (noisily) gone out of the room (noisily).

(19) **Non-lite V manner adverbs**

a. *Verticalement, le pétrole a surgi du sol.
Vertically, the oil has risen from the ground.

b. *Le pétrole s'est mis à verticalement surgir du sol.
The oil has started to vertically rise from the ground.

c. Le pétrole a (?verticalement) surgi (verticalement) du sol.
The oil has (vertically) risen (vertically) from the ground.

(20) **Lite V manner adverbs**

[19]Moreover, there is a lot of variation regarding the classification of individual adverbs, although there is a consensus as to what the classes are. The judgments given here are those of the authors unless otherwise indicated.

[20]The extension of the class of VP manner adverbs seems to be particularly subject to variation. Some speakers, among whom the second alphabetical author of this text, have no adverb in this class. This is why this class is not taken into account in Abeillé and Godard (1997).

a. *Bien, Jean a classé ses fiches.
Well, Jean has filed his cards

b. Jean a décidé de bien classer ses fiches.
Jean has decided to well file his cards

c. Jean a (bien) classé ses fiches (*bien).
Jean has (well) filed his cards (*well)

It is doubtful that these distributional restrictions can be linked to a semantic classification of manner adverbs (see section 6). Notice first the contrast between *silencieusement* and *bruyamment*, which do not have the same distribution despite clear semantic similarity. Since VP (or V) manner adverbs cannot be incidental, and the S-initial position is associated with incidental occurrence, it is tempting to trace the specific behavior of S-manners simply to their ability to occur as incidentals. This implies that we should not distinguish between S- and V/VP-manners when they are postverbal integrated adverbs. Second, although many resultative adverbs pattern like *verticalement*, not all of them do (e.g. *lourdement* 'heavily' patterns like *bruyamment* under its resultative reading). Finally, the class of adverbs with the same distribution as *bien* is clearly the class of 'lite' manner adverbs in the sense of Abeillé and Godard (1997, 2000), and 'liteness' appears to be an arbitrary property of adverbs, from a syntactic point of view.[21]

**Relation to other classifications** In the literature on the syntax of adverbs, there is a long tradition of splitting adverbs into two classes: 'S-adverbs' vs. 'VP-adverbs', (Jackendoff, 1972; Molinier and Levrier, 2000, inter alia) or 'Higher adverbs' vs. 'Lower adverbs' (Cinque, 1999). In the context of the present discussion, it becomes clear that this type of classification blurs two distinctions. Many classifications (e.g. Schlyter 1977, Molinier and Levrier 2000) take the possibility of appearing in sentence-initial position as a necessary condition for being classified as an S-adverb. Since almost all S-initial adverbs are incidentals, S-adverbs are all possible incidentals for these approaches. On the other hand, Cinque (1999) takes the possibility of occurring after the past participle as a criterion for lower adverbs. What he has in mind is not the distinction between possible incidentals and obligatorily integrated adverbs, since he explicitly places incidentals outside the scope of

[21]Two properties show that these adverbs are 'lite': (i) although they can occur before the infinitive, they cannot modify a coordination of VPs (hence, they adjoin to the lexical V rather than the VP); (ii) although they cannot occur in zone 4 bare, they can occur there if modified by another adverb. See Abeillé and Godard (1997, 2000, 2001) for details. Lite adverbs belong to one of three classes: manners, degrees and negations. We leave the question of a possible semantic motivation for further study.

his study (1999: 32). Rather, in the present terms, Cinque's distinction seems to be one made between those (integrated) adverbs which can occur in zone 4 and those which cannot, a distinction which is relevant for French adverbs.

The preceding discussion shows that the full distribution of adverbs cannot be accounted for unless both distinctions are made and they are clearly separated. Labeling some adverb classes as 'sentential' is misleading at best: incidentals are not 'sentential' in any clear sense, since they can occur in every position where integrated adverbs are possible. And integrated, pre-complement adverbs are not 'sentential' either, in any clear sense of the word, since they typically do not occur in sentence-initial position with an integrated prosody. Moreover, as shown by the split between V/VP manners and S-manners, there is no straightforward explanation for either of the two distinctions in semantic terms.

## 3 Relative positions

Constraints on the relative positions of adverbs are usually interpreted in terms of scope: a generalization akin to that proposed in 21 is assumed by most authors (e.g. Jackendoff, 1972; Schlyter, 1977; Cinque, 1999):[22]

(21) If adverbs A and B occur in the same syntactic domain, A precedes B iff A takes scope over B.

If this generalization is correct, then the study of relative positions can serve as an important testing ground for theories of adverb positioning. In a semantics-based theory such as that of Ernst or Shaer, it is predicted that the possible orders for pairs of adverbs follow from their semantic type: adverb A can precede adverb B iff the input type of A is the output type of B (or some type derivable from the output type of B by lifting). In a syntax-based theory such as Cinque's, it is expected that for at least some pairs of adverbs A and B, A will be unable to precede B despite the fact that B's semantic output type is compatible with A's input type.

In this context, it is crucial to know to what extent generalization 21 is correct. In this section, we present the results of a thorough examination of constraints on the relative positions of adverbs in French. First,

[22]Cinque (1999) leaves room for exceptions to this generalization, by assuming that an adverb can be found to the left of another adverb, while having narrow scope, if a constituent containing the adverb is moved to the left. For an account of the distribution of French manner adverbs based on Cinque's theory of adverbs, see Kampers-Manhe (2001).

we redefine 21, in order to take into account the distinction between incidental and integrated adverbs, whose scopal properties are crucially distinct. Second, we show that the generalizations that we obtain do not hold for all adverb classes.

### 3.1 Relative positions and occurrence types

On the basis of pairs of adverbs whose scopal ordering is uncontroversial, such as modals and manners, we find that the correct generalizations are as in 22. Note that the only case where 21 is respected is when two adverbs are both integrated; since (i) an incidental adverb can follow an integrated adverb and still respect 22i, and (ii) 22iii is completely insensitive to order:

(22) i. Incidental adverbs take scope over integrated adverbs.
ii. Scope among integrated adverbs follows linear order.
iii. Scope among incidental adverbs is syntactically unconstrained.

**One incidental, one integrated** Sentences containing both an incidental and an integrated adverb initially seem to support generalization 21. However, this is simply due to the fact that incidental positions tend to precede integrated positions. Once sentence-final incidentals are taken into account, it becomes clear that it is the difference in occurrence type, and not the linear order, which correlates with scope.

(23) a. Probablement, Jean a calmement répondu à la question.
Probably, Jean has calmly answered the question
b. *Calmement, Jean a probablement répondu à la question.

(24) a. Jean a calmement répondu à la question, probablement.
Jean has calmly answered the question, probably
b. *Jean a probablement répondu à la question, calmement.

**Two integrated occurrences** For integrated occurrences, scope genuinely follows order in most cases.[23] However, as we will see in section 3.2, this does not hold for all adverbs.

(25) a. Jean a probablement calmement répondu à la question.
Jean has probably calmly answered the question
b. *Jean a calmement probablement répondu à la question.[24]

[23]Of course, this generalization does not as such preclude one from reducing order facts to hierarchical structure, *à la* Cinque (1999). Since Cinque explicitly excludes incidentals from his study, it is hard to evaluate how he would account for the two other generalizations.

[24]We consider here sentences with both adverbs before the past participle, since modals cannot follow it. Of course, 25a is fine, and even more natural, with *calmement* after the participle.

**Two incidental occurrences** Probably more surprising is the fact that the scope of pairs of incidentals seems to be completely unconstrained in syntax.[25] Thus pairs of incidental adverbs do not respect 21 in any interpretation.

(26) a. Probablement, Jean, calmement, aura répondu à la question.
b. Calmement, Jean aura, probablement, répondu à la question.

### 3.2 Relative positions and lexical classes

Now that the generalizations in 22 have been established, it remains to be verified that various lexical classes of adverbs do indeed respect the constraints on distribution imposed by them. We have thus examined a few pairs of adverbs for each of the $10 \times 10 = 100$ pairs of classes considered in this study.[26] For each pair of adverbs, we examined sentences containing a sentence-initial incidental and a postverbal integrated adverb. Whenever an adverb could not be incidental, we turned to sentences with two integrated occurrences.[27] For reasons of space, it is of course impossible to report the detailed data here: 27 summarizes the constraints on order we found to be valid; all pairs of classes not mentioned in 27 are possible with both orders.

(27) **Constraints on the relative order of integrated adverbs**
i. Evaluatives must precede all other adverbs except time adverbs and connectives.
ii. Manner and degree adverbs must follow all other adverbs except time adverbs.
iii. Modal adverbs must precede agentive, frequency and duration adverbs.

As the reader can see, the order of adverbs is much less constrained than is usually assumed: for many adverb class pairs, both orders are possible. In the following paragraphs, we discuss some of the more interesting interactions of these order constraints with scope properties.

**Predictable rigid ordering** For some pairs of adverbs, we find a rigid ordering which follows directly from the generalizations in 22 and standard assumptions on semantic types. For instance, the data discussed in section 3.1 follow directly from the assumption that modal

[25] Bonami (1999:61–68). This constraint is noted by Jackendoff (1972) with reference to sentence-final incidentals, and by Schlyter (1977) with respect to incidentals after the negation.

[26] We leave aside speech act adverbs, which are always incidentals.

[27] Thus we presuppose that the set of pairs of adverbs is partitioned in the same way by the two contexts. Although this has not been tested thoroughly, it seems to be generally correct. Note that part of the data in this paragraph was difficult to establish, and may deserve extensive discussion.

adverbs are proposition modifiers whereas manner adverbs modify some component of the described proposition (either an eventuality or an eventuality description; see section 5). In other cases, an observed rigid ordering can help in deciding on the semantic type of some less often studied adverb class. For instance, the fact that evaluatives must precede almost all other adverbs,[28] including modals, seems to preclude Wyner's (1994) analysis of evaluatives as predicates of events — except if one is ready to abandon the classical analysis of modals as propositional operators.

(28) a. Heureusement, Paul a vraisemblablement/intelligemment/fréquemment/longtemps/joyeusement accepté de venir.
Fortunately, Paul has likely/intelligently/frequently/for a long time/ happily accepted to come here.

b. ?? Vraisemblablement/Intelligemment/Fréquemment/Longtemps/ Joyeusement, Paul a heureusement accepté de venir.

**Correlation of scope and order** In some cases, a pair of adverbs is possible with both orders, with a clear impact on scope. A straightforward example is that of frequency and duration adverbs. In 29a, the duration adverb *longtemps* measures the global event consisting of an iteration of leavings, whereas in 29b it measures each individual event:

(29) a. Longtemps, il s'est souvent absenté.
For a long time, he often went away

b. Souvent, il s'est longtemps absenté.
Often, he went away for a long time

A similar situation is found, for example, with agentives and durations. Whereas 30a reports that Paul's long term plans were clever, 30b tells us about the duration of Paul's cleverness:

(30) a. Intelligemment, Paul a longtemps évité les débats politiques, et peut aujourd'hui construire sa popularité.
Intelligently, Paul has for a long time avoided political fighting, and can today build his popularity

b. Longtemps, Paul a intelligemment évité les débats politiques, et s'est consacré à son œuvre.

These examples are important for the present discussion on two counts. First, although the possibility of free order is predicted by the generalizations in 22 (as long as some adverbs are of type $\langle x, x \rangle$, whatever $x$ is), that possibility is clearly excluded by Cinque's (1999)

[28]That is, all but time adverbs and connectives; see below.

approach, under which all adverbs should be strictly ordered.[29] This problem with Cinque's approach does not automatically extend to all syntactic approaches to adverb ordering; see Nilsen (2001) for an example of a syntactic approach to adverb ordering which does not presuppose the precedence relation on adverbs to be a linear order.

Second, in some cases, the observed scope-order correlation is unexpected given standard assumptions about the semantic type associated with some adverb classes. Consider the case of time and evaluative adverbs. It is standard to assume that time adverbs are predicates of events, while evaluatives are propositional operators. Against this background, it is surprising to notice that a time adverb may outscope an evaluative, as shown by 31.

(31) a. Bientôt, le château serait malheureusement vendu, mais nous serions fort heureusement à l'abri du besoin.
Soon, the castle would unfortunately be sold, but our financial difficulties would fortunately be over

b. Heureusement, le château serait bientôt vendu, et aménagé un peu plus tard en résidence collective.
Fortunately, the castle would soon be sold, and converted a little later into a condominium

These data seem to favor a propositional analysis of time expressions (even within Davidsonian assumptions; see (Katz, 2000) for a different argument to the same effect).

**Independence of scope and order** In the context of the present discussion, it is somewhat surprising to realize that some adverb pairs accept both orders, with no effect whatsoever on scope. This is quite often found when one of the adverbs is a connective: except if the other adverb is a manner or degree adverb 33, the connective always takes wide scope, irrespective of its position. That the connective takes wide scope is clear from examples like 32a: *donc* states a consequence relation between some previously established proposition and the proposition that they probably reacted in a certain way, not the proposition that they (definitely) reacted in a certain way.

(32) a. Probablement, ils ont donc réagi à la provocation d'une manière violente.
Probably, they have therefore reacted to the provocation in a violent way

[29]Notice that for Cinque, postulating that the initial adverb in 29a, 29b, 30a or 30b is topicalized is not an option, since it is ruled out by the principle of Relativized Minimality.

b. Donc, ils ont probablement réagi à la provocation de manière violente

(33) a. Ils ont donc violemment réagi à la provocation.
They have therefore violently reacted to the provocation

b. * Ils ont violemment donc réagi à la provocation.

These data are very puzzling for two reasons. First, to account for 32, one would like to assume that connectives are somehow exempt from all syntactic constraints on scope (and thus behave as a special class which is to be distinguished from all other adverbs). But the data in 33 must be accounted for: why are manners and degrees ordered with respect to connectives in the VP?[30]

Second, it is tempting to link the behavior of connectives to their parenthetical status (see section 4.3). But again, connectives appear to be an exception even among parentheticals: evaluatives and agentives do not occur on the right of an integrated adverb they take scope over (see e.g. 28). Thus it seems that the only way to account for the data is to relativize the generalizations in 22 to a subset of the set of adverb pairs.

**Conclusion** The generalizations on scope-order correlations stated in 22 cannot be taken for granted, even if they capture a relevant tendency: there are clear cases of adverbs which take scope irrespective of their position in the sentence. Morever, even when the generalizations are respected, they can present a challenge to standard semantic analyses of some adverb classes, as was seen in the case of time and evaluative adverbs.

## 4 Lexical semantic properties

In this section, we review a number of well-known lexical properties of (sub)classes of adverbs and observe how they apply to the French data. The consequences of our findings are discussed in section 5.[31]

---

[30]This behavior occurs even when one adverb is initial (see i). Thus one solution would be to assume that the data in 33 follow from ordering rather than scope constraints. This is the case when postverbal connectives are in zone 3, while manners are in zone 4, see fn 18. This would leave intact the generalization on the scopal independence of connectives.

(i) *Silencieusement, les enfants sont donc sortis de la pièce.
Silently, the children have thus gone out of the room.

[31]We have left aside a number of interesting properties which are often taken to be classificatory criteria, but which we have found to raise more questions than they solve. For instance, although the relative positions of adverbs and negation are intriguing and interesting, they seem to cut through well-established semantic classes. For instance, punctual time adverbs may not precede negation, but exten-

### 4.1 Intensionality

Traditionally, two properties are taken to be characteristic of intensional contexts: (i) Non-substitutivity of coreferential descriptions, e.g. *John thinks Mary is stupid* and *Mary is the new Nobel Prize for physics* do not entail *John thinks the new Nobel Prize for physics is stupid*; (ii) Unspecific readings of indefinites, e.g. *John seeks a book about information structure* does not entail that *There is a book about information structure that John seeks.* As noted by Zimmerman (1993), these two properties are in principle independent, although any one of the two justifies an intensional analysis.[32] A number of adverb classes exhibit one or the other characteristic properties of intensional operators. In the following, we only discuss those adverb classes for which an intensional analysis has been suggested in the literature; we admit without discussion that speech-act, frame, frequency, duration, manner, and degree adverbs are extensional.

**Modal adverbs** fall into two subclasses with respect to intensionality tests. On the one hand, all modal adverbs exhibit unspecific readings of indefinites. This is shown by the coherence of the sentences in 34. On the other hand, the substitutability of coreferring descriptions is dependent on the modal base: alethic or deontic interpretations of modals disallow substitution, whereas epistemic interpretations allow it 35:

(34) a. Jean a nécessairement tué un homme, mais il n'y a pas d'homme (en particulier) que Jean ait nécessairement tué.
Jean has necessarily killed a man, but there is no man (in particular) that Jean has necessarily killed

b. Jean a probablement/peut-être tué un homme, mais il n'y a pas d'homme (en particulier) que Jean ait probablement/peut-

ded time adverbs can (i–ii). Similarly, as observed by (Schlyter 1977, Molinier and Levrier 2000), necessity modals can follow the negation, but possibility modals cannot (iii–iv).

(i) Auparavant, il n'allait pas à Paris.
Before, he NE went not to Paris

(ii) *Bientôt, il n'ira pas à Paris
Soon, he NE will-go not to Paris

(iii) Jean n'a pas forcément compris la question
Jean NE has not neccesarily understood the question

(iv) *Jean n'a pas peut-être compris la question
Jean NE has not perhaps understood the question

Likewise, we did not follow Molinier and Levrier in taking the distribution of adverbs in cleft sentences as a criterion, since (i) the data is very intricate and (ii) its interpretation is difficult, in the absence of a clear understanding of the interpretive effects of clefting on non-nominal expressions.

[32]See Moltmann (1997) for a discussion of further properties of intensional predicates, which we cannot go into here.

être tué.
Jean has probably/perhaps killed a man, but there is no man (in particular) that Jean has probably/perhaps killed

(35) a. Le nombre de solutions de cette équation est nécessairement pair.
The number of solutions for this equation is necessarily even.
Le nombre de solutions de cette équation est le nombre de livres que Paul a lus depuis le début de l'année.
The number of solutions for this equation is the number of books that Paul has read since the beginning of the year
$\not\Rightarrow$ Le nombre de livres que Paul a lus depuis le début de l'année est nécessairement pair.
The number of books that Paul has read since the beginning of the year is necessarily even

b. La commission est obligatoirement présidée par le vice-président.
The committee is obligatorily chaired by the vice-president
Le vice-président est le doyen de l'assemblée.
The vice-president is the oldest member of the assembly
$\not\Rightarrow$ La commission est obligatoirement présidée par le doyen de l'assemblée.
The committee is obligatorily chaired by the oldest member of the assembly

c. Marie connaît forcément son fils.
Marie obligatorily knows her son
Le fils de Marie est le patron de Jean.
Marie's son is Jean's boss
$\Rightarrow$ Marie connaît forcément le patron de Jean.
Marie obligatorily knows Jean's boss

**Adverbs of attitude towards a state of affairs** Perhaps the most celebrated example of an intensional adverb is *volontairement* 'intentionally'. As Thomason and Stalnaker (1973) show, this adverb is peculiar in passing the intensionality tests for complement positions, but not for the subject position.

(36) a. Jean a volontairement insulté Marie.
Jean has intentionally insulted Marie
Marie est la femme du président.
Marie is the wife of the president
$\not\Rightarrow$ Jean a volontairement insulté la femme du président.
Jean has intentionally insulted the wife of the president

b. Marie a volontairement insulté Jean.
Marie has intentionally insulted Jean
Marie est la femme du président.
Marie is the wife of the president
⇒ La femme du président a volontairement insulté Jean.
The wife of the president has intentionally insulted Jean

Other adverbs with the same property include *(in)volontairement, fortuitement, par hasard*, etc. Thomason and Stalnaker conclude that *volontairement* and similar adverbs are (intensional) property modifiers. In a more descriptive approach, we can note that these adverbs always express the attitude of an agent towards a state of affairs; for instance in 36a *volontairement* tells us what responsibility Jean has in the bringing about of a state of affairs where he insulted Marie.[33]

An analysis along these lines is provided by Landman (2000), who proposes to treat these adverbs as relations between an individual, an event, and an (intensional) relation specifying what aspect of the event the individual relates to in the way specified by the adverb. [34]

**Agentive adverbs** The status of agentive adverbs with respect to intensionality tests is less than clear. As Wyner (1997) notes, in some cases the adverb seems to disallow substitution of coreferring descriptions:

(37) a. Intelligemment, Marie a mis sa robe préférée pour la réception.
Cleverly, Marie has put on her favorite dress for the reception

b. La robe préférée de Marie est la même que la robe de la Reine.
Marie's favorite dress is the same as the Queen's dress
⇏ Intelligemment, Marie a mis la même robe que la Reine pour la réception.
Cleverly, Marie has put on the same dress as the Queen for the reception

[33] Most of these adverbs can occur in sentences with a non-agentive head verb. However, in such cases, there is a strong feeling that some unexpressed but salient agent is responsible (or not responsible, depending on the lexical semantics of the adverb) for the expressed state of affairs. Notice the contrast between (i) and (ii): (ii) is odd because one does not see how some agent could be held responsible of the fact that it rains.

(i) La bombe est tombée sur cette ville par hasard
The bomb fell on this town by chance

(ii) ?? La pluie est tombée sur cette ville par hasard
The rain fell on this town by chance

[34] Although Landman presents his analysis as an analysis of *subject-oriented adverbs*, it is clear that it applies only to those adverbs in the *volontairement* class, and not to those Geuder (2000) dubs *agentive adverbs*, which are not intensional, as shown below.

However, this impression can be shown to follow from the context-dependence of agentive adverbs, rather than from genuine intensionality (Geuder, 2000:168). According to Geuder, 37 tells us nothing about intensionality because 37 cannot be taken as an unsituated inference pattern, but only as a situated discourse. Let us see why. In a sentence such as 37a, *intelligemment* states that Marie has some (unexpressed) goal which can be wisely fulfilled by wearing her favorite dress; stereotypically, the hearer will probably interpret that Marie's goal is to be seen in a favorable light at the party. However, the information in 37b strongly suggests that this is not a good way to fulfill the goal, hence the judgment that 37c does not follow. What is crucial here is that from a discourse perspective, the (situated) interpretation of 37b is contradictory with the (situated) interpretation of 37a: once 37b is known, it can no longer be sustained that 37a is true (compare the case of a genuine intensional predicate: knowing that the second sentence of 36a is the case changes nothing as to whether the first is true). Thus 37 cannot be considered to be an abstract inference pattern. This line of analysis suggests that agentive adverbs are not intensional predicates at all, but extensional predicates which are highly sensitive to the context in which they are evaluated.

Elaborating on Geuder's observations, one can see clearly why agentive adverbs could be confused with intensional predicates: in both cases, an inference fails because we are dealing with an imperfect information state. The difference is that, in the case of intensional predicates, the evaluation is sensitive to the information state of an agent mentioned in the sentence, whereas agentive adverbs are sensitive to the information state of the discourse participant.

**Evaluative adverbs** can also be mistaken for intensional predicates, as the following example shows:

(38) a. Heureusement, Œdipe a épousé Jocaste.
Fortunately, Œdipe has married Jocaste
b. Jocaste est la mère d'Œdipe.
Jocaste is Œdipe's mother
$\not\Rightarrow$ Heureusement, Œdipe a épousé sa mère.
Fortunately, Œdipe has married his mother

However this case is similar to the preceding one. Eckardt (1998) suggests that evaluative adverbs are focus-sensitive operators. On its most salient reading, 38a would have a (semantic) focus on *Jocaste* and state that it is happier for Œdipus to have married Jocaste than it would have been to marry alternative possible wives. However 38b gives information which strongly suggests that 38a is not true.

Even if one is not willing to endorse Eckardt's focus-based analysis, it is clear that we are dealing with a case similar to that of agentive adverbs: the failure of the inference is not due to intensionality, but to the incompatibility of what is conveyed by the two premises (within accepted social norms).

### 4.2 Veridicality

We call *veridicality* the property an adverb has if any sentence containing this adverb entails the sentence obtained when the adverb is suppressed (Giannakidou, 1998).[35] Veridicality is a basic property which has been extensively discussed in the literature since Davidson (1967), because it is a precondition any adverb must meet if it is to be analyzed as a Davidsonian predicate of events. Most adverb classes contain only veridical adverbs. There are only three classes which contain unmistakable non-veridical adverbs: the class of modals, the class of quantification adverbs and the class of degree adverbs (more precisely, the subclass of *completion adverbs*; see chapter 12 of this book).

(39) a. Jean est probablement venu. $\not\Rightarrow$ Jean est venu.
Jean has probably come  Jean has come

b. Jean est forcément venu. $\Rightarrow$ Jean est venu.
Jean has obligatorily come  Jean has come

(40) a. Jean n'est jamais venu. $\not\Rightarrow$ Jean est venu.
Jean never came  Jean came

b. Jean est rarement venu. $\Rightarrow$ Jean est venu.
Jean rarely came  Jean came

(41) a. Jean a partiellement lu ton livre. $\not\Rightarrow$ Jean a lu ton livre.
Jean has partially read your book  Jean has read your book

b. Jean a entièrement lu ton livre. $\Rightarrow$ Jean a lu ton livre.
Jean has entirely read your book  Jean has read your book

---

[35]We avoid speaking of *factivity*, since this term has been used with so many different senses; in the context of *factive verbs*, factivity is really presupposition of the complement, whereas Wyner (1994) calls agentive adverbs 'factive', although these do not presuppose their argument. This is clear from the following contrast (remember that presuppositions project out of the antecedent of a conditional):

(i) Si Jean regrette d'avoir parlé à Marie, il le dira. $\Rightarrow$
Jean a parlé à Marie.
If Jean regrets having spoken with Marie, he will say so $\Rightarrow$
J. has spoken to M.

(ii) Si Jean a intelligemment parlé à Marie, il le dira. $\not\Rightarrow$
Jean a parlé à Marie.
If Jean has intelligently spoken to Marie, he will say so $\not\Rightarrow$
J. has spoken to M.

A further class of potentially non-veridical adverbs is that of frame adverbs. The inference in 42 does seem to be invalid:

(42) Sémantiquement, cette question ne présente aucun intérêt.
Semantically, this question is of no interest.
$\not\Rightarrow$ Cette question ne présente aucun intérêt.

However, asking whether frame adverbs are veridical might be beside the point. As Bartsch (1987) emphasizes (see also Bellert 1977), frame adverbs make explicit the "domain" (or "perspective" in Bartsch's terms) in which a sentence is to be evaluated. In the absence of a frame adverb, the domain is left implicit, but this does not mean that the interpretation is domain-independent. Thus the second sentence in 42 can be taken to contain a covert frame adverb (which might be glossed as "in no way"). If this is the case though, 42 is not really a veridicality test for the frame adverb, since suppressing it implies a change of domain.

## 4.3 Compatibility with speech act types

Most studies of adverbs focus only on the analysis of assertive sentences. In this section, we consider the occurrence of adverbs in interrogatives and imperatives. We start with integrated occurrences, and then consider the sentence-initial incidental position.

**Integrated occurrences** The distribution of adverbs in integrated position in interrogatives and imperatives is quite simple. Most adverbs can occur in interrogatives and imperatives; the exceptions are as follows. Speech act adverbs are excluded, just as in declaratives. In addition, evaluatives (43), modals,[36] habituals (44), and agentives (45) are excluded from imperatives.

(43) a. Qui est bizarrement déjà arrivé?
Who is strangely already arrived

b. *Arrive heureusement à l'heure!
Be fortunately on time

(44) a. Qui est probablement venu? Qui arrive habituellement à l'heure?
Who has probably come Who is habitually on time

[36]Note that necessity modals occur naturally in yes–no questions (Schlyter 1977, Molinier & Lévrier 2000):

(i) Jean va-t-il forcément à Paris?
Is Jean going obligatorily to Paris

(ii) ?? Jean va-t-il probablement/peut-être/évidemment à Paris?
Is Jean going probably/perhaps/evidently to Paris?

b. *Arrive probablement/ habituellement à l'heure!
Be probably/ habitually on time

(45) a. Paul a-t-il méchamment refusé de répondre?
Did Paul nastily refuse to answer

b. ?Quand on vous demandera votre accord, refusez méchamment de signer.
When your agreement will be required, nastily refuse to sign.

It is clear that modals and habituals and agentives are excluded from imperatives for reasons which have to do with their lexical semantics. It does not make sense to give modal orders, and habits are not the kind of things one can be ordered to have.Geuder (2000) proposes that agentive adverbs indicate that the described event manifests a disposition of the agent. Under this analysis, it becomes clear why agentives are strange in imperatives: it does not make sense to order an agent to have a disposition, but the sentences are marginally acceptable if understood as requesting the agent to *act as if* he had a disposition; thus 45b is felicitous only if understood as ordering the agent to *look* mean, not to *be* mean.

**S-initial occurrences** The examination of the occurrence of adverbs before sentences expressing speech act types other than assertion is relevant to their semantic classification because the adverb seems to take scope over the speech act, in some cases at least. This is seen most easily in the case of connectives such as *donc*:[37] in 46a, *donc* states that the speaker's asking the question is a consequence of the first sentence; and in 46b, that the speaker's giving the order is explained by the fact that we are late. Speech act adverbs have the same distribution and similar readings:[38]

(46) a. Jean déteste Marie. Donc, viendra-t-il à son anniversaire?
Jean hates Marie. Therefore, will he come for her birthday party

b. Nous sommes en retard. Donc, dépêche-toi!
We are late. Therefore, hurry up

[37]Some connectives, such as *de ce fait*, have a more restricted distribution (Jayez and Rossari, 1998):

(i) Il fait froid. Donc/* De ce fait, ferme la porte.
It is cold. Therefore/Hence, close the door

[38]See Schreiber, 1972; Mittwoch, 1977. Interestingly, speech act adverbs in front of interrogatives are ambiguous between a 'query-oriented' and a 'response-oriented' meaning: 47a can either mean that the speaker is honest in asking the question, or that he requests the answer to be honest.

(47) a. Honnêtement, Paul viendra-t-il?
Honestly, will Paul come

b. Franchement, fais un effort!
Frankly, try harder

Frames and some time adverbs are also possible before an interrogative or imperative, but with a different type of reading: in 48a, *légalement* does not qualify the speech act itself, but is part of the *content* of this act:[39]

(48) a. Légalement, qui est responsable de cela?
Legally, who is the person in charge

b. Officiellement, tenez-vous à l'écart de ce groupe.
Officially, keep away from this group

(49) a. Demain, qui vient à la réunion?
Tomorrow, who is coming to the meeting

b. Demain, prends soin du chat.
Tomorrow, take care of the cat

Finally, among adverbs of quantification, only habituals are possible before interrogatives (Schlyter 1977, Molinier and Levrier, 2000), and neither habitual nor frequency adverbs are possible before imperatives.[40]

In interrogatives, the resulting reading is one where the adverb is integrated in the semantic content, rather than qualifying the question act.

(50) a. Habituellement, qui s'occupe de gérer les candidatures?
Habitually, who takes care of the applications

b. *Souvent, qui arrive à l'heure?
Often, who is on time

(51) a. *Habituellement, arrive à l'heure quand tu prends le train!
Habitually, be on time whan you take the train

b. *Souvent, arrive à l'heure quand tu prends le train!
Often, be on time when you take the train

[39]The fact that the frame adverb is part of the content of the question is shown by the fact that the question with the adverb and the corresponding question without the adverb do not necessarily have the same true answers.

[40]Some non-adverbial frequency adjuncts can occur before an imperative in some contexts. We leave this puzzling fact for future study.

(i) Au moins une fois par mois, mettez à jour votre antivirus.
At least once a week, update your antivirus program

Evaluative, modal, agentive, manner and time adverbs cannot occur before an interrogative or imperative.

These data suggest that some adverbs can take scope 'higher' than the semantic content of the clause they occur in, over a covert speech act operator. Although this fact is well-known and could be easily integrated in a model of grammar, what is mysterious is why only a restricted set of adverb types allows this type of reading. For instance, it would certainly make sense for a sentence such as 52a to have a meaning similar to that of 52b, interpreting *gentiment* as an agentive adverb over the speech act; yet this is not possible.

(52) a. *Gentiment, qui viendra demain à la réunion?
b. I am kind to ask you who will come to the meeting tomorrow.

### 4.4 Parentheticality

Parentheticality, which was introduced in section 2.1, is of course relevant to semantic classification. If we apply the criteria discussed in chapter 13 of this book to the adverb classes under discussion, it turns out that there are four classes of parentheticals: connectives, speech acts, evaluatives and agentives.

(53) A: Marie vient de perdre son boulot. Donc, elle est déprimée.
Marie just lost her job. Therefore, she is depressed
B: *C'est faux, ce n'est pas pour cette raison qu'elle est déprimée.
This is false, it is not for this reason that she is depressed

(54) A: Honnêtement, j'ai détesté ce film.
Honestly, I hated that movie
B: *C'est faux, tu es malhonnête quand tu dis ça.
This is false, you are dishonest to say that

(55) A: Jean a heureusement sauvé l'honneur de son équipe.
Jean has fortunately saved his team's honor
B: *C'est faux, ce n'est pas une bonne nouvelle.
This is false, this is not good news

(56) A: Jean a méchamment refusé de répondre.
Jean has unkindly refused to answer
B: *C'est faux, ce n'était pas méchant de sa part.
This is false, it was not unkind on his part

## 5 Semantic types and pragmatic roles for adverbs

In this section, we take stock of the properties described in the preceding sections, briefly discussing the consequences for each adverb class.

It is important to distinguish the *semantic type* of an adverb from its *pragmatic role*. We take *semantic type* in its usual sense: the semantic type classifies the adverb as to what kind of semantic object it takes as input and what kind of semantic object it outputs. By *pragmatic role*, we mean the role the adverb plays in the overall contribution of an utterance to the context: the adverb may effect an independent speech act by (i) taking the primary speech act as its argument or (ii) making a comment on some part of the semantic content; or the adverb may be inserted into the semantic content. As we will see shortly, the two notions do not coincide, since adverbs of the same semantic type may have different pragmatic roles.

Throughout this section, we follow Ginzburg and Sag (2000) in assuming that the different speech act types do not have the same type of descriptive content (*contra* Searle 1969): although assertions take a *proposition* as content, queries take a *question*, and orders take an *outcome*.[41] On the other hand, we assume that a discourse consists of a set of propositions corresponding to the speech acts the discourse consists of: for each speech act, there is a proposition that some agent asserted/queried/ordered some semantic content. These two hypotheses will play an important role in our account of parentheticals.

## 5.1 Parentheticals

Parenthetical adverbs have the specific property of not being inserted in the main semantic content of the utterance. As shown in chapter 13 of this book, they serve to convey conventional implicatures about (parts of) the main semantic content. In this paragraph we argue that all parentheticals except agentive adverbs have the same semantic type, which is that of a propositional operator, but that they have subtly different pragmatic roles. We consider each class in turn.

**Connectives** have two distinctive properties. First, they escape syntactic constraints on scope (see section 3.2). Second, they can take scope over a query or order speech act (see section 4.3). It should be noted that it is not always easy to determine whether the connective takes scope over the speech act or the (propositional) content. However, that both possibilities do exist is shown by the following two examples. On the one hand, in 57a, there are no speech acts for *donc* to relate, since the related sentences are embedded under a propositional attitude predicate. On the other hand, in 57b, *mais* states a contrast relation between the *forms* of two utterances, and not their content — and must take scope over the speech act to have access to that type of

[41] Of course, adopting Ginzburg and Sag's general hypothesis does not commit us to the particular ontological views they defend.

information.[42]

(57) a. Jean ne sait pas encore que Marie est furieuse contre lui, et qu'elle refusera donc de l'aider.
Jean does not know yet that Marie is angry at him, and that she will thus refuse to help him.

b. Il n'a pas eu un *infractus*, mais un *infarctus*.
He did not have an *infraction* but an *infarction*.

These data can be accounted for by assuming that connectives always take a propositional argument (which it relates to some other proposition of the discourse context). However, the propositional argument of a connective can have two distinct sources: it can be either the semantic content of the sentence, as in 57a; or directly the proposition stating the speech act it expresses, as in 46 and 57b.

**Speech act adverbs** are similar to connectives in taking as their argument the speech act conveyed by an utterance. Where they differ is that they always take the speech act, and never the semantic content, as their argument, even in assertive sentences; 58 contrasts with 57a: 58 means that the speaker's utterance is frank, not that the conveyed proposition is:[43]

(58) Franchement, je n'ai pas confiance en lui.
Frankly, I don't trust him

**Evaluative adverbs** are complementary to speech act adverbs: although they are parentheticals, they seem never to take a speech act as their argument (for instance, *Heureusement, il est venu*, cannot mean 'Fortunately, I tell you that he came'). Moreover, they fail to occur before a non-assertive sentence (**Curieusement, qui est déjà arrivé?* 'Strangely, who is already arrived'), although they occur within an interrogative (see section 4.3). This can be taken to indicate that evaluatives take a proposition argument. If one follows Ginzburg and Sag (2000), interrogatives contribute a question, which is an abstract object

[42] As should be clear from these examples, the different possible pragmatic roles are highly dependent on the connective one considers. As already pointed out in fn 37, some connectives cannot take scope over the speech act; others, such as reformulatives, always say something about the form of the utterance, and thus always take scope over the act. See Jayez and Rossari (1998) for some relevant data.

[43] Mittwoch (1977) shows quite clearly, on the basis of examples such as (i), that speech act adverbs can take as their argument a sub-speech act corresponding to a sub-utterance. Although this issue has important consequences for the construction of a syntax-semantics interface for adverbs, it does not hinge on semantic typing as such.

(i) I voted for John because, frankly, I don't trust Bill.

built out of an (open) proposition. Thus the data could be accounted for by assuming that evaluatives can take the open proposition which is part of a question as their argument, but that this is impossible in sentence-initial position (because there, they must scope over the full content of the sentence). Since imperatives are supposed to denote *outcomes*, and outcomes are not built out of propositions, evaluatives are excluded from imperatives whatever their position.[44]

**Agentive adverbs** have a status somewhat different from that of other parentheticals. Noting that, unlike evaluatives, they are not compatible with disjunctive or implicative sentences (both adverbs are compatible with negative and conjunctive sentences), Geuder (2000) argues that their argument is not a proposition *stricto sensu.*

(59) a. Heureusement/Gentiment, Paul a téléphoné à Marie et il a écrit à Jean.
Fortunately/Kindly, P. has phoned M. and he has written to J.

b. Heureusement/Gentiment, Paul n'est pas allé à Paris.
Fortunately/Kindly, P. did not go to Paris.

c. Heureusement/ ??Gentiment, Paul a téléphoné à Marie ou écrit à Jean.
Fortunately/Kindly, P. phoned M. or wrote to J.

d. Heureusement/??Gentiment, si Paul téléphone à Marie, il lui demandera son avis.
Fortunately/Kindly, if P. phones M., he will ask for her advice

Moreover, as observed in section 4.3, agentives do occur in questions. These data suggest that the argument of agentives is not a proposition, but some abstract object which serves in the construction of the content of assertions, questions and orders. The exact nature of this object is open to debate.[45]

---

[44]Moreover, these data give a further argument against Wyner's (1994) analysis of evaluatives as event predicates: not all sentences have a descriptive content of the proposition type, but all (eventive) sentences have a content built around the description of an event. If evaluatives were event predicates, it would thus be expected that they occur in all speech act types. The same applies to an analysis where they take states of affairs arguments, see fn 45.

[45]This object cannot be an eventuality (Eckardt 1998). It is not a fact either, at least under the ordinary meaning of *fact*, since agentive adverbs occur in non-veridical contexts. One likely candidate is the *state of affairs* or *infon* posited by Situation Theory (Devlin, 1991); see Ginzburg and Sag (2000) for a recent theory of declaratives, interrogatives and imperatives which rests on the notion of a state of affairs as a building block found in the semantic contents of the three speech act types.

### 5.2 Nonparentheticals

All nonparenthetical adverbs share the same pragmatic role: they are inserted in the semantic content of the clause. As for their semantic types, the data presented above are not always sufficient for us to decide, but support the following observations.

Modal and duration adverbs are analyzed as usual. **Modals** are propositional operators.In the absence of type-shifting, and assuming that ordinary declarative sentences express an existential claim about an eventuality, this entails that any adverb which expresses some property of the described eventuality or otherwise participates in the eventuality description provided by the sentence must scope below the modal adverb. Hence, given the general correlations between scope and order noted in section 3.2, this type assignment gives us a simple account of the broad order data concerning modals. **Duration adverbs** are usually taken to be either predicates of events, or eventuality description modifiers. The fact that they enter into scope-order correlations with adverbs like frequency adverbs indicates that they are or can be lifted to eventuality description modifiers (see 29).

The free distribution of frame and time adverbs presents a challenge, which is recognized, but not solved. On the one hand, **frames** (Bartsch 1987) seem to participate in the very makeup of properties (that is, it is not possible to tell the extension of a property without first determining in which "domain" one is evaluating it). On the other hand, they occur in all positions and accept virtually any relative order with other adverbs. Thus, they enter into scope-order correlations with modals, as well as with agentive, frequency, duration and time adverbs. Similarly, **time adverbs** can occur in all zones, as incidentals or integrated adverbs, and can precede and follow the adverbs in all other classes (with or without a scope effect). This suggests that adverbs of these two classes are either (i) highly polymorphic,[46] or (ii) subject to specific interface constraints which differ from those imposed on other adverb classes.

Finally, the relationship between frequency and habitual adverbs as well as that between manners and degrees presents problems which are not usually discussed explicitly. **Frequency adverbs** are standardly taken to be generalized quantifiers over eventualities and/or tuples (de Swart, 1991). In more recent studies which take tense into account (e.g. de Swart and Molendijk, 1999), they are given a more elaborate type: they take two eventuality descriptions and provide a third,

[46]See Katz (1999) for a recent defense of a propositional analysis of time expressions.

new eventuality description. Leaving aside the first argument of frequency adverbs, which is filled by contextually-determined material, this turns frequency adverbs into (contextually-dependent) eventuality description modifiers. It is customary to extend the analysis from pure frequency adverbs to **habitual adverbs** (Krifka *et al.* 1995); however, the distributional data in French do not favor such a parallel analysis at all: for instance, habitual but not frequency adverbs occur before questions; frequency but not habitual adverbs can follow negation (see above, section 4.3 and fn 31). Thus the type of habitual adverbs remains something of a mystery as long as these properties have not been given an explanation.[47]

Although there is a well-established analysis for **manner adverbs** as predicates of events (Davidson, 1967), comparison with some **degree adverbs** presents an interesting challenge. The main argument Davidson provides for his analysis is the systematic veridicality of manner adverbs: if they are predicates of events whose contribution gets conjoined to that of the verb, then veridicality follows directly. On the other hand, among degree adverbs, some completion adverbs such as *partially* are clearly not veridical (see section 4.2). Thus if veridicality is taken to support a Davidsonian analysis for manners, it must in turn be taken to preclude such an analysis for degrees. This result is surprising, since their distribution is very similar: we would expect manners and degrees to have the same semantic type.[48]

Geuder (2000) puts forth a simple but effective argument in favor of the Davidsonian analysis for manner adverbs. It is uncontroversial that 60a and 60b have the same truth conditions, and that *passionately* is derived from *passionate*. It is also uncontroversial that in 60a, the NP *the kissing (of John by Mary)* refers to a particular (call it an event) of which the adjective *passionate* is predicated. If this is the case, then one does not see how the lexical relation between the words *passionate* and *passionately* could be explained except by postulating that *passionately* also predicates a property of an event.

(60) a. The kissing (of John by Mary) was passionate.
b. Mary kissed John passionately.

While Geuder's argument is quite convincing, the surprising fact is that it carries over directly to completion adverbs. 61a and 61b enter

[47] On the basis of their distributional properties, Schlyter (1977) groups habituals with frames and extended time adverbs rather than with frequency adverbs.

[48] This similarity is confirmed by the naturalness of the coordination of manners and degrees:

(i) Paul a lu consciencieusement mais partiellement le manuscrit
Paul read the manuscript seriously but partially

into just the same relation as 60a and 60b. Thus, if we follow Geuder, we have to assume that completion adverbs are really predicates of events.

(61) a. The destruction (of the city by the bombs) is partial.

b. The bombs partially destroyed the city.

It thus seems that something is wrong with the tests for semantic types: either both adverbs are predicates of events, and veridicality cannot be taken to be a necessary property of adverbs expressing predicates of events; or veridicality IS a necessary property of predicates of events, but then we have no analysis for the relation between *partial* and *partially*.

## 6 Classes of manner adverbs

In the previous pages, we have considered broad adverb classes, leaving aside more refined partitions. However, manner adverbs are worth a closer look, because of their clear lack of homogeneity and of their frequent polysemy. We summarize what can be found about the various subclasses, taking advantage of recent work on the topic, to which we refer the reader for more elaborate discussion (in particular, Eckardt 1998, Geuder 2000).

### 6.1 Agent-oriented manner adverbs

Agent-oriented manner adverbs (called 'subject-oriented' in e.g. Schlyter 1977, Milner 1978, Molinier & Levrier 2000), such as *intelligemment* 'intelligently', *attentivement* 'attentively', *adroitement* 'skillfully/cleverly', *sottement* 'stupidly', *soigneusement* 'in a tidy way/carefully', are derived from adjectives that predicate both of individuals and processes; the adverb itself seems to take these two arguments. Sentence 62a can be paraphrased as "Patrice has been careful in tidying his room", and its predicative structure is represented as 62b (Eckardt, 1998: 10):

(62) a. Patrice a rangé soigneusement sa chambre.
Patrice has carefully tidied his room

b. $\mathsf{ranger}(\mathsf{p}, \mathsf{la\text{-}chambre}, e) \wedge \mathsf{soigneux}(\mathsf{p}, e)$

The individual argument is an agent, as shown by the fact that these adverbs fail to modify verbs such as *savoir* 'to know', *souffrir* 'to suffer', *craindre* 'to fear'. The agent is usually the subject but not obligatorily so (see the well-known case of passives, which allow these adverbs, discussed in e.g. Mc Connell-Ginet 1982).

There is a close relation betwen agent-oriented manners and agentives, which has been studied in particular in Geuder (2000): not all agent-oriented manners have an agentive alternate, but all agentives correspond to an agent-oriented manner adverb. As is well-known, the two interpretations are distinguished by their paraphrases, and their position relative to negation (agentives but not agent-oriented manners can precede negation). Crucially, Geuder argues that agentives take an abstract argument (akin, although not identical to a proposition) rather than an event (see section 5.1), and that manner adverbs are derived from agentives, while the basic lexical meaning, inherited from the adjective, remains the same: the adjective denotes a disposition, whose manifestations are foregrounded in the manner interpretation, and backgrounded in the agentive one; in both cases, there is an appeal to a set of alternatives (worlds or courses of events), based on scripts and chains of causality.

Agent-oriented manners can usually occur S-initially, although there is speaker variation regarding specific items.[49] Interestingly, in that position, when a form can be either a manner or an agentive, it is always interpreted as agentive.[50] The adverb is a manner in 63a, and agentive in 63b:

(63) a. % Attentivement, Max a écouté les explications de Paul.
Attentively, Max listened to Paul's explanations
b. Intelligemment, Max a écouté les explications de Paul.
Cleverly, Max listened to Paul's explanations

## 6.2 Mental states

Mental states (or 'psychological adverbs'), such as *calmement* 'calmly', *tristement* 'sadly', have recently been recognized as a semantic class (e.g. Geuder 2000, Shaer 1998). Geuder argues that such forms give rise to two different readings, a pure manner one, and another one, where the adverb takes two arguments, a state and an individual (similarly

[49]There is a scope difference depending on the adverb position. To borrow Eckardt's formulation, the sentence-initial manner can only modify the 'big event' associated with the whole sentence while the postverbal manner modifies either the big event or parts of it (see Creswell 1978, Eckardt 1998, Mc Connell-Ginet 1982, Thomason & Stalnaker 1973). Note that not all S-manners (see section 2.3) are agent oriented (see, e.g. *Lentement, la vérité se fit jour*, 'Slowly, the truth came to light'), and not all agent-oriented adverbs can occur S-initially (see the variation in 63a).

[50]This phenomenon could be treated as a variety of *blocking*: just as the existence of a synthetic morphological form can block the use of an analytic one, the existence of an agentive reading seems to block the manner interpretation in sentence-initial position. The preference may be linked to the incidental vs. integrated status of the adverb, since an adverb like *intelligemment* is ambiguous when integrated in postverbal position. If the analogy with blocking is pursued, this would mean that incidental occurrence is felt as more constrained than the integrated one.

to agent-oriented manner adverbs; see 62b); in addition, a relation is established between the state of the individual and the event associated with the sentence (the state motivates an event, or is caused by it). However, on the basis of French, it is not so clear that these adverbs should be recognized as ambiguous in the same way as agent-oriented adverbs are ambiguous between a manner and an agentive reading.

Mental states can precede the negation when they are sentence-initial. However, this is not the case if the adverb is integrated and postverbal. We contrast the mental state in (64a,b) with the agentive in (65a,b):

(64) a. Joyeusement, Paul n'est pas allé au travail.
Merrily, Paul has not gone to work

b. ?? Paul n'est joyeusement pas allé au travail.
Paul NE-has merrily not gone to work

(65) a. Intelligemment, Paul n'a pas répondu à la question.
Cleverly, Paul NE-has not answered the question

b. Paul n'a intelligemment pas répondu à la question.
Paul NE-has cleverly not answered the question

In addition, we find that mental states do not occur easily after the negation if they are incidentals, unlike agentives (* *Paul n'est pas allé, joyeusement, au travail), although they can be incidental in the VP (Paul est allé, joyeusement, au travail*). If the relational interpretation, which is required for the adverb having scope over the negation, is confined to sentence-initial incidental adverbs, a natural question to ask is whether such adverbs are ambiguous, or whether the relational interpretation does not arise from their use as 'unmarked' sentence adjuncts (no conjunction): it is well-known that such sentence-initial adjuncts give rise to interpretations which involve an implicit predicate not contributed by the lexical content of the adjunct (see for instance Stump (1985) *à propos* causal predicates in absolute constructions, and Krifka et al. (1995) on adjunct clauses providing a restrictor for an implicit adverb of quantification).

It is tempting to include adverbs such as *(in)volontairement* '(un)willingly' among mental states. However, this is not a desirable move, for two reasons: (i) they can precede the negation, in zone 3 as well as zone 1, without any special effect or inference; (ii) they are intensional, which mental states are not (see section 4.1). These adverbs are not manner adverbs but constitute a class by themselves (called above 'adverbs of attitude towards a state of affairs').

### 6.3 Resultative adverbs

Resultative adverbs (also called 'adverbes verbaux de contenu' in Schlyter 1977, and 'object-oriented', e.g. Laezlinger 1998) do not modify the main event associated with the sentence, but, rather, a sub-eventuality, that is a state resulting from it (Eckardt 1998, Geuder 2000):

(66) a. Luc veut meubler confortablement son studio.
Luc wants to furnish comfortably his studio

b. La police a blessé mortellement un manifestant.
The police has wounded fatally a demonstrator

Despite initial impressions, the adverb does not really predicate of the direct object: the wound is fatal, not the demonstrator. However, Geuder proposes that such adverbs have an individual argument: an implicit object, resulting from the event, and present in the lexical description of the verb. This would explain for instance why there is a complementary distribution of the adverb and the direct object denoting the result of the action with a verb of creation like *creuser* 'to dig':

(67) Il creusa un trou/profondément/* un trou profondément.
He dug a hole/deeply/a hole deeply

Like V-manner adverbs, resultatives fail to occur sentence-initially or more generally as incidentals:

(68) a. * Profondément, Paul creusa, pour trouver la roche.
Deeply, Paul dug, to find the rock

b. ?? Paul creusa, profondément, pour trouver la roche.

It is an open question whether such adverbs should be considered as ordinary (V-)manner adverbs, or as forming a semantic class by themselves, as suggested by Geuder.

### 6.4 V-adverbs

V-adverbs modify the event, with no shift towards taking the participants as arguments (*affirmativement* 'affirmatively', *artisanalement* 'by craftsmen', *profitablement* 'profitably'). Like agent-oriented manners, they can be paraphrased by 'in a adj way', but they differ from the former in a number of ways. Unlike (many) agent-oriented manners, most adverbs of this class (85% of them according to Molinier & Levrier 2000) cannot occur S-initially or be incidentals at all:

(69) a. Les enfants ont bruyamment applaudi le clown.
The children applauded the clown noisily

b. ?? Bruyamment, les enfants ont applaudi le clown.

c. ?? Les enfants ont, bruyamment, applaudi le clown.

While some of them derive from adjectives which can be predicated of human beings, like *agréablement* 'nicely', or *bruyamment*, they do not always give rise to a paraphrase with the adjective (Molinier & Levrier):

(70) Max joue agréablement de la mandoline.
Max plays the mandoline nicely.
# Max is nice in playing the mandoline

They do not regularly alternate with a 'higher adverb' as agent-oriented manners do, although they may be polysemous, a phenomenon which involves most adverb classes: speech acts, like *franchement* 'frankly', connectives, like *parallèlement* 'in parallel with', frames like *intérieurement* 'inwardly', evaluatives, like *bizarrement* 'strangely', or resultatives like *élégamment* 'elegantly', if resultatives are a distinct class.

## 7 Conclusions

In this chapter, we show that an adequate classification of adverbs must take into account the distinction between incidental and integrated adverbs, for several reasons: the positions in the sentence are not the same for the two types of occurrence; moreover, the correlations between scope and position do not obey the same constraints in the two cases. Regarding the type of adverbs, we point out a number of unsettled issues. Certainly, a broad classification must distinguish among adverbs depending on the semantic object they take as argument; however, the distributional data do not always give us a clear picture in this respect. In some cases, the various tests used to determine adverb type give incoherent results.

Particularly clear instances are degree and manner adverbs, which should have the same type since they are distributionally so similar, but which do not pattern similarly with respect to veridicality, the standard test for a Davidsonian analysis; similarly for frame and time adverbs, whose distribution does not seem to be explainable in terms of a unique type assignment. In other cases, the distribution is underdetermined by the broad semantic types we have at our disposal, and it is not clear how one could account for it without syntactic stipulation. This is the case e.g. for connectives, which seem to obey distinct syntax-semantics interface principles; or for speech act adverbs, which are the sole adverbs occurring only as incidentals.

Many recent studies of adverbs attempt to derive the grammar of adverbs from independent principles. This is the case for Cinque (1999), who attempts to deduce the distribution of adverbs from an independently postulated sentence structure (in the form of a hierarchy of functional categories). This is also the case in semantics-driven approaches such as Jackendoff (1972) or, more recently, Ernst (1998) and Shaer (1998), which try to reduce the distribution of adverbs to their semantic type plus some general interface principles. What this chapter has shown is that the grammar of adverbs is not trivial: unsurprisingly, adverbs obey a complex pattern of syntax-semantics correlations, which result from general interface principles, properties of specific semantic classes, or idiosyncratic individual behavior — just as the lexical items in any other category.

## References

Abeillé, A. and D. Godard. 1997. The syntax of French negative adverbs. In Forget et al. (1997), pages 1–27.

Abeillé, A. and D. Godard. 2000. French word order and lexical weight. In Borsley (2000), pages 325–360.

Abeillé, A. and D. Godard. 2001. On a class of French lite adverbs. In Camps and Wiltshire (2001), pages 9–25.

Alexiadou, A. 1997. *Adverb Placement.* Amsterdam: John Benjamins.

Bartsch, R. 1976. *The grammar of Adverbials.* Amsterdam: North Holland.

Bartsch, R. 1987. The construction of properties under perspectives. *Journal of Semantics* 5:293–320.

Bellert, I. 1977. On semantic and distributional properties of sentential adverbs. *Linguistic Inquiry* 8:337–351.

Bok-Bennema, R., B. de Jong, B. Kampers-Manhe, and A. Molendijk, eds. 2001. *Adverbial Modification.* Amsterdam–Atlanta: Rodopi.

Bonami, O. 1999. *Les constructions du verbe: le cas des groupes prépositionnels argumentaux.* Ph.D. thesis, Université Paris 7.

Borsley, R., ed. 2000. *The Nature and Function of Syntactic categories*, vol. 32 of *Syntax and Semantics.* New York: Academic Press.

Camps, J. and C. Wiltshire, eds. 2001. *Syntax, semantics, and L2 acquisition in Romance.* Amsterdam: John Benjamins.

Carlson, G. and F. J. Pelletier, eds. 1995. *The Generic Book.* Chicago: The University of Chicago Press.

Cinque, G. 1990. *Relativized Minimality.* Cambridge: MIT Press.

Cinque, G. 1999. *Adverbs and Functional Heads: A Cross-Linguistic Perspective.* Oxford: Oxford University Press.

Copestake, A., D. Flickinger, C. Pollard, and I. Sag. 2000. Minimal recursion semantics: an introduction. Unpublished manuscript.

Cori, M. and J.-M. Marandin. 1995. Discontinuity without discontinuous trees. In Morrill and Oehrle (1995).

Cresswell, M. J. 1978. Adverbs of space and time. In Guenthner and Schmidt (1978).

Davidson, D. 1967. The logical form of action sentences. In Rescher (1967).

De Swart, H. 1991. *Adverbs of Quantification: A Generalized Quantifier Approach*. Ph.D. thesis, University of Groningen. [published by Garland, New York, 1993].

De Swart, H. and A. Molendijk. 1999. Negation and temporal structure of narrative discourse. *Journal of Semantics* 16:1–42.

Devlin, K. 1991. *Logic and Information*. Cambridge: Cambridge University Press.

Ducrot, O. 1972. *Dire et Ne Pas Dire*. Paris: Hermann.

Eckardt, R. 1998. *Adverbs, Events, and Other Things*. Tübingen: Niemeyer.

Ernst, T. 1998. The scopal basis of adverb licensing. In Tamanji and Kusumoto (1998), pages 127–142.

Espinal, M. T. 1991. The representation of disjunct constituents. *Language* 67:726–762.

Forget, D., P. Hirschbühler, F. Martineau, and M.-L. Rivero, eds. 1997. *Negation and polarity: Syntax and Semantics*. Amsterdam: John Benjamins.

Fuchs, C., ed. 1996. *La place du sujet en franccais contemporain*. Gand: Duculot.

Geuder, W. 2000. *Oriented adverbs. Issues in the lexical semantics of event adverbs*. Ph.D. thesis, University of Tübingen.

Giannakidou, A. 1998. *Polarity Sensitivity as (non) Veridical Dependency*. Amsterdam: John Benjamins.

Ginzburg, J. and I. A. Sag. 2000. *Interrogative Investigations*. Stanford: CSLI Publications.

Greenbaum, S. 1969. *Studies in English Adverbial Usage*. London: Longman.

Grevisse, M. 1969. *Le Bon Usage*. Gembloux: Duculot.

Guenthner, F. and S. J. Schmidt, eds. 1978. *Formal Semantics and Pragmatics for Natural Languages*. Dordrecht: Reidel.

Guimier, C. 1996. La place du sujet clitique dans les énoncés avec adverbe initial. In Fuchs (1996).

Horn, L. 1989. *A Natural History of Negation*. Chicago: The University of Chicago Press.

Jackendoff, R. 1972. *Semantic Interpretation in Generative Grammar*. Cambridge: MIT Press.

Jayez, J. and C. Rossari. 1998. Pragmatic connectives as predicates. In Saint-Dizier (1998), pages 285–319.

Kampers-Manhe, B. 2001. Le comportement syntaxique des adverbes de manière. In Bok-Bennema et al. (2001).

Katz, G. 2000. Anti neo-davidsonianism. In Tenny and Pustejovsky (2000).

Krifka, M., F. J. Pelletier, G. N. Carlson, A. ter Meulen, G. Link, and G. Chierchia. 1995. Genericity: an introduction. In Carlson and Pelletier (1995).

Laezlinger, C. 1998. *Comparative studies in word order variation*. Amsterdam: John Benjamins.

Landman, F. 2000. *Events and Plurality*. Dordrecht: Kluwer.

Marandin, J.-M. 1998. Grammaire de l'incidence. ms. CNRS Université Paris 7.

Mc-Connell-Ginet, S. 1982. Adverbs and logical form. *Language* 58:144–184.

Milner, J.-C. 1978. *De la syntaxe à l'interprétation*. Paris: Le Seuil.

Mittwoch, A. 1977. How to refer to one's own words: Speech-act modifying adverbials and the performative analysis. *Journal of Linguistics* 13(2):177–189.

Molendijk, A. and H. de Swart. 1998. Frequency and tense use in French. *Belgian Journal of Linguistics* 12:43–60. Tense and Aspect. Vogeleer and De Mulder and Depraetere, eds.

Molinier, C. and F. Lévrier. 2000. *Grammaire des adverbes. Description des formes en* –ment. Geneva: Droz.

Moltmann, F. 1997. Intensional verbs and quantifiers. *Natural Language Semantics* 5:1–52.

Moore, S. and A. Winner, eds. 1991. *Proceedings from Semantics and Linguistic Theory 1 [= Cornell Working Papers in Linguistics 1]*.

Morrill, G. and R. Oehrle, eds. 1995. *Proceedings of Formal Grammar'95*.

Nilsen, Ø. 2001. Adverb order in Type Logical Grammar. In Van Rooy and Stokhof (2001).

Nilsen, Ø. 2003. *Eliminating positions*. Ph.D. thesis, Utrecht University.

Parsons, T. 1990. *Events in the Semantics of English*. Cambridge: MIT Press.

Rescher, N., ed. 1967. *The Logic of Decision and Action*. Pittsburgh: U. of Pittsburgh Press.

Sag, I. A. and A. Szabolcsi, eds. 1992. *Lexical Matters*. Stanford: CSLI.

Saint-Dizier, P., ed. 1998. *Predicative Forms in Natural Language and in Lexical Knowledge Bases*. Dordrecht: Kluwer.

Schlyter, S. 1977. *La place des adverbes en* –ment *en français*. Ph.D. thesis, Universität Konstanz.

Schreiber, P. A. 1972. Style disjuncts and the performative analysis. *Linguistic Inquiry* 3:321–347.

Searle, J. 1969. *Speech Acts*. Cambridge: Cambridge University Press.

Shaer, B. 1998. Adverbials, functional structure and restrictiveness. In Tamanji and Kusumoto (1998), pages 391–407.

Stump, G. 1985. *The Semantic Variability of Absolute Constructions*. Dordrecht: Reidel.

Tamanji, P. N. and K. Kusumoto, eds. 1998. *NELS 28*.

Tenny, C. 2000. Core events and adverbial modification. In Tenny and Pustejovsky (2000), pages 285–334.

Tenny, C. and J. Pustejovsky, eds. 2000. *Events as Grammatical Objects. The Converging Perspectives of Lexical Semantics, Logical Semantics and Syntax*. Publication Lecture Notes. Stanford, CA: CSLI.

Thomason, R. and R. Stalnaker. 1973. A semantic theory of adverbs. *Linguistic Inquiry* 4:195–220.

Van Hout, A., H. de Swart, and H. Verkuyl, eds. 2002. *Proceedings of the Conference Perspectives on Aspect*. Utrecht University.

Van Rooy, R. and M. Stokhof, eds. 2001. *Proceedings of the Amsterdam Colloquium 2001*. University of Amsterdam.

Wyner, A. 1994. *Boolean Event Lattices and Thematic Roles in the Syntax and Semantics of Adverbial Modification*. Ph.D. thesis, Cornell University.

Wyner, A. 1997. On factive adverbials. Talk presented at The *Sinn und Bedeutung* conference, Berlin.

Zimmerman, T. 1993. On the proper treatment of opacity in certain verbs. *Natural Language Semantics* 1:149–179.

12

# Adverbs and Quantification *

Anne Abeillé, Jenny Doetjes, Arie Molendijk, and Henriëtte de Swart

## 1 Introduction

In this chapter, we deal with two types of adverbs that can have a quantificational interpretation: frequency adverbials that quantify over times or events (*souvent* 'often', *parfois* 'sometimes', *de temps en temps* 'from time to time' and degree adverbs, that can have a quantificational effect (*beaucoup* 'a lot', *trop* 'too much', *complètement* 'completely'.[1] We will ignore scalar adverbs other than degree adverbs (*encore* 'still/yet/ again', *déjà* 'already', which have been studied by Victorri and Fuchs (1996), Gosselin (1996) and others. Durational adverbials like *longtemps* 'for a long time', *en deux heures* 'in two hours' are also left aside here (but see Part III on tense and aspect).

In section 2 we address the semantics of the different types of quantificational and degree adverbs in some detail. Section 3 deals with the interface with syntactic properties, and in particular with the syntactic polymorphism of these adverbs.

## 2 Some semantic properties

We show that frequency and iterative adverbs can be analyzed as quantifiers and that this analysis does not hold for degree adverbs in general.

*For comments and discussion, we thank O. Bonami, J.-M. Marandin, P. Caudal and, in particular, D. Godard, responsible for the Adverb group.
Jenny Doetjes gratefully acknowledges the support from NWO (grant #355-70-003).

[1]We leave aside the pragmatics of degree adverbs (*peu* 'little', *à peine* 'hardly' etc.), see Ducrot (1980), Jayez (1987).

*Handbook of French Semantics.*
Francis Corblin and Henriëtte de Swart (eds.).
Copyright © 2004, CSLI Publications.

We propose a unitary analysis of degree adverbs as scale modifiers.

## 2.1 Counting versus comparison on a scale

The difference between frequency adverbs (like *souvent*, *toujours*) and degree quantifiers (like *beaucoup*) can be characterized as a counting of events versus a comparison on a scale.[2] Frequency and iterative adverbs have a count interpretation: they say something about the number of times something has happened. For frequency adverbs this number is usually related to other times or events, whereas iterative adverbials like *deux fois* ('twice') are typically non-relational (cf. de Swart 1991, Doetjes 2002 and 2.2 below). Degree quantifiers do not impose a count interpretation. This is particularly clear in the following sentence, uttered by a farmer complaining about the dryness:

(1) Il a plu souvent, mais il n'a pas plu beaucoup
'It rained often, but it did not rain a lot'

Obviously, the number of times it rained could, but need not imply anything about the total amount of rain.

In some contexts, degree quantifiers and frequency adverbs are almost synonymous:

(2) a. Jean va beaucoup au cinéma
b. Jean va souvent au cinéma
'Jean goes to the movies a lot/ goes often to the movies'

Note that in this example, the VP denotes a count predicate, which implies that the scale *beaucoup* refers to is defined in terms of natural numbers. In this respect 2 differs from 1, which contains the mass predicate *pleuvoir* 'to rain'.

In yet other contexts, frequency adverbs and degree adverbs have a completely different meaning (cf. Obenauer 1984, 1994):

(3) a. Jean a beaucoup apprécié ses conseils
'Jean appreciated his advice a lot'
b. Jean a souvent apprécié ses conseils
'Jean often appreciated his advice'

*Beaucoup* in 3a functions as an intensifier measuring the degree of appreciation, whereas *souvent* in 3b reports on the frequency of the situation in which Jean appreciated his advice. This confirms that degree

---

[2]We will use the descriptive term 'degree quantifier' for degree adverbs such as *beaucoup* that can be used as degree modifiers in the nominal system as well. See also Part 1 on determiners, chapter 6. In subsection 2.3 below, we will discuss two more types of degree adverbs.

adverbs like *beaucoup* can, but need not have a quantificational meaning, whereas frequency adverbs like *souvent* necessarily involve quantification over events.

As count quantifiers, frequency expressions such as *souvent* 'often' and *quelquefois* 'sometimes' are viewed as the adverbial counterparts of determiners like English *many* and *few*. These determiners impose countability and plurality on the noun phrase they modify (*many books* vs. *#many sand*, *#many book*). Frequency adverbs similarly depend on countability and plurality (de Swart 1991, 1995). Accordingly, Doetjes (2002) analyzes *souvent* and *quelquefois* as composite expressions involving a quantifier Q and a plural classifier *fois* 'times'. This classifier, which is covert in *souvent* and overt in *parfois*, *quelquefois*, is the source of the count character of the frequency expression, and encodes the plurality of the domain of quantification.

Degree quantifiers are interpreted with respect to a scale provided by the expression they modify (see Doetjes 1997, 2002, and below). Whether the interpretation is count or non-count depends on this scale. Verbal predicates denote a partially ordered domain of events or situations by analogy with the denotation of nominal predicates as a partially ordered domain of individuals or masses (see, among others, Link 1983, for NP denotations and Bach 1986, Krifka 1986, 1992 for an extension of such a system to the verbal domain).[3] An expression like *beaucoup* tells us to take into account those sets of objects, masses or degrees the quantity of which exceeds a certain contextually given norm. The application of *beaucoup* to a count predicate as in *beaucoup aller au cinéma* 'to go to the movies a lot' gives us all possible sets of more than $n$ visits to the cinema, where the value of $n$ depends on the context. The combination of *beaucoup* with a mass predicate as in *danser beaucoup* 'to dance a lot' denotes a collection of possible 'masses' of dancing the quantity of which exceeds a contextually given norm. In the context of scalar verbs such as *apprécier* 'to appreciate', the degree expression is understood with respect to the intensity scale that is part of the lexical meaning of the verb. We conclude that the meaning of degree adverbs is so versatile, because the notion of degree can involve amounts, numbers or a scale of intensity. The result is that the interpretation of *beaucoup* depends on the context in which it is used: a mass predicate such as *pleuvoir* in 1, a count predicate such as *aller au cinéma* in 2 or an abstract scalar predicate such as *apprécier*

[3]Given the similarity of the nominal and the verbal system in this respect, it is not surprising to find that degree adverbs can modify both nominal and verbal projections. The syntactic distribution of degree adverbs, which is largely dependent on their semantic properties, will be discussed in section 3 below.

in 3.

## 2.2 Habitual and non-habitual interpretations

Within the class of adverbs that quantify over times, we distinguish between frequentative and iterative or cardinal count adverbials. As the criterion of compatibility with imperfective tenses shows, frequentative adverbs can have a habitual interpretation, but iterative adverbs cannot. We will see that a similar distinction exists within the class of degree adverbs that can have a quantificational meaning.

Frequency adverbs like *toujours* 'always', *souvent* 'often', *quelquefois* 'sometimes', *jamais* 'never', etc. are compatible with all the French tenses, including the Présent and the Imparfait (the imperfective past tense of French), as pointed out by Ducrot (1979), Hoepelman & Rohrer (1981), Kleiber (1987), de Swart (1991), Molendijk & de Swart (1998), Doetjes (2002).[4] In this respect they differ from cardinal count adverbs such as *trois fois* 'three times', which are incompatible with a non-narrative Présent or an Imparfait, unless they are embedded under a frequency adverb 4c or an expression like *par semaine/chaque semaine* that makes their interpretation dependent on a recurrent time interval (4d,e):

(4) a. Jean danse / dansait souvent / de temps en temps
'Jean dances$_{\text{PRES}}$ / danced$_{\text{IMP}}$ often / from time to time'
b. #Jean danse / dansait trois fois
'Jean dances / danced three times'
c. Jean danse / dansait toujours trois fois
'Jean always dances / danced three times'
d. Jean danse / dansait trois fois par semaine.
'Jean dances / danced three times a week'
e. Chaque semaine, Jean danse / dansait trois fois.
'Every week, Jean dances/danced three times'

The French Imparfait is an imperfective tense that bears on non-quantized, mass-like eventualities (Hoepelman & Rohrer 1981, de Swart 1998), whereas the present tense is compatible with states only (Landeweerd 1998, de Swart to appear). Sentences modified by a frequency adverb denote homogeneous situations that have divisive and cumulative reference, so they describe non-quantized eventualities (Kleiber 1987). In the present tense, frequentative sentences get a habitual-like interpretation, which describes a state (de Swart 1998). This explains the well-formedness of 4a. However, sentences modified

[4]Consult Part III, on tense and aspect, for more on the semantics of the Imparfait and other French tenses.

by an iterative adverbial denote non-homogeneous eventualities, just as NPs such as *deux livres* 'two books' have quantized, rather than cumulative reference. As a result, they are incompatible with imperfective tenses like the Imparfait and the Présent 4b. If the iterative adverbial is embedded under a frequency adverb, the sentence describes a frequentative situation, so 4c patterns like 4a. The modifier *par semaine* in 4d introduces an interval with respect to which the cardinal adverbial *trois fois* is interpreted. The addition of the modifier *par semaine* creates a sentence with a frequentative meaning along similar lines as the explicit quantifier over intervals in 4e, because it introduces a recurrent period of time (cf. de Swart 1991).

Most degree quantifiers are compatible with a non-narrative present tense, as in 5:

(5) Il danse beaucoup
'He dances a lot'

However, *un peu* behaves in ways similar to cardinal count adverbs in the sense that it is incompatible with a habitual reading unless it is modified by a quantifier over intervals such as *tous les après-midi*:[5]

(6) a. Il dort un peu
'He is half asleep'
NOT: 'He has the habit of sleeping now and then'

b. Il dort un peu tous les après-midi
'He has the habit of sleeping a bit every afternoon'

The contrast between 5 and 6 shows that the opposition between 4a and 4b shows up between two types of degree quantifiers as well. This implies that degree quantifiers have a subclass that can express habitual (homogeneous) interpretations, and a subclass that cannot (cf. Doetjes 1997, 2002).

## 2.3 Dependent readings and relational readings

Within the class of frequency adverbials, we establish a distinction between 'dependent' and 'independent' ones (cf. Molendijk & de Swart 1998). Compare the fragments in 7 and 8:

[5] *Par semaine* 'per week' depends on countability. Only countable expressions (*trois fois, deux livres* etc.) can be modified by *par* + time unit. The degree quantifier *un peu* always modifies mass expressions (cf. *un peu de vin* 'a bit of wine' vs. #*un peu de livres* 'a bit of books', which explains why we cannot combine *un peu* with *par semaine* in contexts like 6b. *Tous les après-midi* 'all afternoons' has the same semantic effect of introducing a recurrent period of time as a *par semaine* modifier, but it does not require a count interpretation of the modifiee, so it can be used to illustrate the similarity between *un peu* and cardinal count adverbs as far as their lack of habitual interpretation is concerned.

(7) Pauline et Jean jouent dans le jardin. Il la taquine *souvent / parfois*. Mais maintenant (qu'ils jouent dans le jardin), il ne la taquine pas.
'Pauline and Jean play in the garden. He teases her often / sometimes. But now (that they play in the garden), he does not tease her.'

(8) Pauline et Jean jouent dans le jardin. *De temps en temps*, ils s'assoient dans l'herbe. #Mais maintenant (qu'ils jouent dans le jardin), ils ne s'assoient pas dans l'herbe.
'Pauline and Jean play in the garden. From time to time, they sit down in the grass. But now (that they play in the garden), they do not sit down in the grass'

The interpretation of *souvent/parfois* is not dependent on what is referred to in the first sentence. That is, the situation of playing in the garden does not provide the domain of quantification for the set of events the adverb quantifies over. So the second sentence means that, in general, Jean often/sometimes teases Pauline. The third sentence does not lead to a contradiction in this context. The situation is different in 8. *De temps en temps* is a dependent quantifier that refers to a contextually determinable situation, which it qualifies globally. This means that, in relation to the current situation of playing in the garden, Pauline and Jean sit down in the grass from time to time. Given that the first sentence provides the domain of quantification for the adverbial quantifier in the second sentence, the combination with the third sentence leads to a contradiction.

Degree quantifiers behave in the same way as the dependent frequency adverbials:

(9) Pauline et Jean passent leur vacances au bord de la mer. Ils lisent beaucoup. #Mais maintenant (qu'ils passent leurs vacances au bord de la mer) ils ne lisent pas.
'Pauline and Jean are on vacation at the sea side. They read a lot. But now (that they are on vacation at the sea side) they don't read

A further observation about the dependent/non-dependent contrast is that the fragments in 8 and 9 are fine once we add *normalement* 'normally' or *en général* 'in general' in front of the sentence containing the dependent adverb, as in 9':

(9') En général, Pauline et Jean passent leur vacances au bord de la mer. Ils lisent beaucoup. Mais maintenant (qu'ils passent leurs vacances au bord de la mer) ils ne lisent pas.

'In general, Pauline and Jean spend their vacation at the sea side. They read a lot. But now (that they are on vacation at the sea side) they don't read'

The interpretation we obtain for 9' is the one in which most vacations are characterized by heavy reading, but not this one. Accordingly, we can characterize dependent adverbials as anaphoric expressions that can either find a local antecedent (as in 9), or depend on a binding quantifier (as in 9') (cf. Partee 1991, 1995).

Dependency and independency are related to the availability of a so-called relational reading (de Swart 1991). The sentence in 10 is ambiguous between a relational (a) and a non-relational reading (b):

(10) Quand elle est à Paris, Pauline va souvent au Louvre
a. 'Many of the times she is in Paris, Pauline goes to the Louvre'
b. 'Whenever she is in Paris, Pauline often goes to the Louvre'

In the relational reading (a), the *quand*-clause provides the restrictor on the quantifier, and in the non-relational reading (b), the *quand*-clause provides the domain of quantification within which the quantifier operates. Interestingly, the dependent expressions lack a relational reading, and are always interpreted on a par with the (b) reading of 10 (Doetjes 2002):

(11) a. Quand il est à Paris, Paul va beaucoup au Louvre
'Whenever he is in Paris, Paul goes to the Louvre a lot
b. Quand il est à Paris, Paul va de temps en temps au Louvre
'Whenever he is in Paris, Paul goes to the Louvre now and then'

At this point, the question arises why independent frequency adverbs like *souvent* 'often' allow for relational readings, whereas the dependent ones do not. According to de Swart (1991), adverbs like *toujours* 'always', *souvent* 'often', etc. are to be interpreted as generalized quantifiers, that is, they denote relations between sets of eventualities. Adverbs like *souvent* 'often' and *parfois* 'sometimes' have derived non-relational readings in which they function as modifiers, because they are weak quantifiers. Following Keenan (1987, 1989), weakness of generalized quantifiers is related to intersectivity, which implies that the relation between two arguments reduces to a claim about the cardinality of the intersection of the two sets.[6] Although this makes it possible to derive a non-relational reading for an independent frequency adverb

[6]For more on generalized quantifier theory, and issues about weakness and strength, see chapter 1, Generalized Quantifiers, dynamic semantics and French determiners.

like *souvent* 'often', it does not explain why the relational reading is blocked for a dependent frequency adverb like *tout le temps* 'all the time' or a degree adverb like *beaucoup* 'a lot'.

Doetjes (1997, 2002) proposes that frequency adverbs like *souvent* 'often' and *quelquefois* 'sometimes' contain a hidden classifier *fois* 'times'. Following Von Fintel (1994), she assumes that *souvent* contains a hidden domain variable that provides the restrictor on the quantifier. She identifies this hidden domain variable with the covert *fois* within the independent frequency adverb. In the relational reading this hidden *fois* behaves like an anaphor, the contents of which can be identified by a *quand*-clause. As such this element plays a crucial role in obtaining the relational reading. As the element *fois* is not present in degree adverbs like *beaucoup* 'a lot', we do not expect degree adverbs to support a relational reading.

This leaves the case of dependent frequency adverbials like *tout le temps* 'all the time'. We argued above that these are anaphoric expressions as well. However, unlike *toujours* 'always' and *souvent* 'often', they do not try to recover the content of the restrictor from the context, but the domain of quantification within which they quantify. If we combine the dependent frequency adverbial with a *quand*-clause as in 11b, the *quand*-clause provides the domain of quantification, not the restrictor, so we obtain a non-relational interpretation in which some events of going to the Louvre occur within each visit.

Finally, it has been pointed out that iterative adverbials only get a non-relational reading in contexts like 12a (cf. de Swart 1991), although a relational reading seems to be marginally available in examples like 12b:

(12) a. Quand il est à Paris, il va au moins trois fois au Louvre
'When he is in Paris, he goes to the Louvre at least three times'

b. Deux fois, quand il a été à Paris, Paul est allé au Louvre
'Twice, when he has been in Paris, Paul has gone to the Louvre'

Just like dependent frequency adverbials like *de temps en temps* 'now and then', iterative count adverbials like *deux fois* 'twice' use the anaphoric nature of *fois* to recover the domain of quantification, rather than the restrictor. The general incompatibility of cardinal adverbials with the Présent (see section 2.2 above) reinforces the dependent reading of 12a, because the sentence involves a hidden habitual operator. Note that syntactic position may have an influence on semantic scope, as illustrated by 12b. In this case, the anaphoric *fois* finds its antecedent in the preceding context, which brings both the *quand*-clause and the main clause under the scope of the cardinal count adverbial.

## 2.4 Three classes of degree adverbs

So far, we have concentrated on degree quantifiers like *beaucoup* that can get a reading very similar to frequency adverbs. Other degree adverbs, such as *légèrement* 'slightly', *complètement* 'completely', cannot get such a reading. In this section, we distinguish three subclasses of degree adverbs: in addition to degree quantifiers, there are intensity and completion adverbs.

We follow Kennedy (1999) and Kennedy and McNally (1999) who analyze degree adverbs as scale modifiers. In their view, gradable predicates (adjectives or verbs) denote a relation between a given object and a set of degrees called a scale. An adjective like *grand* 'big' for instance, associates an object with a scale of size with a default value. A verb like *souffrir* 'suffer' associates an experiencer with a scale of pain with a default value. The degree adverb modifies this default value: *très* 'very' or *beaucoup* 'a lot' "boosts" the default value, *peu* 'little' lowers it, while *plus* 'more' introduces a relation with another scale (and with another default value).

Degree quantifiers (like *trop, beaucoup*) do not specify the type of scale they modify: it can be a scale of quantity or of intensity. They can thus be interpreted as quantifiers (13a,c) or intensifiers (13b):

(13) a. Max va trop au cinéma.
'Max goes too–much to the movies'
b. Max aime trop le cinéma.
'Max likes the movies too–much'
c. Max a trop de soucis / trop de peine.
'Max has too–many worries / too–much grief'

In 13b the intensity scale is lexically provided by the verbal predicate, which is gradable. In 13a a scale is contextually provided by a hidden temporal quantifier (number of times), and the interpretation is iterative. In 13c, the scale is provided by the mass noun (which denotes a cumulative predicate) or by the plural in the case of count nouns.

Other degree adverbs have a different behavior: they select the type of scale they modify. This is the case for what we call 'intensity' adverbs: adverbs like *faiblement* 'lightly', *extrêmement* 'extremely' only modify gradable, cumulative predicates, which are associated with a scale of intensity. They cannot be used with count predicates and cannot trigger an iterative interpretation (14c).

(14) a. Max appuie légèrement / intensément sur la table.

'Max slightly / intensely presses the table'

b. Un garçon faiblement / prodigieusement intelligent.
'a boy lightly / incredibly intelligent'

c. #Max va faiblement / prodigieusement au cinéma.
'Max goes to the movies lightly / incredibly'

If one wants to take a closer look at the lexical semantics of intensity adverbs, two further properties may be mentioned. Degree adverbs may point to a specific portion of the scale, and thus only combine with predicates with a typical high (or low) default value. *Stupide* 'stupid' or *détruit* 'destroyed' have a typical high value (their default value is the maximum on the scale), while *réveillé* 'awake' or *effleuré* 'touched lightly' have a typical low value (they are by default associated with a minimal value on the scale). They are thus only appropriate with degree adverbs pointing to the same portion of scale (cf. Caudal 1999).

(15) a. extrêmement / #légèrement stupide, détruit
'very / little stupid / destroyed'

b. légèrement / #intensément effleuré
'slightly / intensely touched'

Some intensity adverbs further select predicates with a (culturally) positive evaluation (cf. 16a,b), while others select predicates with a (culturally) negative evaluation (cf. 16c) (cf. Molinier, Lévrier 2001):

(16) a. merveilleusement belle / #laide
'wonderfully beautiful/ugly'

b. atrocement #belle / laide
'horribly beautiful / ugly'

The adverbs in 16 can be analyzed as contributing an evaluation (the speaker's point of view) on top of their degree interpretation.[7]

A third subclass of degree adverbs is provided by so-called 'completion' adverbs, like *complètement* 'completely', *partiellement* 'partly', etc. As observed by Tenny (2000), they can only modify telic predicates, which are verbs with an incremental theme (17b), or denoting a change of state (17c):

(17) a. #Jean a complètement apprécié ses conseils.
'Jean appreciated his advice completely'

b. Jean a complètement compris le texte.
'Jean understood the text completely'

[7] As noted in Molinier (1990), such adverbs only function as degree adverbs in combination with adjectives. In combination with verbal predicates, they behave like manner adverbs (*chanter merveilleusement* 'sing marvelously', cf. chapter 11 of this Part for more on manner adverbs.

c. Jean a complètement noirci le tableau
'Jean has completely darkened the board

They are typically analyzed as specifying the degree to which a situation type has been realized (Parsons 1990, Moltmann 1998, Vanden Wyngaerd 2001, Piñón 2002). Unless the adverb indicates complete realization of the event, they are non-veridical in the sense that 18a does not entail 18b (cf. Thomason and Stalnaker 1974 and chapter 11 of this Part):

(18) a. Jean a partiellement lu le livre.
'Jean has partly read the book'

b. Jean a lu le livre.
'Jean has read the book'

If we associate 18b with a standard degree of realization, and interpret *partiellement* as indicating a lower degree of realization of the event, we can explain why the inference does not hold (cf. Piñón 2002 for details).

This analysis is still insufficient to account for the distribution of intensity and completion adverbs with adjectives:

(19) a. un homme extrêmement / *complètement grand
'a man extremely / completely tall'

b. un verre #extrêmement / complètement vide
'a glass extremely / completely empty'

Another distinction is required. Following Kennedy (1999), adverbs of completion change the default value on a scale, just like other degree adverbs, but, unlike other degree adverbs, they select a closed (as opposed to semi-open) scale. This provides a unitary explanation for their distribution in the adjectival and the verbal domains, since telic predicates are the only verbs with a closed scale.

Scales can be semi-open (with a minimal value and no maximal value) or closed (with a minimal value and a maximal value). The scale associated with *grand* 'big' or *apprécier* 'appreciate') is semi-open, while the scale associated with adjectives like *vide* 'empty' is closed, because there is an inherent maximum. Similarly, the scale associated with *comprendre le texte* is closed, because the process has a natural endpoint.[8] The fact that adverbs like *complètement* 'completely' select

[8]In the terms of Part 3 on tense and aspect, *comprendre* is a dynamic, [+ADD TO] verb that builds a path structure. When the verb combines with a bounded, [+SQA] object, the path is inherently bounded. In this way, we can relate terminativity of the VP with the notion of a closed scale.

a closed scale explains the contrast between 17a (open scale predicate) and 17b,c (closed scale predicates).

According to Kennedy (1999) and Kennedy and McNally (2000), degree adverbs are typically used with open scales. In fact, we find that adverb classes differ on this point. All degree quantifiers are compatible with an open scale predicate. Certain degree quantifiers, like *suffisamment* or *davantage*, are also compatible with closed scale predicates (and are thus insensitive to the open/closed character of the scale):

(20) a. Jean a suffisamment / davantage apprécié ses conseils.
'Jean appreciated his advice sufficiently / more'

b. Jean a suffisamment / davantage compris le texte
'Jean has understood the text sufficiently / more'

On the other hand, completion adverbs select a closed scale, hence their behavior in 19: *complètement* 'completely' does not combine with a open scale predicate like *grand* 'big' (19a). Intensity adverbs usually select predicates with an open scale, hence their occurrence in 14a,b and 19a: *extrêmement* 'extremely' does not combine with a closed scale predicate like *vide* 'empty' (19b).

Summing up, we have established a distinction between adverbs (or adverbials) quantifying over times and degree adverbs. Within the first class, we find frequency (*souvent* 'often') and iterative adverbials (*deux fois* 'twice'). We find independent interpretations for some frequency adverbials (*toujours* 'always', *souvent* 'often'), but not for others (*de temps en temps* 'now and then'). Independent adverbs can establish a relational reading. Within the class of degree adverbs, we defined three subclasses: degree quantifiers (*beaucoup* 'a lot'), intensity adverbs (*légèrement* 'slightly', *prodigieusement* 'incredibly') and adverbs of completion (*complètement* 'completely'). All degree adverbs change the default value of the scale associated with the predicate they modify. Degree quantifiers are insensitive to the kind of scale, and can have a quantification-like interpretation. Adverbs of completion require the predicate they modify to be associated with a closed scale. Intensity adverbs only modify predicates associated with a scale of intensity. They usually combine with open-ended scales, sometimes requiring a particular portion of the scale (*extrêmement* 'extremely' vs. *légèrement* 'slightly'), or a negatively/positively defined scale (merveilleusement 'wonderfully' vs. *affreusement* 'horribly').

## 3 Interface with syntactic properties

Frequency adverbs and degree adverbs typically show up in combination with different syntactic classes: on the whole, these adverbs select the category they modify on a semantic rather than a syntactic basis. Frequency adverbs attach to categories denoting an event; degree adverbs attach to categories denoting a relation between an object and a scale. We examine the pairs *très/beaucoup* 'very'/'a lot', *si/aussi* 'so' / 'so much' which constitute apparent counter-examples to this syntactic polymorphism. We show that the positions of degree adverbs, and those of degree quantifiers in particular, are more constrained than those of frequency adverbs, and propose that degree quantifiers are unique in not projecting (unary) adverbial phrases.

### 3.1 Syntactic polymorphism

Frequency adverbs (*souvent*) and degree adverbs (*trop*) modify verbs (or VPs), adjectives (or APs) and other adverbs (or AdvPs), as well as predicative nominals (bare Ns or NPs):

(21) a. Jean dort souvent / trop
'Jean sleeps often / too much'
b. Un homme [souvent / trop ivre]
'A man often / too drunk'
c. parfois / trop difficilement
'Sometimes / too uneasily'
d. Un enfant [souvent ami avec des plus grands]
'A child often friends with bigger ones'
e. Paul a [trop peur]
lit. Paul has too much fear = 'is too frightened'

There are further semantic restrictions on admissible combinations. As argued in 2.2 above, frequency adverbs imply a plurality of events, so they do not quantify over 'once-only' events, which explains the infelicity of sentences like 22a, as opposed to 22b (cf. de Swart 1991, 1995):

(22) a. ??Jean a souvent beaucoup d'enfants.
'Jean often has many children'
b. Les pauvres ont souvent beaucoup d'enfants.
'The poor often have many children'

Besides semantic restrictions, there are also syntactic constraints. Although frequency adverbs are interpreted as quantifiers over times or events, they cannot modify event-denoting nouns:

(23) a. *La destruction souvent de cette ville 'The destruction often of this town'
b. La destruction fréquente de cette ville 'The frequent destruction of this town'

In addition, degree quantifiers modify indefinite NPs of the form 'de NP'. Following Miller (1991) and Doetjes (1997) we analyze the degree adverb as left adjoined to the 'de NP' (24a),[9] a position where other degree adverbs fail to occur (24b,c):

(24) a. trop / plus de pommes / de peine
'too much / more of apples / of grief'

b. *faiblement / *prodigieusement de pommes / de peine
'lightly/ incredibly of apples / of grief'

c. *complètement / *entièrement de pommes / de peine
'completely / entirely of apples / of grief'

The ungrammaticality of 24c is expected from a semantic point of view: adverbs of completion require a closed scale to be associated with their modified category, but the quantity denoted by 'de NP' is open. On the other hand, intensity adverbs are not acceptable in this construction, even with a gradable predicate such as *peine* 24b, indicating that the constraint is syntactic rather than semantic in nature.[10]

The constraints over the modified category are thus both semantic and syntactic in nature. Frequency adverbs modify stage level predicates denoting plural sets (including predicative NPs) but fail to modify event-denoting NPs. Degree adverbs other than degree quantifiers fail to modify indefinite NPs, even when they provide the right type of scale. Frequency adverbs are syntactically polymorphic, but always modify the same type of semantic object, whereas the polymorphism of degree adverbs is both syntactic and semantic: they underspecify the kind of relation they semantically modify (provided this relation associates an object with a scale).

---

[9]The status of *de* is a matter of debate. It is not a preposition, because extraction is allowed out of the 'de NP' while it is impossible out of PPs:

(i) a. J'ai lu$_{NP}$ [beaucoup de livres de Balzac]
I read many books of Balzac

b. Balzac est un auteur dont j'ai lu beaucoup de livres
Balzac is an author of whom I read a lot of books

(ii) a. Je me souviens$_{PP}$ [de livres de Balzac]
I remember of books of Balzac

b. *Balzac est un auteur dont je me souviens de livres
Balzac is an author of–whom I remember of books

The first *de* is a preposition in (ii) but not in (i), where it can be analyzed as a determiner.

[10]Some speakers accept some mass NPs with intensity adverbs such as *infiniment* 'infinitely' or *extrêmement* 'extremely': % *extrêmement* / *infiniment de peine* 'a lot of trouble'. It is an open question whether such adverbs are used as degree quantifiers in this case.

## 3.2 The syntactic category of degree adverbs

The syntactic polymorphism of degree quantifiers has led some authors to assign them different syntactic categories, depending on the construction in which they occur. Degree quantifiers, when combined with an adjective, have been analyzed as degree words (with a specific category Deg or Q (Jackendoff 1977, Corver 1997), and when combined with an indefinite NP, as predeterminers or complex determiners (Gross 1977). There are good reasons to maintain a unique adverb category.

A syntactic property which sets adverbs apart from other categories in French is their ability to occur between the tense auxiliary and the past participle.[11] Both degree and frequency adverbs occur in this position (25a,b). Syntactically speaking, adverbial expressions like *deux fois* or *de temps en temps* must be characterized as nominal or prepositional phrases. As such, they fail to occur in this position (under unmarked conditions of stress and intonation) (25c):[12]

(25) a. Paul a trop dansé.
'Paul has too much danced'

b. Paul a souvent accompagné son fils à l'école.
'Paul has often accompanied his son to school'

c. *Paul a trois fois / de temps en temps accompagné son fils à l'école.
'Paul has three times / from time to time accompanied his son to school'

Interestingly, this position is allowed even for degree quantifiers interpreted as modifying an indefinite NP (26a) or an adjective (26b):

(26) a. Il a trop bu de vin.
'He has too much drunk of wine'

b. Il a trop été malade ces temps-ci.
'He has too (much) been sick these days'

Examples like 26a have been already described by Kayne (1975), Obenauer (1976), Milner (1978 a,b). They are generally referred to by the term 'quantification at a distance' or QAD, which has been introduced by Obenauer (1983, 1984). Syntactically, it is now generally accepted that the adverb in 26a directly modifies the V (or VP)

[11] See also chapter 11 of this Part.

[12] Pronominal quantifiers (*tout, rien*) also show up in this position. This means that these expressions share the positional properties of adverbs, and should be analyzed as such (see Kayne 1975). This can be represented by a feature [ADV+] present in such NPs, in a decompositional view of categories, or as a mixed category (see Malouf 2000).

rather than moving out of the NP. Semantically, Obenauer (1983, 1984) shows that the distant adverb has a quantity interpretation that involves both the verb and the noun. A sentence like 27a is unacceptable, because the verb *apprécier* is associated with a scale of intensity, not of quantity. Obviously, the nominal construction is quite acceptable in this context (27b):

(27) a. *Jean a beaucoup apprécié de films.
'Jean has a lot appreciated of films'
b. Jean a apprécié beaucoup de films.
'Jean has appreciated a lot of films'

The constraints on suggest that the scale associated with the NP has to be identified with the scale associated with the VP. This results in simultaneous modification of the two scales, as argued by Doetjes (1997), see also chapter 6 of part I. This shows that the degree quantifier is the same item in its adnominal and in its adverbial use.

### 3.3 The pairs *beaucoup / très, si / aussi, tant / autant*

We now look at the specific distribution of degree forms such as *très, beaucoup*, which seem to offer a counter-example to the polymorphism of degree adverbs. Modern French is remarkable in having created a distinction between *beaucoup* and *très*, while losing the ancient form *mult.* It is usually said that *très* and *beaucoup* are in complementary distribution. *Beaucoup* is reserved for verbal forms and nominal expressions of the form 'de NP' while *très* is used for other categories (Gaatone 1981):[13]

(28) a. Jean dort beaucoup / *très
'Jean sleeps a lot / *very'
b. Jean est très / *beaucoup grand / en forme / famille
'Jean is very / *a lot big / in shape / family-prone'
c. *très / beaucoup de pommes / d'argent
very / a lot of apples / money

Similar pairs are *autant / aussi* and *tant/ si. Autant* and *tant* modify verbs and 'de NPs', while *aussi* and *si* modify all non verbal predicative categories.

(29) a. Jean dort autant / *aussi (que Marie)
'Jean sleeps as much as Marie'
b. Jean est aussi / *autant grand / en forme (que Marie)
'Jean is as big / in shape as Marie'

[13]The only adverbs which can be modified by *beaucoup*, and not by *très* are the comparatives: *plus*, *moins* and *mieux*.

c. *si / *aussi / tant / autant de pommes / d'argent
'so / so many apples / so much money'

This syntactic distribution is sometimes assumed to correlate with a semantic distinction: *très, si,* and *aussi* are said to only modify predicates associated with a scale of intensity, while *beaucoup, autant* and *tant* can modify predicates associated with different types of scales, as we have shown above. However, participles denoting events can be modified by both *très* and *beaucoup*, with an iterative interpretation similar to *souvent* 'often' (Authier 1980):

(30) Ce monument est très / beaucoup photographié.
'This building is very / a lot photographed'

Following Doetjes (1997, 2002), we analyze the distribution of such pairs as a case of blocking (see also Di Scullio & Williams 1987).[14] In morphology, it is often assumed that the non existence of one form is due to the mere existence of another form (Aronoff 1976). In many cases, a more constrained form takes precedence over a more general form (cf. Kiparsky's 1973 Elsewhere condition). We analyze *très, si, aussi* as the more constrained forms, in the sense that they can neither be coordinated (31a,d) nor used in isolation (31f), contrary to *beaucoup, autant, tant,* which can be used in coordination contexts (31b,c) and in isolation (31e) (for other syntactic extensions of the notion of blocking, see Poser 1992):

(31) a. ?? Un enfant [très ou trop] intelligent
'A child [very or too] intelligent'

b. Il travaille [beaucoup et même trop]
'He works [a lot and even too much]'

c. Il travaille [autant ou plus] que son frère
'He works [as much or more] than his brother'

d. ?*Il est aussi ou plus grand que son frère
'He is as or more big than his brother'

e. Comment travaillent-ils? – Vraiment beaucoup / Autant.
'How do they work? – Really a lot / As much.

f. Sont-ils grands? – ?? Vraiment très / *Aussi.
'Are they tall? – Really very/ as much'

In that sense, *très, si, aussi* have the properties of weak forms, while *beaucoup, tant, autant* have the properties of strong forms. It is a general tendency in natural languages that weak forms, being more constrained,

[14]Doetjes analyses *beaucoup, tant* and *autant* as adverbs, and *très, si* and *aussi* as heads (selecting an adjectival complement) with a special category Deg.

take precedence over strong forms. Thus, once the weak forms (such as *très*) are specified as combining only with non verbal lexical categories, the impossibility of **beaucoup grand* is explained by the existence of *très grand*. The famous pairs *très/beaucoup, si/aussi* are thus not counter-examples to the syntactic polymorphism of degree adverbs.

### 3.4 Some syntactic constraints on degree adverbs

Turning to the positions of adverbs, we observe that, in a general way, degree adverbs are syntactically more constrained than frequency adverbs. This is particularly true of degree quantifiers, which deserve special attention.

Frequency adverbs occur both as pre- or post-adjectival modifiers, but degree adverbs are restricted to pre-adjectival position:[15]

(32) a. des résultats parfois inférieurs / inférieurs parfois aux prévisions
'results sometimes inferior / inferior sometimes to the expectations'

b. un enfant trop malade / *malade trop.
a child too sick / sick too

c. un enfant prodigieusement doué / ?? doué prodigieusement en musique
a child incredibly gifted / gifted incredibly for music

d. une pièce complètement vide / ?? vide complètement
a room completely empty / empty completely

While both frequency and degree adverbs occur postverbally, only the first can occur in sentence initial position.[16]

(33) a. Souvent / *Trop, Paul voit son frère.
'Often / Too(–much), Paul sees his brother'

b. *Complètement, Paul a assimilé le problème.
'Completely, Paul has understood the problem'

c. #Prodigieusement, Paul a apprécié ce film.
'Tremendously, Paul has appreciated this film'

In addition, degree quantifiers have an exceptional behavior, even among the class of degree adverbs. They do not scramble with complements and cannot be extracted, while frequency, intensity and completion adverbs can:

[15] The post-adjectival adverb may be acceptable if it is incidental rather than integrated (see chapter 21, Prosody and Information in French, for this prosodic distinction).

[16] Sentence 32c is acceptable if the adverb is interpreted as an evaluative adverb.

(34) a. Paul voit souvent son frère / son frère souvent.
'Paul sees often his brother / his brother often'
b. C'est souvent que Paul voit son frère.
'It is often that Paul sees his brother'

(35) a. Paul aime beaucoup / prodigieusement les épinards.
'Paul loves a lot / incredibly spinach'
b. Paul aime les épinards prodigieusement / *beaucoup.
'Paul loves spinach incredibly / a lot'
c. C'est prodigieusement / *beaucoup que Paul aime les épinards.
'It is incredibly / a lot that Paul loves spinach'

To account for such constraints, Abeillé and Godard (2000, 2001) propose that scrambling and extraction are limited to phrases, and ruled out for lexical categories, as the contrast between bare nouns and NPs shows:

(36) a. Paul rend (un vibrant) hommage aux victimes
'Paul paid (a vibrant) tribute to the victims'
b. Paul rend aux victimes un vibrant hommage / *hommage
Paul paid to the victims (a vibrant) tribute
c. C'est *[hommage] / [un vibrant hommage] que Paul a rendu aux victimes
It is (a vibrant) tribute that Paul paid to the victims

This contrast is accounted for if adverbs in general can project adverb phrases by themselves (in the same way as proper names project NPs), while degree quantifiers cannot project such a unary phrase (they are "lite" in Abeillé & Godard's terminology).[17] Thus, we assume, with Sadler and Arnold (1994), Sells (1994), and Abeillé and Godard (2000), that some words can enter the syntax directly, without projecting their own phrase.

Degree quantifiers also have interesting properties regarding left adjunction to verbs or adjectives. There is evidence that they adjoin to the lexical category rather than to the phrase that they modify. They fail to have scope over a coordination of infinitival or adjectival phrases (Abeillé and Godard 2001).[18]

[17]As soon as they are modified, or coordinated (hence no longer lite), they can be scrambled or extracted:
(i) Paul téléphone à son frère [vraiment trop]
'Paul calls his brother [really too much].'

[18]It is impossible to account for the absence of wide scope if they adjoin to a phrase: the constraints on adjunction cannot specify whether this phrase constitutes a coordination or not, and adjuncts have scope (at least) over the category they adjoin to. The data in 38 also show that Corver's (1997) analysis of degree adverbs

(37) a. *Paul craint de trop téléphoner à son frère et écrire à sa mère.
Paul fears too much calling his brother and writing to his mother

b. *Paul évite de beaucoup parler au téléphone et écrire de lettres
Paul avoids much talking on the phone and writing letters

(38) a. *une plante trop [longue à fleurir et difficile à cultiver]
'A plant too long to bloom and difficult to grow'

b. une plante [trop longue à fleurir] et [difficile à cultiver]

c. *une élève plus grande en taille et forte en gym que toi
'A student more tall in height and strong in gym than you'

d. une élève plus grande en taille et plus forte en gym que toi

Sentence 37a is ill-formed because the only possibility for the marker *de* not to be repeated in the second conjunct is that an adverb modifies both conjuncts (see 39a); hence, *trop* cannot have wide scope over the coordination. Sentence 37b is also ill-formed because wide scope is necessary to legitimate the indefinite 'de NP' in the second conjunct (in a construction). Sentence 38a is ungrammatical under this bracketing, and grammatical under that in 38b: it can only mean that the plant is too long to bloom on the one hand, and difficult to grow on the other hand, not that it is too difficult to grow. 38c is difficult because wide scope of *plus* would be necessary to license the shared *que* phrase complement; in the absence of such scope, *plus* must be repeated.

These properties of degree quantifiers are intriguing. Abeillé and Godard's (2001) explanation is that, as lexical adjuncts, degree quantifiers are constrained in adjoining only to lexical heads (cf. Sadler & Arnold 1994, Sells 1994)[19]. However, as we have seen, degree quantifiers can adjoin to indefinite 'de NP', which are phrases. In any case, they contrast with other degree and frequency adverbs, which may have wide scope over a coordination of infinitival or adjectival phrases:[20]

(39) a. ? Il craint de toujours être en retard et rater quelque chose.
'He fears always being late and missing something'

b. % Il craignait de complètement perdre la tête et rater ses examens.

---

as functional heads taking the AP as a complement is not appropriate for French, since it predicts that all degree adverbs can have wide scope over a coordination of APs.

[19]This does not mean that the adverb does not have access to the content of the whole phrase, assuming that heads and phrases share their semantics.

[20]There is speaker variation (indicated by '%') concerning the occurrence of completion adverbs to the left of an infinitival, see chapter 11 of this book. Sentence 39c has two interpretations, corresponding to the wide, or narrow, scope of the adverb.

'He was afraid of completely losing his head and failing his exams'

c. ? une plante souvent / excessivement longue à fleurir et difficile à cultiver
'A plant often / excessively long to bloom and difficult to grow'

We leave open the question of a possible correlation between the syntactic contrast and the semantics of frequency and degree adverbs. It is tempting to relate the absence of degree adverbs in S initial position to the fact that, unlike frequency adverbs, they require access to the lexical semantics of the predicate (the presence and the kind of the scale). However, this does not say anything regarding their position with respect to the head they modify (see 32a vs. 32b,c,d). We also leave open the question of a correlation of the special properties of degree quantifiers with semantics as well as with morphology. As observed by Molinier et Lévrier (2000), Abeillé & Godard (2001), degree quantifiers are usually monomorphematic, while other degree adverbs are *–ment* derived.[21]

## 4 Conclusion

In this chapter, we have discussed the semantic and syntactic properties of different adverbial expressions that are related in various ways to the expression of quantity in the verbal domain. In the first part, we established a distinction between frequency adverbs (*souvent*, *toujours*) and cardinal count adverbs (*deux fois*) on the one hand and degree quantifiers (*beaucoup, énormément, un peu*) on the other hand in terms of countability and plurality of times/events and comparison on a scale. Degree 'quantifiers' like *beaucoup* can, but need not have a quantificational interpretation. Just like other degree adverbs, their interpretation depends on a contextually (or lexically) given scale. In contrast, other degree adverbs like *complètement* or *prodigieusement* never trigger a quantificational interpretation. We argued that such degree adverbs impose constraints on the scale they modify: a closed scale for adverbs of completion like *complètement*, a scale of intensity for adverbs like *prodigieusement*. In the second part, we tried to relate some of these semantic properties to differences in syntactic distribution. We observed that both frequency and degree adverbs are syntactically polymorphic

[21]We found only three *–ment* adverbs uncontroversially productive with 'de NP' (a test of their being degree quantifiers): *tellement, suffisamment* and *énormément* (Schlyter 1977). Molinier and Levrier (2000) and Gross (1977) give more examples, which are not easily accepted by native speakers, although some sound better with an abstract N. A corpus-based enquiry seems indicated.

in the sense that they attach to different syntactic categories. Degree quantifiers are uniquely qualified to occur in contexts of quantification at a distance, because of their extreme syntactic polymorphism. Regarding their positions, degree adverbs are more constrained than frequency adverbs, and, in the verbal and adjectival domains, degree quantifiers are even more constrained than other degree adverbs.

## References

Abeillé, A. and D. Godard. 2000. French word order and lexical weight. In Borsley (2000), pages 325–360.

Abeillé, A. and D. Godard. 2001. On a class of French lite adverbs. In Camps and Wiltshire (2001).

Anderson, S. and P. Kiparski, eds. 1973. *A Festschrift for Morris Halle*. New York: Holt, Rinehart and Winston.

Aronoff, M. 1976. *Word formation in generative grammar*. Cambridge, MA: MIT Press.

Authier, J. 1980. Note sur 'interprétation sémantique de 'très' + participe passé passif. *Cahiers de lexicologie* 37:25–34.

Bach, E. 1986. The algebra of events. *Linguistics and Philosophy* 9:5–16.

Bach, E., E. Jelinek, A. Kratzer, and B. Partee, eds. 1995. *Quantification in Natural Languages*. Dordrecht: Kluwer.

Baüerle, R., C. Schwarze, and A. von Stechow, eds. 1983. *Meaning, Use and Interpretation of Language*. Berlin: Walter de Gruyter.

Bok-Bennema, R., B. de Jonge, B. Kampers-Manhe, and A. Molendijk, eds. 2001. *Adverbial Modification*. Amsterdam: Rodopi.

Borsley, R., ed. 2000. *Syntactic Categories*. New York: Academic Press.

Camps, J. and C. Wiltshire, eds. 2001. *Syntax, semantics, and L2 acquisition in Romance*. Amsterdam: J. Benjamins.

Caudal, P. 1999. *La Polysémie aspectuelle, étude contrastive français-anglais*. Ph.D. thesis, Université Paris.

Corver, N. 1997. The internal syntax of the Dutch extended adjectival projection. *Natural Language and Linguistic theory* 15:289–368.

De Swart, H. 1988. Quelques fois and quelquefois: about iteration and frequency in French. In Hulk and Coopmans (1988), pages 149–158.

De Swart, H. 1991. *Adverbs of Quantification: A Generalized Quantifier Approach*. Ph.D. thesis, University of Groningen. [published by Garland, New York, 1993].

De Swart, H. 1995. (in)definites and genericity. In Kanazawa et al. (1995), pages 171–194.

De Swart, H. 2003. Coercion in a cross-linguistic theory of aspect. In Francis and Michaelis (2003), pages 231–258.

Di Sciullo, A.-M. and E. Williams. 1987. *On the Definition of Word*. Cambridge, MA: MIT Press.

Doetjes, J. 1997. *Quantifiers and selection. On the distribution of quantifying expressions in French, Dutch and English*. Ph.D. thesis, HIL/Leiden University, HAG, The Hague.

Doetjes, J. 2001a. Beaucoup est ailleurs. Expressions de degré et sous-spécification catégorielle. In Bok-Bennema et al. (2001).

Doetjes, J. 2001b. La distribution des expressions quantificatrices et le statut des noms non comptables. In Tasmowski et al. (2001).

Doetjes, J. 2002. Comparing adverbs of quantity. Ms. University of Utrecht.

Ducrot, O. 1979. L'imparfait en français. *Linguistische Berichte* 60:1–23.

Ducrot, O. 1980. *Les Echelles argumentatives*. Paris: Minuit.

Fintel, K. v. 1994. *Restrictions on Quantifier Domains*. Ph.D. thesis, University of Massachusetts at Amherst. Distributed by GSLA.

Francis, E. J. and L. A. Michaelis, eds. 2003. *Mismatch: form-function incongruity and the architecture of grammar*. Stanford: CSLI Publications.

Gaatone, D. 1981. Observations sur l'opposition *très / beaucoup*. *Revue de linguistique romane* 45:74–95.

Gosselin, L. 1996. *Sémantique de la temporalité en français*. Liège: Duculot.

Gross, M. 1977. *Grammaire transformationnelle du français : syntaxe du nom*. Paris: Larousse.

Guimier, C. 1996. *Les adverbes du français: le cas des adverbes en -ment*. Gap: Ophrys.

Hoepelman, J. and C. Rohrer. 1981. On the mass-count distinction and the French imparfait and passé simple. In Rohrer (1981), pages 85–112.

Hulk, A. and P. Coopmans, eds. 1988. *Linguistics in the Netherlands*, Dordrecht. Foris.

Jackendoff, R. 1977. *X-bar Syntax, A study of Phrase structure*. Cambridge, MA: MIT Press.

Jayez, J. 1987. Sémantique et approximation, le cas de presque et à peine. *Lingvisticæ Investigationes* XI(1).

Kanazawa, M., C. Piñón, and H. de Swart, eds. 1995. *Quantifiers, deduction and context*. Stanford: CSLI Publications.

Kayne, R. 1975. *French Syntax. The transformational cycle*. Cambridge, MA: MIT Press.

Kennedy, C. 1999. *Projecting the adjective: the syntax and semantics of gradability and comparison*. New York: Garland.

Kennedy, C. and L. McNally. 1999. From event structure to scale structure: Degree modification in deverbal adjectives. In Mathews and Strolovitsc (1999), pages 163–180.

Kiparski, P. 1973. Elsewhere in phonology. In Anderson and Kiparski (1973).

Kleiber, G. 1987. *Du côté de la référence verbale. Les phrases habituelles*. Bern: Peter Lang.

Krifka, M. 1986. *Nominalreferenz und Zeitkonstitution: Zur Semantik von Massentermen, Pluraltermen und Aspektklassen*. Ph.D. thesis, Munich University, Munich, Germany.

Krifka, M. 1992. Thematic relations as links between nominal reference and temporal constitution. In Sag and Szabolcsi (1992), pages 29–53.

Link, G. 1983. The logical analysis of plurals and mass terms: A lattice-theoretical approach. In Baüerle et al. (1983), pages 302–23.

Malouf, R. 2000. *Mixed Categories in the Hierarchical Lexicon*. Stanford: CSLI Publications.

Mathews, T. and D. Strolovitsc, eds. 1999. *SALT 9*, Ithaca. CLC Publications.

Miller, P. 1991. *Clitics and constituents in Phrase Structure grammar*. Ph.D. thesis, Utrecht University. [published by Garland, New York, 1992].

Milner, J.-C. 1978a. Cyclicité successive, comparatives, et Cross-over en français. *Linguistic Inquiry* 9:673–693.

Milner, J.-C. 1978b. *De la syntaxe à l'interprétation*. Paris: Seuil.

Molendijk, A. and H. de Swart. 1998. Frequency and tense use in French. *Belgian Journal of Linguistics* 12:43–60. Tense and Aspect. Vogeleer and De Mulder and Depraetere, eds.

Molinier, C. 1990. Une classification des adverbes en *–ment. Langue française* 88.

Molinier, C. and F. Lévrier. 2001. *Grammaire des adverbes: descriptions des formes en* –ment. Genève: Droz.

Moltmann, F. 1998. *Parts and Wholes in Semantics*. Oxford: Oxford University Press.

Moore, S. and A. Winner, eds. 1991. *Proceedings from Semantics and Linguistic Theory 1 [= Cornell Working Papers in Linguistics 1]*.

Obenauer, H.-G. 1976. *Etudes de syntaxe interrogative du français*. Tübingen: Niemeyer.

Obenauer, H.-G. 1983. Une quantification non-canonique: la quantification à distance. *Langue française* 58:66–88.

Obenauer, H.-G. 1984. On the identification of empty categories. *The Linguistic Review* 4:153–202.

Obenauer, H.-G. 1994. *Aspects de la syntaxe A-barre. Effets d'intervention et mouvements des quantifieurs*. Ph.D. thesis, Université de Paris VIII.

Parsons, T. 1990. *Events in the Semantics of English*. Cambridge, MA: MIT Press.

Partee, B. 1991. Topic, focus and quantification. In Moore and Winner (1991), pages 159–188.

Partee, B. 1995. Quantificational structures and compositionality. In Bach et al. (1995), pages 541–601.

Piñon, C. 2002. Adverbs of completion with events and degrees. In Van Hout et al. (2002).

Poser, W. 1992. Blocking of phrasal constructions by lexical items. In Sag and Szabolcsi (1992), pages 111–130.

Rohrer, C., ed. 1981. *Time, tense and quantifiers*. Tübingen: Niemeyer.

Sadler, L. and D. Arnold. 1994. Prenominal adjectives and the word – phrase distinction. *Journal of Linguistics* 30:187–226.

Sag, I. A. and A. Szabolcsi, eds. 1992. *Lexical Matters*. Stanford: CSLI.

Schlyter, S. 1977. *La place des adverbes en* –ment *en français*. Ph.D. thesis, Universität Konstanz.

Sells, P. 1994. Sub-phrasal syntax in Korean. *Language Research* 30:351–386.

Tasmowski, L., B. Laca, and G. Kleiber, eds. 2001. *Typologie des groupes nominaux*. Rennes: Presses Universitaires Rennes.

Tenny, C. 2000. Core events and adverbial modifications. In Tenny and Pustejovsky (2000), pages 285–334.

Tenny, C. and J. Pustejovsky, eds. 2000. *Events as grammatical objects*. Stanford: CSLI Publications.

Thomason, R. and R. Stalnaker. 1973. A semantic theory of adverbs. *Linguistic Inquiry* 4(2):195–200.

Van Hout, A., H. de Swart, and H. Verkuyl, eds. 2002. *Proceedings of the Conference Perspectives on Aspect*, OTS Working Papers, Utrecht University.

Vanden Wyngaerd, G. 2001. Measuring events. *Language* 77(1):61–90.

Victorri, B. and C. Fuchs. 1996. *La Polysémie: construction dynamique du sens*. Paris: Hermes.

# 13

# Parentheticals as Conventional Implicatures *

JACQUES JAYEZ AND CORINNE ROSSARI

## 1 Introduction

In his *Logic and conversation*, Grice (1989, chap. 2) proposed a much commented distinction between what is *said* and what is *implied*.[1] This distinction is of particular relevance for constituents that are not the complement or the modifier of another constituent within a sentence, like *heureusement* 'fortunately', *je pense* 'I think' or *d'après Marie* 'according to Mary'. In current usage, such expressions are called *parentheticals*. This is actually misleading. Because many of these expressions are often (see evaluative adverbs such as *heureusement*) or always (see *je pense* 'I think', *paraît-il* 'I hear') prosodically incident, the class of parentheticals tends to be equated with that of expressions which are or can be incidentals. However, the semantico-pragmatic property is clearly distinct from the prosodic property, as shown by Bonami et al., chapter 11: parenthetical adverbs such as *heureusement*, for instance, may occur either as incidents or with an integrated prosody, just like modal adverbs, which we show are not parentheticals. In this paper, we are primarily interested in adverbials that *qualify* an assertion either by modalizing it (modal adverbs) or by signalling that its truth is warranted by a particular source (belief and report expressions). They are particularly puzzling since, although most of them (excluding modals,

*The second author is funded by Swiss FNRS through the project 610–062821.00 *Semantic Typology of French Discourse Markers*

[1] Grice also uses 'suggested' and 'meant'.

*Handbook of French Semantics*.
Francis Corblin and Henriëtte de Swart (eds.).
Copyright © 2004, CSLI Publications.

as we will see) are not a part of 'what is said', they interact with the assertive force of the sentence in which they occur. For instance, sentences with *paraît–il* 'I hear' are certainly less authoritative than the same sentences without the adverbial. We propose that parentheticals fall into the general category of conventional implicatures, that is, constraints on interpretation which are lexically triggered but do not contribute to delineate the referential content of a sentence (the type of situation which the sentence purports to describe). Formally, we capture the distinction between parentheticals and non-parentheticals by distinguishing between two different kinds of updates in the dynamic multimodal multiagent framework of Gerbrandy (1998). The paper is organized as follows: in section 2, we review the different tests and show that they support the distinction we propose. In section 3, we discuss the theoretical status of the distinction. In 3.1, we show that parentheticals must be conventional implicatures, if anything. In 3.2, we characterize the status of conventional implicatures in dynamic semantics. Finally, in 3.3 and 3.4 we present our formal treatment for parentheticals.

## 2 Tests for the distinction

How do we determine that a constituent is part of what is said? We will consider six tests, some of them being mentioned in the literature (see for instance Borillo (1976), Molinier and Lévrier (2000) for French, Wilson (1975), Infantidou (1994), Rouchota (1998) for English).

### 2.1 The *oui/non* test

With *Oui* 'yes' answers, it seems that the speaker can refer to the whole host sentence, including the adverbial. For instance, in (1a,b,c), B's answer can be interpreted as expressing agreement on the choice of the modality.

(1) a. A – Jean a probablement changé de voiture
'John probably got a new car'
B – Oui, c'est même plus que probable
'Yes, it's even more than probable'

b. A – Jean a malheureusement eu un accident
'Unfortunately, John had an accident'
B – Oui, c'est très ennuyeux
'Yes, that's a real problem'

c. A – Jean a eu un accident, paraît–il
'John had an accident, I hear'
B – Oui, je l'ai aussi entendu dire
'Yes, I also heard of that'

However, *non* 'no' is not symmetric to *oui* in all examples.[2]

(2) a. A – Jean a probablement changé de voiture
'John probably got a new car'
B – Non, c'est improbable
'No, it's improbable'

b. A – Jean a malheureusement eu un accident
'Unfortunately, John had an accident'
B1 – Non, ??c'est bien fait pour lui. Il conduit trop vite
'No, he deserves it. He drives too fast'
B2 – Non, ??tu es bien content, avoues-le; tu le détestes
'No, be frank, you are glad of that; you hate him'

c. A – Jean a eu un accident, paraît–il
'John had an accident, I hear'
B1 – Non, personne n'a dit ça
'No, nobody said that'
B2 – Non, ??personne n'était au courant
'No, nobody knew'

In examples (2b), B1's and B2's answers cannot refer to modalities such as 'It is unfortunate that' or 'The speaker A considers that it is unfortunate that'. The case of (2c) is more complex and we return to it in the next section.

## 2.2 The *vrai/faux* test

In this test, one tries to imagine an answer whereby B echoes or opposes directly A's assertion by asserting that what A said is true/false. We illustrate the *C'est faux* ('It's false') case.

(3) a. A – Jean a probablement changé de voiture
'John probably got a new car'
B – C'est faux, c'est improbable
'It's false, it's improbable'

b. A – Jean a malheureusement eu un accident
'Unfortunately, John had an accident'
B1 – ??C'est faux, c'est bien comme ça
'It's false, that is OK'
B2 – ??C'est faux, tu es bien content, avoues–le; tu le détestes
'It's false, be frank, you are glad of that; you hate him'

---

[2] Actually, *oui* has the same behavior as *non*. For instance, if, in (1c), B answers by *Moi aussi* 'Me too', it can only mean 'I had an accident too', not 'I heard it too'.

c. A – Jean a eu un accident, paraît–il
'John had an accident, I hear'
B1 – C'est faux, personne n'a dit ça
'It's false, nobody said that'
B2 – ??C'est faux, personne n'était au courant
'It's false, nobody knew'

In (3a), B takes the modality into account. In contrast, (3b) replicates the observation (2b). B fails to deny that it is unfortunate (for the speaker A) that John had an accident. (3c) exhibits the same contrast as (2c) between a denial based on 'personne n'a dit ça' and 'personne n'était au courant'. B2's answers in (2c) and (3c) are unnatural because they fail to refer to the modality. To interpret these answers, we have to find a discourse relation which might connect *Non* or *C'est faux* with these propositions.[3] Relations like Narration, Elaboration, Contrast, are not good candidates. The most reasonable choices are Justification or Convergence. A Justification relation between $\alpha$ and $\beta$ can be glossed by '$\alpha$ since $\beta$'. A Convergence relation obtains when two propositions point in the same direction (through entailment or implicature). Justification can be signalled by *puisque* and Convergence by *d'ailleurs* (roughly equivalent to 'also' in this context) or *de plus* ('moreover'). (4) illustrates the differences. B1's and B2's answers show that Justification is not possible with the first proposition while Convergence is. B4's answer shows that neither relation is possible with *personne n'était au courant.* This is to be expected since this sentence presupposes that John had an accident, a proposition which is explicitly denied by the first sentence of the answer (*Non* and *C'est faux*). Note that, for Justification to be appropriate with B1, the answer would have to pick up the reportedness modality and produce a meaning like 'It cannot be the case that you heard that since nobody said that'.

(4) A – Jean a eu un accident, paraît–il
'John had an accident, I hear'
B1 – ??Non/C'est faux puisque personne n'a dit ça
'No/It's false since nobody said anything like that'
B2 – Non/C'est faux, d'ailleurs personne n'a dit ça
'No/It's false, also, nobody said anything like that'
B3 – ??Non/C'est faux puisque personne n'était au courant
'No/It's false since nobody knew'
B4 – ??Non/C'est faux, d'ailleurs personne n'était au courant
'No/It's false, also nobody knew'

[3]See Mann and Thompson (1988), Sanders et al. (1992), Lascarides and Asher (1993) for standard repertoires of discourse relations.

## 2.3 The conditional test

Assuming that conditional sentences can have an implicative interpretation of the form $\phi \Rightarrow \psi$, if the modality is integrated into what is said in $\phi$, it may have effects on the truth or relevance of the conclusion $\psi$. For instance, the adjunct *on Tuesday* in *John was in Germany on Tuesday* is a part of what is said because it plays an essential role in the implicative connection of sentences like *If John was in Germany on Tuesday, he was not in San Francisco.* This test is consistent with the idea that the *probablement* modality is a part of what is said but the other two cannot be.

(5) a. Si Jean a probablement changé de voiture, il a probablement aussi acheté une voiture d'occasion
'If John probably got a new car, he also probably bought a second–hand one'

b. Si Jean a probablement changé de voiture, ??il a aussi acheté une voiture d'occasion
'If John probably got a new car, he also bought a second–hand one'

c. Si Jean a malheureusement démissionné, ??alors il est également malheureux que son bras droit ait démissionné
'If John unfortunately resigned, then it is also unfortunate that his assistant resigned'.

In (5a), the *si*–clause is preferably interpreted as echoing some previous judgment. For instance, the speaker echoes what another speaker said or implied. The other possible interpretation, under which the speaker herself introduces the modal judgment, is less natural since it would correspond to a reading like 'If I believe that $\phi$, then $\psi$', where the speaker doubts the existence of her own mental states. (5b) sounds strange because if it is only probable that John got a new car, asserting that it is a second–hand one is too strong. Under the interpretation that the first judgment (it is unfortunate that John has resigned) entails the second (it is unfortunate that his assistant resigned), (5c) is out, because the first modality cannot be integrated into the antecedent and escapes the entailment relation, which is necessary for *aussi* to be justified. The sentence does not means 'If it is unfortunate that ..., then ...'.

*Paraît–il* raises an additional problem. This modality is not compatible with a *si*–clause because it is speaker–centered and means something like 'I heard that'. So, saying *Si Jean a, paraît–il, démissionné* ('If John resigned, I hear') would, at best, amount to saying 'If I heard that John resigned', an improbable case of doubting the existence of one's own perceptions or mental states. To circumvent this problem, one can use another possible interpretation of conditional sentences where the sentence points to a contrast between two propositions. (6a) illustrates the interpretation and (6b) shows that *paraît–il* is compatible with the *si*–clause in this case. (6d) shows that *paraît–il* cannot be a part of what is said and that its interpretation cannot be equated with (6c).

(6) a. Si Marie est grande, Jean est petit
'If Mary is tall, John is short'

b. Si, du moins paraît–il, les impôts augmentent, en revanche, le chômage baisse
'If taxes are increasing, at least according to what I hear, in contrast, unemployment is decreasing'

c. Si j'ai entendu dire que les impôts augmentaient, Jean a entendu dire le contraire. Comment savoir?
'If I heard that taxes are increasing, John heard the contrary. How could we know?'

d. Si, du moins paraît-il, les impôts augmentent, ??Jean a entendu dire le contraire.
'If taxes are increasing, at least according to what I hear, John heard the contrary'

## 2.4 Discourse attachment

The aim of this section is to clarify the illocutionary status of parentheticals. We saw in section 2.2 that attachment problems through discourse relations are responsible for certain differences in acceptability. Asher (2000) proposes that parentheticals are attached to the clause they modify by discourse relations like Comment, Evidence, etc. In Asher's Segmented DRT (SDRT) (Asher, 1993; Lascarides and Asher, 1993), attaching a discourse segment, or *constituent* $\beta$ to another constituent $\alpha$ is only possible in the following two cases, where $\gamma$ denotes the last constituent in the sequential order of discourse:

1. $\alpha = \gamma$.
2. $\gamma$ is subordinated to $\alpha$ *via* a subordination discourse relation.

Attachment can hold between constituents which do not correspond to speech acts in the usual sense (Searle, 1969). For instance, in Asher and Lascarides (1998), the DRSs corresponding to presuppositions can be attached to other constituents.[4]

The attachment properties of parentheticals show that they are not genuine speech acts. Let us consider the triple (7). (7a) connects two

[4] We assume here that presuppositions are not speech acts. For a different view, see Ducrot (1972).

assertions by a Justification relation. The second assertion is presented as a reason to believe that the proposition expressed by the first assertion is true. (7b) and (7c) contain the additional judgment that the situation associated with the first sentence is a good thing. This is the result of inserting an independent assertion in (7b), and a parenthetical adverb in (7c). (7b) is much better if $\beta$ is connected by Explanation to $\gamma$, not to $\alpha$. In other words, the preferred interpretation of the discourse is that the fact that the basketball group voted for Mary is a justification of the assertion that it is a good thing. This suggests that the Comment relation between $\alpha$ and $\gamma$ is *not* a subordination relation but a Coordination relation, which, in SDRT, is predicted to block the attachment of $\beta$ to $\alpha$.

Two observations are in order for (7c). First, the parenthetical is not integrated into what is said since the first sentence cannot be paraphrased by 'It is a good thing that Mary will be elected to head the club'. Assume the contrary; the Justification connection would then be unclear: how could the decision of the basketball group possibly affect the felicity of Mary being elected? Second, the parenthetical is not added in a separate speech act, unlike the parallel judgment in (7b), since we do not observe the same effect in (7c) as in (7b) with respect to attachment. We conclude that, in SDRT, *fortunately* is neither a part of the asserted content nor a separate speech act–based constituent.

(7) a. Mary will be elected to head the club, since the basketball group decided to vote for her

b. Mary will be elected to head the club. ($=\alpha$) This is a good thing. ($=\gamma$) $^{\#}$Since the basketball group decided to vote for her ($=\beta$)

c. Mary will, fortunately, be elected to head the club, since the basketball group decided to vote for her

## 2.5 Interrogatives

If modal adverbs are integrated into what is said, why are they odd in yes–no questions (8a)? One would expect that they combine with the interrogative modality to produce readings like 'Is it probable / likely / etc. that $\phi$?'. Two points should be noted in this respect. First, the combination of parentheticals with the interrogative modality is not uniform. For instance, *heureusement* is out in yes–no questions while *malheureusement* 'unfortunately' is acceptable.[5] Second, the behavior of modal adverbs might be explained by particular scope properties.

[5]See *Est–ce que Jean a, ??heureusement / malheureusement, découvert la réponse?* 'Did John, fortunately / unfortunately find the answer?'.

Molinier and Lévrier (2000) note that four modal French adverbs (*forcément*, *fatalement* 'of necessity', *obligatoirement* 'obligatorily' and *nécessairement* 'necessarily') can occur after the negation marker *pas*, in contrast with other modals (9). They can also occur in questions (8).

(8) a. Est–ce que Jean a ??probablement démissionné?
'Did John probably resign?'

b. Est-ce que Jean a nécessairement / forcément etc. démissionné
'Did John necessarily resign?'

(9) a. Jean n'a (*nécessairement / *forcément etc.) pas (nécessairement / forcément etc.) démissionné
'John did (necessarily) not (necessarily) resign'

b. Jean n'a (probablement) pas (*probablement) démissionné
'John did (probably) not (probably) resign'

(9) indicates that the four mentioned modals can occur in the scope of the main sentential operator, i.e. the negation. If we assume that, in interrogatives, the main operator is a question operator, we can account for the parallelism between (8b) and (9a) in terms of scope. Certain modal adverbs (e.g. *probablement*) must take wide scope, whereas others (e.g., *forcément*) don't follow this rule. This predicts that (8a) means something like 'It is probable that (did John resign?)', hence its oddity. If this conjecture is right, the question test pertains to the scope problem, not to the 'said' vs. 'implied' distinction. The reader is referred to Ferrari (1995) for a more systematic treatment of similar scope problems.

## 2.6 Declarative verbs

Following Bach (1994), an expression is part of what is said if it can occur in the complement clause of a declarative verb, and conversely, is not part of what is said if it cannot. The test is based on the behavior of speech act adverbs such as *frankly*, which are uncontroversially parentheticals, see (10a). However, the test is not convincing. First, as shown in (10b), the French equivalent is acceptable for many speakers. Second, it conflicts with the other tests that we have discussed, since evaluative adverbs or reportive incidentals are perfectly acceptable, as shown by (10c). Speakers who reject (10b) seem to restrict the relevance of speech act adverbs to the actual speech act, to the exclusion of a reported speech act.

(10) a. Mary said that *frankly John is incompetent

b. Marie a dit que, (??)franchement, Jean était incompétent

c. Marie a dit que Jean était, malheureusement / paraît–il, malade
lit.: Mary said that John was, unfortunately / she hears, ill

Summarizing, we see that (i) two tests (declarative clause embedding and interrogatives) are not significant and (ii) the other four support the hypothesis of a difference between modals and parentheticals. Specifically, modals are interpreted as a part of the assertion while parentheticals are not. So the question naturally arises of the exact nature of their contribution. Rossari (2002) has independently provided a convergent analysis for causal parentheticals and non–parentheticals.

## 3 The contribution of parentheticals

### 3.1 Parentheticals convey conventional implicatures

If parentheticals are not part of the assertion, the semantic options left to us are: (i) they introduce presuppositions, (ii) they introduce implicatures. The first possibility is unlikely. Parentheticals like *paraît–il* or *I hear* do not pass the standard tests that detect presuppositions (Soames, 1989; Geurts, 1999). Some of them, e.g. *heureusement* 'fortunately' are considered as 'factive' (Bartsch, 1975). The term may be misleading since it suggests an analogy with factive verbs (see Bonami et al. (chapter 11, this volume) for a discussion). However, factivity–preserving environments for factive verbs do not have the same effect on the adverbs mentioned.

(11) a. Est–ce que tu sais que Marie a réussi son examen?
'Do you know that Mary passed her exam?'

b. Est-ce que, malheureusement, Marie aurait raté son examen?
'Would Mary have –unfortunately– failed her exam?'

While (11a) still carries the presupposition that Mary passed, this is not the case for (11b). The adverb only applies to possible events (of Mary failing). As to *paraît–il*, it is not compatible with questions.

Certain parentheticals correspond to detachable lexical material. One can suppress *fortunately* in *Fortunately, John was elected* without changing the truth–conditions of the sentence. This is less clear for *I hear*. *John was elected, I hear* is more cautious than *John was elected.* However, as shown in section 2, the judgments of truth and falsity ignore the parenthetical, a fact which suggests that its contribution to the truth of the sentence is only indirect. A parenthetical cannot be 'cancelled'. For instance, *If John has a son, his son is certainly proud of his father* suspends the presupposition that John has a son, that is, cancels the default effect of 'his son'. In contrast, *If it is really a good thing that John was elected, then, fortunately, he was elected* is hardly interpretable. According to Grice (1989), the two properties of detachability and non–cancellability are the hallmark of conventional implicatures, and we may assume as a starting point that parentheticals trigger such implicatures.[6]

### 3.2 The status of conventional implicatures

What is the Gricean status of implicatures? Grice proposes that discourse markers like *therefore* convey the implicature that there is a consequence relation between two propositions. Similarly, one might say that *paraît–il* conveys the implicature that the speaker heard that $\phi$, where $\phi$ is the asserted content.

(12) Marie a, paraît–il, réussi son examen
'Mary passed her exam, I hear':
assertion: 'Mary passed her exam'
implicature: 'I heard that Mary passed her exam'

The problem with Grice's approach is that implicatures are mostly described in a negative way (as 'non–assertions'). In this respect, their contribution to the sentence meaning remains somewhat obscure. How is it, for instance, that one cannot deny implicatures? After all, if they simply had a different content from assertions, one could deny this content.[7]

Grice was actually aware of the problem (Grice, 1989, chap. 5). He proposes that conventional implicatures are associated with non–central speech acts which rely on the execution of other, more central ones. For instance, the act of adding (e.g. associated with 'moreover') only makes sense if there are two assertions ('A moreover B' supposes 'A' and 'B'). Grice notes that the dependence of the non–central speech act $X$ upon the central one(s) should be described in a way that accounts for the impossibility of using $X$ for 'saying' something. One must also keep in mind that the central ingredient in Grice's analysis of linguistic meaning is intention. Roughly speaking, by asserting that $\phi$ the speaker $a$ intends to make the hearer believe that $\phi$ and believe that $a$ believes $\phi$ through the identification of this very intention. We ignore the type of circularity involved in this definition (see Barwise and Moss (1996) on this topic), but we retain the idea of an intentional pro-

[6] Generally speaking, recent literature on presuppositions (Beaver, 2001; Geurts, 1999) shows that attempts to put presuppositions and implicatures on a par (Gazdar, 1979; Karttunen and Peters, 1979) are misguided.

[7] Rouchota's 1998 and Asher's 2000 skepticism as to the standard Gricean approach stems partly from the fact that Grice did not really provide an account of conventional implicatures.

cess. Together, intentionality and non–centrality suggest the following picture. The information communicated by a speaker $a$ is partitioned into:

1. what is said (= asserted), that is, what the speaker intends to be added to the common ground, and

2. what is conventionally implied, that is, what the speaker intends to be added to the hearers' beliefs with respect to what the speaker believes.

Note that, in the second case, the speaker certainly intends in certain cases to convince the hearers that the implicature is true. But this would be achieved in an indirect way, through the fact that the hearers espouse the speaker's belief because they trust her. To paraphrase what Stalnaker (1973) observed for presuppositions in such cases, the speaker 'may want to communicate a proposition indirectly'. We then distinguish between the following two kinds of effect for an assertive speech act.

**Definition 1** Let $A$ be an assertive speech act whereby $a$ asserts that $\phi$ and conventionally implicates that $\psi$ in the presence of $b$, then the effect of $A$ on $b$ includes at least the two following updates:
1. If $b$ trusts $a$ on $\phi$, she updates her belief state with $\phi$ and with the proposition that $a$ believes $\phi$,
2. if $b$ trusts $a$ on $\psi$, she updates her belief state with the proposition that $a$ believes $\psi$.
The update in (1) is the *intended effect* of the speech act $A$.

How can we account for the behavior of denials like *C'est faux* 'It's false' ? Adjectives like *true* 'true' and *faux* 'false' select for propositional entities. So, in themselves, they cannot tell apart asserted and implied propositions. This suggests that it is the demonstrative pronoun *c'* 'this, that' that selects the asserted proposition. This is confirmed by the fact that, with other adjectives, the same effect obtains.

(13) A – Jean a raté son examen, il paraît
'John failed his exam, I hear'
B – C'est malheureux / étonnant
'It's unfortunate / surprising'
= 'It is unfortunate / surprising that John failed his exam'

More generally, it seems that anaphors on non–asserted material are impossible or marginal. This is evidenced by anaphoric pronouns and by the *linking law* of Ducrot (1972),[8] which says that discourse markers cannot exploit presupposed material.

(14) a. Jean a raté son examen, il paraît. Je m'y attendais
'John failed his exam, I hear. I expected that'
= 'I expected that he would fail his exam'
≠ 'I expected that I would hear that he failed his exam'

b. Jean a cessé de fumer. ??Pourtant, il connaissait les risques
'John stopped smoking. Yet he was aware of the risks'
≠ 'John was smoking, yet he was aware of the risks'

In (14a), the clitic pronoun *y* cannot refer to the reportive modality. In (14b), the oppositive discourse marker cannot refer to the presupposition that John has been smoking for some time.

Summarizing, our proposal amounts to keeping the truth–conditional and the epistemic status of implicatures separate. Being propositions, implicatures can correspond (or not) to the facts. Then, they are truth–conditional, and we agree with Asher (2000) on this point. Moreover, implicatures are 'dynamic', that is, they can be added to the belief states of the discourse participants. In these two respects, implied propositions do not differ from asserted propositions. However, in contrast to asserted propositions, implied propositions are not added to the common ground. So, although they are dynamic, their epistemic *locus* is different, as evidenced by the impossibility of referring to them through anaphoric markers (pronouns, discourse markers).

## 3.3 Problems with standard dynamic semantics

Following Stalnaker (1978) and Veltman (1996) in particular, we model assertions as information updates. Given a set of epistemic alternatives for an agent $a$, an assertion that $\phi$ may lead $a$ to eliminate the alternatives that are not consistent with $\phi$. Such approaches are not entirely appropriate to our goals for two reasons. First, they are not concerned with embedded belief, making it difficult to represent what agents believe about others' beliefs. We will take this aspect into account by using a multiagent representation system.

Second, they do not make room for *modal* updates. Consider Veltman's approach. An agent believes that $\phi$ iff $\phi$ is true in every epistemic alternative available to the agent. In contrast to 'ordinary' propositions, which give rise to eliminative updates, modal propositions such as $Might\ \phi$ are static. At a given information state, they are simply

[8] *Loi d'enchaînement* in French. We assume here that presuppositions are not asserted and that apparent evidence to the contrary can be disposed of along the lines of Von Fintel (2001).

true or false. $Might\phi$ is true at $S$ iff $\phi$ is true in at least one $s \in S$. The update of $S$ with $Might\phi$ succeeds if $Might\phi$ is true at $S$. Otherwise, it 'fails', that is, it produces the absurd information state $\emptyset$. However, updates triggered by modal sentences are intuitively perceived as adding information, and are thereby not reducible to formula testing. For instance, in (15), a possible interpretation is that the speaker, having learned that John's decision has not been approved by the committee, updates her information state with the proposition that John will *probably* resign.

(15) La décision de Jean n'a pas été approuvée par le comité ? Alors, il va probablement démissionner
'John's decision has not been approved by the committee? Then, he is probably going to resign'

We noted in the introduction that parentheticals qualify assertions. In other terms, they somehow *affect* the content with which the discourse is updated. For instance, in (16b), the update concerns what is said, i.e. the proposition that John has resigned; however, there is a strong feeling that what is said in (16b) is, in some sense, weaker than what is said in (16a), where there is no qualification by *paraît–il.*

(16) La décision de Jean n'a pas été approuvée,
'John's decision has not been approved,'

a. donc il a démissionné
'so he resigned'

b. donc il a, paraît–il, démissionné
'so he resigned, I hear'

### 3.4 Extending the standard semantics

We extend update–based approaches in two directions. First, we consider sets of agents communicating their belief states to each other. This can be done in multiagent dynamic epistemic logic, e.g. Gerbrandy (1998) or Van Ditmarsch (2002). Second, to cope with modal updates, we admit partiality in the semantics. In ordinary possible worlds, every proposition is either true or false. We let partiality in through undetermined propositions. For space reasons, we will consider only a simplified version of Gerbrandy (1998) approach, based on finite *possibilities.*

**Definition 2 Possibilities**
Let $\mathcal{P}$ be a set of propositions, $\mathcal{A}$ a finite set of agents ($a$, $b$, etc.) and $\mathcal{M}$ a finite set of unary modal operators. A *possibility* based on $\mathcal{P}$ and $\mathcal{A}$ is a function $\pi$ which assigns to each proposition of $\mathcal{P}$ one of the values 0, 1, or ? and to each pair $\langle x, M_i \rangle$, with $x \in \mathcal{A}$ and $M_i \in \mathcal{M}$, a

set of possibilities, called an *information state* or i.s. ($s$, $s'$, etc.). We define $\amalg$ to be the following special ('undefined') possibility: $\amalg(p) = ?$ for every $p \in \mathcal{P}$, $\amalg(\langle x, M_i \rangle) = \{\amalg\}$ for every $\langle x, M_i \rangle$. $\pi \upharpoonright \mathcal{P}$ is the *root* of $\pi$.

$\amalg$ is used to stop possibility expansion. A 'preterminal'[9] possibility $\pi$ returns $\amalg$ for any $\langle x, M_i \rangle$ argument. Preterminal possibilities 'measure' the introspective power of agents. The undefined possibility makes every formula undefined ($\amalg \models^{?} \phi$ for every $\phi$). To simplify the semantic definition of truth and the definition of updates, we consider only *normal* possibilities, that is, possibilities where no i.s. contains $\amalg$, except, possibly, for the 'terminal' i.s. $\{\amalg\}$.

**Definition 3** A possibility $\pi$ is *normal* iff it contains no subpossibility $\pi'$ such that $\pi'(\langle x, M_i \rangle) = s$, $\amalg \in s$ and $s \neq \{\amalg\}$, for some $\langle x, M_i \rangle$.

A possibility $\pi$ is *limited* if it ends in $\amalg$ 'everywhere'. A limited possibility is pictured in figure 1 below.

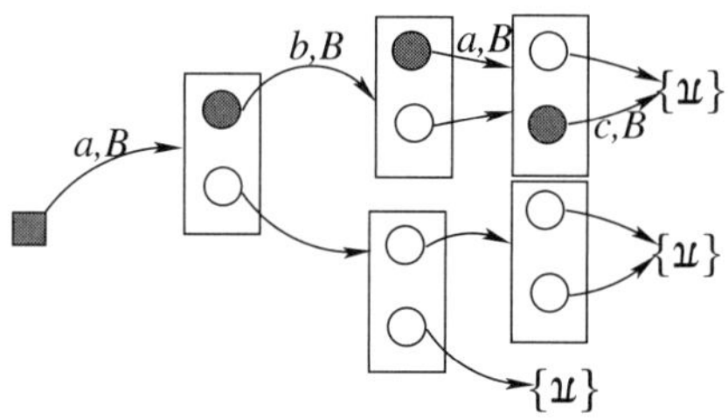


FIGURE 1 A limited normal possibility

More technically, consider the possibility $\pi$; all its branches are streams of the form $\langle r, \pi_1, \pi_2, \ldots \rangle$, where $r$ is the root of $\pi$, $\pi_1$ is one of the possibilities of $\pi(\langle x, M_i \rangle)$, for some $x \in \mathcal{A}$ and some $M_i \in \mathcal{M}$, $\pi_2$ is one of the possibilities in $\pi_1(\langle y, M_j \rangle)$ for some $y$ and some $M_j$, etc. In figure 1, the grey square (the root) and circles determine a branch. A possibility is *limited* when all its branches are of the form $\langle r, \pi_1, \ldots, \pi_n, \amalg, \amalg, \ldots \rangle$, that is when every branch has a finite head before the infinite subbranch $\langle \amalg, \amalg, \ldots \rangle$. Labelled branches are the streams of the form:
$\langle r, \langle x_1, M_1 \rangle, \pi_1, \langle x_2, M_2 \rangle, \pi_2, \ldots, \langle x_n, M_n \rangle, \amalg, \langle x_{n+1}, M_{n+1} \rangle, \amalg, \ldots \rangle$.
They correspond to all the paths in the possibility with agent–operator pairs as labels. In figure 1, the grey square and circles connected by the arrows correspond to the labelled branch $\langle r, \langle a, B \rangle, \pi_1, \langle b, B \rangle, \pi_2, \langle a, B \rangle, \pi_3,$

[9] 'Preterminal' and 'terminal' are used metaphorically. Actually, the 'terminal' $\amalg$ cycles infinitely into itself.

$\langle c, B\rangle, \bot\!\!\!\bot, \ldots\rangle$. In order to be able to use standard recursion instead of corecursion (Barwise and Moss, 1996), we consider only limited normal possibilities. To define updates, we need the notion of truth at a possibility. We assume the standard definitions of truth for partial modal logic (Jaspars and Thijsse, 1996).

**Definition 4 Semantics for possibilities**
Let $\phi$ be a formula; $\bot\!\!\!\bot \stackrel{?}{\models} \phi$; $\phi$ is true, false or undefined at $\pi \neq \bot\!\!\!\bot$, in symbols $\pi \models \phi$, $\pi \mathrel{=\!\!|} \phi$, $\pi \stackrel{?}{\models} \phi$ iff:

1. The main connective/operator of $\phi$ is non–modal and the truth–values of the subformulas in $\phi$ given by $\pi$ obey the standard definition for partial logic.[10]
2. $\pi \models (\mathrel{=\!\!|})\Box_a\psi$ iff $\pi' \models \psi$ for every $\pi' \in \pi(\langle\Box, a\rangle)$ ($\pi' \mathrel{=\!\!|} \psi$ for some $\pi' \in \pi(\langle\Box, a\rangle)$).
3. $\pi \models (\mathrel{=\!\!|})\Diamond_a\psi$ iff $\pi' \models \psi$ for some $\pi' \in \pi(\langle\Diamond, a\rangle)$ ($\pi' \mathrel{=\!\!|} \psi$ for every $\pi' \in \pi(\langle\Diamond, a\rangle)$).

Our next task is to define updates. Since possibilities admit of indetermination ($\stackrel{?}{\models}$), adding the information that $\phi$ may suppress some indetermination but is not deterministic in the general case; hence the following definition for possibilities.

**Definition 5 Updates**
A. If $\pi \models \phi$, $\pi \dot{+} \phi = \{\pi\}$. If $\pi \stackrel{?}{\models} \phi$, $\pi \dot{+} \phi$ is the set such that $\pi' \in \pi \dot{+} \phi$ iff:

1. if $\pi \models \psi$, $\pi' \models \psi$ for any $\psi$,
2. if $\pi \mathrel{=\!\!|} \psi$, $\pi' \mathrel{=\!\!|} \psi$ for any $\psi$,
3. if $\phi = \psi \,\&\, \chi$, $\pi' \in (\pi \dot{+} \psi) \dot{+} \chi$,
4. if $\phi = \psi \vee \chi$, $\pi' \in \pi \dot{+} \psi$, or $\pi' \in \pi \dot{+} \chi$, or $\pi' \in (\pi \dot{+} \psi) \dot{+} \chi$,
5. if $\phi = \neg\psi$, $\pi' \in \pi \dot{+} \psi^{\neg}$, where $\psi^{\neg}$ is the result of pushing $\neg$ one step inward (i.e. $(\psi_1 \,\&\, \psi_2)^{\neg} = \neg\psi_1 \vee \neg\psi_2$, etc.),
6. if $\phi = \Box_a\psi$, $\forall\pi'' \in \pi(\langle\Box, a\rangle)(\pi'(\langle\Box, a\rangle) \in \pi'' \dot{+} \psi)$,
7. if $\phi = \Diamond_a\psi$, $\exists\pi'' \in \pi(\langle\Box, a\rangle)(\pi'(\langle\Box, a\rangle) \in \pi'' \dot{+} \psi)$,
8. $\pi'$ does not differ from $\pi$ except as a consequence of applying 3, 4, 5, 6, 7.

B. If $\Pi$ is a set of possibilities, $\Pi \dot{+} \phi$ is $\{\pi' \mid \pi' \in \pi \dot{+} \phi \text{ for some } \pi \in \Pi\}$.

For instance, if every $\pi''$ in $\pi(\langle\Diamond, a\rangle)$ $\stackrel{?}{\models} \phi$, every $\pi'$ is such that some possibility in $\pi'(\langle\Diamond, a\rangle)$ is a member of $\pi'' \dot{+} \phi$ for some $\pi''$. We are

---

[10] E.g., $\pi \stackrel{?}{\models} A \vee B$ iff $\pi \stackrel{?}{\models} A$ and $\pi \stackrel{?}{\models} B$, etc. As usual, $\pi \stackrel{?}{\models} \phi$ iff $\pi \not\models \phi$ and $\pi \not\mathrel{=\!\!|} \phi$. This extends to modal formulas.

specifically interested in belief updates, where the intended effect of asserting $\phi$ is that every agent believes $\phi$, or equivalently that the i.s. at $\pi(\langle x, B\rangle)$ satisfies $\phi$ for any $x \in \mathcal{A}$. It is also common knowledge that every agent believes that every other agent believes that $\phi$. Therefore, for any $x$ and $y$ in the set of agents, any $\langle x, B\rangle$ link from a possibility in $\pi(\langle y, B\rangle)$ leads to a state where $\phi$ holds. We ignore updates that go beyond the introspective power of agents. In practice, this means that we update the initial possibility with every expression of the form $B_{x_1} B_{x_2} \ldots B_{x_n} \phi$ that does not force us to update the $\langle \perp\!\!\!\perp, \perp\!\!\!\perp, \ldots\rangle$ sub-branches. For instance, in figure 1, we will not update with $B_a B_b B_a B_c \phi$ because this would force us to update $\{\perp\!\!\!\perp\}$. Analogously, we will not update with $B_a(W_a W_b B_b)$, where $\phi$ is the modal expression $W_a W_b B_b$. This shows that, if $\phi$ is sufficiently complex, any update will be impossible, unless we increase the introspective power of agents.

**Definition 6 Belief updates**
The multiagent *assertive* belief update of $\pi$ with $\phi$, in symbols $\pi \oplus \phi$ is the set $(\ldots(\pi \dot{+} \beta_1) \dot{+} \ldots) \dot{+} \beta_k$ where the $\beta_i$'s are all the expressions of the form $B_{x_1} \ldots B_{x_m} \phi$ such that updating $\pi$ with them does not force us to update $\perp\!\!\!\perp$.

Since $\mathcal{A}$ and $\mathcal{M}$ are finite, the set of $\beta_i$'s is finite too. Common belief updates correspond to assertions. Note that, in (6), we have disregarded the possibility that an agent may be insincere and does not update her own information states with $\phi$. Should this be taken into account, we would modify definition (6) by excluding all branches $B_a \phi$, $B_a B_a \phi$, that is $(B_a)^n \phi$ from the update procedure.

For implicatures, we need updates that do not apply to the hearers. For instance, for two agents $a$ and $b$, if $a$ implies that $\phi$, the only directly intended effect is that $b$ believes that $a$ believes $\phi$, not that $b$ himself believes $\phi$. We use a definition parallel to (6), except for the fact that the belief expressions all end with $B_a \phi$. The non–sincerity of $a$ may be mimicked by excluding $(B_a)^n \phi$ branches, as in the previous case.

**Definition 7** The multiagent $a$–centered implicative belief update of $\pi$ with $\phi$, in symbols $\pi \oplus_a \phi$ is the set $(\ldots(\pi \dot{+} \beta_1) \dot{+} \ldots) \dot{+} \beta_k$ where the $\beta_i$'s are all the expressions of the form $B_{x_1} \ldots B_{x_m} B_a \phi$ such that updating with them does not force us to update $\perp\!\!\!\perp$.

Modal adverbs such as *probablement* 'probably' give rise to assertive modal updates of the form $\pi \dot{+} Prob\ \phi$. Parentheticals behave differently. They give rise to two updates. The implicature they convey enters a speaker–centered implicative belief update (def. 7). The assertion they qualify enters an assertive belief update (def. 6). However, in contrast to non–qualified assertions, the asserted content is modalized in a way that reflects the hedging profile of the parenthetical. For instance, $\phi$, *paraît–il* 'I hear' gives rise to an implicative update with the proposition that the speaker heard that $\phi$ and to an assertive update with the (modal) proposition that is true only in these worlds where what the speaker heard about $\phi$ is true. More generally,

**Definition 8** If $a$ reports that $\phi$ from the source $\sigma$, the modal formula $AGR_{\sigma}\phi$ ('$\phi$ if one agrees with $\sigma$') is true at $\pi$ iff $\phi$ is true everywhere at $\pi(\langle\sigma, AGR\rangle)$, which corresponds to the worlds where what $\sigma$ says about $\phi$ is true.

When the speaker uses *paraît–il* or *d'après* X 'according to X', she triggers an assertive update with $AGR_{\sigma}\ \phi$ or $AGR_{\mathrm{X}}\ \phi$, $\sigma$ being an unknown source of information.

## 4 Conclusion

In this chapter, we have considered the status of parentheticals that qualify assertions, contrasting them with modal adverbs. We have argued that they are not part of what is said and that they trigger conventional implicatures *à la* Grice. We have proposed to represent such implicatures as updates of the mutual information that concerns the hearer's beliefs and have shown how this can be done in a finitist version of Gerbrandy's theory of possibilities. However, we have also taken into account the fact that, as qualifiers of assertions, such parentheticals contribute to the update of the common ground in a specific way. The distinction between the propositional content of an epistemic update and its *locus* allows us to make room for different dimensions of update and to solve the Gricean problem of non–central speech acts.

## References

Asher, N. 1993. *Reference to Abstract Objects in Discourse.* Dordrecht: Kluwer.

Asher, N. 2000. Truth conditional discourse semantics for parentheticals. *Journal of Semantics* 17:31–50.

Asher, N. and A. Lascarides. 1998. The semantics and pragmatics of presupposition. *Journal of Semantics* 15:239–299.

Bach, K. 1994. Conversational implicature. *Mind and Language* 9:124–162.

Bartsch, R. 1975. *Adverbial Semantics. The Grammar of Adverbials.* Amsterdam: North–Holland.

Barwise, J. and L. Moss. 1996. *Vicious Circles.* Stanford: CSLI Publications.

Beaver, D. 2001. *Presupposition and Assertion in Dynamic Semantics.* Stanford and Amsterdam: CLSI Publications and FoLLI.

Bezuidenhout, A. and M. Reimer, eds. 2001. *Descriptions and Beyond*. Oxford: Oxford University Press. To appear.

Borillo, A. 1976. Structure et valeur de l'interrogation totale en français. Thèse d'état, Université de Toulouse–Le–Mirail.

Cole, P., ed. 1978. *Pragmatics*, vol. 9 of *Syntax and Semantics*. London: Academic Press. Also in (Stalnaker 1999), chapter 4.

Doherry, P., ed. 1996. *Partiality, Modality and Nonmonotonicity*. CSLI Publications.

Ducrot, O. 1972. *Dire et Ne Pas Dire*. Paris: Hermann.

Ferrari, A. 1995. *Connessioni. Uno Studio Integrato della Subordinazione Avverbiale*. Geneva: Slatkine.

Gabbay, D. and F. Hunter, eds. 1989. *Handbook of Philosophical Logic*, vol. IV. Dordrecht: Reidel.

Gazdar, G. 1979. *Pragmatics: Implicature, Presupposition and Logical Form*. New York: Academic Press.

Gerbrandy, J. 1998. *Bisimulations on Planet Kripke*. Ph.D. thesis, ILLC, University of Amsterdam.

Geurts, B. 1999. *Presuppositions and Pronouns*. Amsterdam: Elsevier.

Grice, H. P. 1989. *Studies in the Way of Words*. Harvard: Harvard University Press.

Ifantidou, E. 1994. *Evidentials and Relevance*. Ph.D. thesis, University College London.

Jaspars, J. and E. Thijsse. 1996. Fundamentals of partial modal logic. In Doherry (1996), pages 111–141.

Jucker, A. H. and Y. Ziv, eds. 1998. *Discourse Markers. Description and Theory*. Amsterdam: John Benjamins.

Karttunen, L. and S. Peters. 1979. Conventional implicature. In *Presupposition*, vol. 11 of *Syntax and Semantics*, pages 1–56. New York: Academic Press.

Lascarides, A. and N. Asher. 1993. Temporal interpretation, discourse relations and commonsense entailment. *Linguistics and Philosophy* 16:437–493.

Mann, W. and S. Thompson. 1988. Rhetorical structure theory: Toward a functional theory of text organization. *Text* 8:234–281.

Marandin, J.-M. 1998. Grammaire de l'incidence. URA 1024 CNRS and UNiversity of Paris 7.

Molinier, C. and F. Lévrier. 2000. *Grammaire des adverbes. Description des formes en* –ment. Geneva: Droz.

Munitz, M. and P. Unger, eds. 1973. *Semantics and Philosophy*. New York: New York University Press. Also in (Stalnaker 1999), chapter 2.

Rossari, C. 2002. L'expression des attitudes et les opérateurs de cause. In Somolinos (2002). To appear in a special issue of *Theleme*.

Rouchota, V. 1998. Procedural meaning and parenthetical discourse markers. In Jucker and Ziv (1998), pages 97–126.

Sanders, T. J., W. P. Spooren, and L. G. Noordman. 1992. Toward a taxonomy of coherence relations. *Discourse Processes* 15:1–35.

Searle, J. 1969. *Speech Acts*. Cambridge: Cambridge University Press.

Soames, S. 1989. Presupposition. In Gabbay and Hunter (1989), pages 553–616.

Somolinos, A. R., ed. 2002. *Des mots au discours: études de linguistique française*. Madrid: Editorial Complutense. To appear in a special issue of *Theleme.*

Stalnaker, R. 1973. Pragmatic presuppositions. In Munitz and Unger (1973), pages 197–214. Also in (Stalnaker 1999), chapter 2.

Stalnaker, R. 1978. Assertion. In Cole (1978). Also in (Stalnaker 1999), chapter 4.

Stalnaker, R. 1998. *Context and Content*. Oxford: Oxford University Press.

Stalnaker, R. 1999. *Context and Content. Essays on Intentionality in Speech and Thought*. Oxford: Clarendon Press.

Van Ditmarsch, H. 2002. Description of game actions. *Journal of Logic, Language and Information* 11:349–365.

Veltman, F. 1996. Defaults in update semantics. *Journal of Philosophical Logic* 25:221–261.

Von Fintel, K. 2001. Would you believe it? The king of France is back (Presuppositions and truth–value intuitions). In Bezuidenhout and Reimer (2001). To appear.

Wilson, D. 1975. *Presuppositions and Non Truth–Conditional Semantics*. New York: Academic Press.

# Part III

# Tense and Aspect

14

# Tense and Aspect in Sentences

Henk Verkuyl, Co Vet, Andrée Borillo, Myriam Bras, Anne Le Draoulec, Arie Molendijk, Henriëtte de Swart, Carl Vetters, and Laure Vieu

## 1 Introduction

In this chapter, we introduce the notions that are necessary to understand the organization of temporal information expressed by sentences in natural language, in particular French. We separate the notion of tense from some aspectual notions which are captured under the general label of *aspectuality*. We show that to understand the intricacies of the French tense system one should distinguish between two sorts of aspectual information, namely predicational aspect and grammatical aspect. The former has to do with how a predication provides information about the way an eventuality is construed, while the latter receives an intermediate position between tense and predicational aspect.

Sentences like (1a) are generally understood as pertaining to an eventuality located in the past of the utterance time of the sentence and sentences like (2a) as locating the same eventuality in the future.

(1) a. Chantal écrivit une lettre.
'Chantal wrote a letter.'
b. PS(Chantal écrire une lettre)

(2) a. Chantal écrira une lettre.
'Chantal will write a letter.'
b. FUT(Chantal écrire une lettre)

The positioning of the eventuality in time is attributed to the pres-

*Handbook of French Semantics.*
Francis Corblin and Henriëtte de Swart (eds.).
Copyright © 2004, CSLI Publications.

ence of tense. Both sentences provide information about the temporal position of the eventuality as related to the point of speech or to some other point of time with respect to which Chantal's writing is in the past or in the future. For obtaining this, one may use the Passé Simple in (1a) and the Futur Simple in (2a).

One way of accounting for this is to treat tense as an operator taking a tenseless sentence in order to speak about what (1a) and (2a) have in common. An appropriate metaphor is to compare the tenseless part of (1b) and (2b) with a part of a musical score and the tense operators as bringing about the performance of it in real time. The tenseless part will be interpreted as referring to an abstract semantic object which by tense is mapped onto the real time axis providing it with a location that plays a role in the discourse of which (1a) or (2a) is a part.[1] After all, Chantal will have written more than one letter in her life, so what she did if sentence (1) is true, may be repeated if (2) will become true. The tenseless part of (1b) and (2b) will be central in the present section, in § 3 the tense operators will be discussed in detail.

The notion of location in the past does not suffice because sentence (3a) with the Imparfait, and (3b), with the Passé Composé, also locate the eventualities in the past, whereas (4) provides another way of talking about the future occurrence of the eventuality by using the Futur Périphrastique.

(3) a. Chantal écrivait une lettre.
'Chantal was writing a letter.'

b. Chantal a écrit une lettre.
'Chantal has written/wrote a letter.'

(4) Chantal va écrire une lettre.
'Chantal is going to write a letter.'

So, additional tools are necessary to distinguish between the three past tense forms and the two future tense forms. This is precisely the point where the notion of aspectuality may help.

## 2 Aspectuality

### 2.1 Introduction

Central to the notion of aspectuality is the notion of completion, irrespective of the location of an eventuality (cf. (Comrie, 1976, 18ff).)

[1]By speaking of real time we do not take the realist position in the philosophical discussion between realists and nominalists. For us the real time of (1a) is the time in which Chantal made the event happen, a time that can be related to some other reference point from which the existence of the event can be taken for granted.

Here we show that there are three ways in which this notion can be understood. The first one is visible if we say at time $t$ that an eventuality $e$ is in the past of $t$, so that at $t$ it is "behind us": no part of $e$ takes place at $t$. In this case $e$ is completed with respect to $t$. This sense of completion is not applicable to eventualities in the present or future of $t$. The second way of interpreting the notion of completion is tied to the difference between the Imparfait as used in (5a) and the Passé Simple as applied in (5a).

(5) a. Pierre entra. Chantal rangeait ses papiers.
'Pierre entered (PS). Chantal ordered (IMP) (= was ordering) her papers.'

b. Pierre entra. Chantal rangea ses papiers.
'Pierre entered (PS). Chantal ordered (PS) her papers.'

The former locates the entering somewhere in the middle of Chantal's ordering her papers, whereas the latter locates the ordering after Pierre's entering. Here it is not unreasonable to associate the Imparfait with a notion of presenting an eventuality as incompleted (at the time) and the Passé Simple with the notion of presenting an eventuality as completed. The third way to understand completion concerns the constituency of an eventuality itself: there is a clear difference, for example between sleeping and discovering a treasure, in the sense that one can easily speak of an eternal sleep, whereas discovering a treasure is somehow inherently associated with the sense of completion. As we shall point out, it is possible to tell the three notions apart.

The need to make a distinction between the different sorts of completion inevitably leads to extending the scope of our analysis so as to include the Russian sentences in (6), which show a well-known opposition between the so-called imperfective and perfective aspect, which cannot be ignored in the discussion about the French Imparfait and the Passé Simple.

(6) a. Chantal pisala pismo.
Chantal imp-write letter
'Chantal was writing/wrote at a/the letter.'

b. Chantal napisala pismo.
Chantal pf-write letter
'Chantal wrote a/the letter.'

Sentence (6a) is said to present Chantal in a past situation in which she was writing a or the letter, but it may also be used to express more generally that she had the intention to do so. Sentence (6b) clearly pertains to a unique event that took place sometime in the past resulting in a letter that was completed.

In the long tradition in which aspect has been studied, scholars have always associated Russian aspect with the notion of viewpoint.[2] Yet, it has become customary to analyze sentences like (6) semantically in two ways. Many scholars associate the presence of the perfective prefix in (6b) as the explicit introduction of a viewpoint outside the event described in the past, which contributes to the sense of completion. The absence of a perfective prefix in (6a) associates the verb form *pisala* with a point of view located inside an eventuality.

At the end of the nineteenth century a distinction emerged between grammatical aspect (= the viewpoint aspect just discussed) and lexical aspect, mostly called the Aktionsart of the verb. Verbs were said to express a sense of boundedness. For example, *pisat'* (write) in both (6a) and (6b) was taken as pertaining to some action that in itself is bounded, that is, by its own lexical meaning. This sense of lexical boundedness was said to be absent in verbs like *derzhat'* (hold), *véshat'* (hang), *nenavidet'* (hate), etc.

In Verkuyl (1972), it was argued that for the English glosses of the sentences in (6b) it does not make sense to assign the sense of boundedness to the verb *write*, because it is clear that the arguments of the verb should be involved: writing a letter may be considered as something inherently bounded but this is not the case for writing letters. In order to be able to speak about the contribution of the arguments of the predication to the interpretation of temporal structure, we will use the term *predicational aspect* for the information scattered around in the verb and its arguments in the English glosses of (6). The general idea, which also applies to French, is that whatever Aktionsart turns out to be, it does not make sense to treat it lexically. Verkuyl's (1972) central thesis was that the English tenseless sentence in the gloss of (6b) *Chantal write a letter* expresses boundedness due to the fact that *Chantal* and *a letter* pertain to bounded entities. Thus boundedness is taken as a property of a tenseless predication. It is the interplay between the temporal information provided by the verb and the arguments that makes the eventuality discernible so that it can be seen as a discrete unit distinguished from processes and states. The sense of boundedness is absent in *Chantal wrote letters* or *Nobody wrote a letter* even though the eventualities themselves are located in the past.

Given the correctness of a compositional view on the expression of boundedness, one could argue that the choice between saying the

[2]Even the term *vid* (aspect) in *vid sovershénn'iy* (completed aspect) and *vid nesovershénn'iy* (incompleted aspect) is derived from the Latin *videre* (see).

bounded *Chantal write some letters* and the unbounded *Chantal write letters* is a matter of viewpoint. Both predications may pertain to the very same situation and it may be argued that it is the speaker who, by the choice of the constituents, presents the tenseless sentence as bounded or unbounded. Which is to say that the choice of the speaker as to how to present the information is decisive for the choice of the elements making up predicational aspect compositionally.

The discussion about whether or not viewpoint aspect and predicational aspect can be identified is still going on in the literature.[3] In the present chapter, however, we will not identify viewpoint aspect and predicational aspect, because the French tense system is so rich that not all forms can be covered on the basis of temporal location alone. So, in our analysis we will work with the triple ⟨Tense, Grammatical Aspect, Predicational Aspect⟩ rather than with only the pair ⟨Tense, Aspect⟩. This enables us to have sufficient room to deal with factors that in some languages turn out to be neither tense nor predicational aspect in the sense just defined. As a consequence, we have room to analyze sentences like (3a) *Chantal écrivait une lettre* as in (7):

(7) PAST(ASP(Eventuality description))

where the aspectual operator ASP modifies the aspectual information as expressed by the eventuality description and where PAST is analyzed as the "pure" tense part of what is expressed by *-ait* locating the eventuality in the past at the moment of speech.

## 2.2 Aspectual tests and boundedness

There are well-established tests bringing out aspectual differences between sentences like (6a) and (6b). Consider the opposition in:

(8) a. Ivan pisal pismo čas
Ivan imp-write letter for an hour
'John was writing/wrote at a/the letter for an hour'

b. #Ivan napisal pismo čas
lit: #Jean wrote a/the letter for an hour

In (8a) the adverbial *čas* expressing a duration is compatible with the rest of the sentence. This is not the case in (8b). The #-sign says that the single event interpretation of the predication is blocked. If the sentences have an interpretation, then they express either a sort of

[3] Among those who deny the usefulness of a distinction between the two are Comrie (1976), Verkuyl (1972) and recently Kabakčiev (2000). Verkuyl (1972) turned it into a strategical point: deny the existence of the distinction until it can be shown to be useful. It is still debatable whether or not the distinction makes sense for Germanic languages.

forced repetition or stretching out of the process, which in French is visible in sentences like (9).

(9) #Jean a rempli la bouteille pendant une heure
#'John filled the bottle for an hour'

There is a complementary test given in (10).

(10) a. *Ivan pisal pismo za čas
lit: *John was writing/wrote at a letter in an hour
b. Ivan napisal pismo za čas
Ivan pf-write letter in an hour
'John wrote a letter in an hour'

The Russian (10a) and its English translation are not acceptable, whereas (10b) and its counterpart both express that it took an hour for John to write a letter.

The two tests reveal an interesting point. One has to establish whether the tests apply to grammatical aspect or to predicational aspect. In Germanic languages one could argue that the test is restricted to the latter. In Slavic such an argument is quite hard to establish. As we shall indicate below, for French the test is even more complicated because of the interaction between predicational aspect and grammatical aspect and grammatical aspect in a number of tense forms.

## 2.3 Predicational aspect

In Verkuyl (1993) an easy format was developed for describing the contribution of the elements of a predication to aspectual information. This scheme was applied to Germanic languages. It is exemplified in (11) with respect to French, where it also appears to hold.[4]

(11) a. Chantal écrire une lettre
'Chantal write a letter'
$[_{\text{NP}}\ +\text{SQA}] + [_{\text{VP}}\ [_{\text{V}}\ +\text{ADDTO}] + [_{\text{NP}}\ +\text{SQA}]] \Rightarrow$ terminative
b. Chantal écrire des lettres
'Chantal write letters'
$[_{\text{NP}}\ +\text{SQA}] + [_{\text{VP}}\ [_{\text{V}}\ +\text{ADDTO}] + [_{\text{NP}}\ -\text{SQA}]] \Rightarrow$ durative
c. Des retraités écrire une lettre
'Pensioned-off people write a letter'
$[_{\text{NP}}\ -\text{SQA}] + [_{\text{VP}}\ [_{\text{V}}\ +\text{ADDTO}] + [_{\text{NP}}\ +\text{SQA}]] \Rightarrow$ durative
d. Chantal tenir une lettre à la main
'Chantal hold a letter in her hand'

[4]Roughly, SQA assigned to an NP stands for 'Specified Quantity of A', where A is the denotation of the head noun; [+ADDTO] assigned to a V stands for the lexical property of nonstativity. The two notions will be discussed in more detail shortly.

$$[_{NP}\ +\text{SQA}] + [_{VP}\ [_{V}\ -\text{ADDTO}] + [_{NP}\ +\text{SQA}]] \Rightarrow \text{durative}$$

The general idea is that the "local" information of the verb, represented as [±ADDTO], and its arguments, represented by [±SQA], comes together at a higher phrase level: the VP and the S, where the complex features [+TERMINATIVE] or [-TERMINATIVE] are formed. We will use the pair *terminative* vs. *durative* for the binary aspectual opposition that arises at the level of the VP and the S. Another term for *terminative* is *telic* as opposed to *atelic*.

As pointed out in Verkuyl (1972):60, [±SQA] cannot be equated with the feature [±DEFINITE] because *une lettre* is [−DEFINITE] but [+SQA], whereas *the wine* in sentences like *She drank the wine (and not the beer)* is [+DEFINITE] but [−SQA] in the interpretation where *the wine* pertains to the whole category (cf. *The whole evening she drank the Bordeaux ignoring the beautiful Gigondas*). Of course, *She drank the wine* may pertain to a situation in which *the wine* refers to, say, a glass of wine and in that case the NP receives the feature [+SQA]. It can be predicted that on that interpretation *She drank that wine for hours* the sentence receives a #-sign blocking the single event reading. The essence of the SQA-notion is that the semantic object denoted by a [+SQA]-NP is discernible as a discrete object or portion of substance.

As to the feature [+ADDTO], it simply expresses nonstativity or dynamicity. The label has been chosen to express that the predication is structured in such a way that the verb and its internal argument provide so-called Path-information. The temporal information expressed by *écrire une lettre* can be conceived of as a process starting at some point zero (the beginning of the eventuality) which in the case of the presence of *une lettre* in (11a) develops in such a way that it terminates at the point at which the letter is finished. In the case of (11b) the [-SQA]-information provided by *des lettres* does not stop the process evoked by the verb and so the sentence is to be interpreted as durative: there is no way to delimit the dynamicity expressed by the verb. An aspectual "leakage" also occurs in (11c) where the plural *des retraités* prevents the NP from applying to a specified quantity. The resulting interpretation applies to something that used to be the case. In (11d), it is the stative verb *tenir* (hold) that causes the predication to become durative. A nonstative verb is taken as building temporal structure. The use of the label [+ADDTO] for nonstative verbs underscores that a Path is built up by information provided by the internal argument. We will come back to this point below.

The four logical possibilities of the feature system shown in (11) demonstrate the so-called Plus-Principle, which says that one minus-value suffices to make a sentence durative. It also expresses that terminativity is the marked case: all values need to have a plus-value in order to delimit an eventuality with respect to the rest of the world, to make it discernible as an entity.[5] The semantic feature system is just for convenience: all the values involved have a precise formal-semantic definition along the lines worked out above in explaining the interpretation of the two features involved. (cf. Verkuyl (1993))

The differences between durative and terminative predications show up in the comparison of sentences like (12).

(12) a. Chantal a écrit une lettre en quarante minutes.
'Chantal has written a letter in 40 minutes'

b. *Chantal a écrit des lettres en quarante minutes
lit: Chantal has written letters in 40 minutes

c. ??Chantal a tenu une lettre à la main en quarante minutes
lit: Chantal has held a letter in her hand in 40 minutes

Sentence (12a) says that it took Chantal forty minutes to accomplish her task. This interpretation is excluded in (12b) and (12c). In the same way the following three sentences show that the differences between (11a) and (11b-d) concern the predication itself rather than the viewpoint from which the eventuality is presented.

(13) a. #Chantal a écrit une lettre pendant quarante minutes
'Chantal has written a letter for 40 minutes.'

b. Chantal a écrit des lettres pendant quarante minutes
lit: Chantal has written letters for 40 minutes

c. Chantal a tenu une lettre à la main pendant quarante minutes
'Chantal has held a letter in her hand for 40 minutes'

Whereas (13b) reports on the activity of writing letters and (13c) on a certain state lasting forty minutes, (13a) cannot be interpreted "normally": one is forced to break away from the need to interpret the predication as pertaining to a bounded eventuality as in:

(14) ?Chantal a écrit une lettre pendant quarante minutes sans jamais la finir
lit: Chantal has written a letter for 40 minutes without ever finishing it

In this case *une lettre* cannot be interpreted as a [+SQA] because it does not refer to a discrete semantic object, as in the regular cases.

[5]Given the three features there are eight possible configurations. We leave out the four other durative constructions in which there are two or more minus-features.

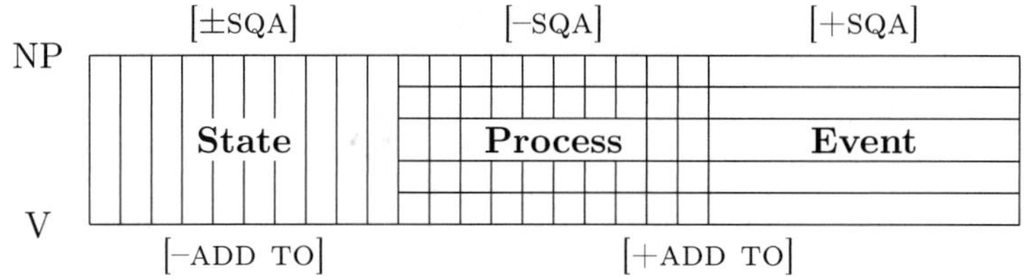


FIGURE 1 Construal of three aspectual classes

## 2.4 Aspectual classes

At this point we should say something more about aspectual classes. In the literature there are two main classifications, both based on Aristotle. The first one is due to Vendler (1957), who distinguishes between States, Activities, Accomplishments and Achievements. The second one emerged in the seventies and is harder to attribute to one person: it distinguishes between states, processes and events.[6] There is some overlap between the classifications. States occur in both, and Vendler's Activities are more or less the same as what Processes are in the second classification. The difference is found in Vendler's distinction between Accomplishments (roughly process+termination) and Achievements (point-events), which is not made in the other classification.

In Verkuyl (1993) it was shown that if one takes aspectual classes as being formed on the basis of the structural information conveyed by a sentence, the tripartition is predicted on the basis of the feature-system in (11) as shown by (15).

(15) a. Chantal manger un sandwich
'Chantal eat a sandwich'
$[_{\text{NP}}\ +\text{SQA}] + [_{\text{V}}\ +\text{ADDTO}] + [_{\text{NP}}\ +\text{SQA}] \Rightarrow$ event

b. Chantal manger du pain
'Chantal eat bread'
$[_{\text{NP}}\ +\text{SQA}] + [_{\text{V}}\ +\text{ADDTO}] + [_{\text{NP}}\ -\text{SQA}] \Rightarrow$ process

c. Chantal mastiquer son pain
'Chantal chew her bread'
$[_{\text{NP}}\ +\text{SQA}] + [_{\text{V}}\ -\text{ADDTO}] + [_{\text{NP}}\ +\text{SQA}] \Rightarrow$ state

It is easy to derive an ontological classification on the basis of this, as shown in Figure 1. It is important to underline that the point of departure for this ontological tripartition is to be found in the language: the information provided in a predication determines to which ontological class the speaker is committed to report on.

[6]Early references are Comrie (1976), Mourelatos (1978) and Bach (1986).

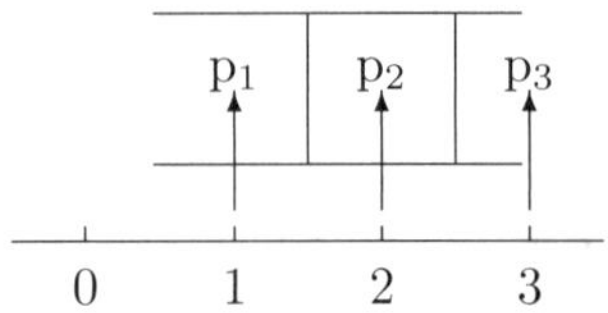


FIGURE 2 to order three pastis (successively)

Events are equated here with terminative semantic objects. The difference between Accomplishments and Achievements is not relevant for the sentences under consideration. Therefore, we will make use of the tripartition, because, in our view, it expresses a language filter on reality. A speaker has the choice between describing one and the same situation by (15a), (15b) and (15c). So our ontological claims with respect to the notion of aspectual class are minimal. What is maximal is that by using certain elements and organizing them properly into larger units a speaker is able to create referents for the discourse connected with the information as given. That is, after having said (15b) we dispose of information concerning a process, whereas after (15a) we have a potential discourse referent which is to be taken discretely.

## 2.5 Aspectual Structure and Predication

The combinatorial schemes in (15) express an asymmetry between the internal and the external argument. That is, the verb and its internal arguments have closer ties as far as temporal structure is concerned. This is particularly visible as soon as the internal argument is a plural NP. Consider the sentence in (16a).

(16) a. Riri a commandé trois pastis
'Riri ordered three pastis'

b. TENSE(Riri commander trois pastis)

As suggested above, the VP *commander trois pastis* of the tenseless sentence introduces a Path made up by the [+ADDTO]-information contributed by the Verb and by the complex [+SQA)]-information contributed by the NP *trois pastis*. Why complex? One answer is that (16) underinforms us as to what happened giving us a well-determined set of combinatorial possibilities one of which is given in Figure 2. This is the possibility compatible with the situation in which Riri ordered his pastis consecutively. The natural numbers at the bottom line are counting points dividing the set P of three pastis into three parts.

The dynamicity of the Verb is provided by the counting mechanism. Another way of speaking says that a nonstative verb is associated with

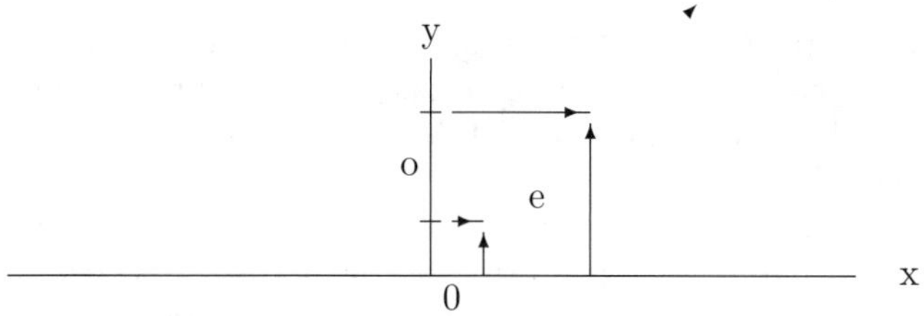


FIGURE 3 Temporalizing by mapping

**N**, the infinite set of natural numbers. So, if the verb is not restricted by its internal argument one may enumerate indefinitely. In this case, the counting comes to a stop because there is a specified quantity of pastis available for the values of the function connecting the verbal information with the NP-information. This makes the VP terminative. Now, Riri could have ordered the three pastis in a different way. Another way of putting this is to say that the predication was satisfied in a different way. We never know what happened unless we are informed later on in the discourse. Verkuyl (1993, 1999) presents a formal-semantic machinery covering the underdeterminedness expressed by (16).

In view of the discussions to follow in this part we now discuss (briefly) two views on predicational structure that are quite popular. Krifka's work (1987; 1989; 1998) is characterized by a mereological approach to temporal structure which boils down to taking *three pastis* in(16a) as a singular (complex) object, that is, as a complex individual. More concretely, Krifka generalizes over the sentences *Riri ordered a pastis* and *Riri ordered three pastis* by modelling the latter on the former. In his mereological approach Krifka (1989) projects the information of an NP on the y-axis of a cartesian product and the process side of the event on the horizontal x-axis. In this way one can register the development of an event from its origin to its culmination point. This is done in cases like *Riri drank a glass of wine*, *Riri ordered a pastis*, *Riri ordered pastis*, but also in *Riri ordered three pastis*, etc., because, as said, mereologically the plural NP *three pastis* is taken as an object.

An advantage of Krifka's mereological position over the Boolean position is that his mapping is more natural in sentences like *Riri drank a pastis.* Krifka's idea is that the process of drinking is related to emptying the glass with pastis. This mapping is what determines the coming into existence of an event, as illustrated in Figure 3. On the Boolean approach, this is not (yet) really possible for a single object: inspection has to go in one swoop, so to speak, because an individual is to be taken as a singleton, which is an indivisible unit. However, in the case of plural NPs the plural approach is more adequate because it takes into account the combinatorial possibilities that are available: it is really directed towards quantificational information as a means of shaping a discernible unit.

The second view is discussed here because it plays an important role in DRT. Kamp and Reyle borrow the structure of events from Moens and Steedman (1987), who introduce the scheme in Figure 4 as part of the ontology without tying the notion of culmination to the presence of specific information contributed by the NP. A lot of scholars find

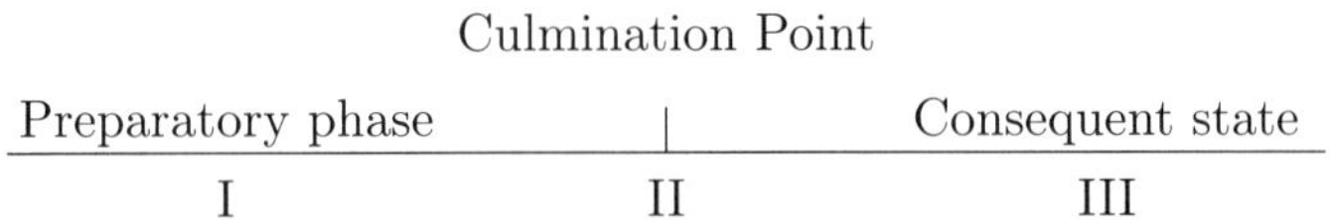


FIGURE 4 Phasal structure

this scheme attractive because it provides a way to distinguish the consequent state, which can be seen as a state resulting from the event itself. For example, Kamp and Reyle analyze sentences like (17) as in Figure 5.

(17) Mary has written the letter
[PRES[ PERF[Mary write the letter]]]

According to Kamp and Reyle, sentences in the Perfect are stative, so the Perfect could be taken as denoting a function PERF: $\mathcal{E} \rightarrow S$, mapping any kind of eventuality onto a state. In their view, the Perfect introduces the consequent state which starts when the eventuality ends. This is represented in Figure 5. The condition $e \supset\subset s$ ($e$ 'abuts' $s$)

n e s t x y

t = n
Mary(x)
the-letter(y)
s ∘ t
e ⊃⊂ s
e: [write(x,y)]

FIGURE 5 Mary has written the letter

means that the consequent state starts right at the end of the event. The consequent state provides the variable $t$ for the Present tense to operate on, because $s$ results from the application of PERF. If the resulting state $s$ holds now, one can be sure that the event $e$ took place in the past of the speech time, and so the consequent state has current relevance. It should be emphasized here that this analysis may hold for English, but not so much for the French Passé Composé, as we shall see shortly.

### 2.6 Conclusion

Tense, viewpoint aspect and predicational aspect are seen as three factors determining the temporal information expressed by sentences. The Verb as the main contributor to the predication needs information from its arguments to be able to express boundedness or unboundedness. This process of building up complex information can be separated from its location in the real time structure of the discourse of which the sentence in question is part. Tense is seen as providing information about the position of the eventuality with respect to other points that already have been identified, such as the point of speech or points introduced by eventualities. Viewpoint aspect can be seen as an instruction about the way the eventuality is to be located with respect to other points in the information structure developing in discourse.

## 3 Tense

### 3.1 Introduction

The notion of tense is not unequivocally defined. This makes it rather difficult to agree on elementary things such as the number of French indicative tenses. Practical grammars of French generally restrict themselves to the eight tense forms of Table 1, whereas (more) scientific grammars end up with a larger number.[7] The structure underlying Table 1 is clearly based on the opposition between simple forms and composed forms, which are tense forms containing the auxiliary verb *avoir* (have) or the auxiliary verb *être* (be).[8] The opposition between simple and composed is visible in the two columns of the matrix in Table 1. Its rows suggest a tripartition: Present, Past and Future. The Past is subdivided into two forms which are generally distinguished on the basis of an aspectual opposition.

Table 1 does not give a complete indicative tense system, because the verb *avoir* itself also has eight tense forms, some of which occur in the so-called overcomposed forms (formes surcomposées) in scientific

[7] *L'Art de conjuguer* (Didier Hatier), *Conjugaison* (Larousse), Le Robert Micro (Dictionnaires Robert) are instances of the first category; Grevisse (1964) and Riegel et al. (1994) are instances of the second.

[8] To keep our tables simple our examples are restricted to forms with *avoir*, but in the running text forms with *être* are also given.

| | Simple Form | Composed Form |
|---|---|---|
| Present | **Présent**<br>Elle dort | **Passé Composé**<br>Elle a dormi |
| Past1 | **Imparfait**<br>Elle dormait | **Plus-que-parfait**<br>Elle avait dormi |
| Past2 | **Passé Simple**<br>Elle dormit | **Passé Antérieur**<br>Elle eut dormi |
| Future | **Futur Simple**<br>Elle dormira | **Futur Antérieur**<br>Elle aura dormi |

TABLE 1 Tenses according to practical grammars

grammars. The tense forms in Table 1 are complemented by the forms *Elle a eu terminé* (lit: She has had finished) and *Elle avait eu terminé* (lit: she had had finished) as in (18).

(18) a. Quand il a eu terminé, il a bourré sa pipe
lit: When he has had finished, he has filled his pipe
b. Il a eu bourré sa pipe en un rien de temps
lit: He has had filled his pipe in less than no time
c. Quand il avait eu terminé, il avait bourré sa pipe
lit: When he has had finished, he had filled his pipe
d. Il avait eu bourré sa pipe en un rien de temps
lit: He had had filled his pipe in less than no time

The sentences (18a,b) exemplify the Passé Surcomposé, (18c,d) the Plus-que-Parfait Surcomposé. The overcomposed forms are used in spoken language and they are only possible in two sorts of contexts: in temporal clauses and in combination with adverbials denoting a very short period of time. There is a firm consensus on the marked status of the overcomposed forms—they appear under quite restricted conditions—but it should be added that this also holds for the Passé Antérieur, as shown in (19).[9]

(19) a. Quand il eut terminé, il bourra sa pipe
lit: When he had (PA) finished, he filled his pipe
b. Il eut bourré sa pipe en un rien de temps
lit: He had (PA) finished in less than no time

The Passé Simple is highly marked as well: it has been replaced or is in the process of being replaced by the Passé Composé in the oral and even in the written language. Its position is mainly maintained in

[9] As the gloss indicates, the *eut*-part of the Passé Antérieur is itself the Passé Simple of *avoir*.

written French. So, Table 1 seems to give a fairly adequate account of what people learning French need in the first place. The more complex tenses are relegated to the domain of scientific grammars.

Two other forms present themselves in French: *Elle va dormir* (lit: She goes sleep) and *Elle allait dormir* (lit: She went sleep). The tense forms with *aller* (go) are as composed as the *avoir*-forms. According to some scholars, they express (roughly) a more immediate future than the simple future forms, but as pointed out in Vet (1994) this position cannot be maintained (cf. Lorenz (1989a) and Lorenz (1989b) for some discussion). From the analytical point of view of the present chapter it would be wrong to ignore these forms for the simple reason that if one includes the *avoir*-forms, there is no argument to expel the forms with *aller*. These forms have undergone a grammaticalisation process: their use is restricted to the Present and Imparfait only.

A final preliminary remark should be made. The Futur du Passé *Elle dormirait* (She would sleep) and the Futur Antérieur du Passé *Elle aurait dormi* (She would have slept) are generally considered as conditional, non-indicative tense forms. In the practical grammars mentioned earlier they are put under the label of *Conditionnel*, as Conditionnel Présent and Conditionnel Passé. However, from the same analytical point of view just mentioned there is no reason to expel these forms from the indicative forms. On the contrary, as we will show, both the Futur du Passé and the Futur Antérieur du Passé play an important role in a system of oppositions underlying the French tense system. In fact, one could better argue against the usefulness of the term *indicative* than drop the two future anterior forms. Moreover, there are contexts in which it would be misleading to speak of a conditional, as in (20b).

(20) a. À huit heures, Pierre bourrera/aura bourré sa pipe
lit: At eight o'clock Pierre will/will have filled his pipe

b. Elle savait que, à huit heures, Pierre bourrerait/aurait bourré sa pipe
lit: She knew that at eight o'clock Pierre would/would have filled his pipe.

Comparing the interpretation of the forms in (20a) and (20b), we have no reason to locate the *bourrerait/aurait bourré*-forms outside the domain of the indicative tense and to put the *bourrera/aura bourré*-forms inside. The measure of uncertainty with respect to what Pierre planned to do is as great in (20a) as it is in (20b).

Given the richness of the French tense system it is necessary to see how it can be described systematically. In the next section, we will discuss some proposals that have been made.

### 3.2 Reichenbach's tense system

There is a widespread intuition that the time axis should be divided into Past, Present and Future and that an eventuality E reported by a sentence can be earlier, simultaneous or later with respect to the speech point S. A system expressing only this tripartition, as in Figure 6, would

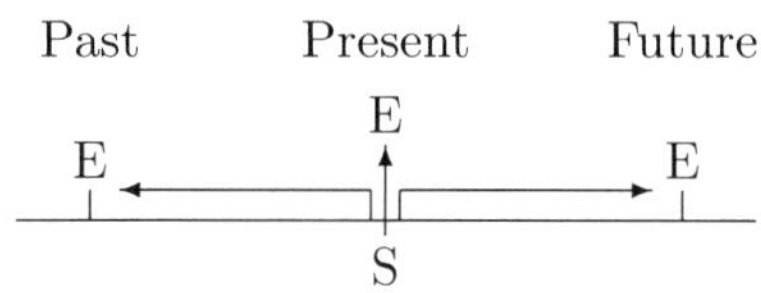


FIGURE 6 A tripartition

account for three relations between S and E: E < S for a Simple Past, e.g. *dormit* (slept), E = S for the Simple Present, e.g. *dort* (sleeps), and S < E for the Simple Future, e.g. *dormira* (will sleep).

However, French and many other languages express more complex relations, as we have illustrated above. To account for the richness of the Germanic and Romance languages, Reichenbach (1947) introduced an auxiliary orientation point R, which he used as an intermediate point of reference. Rather than having a direct relation between S and E, Reichenbach applied the above tripartition to the relation between S and R and on top of that he introduced a similar tripartition to account for the relation between E and R. Schematically this leads to temporal configurations like the ones in Figure 7. This insight gave rise

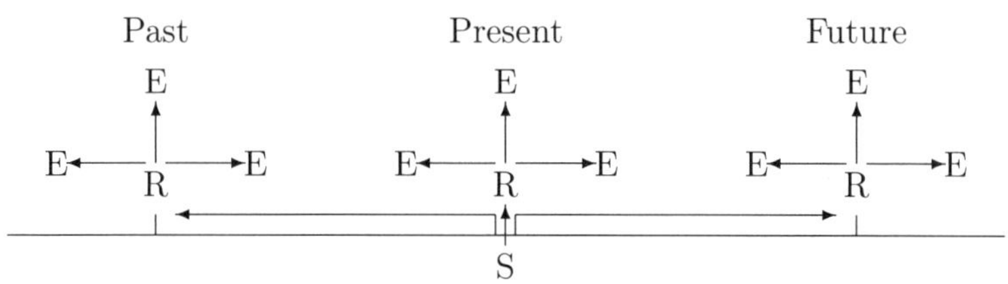


FIGURE 7 Nine configurations on the basis of two tripartitions

to a system with nine positions for tenses in a matrix shown in Table 2, in which we have put the French tense forms.[10]

We have given each of the nine cells a number in order to refer to individual cells. Reichenbach uses the term Simple in the Cells 4, 5

[10]At some point Reichenbach also discusses part of the French system, comparing it with the English system that he described.

| | Past<br>R – S | Present<br>R,S | Future<br>S – R |
|---|---|---|---|
| Anterior<br><br>E – R | 1. Anterior Past<br>(Past Perfect)<br>E – R – S<br><br><br>*avait dormi* | 2. Anterior Present<br>(Present Perfect)<br>E – R,S<br><br><br>*a dormi* | 3. Anterior Future<br>(Future Perfect)<br>E – S – R<br>E, S – R<br>S – E – R<br>*aura dormi* |
| Simple<br>E,R | 4. Simple Past<br>E,R – S<br>*dormit, dormait* | 5. Simple Present<br>E,R,S<br>*dort* | 6. Simple Future<br>S – R,E<br>*dormira* |
| Posterior<br><br>R – E | 7. Posterior Past<br><br>R – E – S<br>R – S,E<br>R – S – E<br>*dormirait,*<br>*allait dormir* | 8. Posterior Present<br>(Present Future)<br>S,R – E<br><br><br>*dormira,*<br>*va dormir* | 9. Posterior Future<br><br>S – R – E<br><br><br>**dormira*<br>**ira dormir* |

TABLE 2 Reichenbach's matrix for French tense forms

and 6 as expressing "coincidence of R and E" (p. 297). He observes that there is no traditional name for the Posterior Past (we would say Future in the Past) and for the Posterior Future.

Over de last few decades it has become clear that there are problems with the system in Table 2. The root of these problems appears to be the 3×3 set up of the system. The tenses of Germanic and Romance languages cannot be described correctly on the basis of the system demonstrated in Table 2. The use of auxiliary points like R, however, has turned out to be very fruitful and the general agreement nowadays is certainly that tenses involve some kind of auxiliary points in order to account for the structure they introduce.

### 3.3 Problems with Reichenbach's system

In spite of Reichenbach's innovative contribution to the discussion on tense systems, there are severe problems with his system. We will discuss them as far as they are relevant for the purpose of describing the French tense system and then discuss some systems that offer solutions.

**Problems with the Posterior Future.** The 3×3-system predicts the existence of a tense form in Cell 9 that is capable of expressing the configuration S – R – E as the exact mirror image of the Plus-que-Parfait in Cell 1 which expresses E – R – S. However, the tense form *dormira* does not express that configuration. Reichenbach not only fails to capture this empirical fact, he also predicts that there is a tense form that should express future posteriority.

The system is also unable to explain why a theoretically possible tense form in which the Futur Simple (FS) and the Futur Périphrastique (FP) are combined is unacceptable in French, as shown in (21c):

(21) a. Pierre va entrer dans sa chambre
Pierre goes enter (FP) his sleeping room
Pierre is going to/will enter his sleeping room

b. Pierre entrera dans sa chambre
Pierre will enter (FS) his sleeping room

c. *Pierre ira entrer dans sa chambre
lit: Pierre will go enter (FS+FP) his sleeping room

Reichenbach explained his system (mainly) with the help of the English tense forms using periphrastic forms for the future (*He will sleep*, *he would sleep*, etc.) and for the anterior forms (*He has slept*, *he had slept*, etc). So, there is no way to determine how he would handle a tense system distinguishing between periphrastic and non-periphrastic forms.

**The problem of allotopy** In Table 2, two tenses are associated with three configurations: the Anterior Future and the Posterior Past.[11] It is caused by the fact that in the 3×3-system S and E do not relate directly to one another. This means that in the Anterior Future where R is posterior to S, E may not only be located later than S, but also at S itself or before S. The same applies mutatis mutandis to the Posterior Past. Given the fact that the other seven tense cells in Table 2 have just one configuration, one could say that Reichenbach predicts that the Anterior Future and Posterior Past are three-way ambiguous. This is counterintuitive because the only meaning of the Futur du Passé is that R is anterior to S and that E is posterior to R, the relation between S and E being irrelevant, as shown by (22).

(22) Pierre avait dit qu'il terminerait son travail le 20 mars.
'Pierre had said that he would finish (FDP) his work the 20th of March'

(22) can be used when the 20th of March precedes S, but also when it follows S. It is part of the meaning of the Futur du Passé to be flexible with respect to the position of E with respect to S.

To have three different configurations for the Futur Antérieur (cell 3) is not correct either, but for a different reason. It is impossible to

[11] The notion of *allotopy* for this was coined in Verkuyl and Le Loux-Schuringa (1985) analogous to the well-known notion of allomorphy.

find examples in which the eventuality E is anterior or simultaneous to S, so that the only possible configuration is S – E – R:

(23) Jeanne me dit qu'elle aura terminé son travail le 8 septembre.
'Jeanne tells me that she will have finished (FA) her work the 8th of September.'

(23) cannot be used if the 8th of September is anterior to S or if S is included in that day. Sentence (24) is a clear example of why Reichenbach's configuration E – S – R cannot lead to an acceptable result:

(24) *Jeanne me dit qu'elle aura terminé son travail hier à 8 heures. lit: Jeanne to-me says that she will have finished her work yesterday at 8 o'clock.

The reason for the unacceptability of (24) is undoubtedly caused by the fact that by the use of *hier* it is clear that Jeanne finished her work yesterday. If an eventuality is in the past, one has to use a past tense rather than predict that something will have happened in the future.

**The problem of the missing tense cell.** Romance and Germanic languages possess a tense form which is capable of indicating the past of the Anterior Future. That is, the French Futur Antérieur form *aura dormi* (will have slept) has a corresponding past form *aurait dormi* (would have slept), called the Futur Antérieur du Passé. Its use can be understood by comparing sentences like (25) and (26).

(25) Pierre dit qu'il *aura terminé* son travail à 8 heures.
'Pierre said that he will have finished (FA) his work at 8 o'clock'

(26) Pierre avait dit qu'il *aurait terminé* son travail à 8 heures.
Pierre had said that he would have finished (FADP) his work at 8 o'clock

Reichenbach cannot provide a cell in the matrix for this form because a proper analysis of (26) would require an extra point of reference. On the assumption that pastness can be expressed by the relation S' – S (as we shall argue for later on), the most appropriate representation would be something like S' – E – R – S, where the S' – E – R-part expresses the close correspondence with the Futur Antérieur-structure S – E –R. In other words, one could introduce a sort of auxiliary point of speech to which one "goes back" in order to be in the position to use the Futur Antérieur du Passé. It is clear that such an extension of the system would require a radical change of its 3×3 set up.

**A problem of ambiguity** Reichenbach predicts that *dormira* (will sleep) is ambiguous because it occurs in cells 6 and 8 of Table 2 on the basis of the difference between S,R and S – R. As we will see, this is not a correct treatment of the Futur Simple. It is more plausible to associate the periphrastic form *va dormir* with the Present (S,R) and to restrict S – R for *dormira*. We will come back to that point.[12]

The problems discussed above strongly suggest that there is something fundamentally wrong with Reichenbach's tense system, both systematically and empirically. His treatment of tense in terms of systematic relations between points like E, S and R has shown to be certainly fruitful, but many languages, including French, require quite a different organization. It turns out to be counterproductive to force the French tense system into the matrix of Table 2. Rather than having a simple matrix crossing two tripartitions (Past-Present-Future and Anterior-Simultaneous-Posterior) French can be characterized by its having two parallel subsystems, the deictic one having the point of speech S as its origin and the anaphoric one originating in some other perspective point S' related to S and located before S. This boils down to acknowledging that there is a crucial difference between orientation on the point of speech and orientation on a point of reference in the past.

### 3.4 The proposals by Imbs, Martin and Vet

Reichenbach's tripartition Past, Present and Future is found in some influential work on French tenses without there being a direct influence, as in Imbs (1960) and Martin (1971). Imbs proposes the system represented in Table 3.[13] The term *Simultaneous* is not used by Imbs, but added by us. Imbs makes exactly the same primary division of the time axis as Reichenbach. Then he adds three relations with respect to these three times: Anterior, Simultaneous and Posterior. This system also yields nine tense positions. It is interesting, however, to note that Imbs uses periphrastic forms to complete the Present time column: *venir de* + $V_{inf}$ (literally: come from $V_{inf}$) and *aller* + $V_{inf}$ (go + $V_{inf}$).

Imbs' system obviously presents the same flaws as Reichenbach's: no position for the Futur Antérieur du Passé and an empty position for the Posterior Future.[14] But there are other problems, for example the periphrastic forms *venir de* + $V_{inf}$ and *aller* + $V_{inf}$ can only be used

[12] Actually, Reichenbach writes in a footnote on page 296: "The distinction between the French future forms *je vais voir* and *je verrai* may perhaps be regarded as representing the distinction between the order S,R – E and the order S – R,E." But this would mean that the set up of the whole system would have to be adapted, as we shall point out.

[13] We have adapted the table in order to facilitate a comparison with Reichenbach's system.

[14] This observation has also been made by Martin 1971:147.

| | Past | Present | Future |
|---|---|---|---|
| Anterior | Passé Antérieur<br>Plus-que-Parfait<br>Formes<br>Surcomposées | venir de + Inf. | Futur Antérieur |
| Simultaneous | Passé Simple<br>Imparfait<br>Passé Composé | Présent | Futur Simple |
| Posterior | Futur du Passé | aller +Inf. | — |

TABLE 3 Imbs' tense system

in the Présent and the Imparfait. So in the Past-column of Table 3 there should also be a subsystem, parallel to that of the Present. The second row of Table 4 shows that such a subsystem does not exist in the future, while the third and fourth row show that the periphrastic

| | | |
|---|---|---|
| venait de + $V_{inf}$ | Imparfait | allait + $V_{inf}$ |
| *viendra de + $V_{inf}$ | Futur Simple | *ira + $V_{inf}$ |
| *vint de + $V_{inf}$ | Passé Simple | *alla + $V_{inf}$ |
| *est venu de + $V_{inf}$ | Passé Composé | *est allé + $V_{inf}$ |

TABLE 4 The restricted use of periphrastic tense forms

auxiliaries can neither occur in the Passé Simple(*vint de + $V_{inf}$ = came-PS from doing) nor in the Passé Composé form (**est venu de* + $V_{inf}$ = has come from doing). Imbs' system does not account for these facts. Table 4 shows that the Présent and the Imparfait play a central role in the tense system and that the Imparfait differs from the Passé Simple and Passé Composé in that the latter cannot be used in the periphrastic forms with *aller* and *venir de*. Note finally that the overcomposed forms in Table 3 are in the wrong position. They should not appear in the cell of the Anterior Past. Imbs' insight that the periphrastic forms should be included in the analysis of the French tense system, however, is important.

(Martin, 1971, 154-155) presents two quite different tense systems, one for written and one for spoken French. The hypothesis that there are two tense systems in French is justified by the fact that the Simple Past and the Anterior Past are almost exclusively used in written French. In spoken French the Passé Composé and the Passé Surcomposé are used instead of the Passé Simple and the Passé Antérieur. The system of the written register in Figure 8 resembles Reichenbach's and

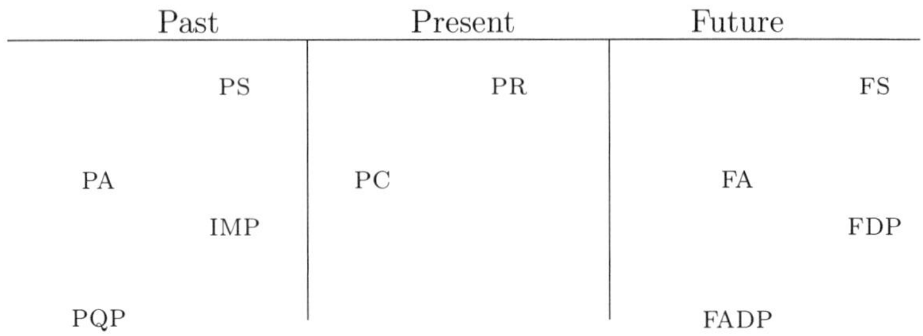


FIGURE 8 Martin's tense system for written French

Imbs' systems in that the time axis is divided into past, present and future. The Présent is the central tense of the system. The Imparfait and Passé Simple are past tenses occupying the same position in the system and placing the eventuality before the present. Figure 8 suggests that the Futur du Passé positions the eventuality after the present but this is not necessarily true because the eventuality can also have taken place before the present. The oblique lines indicate that the contrast between the verbal forms is not temporal but aspectual. Martin uses the term *accomplished aspect* in this connection, but we will call it *retrospective aspect* to avoid any association with Vendler's term *accomplishment*.

Figure 9 represents Martin's system of spoken French. It consists of two parallel subsystems, one with the Présent as its central tense form and one with the Imparfait as its center. The arrows pointing back

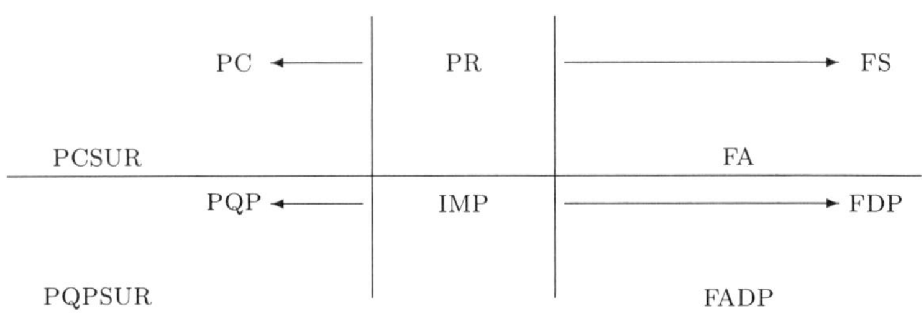


FIGURE 9 Martin's tense system for spoken French

represent a strict tense relation, that is, the relation of anteriority and posteriority, whereas the oblique lines express retrospective aspect.[15]

[15]The arrows do not occur in Figure 8, where we must assume that anteriority

Note that in Figure 8 the relation between the Présent and Passé Composé expresses retrospective aspect, whereas in Figure 9 it expresses tense. So, in Martin's view the Passé Composé has undergone a shift from aspect to tense in the process of replacing the Passé Simple.

By its parallelism the system in Figure 9 is intuitively more satisfactory than what Martin proposed in Figure 8. This can be made clear by Table 5. The tenses at the left-hand side of the equation sign take

| | | | |
|---|---|---|---|
| PR : PC | = | IMP: PQP | simultaneity vs. anteriority |
| PC : PCSUR | = | PQP: PQPSUR | eventuality vs. retrospective asp. |
| PR : FS | = | IMP: FDP | simultaneity vs. posteriority |
| FS : FA | = | FDP: FADP | eventuality vs. retrospective asp. |

TABLE 5 Parallelisms

the speech time S as their perspective point. They form the deictic subsystem of the whole tense system. The right-hand side of the equation sign forms a subsystem whose tenses take some point anterior to S as their perspective point. This subsystem is anaphoric.

Vet (1980) takes Martin's tense system as represented in Figure 9 as the starting point for his system. In his view, the main perspective point can be simultaneous with the speech point (S) or lie before it (S'). The temporal relations of anteriority, simultaneity and posteriority are made with respect to these two points, giving rise to a system of six tenses. In Vet (1980) only the tense system of spoken French is described. In the system that we now present in order to discuss the French tense system, we follow Martin's distinction between forms expressing tense and those expressing aspect. We do this with the help of Figure 10, which expresses Vet's adaptation of Martin's views.[16] The subsystems **1a** + **2** without the Plus-que-Parfait Surcomposé and perhaps the Futur Périphrastique du Passé represent the tense system of written French, while the systems **1b** + **2** with all the forms constitute the tense system of spoken French. Each of the subsystems has a distinct function in language use: the subsystems **1a** and **1b** are deictic systems: the tenses of these systems establish a relation to S. Subsystem **2** is anaphoric because the tenses of this system need to establish a relation with some temporal antecedent. The main perspective point S' of subsystem **2** is dependent on another point previously introduced in

and posteriority are defined in terms of occurring at the same level as PR.

[16]The periphrastic form *vient de*+ Inf (comes from doing) also occupies the PC-position in the subsystems 1a and 1b. Analogously, the form *venait de* + Inf occupies the PQP-position in subsystem 2.

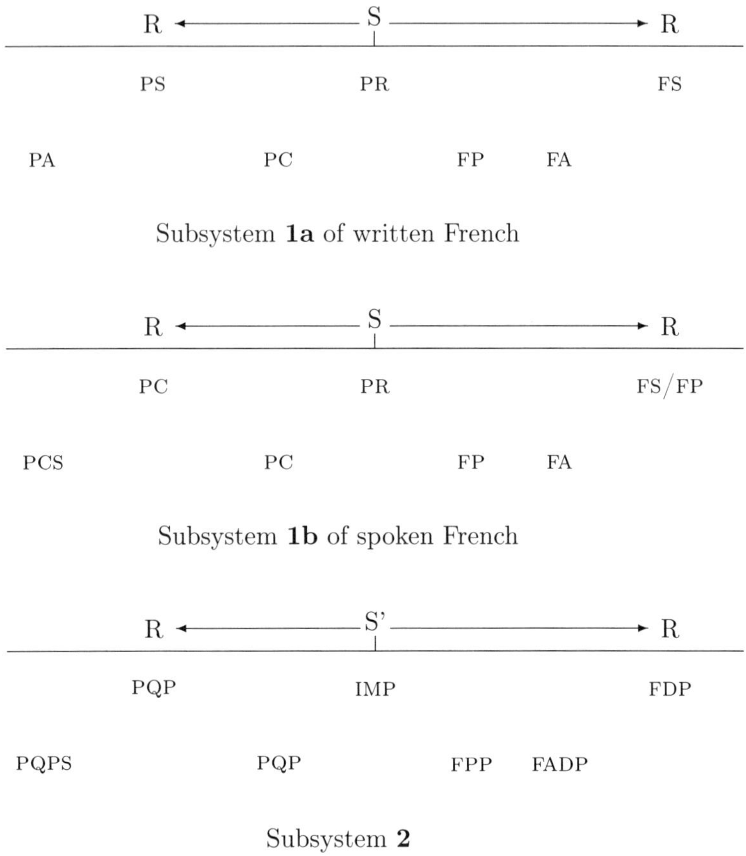


FIGURE 10 Three subsystems

the discourse by which it obtains the status that S has in the systems **1a** and **1b** (cf. Kamp and Rohrer (1983)).

### 3.5 Subsystem 1a

Let us have a closer look at subsystem **1a**, which belongs to the written register of French. Passé Simple, Présent and Futur Simple indicate that the eventuality referred to by the sentence lies before S, at S or after S as illustrated by the following example:

(27) Il fut, est et sera mon meilleur ami.
'He was (PS), is (PR) and will be (FS) my best friend.'

The rest of the forms of this subsystem, the Passé Antérieur, Passé Composé and Futur Antérieur, express retrospective aspect. At this point, it should be emphasized that it is possible to interpret the notion of retrospective aspect in terms of the relation between E and R (cf. section 3.8, Table 6). A strict interpretation of Martin's view is that at R there is evidence that an eventuality E, as described by the sentence's predication occurred before R.[17] Let us look at some examples:

(28) Pierre a abattu le vieux chêne.
'Pierre has cut down (PC) the old oak.

(29) Je vois que Pierre a abattu le vieux chêne.
'I see that Pierre has cut down (PC) the old oak

Sentence (28) can be said when the speaker sees the oak lying on the ground at S, as in (29), where the use of the Passé Composé implies that the result or some traces of the eventuality 'abattre le vieux chêne' are perceptible at S. The Passé Composé of (28) and (29) behaves as a present tense and can alternate with the present tense in (30). The Passé Simple cannot be used in this context:

(30) Je vois que Pierre abat /a abattu /*abattit le vieux chêne.
'I see that Pierre is cutting down (PR)/*has cut (PC)/cut down (PS) the old oak.'

The form *a abattu* describes, just like the Présent, a situation that is simultaneous to S.

The retrospective form of the Passé Simple, the Passé Antérieur, can only be used in two contexts: in adverbials introduced by *quand* 'when', *dès que* 'as soon as', etc. and in sentences containing an adverbial referring to a very small stretch of time. For example:

(31) Dès que Chantal eut terminé son travail ($E_1$), elle rentra chez elle ($E_2$).
'As soon as Chantal had finished (PA), she went home (PS).'

(32) Chantal rentra chez elle ($E_1$). Elle eut terminé son travail ($E_2$) en un rien de temps.
'Chantal went home (PS). She had finished (PA) her work in no time.'

Sentence (31) states that the result of $E_1$ was obtained before Chantal went home. Sentence (32) says that Chantal went home and that she had finished her work there very soon afterwards.

Since the early eighties it has been generally accepted that the use of the Passé Simple in discourse moves the R forwards to a following

[17]This implies that E,R expresses that at R the event is taking place or that it has terminated. We come back to this in more detail later on.

position separated from the earlier one. This insight is due to Kamp and Rohrer (1983) and has become standard in the literature on discourse, in spite of some counterevidence. It will be discussed in detail in chapter 15. As the Passé Antérieur can be seen as closely related to the Passé Simple, we may expect an R-shift in (32). This can be made visible in Figure 11, where the two tense configurations are brought together with S as the point of connection. The point $R_1$ at which

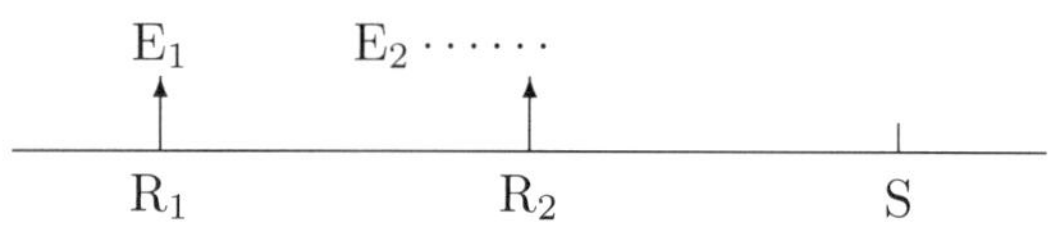


FIGURE 11

the completed eventuality $E_1$ is located cannot serve as the point from which the location $E_2$ can be computed with respect to $E_1$. The Passé Antérieur creates its own reference point $R_2$. Note that there is a difference between (32) and (33) in which the second sentence contains a Passé Simple.

(33) Marie rentra chez elle ($E_1$). Elle termina son travail ($E_2$) en un rien de temps.
'Marie went home (PS). She finished (PS) her work in no time.'

Rather than having Figure 11, we obtain Figure 12. The difference

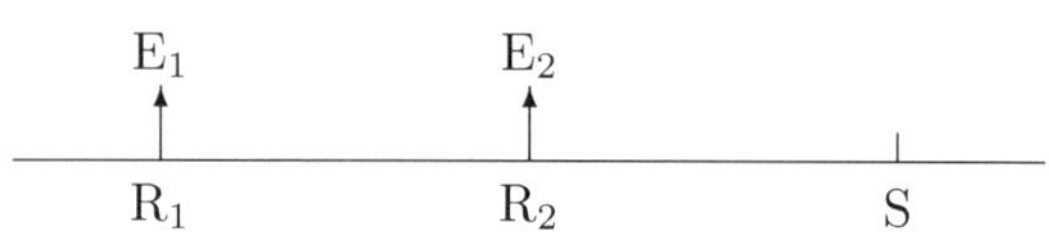


FIGURE 12

between the configurations in Figure 11 and Figure 12 is rather subtle but clearly present. Jumping forwards from $R_1$ to $R_2$ in Figure 11 yields the interpretation of getting a result in no time, because $E_2$ has already taken place in the past. In Figure 12 the temporal actualization of the event is put in the foreground: the second sentence in (33) says that $E_2$ has taken place at $R_2$. Note also that in (31) and (32) the Passé Antérieur cannot be replaced by the Pluperfect, the former creating its own reference point whereas the Pluperfect gives the instruction to look for an existing reference point in the preceding context. Compare (33) to (34) (see also (Vet and Molendijk, 1986, 153)).

(34) Chantal rentra chez elle ($E_1$). Elle avait terminé son travail ($E_2$) en très peu de temps
'Chantal went home (PS). She had finished (PQP) her work in a very short time.'

The fragment of (34) has only one reference point, the one introduced by the Passé Simple of the first sentence. This is shown in Figure 13. The Passé Simple of the first sentence in (34) creates the reference point

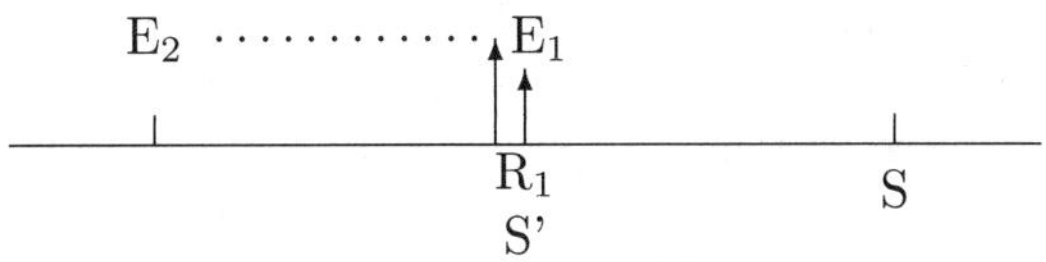


FIGURE 13

$R_1$ which is simultaneous with $E_1$. The result of $E_2$ is viewed from the perspective point S' which takes the R of $E_1$, i.e. $R_1$, as its temporal antecedent. From that point the result of $E_2$ is visible. The contrast between (33) and (34) is clear: the result of the finishing of the work in (33) is later than Chantal's coming home, whereas in (34) this result is true at $R_1$ and therefore $E_2$ precedes $E_1$.

The Futur Antérieur of subsystem 1a is the accomplished variant of the Futur Simple. Compare:

(35) a. A huit heures Chantal finira son travail.
'At eight o'clock Chantal will finish (FS) her work.'
b. A huit heures Chantal aura fini son travail.
'At eight o'clock Chantal will have finished (FA) her work.'

In (35a) the eventuality 'finish her work' takes place at eight o'clock, whereas in (30b) the result of the eventuality 'finish her work' is available at eight o'clock. Subsystem **1a** has another E – R-form, the Periphrastic Future. This is the mirror image of the Passé Composé of this system (see (29) above). Compare (36a) and (36b).

(36) a. Jean va abattre le vieux chêne.
lit: Jean goes cut down (FP) the old oak
'Jean is going to cut down the old oak'
b. Je vois que Jean va abattre le vieux chêne.
'I see that Jean is going to cut down (FP) the old oak.'
c. *Je vois que Jean abattra le vieux chêne.
lit: I see that Jean will cut down (SF) the old oak.

(36b) shows that there is something to see at S. What can be seen is the 'preparatory phase' of a future eventuality. The Simple Future cannot be used in the context of (36b). In (36c) the speaker cannot see anything at S, simply because one cannot see future eventualities.[18]

### 3.6 Subsystem 1b

The difference between subsystems **1a** and **1b** is that the Passé Composé has undergone a semantic extension in spoken French. The existence of an eventuality anterior to S was already presupposed in the aspectual use of the Passé Composé. The extension of its sense means that this form can indicate that focus is either on the aftermath of an eventuality anterior to S or on the eventuality anterior to S. Such choice of focus also holds for the Futur Périphrastique. The aspectual use of this form presupposes the existence of a future eventuality. In the current usage of the Futur Périphrastique focus can switch from the preparatory phase of a future eventuality to the future eventuality itself. In other words Passé Composé and Futur Périphrastique can express either that the resultative or the preparatory phase of an event is true at S or that there is an eventuality before or after S respectively, cf. Vet (2001). A more detailed semantic description of the Passé Composé is given in section 4 in chapter 15.

The overcomposed Passé Composé (Passé Surcomposé) is used in exactly the same contexts as the Passé Antérieur, as a comparison between (37) and (38), and between (31) and (32) indicates.

(37) Dès que Marie a eu terminé son travail ($E_1$), elle est rentrée chez elle ($E_2$).
lit: As soon as Marie has had finished (PCS), she has gone (PC) home.
'As soon as Marie had finished her work, she went home.'

(38) Marie a eu terminé son travail ($E_2$) en un rien de temps.
lit: Marie has had finished (PCS) her work in no time.
'Marie had finished her work in no time.'

The rule for the interpretation of the Passé Composé is very simple. In the case of S,R, the Passé Composé has the aspectual (retrospective) reading, when R – S, we have the tense reading of this form. This is the case in (32) and (33). The two perfects in the Passé Surcomposé have two different functions:

(39) PCS: PRES[$\text{PERF}_1$[$\text{PERF}_2$[Verb]]]

The PRES + $\text{PERF}_1$ is a tense marker: it places the eventuality at R – S and $\text{PERF}_2$ is the retrospective aspect marker, telling the hearer that the focus is not on the eventuality itself, but on its aftermath. So the

[18](36c) is acceptable if *voir* is taken metaphorically as 'understand', 'realize'.

Passé Surcomposé does not indicate a past in the past, but a result at R earlier than S, just as the Passé Antérieur in (40):

(40) PA: PS[PERF[Verb]]

Here the Passé Simple places the eventuality at R – S and PERF yields the aspectual (retrospective) reading. The semantic interpretation of the two forms is the same.

The Futur Périphrastique of subsystem **1b** also has the same possibilities as the Passé Composé: it can express (prospective) aspect or future tense. The latter meaning is the result of a sense extension. In its aspectual use it cannot be replaced by the Futur Simple, as illustrated by (36c), in its temporal use it can, witness (41a, b):

(41) a. L'an prochain nous passerons nos vacances en Ecosse.
'Next year we will spend (FS) our holidays in Scotland.'
b. L'an prochain nous allons passer nos vacances en Ecosse.
'Next year we will spend (FP) our holidays in Scotland.'

The aspectual or tense reading of the Periphrastic Future depends on the current reference point: when S,R is the case, one obtains the aspectual one (prospective), when S – R, as in (41b), the future tense reading shows up. See (36a,b) above and (42a,b).

(42) a. Cet homme va mourir. Appelez le docteur!
'That man is going to die (FP). Call the doctor!!'
b. ??Cet homme mourra. Appelez le docteur!
lit: That man will die (FS). Call the doctor!!

The Futur Périphrastique has two possible readings (prospective aspect and future tense) whereas the Futur Simple can only function as tense. It is not true, however, as some grammars of French claim, that the Futur Périphrastique is exclusively used in spoken French and the Futur Simple in written French. Both forms are used in both registers. It is true that the Futur Périphrastique is slightly more frequent in spoken French and the Futur Simple more often used in written French. But this is only a tendency as pointed out by Lorenz (1989a) and Lorenz (1989b). They also observe that the Simple Future has a preference for negative contexts. The latter tendency of European French has become a rule in Québécois French, where the Futur Simple has become a negative polarity item and is used exclusively in negative contexts (cf. Deshaies and Laforge (1981)).

### 3.7 Subsystem 2

This system exactly mirrors subsystem **1b**, with the only difference that the central orientation point S' is dependent on a temporal antecedent previously identified by the context. The forms of this system have the same verb endings (*-ais*, *-ait*, etc.). The function of these forms in discourse is to provide background information or explanations about facts that were presented in the preceding context.[19] This is true of the Imparfait, but also of the other tenses of subsystem **2**. Compare:

(43) Marie entra dans la cuisine ($E_1$). Pierre faisait la vaisselle ($E_2$).
'M. entered (PS) the kitchen. P. was washing (IMP) the dishes.'

(44) Marie entra dans la cuisine ($E_1$). Pierre avait fait la vaisselle ($E_2$).
'M. entered (PS) the kitchen. P. had washed (PQP) the dishes.'

(45) Marie entra dans la cuisine ($E_1$). Pierre allait faire la vaisselle ($E_2$).
'M. entered (PS) the kitchen. P. was going (FPP) to wash the dishes.'

The Futur du Passé is used in subordinate clauses or in reported speech.

(46) Marie pensait que Pierre terminerait son travail avant huit heures.
'Marie thought that Pierre would finish his work before 8 o'clock.'

(47) Sa décision était prise: il terminerait le travail avant huit heures.
'He had taken his decision: he would finish the work before 8 pm'

The Plus-que-Parfait Surcomposé is used in the same contexts as the Passé Surcomposé.

(48) Quand il avait eu terminé son travail, il était rentré chez lui.
When he had had finished (PQPS) his work, he had gone (PQP) home.
'When he had finished his work, he had gone home.'

(49) Pierre avait réalisé que Marie avait eu terminé son travail en un rien de temps.
Pierre had realized (PQP) that Marie had had finished (PQPS) her work in no time.
'Pierre had realized that Marie had finished her work in no time.'

### 3.8 Organizing the subsystems in a matrix

The above exercise has demonstrated several uses of the French tense forms with the help of Figure 10 which represents Vet's way of interpreting Martin's system and improving on some inconsistency in the set up of the whole system. Figure 10, however, has been shown to raise questions about how it relates to what is expressed in a Reichenbachian system. Moreover, one of the two main authors of the present section has argued that a binary tense system along the lines of the

[19] See Kamp and Rohrer (1983), Vet and Molendijk, (1986) and chapter 15.

Dutch grammarian Te Winkel has the virtue of revealing two parallel subsystems much in the way discussed above.[20] This system, which by its 3×2-set up turns out to be very natural for English and Dutch with their eight tenses, runs into the problem that Romance languages have an overt future tense form. This need not lead to abandoning a binary approach for Romance languages but here we settled on a format that harbours both the insights about the parallelism and the fundamental distinction between deictic and anaphoric in a more standard way, accepting the Reichenbachian heritage in spite of the severe objections raised against the 3 × 3-approach.

Therefore we aim at a Table in which the parallelism between the two subsystems **1** + **2** comes out in a striking way. The first We also insert the periphrastic forms which have not been discussed in the presentation of the subsystems **1** + **2**. The relation between *allait dormir* and *dormait* is parallel to the relation between *va dormir* and *dort*. The forms take the same cells in the system. But the former two take the same position in subsystem **1a** as the latter in **2**. The same applies to *aura dormi* and *aurait dormi*, among many others.[21]

It is time now to comment on the gray blocks in Table 6. In order to achieve the aspectual interpretation of the bottom tense forms in **1a** and **2** we have coloured the blocks in gray which is taken to be equivalent to the dotted representations in Figures 11 and 13.[22] In the Reichenbachian context of using the points E and R, the Martin/Vet position imposes a specific interpretation on the representations E,R on the one hand and E – R and R – E on the other. In the literature one often finds analyses in which E,R is taken as 'E is taking place at R', which implies that E – R expresses that E took place before R.[23] On the

[20]This binary system has been described in detail in Verkuyl and Le Loux-Schuringa (1985); in Verkuyl (2001) it was shown that this system is compositional in the formal semantic sense. The basic idea is that there is a primary division between Present and Past. At each of these points another division can be applied: Synchronous and Posterior. Each of the four points thus obtained is subjected to the third division between Incomplete(d) and Complete(d). This provides a Present system of four forms and a Past system of four forms, where Past is to be taken as 'Present in the Past'.

[21]We do not take into account the forms with *venir de*+ infinitive. *Il vient de*+inf. would have the configuration E–R,S and *il venait de*+inf. would have E–R,S'.

[22]As discussed in Verkuyl and Le Loux-Schuringa (1985), a repeated 2 × 3-system was proposed for Dutch in Kollewijn (1892), the only difference between Kollewijn's first subsystem and subsystem **1a** being that Kollewijn considered the relation introduced by the auxiliary *hebben* (have) as a tense relation, whereas Martin and Vet put heavy emphasis on the aspectual nature of this relation.

[23]For example, Boogaart (1999), among many others. This interpretation is actually not present in Reichenbach (1947) itself, as should be clear from the attempt to distinguish the French Imparfait from the Passé Simple on the basis of putting

| 1a | **Past**<br>R – S | **Present**<br>R,S | **Future**<br>S – R |
|---|---|---|---|
| E,R | Passé Simple<br>E,R–S<br>*dormit* | Présent<br>E,R,S<br>*dort* | Futur Simple<br>S–R,E<br>*dormira* |
| | | Futur Périphrastique<br>S,R–E<br>*va dormir* | |
| Acc.<br>E-R | Passé Antérieur<br>E–R–S<br>*eut dormi* | Passé Composé<br>E–R,S<br>*a dormi* | Futur Antérieur<br>S–E–R<br>*aura dormi* |
| **2** | **Past in the Past**<br>R – S' | **Present in the Past**<br>R,S' | **Future in the Past**<br>S' – R |
| E,R | Plus-que-Parfait<br>E,R – S'<br>*avait dormi* | Imparfait<br>E,R,S'<br>*dormait* | Futur du Passé<br>S' – R,E<br>*dormirait* |
| | | Futur Périphrastique du Passé<br>S',R – E<br>*allait dormir* | |
| Acc<br>E-R | | Plus-que-Parfait<br>E – R,S'<br>*avait dormi* | Futur Antérieur du Passé<br>S' – E – R<br>*aurait dormi* |

TABLE 6 The tense system for written French

Martin/Vet line of thinking, the relation between E and R should be seen as completely neutral with respect to predicational aspect. That is, R is not a point at which one could decide whether or not the eventuality is taking place "by looking at it". So the configuration E,R in the cell of the Passé Simple in Table 6 does not express that the sleeping was going on at R: *Elle dormit* means that the eventuality is presented as completed. The subsystems **1b** and **2** can be put together in Table 7. The Passé Composé has obtained two configurations, one of them suppressing the Passé Simple. There is also a striking feature in the system that did not appear in Martin's work: the Plus-que-Parfait is taken as ambiguous, because it receives both E,R – S and E – R,S. According to Vet, there are two ways of using the Plus-que-Parfait. On the E,R – S' – S interpretation the perspective point S' is in the past, from where a point R is contrued coinciding with the event E.

R,E in an extended interval (1947:291) in the former case.

| 1b | Past<br>R – S | Present<br>R,S | Future<br>S – R |
|---|---|---|---|
| E,R | Passé Composé<br>E,R – S<br>*a dormi* | Présent<br>E,R,S<br>*dors* | Futur Simple<br>S – R,E<br>*dormira*<br>Futur Périphrastique<br>S – R,E<br>*va dormir* |
| | | Futur Périphrastique<br>S,R – E<br>*va dormir* | |
| E-R | Passé Surcomposé<br>E – R – S<br>*a eu dormi* | Passé Composé<br>E – R,S<br>*a dormi* | Futur Antérieur<br>S – E – R<br>*aura dormi* |
| **2** | **Past in the Past**<br>R – S' | **Present in the Past**<br>R,S' | **Future in the Past**<br>S' – R |
| E,R | Plus-que-Parfait<br>E,R – S'<br>*avait dormi* | Imparfait<br>E,R,S'<br>*dormait* | Future in the Past<br>S' – R,E<br>*dormirait* |
| | | Futur Périphrastique du Passé<br>S',R–E<br>*allait dormir* | |
| E-R | Plus-que-Parfait Surcomposé<br>E – R – S'<br>*avait eu dormi* | Plus-que-Parfait<br>E – R,S'<br>*avait dormi* | Futur Antérieur du Passé<br>S' – E – R<br>*aurait dormi* |

TABLE 7 The tense system for spoken French

On Martin's view this would be a more temporal interpretation of the Plus-que-Parfait. The aspectual interpretation would be obtained in E–R,S'–S, where R coincides with the root of the secondary system S' yielding its aspectual reading.

### 3.9 The current usage of French tenses

The distinction we have drawn between the subsystems **1a** and **1b** in Table 6 and Table 7 represents a stage of the language that does not exist anymore at least not in its pure form. In written French, even in literature, authors avoid the exclusive use of system **1a**. Instead of a constant use of the Passé Simple as was usual in the nineteenth century (cf. Flaubert), authors use the historic present, the Plus-que-Parfait, the Passé Composé and the Passé Simple. It seems to us that in written

French subsystems **1a** and **1b** have merged (see Vet 1999). We cite here a fragment given by Waugh and Monville (1986: 809-10):

(50) ... Le ministre des affaires étrangères du président Bourguiba, M. Beji Caid Essebsi, a avancé deux arguments pour justifier sa position: les raisons qui ont motivé l'exclusion de l'Egypte a-t-il déclaré, n'ont pas disparu, et d'ailleurs, ajouta-t-il, la question ne devrait même pas être débattue puisqu'elle ne figurait pas à l'ordre du jour... (Eric Rouleau, Le Monde 1.20.84)
'The minister of Foreign Affairs of President Bourguiba, Mr. Beji Caid Essebsi, put forth (PC) two arguments to justify his position: the reasons why Egypt was excluded, he declared (PC), have not disappeared and by the way, he added (PS), the question should not even be debated since it was not on the agenda...' (translation by Waugh and Monville)

What is also new is that the use of the tenses of subsystem **1a** is no longer obligatory. Even in literature authors use exclusively the tenses of subsystem **1b**. *L'étranger* by Albert Camus is one of the first examples, as discussed in chapter 15. This would be the last stage of a language change in which subsystem **1a**, and particularly the Passé Simple and Passé Antérieur of this system disappear. Such a change, however, is not yet totally completed. In normal spoken French subsystem **1a** is never used, its use is restricted to very official discourse or in the speech of teachers of history. It may be expected that subsystem **1a** will disappear from the language and that **1b** and **2** form the new system. This is already the practice for the majority of the French-speaking population.

## 4 Conclusion

The problems one encounters in describing the indicative tense system of French are threefold. First the current system is changing: subsystem **1a** is becoming more and more obsolete. Secondly, some of the composed forms (the Passé Composé and the Pluperfect) originally used for expressing retrospective aspect, have developed into tenses, without losing the possibility to express aspect in appropriate contexts. This shift first took place in spoken French, but extends nowadays to written French. The same meaning shift led to the creation of the Passé Surcomposé, which replaces the Passé Antérieur in spoken language, and of the Plus-que-Parfait Surcomposé whereas the Futur Antérieur and Futur Antérieur du Passé continued to express retrospective aspect only. Thirdly, the Futur Périphrastique, which originally expressed only prospective aspect, has become a future tense, again without losing its aspectual meaning in appropriate contexts. The same is true for the Futur Périphrastique du Passé. Contrary to what happens with the Passé Simple and the Passé Antérieur, the Futur Simple and Futur du Passé are not disappearing from spoken French (nor from the written register). So the Passé Composé and the Plus-que-Parfait have an extended meaning (comprising both aspect and tense) and the same extension characterizes the Futur Périphrastique and the Futur Périphrastique du Passé. Stense) and the same extension characterizes the Futur Périphrastique and the Futur Périphrastique du Passé.

The system presented in Table 8, in which Table 6 and Table 7 are taken together, has some obvious advantages over Reichenbach's system. First, there is no place for Posterior Future. This is a systematic gap in natural languages and the system predicts the absence of such a tense. Secondly, there is room for the Futur Antérieur du Passé, which Reichenbach's system could not account for. The system correctly predicts that there are six forms expressing retrospective aspect based on E – R. It is also possible to explain why the periphrastic future only appears in two forms (the Futur Périphrastique and the Futur Périphrastique du Passé). Prospective aspect can only be expressed at S or S' and not at one of the R's of the system. In contexts in which S – R or S' – R the Futur Périphrastique-forms always express tense.

| 1 | **Past**<br>R – S | **Present**<br>R,S | **Future**<br>S – R |
|---|---|---|---|
| E,R | Passé Simple<br>E,R – S<br>*dormit*<br>Passé Composé<br>E,R – S<br>*a dormi* | Présent<br>E,R,S<br>*dors* | Futur Simple<br>S – R,E<br>*dormira*<br>Futur Périphrastique<br>S – R,E<br>*va dormir* |
| E-R | Passé Antérieur<br>E – R – S<br>*eut dormi*<br>Passé Surcomposé<br>E – R – S<br>*a eu dormi* | Futur Périphrastique<br>S,R – E<br>*va dormir*<br>Passé Composé<br>E – R,S<br>*a dormi* | Futur Antérieur<br>S – E - - R<br>*aura dormi* |
| **2** | **Past in the Past**<br>R – S' | **Present in the Past**<br>R,S' | **Future in the Past**<br>S' – R |
| E,R | Plus-que-Parfait<br>E,R – S'<br>*avait dormi* | Imparfait<br>E,R,S'<br>*dormait* | Futur du Passé<br>S' – R,E<br>*dormirait*<br>Futur Périphrastique du Passé<br>S' – R,E<br>*allait dormir* |
| | | Futur Périphrastique du Passé<br>S',R – E<br>*allait dormir* | |
| E-R | Plus-que-Parfait Surcomposé<br>E – R – S'<br>*avait eu dormi* | Plus-que-Parfait<br>E – R,S'<br>*avait dormi* | Futur Antérieur du Passé<br>S' – E – R<br>*aurait dormi* |

TABLE 8 The current system as a whole

## References


ACL. 1987. *Proceedings of the 25th Annual Meeting of the Association for Computational Linguistics*, Stanford University. ACL.

Bach, E. 1986. The algebra of events. *Linguistics and Philosophy* 9:5–16.

Bartsch, R., J. van Benthem, and P. van Emde Boas, eds. 1989. *Semantics and Contextual Expression*, vol. 11 of *Groningen-Amsterdam Studies in Semantics*. Dordrecht: Foris Publications.

Bäuerle, R., C. Schwarze, and A. von Stechow, eds. 1983. *Meaning, Use and Interpretation of Language*. Berlin and New York: Mouton de Gruyter.

Boogaart, R. 1999. *Aspect and temporal ordering. A contrastive analysis of Dutch and English*. Ph.D. thesis, Free University, Amsterdam.

Comrie, B. 1976. *Aspect*. Cambridge Textbooks in Linguistics. Cambridge: Cambridge University Press.

Deshaies, D. and E. Laforge. 1981. Le futur simple et le futur proche dans le français parlé dans la ville de Québec. *Langues et Linguistique* 7:21–37.

Grevisse, M. 1964. *Le Bon Usage. Grammaire française avec des remarques sur la langue française d'aujourdhui*. Gembloux & Paris: J. Duculot & A. Hatier. Huitième edition revue.

Imbs, P., ed. 1960. *L'emploi des temps verbaux en français moderne: essai de grammaire descriptive*. Paris: Klincksieck.

Kabakčiev, K. 2000. *Aspect in English. A "Common-Sense" View of the Interplay between Verbal and Nominal Referents*, vol. 75 of *Studies in Linguistics and Philosophy*. Kluwer Academic Publishers.

Kamp, H. and C. Rohrer. 1983. Tense in texts. In Bäuerle et al. (1983), pages 250–269.

Kollewijn, R. 1892. Het systeem van de tijden der werkwoorden. *Taal en letteren* 2:141–147.

Krifka, M. 1989. Nominal reference, temporal constitution and quantification in event semantics. In Bartsch et al. (1989), pages 75–115.

Kronning, H., C. Noren, B. Novèn, G. Ransbo, L.-G. Sundvell, and B. Svane, eds. 2001. *Langage et références: mélanges offerts à Kerstin Jonasson à l'occasion de ses soixante ans*. Uppsala: Actas Universitatis Uppsaliensis.

Lo Cascio, V. and C. Vet, eds. 1986. *Temporal Structure in Sentence and Discourse*, vol. 5 of *Groningen-Amsterdam Studies in Semantics*. Dordrecht: Foris Publications.

Lorenz, B. 1989a. *Die Konkurrenz zwischen dem* futur simple *und dem* futur périphrastique *im gesprochenen Französisch der Gegenwart*. Münster: Kleinheinrich.

Lorenz, S. 1989b. *Die Konkurrenz zwischen dem* futur simple *und dem* futur périphrastique *im geschriebenen Französisch der Gegenwart*. Münster: Kleinheinrich.

Martin, R., ed. 1971. *Temps et aspect. Essai sur l'emploi des temps narratifs en moyen français.*. Paris: Éditions Klincksieck.

Moens, M. and M. Steedman. 1987. Temporal ontology in natural language. In ACL (1987), pages 1–7.

Mourelatos, A. P. 1978. Events, processes and states. *Linguistics and Philosophy* 2:415–434.

Reichenbach, H. 1947. *Elements of Symbolic Logic*. New York: The Macmillan Company, first free press paperback edition 1966 edn.

Riegel, M., J.-C. Pellat, and R. Rioul. 1994. *Grammaire méthodique du français*. Paris: Presses universitaires.

Vendler, Z. 1957. Verbs and times. *The Philosophical Review* 66:143–160.

Verkuyl, H. J. 1972. *On the Compositional Nature of the Aspects*, vol. 15 of *FLSS*. Dordrecht: D. Reidel Publishing Company.

Verkuyl, H. J. 1993. *A Theory of Aspectuality. The Interaction between Temporal and Atemporal Structure*, vol. 64 of *Cambridge Studies in Linguistics*. Cambridge: Cambridge University Press.

Verkuyl, H. J. 1999. *Aspectual Issues. Structuring Time and Quantity*, vol. 98 of *CSLI Lecture Notes*. Stanford, California: CSLI Publications.

Verkuyl, H. J. 2001. On the compositionality of tense: merging Reichenbach and Prior. Unpublished paper.

Verkuyl, H. J. and J. A. Le Loux-Schuringa. 1985. Once upon a tense. *Linguistics and Philosophy* 8:237–261.

Vet, C. 1980. *Temps, aspects et adverbes de temps en français contemporain*. Geneva: Droz.

Vet, C. 1994. Future tense and discourse representation. In Vet and Vetters (1994), pages 49–76.

Vet, C. 2001. Deux cas de polysémie: le passé composé et le futur periphrastique. In Kronning et al. (2001), pages 697–686.

Vet, C. and A. Molendijk. 1986. The discourse functions of the past tenses of French. In Lo Cascio and Vet (1986), pages 133–159.

Vet, C. and C. Vetters, eds. 1994. *Tense and Aspect in Discourse*, vol. 75 of *Trends in Linguistics. Studies and Monographs*. Berlin and New York: Mouton de Gruyter.

15

# Meaning and Use of Past Tenses in Discourse

ARIE MOLENDIJK, HENRIËTTE DE SWART, CARL VETTERS, ANDRÉE BORILLO, MYRIAM BRAS, ANNE LE DRAOULEC, LAURE VIEU, HENK VERKUYL, AND CO VET

## 1 Overview

Chapter 14 developed an analysis of the tense system of French as a whole, and considered the relations between the various tenses. In this section, we exploit and extend that system in order to provide an analysis of the three main past tenses of French—Passé Simple, Imparfait and Passé Composé—at the discourse level. We start from the observation that the tense system developed in chapter 14 does not give a straightforward account of the alternation between Passé Simple and Imparfait in written discourse, Passé Composé and Imparfait in spoken discourse, or Passé Simple, Passé Composé and Imparfait in 'mixed' discourses such as Vet's newspaper corpus (cf. Vet 1999). One reason is that the representations of the different tenses appeal to a reference point R. Chapter 14 claims that the Imparfait is anaphoric, because subsystem 2 involves a perspective point S' that depends for its reference on another point previously introduced in the discourse.[1] Obviously, we need a resolution procedure to determine what functions as the current reference point in the discourse. The second point is that

[1]The best way to understand the difference between the original Reichenbachian configurations and those of subsystem 2 in Table 8 is to take S' in subsystem 2 as the original Reichenbachian R.

*Handbook of French Semantics.*
Francis Corblin and Henriëtte de Swart (eds.).
Copyright © 2004, CSLI Publications.

the system as presented in Figure 10 and Table 6, 7 above is essentially temporal in nature, and remains neutral with respect to (im-)perfective aspect. According to Table 6, both Passé Simple and Imparfait involve a relation E,R. Although this relation might correspond with 'E taking place at R' for the Imparfait, that is not appropriate for the Passé Simple, which presents the eventuality as completed. In the following, we acknowledge that the Passé Simple, Imparfait and Passé Composé are all past tenses, but base part of their different behavior at the discourse level on aspectual differences.

The organization of this section is as follows. We first motivate the treatment of the Passé Simple/Imparfait opposition as an aspectual contrast (section 2), and then complement the system developed so far with a discourse-oriented aspectual analysis of the opposition between the Passé Simple and Imparfait (section 3) in written discourse. This part focuses on the choice of the temporal antecedent of a sentence, and the temporal relation established between the eventuality and the reference time. Section 4 extends the analysis to the narrative use of the Passé Composé in spoken language. The temporal structure of 'mixed' discourses involving Passé Simple, Passé Composé and Imparfait will not be addressed here. For now, we concentrate on discourse structures that can be derived with purely temporal-aspectual properties. In chapter 16 below, we see that a full discourse analysis needs to appeal to rhetorical structure, which implies lexical and world knowledge.

## 2 The PS/IMP opposition as an aspectual contrast

### 2.1 An analysis in terms of aspectual operators

The dominant view in the literature, and one we follow seems to be that the opposition between Passé Simple and Imparfait is aspectual in nature. One line of work involves an extension of the analysis of the Slavic perfective/imperfective contrast (cf. section 2.2) to the Romance languages. This has led to the introduction of two aspectual operators: a perfective and an imperfective operator for the Passé Simple and the Imparfait respectively (cf. Comrie (1985); Smith (1991); Vet (1994); Verkuyl (2001)). The perfective indicates that the assertion presents the process as completed, including the beginning point and the endpoint. The prototypical interpretation of the imperfective is to present the process as already started, and susceptible to continuing further. The contrast is illustrated by pairs of sentences like (1):

(1) a. Chantal écrivit une lettre.
'Chantal wrote (PS) a letter'

b. Chantal écrivait une lettre.
'Chantal wrote (IMP) a letter'

Sentence (1a) in the Passé Simple describes the event of Chantal writing a letter from the outside; it is a completed process, i.e. there is a (complete) letter. (1b) describes the process of writing from the inside, as an ongoing event, so the letter is not (yet) completed.

Analyses in terms of external versus internal point of view are insightful, but tell us little about the way past tense sentences hang together in more complex structures. An example of the different roles of the Passé Simple and Imparfait is given in (2) (from Molendijk (1990)):

(2) a. Le général attaqua l'ennemi, qui se retirait.
'The general attacked (PS) the enemy, who withdrew (IMP)'

b. Le général attaqua l'ennemi, qui se retira.
'The general attacked (PS) the enemy, who withdrew (PS)'

In (2a), the withdrawal was already under way when the general attacked. In (2b), the withdrawal followed the attack. The aspectual contrast or difference in point of view between the Passé Simple and Imparfait thus leads to differences in temporal structure, and it is this impact of the tenses on the temporal relations between sentences that we address in this section.

## 2.2 An analysis in terms of aspectually sensitive tense operators

All the analyses discussed so far rely on a clearcut distinction between *predicational aspect* (alternatively called Aktionsart or aspectual class or situation type) and *grammatical aspect* (alternatively called point of view or viewpoint aspect). They can be opposed to analyses in which the distinction between predicational and grammatical aspect is blurred, such as Kamp and Rohrer (1983), Partee (1984) and Hinrichs (1986). Kamp and Rohrer take Passé Simple sentences to refer to events, and Imparfait sentences to describe states, independently of the predicational aspect of the sentence. This analysis suggests that predicational aspect either does not influence the denotation of the sentence as a whole, or is in some sense 'overruled' by the contribution of grammatical aspect. This view is motivated by the temporal structure of narrative discourse, where we observe differences between states and events. Events move the story line forward, whereas states typically provide background information. We can see this contrast at work in the relation between the two sentences in (2) above, or in discourses like (3):

(3) a. Pierre rentra. Marie téléphonait.
'Pierre came (PS) home. Marie called (IMP).'
b. Pierre rentra. Marie téléphona.
'Pierre came (PS) home. Marie called (PS).'

In (3a), Marie was already on the phone when Pierre came home, whereas the preferred interpretation of (3b) is that Marie called (right) after Pierre came home. If the Passé Simple sentence denotes an event, and event sentences generally move time forward, we can explain why (3b) leads to temporal succession. If the Imparfait sentence denotes a state, and states usually don't move time forward, we can explain why there is temporal overlap in (3a).

The examples in (2) and (3) present minimal pairs, where the only difference resides in the tense choice, so the predicational aspect does not seem to play a role in this contrast. If only the output type matters at the discourse level, it is less important to know whether the sentence denotes a state because it just has the predicational aspect of a state, or because it is a derived (progressive or imperfective) state. Given that Kamp and Rohrer (1983), Partee (1984) and Hinrichs (1986), etc. are mostly interested in the temporal structure of the discourse, the emphasis on the denotation of the sentence as a whole seems justified. The drawback of this focus on output type is that we do not gain insight into the way specific meaning effects result from the combination of predicational aspect, aspectual operators, and tense operators.

The aim of De Swart (1998) is to develop a compositional analysis of predicational aspect and grammatical aspect which preserves insights from the two approaches described, and which can serve to describe the discourse semantics of the French past tenses. Her system crucially relies on the assumption that the semantic structures underlying predicational and grammatical aspect are the same, and can be captured by introducing states, processes and events as ontological entities into the model. De Swart adopts (4) as the temporal-aspectual structure of a sentence:

(4) [ Tense [ Aspect* [Eventuality description] ] ]

The notion of eventuality description corresponds to the one used in schema 7 in section 2.1. It will be taken as applying to the three different sort of eventualities distinguished in Figure 1, section 2.4. Aspectual operators take an eventuality of a certain type and yield an eventuality of a different type, the Kleene star indicating that one can have zero, one or more aspectual operators. Tense operators introduce existential closure over a set of eventualities, and map the resulting event via its location time onto the time axis relating it to the speech time.

In Vet (1994), (1a) and (b) get the representation in (5a) and (b) respectively:

(5) a. [PAST[ PERF [Anne write a letter]]]
 b. [PAST[ IMP [Anne write a letter]]]

The position of PERF/IMP in between the predicate-argument structure and the tense operator defines these operators as aspectual operators in the sense of (4). Unlike Vet, de Swart does not define the semantics of the Passé Simple and the Imparfait in terms of aspectual operators, but develops an analysis of these tenses as aspectually sensitive tense operators. Both the Passé Simple and the Imparfait are past tenses, but the former presupposes events (quantized eventualities), and the latter homogeneous, non-quantized eventualities (states or processes).

De Swart offers three reasons to prefer an analysis in terms of tense operators over aspectual operators. Unlike well-established aspectual operators like the Perfect (in French, English, and other languages), and the English Progressive, there is no morphology corresponding to the perfective/imperfective contrast in French. There is one verbal ending that encodes both temporal and aspectual information, e.g. the Imparfait form écriv*ait* of the verb 'to write' encodes both past tense + imperfective aspect in the ending-*ait*.[2] Similarly, the Passé Simple form écriv*it* of the same verb, encodes both past tense + perfective aspect in the ending *-it*. If it is impossible to (morphologically) separate the aspectual from the temporal information, maybe we should try to account for that by locating the aspectual difference within the tense operator. This is confirmed by the fact that the Passé Simple/ Imparfait contrast is not found elsewhere in the tense system, whereas the Perfect, the Progressive, but also the Slavic perfective/imperfective contrast are available not only in the past tense, but also in the present and/or future tense. Finally, statistics about tense distribution in actual texts indicate that the default tense choice for event-like propositions is the Passé Simple, whereas the Imparfait is mostly used for stative/process-like propositions. In the default cases, the tense does not make a strong aspectual contribution, which raises problems for an operator-based analysis. However, if we take the Passé Simple to be the past tense operator for event-like propositions, and the Imparfait the past tense operator for stative/process-like propositions, the statistical preference reflects that a presuppositional operator likes to see its presupposition satisfied. Thus, if we combine the Passé Simple with

[2]Note that our assumption that the Imparfait is a past tense is not entirely uncontroversial, cf. Damourette and Pichon (1936) and Le Goffic (1995) for alternative approaches.

a proposition whose predicational aspect indicates that it denotes an event, the Passé Simple does not contribute anything beyond the claim that the event is located in the past. It follows that there is no semantic difference between the French sentence (6a), and its English counterpart (6b), even though the French Passé Simple has been claimed to be perfective, whereas the English Simple Past is aspectually neutral according to Hinrichs (1986):

(6) a. Anne écrivit (PS) une lettre.
 b. Anne wrote (PS) a letter.

Similarly, the combination of the Imparfait with a state-denoting proposition does nothing but confirm the stative nature of the proposition, which leads to the equivalence of sentences like (7a) and its English counterpart (7b):

(7) a. Anne savait (IMP) la réponse.
 b. Anne knew (SP) the answer.

If we take these intuitions seriously, we don't need an aspectual operator to get the interpretation of sentences like (6a) and (7a) right. In de Swart's analysis, these sentences get the representations in (8a) and (b) respectively:

(8) a. Anne écrivit (PS) une lettre.
 [ PAST [Anne write a letter]]
 b. Anne savait (IMP) la réponse.
 [ PAST [Anne know the answer]]

In sum, both the Passé Simple and Imparfait are past tense operators. They only differ in their input conditions: the Passé Simple presupposes event-denoting eventuality descriptions, and the Imparfait applies to state-denoting eventuality descriptions. The interpretation of these sentences in the framework of Discourse Representation theory developed by Kamp and Reyle (1993) is worked out in De Swart (1998). This leads to the Discourse Representation Structures in Figure 1 and Figure 2.

One of the interesting features of the treatment of the Passé Simple and the Imparfait as aspectually sensitive past tense operators is that this approach allows us to bridge the gap between a compositional analysis of aspect at the sentence level, and the view that an important role of tenses is to give instructions about how to build the temporal structure of the discourse. If the Passé Simple and the Imparfait are past tense operators that apply to (quantized) events and (homogeneous) states/processes respectively, and if events move time forward,

| n s t x y |
|---|
| $t \prec n$<br>Jeanne(x)<br>Answer(y)<br>$s \circ t$ |
| s: [ x know y ] |

FIGURE 1 DRS for *Anne savait la réponse*

| n e t x y |
|---|
| $t \prec n$<br>Jeanne(x)<br>Letter(y)<br>$e \subseteq t$ |
| e: [ x write y ] |

FIGURE 2 DRS for *Anne écrivit la lettre*

but states do not, we have the starting point of an analysis that accounts for the behavior of the French past tenses at the discourse level. We will say more about tenses at the discourse level in section 3. But let us first examine some more complex examples.

The treatment of examples like (8a) and (b) needs to be extended to pairs of examples like (2a,b) and (3a,b) above, which are identical except for the tense choice. This implies that the Passé Simple and Imparfait do not only apply to propositions whose predicational aspect is of type event or state respectively. This is where we really see the aspectual sensitivity of the tense operator at work. Sentences like (9a) and (10a) present a conflict between the aspectual type of the eventuality description and the input requirements of the tense operator.

(9) a. Jeanne sut la réponse.
    b. [ PAST [ $C_{se}$ [ Jeanne know the answer ] ]

(10) a. Jeanne écrivait une lettre.
    b. [ PAST [ $C_{eh}$ [Jeanne write a letter ] ]

In order to interpret such sentences, De Swart (1998) appeals to the notion of coercion, as used by Moens (1987), Pustejovsky (1995). Coercion is a general process of contextual reinterpretation. In the context of our aspectual theory, implicit aspectual operators coerce the eventuality into the appropriate type: the coercion operator $C_{se}$ in (9b) reflects a hidden aspectual transition that maps the stative description onto an event. One possibility for (9b) is to derive an inchoative reading, where Jeanne (suddenly) knew the answer. Similarly, the coercion operator $C_{eh}$ in (10b) reflects a hidden transition from events to homogeneous eventualities (states or processes). A plausible interpretation for (10b) is a process or progressive interpretation in which Jeanne is in the middle of writing a letter. The interpretation of (9a) and (10a) in DRT is given in Figure 3 and Figure 4.

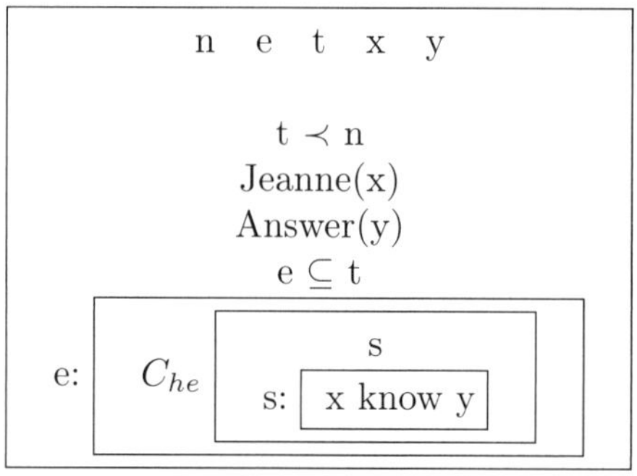


FIGURE 3 DRS for *Anne sut la réponse.*

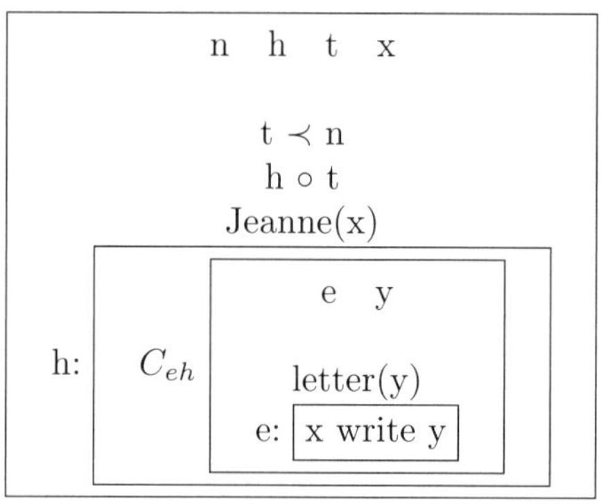


FIGURE 4 DRS for *Anne écrivait la lettre.*

Coercion involves building complex eventuality descriptions in this approach, so all pieces of semantic information remain visible in the representation. Coercion operators only appear when they are triggered by a conflict between the aspectual input of an operator, and the aspectual nature of the argument. They are always semantically underspecified, and should be seen as 'superoperators' that correspond to a family of implicit aspectual transitions. The preferred interpretation depends on context and situation, compare (11a) and (b):

(11) a. Le lendemain, je faisais mes courses chez l'épicier quand je rencontrai Jean.
'The next day, I got (IMP) my groceries at the store when I ran (PS) into Jean.'

b. A cette époque-là, je faisais mes courses chez l'épicier du coin.
'In those days, I got (IMP) my groceries at the local store.'

The same combination of predicational aspect with the Imparfait leads to a progressive interpretation in one context (11a) and to a habitual interpretation in another (11b). Similar observations can be made about the Passé Simple. The combination of the Passé Simple with the verb *être* ('to be') leads to an inchoative interpretation ('Louis XIV became king') in (12a), and a bounded interpretation in (12b) ('Louis XIV was king for a bounded period of time'):

(12) a. En 1643, Louis XIV fut roi.
'In 1643, Louis XIV was (PS) king.'

b. Louis XIV fut roi de 1643 à 1715.
'Louis XIV was (PS) king from 1643 to 1715.'

The two examples use the same tense form, but the underspecified nature of the coercion operator leads to different interpretations, depending on the context. Both inchoative and bounded interpretations satisfy the input conditions on the Passé Simple, because they lead to quantized eventualities.

Although it is possible to formulate rules that block a bounded or inchoative interpretation in certain contexts (cf. Vet (1980); Vikner (1985)), it is difficult to account for the interpretational variability of the Passé Simple and the Imparfait in terms of an aspectual operator, because aspectual operators like the Perfect or the Progressive typically have one, well-defined meaning rather than a family of interpretations. In the literature, we find attempts to derive the different interpretations from one core meaning. For instance, Verkuyl (1995) derives the habitual meaning from the progressive meaning of the Imparfait. Under an analysis in terms of coercion, interpretational variability is not a problem: different interpretations are allowed depending on context and situation, as long as the aspectual input conditions of the tense operator are satisfied. More specifically, the analysis predicts that special meaning effects such as inchoativity, habituality, etc. only show up in contexts that involve coercion operators, not in default cases.

The analysis of the Passé Simple and the Imparfait in terms of aspectually sensitive tense operators also helps to account for the contrast noted in section 1 between (13a,b) and (c), that we will discuss along with the contrast between (14a/b) and (c):[3]

(13) a. #Jean écrivait/écrivit une lettre pendant une heure.
lit: 'Jean wrote (IMP/PS) a letter for an hour'
b. #Jean écrivait une lettre en une heure.
lit: 'Jean wrote (IMP) a letter in an hour'
c. Jean écrivit une lettre en une heure.
lit: 'Jean wrote (PS) a letter in an hour'

(14) a. #Jeanne dormait pendant une heure.
lit: 'Jeanne slept (IMP) for an hour'
b. #Jeanne dormit en une heure.
lit: 'Jeanne slept (PS) in an hour'
c. Jeanne dormit pendant une heure.
lit: 'Jeanne slept (PS) for an hour'

Following De Swart (1998), we interpret durational adverbials introduced by *en* and *pendant* as eventuality description modifiers with different input conditions: *en* applies to events, whereas *pendant* applies to homogeneous eventualities (states or processes). The output type of both sorts of durational adverbials is the same: both describe sets of events. For [*en une heure* [event]] this is to be expected, as the underlying eventuality is already an event. For [*pendant une heure* [state/process]], this is the result of the boundedness imposed by the *pendant* adverbial. The *en*-adverbial is thus an aspectual operator that maps events onto events, whereas the *pendant*-adverbial maps states/processes onto events. Given that tense operators take wide scope over aspectual operators in both the system of chapter 14 and in De Swart (1998), we can explain the contrasts in (13) and (14). Both (13c) and (14c) are grammatical under the single-event reading, because the durational adverbial applies to an eventuality description of the right aspectual type, and so does the tense operator (the Passé Simple locates an event in the past). (13a) and (14b) fail because the eventuality description does not satisfy the aspectual input conditions of the durational adverbial. (13b) and (14a) fail because the aspectual input conditions on the tense operator are not met. Obviously, the

[3]The #-sign means that the sentence is not ungrammatical, but is not acceptable under a single event reading, cf. also chapter 14

sentences are not ungrammatical, because we can coerce the input, and obtain a felicitous reading in the right context (e.g. an iterative or habitual reading for 13a,b, an inchoative reading for 14b). This is why we mark them with #, rather than ∗.

### 2.3 A comparison of the French and English past tenses

The analysis of the Passé Simple and the Imparfait as aspectually sensitive tense operators sheds new light on the contrast between these tenses and the Simple Past (SP) and the Progressive (PROG) in English. English-speaking learners of French and French-speaking learners of English often start from the following misleading equivalencies:

| | | |
|---|---|---|
| Passé Simple | = | Simple Past |
| Imparfait | = | Past Progressive |

This simplistic scheme cannot be maintained. It is true that, as a general rule, sentences in the Past Progressive (PPROG) (15a) can be translated in French by Imparfait sentences (15b):

(15) a. Jean was preparing (PPROG) a meal. He was singing (PPROG).
b. Jean préparait (IMP) un repas. Il chantait (IMP).

The Past Progressive cannot always be used to translate the Imparfait. The main reason for this is that the Imparfait can be used in non-singulative sentences (16a) and in sentences describing permanent states or properties (17a), whereas in the vast majority of cases, the Past Progressive presents one single eventuality as 'going on' at a given moment in time (singulative use):

(16) a. Chaque jour, il venait (IMP) me voir.
b. He came (SP)/*was coming (PPROG) to see me every day.

(17) a. Jean avait (IMP) les yeux bleus.
b. Jean had (SP)/*was having (PPROG) blues eyes.

So the French Imparfait has a larger distribution than the English Past Progressive. We can explain this if we assume with De Swart (1998) that the Progressive is an aspectual operator that maps processes/events onto states that describe the process/event as being in progress, whereas the Imparfait more generally locates a homogeneous eventuality in the past. This can be either a lexical state or process, or an event that has been coerced into a homogeneous eventuality.

The opposite is true for the relation between the French Passé Simple and the English Simple Past. The Passé Simple is more constrained than the Simple Past, which can be rendered in French by the Passé

Simple and the Imparfait. The 'correct' choice depends on many factors that will be discussed in the following sections. In (18a) we find only Simple Past forms. In (18b) we observe that the first Simple Past is translated by a Passé Simple, all the others by Imparfait forms:

(18) a. Garcia *escorted* Ruth to the front door. The Dobermans *panted* after her. She *excuded* some new scent of triumph, freedom and fear, all mixed. They *found* it heady. Their noses *ruffled* up under the sage-green smock.
(Fay Weldon, *The Life and Loves of a She-Devil*, Hodden and Stoughton Publishers, p. 74)

b. Garcia *raccompagna* (PS) Ruth jusqu'à la porte d'entrée. Les dobermans *haletaient* (IMP) derrière elle. Elle *dégageait* un nouveau parfum, de triomphe, de liberté et de peur, tout emmêlé. Qu'ils *trouvaient* (IMP) entêtant. Leurs truffes froncées *s'insinuaient* (IMP) sous sa robe vert cendrée
(Translated by Isabelle Reinharez : La Diable, Editions Deux Temps - Tierce, p. 88 - ex. a.-b. quoted by Trévise 1994: 58)

Moreover, certain verbs of position, like *to hang, to stand, to sit, to lie* and a verb like *to wear* are more frequent in the Simple Past than in the Past Progressive. As pointed out by Dowty (1979, 1986), they are lexically ambiguous between a stative and a non-stative interpretation. So the Past Progressive is not 'needed' in order to obtain a stative reading. In French, on the other hand, the use of the Imparfait is quite normal (in the French counterparts of these verbs), the Passé Simple being excluded in many contexts:

(19) a. Jean entered the room. The President sat behind his desk. He wore a yellow sweater.

b. Jean entra. Le Président était (IMP) / #fut (PS) à son bureau. Il portait (IMP)/ #porta (PS) un pull jaune.

This can be explained if we assume that the English Simple Past is aspectually 'transparent' in the sense that it applies to eventualities of any aspectual type, and it preserves the aspectual nature of the eventuality it applies to (cf. Hinrichs 1986). The French Passé Simple on the other hand always locates an event in the past, so it is not appropriate in the context of (19b). We will come back to the contrast in (19) once we have specified the discourse semantics of the Passé Simple (cf. section 3.4 below).

The analysis in terms of aspectually sensitive tenses provides a link between analyses of the Passé Simple/Imparfait that appeal to the perfective/imperfective contrast, and analyses that focus on the temporal structure of discourse. If events move time forward, but states do not, and Passé Simple sentences always describe events, whereas Imparfait sentences describe states, we can explain the observations made by Kamp and Rohrer (1983) about the temporal structure of French discourse. In section 3, we will argue that the situation is actually more complex. The Passé Simple does not necessarily move time forward, and the Imparfait does not necessarily block progress in time. On the one hand, this has to do with the temporal restrictions on the French past tenses. On the other hand, this has to do with a more general view of the relations between states, processes and events than just narrativity and background. Before we address the more general issues of rhetorical structure (cf. chapter 16), we study the temporal restrictions on the Passé Simple and the Imparfait, and propose a discourse semantics for each tense.

## 3 Passé Simple and Imparfait at the discourse level

### 3.1 Discourse semantics of the Passé Simple

According to many grammarians, the main function of the Passé Simple at the discourse level is to express narrativity, as in (2b), (3b) or (20):

(20) Il se leva et monta dans sa chambre.
'He got up (PS) and went (PS) to his room.'

Narrativity leads to temporal succession. The important insight of Kamp and Rohrer (1983) was that we can capture the discourse semantics of the Passé Simple and the Imparfait in a formal semantic theory based on the principles of Reichenbach (1947). Both the Passé Simple and the Imparfait are past tenses, so they correspond to the Reichenbachian schema E,R-S in chapter 14. Kamp and Rohrer's discourse semantics relies on three assumptions. The first one is that Passé Simple sentences denote events, and Imparfait sentences denote states. We have seen in section 2.2 above how we can obtain this result in a compositional semantics that takes sentence-internal structure seriously. Second, the aspectual difference between states and events is reflected in the relation between E and R. According to Kamp and Rohrer, events are included in their reference time, whereas states include or overlap with their reference time. Finally, the reference time moves forward with the story line. Changes in the reference time thus reflect narrativity. This leads to the following rule for the discourse semantics of the Passé Simple (Kamp and Rohrer, 1983, p. 253-4):[4]

---

[4]For ease of exposition, we follow Kamp and Reyle's convention of using small $e$ for events, $r$ for reference time, and $n$ for the speech time ('now').

(21) **Rule for Passé Simple sentences**

(i) The sentence $S_j$ introduces a new event $e$;

(ii) $e$ lies before the speech time $n$;

(iii) $e$ temporally follows the current reference point $r$ (where $r$ coincides with the event introduced by the last Passé Simple sentence $S_i$ preceding $S_j$);

(iv) the current reference point $r$ is reset at $e$.

(21i) reflects the aspectual nature of Passé Simple sentences and (21ii) reflects their past tense character. The discourse behavior of the Passé Simple is governed by (21iii). Given that the Passé Simple resets the reference time (iv), the next event will be located later in time than the current event. This rule correctly accounts for the observation that sequences of sentences in the Passé Simple such as (20) (but also 2b and 3b above) typically describe events that happen one after another.

Kamp and Rohrer themselves observe that not all occurrences of the Passé Simple exhibit the same clear-cut temporal ordering as (20) above. They provide the following examples in which $e$ does not follow the last event already mentioned:

(22) Marie chanta et Pierre l'accompagna au piano.
'Marie sang (PS) and Pierre accompanied (PS) her at the piano.'

(23) L'année dernière Jean escalada le Cervin. Le premier jour il monta jusqu'à la cabane H. Il y passa la nuit. Ensuite il attaqua la face nord. Douze heures plus tard il arriva au sommet.
'Last year Jean climbed (PS) mount Cervin. The first day he reached (PS) mountain cottage H. He spent (PS) the night there. Next he attacked (PS) the north side of the mountain. Twelve hours later he reached (PS) the top.'

(24) L'été de cette année-là vit plusieurs changements dans la vie de nos héros. François épousa Adèle, Jean-Louis partit pour le Brésil et Paul s'acheta une maison à la campagne.
'The summer of that year saw (PS) several changes in the lives of our heroes. François married (PS) Adèle, Jean-Louis went (PS) to Brazil and Paul bought (PS) a house in the countryside.'

In (22), there is one event consisting of two parallel subevents that take place at the same time. In (23) and (24), the first sentence mentions an event which is divided into separable episodes. In (23), these episodes are temporally ordered; in (24), the temporal relationship between them is left unresolved. According to Kamp and Rohrer, (22)-(24) show that only a weak version of the Passé Simple rule accounts for all cases. They propose to replace (21) by (25) (Kamp and Rohrer, 1983, p. 261).

(25) **Rule for Passé Simple sentences** (revised)

(i) the sentence $S_j$ introduces a new event $e$;

(ii) $e$ lies before the speech point $n$;

(iii) $e$ may not entirely precede the event or time which currently functions as $r$;

(iv) the current reference point $r$ is reset at $e$.

(25iii) allows all the temporal structures in (20) and in (22-24), but blocks the inverse temporal order between two sentences. This seems to be correct in view of examples like the following (see Kamp and Rohrer (1983), Molendijk and De Swart (1999), Saussure (2000)):

(26) a. Jean se cassa la jambe. # Il se jeta par la fenêtre.
'Jean broke (PS) his leg. He jumped (PS) out of the window.'

b. Jean épousa une princesse. # Il la rencontra à Fatu-Hiva.
'Jean married (PS) a princess. He met (PS) her in Fatu-Hiva.'

These sequences are infelicitous under the interpretation in which the event of the second sentence precedes the one introduced by the first sentence. This temporal feature of the Passé Simple clearly opposes this tense form to the Simple Past of English, which can be used in explicative contexts that involve inverse temporal order:

(27) a. Jean broke his leg. He jumped out of the window.

b. Jean married a princess. He met her in Fatu-Hiva.

Often, utterances quoted to exemplify inverse temporal order also permit a linear interpretation, as in (28):

(28) a. Jane left me. She fell in love with somebody else.
(Caenepeel and Moens 1994)

b. Max fell. John pushed him. (Lascarides and Asher 1993)

A priori the possibility that Jane met someone after she left me or that, when John fell, Max grabbed the occasion to push him over the edge is not excluded. But the point is that these discourses allow an interpretation in terms of inverse temporal order (Jane left me after she fell in love with somebody else, John's pushing caused Max to fall), that is unavailable for their French translations in (29):

(29) a. Jeanne le quitta. Elle tomba amoureuse de quelqu'un d'autre.
'Jeanne left (PS) him. She fell (PS) in love with someone else.'

b. Max tomba. Jean le poussa.
'Max fell (PS). Jean pushed (PS) him.'

Thus, the Passé Simple constrains the temporal ordering of the events more severely than the English Simple Past does. Smith (1993) concludes from examples like (27) and (28) that there is no need to complicate the semantics of tenses; there is only a need for appropriate pragmatic rules. Similar ideas led Lascarides and Asher (1993) to abandon the idea of exploiting the Reichenbachian notion of reference time to account for the temporal structure of narrative discourse, and develop an account in terms of rhetorical structure instead. The examples in (20), (22-24), (29) and (31) show that the picture for the Passé Simple is more complicated. On the one hand, certain temporal structures (in casu, inverse temporal order) are blocked by the tense form. On the other hand, the Passé Simple allows more than just progress in time, and the choice between the different temporal configurations is driven by rhetorical structure, as we will argue in chapter 16 below.

Moeschler (2000) claims that (25iii) is still too strong, for the insertion of *parce que* 'because', *car* 'for' etc. in certain sequences of type Passé Simple + Passé Simple can lead to an explicative, inverse temporal order reading. Here is an example:

(30) Il heurta du pied le corps de son camarade [. . . ]. Un tremblement le prit, car il vit que le Pharaon était en colère. (Théophile Gautier, Le roman de la Momie, http://mercator.ens.fr/home /letourne/ gautier/ gautier.html. bnf.fr/MetaPrincipal.htm)
'His feet touched (PS) the dead body of his friend. He got (PS) the shivers, for he saw (PS) that the Pharaoh was in anger.'

In this example, the temporal order does not match the linguistic order, for the seeing temporally precedes the getting the shivers, even though it is reported by a later sentence. This suggests that causal conjunctions and connectors facilitate the inverse temporal reading. More examples along these lines are the following:

(31) Le singe s'échappa. Nous ne le retrouvâmes plus, car il disparut dans la forêt épaisse.
'The monkey escaped (PS). We NEG found (PS) it anymore, for it vanished (PS) into the thick forest.'

(32) Les passagers descendirent. En effet, la porte se débloqua finalement.
'The passengers got (PS) out because the doors finally opened' (PS).

(33) Jean se réveilla quand la voiture s'arrêta.
'Jean woke (PS) up when the car stopped (PS).'

The question that arises at this point is whether or not the claim made in (25) about the constraint imposed by the Passé Simple on temporal ordering can be maintained. And if not, what explains the difference between the Passé Simple and the Simple Past in the availability of inverse temporal order? We think that the intuition that the Passé Simple blocks inverse temporal order in cases like (26) and (29) is strong enough for us to maintain the claim about the ban on inverse temporal order. But note that (25iii) claims that $e$ may not entirely precede the event or time **that currently functions as** $r$. For a fuller account, we need a better understanding of what must be considered the reference point $r$ of a sentence $S_j$ with respect to which the eventuality reported by $S_j$ must be located on the time-axis.

In Hinrichs (1986) it is argued that subordinate clauses introduced by a temporal connective like *when* are always processed first, and thus provide the reference time for the main clause. This is sufficient to account for the well-formedness of (33).[5] In order to deal with the other cases, Molendijk and Vet (1995) and Molendijk and De Swart (1999) broaden the notion of reference time to that of 'temporal antecedent'. They argue that the selection of the temporal antecedent of $S_j$ is severely constrained: it must correspond to an earlier sentence $S_i$ such that the 'rhetorical relationship' (taken in the sense proposed by Lascarides and Asher (1993), see chapter 16 below) that can be established between $S_j$ and $S_i$ by virtue of pragmatic or textual knowledge does not conflict with what is (temporally) expressed by the tense form occurring in $S_j$. For an example like (31), this means that the temporal antecedent of the last sentence of (31) *il disparut dans la forêt* cannot be the immediately preceding sentence *nous ne le retrouvâmes plus*, for the disappearance into the forest precedes the not-finding. The causal connective *car* implies partial or complete anteriority, along the lines of Lascarides and Asher (1993). Identification of the temporal antecedent of the last sentence of (31) with the first sentence of the discourse does not create a conflict betweeen rhetorical structure and tense form. The rhetorical relationship between the escape and the vanishing is of type Narration (Lascarides and Asher (1993), Asher and Bras (1993), see also chapter 16 below), and Narration implies posteriority. Obviously, the temporal relation of posteriority is quite compatible with the semantics of the Passé Simple (cf. 25iii).

This analysis explains why we can add an adverb like *aussitôt* 'immediately', which expresses forward movement in time. The temporal structure of (34) (with *aussitôt*) is identical to that of (31) (without *aussitôt*):

[5]Hinrichs' view is modified by De Swart (2001) in view of data where this view conflicts with topic-focus articulation, but she maintains the possibility that a *quand*-clause provides the reference time for the main clause as in (33).

(34) Le singe s'échappa. Nous ne le retrouvâmes plus, car il disparut aussitôt dans la forêt épaisse.
'The monkey escaped (PS). We NEG found (PS) it anymore, for it vanished (PS) immediately into the thick forest.'

We conclude that temporal and rhetorical relations between sentences are to be teased apart in contexts like these, and refer to Molendijk and De Swart (1999) for more discussion.

The argumentation extends to the examples in (30) and (32). For instance, the temporal antecedent of *il vit que ...*, the last sentence of (30), is not the preceding sentence *un tremblement le prit*, but the earlier sentence *il heurta du pied le corps de son camarade.* If we take the time of feet-touching as the reference time $r$, then the third sentence does not express anteriority with respect to the current $r$ (which would cause problems for the rule in 25iii above), but posteriority (which we know is compatible with the discourse semantics of the Passé Simple). On the basis of these observation, we propose to further modify the clauses (iii) and (iv) in the rule for the Passé Simple:

(35) **Rule for Passé Simple sentences** (second revised version)

(i) the sentence $S_j$ introduces a new event $e$;

(ii) $e$ lies before the speech point $n$;

(iii) $e$ may not entirely precede the past time event or time which currently functions as $r$ or - more generally - as the temporal antecedent.

(iv) The temporal antecedent is provided by another sentence $S_i$ with which $S_j$ establishes a rhetorical relation *Rhet* such that the temporal relationship that is associated with *Rhet* does not conflict with what may be (temporally) expressed by the Passé Simple: non-anteriority.

Note that this rule does not take into account the so-called 'deictic' or 'autonomous' use of the Passé Simple, illustrated in (36):

(36) En 1869, Dumoulin visita Paris. Ses récitals eurent un succès formidable. Certes, ses symphonies - car Dumoulin fut un grand compositeur de musique orchestrale - étaient appréciées d'un Liszt et d'un Wagner, mais la société parisienne admirait surtout ses compositions pour piano.
'In 1869, Dumoulin visited (PS) Paris. His recitals had (PS) an enormous success. Certainly, his symphonies - for Dumoulin was (PS) a great composer of orchestral music - were (IMP) appreciated by people like Liszt and Wagner, but Parisian society especially admired (IMP) his compositions for piano.'

In this fragment, it is not possible to establish discourse relations between the sentence *car Dumoulin fut un grand compositeur de musique orchestrale* and the other sentences. Intuitively, the temporal antecedent of the sentence corresponds with the speech time $n$: the sentence does not situate the event in the time of the story (situated around 1860), but simply places this fact before the speech time. Thus the event narrated in the Passé Simple is presented in isolation of its textual environment to the point that it expresses a pure and simple 'past' in the sense of Molendijk (1990), Molendijk and De Swart (1999). As a non-anaphoric use of the Passé Simple, it does not require a special discourse semantics, and we will ignore this use in the following.

The rule for the Passé Simple will have to be modified one more time, but the motivation for that final revision comes from a comparison with the interpretation of the Imparfait in section 3.4 below. So let us move to the rule for the Imparfait first.

### 3.2 Discourse semantics of the Imparfait

Sentences in the Imparfait are traditionally taken to describe background information that does not move the story forward, as in (37):

(37) a. Je rencontrai son ami Jean. Il avait 20 ans. Il avait les yeux bleus.
'I met (PS) his friend Jean. He was (IMP) 20 years old. He had (IMP) blue eyes.'

b. Jean entra dans son bureau. Il était fatigué. Il avait mal à la tête.
'Jean entered (PS) his office. He was (IMP) tired. He had (IMP) a head-ache.'

The Imparfait sentences in (37a) describe individual-level predicates and give background information of a more permanent nature. The Imparfait sentences in (37b) describe stage-level predicates, which give background information relevant to the situation at hand. In both cases, we have stative descriptions that do not imply narrativity or temporal progression. Kamp and Rohrer therefore take sentences in the Imparfait to denote states, and propose the following rule for the Imparfait (Kamp and Rohrer, 1983, p.253):

(38) **Rule for Imparfait sentences**

(i) the sentence $S_j$ introduces a new state $s$;
(ii) $s$ is located before the moment of speech $n$;
(iii) $s$ temporally contains the current reference point $r$ (where $r$ normally coincides with the event that was introduced by the last Passé Simple sentence preceding $S_j$).

(38i) and (ii) are consistent with the interpretation of the Imparfait as a past tense that applies to homogeneous eventualities (see section 2.2 above).[6] Clause (38iii) constrains the temporal relation between the state and the reference time to a relation of inclusion. Note moreover that the Imparfait, unlike the Passé Simple, does not introduce a new reference time. As a result of the orientation towards the current reference time, the Imparfait does not move the story line forward, but establishes a relation of temporal overlap with the last Passé Simple sentence. The discourses in (37) show that a sequence of Imparfait sentences can be oriented towards one particular event described by a Passé Simple sentence.

However, as Kamp and Rohrer themselves admit, (38iii) is too strong. They provide the following counter-example:

(39) Jean tourna l'interrupteur. La lumière éclatante l'éblouissait.
'Jean switched (PS) on the light. The bright light blinded (IMP) him.'

It is clear that *la lumière l'éblouissait* 'the light blinded him' does not temporally contain *Jean tourna l'interrupteur* 'Jean turned on the light'.[7] A similar example is discussed in Hinrichs (1986) for English:

(40) Max switched off the light. The room was pitch dark around him.

Hinrichs proposes a revision of Kamp and Rohrer's rule for the introduction of reference times. He suggests that every event introduces a new reference time following the event in time. Subsequent state sentences can then be oriented towards that new reference time, and thus describe a situation later in time than the event of the previous sentence. In metaphorical terms, Kamp and Rohrer's analysis can be described as an attempt to 'pull' the reference time forward, whereas Hinrichs' analysis 'pushes' the reference time forward. However, Hinrichs' revision does not help to account for the 'mirror images' of (37) and (40) in (41):

(41) a. Max switched on the light. The room was pitch dark around him.

---

[6] Kamp and Rohrer adopt an ontology of states and events, whereas De Swart (1998) adopts a three-way ontology of states, processes and events. If we leave processes out of the discussion for the time being, we can see that the analyses are very similar indeed.

[7] *tourner l'interrupteur* literally means 'turning the switch', so the first sentence could mean either 'Jean switched on the light' or 'Jean switched off the light'. The second sentence of (39) cancels a reading implying that 'Jean tourna l'interrupteur' causes the room to be dark.

b. Max rentra. Le soleil lui brûlait les épaules.
   'Max went (PS) back in. The sun burned (IMP) his shoulders.'

In (41a), the room being pitch dark is the motivation for Max to switch on the light, so it describes a situation leading up to the event. Similarly, the Imparfait sentence in (41b) describes a state of the sun burning Max's shoulders, leading him to go back into the house subsequently.

In view of examples like (37) and (41), certain French linguists explicitly abandon the simultaneity hypothesis of the Imparfait (Berthonneau and Kleiber (1993, 1994, 1998, 1999)).[8] Landeweerd (1998) proposes a minimal revision of the simultaneity hypothesis. She replaces simultaneity by left adjunction and right adjunction. She suggests that an Imparfait sentence normally cannot be temporally separated from its temporal antecedent (reference point). That is, it does not permit a gap between the Imparfait eventuality and its antecedent. The examples in (42-44) and (45-47) illustrate the contrast:

(42) Jean se mit en marche. Il boitait fortement.
'Jean started (PS) walking. He limped (IMP) heavily.'

(43) Marie mit sa nouvelle robe. Elle lui allait très bien.
'Marie put on (PS) her new dress. She looked (IMP) very nice in it.'

(44) Jean attrapa une contravention. Il roulait trop vite.
'Jean got (PS) a ticket. He drove (IMP) too fast.'

(45) Jean sortit sous la pluie. ?Il était tout mouillé.
'Jean went(PS) out in the rain. He was (IMP) soaking wet.'

(46) Le mannequin monta dans la voiture. ?Son parfum empestait la voiture.
'The model got (PS) into the car. She poisoned (IMP) the air with her perfume.'

(47) Jean attrapa une contravention. ?Il brûlait un feu rouge.
'Jean got (PS) a ticket. He ran (IMP) a red light.'

In (42) and (43) the situation referred to by the second sentence is available immediately after the occurrence of the event reported by the first sentence: as soon as Jean starts walking, he is limping; as soon as Marie puts on her new dress, it is true that she looks nice in it. In (45) on the other hand, there is a gap between going out in the rain and being soaking wet. Similarly, the air is not poisoned right away when

[8]Berthonneau and Kleiber develop an analysis in terms of an 'imparfait méronomique'. We will not discuss this theory here, but see Molendijk (1996) for a critical discussion.

the model gets in (46). The contrast between (41b), (44) and (47) is similar, but relates to left adjunction, rather than right adjunction.

The proposal in Landeweerd (1998) weakens the semantics of the Imparfait. Alternatively, we can try to maintain temporal overlap, but adapt the notion of reference time. Molendijk (1993) argues that the temporal antecedent of a sentence $S_j$ need not be explicitly mentioned, but may correspond to an implication or presupposition of an earlier $S_i$. In this approach, (41b) and (44) take the temporal presupposition of their first sentence as the temporal antecedent, whereas (39), (42) and (43) take the temporal implication of the first sentence as the temporal antecedent.

Note that temporal presuppositions and implications are respectively left and right adjoined to the event time. In other words, the time of the presupposition/implication and the event time 'abut': there is no gap between them (cf. chpater 16 below for more on the 'abut' relation in a DRT framework). In this sense, the explanations in terms of left/right adjunction (Landeweerd) and temporal presupposition/implicature (Molendijk) amount to the same thing, but use different tools (temporal semantic relation established by the Imparfait and definition of temporal antecedent respectively) to obtain this result. In the revised version of the discourse rule for the Imparfait, we implement Molendijk's approach, rather than Landeweerd's proposal, because we exploit the extended notion of temporal antecedent in the discourse semantics for the Passé Simple as well (see section 3.4 below. Accordingly, we replace the Imparfait rule given in (38) by (48):

(48) **Rule for Imparfait sentences** (final version):

(i) the sentence $S_j$ introduces a new state $s$;

(ii) $s$ is located before the moment of speech $n$;

(iii) $s$ temporally contains the temporal antecedent (relationship of global simultaneity)

(iv) the temporal antecedent of $S_j$ is provided by another sentence $S_i$ (or the implication/presupposition of $S_i$) with which $S_j$ establishes a rhetorical relation *Rhet* such that the temporal relationship that is associated with *Rhet* does not conflict with what is temporally expressed by the Imparfait: global simultaneity.

We will see that temporal presuppositions and implications also play a role in the discourse semantics of the Passé Composé. For all tenses it is obvious that a further analysis in terms of rhetorical structure is required to fine tune the temporal structure (see chapter 16 below).

### 3.3 The narrative Imparfait

There exists a long-standing problem in French aspectology concerning the so-called narrative or 'picturesque' use of the Imparfait: this tense form may unexpectedly advance narrative time. Here is an instantiation of this use:

(49) Le commandant se jeta sur l'interphone et hurla qu'il avait à parler à Mr Chisnutt. Trois minutes plus tard, Mr Chisnutt se présentait chez le commandant (Molendijk 1990).
'The commander threw (PS) himself on the intercom and shouted (PS) that he had (IMP) to see Mr. Chisnutt. Three minutes later, Mr. Chisnutt presented (IMP) himself at the commander's office.'

As far as aspectual class is concerned, the third clause of (49) is characterized as an event. The description of events with the Imparfait normally leads to a progressive or a habitual interpretation under the influence of coercion (cf. section 2.2 above). However, in (49) the third clause seems to be event-denoting, even though it is in the Imparfait, and the temporal structure of the discourse is that of narrative order rather than simultaneity. This suggests that the narrative Imparfait follows the rule for the Passé Simple, rather than for the Imparfait.

Bres (1998) and Gosselin (1999), following Tasmowski-De Rijck (1985), provide 'literary' examples in which the narrative Imparfait combines with bounding adverbial complements:

(50) Tous deux se mirent à aller à côté l'un de l'autre, sans rien se dire. Ils arrivèrent à une route pavée [...]. Là [...] ils marchaient longtemps [...] (E. et J. de Goncourt, quoted by Bres (1998))
'Both started (PS) to walk side by side, without talking to each other. They reached (PS) a paved road. There, they walked (IMP) a long time.'

(51) Les deux hommes erraient ainsi quelques instants, gênés, bousculés (M. Allain, *Le train perdu*, quoted by Gosselin (1999)).
'That way, the two men wandered (IMP) a little while (literally: some moments), perplexed, bewildered.'

The combination with bounding adverbial complements is relevant, because these normally require the Passé Simple rather than the Imparfait. In § 2.2 above, we argued that they turn an unbounded eventuality (state or process) into a quantized event. However, there are strong indications that the narrative Imparfait cannot be identified with the Passé Simple. Molendijk (1990) and Berthonneau and Kleiber (1999) point out that the narrative Imparfait generally establishes a rather specific (non-temporal) relationship with the preceding discourse. In (49) for example, the Imparfait *se présentait* 'presented himself' presents the arrival of Mr Brown as something that could be expected on the basis of the information given by the preceding discourse. If we replace *Mr Chisnutt* in (49) by *Mr Brown*, a person whose arrival cannot be expected on the basis of the information in the discourse, the discourse would not be quite natural. We can only obtain a natural use of the Imparfait if the sentence contains an expression indicating surprise. In (52), a cleft construction is used to that effect:

(52) Le commandant se jeta sur l'interphone et hurla qu'il avait à parler à Mr Chisnutt. Trois minutes plus tard, c'était Mr Brown qui se présentait chez le commandant.
The commander threw (PS) himself on the intercom and shouted (PS) that he had (IMP) to see Mr. Chisnutt. Three minutes later, it was Mr. Brown who presented (IMP) himself at the commander's office.

Tasmowski-De Rijck (1985), Berthonneau and Kleiber (1999) and others observe that sentences in the narrative Imparfait often contain a temporal adverb like *trois minutes plus tard*, that pushes the reference time forward (cf. chapter 16 below for more on temporal adverbs). In many contexts, the temporal adverb cannot be omitted (cf. (53a) and (b), discussed by Berthonneau and Kleiber (1999)):

(53) a. Pour la première fois de sa vie, il ne s'ennuya pas au théâtre et il passa la nuit avec des filles. Six mois plus tard il se remariait. (Maupassant)
'For the first time of his life, he NEG was not bored in the theatre, and he spent (PS) the night with girls. Six months later, he remarried (IMP).'

b. Pour la première fois de sa vie, il ne s'ennuya pas au théâtre et il passa la nuit avec des filles. #Il se remariait ( Berthonneau and Kleiber (1999)).
'For the first time of his life, he NEG was not bored in the theatre, and he spent (PS) the night with girls. He remarried (IMP).'

This observation provides the key to the narrative Imparfait. Temporal adverbs like *six mois plus tard* shift the reference time (cf. Kamp and Reyle 1993, de Swart 2001). Accordingly, we can maintain an interpretation in terms of simultaneity with the current reference time. This allows us to preserve the discourse semantics of the Imparfait (cf. 48 above). Note that in those cases where no temporal adverb is present, some other element seems to take care of shifting of the reference time:

*là* in (50) or *ainsi* in (51). Space and time are intimately connected Asher and Bras (1993), and the (spatial) reference *là* makes to the location of the road in (50) allows the (temporal) reference to shift to the moment the road has been reached.

Although the combination with durative adverbs in (50) and (51) shows that the imperfectivity of the Imparfait is challenged by the boundedness of *longtemps* or *quelques instants*, we observe that these adverbs are not as strongly bounded as 'authentic' quantized duration complements like *de 5h à 8h* 'from 5 to 8' or *pendant 45 minutes* 'for 45 minutes'. These remain odd in the Imparfait (in a single event reading), even in a context that favors a narrative use of the Imparfait:[9]

(54) ?Les deux hommes erraient ainsi deux minutes, gênés, bousculés.
'That way, the two men wander (IMP) for two minutes, perplexed, bewildered.'

So even if it might be reasonable to think that the Imparfait is developing into 'some kind of Passé Simple', we conclude that this development is not quite completed.

### 3.4 Final remarks about the discourse semantics of the Passé Simple and the Imparfait

Now that we have established the discourse semantics of the Imparfait, we need to make some final modifications to the rule for the Passé Simple. The first observation here is that the temporal antecedent of the Passé Simple can also be implicit, rather than explicit:

(55) Il se mit à marcher. (Soudain), il s'enfonça dans la neige jusqu'aux chevilles.
'He started (PS) walking. (Suddenly), he sank (PS) away in the snow up to his ankles.'

In (55a), the second Passé Simple event is temporally oriented towards the time of walking, which we construe as the temporal implication of the first sentence: *à un moment donné de la marche, il s'enfonça ...* 'at some point during the walk, he sank away ... '. So not only Imparfait sentences, but also Passé Simple sentences may take the temporal implication of an earlier sentence as their antecedent.

The second observation is that the current formulations of the discourse rules for the Passé Simple and the Imparfait overlap. If the Passé

[9] Tasmowski-De Rijck (1985) does provide examples of such use of the Imparfait: *et le jour du championnat, Jean courait trois heures; le lendemain, Jean faisait son devoir en une 1/2 heure (chose qui ne se reproduisit plus par la suite).* This use remains exceptional, however, and is judged unnatural by many native speakers of French.

Simple tolerates all temporal relations except inverse order, we predict that both Passé Simple and Imparfait can express simultaneity. We think this semantics for the Passé Simple clause (35iii) is too weak. In the cases that Kamp and Rohrer discuss to motivate a rule weaker than posteriority, the Passé Simple focusses on some part of the interval referred to by a preceding past tense sentence. For instance, the second sentence of (23) above, repeated here as (56) expresses partial simultaneity with respect to the first sentence:

(56) L'année dernière Jean escalada le Cervin. Le premier jour il monta jusqu'à la cabane H. Il y passa la nuit. Ensuite il attaqua la face nord. Douze heures plus tard il arriva au sommet.
'Last year Jean climbed (PS) mount Cervin. The first day he reached (PS) mountain cottage H. He spent (PS) the night there. Next he attacked (PS) the north side of the mountain. Twelve hours later he reached (PS) the top.'

Similar remarks apply to the second, third and fourth sentence of (24). So both the Imparfait and the Passé Simple can be used to express temporal overlap. But where the Imparfait normally expresses global simultaneity, the Passé Simple expresses (proper) temporal inclusion (see Molendijk 1990). (57) illustrates the contrast:

(57) Pierre et Marie se promenaient dans la rue. Pierre expliquait à sa femme les conditions de vie sur Mars et lui indiqua la Planète Rouge (Molendijk 1990).
'Pierre and Marie walked (IMP) down the street. Pierre explained (IMP) to his wife the conditions of life on Mars and pointed (PS) towards the Red Planet.'

The Imparfait form *expliquait* 'explained' expresses global simultaneity with the time of the walking, whereas the Passé Simple form *indiqua* 'pointed towards' indicates proper inclusion. An example like (22) above is not an exception to this rule. It normally occurs in contexts like (58):

(58) Le rideau s'ouvrit. Tout le monde se tut. Marie chanta. Pierre l'accompagna au piano.
'The curtain rose (PS). Everybody stopped (PS) talking. Marie sang (PS). Pierre accompanied (PS) her at the piano.'

(58) locates both the singing and the playing as posterior to *tout le monde se tut* 'everybody stopped talking'. These observations lead us to propose the following revision of the rule for the Passé Simple:

(59) **Rule for sentences in the Passé Simple** (final version)

(i) the sentence $S_j$ introduces a new event $e$;

(ii) $e$ lies before the speech point $n$;

(iii) For non-deictic (anaphoric) uses, $e$ is posterior to the temporal antecedent, or is temporally included in it.

(iv) The temporal antecedent of $S_j$ is provided by another sentence $S_i$ (or its implication/presupposition) with which $S_j$ establishes a rhetorical relation *Rhet* such that the temporal relationship that is associated with *Rhet* does not conflict with what may be temporally expressed by the Passé Simple: posteriority or (proper) temporal inclusion.

We are now in a position to explain why (19b) above, repeated here as (60), is odd. (Note that the rule given in (35) does not exclude it):

(60) Jean entra. Le président #fut à son bureau. Il #porta un pull jaune.
Jean entered (PS) the room. The president sat (PS) (lit: was) behind his desk. He wore (PS) a yellow sweater.

In (60), the use of the Passé Simple forms *fut* 'was' and *porta* 'wore' is infelicitous, because we assume there is a relation of global simultaneity between *le Président être à son bureau* 'the President sit behind his desk' and *il porter un pull jaune* 'he wear a yellow sweater' and these form the background to (so are also globally simultaneous with) *Jean entrer* 'Jean entrer', whereas the Passé Simple permits only posteriority or proper temporal inclusion.

None of what has been said so far applies to the Simple Past of English. Lascarides and Asher (1993) argue that this tense form does not impose particular constraints on temporal ordering. So (at least part of) the explanation of the difference between (60) (unnatural) and its English equivalent (61) (perfectly acceptable) can be explained by the absence of these constraints in English:

(61) Jean entered the room. The president sat behind his desk. He wore a yellow sweater.

In the preceding sections, we have seen that there are important differences between the simple past tenses of French and English. It can easily be shown that the same observation applies to the present perfect tenses of both languages: the Passé Composé of French and the Present Perfect of English. The study of these tense forms is the topic of the next section.

## 4 The semantics of the Passé Composé

Although the English term 'present perfect' suggests that the Present Perfect is not part of the past tense system of the language, this cannot be the full story for the French Passé Composé. The contrast between Passé Simple and Imparfait only exists in the written language of standard modern French. In the spoken language, the Passé Composé has replaced the Passé Simple. Of course the Passé Composé also exists in the (standard) written language, but only in its true resultative use (cf. chapter 14). Thus a system with an opposition between three tenses (Passé Simple, Imparfait, (resultative) Passé Composé) has developed into a system with an opposition between two tenses (Imparfait and (resultative/narrative Passé Composé). This has led to the claim in Vet (1992) and Vet (1999) that the Passé Composé has developed into a perfective past tense, similar to the Passé Simple, while also maintaining its traditional interpretation as a (resultative) perfect.

A discourse semantic study of the use of the narrative Passé Composé in Camus' novel *L'étranger*, carried out by De Swart and Molendijk (2002) suggests that the temporal structure of stories told in the Passé Composé is quite different from that of Passé Simple discourses, which leads us to claim that the Passé Composé may be on its way to developing into a perfective past, but it isn't quite there yet. In this section, we explore the temporal, aspectual and discourse-semantic properties of the Passé Composé. The analysis of time adverbials in chapter 16 below will lead us to re-consider the role of time adverbials in the temporal structure of a Passé Composé discourse.

### 4.1 A temporal analysis of the perfect

The difference between the Simple Past (SP) in (62a) and the Present Perfect (PP) in (62b), has been analyzed by Reichenbach (1947) as follows:

(62) a. Sara left the party. SP: E,R-S
b. Sara has left the party. PP: E-R,S

In (62a) as well as in (62b), the event E of Sara's departure is located before the speech time S on the time axis. The main difference between the two sentences is that (62b) does not only look at the past, but maintains the importance of S, whereas (62a) only reports the leaving. Reichenbach explains the difference in perspective in terms of his notion of reference time R. For the Simple Past, the reference time coincides with the past event E, whereas for the Present Perfect, the reference time coincides with the moment of speech S.

The Reichenbachian structure E-R,S has been used to explain various properties of the English Present Perfect. It has been claimed that locating time adverbialsadverbial modify the reference time R, rather than the event time E. Given that R coincides with S, we expect the

Present Perfect to be compatible with deictic adverbials only, which seems to be confirmed by the contrast between (63a) and (b):

(63) a. *Sara has left at six o'clock.
b. Sara has left this afternoon.

Furthermore, we expect the Present Perfect to be an inappropriate tense to tell a story, for narrative contexts require the perspective to shift to the sequence of events, rather than on S. In Boogaart (1999) the occurrence of a tense in a subordinate clauses introduced by *when* are used to test for narrative use. The Present Perfect cannot be used in this context (64a), whereas the Simple Past can (64b) confirms that the former is not a narrative tense, but the latter is:

(64) a. *When John has seen (PP) me, he has got (PP)/got (SP) frightened.
b. When John saw (SP) me, he got (SP) frightened.

The fact that the Reichenbachian analysis of the English Present Perfect can be exploited to explain the restrictions of this tense on locating time adverbials and its infelicitous use in narrative contexts is a nice result. However, the analysis raises problems for other cases. The Pluperfect combines with locating time adverbials that can either modify the reference time R or the event time E, cf. the ambiguous (65):

(65) Sara had left at six o'clock.
a. At six o'clock (it became clear that) Sara had already left.
b. (At some point in time it became clear that) Sara had left at six o'clock.

The Pluperfect also has a narrative use in *when*-clauses:

(66) When John had crossed the street, he entered a shoe store.

One way of getting around the problem of the Pluperfect is to assume that this tense is ambiguous between a perfect in the past and a past in the past (cf. Kamp and Reyle 1993: 598-601). Although this is a perfectly legitimate solution to the problem, it implies that the 'strong' interpretation of the Reichenbachian analysis for English (i.e. the view that the Reichenbachian analysis explains the observations made with respect to (63) and (64) is not supported by other perfect tenses besides the Present Perfect).

If we compare the English Present Perfect to the Dutch Voltooid Tegenwoordige Tijd (VTT) and the French Passé Composé (PC), we see that the French and Dutch perfect tenses easily combine with locating time adverbials, as illustrated in (67a) and (b), which are literal translations of (63a):

(67) a. Sara is om zes uur vertrokken. [Dutch]
b. Sara est partie à six heures. [French]

Furthermore, the French Passé Composé freely occurs in subordinate clauses introduced by 'when', but its English and Dutch counterparts do not, compare (64a) with (68a) and (b):[10]

(68) a. *Toen Jan me heeft gezien (VTT) is hij bang geworden (VTT)/ werd hij bang (OVT). [Dutch]
b. Quand Jean m'a vu (PC), il a eu peur (PC). [French]

There are two ways we can go about these cross-linguistic differences. We might assume that Dutch and French are exceptional, and the English Present Perfect is the only tense that provides a perfect illustration of the Reichenbachian schema E-R,S. Thus Vet (1992; 1999, 2001) proposes that the French Passé Composé is ambiguous or polysemous between a present perfect and a simple past tense. The other option is that we maintain the characterization of the Dutch Voltooid Tegenwoordige Tijd and the French Passé Composé as perfects that obey the Reichenbachian schema E-R,S, and explain the restrictions that various languages impose on the compatibility with time adverbials and the narrative use of the tense in a different way. In De Swart and Molendijk (2002) and De Swart (2003), the second option is explored. These papers assume the Dutch and English tenses are subject to additional constraints. The English PP blocks any temporal relation whatsoever with the event time E. The Dutch VTT resists temporal relations between E and other eventualities (but not other times, as indicated by time adverbials). The French PC is not subject to any further constraints, which guarantees that it freely combines with time adverbials and occurs in narrative contexts. However, it remains a perfect in the sense that the event in the past is viewed from the speech time S. Accordingly, we propose the following semantic rules for the perfect in English, Dutch and French:

(69) Semantics of the English PP
(i) E-R,S
(ii) E@X where @ is any temporal relation, and X is a moment other than R or S, or an event.

(70) Semantics of the Dutch VTT
(i) E-R,S

[10]Note that (68a) is not ungrammatical in certain dialects of Dutch, especially in Flanders (C. Vetters, p.c.). In these dialects, the Onvoltooid Verleden Tijd (OVT) is losing its narrative ground to the VTT, possibly under the influence of French.

(ii) E@X where @ is any temporal relation, and X is an event.

(71) Semantics of the French PC

(i) E-R,S

These rules allow us to maintain the Reichenbachian schema for the perfect in all three languages. They give a weak interpretation of the Reichenbachian analysis in which the restrictions on the English PP do not follow from the schema E-R,S itself, but are formulated as additional constraints on the tense form. This allows counterparts of the Present Perfect in other languages to be less constrained perfects. Independent support for this view comes from an analysis of the English, Dutch and French Pluperfect. For all these tenses, we can maintain the traditional Reichenbachian schema E-R-S. Without any further constraints, we would then derive the properties of the English Pluperfect illustrated in (65) and (66) above. Thus we don't need to posit an ambiguity between perfect in the past and past in the past. We will not elaborate this point, but concentrate on the consequences of this cross-linguistic analysis of the Present Perfect for the Passé Composé.

### 4.2 An aspectual analysis of the perfect

The Reichenbachian schema of the perfect focusses on the temporal location of the eventuality, and of the reference time, the time from which the eventuality is viewed. It does not say anything about the aspectual nature of the perfect. A more aspectually oriented definition of the perfect has been proposed by Kamp and Reyle (1993), and adopted by De Swart (1998) and others. This definition is tense neutral (it generalizes over the present, past and future perfect), and it assumes that the perfect operates on an eventuality $e$ and introduces the result state $s$ of that eventuality as immediately following $e$. The notation is $e \supset\subset s$, which means that $e$ and $s$ 'abut', i.e. they touch on the time axis (so there is no temporal 'gap' between them), but they do not overlap. It is the result state that is located in time by the tense operator (present, past or future), so this analysis confirms that the perspective on the event reported in the present perfect remains at the speech time S. As pointed out by De Swart (2003), this definition requires the perfect to operate on a quantized event. Without a final boundary on the event, it is impossible to define the consequent state, so the perfect must presuppose a non-homogeneous eventuality. It is this property which allows the perfect in many languages to grammaticalize into a perfective past tense when the accent shifts from the resulting state to the underlying event (Bybee et al., 1994).The grammaticalization approach can be taken to support the claim that the narrative Passé

Composé in French is a perfective past (Vet 1992; 1999, 2001). However, we can also adopt a weaker position, stating that a sentence reported in the Passé Composé describes a quantized event. At the discourse level, sentences in the PC alternate with sentences in the Imparfait describing unbounded states or processes (cf. § 2.2 above), in ways similar to the alternation between the Passé Simple and Imparfait. However, looking at the discourse semantics of the Passé Composé, we observe that it is quite different from the rule for the discourse interpretation of the Passé Simple, given in § 3 above.

### 4.3 The discourse semantics of the Passé Composé

If we adopt the idea that we can use the Passé Composé to tell a story, even if this verb form is oriented towards the speech time S, we have to start by making an inventory of the temporal relations that can be established between two sentences in the Passé Composé at the discourse level. We analyzed the temporal structure of the first two chapters of *L'étranger* by Albert Camus, and use this as our corpus. The data suggest that in principle any temporal relation can be established between two sentences in the Passé Composé: posteriority, overlap (simultaneity, inclusion), and temporal inversion. Here are some examples illustrating each of these cases:[11]

(72) Posteriority

a. Il est sorti, est revenu, a disposé des chaises. Sur l'une d'elles, il a empilé des tasses autour d'une cafetière. (p. 18)
'He went (PC) in and out, arranging chairs. On one of them he stacked (PC) some cups round a coffee-pot.'

b. Nous avons traversé une cour où il y avait beaucoup de vieillards, bavardant par petits groupes. (...) A la porte d'un petit bâtiment, le directeur m'a quitté: (...) (p. 13)
'We crossed (PC) a courtyard where there were lots of old people, chatting in little groups. (...) At the door of a small building the warden stopped (PC).' (...).

c. La garde s'est levée et s'est dirigée vers la sortie. (p. 14)
'The nurse stood up (PC) and went (PC) towards the door.'

The posteriority expressed by examples like (72) is an important argument in favor of the treatment of the Passé Composé as a narrative

[11]Camus' novel first appeared in 1942. We use the following editions for reference: *L'étranger*, collection Folio, Gallimard (1957). *The outsider*, Penguin Books (1982) is translated from the French by Joseph Laredo. We use the official translation of *L'étranger* to gloss the meaning of the French examples unless specified otherwise. We add information about the tense use of the French original (in particular PC for Passé Composé and IMP for Imparfait).

tense on a par with the Passé Simple (cf. Vet 1992; 1999). But other temporal relations are possible:

(73) Overlap (simultaneity, inclusion)

a. Mais j'ai attendu dans la cour, sous un platane. Je respirais l'odeur de la terre fraîche et je n'avais plus sommeil. J'ai pensé aux collègues du bureau. (p. 23)

'But I waited (PC) in the courtyard, under a plane tree. I breathed (IMP) in the fresh smells of the earth, and I no longer felt (IMP) sleepy. I thought (PC) of my colleagues at the office.'

b. Les tramways suivants ont ramené les joueurs que j'ai reconnus à leurs petites valises. Ils hurlaient et chantaient à pleins poumons que leur club ne périrait pas. Plusieurs m'ont fait des signes. L'un m'a même crié: "On les a eus." (p. 39)

'The next few trams brought (PC) back the players; I recognized (PC) them by their little suitcases. They were yelling (IMP) and singing (IMP) at the tops of their voices that their team would never die. Several of them waved (PC) to me. One of them even shouted (PC) to me, 'We trashed them."

c. Aujourd'hui j'ai beaucoup travaillé au bureau. Le patron a été aimable. Il m'a demandé si je n'étais pas trop fatigué et il a voulu savoir aussi l'âge de maman. (p. 43)
'I worked (PC) hard at the office today. My boss was (PC) kind. He asked (PC) me if I wasn't (IMP) too tired and he also wanted (PC) to know how old mother was.'

(73a) suggests that the protagonist Meursault is thinking of his colleagues while he is waiting in the courtyard. In (73b) there is global simultaneity between *ramener, faire des signes* and *crier*. In (73c), *être aimable* is temporally included in *travailler beaucoup*.

It has been pointed out by Saussure (1996), Molendijk and De Swart (1999) and others that the Passé Simple blocks temporal inversion. However, this constraint does not extend to the Passé Composé. In *L'étranger* we find several examples of inverse temporal order:

(74) Temporal inversion

a. *J'ai pris* l'autobus à deux heures. Il faisait très chaud. *J'ai mangé* au restaurant, chez Céleste, comme d'habitude. Ils avaient tous beaucoup de peine pour moi et Céleste m'a dit: "On n'a qu'une mère". Quand je suis parti, ils m'ont accompagné à la porte. J'étais un peu étourdi parce qu'il a fallu

que je monte chez Emmanuel pour lui emprunter une cravate noire et un brassard. Il a perdu son oncle, il y a quelques mois. *J'ai couru* pour ne pas manquer le départ. (...) (p. 10)
'I caught (PC) the two o'clock bus. It was (IMP) very hot. I ate (PC) at Céleste's restaurant, as usual. They all felt (IMP) very sorry for me and Céleste told (PC) me, "There's no one like a mother" . When I left (PC), they came (PC) to the door with me. I was (IMP) in a bit of a daze because I had (PC) to go up to Emmanuel's place to borrow a black tie and armband. He lost (PC) his uncle, a few months ago.
I had to run for the bus.' (p. 10)

b. J'ai retourné ma chaise et je l'ai placée comme celle du marchand de tabac parce que j'ai trouvé que c'était plus commode. (p. 39)
'I turned (PC) my chair round like the tobacconist's because I found (PC) it more comfortable that way.'

The explicative structure of (74c) can be treated in ways similar to the examples with *car* in section 3.1 above (e.g. 30, 31). But the temporal structure in (74a) could not be obtained with the Passé Simple. World knowledge tells us that lunchtime is before two o'clock, so the events reported by *j'ai pris l'autobus* and *j'ai mangé au restaurant* are presented in the inverse temporal order. That inverse order is triggered by *j'ai couru* in the next paragraph, where we return to the time of taking the bus.

The fact that the French Passé Composé allows temporal inversion in the absence of causality means that this tense imposes a weaker constraint on discourse structure than the English Simple Past (cf. Lascarides and Asher (1993))at this point is how the Reichenbachian structure E-R,S and the aspectual structure $e \supset\!\subset s$, in combination with the possibility of coercion, can be complemented with a discourse semantics of the Passé Composé. We find this impossible to state in a purely temporal framework, and argue that we need to appeal to a theory like SDRT (Segmented Discourse Representation Theory) to define the discourse semantics of the perfect. Given that this framework will be introduced in chapter 16, we will not spell out the discourse semantics of the Passé Composé until then.

## 5 Conclusion

In this chapter, we have developed a compositional semantics of the Passé Simple, the Imparfait and the Passé Composé at the sentential level. This semantics provided the input for the study of these tense forms at the discourse level. We formulated rules for the discourse semantics of the Passé Simple and the Imparfait that are dependent on rhetorical structure. As far as the narrative Passé Composé is concerned, we conclude that it cannot be determined purely by the temporal properties of this tense form. Accordingly, we extend our semantics of these three tenses with a rhetorical dimension in chapter 16.

## References

Asher, N. and M. Bras. 1993. The temporal structure of French texts within segmented discourse representation theory. In Aurnague et al. (1993).

Aurnague, M., A. Borillo, M. Borillo, and M. Bras, eds. 1993. *Semantics of Time, Space and Movement*, vol. 4, Toulouse.

Bäuerle, R., C. Schwarze, and A. von Stechow, eds. 1983. *Meaning, Use and Interpretation of Language*. Berlin and New York: Mouton de Gruyter.

Berthonneau, A.-M. and G. Kleiber. 1993. Pour une nouvelle approche de l'imparfait: l'imparfait, un temps anaphorique méronomique. *Langages* 112:55–73.

Berthonneau, A.-M. and G. Kleiber. 1994. Imparfait de politesse: rupture ou cohésion. *Travaux de linguistique* 29:59–92.

Berthonneau, A.-M. and G. Kleiber. 1998. Imparfait, anaphore et inférences'. *Cahiers Chronos* 3:53–65.

Berthonneau, A.-M. and G. Kleiber. 1999. Pour une réanalyse de l'imparfait de rupture dans le cadre de l'hypothèse méronomique. *Cahiers de praxématique* 32:119–166.

Bertinetto, P. M., V. Bianchi, J. Higginbotham, and M. Squartini, eds. 1995. *Temporal Reference, Aspect and Actionality*, vol. I. Semantic and Syntactic Perspectives. Rosenberg and Sellier.

Boogaart, R. 1999. *Aspect and temporal ordering. A contrastive analysis of Dutch and English.* Ph.D. thesis, Free University, Amsterdam.

Bres, J. 1998. L'imparfait narratif n'existe pas, je le rencontrais. Unpublished talk given at the 3rd Colloque Chronos, Valenciennes, October 1998.

Bybee, J., R. Perkins, and W. Pagliuca. 1994. *The evolution of grammar. Tense, aspect and modality in the languages of the world.* Chicago: University of Chicago Press.

Caenepeel, M. and M. Moens. 1994. Temporal structure and discourse structure. In Vet and Vetters (1994), pages 5–20.

Caudal, P. 2000. *La polysémie aspectuelle: contraste français - anglais*. Ph.D. thesis, University of Paris VII.

Chevalier, J.-C., C. Blanche-Benveniste, M. Arrivé, and J. Peytard. 1994. *Grammaire du français contemporain*. Paris: Larousse.

Comrie, B. 1985. *Tense*. Cambridge Textbooks in Linguistics. Cambridge: Cambridge University Press.

Damourette, J. and E. Pichon. 1936. *Des mots à la pensée. Essai de grammaire de la language française*. Paris: D'Atrey.

De Mulder, W., L. Tasmowski-De Rijck, and C. Vetters, eds. 1996. *Anaphores temporelles et (in-)cohérence*, vol. 1 of *Cahiers Chronos*. Amsterdam: Rodopi.

De Swart, H. 1991. *Adverbs of Quantification: A Generalized Quantifier Approach*. Ph.D. thesis, Rijksuniversiteit Groningen, Groningen. published by Garland, New York, 1993.

De Swart, H. 1998. Aspect shift and coercion. *Natural language and linguistic theory* 16:347–85.

De Swart, H. 2001. Discourse properties of the perfect in French, English and Dutch. *GAGL, special issue with proceedings of the conference 'Making sense: from lexeme to discourse', University of Groningen* 44:195–212.

De Swart, H. 2003. Coercion in a cross-linguistic theory of aspect. In Francis and Michaelis (2003), pages 231–258.

De Swart, H. and A. Molendijk. 2002. Le passé composé narratif: une analyse discursive de *L'étranger* de camus. In Laca (2002), pages 193–211.

Dowty, D. 1979. *Word Meaning and Montague Grammar. The Semantics of Verbs and Times in Generative Semantics and in Montague's PTQ*, vol. 7 of *Synthese Language Library*. Dordrecht: D. Reidel Publishing Company.

Dowty, D. 1986. The effects of aspectual class on the temporal structure of discourse: Semantics or pragmatics? *Linguistics and Philosophy* 9:36–61.

Francis, E. J. and L. A. Michaelis, eds. 2003. *Mismatch: form-function incongruity and the architecture of grammar*. Stanford: CSLI Publications.

Gosselin, L. 1999. Le sinistre fantômas et l'imparfait narratif. *Cahiers de praxématique* 32:19–42.

Guillemin-Flescher, J. 1981. *Syntaxe comparée du français*. Paris: Ophrys.

Hinrichs, E. 1986. *A Compositional Semantics for Aktionsarten and NP Reference in English*. Ph.D. thesis, Ohio State University, Columbus, Ohio.

Kamp, H. and U. Reyle. 1993. *From Discourse to Logic. Introduction to Modeltheoretic Semantics of Natural Language, Formal Logic and Discourse Representation Theory*, vol. 42 of *Studies in Linguistics and Philosophy*. Dordrecht: Kluwer Academic Publishers.

Kamp, H. and C. Rohrer. 1983. Tense in texts. In Bäuerle et al. (1983), pages 250–269.

Kronning, H., C. Noren, B. Novèn, G. Ransbo, L.-G. Sundvell, and B. Svane, eds. 2001. *Langage et références: mélanges offerts à Kerstin Jonasson à l'occasion de ses soixante ans*. Uppsala: Actas Universitatis Uppsaliensis.

Laca, B., ed. 2002. *Temps et Aspect: de la morphologie à l'interprétation*. Paris: Presses Universitaires de Vincennes.

Landeweerd, R. 1998. *Discourse Semantics of Perspective and Temporal Structure*. Ph.D. thesis, University of Groningen, Groningen.

Lascarides, A. and N. Asher. 1993. Temporal interpretation, discourse relations and commonsense entailment. *Linguistics and Philosophy* 16:437–493.

Le Goffic, P. 1995. La double incomplétude de l'imparfait. *Modèles linguistiques* 16:133–149.

Michaelis, L. 1994. The ambiguity of the English present perfect. *Journal of Linguistics* 30:111–157.

Moens, M. 1987. *Tense, aspect and temporal reference*. Ph.D. thesis, University of Edinburgh.

Moeschler, J. 2000. L'ordre temporel dans le discours: le modèle des inférences directionnelles. *Cahiers Chronos* 6:1–11.

Molendijk, A. 1990. *Le passé simple et l'imparfait: une approche reichenbachienne*. Amsterdam: Rodopi.

Molendijk, A. 1993. Temporal anaphora and tense use in French. In P. Dekker and M. Stokhof, eds., *Proceedings of the 9th Amsterdam Colloquium*, pages 427–445. Amsterdam, ILLC.

Molendijk, A. 1996. Anaphore et imparfait: la référence globale à des situations présupposées ou impliquées. In De Mulder et al. (1996), pages 109–123.

Molendijk, A. and H. De Swart. 1999. L'ordre discursif inverse en français. *Travaux de linguistique* 39:77–96.

Molendijk, A. and C. Vet. 1995. Interprétation, référence et cohésion. In Vet (1995), pages 63–88.

Partee, B. 1984. Nominal and temporal anaphora. *Linguistics and Philosophy* 7:243–286.

Plénat, M., M. Aurnague, A. Condamines, J.-P. Maurel, C. Molinier, and C. Muller, eds. 1999. *L'emprise du sens. Structures linguistiques et interprétations. Mélanges de syntaxe et de sémantique offerts à Andrée Borillo*. Amsterdam: Rodopi.

Pustejovsky, J. 1995. *The generative lexicon*. Cambridge, MA: The M.I.T. Press.

Reichenbach, H. 1947. *Elements of Symbolic Logic*. New York: The Macmillan Company, first free press paperback edition 1966 edn.

Saussure, L. d. 1996. Encapsulation et référence temporelle d'énoncés négatifs au passé composé et au passé simple. *Cahiers de linguistique française* 18:219–242.

Saussure, L. d. 2000. Quand le temps ne progresse pas avec le passé simple. *Cahiers Chronos* 6:37–48.

Smith, C. S. 1991. *The parameter of Aspect*, vol. 43 of *Studies in Linguistics and Philosophy*. Dordrecht: Kluwer Academic Publishers.

Smith, N. 1993. Observations sur la pragmatique des temps. *Langages* 112:26–38.

Tasmowski-De Rijck, L. 1985. L'imparfait avec et sans rupture. *Langue française* 67:59–77.

Touratier, C. 1998. L'imparfait, temps du passé non marqué. *Cahiers Chronos* 2:21–28.

Trévise, A. 1994. *Le prétérit anglais*. Paris: Nathan.

Verkuyl, H. J. 1995. Indices and habituality. In Bertinetto et al. (1995), pages 195–217.

Verkuyl, H. J. 2001. On the compositionality of tense: merging Reichenbach and Prior. Unpublished paper.

Vet, C. 1980. *Temps, aspects et adverbes de temps en français contemporain*. Geneva: Droz.

Vet, C. 1992. Le passé composé: contextes d'emploi et interprétation. *Cahiers de Praxématique* 19:37–59.

Vet, C. 1994. Petite grammaire de l'Aktionsart et de l'aspect. *Cahiers de Grammaire* 19:1–17.

Vet, C., ed. 1995. *Sémiotiques: Théories sémantiques et modélisation*. Paris: Didier Erudition.

Vet, C. 1999. Le passé simple, le passé composé et les règles d'interprétation discursive. In Plénat et al. (1999), pages 323–336.

Vet, C. 2001. Deux cas de polysémie: le passé composé et le futur periphrastique. In Kronning et al. (2001), pages 697–686.

Vet, C. and C. Vetters, eds. 1994. *Tense and Aspect in Discourse*, vol. 75 of *Trends in Linguistics. Studies and Monographs*. Berlin and New York: Mouton de Gruyter.

Vetters, C. 1996. *Temps, aspect et narration*. Amsterdam: Rodopi.

Vetters, C. and W. D. Mulder. 2000. Passé simple et imparfait: contenus conceptuel et procédural. *Cahiers Chronos* 6:13–36.

Vikner, S. 1985. Reichenbach revisited: One, two or three temporal relations? *Acta Linguistica Hafniensis* 19:81–95.

Weinrich, H. 1973. *Tempus. Besprochene und erzählte Welt*. Stuttgart: Verlag W. Kohlhammer.

16

# Tense, Connectives and Discourse Structure

ANDRÉE BORILLO, MYRIAM BRAS, ANNE LE DRAOULEC, LAURE VIEU, ARIE MOLENDIJK, HENRIËTTE DE SWART, HENK VERKUYL, CO VET, AND CARL VETTERS

Preceding chapters have shown that tense, grammatical and predicational aspect are very important clues in the process of temporal interpretation of sentences (chapter 14) and discourse (chapter 15). The present chapter investigates the interaction of tense with other temporal markers in the discourse, in particular temporal adverbials, and more specifically connectives, the linguistic elements that are used for connecting discourse segments.

Section 1 presents temporal adverbials from the point of view of their contribution to the structuring of discourse: they can have the role of connecting sentences thus contributing to the temporal discourse structure. On the basis of this, section 2 discusses a formal theory which aims at accounting for discourse structure, SDRT. Section 3 presents an application of standard SDRT to French data providing an account of the way in which temporal markers interact with discourse structure. Two connectives, namely *puis* ('then, afterwards') and *un peu plus tard* ('a bit later'), will be analyzed in more detail in order to display the often subtle differences in the behavior of these connectives, when different discourse relations hold. Section 4 will apply some of these insights to the role of time adverbials in a discourse in the Passé Composé.

*Handbook of French Semantics.*
Francis Corblin and Henriëtte de Swart (eds.).
Copyright © 2004, CSLI Publications.

## 1 Temporal adverbials and discourse connectives

Temporal connectives have a mixed character, for they belong both to the category of temporal adverbials and to the category of discourse connectives. We show how, for at least some elements, there is a natural extension from one function to the other.

We call *temporal adverbial* any kind of adverbial element or expression that has to do with temporal reference or expresses a temporal relation. Since we are not interested in morphological or lexical properties but in grammatical or discursive functions, no difference will be made between adverbs like *maintenant* ('now'), *demain* ('tomorrow'), *récemment* ('lately'), nominal phrases such as *le mois dernier* ('last month'), *le jour suivant* ('the following day'), prepositional phrases such as *depuis trois jours* ('for three days'), *dans la journée* ('during the day'), *à sa naissance* ('at his birth'), infinitival phrases such as *avant de partir* ('before leaving'), or conjunctive sentences such as *dès qu'il comprit* ('as soon as he understood'). So we consider as a temporal adverbial any temporal unit of the sentence that has an adverbial function, that is, any constituent that does not belong to the argumental structure of the sentence and refers to its temporal setting. But other distinctions do have to be made since, within the sentence, these temporal adverbials may be peripheral to the clause or integrated to some extent into its structure.

In studies on adverbials, different classifications have been proposed, depending on the properties that were highlighed: the position of the adverbial within the sentence, adverbial scope with respect to other constituents of the sentence, its application to the sentence content, etc. Among the criteria most often advocated, we will retain those we consider most appropriate for the category of temporal adverbials as a whole, and the category of temporal connectives in particular.

In the general classifications of adverbials developed by Quirk and Greenbaum (1973) for English, or Melis (1983), Guimier (1996), Lévrier and Molinier (2000), Nølke (2001), and chapter 11 (this volume) for French, temporal adverbials are always treated apart, as they don't fit well within the general framework defined for adverbials. For some of the authors, they are even explicitly considered as a special category, together with space adverbials (Nølke 2001: 260). In fact, the distinctions made to organize these general classifications cannot be directly exploited for temporal adverbials. Not only do they differ markedly from one author to another, but basically, they don't seem to apply successfully to temporal adverbials taken as a whole.

### 1.1 General view of temporal adverbials

The term *temporal adverbial* has a very loose and underdetermined status. Under the same form, an adverbial can fulfill different functions. Unless we talk of homonymy as some authors are inclined to do (Lévrier and Molinier (2000)), it is appropriate to isolate the different functions that temporal adverbials can fulfill within the sentence or across two sentences. For example, one can see that a temporal adverbial such as *tout de suite, aussitôt* or *immédiatement* ('at once, immediately') is taken as a manner adverbial in (1) and as a temporal connective in (2).[1]

(1) Le téléphone sonna mais il ne se leva pas immédiatement pour répondre.
'The phone rang but he did not get up immediately to answer.'

(2) Les cloches se mirent à sonner. Immédiatement, ce fut le branle-bas dans le village
'The bells started ringing. Immediately, the whole village was in a turmoil.'

If we consider things at the most general level, the only common property that can be retained for the whole set of temporal adverbials is a semantic one: these adverbials provide explicit information for the temporal anchoring of eventualities presented and described in sentences and so they contribute to a coherent discourse. Their role is to introduce a new temporal referent or to create a relation with a temporal referent already given or calculated in a preceding sentence.

### 1.2 Temporal adverbials within the general system of adverbs

Temporal adverbials count as integrated adverbials, for they can be extracted, restricted, etc. as shown in (3):[2]

(3) Ce n'est que le lendemain qu'il a téléphoné.
'It was only the day after that the telephoned.'

---

[1] *Immédiatement* expresses some sort of consecutivity (quick reaction.)

[2] *Le lendemain* ('the day after') is an anaphoric time location adverbial, but it would be the same with deictic adverbials *lundi prochain* ('next Monday'), *dans trois jours* ('within three days') or with iterative or frequency adverbials, *chaque matin* ('every morning'), *souvent* ('often'), etc. Not all adverbials behave alike. Some frequency adverbials like *parfois* ('sometimes'), *quelquefois* ('sometimes'), *jamais* ('never'), *toujours* ('always') resist extraction and restriction, and others like *constamment* ('constantly'), *rarement* ('rarely'), *continuellement* ('continuously'), cannot be detached at the head of a negative sentence. Cf. chapter 12 (this volume) for more on adverbs of quantification.

But in an initial detached position, their function seems to be different, as their scope extends to the whole proposition and not only to the predicate in this position:

(4) Le lendemain, il n'a pas téléphoné.
'The day after, he did not telephone.'

(5) Il n'a pas téléphoné le lendemain (mais trois jours après)
'He did not telephone the day after (but three days after).'

Accordingly, we distinguish between the exophrastic function of an adverbial in an initial detached position, which involves application to the whole proposition, and the endophrastic function for other positions and other kinds of applications within the sentence.

Within the large category of temporal adverbials, there is a small group of adverbials known as 'relational temporal adverbials' (Nøjgaard 1992–1995) that is to be distinguished on the basis of both their syntactic and their semantic properties. Among them there are items such as *auparavant* ('before') *entretemps* ('meanwhile'), *par la suite* ('afterwards'), *sur ce, après quoi* ('whereupon'), *dès lors* ('from that time'), *ensuite* ('then'), *enfin* ('lastly'), *puis* ('then'), etc. The function of these adverbials is primarily to act as relational elements that establish a transphrastic relation between their host sentence and the preceding sentence — or a preceding segment of text larger than a sentence. Their semantic content does not provide temporal reference; they mainly express chronological order — anteriority, simultaneity or posteriority — with a situation described in a preceding sentence:

(6) Il décida de réserver une place mais auparavant, il tint à vérifier l'horaire.
'He decided to book a seat but before, he wanted to check the time-table.'

Sometimes, they can be used with an endophrastic function: they may be placed within the sentence, even in a position adjacent to the verb and they can be questioned with *quand?* ('when?') or be extracted in a cleft sentence with *c'est... que*:

(7) Il entendit un grand bruit et ce n'est qu'ensuite qu'il vit de la fumée sortir par la fenêtre.
'He heard a big noise and it was only after that he saw some smoke coming out of the window'.

Frequently, they appear detached at the head of the sentence. This position is obligatory or quasi-obligatory for those that we call *pure linking adverbials*: *sur ce, après quoi* ('whereupon'), *puis* ('then'), *en-*

*fin* ('lastly'), etc. So, on account of their exophrastic function and of their relational link with a preceding context, this small group of adverbials can be considered as belonging to a larger category of temporal adverbials, that we call *transphrastic temporal adverbials.*[3]

### 1.3 Transphrastic temporal adverbials

A subset of the transphrastic adverbials is of particular interest to us. This subset consists of adverbials that establish a a temporal connection with the preceding context. We establish a distinction between relational adverbials, referential anaphoric adverbials and aspectual-temporal adverbials.

**Relational temporal adverbials.** Relational temporal adverbials act primarily as linking elements. Some of them calculate the time interval between two eventualities: *deux jours après* ('two days after'), *deux ans avant* ('two years before'):

(8) Dimanche, elle lui écrivit pour l'inviter mais deux jours après, elle lui téléphona pour annuler l'invitation (i.e. deux jours après avoir écrit).
'(On) Sunday, she wrote him to invite him but two days later she telephoned to cancel the invitation (i.e. two days after writing)'

Others do not express a time interval at all but only chronological order: *ensuite*('then'), *auparavant* ('before'), etc. Among them we find the so-called *discourse connectives* (cf. section 3 below).

**Referential anaphoric adverbials.** Referential anaphoric adverbials semantically introduce a temporal referent that is anchored to a reference point that is already identified, but that is necessarily different from the moment of speech, *le lendemain* ('the day after'), *la semaine suivante* ('the following week'), *l'année précédente* ('the preceding year'):

(9) Dimanche, elle lui écrivit pour l'inviter et la lettre arriva le lendemain.
'(On) Sunday, she wrote him to invite him and the letter arrived the day after.'

Note that *le lendemain* (the next day) which normally behaves as a simple anaphoric location adverbial in (9) can occasionally be considered as providing a temporal discursive link in (10).

[3]They establish a backward link outside the sentence. The term 'conjonctifs' (conjuncts) (Lévrier and Molinier (2000)) is not appropriate since it only applies to sentence adverbials.

(10) Elle marcha sous la pluie toute la journée. Le lendemain, elle était clouée au lit avec 40° de fièvre.
'She walked in the rain all day. The day after, she was in bed with a temperature of 40°.'

**Transphrastic function.** The same kind of transphrastic function can be fulfilled, more surprisingly, by adverbials that are not overtly anaphoric but express some kind of temporal modality — the idea of rapidity, suddenness, short interval — such as *soudain* ('suddenly'), *immédiatement* ('immediately'), *tout à coup* ('all of a sudden'), *brusquement* ('suddenly', literally 'abruptly), etc. They are generally considered as a sort of manner adverbials under the name of *aspectual-temporal* adverbials (cf. Guimier (1996)). Their exophrastic function was illustrated in (2) for *immédiatement* ('immediately'), but it would be the same with *brusquement* ('suddenly'):

(11) Il s'arrêta devant la maison. Brusquement, la porte s'ouvrit.
'He stopped in front of the house. Suddenly, the door opened.'

So, when these three kinds of adverbials are initially detached in a sentence with a status of exophrastic adverbials, they establish a temporal transphrastic relation with the preceding sentence or the preceding text segment, a relation through which the eventuality described can be located or chronologically ordered. This temporal relation is to be interpreted as a discourse relation giving these adverbials the status of connectives.

We will now turn to the investigation of the role temporal adverbials may play at the discourse structure level. First, the issue of discourse structure will be addressed more generally with the presentation of SDRT (§ 2). Building on the present section and § 2, we compare the role of two connectives *puis* ('then') and *un peu plus tard* ('a bit later') in section 3. Section 4 treats the role of discourse connectives in stories told in the Passé Composé.

## 2 Discourse Structure

Discourse relations, that is, relations involved in the structuring of discourse, have been treated by many authors. They are known under different names —*rhetorical relations* (Grosz and Sidner (1986b); Mann and Thompson (1987)), *sentence relations* (Quirk and Greenbaum (1973)), *coherence relations* (Hobbs (1985); Sanders et al. (1992))— but the term that will be retained here is *discourse relations*, as used by Lascarides and Asher (1993) and Asher (1993).

Since we need to investigate the interactions between discourse structure and the semantic contribution of the temporal adverbials —as well as that of the tenses, we have chosen a formal theory of the semantic-pragmatic interface, namely Segmented Discourse Representation Theory (SDRT). This section first presents the theoretical framework. We then discuss the discourse relations used to analyze narratives in more detail, with a special focus on the treatment of French past tenses.

## 2.1 SDRT

SDRT is a non-trivial extension of Discourse Representation Theory (DRT) as standardized in Kamp and Reyle (1993) that takes discourse structure —i.e. the relationships between discourse segments— into account and offers a theory of the semantics/pragmatics interface. Only a brief outline of SDRT will be given here.[4]

In SDRT, a discourse is represented by an SDRS. An SDRS is a recursive structure consisting of elementary DRSs—i.e. DRSs representing a single clause—and sub-SDRSs linked together by Discourse Relations, such as Narration, Elaboration, Background, Continuation, Result, Contrast and Explanation. These elementary DRSs and the sub-SDRSs corresponding to complex discourse segments are the *constituents* of the SDRS representing the discourse. We use Greek letters as variables for constituents, and $K_i$ as constants.[5]

DRSs are often represented graphically as "boxes" (compare chapter 15). Thus, the sentence *Paul frappa à la porte* ('Paul knocked at the door') yields the DRS in Figure 1, where the upper part is the *universe of discourse*, that is, the set of discourse referents introduced by the sentence, and the lower part is the set of DRS-*conditions*.

| $x$, $l$, $y$, $e_1$, $n$ |
| --- |
| Paul($x$)<br>$l$ =?<br>porte-de($y, l$)<br>$e_1$ – frapper-à($x, y$)<br>$e_1 \prec n$ |

FIGURE 1 DRS for *Paul frappa à la porte.*

SDRSs are also usually represented as boxes, the universe of discourse

[4]For a thorough presentation, see Asher (1993), Lascarides and Asher (1993), Asher (1996) and Busquets et al. (2001).

[5]An important element of SDRSs is being neglected here, namely the *labels* that distinguish between different occurrences of the same constituent, while representing speech acts to some extent. Discourse relations link *labelled* DRSs and SDRSs, not just the bare constituents, and the Greek letters are variables for labels.

being the set of its constituents, and the conditions being the description of each constituent and the discourse relations that link them. For example in Figure 2 we give a preliminary version of the SDRS for the small text *Paul frappa à la porte. Il entra* (He entered).[6]

| $K_1, K_2$ | |
|---|---|
| $K_1$ : | $x, y, l_1, e_1, n$ <br> Paul($x$) <br> $l_1 = ?$ porte-de($y, l_1$) <br> $e_1$ – frapper-à($x, y$) <br> $e_1 \prec n$ |
| $K_2$ : | $z, l_2, e_2, n$ <br> $z = x$ <br> $l_2 = l_1$ <br> $e_2$ – entrer($z, l_2$) <br> $e_2 \prec n$ |
| Narration($K_1, K_2$) | |

FIGURE 2 Preliminary SDRS for *Paul frappa à la porte. Il entra.*

SDRSs are built up incrementally. SDRT defines a *Glue Logic* and an *Update Function* that together determine a new SDRS for a given SDRS $\tau$ representing the context (the discourse already processed), and a new constituent $\alpha$ representing the information to be integrated into that context. The Glue Logic is embedded in the framework of so-called Commonsense Entailment developed in Asher and Morreau (1991), a logic that exploits both monotonic ($\rightarrow$) and non-monotonic ($>$) conditionals.[7] The Glue Logic is specified by:

- definitions characterizing which constituents in $\tau$ are open for attaching $\alpha$,

[6] This SDRS misses one component: its topic. We will give the right representation of this small text below, where we also explain how it is built.

[7] $\phi > \psi$ means "if $\phi$ then normally $\psi$". From $\phi > \psi$ and $\phi$, Commonsense Entailment (CE) entails $\psi$ 'by default', that is, defeasibly, in the absence of further information regarding the truth value of $\psi$. From $\phi > \psi$, $\phi$ and $\neg\psi$, CE no longer entails $\psi$, but $\neg\psi$. From $\phi > \psi$, $\zeta > \neg\psi$, $\phi \rightarrow \zeta$, $\phi$ and $\zeta$, $\psi$ (and not $\neg\psi$) is inferred (Penguin principle). From $\phi > \psi$, $\zeta > \neg\psi$, $\phi$ and $\zeta$, if $\phi$ and $\zeta$ are logically independent, CE cannot conclude $\psi$ nor $\neg\psi$ (Nixon Diamond).

- axioms detailing what discourse relations may be inferred, on the basis of a variety of linguistic and common knowledge clues, in order to actualize the attachment of $\alpha$ to some open constituent of $\tau$,
- axioms specifying the semantic effects of those discourse relations.

The Update Function is in charge of the proper hierarchization of the Structure and of the resolution of the possibly existing underspecifications (e.g., anaphora and ellipsis).

As far as the ontology of eventualities at the discourse level is concerned, SDRT builds on DRT, and assumes the same Davidsonian approach that considers events and states as individuals in the representation and in the models.

As in chapter 15, we assume that Imparfait sentences introduce state referents (cf. rule 48) and that Passé Simple sentences introduce event referents in the SDRS (cf. rule 35).

SDRT assumes that each event has two associated states: a prestate (presupposition) and a poststate (consequent state or implication). These states are not always explicitly referred to. For example, a poststate is introduced by a Passé Composé verb, but in Passé Simple sentences, both pre- and poststate remain implicit, and don't appear in the DRS. Even when explicitly introduced in the universe of discourse, their semantic content may not be quite clear. Depending on their predicational aspect, some verb phrases may have obvious preconditions and/or postconditions in their lexical semantics or not. For example, *sortir de la maison* ('to leave the house') clearly implies a prestate in which the agent is located in the house, and a poststate in which the agent is no longer in that place. In contrast, the pre-and poststate of a verb like *se promener* ('to stroll') have no definite semantic content. Nevertheless, we still assume that these two states may be described by something like, for the prestate, "is not strolling", and for the poststate, "is not strolling and has strolled". Finally, SDRT assumes that in each basic constituent, one eventuality is designated as the 'main eventuality'.

## 2.2 Discourse Relations

In the following, we only present the discourse relations that will be used to describe the discourse contribution of tenses and connectives: Narration, Result, Explanation, Elaboration, Continuation, Topic (denoted $\Downarrow$), Background and Contrast.

Building on previous work on discourse relations (Hobbs (1985), Grosz and Sidner (1986a) and Mann and Thompson (1987), among others), SDRT distinguishes coordinating relations from subordinating ones. Explanation, Topic and Elaboration are subordinating, and the others coordinating. Only subordinating relations may introduce complex SDRSs. In other words, the Update Function may gather several SDRSs into a new complex SDRS only if these constituents are attached to the same site with the same subordinating relation. On the graphs depicting SDRSs, coordinating relations are usually denoted by horizontal lines and subordinating relations by vertical ones (see, for example, the graph representing the SDRS of (12) below, in Figure 4. Note also that in SDRT several discourse relations may simultaneously link the same two constituents, departing from other discourse approaches, notably RST (Mann and Thompson, 1987).

**Narration.** Narration is a relation which is based on the Gricean pragmatic maxim of manner Be Orderly. Two clauses linked by Narration describe two successive events 'of the same story'. Building on the analyses of Lascarides and Asher (1993), Asher et al. (1995a,b) show that, in the absence of locating adverbials, a relation of Narration between two constituents $\alpha$ and $\beta$, entails a temporal overlap between the poststate $post(e_\alpha)$ of the main eventuality $e_\alpha$ denoted by $\alpha$, and the prestate $pre(e_\beta)$ of the eventuality $e_\beta$ denoted by $\beta$:

**A 1** $Narration(\alpha, \beta) \rightarrow post(e_\alpha) \circ pre(e_\beta)$

A1 aims at capturing the fact that narratives must cohere in the sense that the events linked together by Narration must fit consistently and without significant spatio-temporal gaps, as expressed in Asher (1996) and observed in earlier work on temporal order in narratives, for example in Caenepeel (1989). This does not mean that there should be no interval of time between the two events $e_\alpha$ and $e_\beta$, but rather that no relevant event can occur during this interval. From A1 and uncontroversial ordering assumptions on events and their pre- and poststates, we can deduce a relation of temporal precedence between the events $e_\alpha$ and $e_\beta$: $e_\alpha \prec e_\beta$.[8] Actually, temporal overlap is too weak to fully capture the 'no-significant-gap' constraint. It should be guaranteed that $post(e_\alpha)$ persists (at least) up to the beginning of $e_\beta$, and, conversely, that $pre(e_\beta)$ starts when (or before) $e_\alpha$ ends. So we propose here an improved version of A1, where $\sqcap$ denotes the intersection operator.[9]

**A 2** $Narration(\alpha, \beta) \rightarrow e_\alpha \supset\!\subset (post(e_\alpha) \sqcap pre(e_\beta)) \supset\!\subset e_\beta$

[8] Such as $Event(e) \rightarrow pre(e) \supset\!\subset e \supset\!\subset post(e)$, where $\supset\!\subset$ denotes temporal abutment, as used in DRT, or the 'meets' relation as used in Allen (1984).

[9] We assume that $s_1 \sqcap s_2$, when applicable, that is, when $s_1 \circ s_2$, yields a new state lasting the maximum interval of time during which both $s_1$ and $s_2$ hold, and whose propositional content is the conjunction of $s_1$ and $s_2$'s propositional contents.

For both A1 and A2, it is important to note that the consequent sub-formulas imply more than a temporal ordering between the four eventualities $e_\alpha$, $post(e_\alpha)$, $e_\beta$ and $pre(e_\beta)$. $Post(e_\alpha) \circ pre(e_\beta)$ entails that the propositional contents of these two states are compatible; the consequent of A2 entails in addition that there is no intervening event whose propositional content interferes with that of $post(e_\alpha)$ or of $pre(e_\beta)$. That is, no "relevant" event that ends $post(e_\alpha)$ before $e_\beta$,
starts or prevents $pre(e_\beta)$ from holding right after $e_\alpha$ has ended.

Narration is motivated by the intuition that the elements of a Narration belong to the 'same story', i.e., they must have some common subject matter. To this effect, axiom A3 expresses that the constituents connected by Narration must have a common *topic*.[10]

**A 3** $(\langle\tau,\alpha,\beta\rangle \wedge \mathit{Narration}(\alpha,\beta)) \rightarrow \exists\gamma\,(\mathit{Contingent}(\gamma) \wedge \mathit{Topic}(\gamma,\alpha) \wedge \mathit{Topic}(\gamma,\beta))$

A topic is contingent—that is, not vacuous, not contradictory, not tautological—and it subsumes the constituents of a sub-SDRS, in this case, the constituents linked by Narration. If not already present in the context, it has to be added to the SDRS during the update. A3 and the rules of the underlying logic imply that Narration can be non-monotonically inferred only if such a topic exists or can be built.

To illustrate these structural effects, let us consider the following simple example again:

(12) Paul frappa à la porte. Il entra.
'Paul knocked at the door ($S_1$). He entered ($S_2$).'

This small text clearly tells the story of Paul arriving at someone's home, room or office. Such a 'topic' is inferred only because the two sentences are textually linked together and in this order (try to think of other texts in which either sentence describes an event taking place in a different situation). In SDRT and with axiom A3, attaching the representation $K_2$ of $S_2$ in (12)— which is a DRS, because $S_2$ is a single clause—to that of its first one $K_1$, yields the SDRS structure fully represented in Figure 3. The same information is given as a graph in Figure 4. In the latter figure, $K^*$ is the topic and $\mathcal{K}$ is the complex SDRS consisting of the two DRSs $K_1$ and $K_2$. The oblique dashed lines represent this SDRS or sub-SDRS link.

According to Asher (1996), Narration is inferred "by default" if no other relation can be inferred, that is, if in the discourse there are no

[10] $\langle\tau,\alpha,\beta\rangle$ means that $\beta$ is to be attached to $\alpha$ in the SDRS $\tau$ ($\beta$ follows $\alpha$ in the text structure). Topic is a subordinating discourse relation whose semantics essentially involves subsumption between the topic and the elements of the narrative it summarizes.

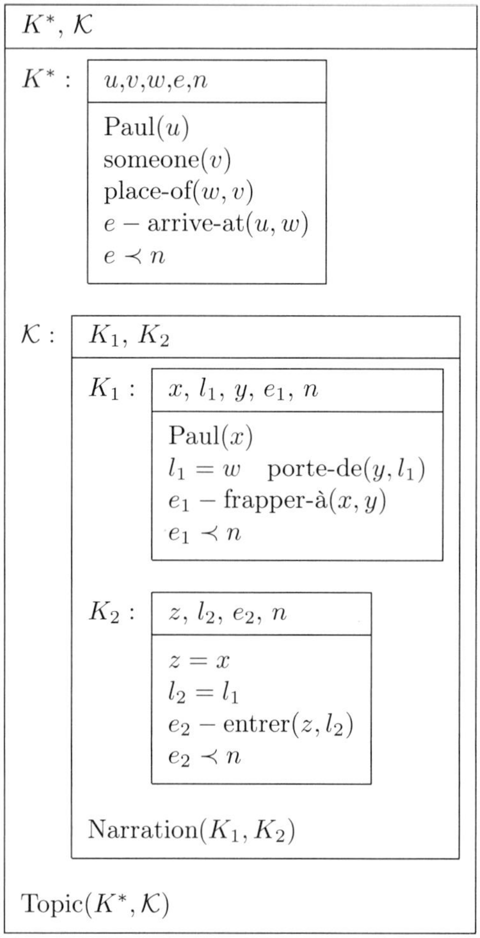


FIGURE 3 SDRS for 12

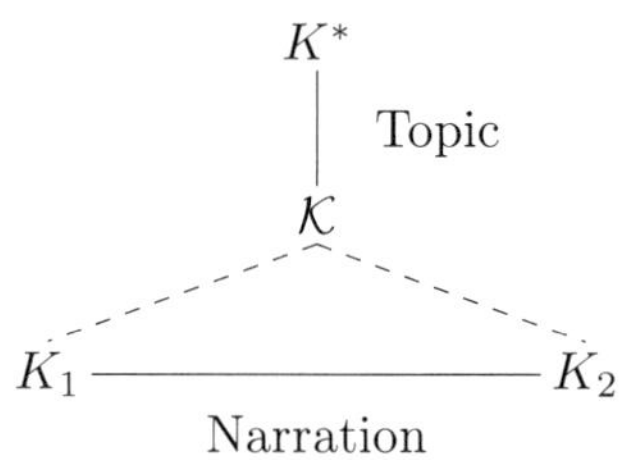


FIGURE 4 Graph representing the SDRS structure of Fig. 3

clues that other axioms could exploit to infer other discourse relations. This results in Axiom 4.

**A 4** $(\langle\tau,\alpha,\beta\rangle \wedge \neg \mathit{Clues\_}\ R_1(\tau,\alpha,\beta) \wedge \neg \mathit{Clues\_}\ R_2(\tau,\alpha,\beta) \wedge \ldots \wedge \neg \mathit{Clues\_}\ R_n(\tau,\alpha,\beta)) > \mathit{Narration}(\alpha,\beta)$

Here $R_1 \ldots R_n$ are all the discourse relations used in SDRT but Narration, and $\mathit{Clues\_}\ R_i(\tau,\alpha,\beta)$ holds whenever the propositional content of $\alpha$ and $\beta$ and the discourse structure of $\tau$ contain clues that could be exploited for inferring $R_i(\alpha,\beta)$.[11]

Narration can be non-monotonically inferred if the predicate *Occasion* holds between the clauses to be related:

**A 5** $(\langle\tau,\alpha,\beta\rangle \wedge \mathit{Occasion}(\alpha,\beta)) > \mathit{Narration}(\alpha,\beta)$

Occasion holds if the two clauses contain clues indicating that their main eventualities are of types that may belong to "the same story". Occasion exploits lexical semantics and shared knowledge in terms of scripts connecting certain event types in sequences in which one event 'naturally' leads to the next. (12) is an example of Narration where Occasion holds, for there is a script in which people knock on the door before entering. This kind of script may be encoded in the following axiom A 6.[12]

**A 6** $(\mathit{frapper\text{-}\grave{a}}(e_\alpha,x,y,\alpha) \wedge \mathit{porte\text{-}de}(y,z,\alpha) \wedge \mathit{entrer}(e_\beta,x,z,\beta)) \rightarrow \mathit{Occasion}(\alpha,\beta)$

In (12), the sequence of events is only typical. Oviously, stronger dependency links between event types like Precondition and Cause also give rise to Occasion—and by non-monotonic inference, Narration. But some of these links are also exploited to infer more specific discourse relations, such as Result.

**Result.** A Result relation between constituents $\alpha$ and $\beta$ expresses the narrator's intention to signify that $\beta$ is a result of $\alpha$ (or $\alpha$ results in $\beta$). It has the semantic effect of implying a causal link between the main eventualities of the constituents it relates:

**A 7** $\mathit{Result}(\alpha,\beta) \rightarrow \mathit{Cause}(e_\alpha,e_\beta)$

The predicate $\mathit{Cause}(e_1,e_2)$—to be read $e_1$ causes $e_2$—implies, among

[11] SDRT explicitly states that there should be a finite set of discourse relations. For present purposes, we restrict the discussion to: Narration, Background, Elaboration, Continuation, Topic, Result, Explanation, and Contrast, for which an SDRT account can be found in the literature.

[12] A DRS-condition $\phi(x_1,\ldots,x_n)$ appearing in the constituent (labelled by) $\alpha$ is written in the Glue Logic with $\alpha$ as an extra argument: $\phi(x_1,\ldots,x_n,\alpha)$

other things, that if $e_1$ and $e_2$ are events, the first temporally precedes the second:

**A 8** $(Cause(e_1, e_2) \wedge Event(e_1) \wedge Event(e_2)) \rightarrow e_1 \prec e_2$

If $e_1$ is an event and $e_2$ a state, $e_2$ immediately follows $e_1$:

**A 9** $(Cause(e_1, e_2) \wedge Event(e_1) \wedge State(e_2)) \rightarrow e_1 \supset\!\subset e_2$

Result may be monotonically inferred on the basis of the presence in $\beta$ of a marker of causation such as *donc* (therefore) in (13).[13]

(13) Max a eu son bac en juillet dernier. Donc il a pu entrer à l'université en septembre.
'Max passed his A-levels last July. Therefore he was able to go to the university in September.'

**A 10** $(\langle \tau, \alpha, \beta \rangle \wedge donc(\beta)) \rightarrow Result(\alpha, \beta)$

Result can also be non-monotonically inferred on the basis of lexical semantics or shared knowledge of the event types in $\alpha$ and $\beta$, as in the well-known examples from Hinrichs (1981) and Hinrichs (1986):

(14) Tarzan poussa Jane. Elle tomba.
'Tarzan pushed Jane. She fell.'

(15) Max éteignit la lumière. Il faisait nuit noire autour de lui.
'Max switched off the light. It was pitch dark around him.'

In (14) and (15), generic script-like information on pushing and falling, and on switching off the light event types and being dark state types that enables one to recover the causal links that the narrator wants to express. The presence of clues indicating a possible causal link is expressed by the predicate *D-Permissible-Cause* where *D-Permissible-Cause*$(\alpha, \beta)$ means that $\alpha$ describes an eventuality which is a possible cause for $\beta$'s main eventuality. For instance, Axiom 11 encodes a plausible piece of shared knowledge.[14]

**A 11** $(push(e_\alpha, x, y, \alpha) \wedge fall(e_\beta, y, \beta)) \rightarrow D\text{-}Permissible\text{-}Cause(\alpha, \beta)$

which is in turn exploited by Axiom 12 to (defeasibly) infer Result:

**A 12** $(\langle \tau, \alpha, \beta \rangle \wedge D\text{-}Permissible\text{-}Cause(\alpha, \beta)) > Result(\alpha, \beta)$

**Explanation.** The classical example (14) is from Lascarides and Asher (1993):

[13] *Donc* has other meanings, which do not denote a "material consequence", but rather a logical or argumentative consequence, as in *Il a réussi à faire l'exercice, donc il a bien compris le cours* ('He succeeded in solving the problem, therefore he understood the class well').

[14] Taking advantage of a well-structured lexicon, such axioms can be generalized, avoiding writing a rather tedious series of axioms, see Asher and Lascarides (1998).

(16) John fell. Max pushed him.

It illustrates the relation of Explanation, Result's inverse relation, that can be triggered by Axiom 13, where *Explanation*$(\alpha, \beta)$ means that $\alpha$ is explained by $\beta$, that is, $\beta$ explains $\alpha$.

**A 13** $(\langle\tau, \alpha, \beta\rangle \wedge \textit{D-Permissible-Cause}(\beta, \alpha)) > \textit{Explanation}(\alpha, \beta)$

In French, it is not possible to express an explanation with a sequence of sentences in the Passé Simple, as shown in chapter 15 (this volume), so we need the following rule:

**A 14** $(\langle\tau, \alpha, \beta\rangle \wedge \textit{PS}(e_\alpha, \alpha) \wedge \textit{PS}(e_\beta, \beta)) \rightarrow \neg\textit{Explanation}(\alpha, \beta)$

but it can be done with a sequence of sentences in the Passé Composé:

(17) Jean est tombé. Paul l'a poussé.
'Jean fell (PC). Paul pushed (PC) him.'

or by a sequence of sentences in the Passé Simple + Imparfait or Passé Composé + Imparfait:

(18) Marie arriva/est arrivée en retard au cinéma. Elle attendait son mari à la maison et c'était lui qui devait garder les enfants.
'Marie arrived (PS/PC) late at the cinema. She was waiting (IMP) for her husband at home and he was the one who had to look after the children.'

Result is a coordinating relation, whereas Explanation is subordinating.

**Elaboration.** Elaboration is a subordinating discourse relations, i.e., a relation that introduces a complex constituent, a SDRS containing a sub-SDRS. A famous example of Elaboration from Kamp and Rohrer (1983) was given in chapter 15, and is repeated here as (19):

(19) L'été de cette année-là vit plusieurs changements dans la vie de nos héros. ($S_1$) François épousa Adèle ($S_{2a}$), Jean-Louis partit pour le Brésil ($S_{2b}$) et Paul s'acheta une maison à la campagne ($S_{2c}$).

$S_1$ is elaborated by the complex $S_2$. It provides the topic for each of the changes described in the following clauses. Between $K_1$, the constituent representing $S_1$, and each of $K_{2a}$, $K_{2b}$ and $K_{2c}$, an Elaboration relation holds. Between $K_{2a}$ and $K_{2b}$, and between $K_{2b}$ and $K_{2c}$, a so-called Continuation relation holds.

Continuation is a rather weak discourse relation. It merely records that all the constituents of a complex SDRS connected to a constituent by a subordinating relation are siblings. It has no temporal effects (cf. also section 4 below). Elaboration implies that the main eventuality of each elaborating clause is a (proper) part of that of the elaborated clause, which in turn implies that there is a (strict) temporal inclusion between them:

**A 15** $\mathit{Elaboration}(\alpha, \beta) \rightarrow \mathit{Part\text{-}of}(e_\beta, e_\alpha)$

**A 16** $\mathit{Part\text{-}of}(e_1, e_2) \rightarrow e_1 \subset e_2$

Elaboration is triggered by the lexical semantics of the event predicates involved, or by shared knowledge on event types and subtypes. The predicate *D-Permissible-Subtype* gathers all these clues allowing to non-monotonically infer Elaboration:

**A 17** $(\langle \tau, \alpha, \beta \rangle \wedge \mathit{D\text{-}Permissible\text{-}Subtype}(\alpha, \beta)) > \mathit{Elaboration}(\alpha, \beta)$

**Contrast.** Contrast is a structural relation, as it is usually triggered by a partial isomorphism on the syntactic trees of the two constituents and the presence of contrasting themes (cf. (Asher, 1993; Asher et al., 2001).

**A 18** $(\langle \tau, \alpha, \beta \rangle \wedge \mathit{Structurally\text{-}similar}(\alpha, \beta) \wedge \mathit{Contrasting\text{-}themes}(\alpha, \beta)) > \mathit{Contrast}(\alpha, \beta)$

It can also be monotonically inferred by the presence of an explicit marker of contrast like *but* or *mais* in French:

**A 19** $(\langle \tau, \alpha, \beta \rangle \wedge \mathit{mais}(\beta)) \rightarrow \mathit{Contrast}(\alpha, \beta)$

Here is an example taken from Asher (1996):

(20) As-tu acheté le livre? Oui, je l'ai acheté, mais je l'ai prêté.
'Did you buy the book? Yes, I bought it but I lent it.'

*Contrast*$(\alpha, \beta)$ implies that $\alpha$ and $\beta$ have incompatible implicatures, i.e., that from the propositional content of $\alpha$ one can derive a fact whose negation can be derived from the propositional content of $\beta$. Contrast has no temporal effects. In (20), both Contrast and Narration are inferred, for the relation between buying and lending triggers a relation of Occasion.

**Background.** This relation is inferred from aspectual discontinuities such as a change of type of temporal referent, e.g. an event followed by a state. In (21), the Passé Simple in $S_1$ introduces an event referent, while the Imparfait in $S_2$ introduces a state referent.

(21) Paul entra. Marie faisait la vaisselle.
'Paul entered (PS) ($S_1$). Mary was doing (IMP) the dishes ($S_2$).'

The triggering axioms for the Background relation when aspectual discontinuities are encountered are the following, where *Background1*$(\alpha, \beta)$ means that $\alpha$ is the foreground and has $\beta$ as background, and *Background2*$(\alpha, \beta)$ means that $\beta$ is the foreground and has $\alpha$ as background:

**A 20** $((\langle\tau,\alpha,\beta\rangle \wedge \mathit{Event}(e_\alpha) \wedge \mathit{State}(e_\beta)) > \mathit{Background1}(\alpha,\beta)$

**A 21** $((\langle\tau,\alpha,\beta\rangle \wedge \mathit{State}(e_\alpha) \wedge \mathit{Event}(e_\beta)) > \mathit{Background2}(\alpha,\beta)$

Background affects the semantic contents of discourse. Axioms 22 and 23 give its temporal effects: enriching the discourse representation with a temporal overlap between the two eventualities.

**A 22** $\mathit{Background1}(\alpha,\beta) \rightarrow e_\alpha \subset e_\beta$

**A 23** $\mathit{Background2}(\alpha,\beta) \rightarrow e_\beta \subset e_\alpha$

Like Narration, Background also has structural effects. When a Background relation holds, a new sort of topic, a *Foreground-Background Pair* (FBP) is built. This new constituent is the fusion of the two constituents linked by the relation, that is, the foreground and the background.[15]

**A 24** $\mathit{Background1}(\alpha,\beta) \rightarrow \exists\gamma \mathit{FBP}(\gamma,[\alpha,\beta])$

**A 25** $\mathit{Background2}(\alpha,\beta) \rightarrow \exists\gamma \mathit{FBP}(\gamma,[\alpha,\beta])$

Asher et al. (1995a) show that examples like (22) can be accounted for with this new FBP structure.

(22) Marie entra dans la librairie. Un homme lisait un journal près de la caisse. Elle s'approcha de lui.
'Marie entered the bookshop ($S_1$). A man was reading a newspaper near the cashdesk ($S_2$). She got closer to him ($S_3$).'

In this example, a Narration relation should temporally order the eventualities of $K_1$ and $K_3$ and, at the same time, the information the background of $K_2$ needs to be used to solve the anaphoric pronoun *lui* in $S_3$.[16] According to Asher (1996), the new constituent $K^*$, the FBP of the complex SDRS constituted of the foreground $K_1$ and the background $K_2$ (sloppily noted $[K_1, K_2]$) becomes a possible attachment site for $K_3$ by Narration, which both yields the right temporal order and enables the right anaphora resolution.

In such a discourse structure, Axiom 2 on Narration makes it possible to infer $e_1 \prec e_3$, for the main eventuality of $K^*$ is $e_1$, according to the first of the following axioms:

**A 26** $(\mathit{FBP}(\gamma,[\alpha,\beta]) \wedge \mathit{Background1}(\alpha,\beta)) \rightarrow e_\gamma = e_\alpha$

**A 27** $(\mathit{FBP}(\gamma,[\alpha,\beta]) \wedge \mathit{Background2}(\alpha,\beta)) \rightarrow e_\gamma = e_\beta$

---

[15] $[\alpha,\beta]$ is short for the complex SDRS constituted of $\alpha$ and $\beta$.
This axiom actually should be written: $\delta = [\alpha,\beta \mid \mathit{Background1}(\alpha,\beta)] \rightarrow \exists\gamma\ \mathrm{FBP}(\gamma,\delta)$, using DRS notation à-la-Muskens.

[16] $K_1$, $K_2$ and $K_3$ are the basic constituents representing $S_1$, $S_2$ and $S_3$, respectively.

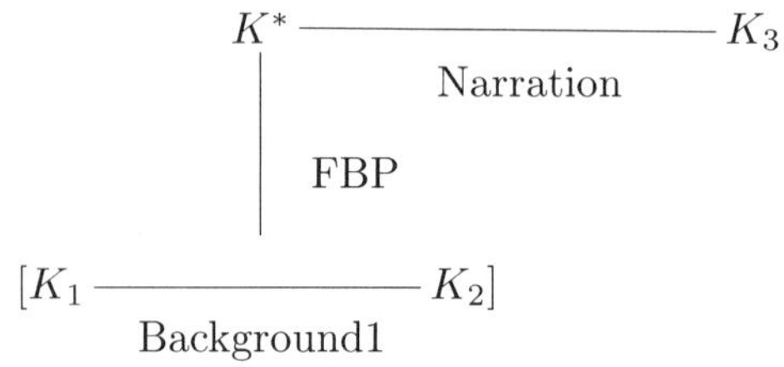


FIGURE 5 The graph of the SDRS representing 22

### 2.3 Conclusion: Tenses and Discourse Relations

In this section, we have proposed an application of SDRT to French narratives. It has been shown how the rules settled on in chapter 15 to deal with past tenses such as the Imparfait, Passé Simple and Passé Composé, can be accounted for in the SDRT framework.

It has been shown that two consecutive sentences in the Passé Simple can yield two possible temporal orderings, namely temporal succession when Narration holds as in (12) or when Result (possibly together with Narration) holds as in (14); and temporal inclusion when Elaboration holds as for the two first sentences of (19). It is also possible to have two Passé Simple sentences bearing no textually expressed temporal ordering, as is the case between two sentences related by a Continuation relation within a complex segment, that, for instance, elaborates a previous topic sentence as in $S_{2a}$, $S_{2c}$ and $S_{2c}$ in (19).

We also explained that a sequence of sentences in the Passé Simple and Imparfait in both orders can yield four possible temporal relations: temporal inclusion, in one direction or another, when Background holds as in (21) (and similarly with an Imparfait sentence before a Passé Simple sentence); temporal succession when Result holds as in (15); temporal precedence when Explanation holds as in (18).

## 3 Connectives, Discourse Structure, and Simple Past Tenses (Passé Simple and Imparfait)

In this section, we compare the behavior of connectives such as *puis* ('then, afterwards') and *un peu plus tard* ('a bit later') in combination with the Passé Simple and the Imparfait in order to find out to what extent they affect Discourse Structure. These two temporal connectives are semantically quite close, since they both express temporal succession, although we have seen in Section 1 that they belong to two different categories of temporal adverbials. *Un peu plus tard* represents the class of adverbials *NP plus tard/après* that establishes a relation of succession between two temporal referents. *Puis* represents the class of pure linking adverbials (cf. section 1).

### 3.1 Connecting two Passé Simple sentences

The comparison starts with *puis* and *un peu/NP plus tard* in cases in which they connect two Passé Simple sentences:

(23) a. L'acide tomba dans le mélange. Une explosion se produisit.
'The acid fell into the mixture. An explosion happened.'

b. L'acide tomba dans le mélange. **Puis** une explosion se produisit.
'The acid fell into the mixture. Then an explosion happened.'

c. L'acide tomba dans le mélange. **Un peu plus tard** une explosion se produisit.
'The acid fell into the mixture. A bit later an explosion happened.'

The three examples all express a relation of temporal succession between the two events. But in (23a), the explosion event is not only interpreted as posterior to, but also as a result of the acid falling event. This interpretation is preserved in (23c), but it is lost in (23b). With *puis*, the events are presented from an external point of view, as if the speaker did not intend to express a resultative link.

Let us now look at (24):

(24) a. La petite fille s'endormit. Il se mit à pleuvoir.
'The little girl fell asleep. It began to rain.'

b. La petite fille s'endormit. **Puis** il se mit à pleuvoir.

c. La petite fille s'endormit. **Un peu plus tard**, il se mit à pleuvoir.

The use of *puis* in (24b) is not as straightforward as the use of *un peu plus tard* in (24c). In order to interpret (24b), one has to imagine a specific context (possibly established in a previous piece of text), for example "the story of a little girl lost in the woods", in which the contribution of each sentence to the coherence of the discourse is more obvious (the rain being a potential nuisance concerning her good sleep). *Un peu plus tard* does not require this kind of constraint.

The difference is less important when the text itself describes two events that are clearly linked together, as in (25):

(25) a. Marie écrivit une longue lettre à son cousin. Elle alla la poster au village voisin.
'Marie wrote a letter to her cousin. She went to the next village and posted it.'

b. Marie écrivit une longue lettre à son cousin. **Puis** elle alla la poster au village voisin.

c. Marie écrivit une longue lettre à son cousin. **Un peu plus tard**, elle alla la poster au village voisin.

No particular context is needed to interpret (25b) and (25a). Nevertheless, the events seem to be more disconnected in (25c) than in (25b) or (25a). The intuitions described above may be accounted for in the SDRT framework developed in section 2 above.

***Puis* and *un peu plus tard* with Narration.** In Bras et al. (2001b), it is argued that *puis* is a rhetorical marker which introduces a relation of Narration:

**A 28** $(\langle\tau, \alpha, \beta\rangle \wedge puis(\beta)) \rightarrow Narration(\alpha, \beta)$

In both (24a) and (24b), a Narration relation is inferred, either by default with A4 for (24a), or due to *puis* with A28 for (24b). To account for the different interpretation in (24c), we hypothesize that *un peu plus tard* blocks Narration. Axiom A2 on Narration states that the intersection of the poststate of $e_\alpha$ and the prestate of $e_\beta$ exists and fills the interval between the two events. This means that the events must fit consistently and without significant spatio-temporal gaps. A2 uses a material implication. That is, if the consequent (the no-significant-gap condition) does not hold, Narration does not hold. A way to test the possibility of a relevant spatio-temporal gap between the two events is to try and insert a third event between $e_\alpha$ and $e_\beta$ that terminates $post(e_\alpha)$ (cf. Caenepeel (1995)). An event whose poststate is incompatible with $post(e_\alpha)$ would be the event of the little girl waking up.

(26) a. La petite fille s'endormit. Il se mit à pleuvoir. *Elle venait juste de se réveiller (She had just woken up.). /*Entretemps elle s'était réveillée (Meanwhile she had woken up.).

b. La petite fille s'endormit. **Puis** il se mit à pleuvoir. *Elle venait juste de se réveiller./*Entretemps elle s'était réveillée.

c. La petite fille s'endormit. **Un peu plus tard**, il se mit à pleuvoir. Elle venait juste de se réveiller./Entretemps elle s'était réveillée.

The test on the temporal effect of Narration fails in (26c). It is successful in (26a) and (26b), as the insertion of an intermediate event appears to be very difficult. Let us insist on the fact that the above examples are built in such a way that the intermediate events actually imply the end of $post(e_\alpha)$, hence involve a temporal *relevant* gap between $e_\alpha$ and $e_\beta$. Otherwise, the adding of another event with *entretemps* poses no problem. For instance, (27 is perfectly acceptable, for the falling of the night does not imply that the little girl is no longer asleep.

(27) La petite fille s'endormit. **Puis** il se mit à pleuvoir. Entretemps la nuit était tombée ('Meanwhile the night had fallen.').

Let us also note that it might be possible to improve (26a) and (26b), by introducing the third event with something like "*Ajoutons/précisons que, entretemps, la petite fille s'était réveillée*" ('Let us add/point out that, meanwhile, the little girl had woken up'). In such a case, however, there is an explicit correction, and so it is not surprising that the temporal effects of Narration should be revised.

The second semantic effect of Narration is the topic requirement A3. A thematic link is required between the two events in (24a) and (24b). Since it is difficult to infer the topic from the propositional contents of the text alone, the requirement entails that the text will be felicitous only when inserted in a larger context providing the topic. The topic requirement is stronger in (24b). This is an indication that *puis* requires more than a simple Narration relation. We leave this aside for now, and turn to the difference between *puis* and *un peu plus tard.* No special context is needed to interpret (24c). This is further evidence for the accuracy of the hypothesis that *un peu plus tard* blocks Narration.

Now, if the relation between the sentence $\beta$ introduced by *un peu plus tard* and the sentence $\alpha$ is not Narration, what is it? Of course, *un peu plus tard* contributes a temporal relation of succession between the events. But apart from this, and as noticed above, the relation between $\alpha$ and $\beta$ does not match the semantic effects of Narration. (24c) being a coherent (acceptable) discourse, another discourse relation must hold.[17] We hypothesize that it should be a relation that only supports temporal precedence, that could be viewed as a kind of 'weak Narration'. In this perspective, Narration is a gradual relation that normally occurs under its "strong form" (what we have been calling Narration up to now), and always at least under its weak form:

**A 29** $Narration(\alpha, \beta) > Strong\text{-}Narration(\alpha, \beta)$

**A 30** $Narration(\alpha, \beta) \rightarrow Weak\text{-}Narration(\alpha, \beta)$

This change implies updating the axioms given earlier: *Narration* has to be replaced by *Strong-Narration* in the axioms A2, A3, A5 and A28, but in A4, the general *Narration* relation predicate remains.

Weak-Narration has no requirement on topic nor does it have the 'no-significant-gap constraint'. The only semantic effect of Weak-Narration is temporal precedence:

[17] In SDRT in a coherent discourse, any constituent must be linked by a discourse relation to some previous constituent. In a two-sentence text, this means that the two constituents representing the two clauses must be linked together.

**A 31** *Weak-Narration*$(\alpha, \beta) \rightarrow e_\alpha \prec e_\beta$

With such limited semantic effects, *un peu plus tard* is obviously compatible with Weak-Narration. It must be noted though, that we do not consider adverbials of this kind as rhetorical markers of this relation. Unlike *puis*, they do not syntactically behave as conjuncts. Moreover, their main semantic contribution materializes compositionally within the constituent itself, specifying not only temporal succession between two temporal referents, but also the length of the temporal interval between these referents.

Let us now return to example (25) in the light of these considerations on the role of *un peu plus tard*. In both (25a) and (25b), a Strong-Narration relation will be inferred: for (25a), Occasion holds and A5 is triggered; for (25b), the presence of *puis* triggers (A28). Unlike (24), Occasion holds in both cases, and thus it is easy to build a topic common to both sentences. The example in (25c) is perfectly all right, but bears a slightly different interpretation: here the strong link between the two events is lost. It is indeed quite possible to introduce an intervening event, as (28a) shows, while this is not possible for the two other examples, viz. (28a) and (28b).

(28) a. Marie écrivit une longue lettre à son cousin. Elle alla la poster au village voisin. *Entretemps, elle l'avait retouchée à plusieurs reprises ('Meanwhile she had altered it several times.)'.

b. Marie écrivit une longue lettre à son cousin. **Puis** elle alla la poster au village voisin. *Entretemps, elle l'avait retouchée à plusieurs reprises.

c. Marie écrivit une longue lettre à son cousin. **Un peu plus tard**, elle alla la poster au village voisin. Entretemps, elle l'avait retouchée à plusieurs reprises.

Therefore, *un peu plus tard* blocks Strong-Narration not only when it could have been inferred by default, but also when Occasion holds. To account for this blocking, the following axioms must be introduced:

**A 32** $(\textit{Narration}(\alpha, \beta) \wedge \textit{un peu plus tard}(\beta)) > \neg\textit{Strong-Narration}(\alpha, \beta)$

**A 33** $(\langle \tau, \alpha, \beta \rangle \wedge \textit{Occasion}(\alpha, \beta) \wedge \textit{un peu plus tard}(\beta)) >$
$\neg\textit{Strong-Narration}(\alpha, \beta)$

A32 will block the inference of Strong-Narration in the absence of other relations (i.e., a Strong-Narration that could have been inferred with A4 and A29). A33 is needed as well for the cases in which Occasion holds. Applying the Penguin Principle, it circumvents a Nixon Diamond schema between A5 and A32 that would preclude the inference of any relation at all (compare footnote 7 above).

Coming back again to (25) we observe that the perception of a difference between (25a) and (25b) on the one hand, and (25c) on the other hand, is certainly also due to a particularity of *un peu plus tard* concerning plans. As a matter of fact, the presence of *un peu plus tard* has the effect of blocking the interpretation that events $e_\alpha$ and $e_\beta$ are part of a plan (a plan in which $e_\alpha$ is intended to lead to $e_\beta$, for example, when $e_\alpha$ is a precondition to $e_\beta$).[18] This difference in terms of planning is more obvious in examples like (29).

(29) a. Marie rejoignit son ami, **puis** lui glissa à l'oreille qu'elle voulait partir.
'Marie rejoined her friend, then she whispered in his ear that she wanted to leave.'

b. Marie rejoignit son ami; **un peu plus tard**, elle lui glissa à l'oreille qu'elle voulait partir.

Example (29a) lends itself to an interpretation in which Marie reaches her friend in order to tell him something. But this plan interpretation is suspended when *puis* is replaced with *un peu plus tard* in (25b).[19]

The difference in behavior evidenced here should be explained at the rhetorical level. It would probably require in some contexts the use of a new relation of 'Planned-Sequence' (not yet introduced in SDRT), allowed by *puis*, and again, blocked by *un peu plus tard*.

***Puis* and *un peu plus tard* with Result.** Let us now come back to (23), that we repeat here for the sake of readability:

(23) a. L'acide tomba dans le mélange. Une explosion se produisit.
b. L'acide tomba dans le mélange. **Puis** une explosion se produisit.
c. L'acide tomba dans le mélange. **Un peu plus tard** une explosion se produisit.

The different interpretations of (23a) and (23c) on the one hand, and of (23b) on the other hand, have to be accounted for. Assuming that there is most probably some piece of shared knowledge on chemicals implying that D-Permissible-Cause holds between the two constituents representing the two clauses, SDRT non-monotonically concludes Result

[18] This at least seems to be true when *un peu plus tard* connects two Passé Simple sentences. As we will note later, things are more complicated when *un peu plus tard* introduces a so-called 'narrative Imparfait'.

[19] Or, for that matter, another adverbial indicating an even shorter temporal separation like *immédiatement après* ('immediately after').

with Axiom 12. As was shown in Bras et al. (2001b), *puis* blocks the non-monotonic inference to Result. SDRT can exploit the logical properties of defeasible reasoning in Commonsense Entailment to explain this blocking, if the presence of *puis* implied some fact incompatible with Result. Axiom 28 together with the semantic effects of Strong-Narration A2 is unable to infer any such fact. Hence an additional axiom is needed:

**A 34** $(\langle \tau, \alpha, \beta \rangle \wedge \mathit{puis}(\beta)) \rightarrow \neg \mathit{Result}(\alpha, \beta)$

or

**A 35** $(\langle \tau, \alpha, \beta \rangle \wedge \mathit{puis}(\beta)) \rightarrow \neg \mathit{Cause}(e_\alpha, e_\beta)$

It is possible to choose between these two solutions and retain A34 by observing that the blocking should be on the rhetorical level only. Indeed, it could be the case that the two events described are actually causally connected, even though the text doesn't tell us anything regarding such a connection. So, our intuition that there is a difference of interpretation between (23b) and (23c) is expressed, in SDRT, by the fact that *puis* blocks the rhetorical relation of Result. For *un peu plus tard*, no such constraint is at stake, so the Result relation will be inferred thus accounting for the intuition of a mere 'delayed' result.

***Puis* and *un peu plus tard* with Contrast.** Let us finally examine cases in which a relation of Contrast is expressed:

(30) a. Il s'en moqua d'ailleurs comme d'une naïveté, **puis** la vanta comme un moyen de contraindre la sottise des petites gens au respect du savoir et de la puissance[...] (Adam, L'enfant d'Austerlitz)
'He mocked it besides as a naïvety, then praised it as a means to compel the stupidity of ordinary people to the respect of knowledge and power[...]'

b. Il s'en moqua d'ailleurs comme d'une naïveté; **un peu plus tard** il la vanta comme un moyen [...]

(31) a. Vaton se tut sous le choc, **puis** bredouilla quelques mots[...] (Malègue, Augustin ou le Maitre est là)
'Vaton went silent under the shock, then he stammered a few words[...]

b. Vaton se tut sous le choc; **un peu plus tard**, il bredouilla quelques mots[...]

In these examples SDRT predicts that a rhetorical relation of Contrast holds between the clauses linked by *puis* or *un peu plus tard*, as the required partial structural isomorphism is accompanied by a lexical opposition of the main predicates (*to mock/to praise*, *to go silent/to stammer*). These opposed predicates describe actions of a same agent, so that the corresponding events are necessarily temporally disjoint. However, neither *puis* nor *un peu plus tard* are redundant in these examples. They emphasize the separation between the two actions, ordering them temporally. Without *puis* or *un peu plus tard*, the temporal succession reading is lost and incoherent discourses are obtained:

(32) Il s'en moqua d'ailleurs comme d'une naïveté; ? il la vanta comme un moyen[...]

The incoherence remains if the temporal adverbials are replaced with the explicit Contrast marker *mais* ('but').[20]

(33) Il s'en moqua d'ailleurs comme d'une naïveté, ? mais la vanta comme un moyen[...]

This actually confirms SDRT axiom A4: Narration cannot be inferred by default (i.e., without Occasion and without any specific marker like *puis*) when other discourse relations, like Contrast, can be triggered[21]. However, SDRT does not at present explain why such discourses are incoherent. It seems that further semantic constraints on the Contrast relation are needed, requiring some explicit temporal separation where the two events cannot occur simultaneously. Now, what is the difference between (30a) and (30b) or between (31a) and (31b)? According to what has been previously shown, it is only in (30a) and (31b), with *puis*, that Strong-Narration is inferred. In (30b) and (31b) the discourse relation of Weak-Narration will be inferred. So the difference between these examples is of the same type as the one we observed for (24) and (25). As an indication of temporal succession is sufficient to admit incompatible situations, both the examples with *puis* and *un peu plus tard* are acceptable. But at the same time as *puis* triggers a separation between the two events in a relation of Contrast, the absence of significant gap associated with it gives a cohesion that *un peu plus tard* does not give. And as was previously seen, the difference in cohesion may be evidenced by a difference of acceptability between (34) and (35)

(34) Il s'en moqua, **puis** la vanta. *Entretemps, il avait réfléchi.
'He mocked it, then he praised it. Meanwhile he had thought

---

[20]The incoherence may disappear only when the reading is not a narrative one, i.e., if the mocking and the praising are no longer considered as temporally ordered. In this case, the use of the Contrast marker focuses on the co-existence of two different features of the object at stake that can be evaluated at the same time: one negatively (as a naïvety) and the other positively (as a restrictive means).

[21]Notice that with Occasion, we may have both Contrast and Strong-Narration relations without *puis*.

things over.'

(35) Il s'en moqua et **un peu plus tard** la vanta. Entretemps, il avait réfléchi.

It can be noticed that the temporal interval between the two events is quantified with *un peu plus tard*, and not with *puis*. Two remarks can be made. First, even with a quantification specifying that the interval is short (*peu* means *little*), *un peu plus tard* does not succeed in giving the 'no-significant-gap' reading that *puis* gives. Second, even though in many contexts, the 'no-significant-gap' constraint imposed by Strong-Narration with *puis* leads to an implicit characterization of this interval, as being rather short, this is by no means necessary. See for instance 36, in which the author felt the need to add a quantification of the interval, using both *puis* and *peu après*.[22] This shows that the 'no-significant-gap' constraint is not a metric notion, but indeed a conceptual one: no relevant event happened in between.

(36) Azarius l'entendit qui enjoignait à l'enfant de dormir. **Puis, peu après**, il la vit qui le surveillait, appuyée au chambranle de la porte. (Roy, Bonheur d'occasion)
'Azarius heard her enjoining the child to sleep. Then, a little later, he saw her watching him, leaning against the doorpost.'

### 3.2 Connecting Passé Simple and Imparfait sentences

**Imparfait sentence linked to a Passé Simple sentence with *puis* or *un peu plus tard*.** In Bras et al. (2001a), a corpus of discourse pieces in which *puis* connects an Imparfait sentence and a Passé Simple sentence, such as 37, is analyzed:

(37) Mme Rieux détourna la tête vers la fenêtre. Le docteur se taisait. **Puis** il dit à sa mère de ne pas pleurer, qu'il s'y attendait, mais que c'était quand même difficile. (Camus, La Peste)
'Mme Rieux turned her head away towards the window. The doctor kept (IMP) silent. Then he told (PS) her mother not to cry, that he was expecting it, but that it was difficult nonetheless.'

In (37), besides the Background relation between the constituents representing the first two sentences, there is both a relation of Contrast and a relation of Strong-Narration between the constituent representing *le docteur se taisait* and the one for *il dit à sa mère...* Actually, in all

---

[22]This is a case for which the analysis correctly predicts Strong-Narration, even though *un peu plus tard* is used, illustrating again the inferential priorities between material
implication and non-monotonic conditional.

the examples following the Imparfait *puis* Passé Simple scheme that are found in the corpus, both Strong-Narration and Contrast hold, leading us back to cases of Contrast we have studied above for the Passé Simple. It is shown in Bras et al. (2001a)

that the relation of Contrast is present in all such examples, as it helps to end the durative situation (associated with the Imparfait) to express a Strong-Narration.[23] (37) can be modified by replacing *puis* with *un peu plus tard*:

(38) Mme Rieux détourna la tête vers la fenêtre. Le docteur se taisait. **Un peu plus tard**, il dit à sa mère de ne pas pleurer, qu'il s'y attendait, mais que c'était quand même difficile.

(38) gets a slightly different interpretation. The silence described by *le docteur se taisait* might have been broken by something else than what is described in *il dit à sa mère de ne pas pleurer*. This would be impossible for (37). The discourse relations inferred for (38), namely Contrast and Weak-Narration, correctly account for this. Again, the distinction between *puis* and *un peu plus tard* is the same as the one seen above for the Passé Simple cases with Contrast.

**Passé Simple sentence linked to an Imparfait sentence with *puis* or *un peu plus tard*.** In Section 2.2 it was shown that two sentences in a sequence Passé Simple - Imparfait without connectives could be linked by three discourse relations: Background, Result or Explanation, if we only consider the possible discourse relations with temporal effects. If we try to link two such sentences with *puis* and *un peu plus tard*, it is obvious that Explanation is not compatible with either *puis* or *un peu plus tard*, as they have opposite temporal effects (precedence vs. succession). In cases of the 'background Imparfait', the standard Imparfaituse, the Imparfait temporally includes some required temporal anchor. In such contexts the behavior of *puis* and *un peu plus tard* is not the same, as shown in (39).[24]

(39) a. Marie promit qu'elle allait réparer la voiture. **Un peu plus tard / un quart d'heure plus tard** elle était plongée dans son roman, affalée sur le canapé.
'Marie promised to go and fix the car. A bit later / a quarter of an hour later, she was-Imparfait immersed in her novel, slumped

[23] The way an event may be linked to a state through a relation of Strong-Narration has not classically been studied in SDRT. The difficulties raised by the attachment, and some propositions to resolve them through an adjustment of the FBP structure (cf. Section 2.2) are presented in Bras et al. (2001a).

[24] See Gosselin (1999) for a similar example where the Imparfait may be paraphrased by *être-IMP en train de V-INF*.

in the sofa.'

b. Marie promit qu'elle allait réparer la voiture. *Puis elle était plongée dans son roman, affalée sur le canapé.

*Un peu plus tard* or *un quart d'heure plus tard* can provide the temporal referent the standard Imparfait requires, while *puis* cannot.[25] It is shown in Asher et al. (2002) that when relational adverbials are quantified with a durative NP, a time $t$ may be introduced, just as with referential adverbials. Pure linking adverbials like *puis* never include a durative NP, and are thus unable to provide such a temporal referent. Without an explicit temporal quantification, relational adverbials such as *plus tard* or *après* come close to *puis*, since no new time referent can be forced in (40), a variant of (39).

(40) Marie promit qu'elle allait réparer la voiture. ***Plus tard**, elle était plongée dans son roman, affalée sur le canapé.

The so-called 'narrative Imparfait' in (41) and (42) also requires a temporal anchor, provided by adverbials of type *NP plus tard/après*, but not by *puis* (cf. chapter 15 for discussion of the Narrative Imparfait).

(41) a. Pierre déclara d'abord que ce livre ne l'intéressait pas. **Peu après**, il le recommandait chaudement à tous ses amis.
'Pierre first claimed (PS) that he was not interested in this book. A bit later, he recommended (IMP) it heartily to all his friends.'

b. Pierre déclara d'abord que ce livre ne l'intéressait pas. ***Puis**, il le recommandait chaudement à tous ses amis.

(42) a. Pour la première fois de sa vie, il ne s'ennuya pas au théâtre et il passa sa nuit avec des filles. **Six mois plus tard**, il se remariait. (Maupassant,*Les bijoux*, quoted by Berthonneau and Kleiber (1999))
'For the first time in his life, he wasn't (PS) bored at the theater and he spent (PS) his night with girls. Six months later, he remarried (IMP).'

b. Pour la première fois de sa vie, il ne s'ennuya pas au théâtre et il passa sa nuit avec des filles. ***Puis** il se remariait.

(43) a. [le commandant (...) se jeta sur l'interphone] et hurla qu'il avait à parler à Mr Chisnutt. **Trois minutes plus tard**, Mr Chistnutt se présentait chez le commandant.
'[The commandant rushed at the intercom] and roared that

[25] This infelicity is not due to the particular discourse relation involved here, i.e., Contrast. We have seen above that *puis* is compatible with the relation of Contrast.

he had to speak to Mr Chisnutt. Three minutes later, Mr Chisnutt appeared at the commandant's.'

b. [le commandant (...) se jeta sur l'interphone] et hurla qu'il avait à parler à Mr Chisnutt. ***Puis** Mr Chistnutt se présentait chez le commandant.[26]

Actually, very rare cases of narrative Imparfait can be found in the corpus, triggered by *puis* (Bras et al., 2001a):

(44) Un grand silence tomba. – Quand nous reviendrons de la guerre, dit enfin M. Pasquier, je vous raconterai les souvenirs de mon voyage en Afrique. Un voyage mirobolant! Il y eut un nouveau silence. **Puis** on entendait un bruit poignant, un bruit terrible, qui semblait sourdre non d'un être, mais de l'épaisseur de la terre. (Duhamel, Le Combat contre les ombres)
'[...] There was (PS) another silence. Then one heard (IMP) a poignant noise, a terrible noise, which seemed to rise not from a being, but from the depths of the earth.'

Nevertheless, such cases studied in Bras et al. (2001a), are rather marked, and not to be considered as counter-examples.

### 3.3 Conclusion

*Puis* and *un peu plus tard* have been compared in order to determine the way they affect the temporal structure and discourse structure of sentences in the Passé Simple and the Imparfait. Both connectives express temporal succession, but *puis* involves a stronger temporal semantics content: $(e_\alpha \supset\!\subset (\text{post}(e_\alpha) \sqcap \text{pre}(e_\beta)) \supset\!\subset e_\beta)$. As far as the discourse structure is concerned, *puis* is a marker of Strong-Narration, involving the notion of telling the 'same story' (topic), whereas *un peu plus tard* blocks Strong-Narration and licences Weak-Narration, involving no more semantic effects than temporal succession. In addition, *puis* blocks Result, while *un peu plus tard* doesn't.

We conclude that a priori temporally equivalent adverbials may have different effects on discourse structure. On the one hand, we see that *puis* is a real discourse relation connective, which is no surprise given its conjunct character. On the other hand, if *un peu plus tard* is not a discourse relation connective, neither is it the purely temporal adverbial

[26]This example is mentioned here as it is one of the examples used by Molendijk (1990) to show that the narrative Imparfait has the characteristic of being 'prepared', i.e. of coinciding with an implication of a preceding sentence.

Examples such as this one justify our claim that the presence of *un peu plus tard* blocks the interpretation that the events it connects are part of a plan: the validity of this claim is limited to cases in which *un peu plus tard* connects two Passé Simple sentences; it doesn't hold when *un peu plus tard* introduces a 'narrative Imparfait'.

that one could expect, since it is capable of blocking some discourse relations, like Strong-Narration, the usual case of Narration. And this is certainly not an obvious fact for an adverbial primarily indicating temporal succession.

The analysis proposed up to now has been restricted to two representative connectives, and to their interaction with two simple tenses. In what follows, the perspective is slightly different: the study focuses on the way a text written in the Passé Composé may appeal to connectives in order to facilitate the interpretation of its temporal structure. In this perspective, a larger range of connectives will be taken into account.

## 4 Connectives, Discourse Structure, and the Passé Composé

At this point, we have all the analytical tools we need to re-examine the temporal structure of discourses in the Passé Composé. In chapter 15 above, building on de Swart and Molendijk (2002, to appear), we claimed that the French Passé Composé respects the temporal structure E-R,S of the Reichenbachian perfect. Furthermore, we claimed that the Passé Composé introduces a quantized event $e$ into the discourse representation structure, and a consequent state $s$, such that $e \supset\!\subset s$. On the basis of a study of *L'étranger* we concluded that any temporal relation could be established between two sentences in the Passé Composé: we found examples of posteriority, simultaneity/overlap and even temporal inversion. The question that remains to be answered is how the temporal structure of a discourse in the Passé Composé is determined. We claim that the temporal structure is parasitic upon the rhetorical structure of the Passé Composé.

### 4.1 From Reichenbach to rhetorical structure

In the Reichenbachian view, the non-anaphoric nature of the perfect is the result of its orientation towards the speech time S. In terms of SDRT, we can say that the perfect creates an Elaboration structure in which the speech time S (or more generally: the utterance situation or writing context) provides the topic, and all sentences in the perfect are elaborations of this topic. Typically, several sentences entertain an Elaboration relation with the Topic at hand, which leads to a relation of Continuation between these sentences. If we find a series of sentences in the perfect, which elaborate a particular speech situation, the rhetorical relation between those sentences is the relation of Continuation as exemplified in Figure 6.

Continuation is a purely rhetorical relation, that does not have temporal implications in and of itself (cf. section 2.2 above). The sen-

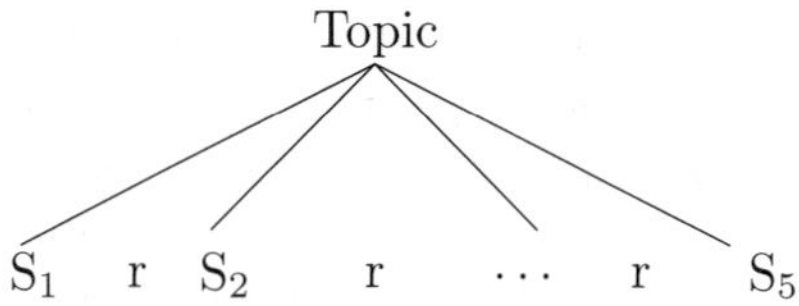


FIGURE 6 Topic, Elaboration, Continuation

tences $S_1 \ldots S_n$ in the perfect thus describe a temporally unordered set of events. We can use this discourse semantics to describe the structure of texts like (45) (English) and (46) (French).[27]

(45) Here then is a letter. You and I long since agreed that letters are nothing. Yours tell me what I knew already or could well imagine, and they frequently departed from the rule which we had laid down that a letter should consist principally of facts.
'Here are my facts. The weather *has been* incomparable. There *have been* many parties on sea and on land. I leave all reunions which *have been abandoned* to conversation only and for which the host *has made* no plans for entertainment.'

(46) La bêtise n'est pas mon fort. J'*ai vu* beaucoup d'individus, j'*ai pris* ma part d'entreprises diverses sans les aimer, j'*ai mangé* presque tous les jours, *j'ai touché* à des femmes.
'Stupidity is not my strong point. I have seen many individuals, I have taken part in several activities that I didn't like, I have eaten almost every day, I have touched women.'

The Topic of the Elaboration in (45) is given by the sentence 'Here are the facts'. The series of sentences in the Present Perfect that follows describes Elaborations of this topic. Although the sentences are related by the rhetorical relation of Continuation, this does not in and of itself induce temporal structure. The set of events is described as a temporally unordered set. Similar remarks can be made about (46). The Topic here is *La bêtise n'est pas mon fort.* The series of sentences in the Passé Composé that follows describes Elaborations of this topic, and collects the events in an unordered set. In both cases the Topic is provided by a sentence in the present tense, which confirms the orientation of the

[27](45) is a passage from (the English translation of) a letter by Clodia Pulcher to the poet Catull, quoted by Weinrich (1973: 74–75)
in his discussion of the English perfect. (46) contains the opening sentences of Paul Valéry's story *La soirée avec M. Teste*; it is quoted by Weinrich (1973: 77) in his discussion of the French perfect.

perfect towards the speech time.

The relation of Continuation does not induce temporal structure, and we see in (45) and (46) that it does not have to have temporal implications. However, Continuation is not incompatible with temporal relations between the events of the Elaboration, as we have seen earlier in this chapter. Now the English Present Perfect and Dutch Voltooid Tegenwoordige Tijd do not allow temporal relations with other events (cf. de Swart and Molendijk, to appear), so we cannot develop temporal structure by means of the Present Perfect or the VTT. The main difference with French then is that we can use the Passé Composé to tell a story, because the relation of Continuation between the perfect sentences can get a temporal dimension. Note that temporal structure is not induced by the Passé Composé (it is 'just' a perfect that introduces a structure of Elaboration), but we know that it does not block temporal structure. Thus we can formulate the discourse semantics of the Passé Composé as:

(47) **Rule for the interpretation of the Passé Composé**

(i) The Passé Composé respects the temporal structure E-R,S

(ii) The Passé Composé introduces a quantized event e into the discourse, and a consequent state $s$, such that $e \supset\!\subset s$.

(iii) A sentence in the Passé Composé takes the speech time S (or the utterance situation) as its Topic, and creates an Elaboration structure. The rhetorical relation between two sentences in the Passé Composé is Continuation;

(iv) Any temporal relation is possible between the events $e$ and $e'$ reported by two sentences in the Passé Composé.

Clause (47i) states that the Passé Composé has the Reichenbachian structure of a perfect. Clause (47ii) states that the Passé Composé locates an event $e$ on the time axis. We can call the Passé Composé a perfective past tense in the sense that the Passé Simple also does this. Clause (47iii) fixes the rhetorical interpretation of the Passé Composé. The Passé Composé does not induce temporal structure, but it does not block it either, so any temporal relation between two sentences in the Passé Composé is permitted (47iv).

## 4.2 How to tell a story in the Passé Composé

The Passé Composé is not responsible for the temporal relations between the events. The analysis of *L'étranger* shows that the temporal structure of a story told in the Passé Composé is driven by lexical semantics and pragmatic (rhetorical) knowledge. Telling a story involves putting a sequence of events in a temporal order. We distinguish three basic cases: posteriority, overlap (simultaneity/inclusion) and temporal inversion. In chapter 15, we showed that any of these three relations can be found between two sentences in the Passé Composé. Our main emphasis will be on posteriority, for that is the essential characteristic of narration. Camus obtains a temporal structure of posteriority by exploiting temporal connectives, the lexical semantics of verbs and adverbials expressing time going by, the existence of temporal presuppositions and implications, and rhetorical structure.

**Connectives** Camus frequently uses connectives like *puis, ensuite, un moment après*, as was already observed by (Weinrich, 1973, 268). (48) is a representative example, but we could have given many others:

(48) J'ai dit au concierge, sans me retourner vers lui: "Il y a longtemps que vous êtes là?" *Immédiatement* il a répondu: "Cinq ans" – comme s'il avait attendu depuis toujours ma demande. *Ensuite* il a beaucoup bavardé. On l'aurait bien étonné en lui disant qu'il finirait concierge à l'asile de Marengo. Il avait soixante-quatre ans et il était parisien. *A ce moment* je l'ai interrompu: "Ah! Vous n'êtes pas d'ici?" *Puis* je me suis souvenu qu'avant de me conduire chez le directeur, il m'avait parlé de maman. (p. 15–16)
'Without turning around, I said (PC) to the caretaker, 'Have you been here long?' Straight away he answered (PC), 'Five years' – as if he'd been waiting (PQP) for me to ask all the time.

After that he chatted (PC) a lot. He'd have been very surprised if anyone had told him he'd end up as the caretaker of the Marengo home. He was (IMP) sixty-four and he came (IMP) from Paris. At that point I interrupted (PC) him, 'Oh, you're not from round here?' Then I remembered (PC) that he'd talked to me about mother.'

If the Passé Composé is not inherently a narrative tense, the frequent use of connectives can be explained by the need to indicate posteriority at the discourse level. In § 3 above, it has been argued that *puis* is a rhetorical marker that introduces a relation of Narration (cf. axiom A28 above). The rhetorical relation of Narration obligatorily leads to succession in time, so the use of connectives like *puis, ensuite, un moment après*, etc. moves the story forward.

**Time goes by** *L'étranger* is full of expressions that mark the passing of time. We find both adverbial (49) and verbal (50) expressions that indicate a period of time going by:

(49) Nous sommes restés *un long moment* ainsi. (p. 20)
We sat (pc) like this for quite some time.

(50) La journée *a tourné encore un peu.* Au-dessus des toits, le ciel est devenu rougeâtre et, avec *le soir naissant*, les rues se sont animées. (p. 39)
'The day advanced (pc) a bit more. Above the roofs the sky began (pc) to redden and with evening approaching, the streets came (pc) to life.'

Moreover, Camus frequently refers to the location of the events on the time axis by means of indications of light or heat. Thus, the day of the funeral is structured in the following way:

(51) Le jour glissait sur la verrière. (...) Quand je suis sorti, le jour était complètement levé. (...) Le soleil était monté un peu plus dans le ciel: il commençait à chauffer mes pieds. (...) Le ciel était déjà plein de soleil.(...) J'étais surpris de la rapidité avec laquelle le soleil montait dans le ciel. (p. 22–28)
'The dawn was creeping (imp) up over the glass roof. (...) When I went (pc) outside, it was (imp) broad daylight. (...) The sun had risen (pqp) a little higher in the sky: it was beginning (imp) to warm my feet up. (...) The sun was (imp) already high in the sky. (...) I was (imp) surprised how rapidly the sun was climbing (imp) in the sky.'

**Presuppositions and implications** Vet (1980) establishes a distinction between transitional and non-transitional verbs. A transitional verb describes the transition between two states, and leads to pre-states and post-states. In *L'étranger*, we find many references to the spatial location of the result state:

(52) Je me suis levé sans rien dire et *il m'a précédé vers* la porte. *Dans l'escalier*, il m'a expliqué (...). (p. 12)
'I stood up (pc) without saying anything and he led (pc) the way to the door. On our way downstairs he explained (pc) (...).'

An action like *précéder quelqu'un vers la porte* (52) implies that one comes closer to the door. The adverbial *dans l'escalier* refers to a location on the other side of the door. Given that movement takes time (cf. Asher et al. 1995), one can interpret *il m'a expliqué* as later in time. The notion of temporal presupposition is not restricted to movement verbs, as the example in (53) illustrates:

(53) La garde est entrée à ce moment. Le soir était tombé brusquement. Très vite, la nuit s'était épaissie au-dessus de la verrière.

Le concierge *a tourné* le commutateur et *j'ai été aveuglé* par l'éclaboussement soudain de la lumière. (p. 17)
'The nurse came (PC) in at that point. Night had fallen (PQP) suddenly. The sky had darkened (PQP) rapidly above the glass roof. The caretaker turned (PC) the light-switch and I was (PC) blinded by the sudden blaze of light.'

(54) shows that we can also exploit presuppositions of transitional verbs to create a structure of temporal succession:

(54) Il a consulté un dossier et m'a dit: (...). *J'ai dit*: (...). Il *a ajouté*: (...). Le directeur m'a *encore* parlé. (p. 11)
'He consulted (PC) a file and told (PC) me, (...) I said (PC), (...) He added (PC), (...) The warden spoke (PC) to me again.'

Both *ajouter* and *encore* in (54) presuppose that something has been said before, so there must be successive speaking events. Just like in the movement cases, the presupposition has a temporal dimension that is exploited to create narrative structure.

**Rhetorical structure** The Passé Composé is a neutral, non-anaphoric tense, and not an inherently narrative tense like the Passé Simple. This implies that the Passé Composé does not give rise to Narration as a default rhetorical relation. However, sentences in the Passé Composé can be related by "strong" Narration, if the predicate Occasion holds between the two clauses, cf. A5 in § 2 above. The idea behind Occasion is that a sequence of sentences reporting a series of events is coherent only if this sequence reflects a 'natural' order of events (cf. Moens (1987); Glasbey (1993); Asher (1996)). World knowledge allows us to see a natural order in sequences of the type question-answer, offer-acceptance/rejection, and in more complex scripts and scenarios. Once we have derived Occassion, we can derive a temporal order of succession. Examples where Camus exploits Occasion are given in (55), (56):

(55) *Je lui ai fait remarquer* qu'en somme il était un pensionnaire. *Il m'a dit* que non. (p. 16)
'I pointed (PC) out to him that even so he was (IMP) still an inmate. He said (PC) no.'

(56) *Il m'a offert* alors d'apporter une tasse de café au lait. Comme j'aime beaucoup le café au lait, *j'ai accepté* et (...) (p. 17)
'He then offered (PC) to bring me a cup of white coffee. I'm (PR) very fond of white coffee, so I accepted (PC) and (...).'

At a more global level, we can use the notion of script in a similar way. Scripts and scenarios have been defined as stereotypical sequences of actions. (57) illustrates the script of getting up in the morning, where we have a 'typical' series of events in a natural order: waking up, getting up, shaving, etc. The sentences are locally connected by Occasion:

(57) En me *réveillant*, j'ai compris pourquoi mon patron avait l'air mécontent quand je lui ai demandé mes deux jours de congé: c'est aujourd'hui samedi. (...) J'ai eu de la peine à *me lever* parce que j'étais fatigué de ma journée d'hier. Pendant que je me *rasais*, je me suis demandé ce que j'allais faire et j'ai décidé d'aller me baigner. (p. 34)
'When I woke up, I understood (PC) why my boss seemed (IMP) unhappy when I asked (PC) him for my two days off: today's a Saturday. (...) I had (PC) trouble getting up because I was (IMP) tired from the day before. While I was shaving (IMP), I wondered (PC)what to do with myself and I decided to go for a swim.'

In sum, temporal relations of posteriority are established by connectives, the lexical semantics of verbs and adverbs, and world knowledge about the 'natural' order of events. The fact that the Passé Composé is not anaphoric, and is not an inherently narrative tense like the Passé Simple is not a barrier for narrative use, because there are other means of creating narration.

Telling a story does not only rely on posteriority relations, it is equally important to describe simultaneity and inverse temporal order. Although indications of the time of the day are frequent in *L'étranger*, they are exclusively used to make time move forward, and they never indicate going back in time. The same is true for transitional verbs, where presuppositions could potentially be exploited to create inverse temporal order, but we found no examples. However, Camus exploits world knowledge and rhetorical structure to express simultaneity and inverse temporal order. We pointed out in chapter 15 that the Passé Composé allows inverse temporal order, as opposed to the Passé Simple. The relevant example is repeated here as (58):

(58) *J'ai pris* l'autobus à deux heures. Il faisait très chaud. *J'ai mangé* au restaurant, chez Céleste, comme d'habitude. Ils avaient tous beaucoup de peine pour moi et Céleste m'a dit: "On n'a qu'une mère". Quand je suis parti, ils m'ont accompagné à la porte. J'étais un peu étourdi parce qu'il a fallu que je monte chez Emmanuel pour lui emprunter une cravate noire et un brassard. Il a perdu son oncle, il y a quelques mois.
*J'ai couru* pour ne pas manquer le départ. (...) (p. 10)
'I caught (PC) the two o'clock bus. It was (IMP) very hot. I ate (PC) at Céleste's restaurant, as usual. They all felt (IMP)very

sorry for me and Céleste told (PC) me, "There's no one like a mother" . When I left (PC), they came (PC) to the door with me. I was (IMP) in a bit of a daze because I had (PC) to go up to Emmanuel's place to borrow a black tie and armband. He lost(PC) his uncle, a few months ago.
I had to run for the bus.' (p. 10)

We infer from (58) that lunch takes place before the protagonist takes the bus, because he had to run for the bus. We posit a relation of Occasion between the event of running, and the event of taking the bus, and capture the structure of the sequence with the following axiom on Inverse Occasion, that we add to the system developed above:

**A 36** $\langle \tau, \alpha, \beta \rangle \wedge \mathit{Occasion}(\beta, \alpha) > \mathit{Narration}(\beta, \alpha)$

Given that Narration implies temporal succession, a relation of Occasion between $\beta$ and $\alpha$ implies inverse temporal Order. Narration implies that no 'relevant' event intervenes between the two events $e_\beta$ and $e_\alpha$. This allows the story to go back in time, without going back to a 'random' earlier time. It also implies that *j'ai mangé au restaurant* cannot take place in between the running and the taking the bus. It cannot be set later, because the 'habit' referred to involves Meursault's lunch with his friends, in the town where he works, rather than the village where the bus takes him (and where his mother's home is situated). Thus, we have to locate the lunch before the bus ride. The rhetorical relation of Continuation between the two sentences *j'ai pris l'autobus à deux heures* and *j'ai mangé au restaurant comme d'habitude* creates a weak rhetorical structure that is nevertheless sufficient to maintain the coherence of the fragment, because both sentences are elaborations of the same topic (the day of the mother's death).

Inverse Occasion is a somewhat strange rhetorical relation from a conceptual point of view: we do not usually tell stories in the reverse order in which they occur. However, examples like (58) suggest that we may exploit the non-anaphoric nature of the Passé Composé and our knowledge of scripts and 'natural' orders of events to construct the intended rhetorical structure after all. The fact that the English Simple Past is quite free in the construction of temporal structure, but blocks Inverse Occasion suggests that the question whether a tense does or does not disallow Inverse Occassion could be the criterion for characterizing it as a narrative tense or not.

## 4.3 Conclusion

We conclude that the French Passé Composé is well on its way to become a perfective past tense, but it is not quite there yet. Its orientation towards the speech time makes it a non-anaphoric tense, which means that it is not in essence a narrative tense. This confirms the traditional view that the Reichenbachian schema E-R,S reflects: that the perfect is not meant for narration. Although the Passé Composé is not blocked in narrative contexts, it can only be used to tell a story if there is a clear deictic dimension. In spoken language, the connection with the speech time is always available. In written language, the connection with the speech time is available in the context of a diary, a newspaper, etc. It need not come as a surprise to learn – much later in *L'étranger* – that we are reading the protagonist's memories of the events preceding his arrest and trial. We claim that the Passé Composé remains a perfect as long as it maintains its clear deictic character. It is not until we start finding the Passé Composé as the standard tense of written, narrative discourse that it can really be characterized as a perfective simple past. The diachronic development of the French language has not yet reached that stage.

## References


Allen, J. 1984. Towards a general theory of action and time. *Artificial Intelligence* 23(2):123–154.

Asher, N. 1993. *Reference to abstract objects in discourse*. Dordrecht: Kluwer.

Asher, N. 1996. Mathematical treatments of discourse contexts. In *Proceedings of the 10th Amsterdam Conference on Formal Semantics*, vol. 1, pages 21–40. Amsterdam: ILLC Publications.

Asher, N., M. Aurnague, M. Bras, P. Sablayrolles, and L. Vieu. 1995a. De l'espace-temps dans l'analyse du discours. *Sémiotiques* 9:11–62. Co Vet ed., Théories sémantiques et modélisation.

Asher, N., M. Aurnague, M. Bras, and L. Vieu. 1995b. Spatial, temporal and spatio-temporal locating adverbials in discourse. In P. Amsili, M. Borillo, and L. Vieu, eds., *Time, Space and Movement. Meaning and Knowledge in the Sensible World, Workshop Notes of the 5th International Workshop TSM'95*, pages A107–119. Toulouse.

Asher, N., M. Aurnague, M. Bras, and L. Vieu. 2002. The syntax and semantics of locating adverbials. *Cahiers de Grammaire* 26:11–35.

Asher, N., D. Hardt, and J. Busquets. 2001. Discourse parallelism, ellipsis and ambiguity. *Journal of Semantics* to appear.

Asher, N. and A. Lascarides. 1998. Bridging. *Journal of Semantics* 15(1):83–113.

Asher, N. and M. Morreau. 1991. Commonsense entailment: A modal theory of nonmonotonic reasoning. In J. Mylopoulos and R. Reiter, eds., *Proceedings of the Twelfth IJCAI*, pages 387–392. Los Altos, CA: Morgan Kaufman.

Berthonneau, A. M. and G. Kleiber. 1999. Pour une réanalyse de l'imparfait de rupture dans le cadre de l'hypothèse anaphorique méronomique. *Cahiers de Praxématique* 32:119–166.

Bras, M., A. Le Draoulec, and L. Vieu. 2001a. Connecteurs et temps verbaux dans l'interprétation temporelle du discours: le cas de *puis* en interaction avec l'imparfait et le passé simple. *Cahiers Chronos* to appear.

Bras, M., A. Le Draoulec, and L. Vieu. 2001b. French adverbial *puis* between temporal structure and discourse structure. In M. Bras and L. Vieu, eds., *Semantic and Pragmatic Issues in Discourse and Dialogue: Experimenting with Current Dynamic Theories*, CRiSPI series. Oxford: Elsevier.

Busquets, J., L. Vieu, and N. Asher. 2001. La SDRT: Une approche de la cohérence du discours dans la tradition de la sémantique dynamique. *Verbum* to appear.

Caenepeel, M. 1989. *Aspect, Temporal Ordering and Perspective in Narrative Fiction.* Ph.D. dissertation, University of Edinburgh, Edinburgh.

Caenepeel, M. 1995. Aspect and text structure. *Linguistics* 33.

Caudal, P., ed. (to appear). *Cahiers Chronos — volume sur le temps et l'aspect.* Amsterdam: Rodopi.

De Swart, H. and A. Molendijk. 2002. Le passé composé narratif: une analyse discursive de *L'étranger* de camus. In Laca (2002), pages 193–211.

De Swart, H. and A. Molendijk. (to appear). In pursuit of the 'perfect' perfect. In Caudal ((to appear).

Glasbey, S. 1993. Distinguishing between events and times: some evidence from the semantics of *then. Natural Language Semantics* 1:285–312.

Gosselin, L. 1999. Le sinistre fantomas et l'imparfait narratif. *Cahiers de Praxématique* 32:19–42.

Grosz, B. and C. Sidner. 1986a. Attention, intention and the structure of discourse. *Computational Linguistics* 12:175–204.

Grosz, B. and C. Sidner. 1986b. Attention, intentions, and the structure of discourse. *Computational Linguistics* 12(3):175–204.

Guimier, C. 1996. *Les adverbes du français. Le cas des adverbes en -ment.* Paris: Ophrys.

Hinrichs, E. 1981. *Temporale Anaphora im Englischen.* Master's thesis, University of Tübingen, Tübingen.

Hinrichs, E. 1986. Temporal anaphora in discourses of English. *Linguistics and Philosophy* 9:63–82.

Hobbs, J. R. 1985. On the coherence and structure of discourse. Report CSLI-85-37, Center for Study of Language and Information.

Kamp, H. and U. Reyle. 1993. *From Discourse To Logic.* Dordrecht: Kluwer.

Laca, B., ed. 2002. *Temps et Aspect: de la morphologie à l'interprétation.* Paris: Presses Universitaires de Vincennes.

Lascarides, A. and N. Asher. 1993. Temporal interpretation, discourse relations, and commonsense entailment. *Linguistics and Philosophy* 16(5):437–493.

Lévrier, N. and C. Molinier. 2000. *Grammaire des adverbes*. Genève-Paris: Drosz.

Mann, W. and S. Thompson. 1987. Rhetorical Structure Theory: A theory of text organization. Reprint Series ISI/RS-87-1190, Information Sciences Institute, Marina del Rey, CA.

Melis, L. 1983. *Les circonstants et la phrase*. Louvain: Presses Universitaires de Louvain.

Moens, M. 1987. *Tense, aspect and temporal reference*. Ph.D. thesis, University of Edinburgh.

Molendijk, A. 1990. *Le passé simple et l'imparfait: une approche reichenbachienne*. Amsterdam: Rodopi.

Nøjgaard, M. 1992. *Les adverbes français*. Copenhagen: Munksgaard. Published between 1992–1995.

Nølke, H. 2001. Les adverbiaux spatio-temporels dans le système adverbial. In H. Nølke, ed., *Le regard du locuteur 2*. Paris: Kimé.

Quirk, R. and S. Greenbaum. 1973. *A University Grammar of English*. London: Longman.

Sanders, T., W. Spooren, and L. Noordman. 1992. Toward a taxonomy of coherence relations. *Discourse Processes* 15:1–35.

Weinrich, H. 1973. *Tempus. Besprochene und erzählte Welt*. Stuttgart: Verlag W. Kohlhammer.

# Part IV

# Negation

17

# French Negative Dependency*

DANIÈLE GODARD

French negation associates a negative expression with clitic *ne*, a situation which we call 'negative dependency' (translating 'association négative', Milner 1979). After defining negations and briefly justifying the analysis of negative words or expressions as the semantic negations, and clitic *ne* as a scope marker, we summarize the constraints on negative dependency. Most of the chapter is then devoted to formal implementations of the dependency in a constraint-based lexicalist framework (HPSG) and in transformational approaches, with explicit discussion of the syntax-semantics interface.

## 1 Definition of negations

The definition of negations is not trivial in French: negative expressions cannot be characterized on a morphological basis, unlike what is usually the case in other Romance languages, and semantic negation seems to be spread over the verbal clitic *ne* and negative items. We give a number of criteria for distinguishing negations, and we briefly explain why *ne* is not generally analyzed as negative in the standard system in modern French, but contributes a scope marker for the negation.

*Section 1.1 has been elaborated by the the members of the 'negation group'. In addition, I wish to thank Anne Abeillé, Olivier Bonami, Robert Borsley, Francis Corblin, Jacques Jayez, Michael Jones, Massimo Poesio, Adam Przepiórkowski, Louisa Sadler and Henriëtte de Swart for their comments.

*Handbook of French Semantics.*
Francis Corblin and Henriëtte de Swart (eds.).
Copyright © 2004, CSLI Publications.

### 1.1 Criteria for negation

Unlike other Romance languages, where negative words tend to begin with an element *n-* inherited from Latin, French does not characterize them morphologically. This is because historically they come from minimizers co-occurring with the phonologically weakened negation *ne* (from Latin *non*), exemplifying a semantic transfer known under the name of 'Jespersen cycle' (Jespersen 1924, and Corblin et al., this volume). We propose here a number of semantic criteria which define (sentential) negation, some of them quite general, and others more specific to French.

**(i)** The co-occurrence of negative expressions and quantifiers or indefinites gives rise to ambiguities. There may be preferred interpretations (as is well-known, 1 and 2 are preferably interpreted as in 1a, 2a), but the following sentences are ambiguous:[1]

(1) Tous les étrangers n'ont pas de carte d'identité.
All the foreigners ne-have not of card of identity.
a. 'It is not the case that all foreigners have an ID'.
b. 'For all foreigners, it is the case that they don't have an ID'.

(2) Aucun des étudiants n'a lu trois livres de cette liste.
None of the students ne-have read three books on this list.
a. 'It is not the case that any of the students has read three books on this list'.
b. 'For three books on this list, it is the case that no student has read them'.

**(ii)** Negative expressions create a domain which licenses object NPs of the form *de N*. Unlike usual indefinites, such NPs do not create scopal ambiguities, but are always interpreted in the scope of the negation (see the contrast between 3a and 3b). The domain is non-local (4). Interestingly, *de N* does not have to be syntactically c-commanded by the negative expression (*personne, aucun*, etc.), as noted in e.g. Valois (1997), see 5; rather, *de N* is the object of a V bearing the clitic *ne* (for short, 'ne-V') or of a V occurring within a complement of a ne-V, see 4.[2]

(3) a. Paul n'a pas lu de journal.
Paul ne-has not read of newspaper
'P. has read no newspaper'

[1]For reasons of space, we do not in general provide both glosses and translations, relying on the closeness of the two languages.

[2]Inverted subjects can also be of the form *de N* (*le jour où ne se présenterait plus de candidat, ...* 'the day when (there) would not be any more candidates').

b. Paul n'a pas lu un journal.
Paul ne-has not read a newspaper
'There is a newpaper that P. has not read'
'P. has read no newspaper'

(4) a. Personne ne voulait que j'achète de journal.
Nobody ne-wished that I bought of newspaper

b. Paul n'a pas eu l'occasion de lire de journal aujourd'hui.
Paul ne-has not had the opportunity of read of newspaper today
'P. did not have the opportunity to read a newspaper today'.

(5) Paul ne donne de leçons aux enfants d'aucun collègue.
Paul ne-gives lessons to-the children of no colleague

**(iii)** Negative expressions create a domain licensing time expression of the form *de* $NP_{time}$ (*de la journée* 'in the whole day', *de tout le mois* 'in the whole month'). Like the object *de N*, it can be found in an infinitive or a subjunctive complement of the ne-V, so the relation is not local:

(6) a. Il ne veut signer aucun papier de tout le mois.
He ne-wants to sign no paper in the whole month

b. Il ne veut pas que tu viennes de tout le mois.
He ne-wants that you come in the whole month

**(iv)** Negative expressions license polarity items (e.g. *lever le petit doigt* 'to lift a finger', *le moindre N* 'the least N', and *grand-chose* 'much'). Unlike *de N* and *de* $NP_{time}$, polarity items occur in contexts other than negation, such as conditionals and questions (see Tovena et al., this volume).

(7) a. Paul n'a pas fait le moindre effort.
'Paul has not made the smallest effort'.

b. Paul fait-il le moindre effort?
'Does Paul make the smallest effort?'

c. * Paul lit-il de journal?
'Does Paul read (of) newspaper?'

**(v)** Negative expressions license elliptical conjuncts of the form *et XP non plus* 'and neither XP':

(8) a. Je ne suis jamais allé à Rome, et à Paris non plus.
I have never been to Rome, and to Paris neither

b. On ne lit plus Molière, et Corneille non plus.
We don't read Molière any longer, and Corneille neither

**(vi)** Negative expressions license the negative conjunction *ni* ('neither'):

(9) a. Personne n'a ni mangé ni bu ni dormi.
Nobody has neither eaten nor drunk nor slept

b. Paul n'a pas mangé ni bu.
'Paul has not eaten nor drunk'

These criteria give the following set of negative words: the NPs *personne* 'nobody', *rien* 'nothing', the NPs or determiners *aucun, nul* 'no', 'none', *pas un* 'not one', the adverbs *pas* 'not', *plus* 'no more', *jamais* 'never', *aucunement, nullement* 'in no way' (the adverbs *guère* and *point* are archaic), the preposition *sans* 'without', and the conjunction *ni* 'neither'. In addition, the pro-S adverb *non*, which can be used as an answer or as an embedded complement sentence (*Paul pensait que non*, 'P. thought that is was not the case'), is also a negative word (see the dialogue: *Marie est-elle venue ? – Non, et Paul non plus*, 'Did Mary come? – No, and neither (did) Paul'). *Ni* has an intricate behavior: in addition to being either a simple or multiple conjunction (see 9b vs 9a), it can either occur in the scope of a negative word, as in 9b, or be negative by itself (as in 9a) (de Swart 2001).

As noted in Corblin (1994, 1996), the criteria allow a clear distinction between the 'logical' negation, on the one hand, and items whose semantics have a negative flavor and can sometimes substitute for negative words, on the other (for instance, lexical opposites such as *heureux/ malheureux* 'happy/ unhappy', *accepter/ refuser* 'accept/ reject', or expressions such as *être loin de* 'to be far from' are not negations).[3]

All these negative expressions are associated with the clitic *ne* on the V,[4] at least in high or careful registers.[5] The (possible) presence of *ne* is recognized as a test for the distinction between sentential negation, where the negation has scope over the whole sentence, and constituent negation (with negations *non (pas)* or *pas*), where it does not. An interesting case in point is when *pas* negates a determiner: the combination of *pas* with *un* has evolved into a complex negative determiner while this has not happened with other quantity expressions (for a discussion, see Knüppel 2001):[6]

---

[3]With lexically incorporated negation, the two terms are usually contraries rather than contradictories, see Horn (1989), in particular, chapter 5.

[4]*Sans* constitutes a principled exception, see below fn 21.

[5]The variation in the occurrence of *ne* in spoken French has often been studied. For a survey of corpus-based studies, see Gadet (2000).

[6]The NP containing the determiner *pas un* is functionally restricted (included in a subject or time adjunct). A possible syntactic difference between 10a and 10b is that *pas* combines with the determiner *un*, while it adjoins to the NP in the other cases. While *pas un* is register neutral, other combinations may be more restricted

(10) a. Pas un candidat ne s'est présenté.
Not one candidate came

b. Pas moins d'une centaine d'artistes (*ne) sont exposés.
Not fewer than a hundred artists are presented

Besides being a pro-S, the negative adverb *non* (possibly reinforced by *pas*) usually called a 'contrastive negation', can also occur before the first member of a coordination (11a); in fact, given the obligatoriness of the coordination, it seems best to analyze *non (pas) ... mais* ('not X but Y') as a binary conjunction, analogous to *both ... and.* Besides being a sentential negative adverb, *pas* can also adjoin to a predicative complement or an adjunct (11b), or occur before the elliptical second member of a coordination (11c):

(11) a. Paul a acheté non un tableau, *(mais une sculpture).
Paul has bought not a picture, but a sculpture

b. Pas encore réveillé, Paul avait du mal à écouter.
Not yet awake, Paul had trouble listening

c. Marie est arrivée, et / mais pas Jeanne.
Marie has arrived, and / but not Jeanne

In the remainder of this chapter, we concentrate on sentential negation, and particularly, on the interaction between *ne* and the negative expressions.

## 1.2 Varieties of *ne*

Semantically, the verbal clitic *ne* comes in three varieties: 'dependency *ne*', when *ne* is associated with a negative expression, 'negative *ne*', or 'expletive *ne*'. From a morphological point of view, they are non-distinct when the host is a finite V. However, expletive *ne* does not occur with an infinitival V(P) (Recourcé 1996):

(12) a. Il ne pense pas cela. (dependency *ne*)
He ne-thinks not that
'He does not think that'

a'. Il pense ne pas revenir.
He thinks ne-not come back
'He is thinking of not coming back'

b. Paul ne savait quoi dire. (negative *ne*)
Paul ne-knew what to say
'Paul did not know what to say'

(for instance *pas beaucoup de N* 'not many N' belongs to spoken French).

b'. ? Il avouait ne savoir quoi dire.
He recognized ne-know what to say
'He recognized not to know what to say'.

c. Je serai épuisé avant qu'il n'ait avoué. (expletive *ne*)
I will-be tired before he ne-admit 'before he admits it'

c'. * Je serai parti avant de n'avouer.
I will be gone before of ne-admit 'before admitting it'

Cases where *ne* is a semantic negation are the remains of an older system, where *ne* was the negative adverb. They divide between a number of fixed forms, verbal (forms of *cesser, oser, pouvoir, savoir*) or idiomatic, and a few productive constructions (for a detailed presentation, see Muller 1991, 227–245).[7] To the two well-known examples of such constructions, *Il y a / voilà / Ça fait / Depuis NP / $Adv_{\text{time}}$ que ... ne-V...* 'There is $NP_{time}$ that S', and relative clauses whose antecedent is a negative NP, one should add sentences with a preposed comparative expression of unequality, modified with *pas*. The two last cases are illustrated in (13a,b):

(13) a. Je ne connais personne qui n'aime Mozart.
I ne-know nobody who ne-loves M.
('who does not love M.')

b. Pas plus aujourd'hui qu'hier, nous n'avons de chances de réussir.
No more today than yesterday, we ne-have chances to succeed

c. Nous n'avons pas plus de chances de réussir aujourd'hui qu'hier.
'We have no more chances to succeed today than yesterday'.

d. Il n'est pas allé à Paris pour faire de la figuration.
He ne-is not gone to P. to do walk-on parts
'He did not go to Paris to do walk-on parts'.

e. * Pas pour faire de la figuration, il n'est allé à Paris.
Not for doing walk-on parts, he ne-went to Paris

The relative clause in 13a contains a negative *ne*, since there are two logical negations (the sentence implies that all the persons known by the speaker like Mozart). The contrast between 13d and 13e shows that a preposed adjunct modified by *pas* cannot be linked to a dependency *ne*. Accordingly, this cannot be the right analysis for 13b, in spite of

[7] These verb forms may have a restricted subcategorization, compared with the positive V or the V negated with *pas*. For instance, the verb *ne-savoir* is specialized for an interrogative complement, while *savoir* negated with *pas* accepts the same subcategorizations as *savoir*.

its equivalence with 13c. We must posit a specific construction for 13b, with a negative *ne* (which is in need of further study).

There are various contexts which license expletive *ne* (see van der Wouden 1994:107–121, and Muller 1991:357–380 and 423–443 for French), which can be easily recognized since there is an equivalent sentence without *ne*. Syntactically, these contexts are not homogeneous: they include the complements of a number of verbs or expressions, meaning 'to be afraid', 'to prevent', 'to deny' or 'to ignore' (the latter only if negated), certain adjuncts (*avant que* 'before', *sans que* 'without', *à moins que* 'unless'), and comparatives. They seem to form a semantically homogeneous class, the precise definition of which we leave aside here.[8]

In the remainder of the paper, we ignore negative and expletive *ne*, and concentrate on negative dependency (ND).[9]

### 1.3 The semantic contribution of *ne* in ND

It is well-accepted nowadays (although not by everyone) that words like *personne, pas* etc. are semantic negations while *ne* is not negative, or even part of the negation proper (see Corblin 1992, 1994, 1996). A number of factors indicate that *ne* itself is not negative in ND. First, the contexts where *ne* alone is negative are restricted, and belong to formal registers (see section 1.2); second, *ne* is often omitted in spoken French; finally, when the sentence contains two negative expressions with a double negation reading (as in *Rien ne naît de rien* 'nothing comes from nothing'), there is only one *ne*: if it were negative or part of the negation, we would have to accept haplology of a crucially semantically potent morpheme. We conclude that French *ne* is not a negation, unlike

[8]Expletive *ne* has been described as being licensed by a subset of monotone decreasing contexts (van der Wouden 1994), or by non-veridical contexts (Knüppel 2001). The second suggestion does not seem to be correct, since the verb *craindre*, following the definitions in Giannakidou (1998), is veridical in (i):

(i) Je crains qu'il ne soit déjà arrivé.
(I am afraid that he ne-has already arrived).

[9]It is interesting to look at *ne* in the focus construction *ne-V... que* ('only'), often included among negations. It cannot be expletive, since there is no equivalent sentence without *ne* (in the register under consideration). But *que* is not a negation since it fails the tests in section 1.1 (see *Paul n'aime que Mozart, et Marie aussi / * non plus* 'Paul likes only Mozart, and Marie too / * neither (does) Marie'). On the other hand, the relation between the ne-V and the focussed constituent (or sequence) has the same properties as the ND (it is not strictly local, cf. *Il ne veut écouter que Mozart* 'He (ne)wants to listen only to Mozart', see section 2.2). We assume that *ne* is a scope marker in this construction as well as in ND (the ne-V can be common to a negation and a *que*-focus, as in *Personne n'écoute que Mozart*, 'Nobody listens only to Mozart'), and that the focussed constituent takes scope in the same conditions as the negations.

its cognates in the other Romance languages.

Instead, we accept the analysis originating in Kayne (1984), where *ne* indicates the scope of the negation: the negation has scope over, and cannot have scope higher than, the sentence where *ne* occurs. This is clearly shown by non-local negative dependency contexts (see section 2); the interpretation differs depending on whether the negative expression is in the same verbal domain as the ne-V or not:

(14) a. Paul accepte de ne recevoir personne.
Paul agrees not to see anybody

b. Paul n'accepte de recevoir personne.
Paul does not agree to see anybody

c. Personne n'accepte de ne rencontrer personne. (DN)
Nobody agrees to see nobody

d. Personne n'accepte de rencontrer personne. (DN or NC)
Nobody agrees to see nobody / to see anybody

While 14a is paraphrased by 'P. agrees that it is not the case that there is someone whom he will receive', 14b is paraphrased by 'It is not the case that there is someone that P. agrees to receive': the negation is interpreted downstairs in 14a, and upstairs in 14b. Moreover, the process of 'negative concord' (NC), through which two negations in the same domain can create a mono-negative interpretation (see Corblin et al., chapter 19, this volume), is possible across the infinitival VP only in the absence of *ne* (14d): 14c is obligatorily interpreted with two semantic negations (DN).

## 2 Constraints on negative dependency

As brought to light by Milner (1979, 1982), the relation between *ne* and the negative expression is not strictly local, but it is certainly bounded. In this section, we review the constraints on ND, comparing them with those on other dependencies. Note that we exclude cases of meta-linguistic negation, where a speaker objects to the content or form of a previous utterance (see e.g. Ducrot, 1972, Horn, 1989, chapter 6): the constraints seem to be relaxed in such cases, but we lack appropriate data and descriptions (see fn 12,13).

### 2.1 Lexical and syntactic constraints

The ND between the ne-V (or the ne-VPinf, see section 3) is local when the negative expression is an argument of the ne-V or modifies a ne-VPinf (see section 3.1). The negative expression can also be the complement of a preposition or an argument within a subject or object

NP, or a predicative AP:[10]

(15) a. Le professeur ne reçoit personne / aucun étudiant.
The professor ne-receives nobody / no student

b. Paul ne va pas / jamais à la plage.
Paul ne-goes not / never to the beach

c. Je ne compte sur personne.
I ne-rely on nobody

d. Les collègues d'aucun des inculpés n'ont fait grève.
The colleagues of none of the accused ne-are on strike

e. Il ne lit les compte-rendus d'aucun de ses spectacles.
He ne-reads the reviews of none of his shows

f. Ils ne sont contents de rien.
They ne-are happy with nothing

The negative expression can also occur within an infinitival VP complement of the ne-V (see 14b,d). There are several constraints on such non-local ND. First, the occurrence of a negative expression in an embedded VP is lexically controlled: not all ne-Vs allow their VP complement to contain a correlated negative expression. For instance, 14b contrasts with a sentence such as **Paul n'avoue avoir vu personne* 'P. ne-recognizes hav(ing) seen nobody'. Unlike e.g. Haïk (1985), Déprez (1997), we do not identify the class of Vs licensing non-local ND in French with that of Restructuring Vs in other Romance languages: even allowing for speaker variation, it is clear that the two classes overlap, but do not coincide. Restructuring Vs (Rizzi 1982 for Italian) comprise modals ('must', 'can', 'want', 'seem', a few conatives), aspectuals ('to begin', 'to go on' etc.), and a few movement verbs. Modals are both Restructuring and non local ND verbs, but there are many more conative verbs, and, more generally, more verbs of attitude towards an action in the class of non-local ND verbs than there are among Restructuring verbs (non-local ND verbs include *accepter / refuser de* 'agree / not-agree', *être prêt / décidé à* 'be ready to', *avoir besoin / envie de* 'to need, wish', *demander à* 'to intend, ask to', which are not good restructuring verbs). On the other hand, movement and aspectual verbs do not license non-local ND in French, in a general way (*aller* 'be going to' is acceptable). The distinction between predicates which allow and predicates which fail to allow non-local ND, seems to be semantically based (their infinitival complement seems to be non-factive), but more

[10]It has been observed that the dependency was more restricted in subject NPs than object NPs. This seems to be of a pragmatic or processual nature rather than a syntactic one (see Muller 1991).

work needs to be done to make this intuition precise. We call verbs allowing non-local ND the 'vouloir-verbs'.

Second, negative adverbs do not participate in non-local ND, which is confined to 'nominal' negations (*personne, nul (N), (N)*, Milner 1979, 1982), see 14 and 16a. This is true not only of preverbal adverbs (16b,c), but also of postverbal adverbs (16d):

(16) a. Cet inculpé n'essaie de convaincre personne.
The accused ne-tries to convince nobody

b. * Paul n'essaie de pas / jamais travailler.
Paul ne-tries to not / never work

c. * Paul ne demande à aucunement être plaint.
Paul ne asks to in-no-way be lamented on

d. * Paul ne demande à se plaindre aucunement.
Paul ne-asks (to) complain in-no-way

Given the behavior of *jamais* (indubitably a quantifier), this intriguing distinction cannot be traced to a putative difference between quantifiers and non-quantifiers. It may be purely syntactic (adverbs are excluded *qua* adverbs) or due to a yet uncovered semantic difference. We leave the question open for further study.

Third, the negative dependency obeys some island constraints (e.g. Milner 1979, 1982, Muller 1991, Déprez 1997, Valois 1997). The negative expression cannot belong to a VPinf subject of a ne-V (compare 17a and 17b), or to an adjunct:[11]

(17) a. * Aujourd'hui, voir personne n'est souhaitable.

b. ? Aujourd'hui, il n'est souhaitable de voir personne.
To-day, it ne-is desirable to see nobody

c. * Paul n'a rencontré des enfants jamais malades
Paul ne-has met children never sick

d. * Paul ne lit des journaux contenant aucune photo
Paul ne-reads newspapers containing no picture

[11]Contrary to Valois (1997), we do not conclude from the acceptability of (i) that the negation is allowed in an adjunct: such PPs can be analyzed as complements (for an analysis of postverbal adverbials as complements, see e.g. Bouma et al. 2001, and section 3.1 below). In any case, one must be able to distinguish between (i) and (ii) (the latter are only acceptable as a metalinguistic negation, and for some speakers).

(i) ? Je ne suis sorti avant personne.
(I ne-went out before nobody)

(ii) * Je ne suis sorti avant de recevoir personne.
(I ne-went out before receiving nobody)

Finally, the negative expression cannot belong to a tensed clause, witness the contrast between 18a and 18b:[12]

(18) La situation est claire. ('The situation is simple')

a. Le patron ne veut tolérer aucun désordre.
The boss ne-wants to tolerate no untidiness.

b. * Le patron ne veut que vous tolériez aucun désordre.
The boss ne-wants that you tolerate no untidiness

c. * Le patron ne veut qu' aucun désordre subsiste.
The boss ne-wants that no untidiness remains

## 2.2 Comparison between dependencies

We compare the constraints on ND first with those on the syntactic sharing of arguments, then with those on negations entering into negative concord, with those between an NPI and its licensor, and finally with those on syntactic unbounded dependencies.

The syntactic sharing of arguments between a predicate and a higher V exists in three cases in French: (i) raising Vs share their subject (or their object) with the subject of their VPinf complement; (ii) a few Vs (auxiliary, causative and perception verbs) share the arguments of their non-finite complement, giving rise to 'complex predicates', (see e.g. Abeillé and Godard 2002,2003); (iii) a larger class of Vs may inherit bare universal quantifiers (*tout, tous, rien*, cf. 'leftward tous' in Kayne 1975). That a subject raising V can function as a ne-V with respect to its negative subject is expected (19a), since it is in fact a case of local dependency; similarly for the head of a complex predicate with respect to an argument of its complement (19b). On the other hand, it is remarkable that the class of verbs which can inherit bare quantifiers is the same as the class of 'vouloir-verbs', that is those verbs which allow non-local ND (see 19c,d vs 19e,f), see Milner (1979, 1982), Déprez (1997).

[12]It is often assumed since Kayne (1984) (although see Déprez's observations), that sentences such as 18b are acceptable. The only contexts where they may seem acceptable in standard French is with a metalinguistic negation, as a denial of a preceding discourse, with stress on the negation and, possibly, exclamative prosody. This corresponds to Muller's comments on the data, although he notes them as acceptable (Muller 1991:353). It seems reasonable to distinguish between the conditions on descriptive and metalinguistic negations (constraints are relaxed on the latter case), and to look for further data regarding the latter, especially if they correspond to spoken discourse, where acceptability judgments are notoriously unreliable. In spoken and non-standard French, it is possible that the domain of a negation can be extended to the matrix clause in such a configuration, with a very small set of Vs, but it is unlikely that *ne* will be present, see fn 13.

(19) a. Personne ne semble être malade.
Nobody ne-seems (to) be sick

b. Il ne l'a entendu donner des conseils à personne.
He ne-him-has heard give advice to nobody

c. Il n'a encore cherché à contacter personne.
He ne-has yet tried to contact nobody

d. Il a tout cherché à comprendre.
He has everything tried to understand

e. * Il n'a reconnu avoir rencontré personne.
He ne-has recognized having seen nobody

f. * Il a tout reconnu avoir compris à ce moment-là.
He has everything recognized having understood then
(putatively 'He has recognized having understood everything then')

Moreover, island constraints are the same with ND and inherited bare quantifiers, since the latter cannot be inherited from a finite clause, or from a subject VPinf, or from an adjunct:[13]

(20) a. ?? Il a tout accepté [que je traduise].
He has everything accepted that I translate

b. [Faire tout] aurait été souhaitable.
(To) do everything would have been desirable

c. * Faire aurait tout été souhaitable.

d. * Paul est tout parti [pour acheter].
P. is everything gone to buy
(P. has gone to buy everything)

We conclude that the constraints on 'left tous' and on ND should be identified. This follows if both phenomena involve the interpretation of a quantifier in a clause higher than that of the verb which subcategorizes for it. In fact, syntactically raised negations and universals are not interpreted in the lower clause, as illustrated in 21. Example 21a illustrates the fact, noted in Milner (1982), that a negative expression cannot be the subject of a raising V if the Vinf is a ne-V; this shows that a negative expression cannot be interpreted lower than where it occurs, contrary to indefinites. The contrast between 21b and 21c shows

[13]Some speakers accept a bare universal quantifier *tous/tout/rien* raised in the higher clause with a very small set of V (*il faut* 'it is necessary', *vouloir* 'to want' are the two usually mentioned), cf. *%Il (ne) faut rien que tu fasses*, lit. It (NE) is-necessary nothing that you do, 'it is not necessary that you do anything'. Unfortunately, it is difficult to test whether this correlates with an extended domain for ND, because such sentences belong to a spoken (or NS) register, where *ne* is usually absent. See also fn 12 and 29.

that the same is true of the universal quantifier. In 21b, the quantifier has scope over *refuser* (the sentence implies that he wants to see no one) while it has scope under it in 21c (which implies that he does not want to see all of them) (Abeillé and Godard 1999):

(21) a. * Personne semble n'être malade.
Nobody seems (to) ne-be sick
b. Le professeur a tous refusé de les recevoir.
The professor has all refused to see them
c. Le professeur a refusé de les voir tous.
The professor has refused to see them all

Turning to the comparison between ND and negative concord (NC), we observe again that the constraints are identical. Thus, for instance, in addition to cases where the two negative expressions are arguments of the same predicate (22a), one of them can be an argument of an N, or the complement of a P (22b,c); it can also occur in a VP complement while the other is in the matrix clause (see 14d), but not in an embedded finite clause. Although words which share the same form as the negative words (*jamais*, *personne*, etc.) can occur (in high registers) in the finite complement sentence (22d,e), they must then be analyzed as NPI (the remains of the older system, see Corblin et al., chapter 19, this volume) rather than negations. Proof of this is that sentence 22d is obligatorily interpreted with one logical negation, while it should be ambiguous if there were NC (as in 14d); moreover, the negative adverb *pas* can license such expressions in the complement S, while it cannot enter into the NC system (at least, in the French of France).

(22) a. Personne ne parle à personne ici. (DN and NC)
Nobody ne-talks to nobody here
b. Personne ne lit les livres d' aucun confrère.
Nobody ne-reads the books of no colleague (DN and NC)
c. Personne ne peut compter sur personne ici.
Nobody ne-can rely on nobody here (DN and NC)
d. Personne n'a prétendu qu'aucun de ses livres ait été compris.
Nobody ne-has claimed that any of his books had been understood (*aucun* = NPI)
e. Paul n'a pas prétendu qu'aucun de ses livres ait été compris.
Paul did not claim that any of his books was understood (*aucun* = NPI)

These data are expected if NC results from the interpretation of two (or more) negative expressions in the same interpretive domain. If verbal, this domain is defined by the occurrence of a ne-V (or ne-VP), to which each negative expression is independently related. It follows that there cannot be any difference between the constraints defining the domain for the ND (between a ne-V and a negation) and for negative concord (which depends on the occurrence of two negative expressions, each of them related to a ne-V).

On the other hand, it is immediately clear that the negative dependency and the relation between an NPI and its licensor are distinct. Thus, for instance, there is no evidence that the NPI dependency is lexically restricted; for instance, verbs of saying allow it, although they prevent negative dependency (19d). In addition, NPIs are perfectly acceptable in an embedded finite clause (see also (22d,e)):

(23) a. Paul n'a pas reconnu avoir acheté quoi que ce soit.
Paul has not recognized having bought anything

b. Personne n'a dit que tu avais acheté quoi que ce soit.
Nobody said that you had bought anything

This result should not come as a surprise: we have analyzed French negative words as negations, rather than NPIs in the general case (although such forms can be NPIs in restricted conditions, in high registers, as is *aucun* in (22d,e)), and everything indicates that negative dependency and licensing of an NPI are two different phenomena. Note that the different behavior of the two negative words in NC, on the one hand, and the pair NPI-licensor, on the other hand, argues against analyses of NC where one of the negations is treated essentially as an NPI.

Finally, the constraints on ND must be compared with those on syntactic unbounded dependencies. The dependencies share two island constraints: neither a gap, nor a negative quantifier can be in a subject VPinf, or embedded in an adjunct. However, the other constraints are clearly different: (i) both dependencies are lexically controlled, but the set of bridge predicates is obviously much bigger than the set of non-local ND verbs; (ii) a gap, but not a negative word, can be in a finite S; (iii) a negative word, but not a gap, can be in a PP. As a consequence, any account of ND which appeals to 'movement' must distinguish between types of movements. Note that the contrast is not between overt and LF movement, since leftward *tous* ('overt') and ND ('covert') are similarly constrained.

To sum up, the domain for ND should be identified with (i) the domain for the syntactic raising of a bare universal quantifier, and (ii) the domain which allows for NC. On the other hand, the dependency between ne and a negation is clearly different from the licensing of an NPI, and from movement dependencies.

## 3 Syntax-Semantics interface

The analysis of French negative dependency must account for the dual nature of negative expressions, which are both quantifiers and negations, and for their interaction with clitic *ne*, which is lexically, syntactically and semantically constrained. Before presenting two different approaches to this syntax-semantics interface problem, it is necessary to describe the syntax of negative adverbs and of the clitic *ne* (negative nominals, NPs or determiners, raise no difficulty).[14]

### 3.1 Basic syntactic properties of negative adverbs

The distribution of French negative adverbs is more complex than is usually assumed: (i) all negative adverbs occur after the Vfin (24a); (ii) all negative adverbs can occur before the Vinf (24b), (29a); (iii) although the non-modified (bare) negative adverbs *pas, plus, jamais* do not occur after Vinf, *aucunement, nullement* can occur, as well as *pas, plus* and *jamais* if they are modified (24c,d); (iv) non-modified postverbal adverbs *pas, plus, jamais* must precede nominal and prepositional complements, *aucunement, nullement* as well as modified *jamais* and *plus* can follow them (24e,f,g), see Abeillé and Godard (1997).[15]

(24) a. Jean ne lit pas / plus / jamais de journaux.
Jean ne-reads not / no-more / never (of) newspapers

b. Jean avoue ne pas / ne plus / ne jamais lire de journaux.
Jean recognizes ne-not / ne-no-more / ne-never read (of) newspapers

c. On lui reproche de ne lire aucunement les journaux.
They fault him with ne-read in-no-way newspapers

d. On lui reproche de ne rendre absolument jamais / pas visite à sa grand-mère.
They fault him with ne-pay absolutely never / not visit to his grand-mother

e. Jean ne rend visite à sa grand-mère * (absolument) jamais.
Jean ne-pay visit to his grand-mother absolutely never

f. On lui reproche de ne rendre visite à sa grand-mère *(absolument) jamais.

g. * Jean ne rend visite à sa grand-mère (absolument) pas.

There are unitary and non-unitary analyses of negative adverbs. In the first approach, the adverb has one position and one grammatical

---

[14]For a description of French negation in DRT, see Corblin (1992, 1994, 1996), Amsili (1994). These works do not contain an explicit account of ND.

[15]In addition, as is well-known, non modified negative adverbs can follow infinitival 'auxiliaries' (see e.g. Emonds 1978, Pollock 1989, Kim and Sag 2002).

function, while the finite and the infinitival verbs are in different positions. In the second approach, the verb is always in the same position, but the adverb has a different position and/or a different grammatical function depending on its position relative to the verb.

There is general agreement that *ne* is a clitic: it never bears stress, and, if hosted by a finite verb, it occurs between the pronominal subject clitic and the series of complement clitics. However, not everyone agrees that French clitics are affixes (hence, part of the word which hosts them) rather than post-lexical clitics (hence, syntactic words by themselves); for recent discussions, see Miller (1992), Miller and Sag (1997), Miller and Monachesi (2003). Even if they are analyzed as affixes, their treatment depends on whether the framework adopts the principle of lexical integrity or not. Since analyses making use of verb movement do not (the morphological expression of tense does not form an independent word in French, while it — or corresponding features — stands alone in Infl, or T), nothing prevents them in principle from adopting the affixal analysis of clitics.

We consider in turn an analysis in a constraint-based lexicalist framework, namely HPSG (Pollard and Sag 1994), and three proposals in configurational frameworks.

## 3.2 An Analysis in constraint-based lexicalism (HPSG)

The HPSG framework distinguishes among different types of grammatical objects corresponding to different kinds of information. We are mainly concerned here with *synsem* objects, that is, syntactic and semantic features which are the value of the feature SYNSEM, and, more precisely, with the features CATegory (for syntactic information), CONTent (for semantic information), and Q-STORE (for unscoped quantificational information). They are part of the description of the two types of signs, words and phrases, which, in addition, also contain other types of information (such as phonology and morphology). Phrases have daughters, divided among a head daughter and non-head daughter(s), words do not have daughters; words have an ARGument STructure, while phrases do not. For phrase structure, we have the usual HEAD-DTR and NON-HEAD-DTRS, to which we add the feature DTRS (whose value is a list concatenating the head daughter with the non-head daughters).

The analysis of ND builds on previous work on French negation in HPSG: the syntax of negative adverbs in Abeillé and Godard (1997), Kim and Sag (2002), the properties of *ne* observed in Recourcé (1996), and the analysis of negative quantifiers in de Swart and Sag (2002), as well as the treatment of ND in Romanian in Ionescu (1999).[16] The problem being at the syntax-semantics interface, we explain the syntax and morpho-syntax of *ne* and negative adverbs, and the treatment of quantification that we adopt, before giving a description of the French negative dependency which correlates the two.

### 3.2.1 The syntax of negative adverbs

We adopt the following syntax:

**(i)** negative adverbs are adjoined to non-finite categories, which include but are not limited to VPinf (cf. 11b,c and 13b), while they are considered complements of Vfin; word order constraints (which we leave aside here) ensure that the negative adjuncts are to the left of the VP, and the complements are to the right of the head V (V denotes a lexical V, and VP a phrase missing a subject).

**(ii)** the clitic *ne* is an affix, the realization of a morpho-syntactic feature [NE+].

As adjuncts, negative adverbs are constrained by the *head-adjunct-phrase* description, which specifies the adjunct for the type of head that it can adjoin to, via the MOD feature whose value is identified with the synsem of the head (see 25a). negative adverbs contain a MOD feature whose value is compatible with VPinf.[17] The specification in 25b relies on the semantic classification of quantifiers, to which we come back shortly; an example is given in 25c, where the branches are annotated with their grammatical function.

(25) a. *head-adjunct-phrase* ⇒

$$\begin{bmatrix} \text{HEAD-DTR} & \boxed{1}\ [\text{SYNSEM}\ \boxed{2}] \\ \text{NON-HEAD-DTRS} & \langle [\text{MOD}\ \boxed{2}] \rangle \end{bmatrix}$$

b. *Adverbs*[CONT*neg-quant-rel*] ⇒ [MOD XP *non-finite*].

[16] For a different analysis of French negation in HPSG, see Richter and Sailer (1999). For a different analysis of negative dependency and negative concord in Polish and Italian in HPSG, see Przepiórkowski and Kupść (1999).

[17] 'XP non-finite' covers non-finite VPs but also non-verbal categories, as required for constituent negation, as in (i).

(i) Jamais malades, les enfants étaient joyeux.
Never sick, the children were happy

(ii) Je cherche non un stylo, mais une craie.
I am looking not for a pen, but for a piece of chalk

c. 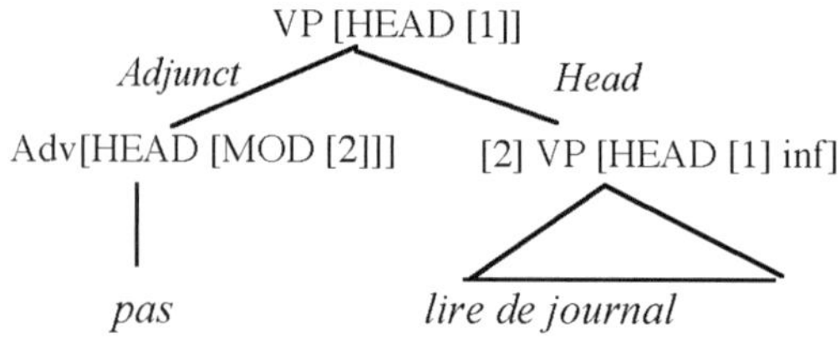


Basic Vs do not usually take adverbs as arguments,[18] but Vs with an 'augmented' argument structure do: the argument structure of basic Vs can be augmented to include adverbials (with a MOD value), roughly if the content of the head which they can modify is identified with that of the V.[19] This analysis allows us to treat negative adverbs as syntactic arguments of the V. A simple constraint, based on the syntactic WEIGHT feature (see e.g. Abeillé and Godard 1997, 2000), is added to deal with the data in (24b–g). While *-ment* negative adverbs as well as modified *pas, plus, jamais* are 'non-light', non-modified *pas, plus* and *jamais* are 'light'. The constraint states that, if a syntactic argument of a V is a light negative adverb, then this V is finite (or an [AUX+], see e.g. Emonds 1978, Pollock 1989, for the data concerning 'auxiliaries').

Since the list of arguments is the concatenation of the subject and the complements, all arguments except for the first one are realized as complements. An example is given in 26.

(26)

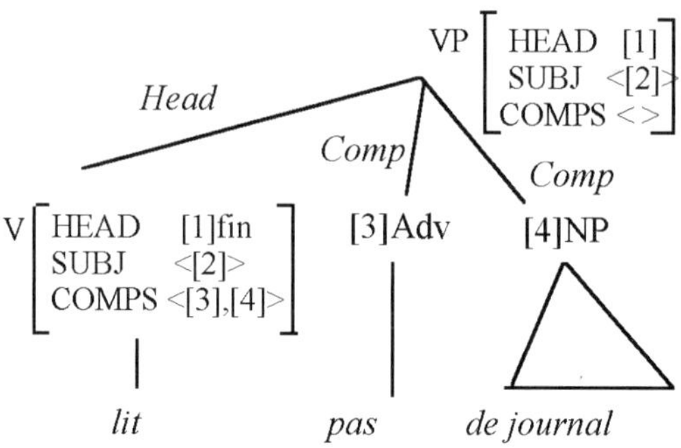


Like other complements, postverbal negative expressions are constrained by the *head-complements-phrase* (a *head-complements-phrase*, for instance a VP, dominates a lexical head and its complements).

[18] There are some which do, such as *se comporter *(bien)* 'to behave well', *traiter NP *(correctement)* 'to treat NP correctly'.

[19] For different implementations of this analysis, see e.g. Abeillé and Godard (1997), Bouma et al. (2001), Kim and Sag (2002).

Both *the head-adjunct-phrase*, and the *head-complements-phrase* are constrained by the Generalized Head Feature Principle (Ginzburg and Sag 2000: 33), which says that the features of a mother phrase and those of its head daughter have identical values, unless they are explicitly said to be different in the description of more specific cases (see the '/' notation for defaults):

(27) Generalized Head Feature Principle (GHFP)

$$\textit{headed phrase} \Rightarrow \begin{bmatrix} \text{SYNSEM} & / \boxed{1} \\ \text{HEAD-DTR} \mid \text{SYNSEM} & / \boxed{1} \end{bmatrix}$$

Let us turn to the analysis of the clitic *ne*. Interestingly, its properties are different depending on the finiteness of the V (Recourcé 1996). With a finite V, *ne* has the same properties as pronominal clitics; in particular, it can only be hosted by a V, and must be repeated on each V in case of coordination of VPs or Vs (see *Paul ne voit personne et *(ne) reçoit aucune nouvelle* 'Paul ne-sees nobody and ne-receives no news', *Paul n'achète et/ ou *(ne) lit aucun journal* 'Paul ne-buys or reads no newspaper'). Moreover, it occurs between the subject and the complement clitics (*Il ne le lit jamais*, He-ne-it-reads never). We extend the analysis of pronominal clitics as lexical affixes (Miller 1992, Miller and Sag 1997) to finite *ne*.

On the other hand, with an infinitival VP, *ne* can be hosted not only by the V (see (14a,c)), but by a bare quantifier or an adverb.[20] If a negative adverb is adjoined to the VPinf, one occurrence of *ne* must precede it. If the negative expression is an argument, *ne* occurs on the first word of the VP. If both types of occurrences are present, there can be one or two occurrences of *ne*, with only a double negation reading in the second case.

(28) a. Il avoue [ne jamais [lire de journal]].
He recognizes (to) ne never read a newspaper

a'. * Il avoue jamais ne lire de journal.

b. Il avoue [[ne beaucoup parler] avec personne].
He recognizes (to) ne a-lot speak with nobody

b'. * Il avoue beaucoup ne parler avec personne.

c. Il prétend ne jamais recevoir personne le dimanche. (NC or DN)
He pretends ne never receive nobody on Sundays

c'. Il prétend ne jamais ne recevoir personne le dimanche. (DN)

[20]For a distinction between adverbs modifying the lexical Vinf (28b) and adverbs modifying the VPinf (28a), see Abeillé and Godard (1997).

The data regarding coordination are also different. If a negative adverb is adjoined to conjoined VPs, *ne* may have wide scope (*Il prétend ne jamais le voir ou recevoir de nouvelles de sa famille* lit. He pretends ne-never see him or receive of news from his family); if the negative expression is an argument of conjoined Vs, the second *ne* is optional (*Il prétend ne voir ou (n') entendre personne* 'He pretends (to) ne-see or (ne)-hear nobody'); if the conjoined VPs each contain a negative expression, *ne* must be repeated (*Il prétend ne voir personne et *(ne) recevoir aucune nouvelle*, lit. He pretends ne-see nobody and ne-receive no news).

We also analyze this infinitival *ne* as an affix (unlike Recourcé 1996), but a phrasal affix — an affix morphologically part of the first word, but triggered by a feature on the VP. This analysis allows us to minimize the distinction between the two types of occurrences, which are both affixes realizing the morpho-syntactic feature [NE+].

If *ne* is an affix, we can also make sense of the curious behavior of *aucunement, nullement*. While such adverbs fail to adjoin to VPinf in a general way (see 29b), they can adjoin to the VP complement of *sans* (see 29a). Since the contrast is correlated with the presence or absence of *ne*,[21] the problem is not adjunction to VPinf, but the combination of the adverb with affixal *ne*, a combination which we propose is excluded on morphological (rather than syntactic) grounds.[22]

(29) a. Ils sont partis sans aucunement se plaindre.
They went away without in-no-way complaining

b. * Ils sont connus pour n'aucunement se plaindre.
They are known for ne-in-no-way complaining

[21] *Sans* is remarkable among prepositions in that it takes a VPinf which does not bear *ne*: *Sans (*ne) se plaindre à personne* (lit. Without ne-complain to nobody), vs *Pour ne se plaindre à personne* (lit. To ne-complain to nobody). This is expected in our analysis. As shown in de Swart and Sag (2002), *sans* constrains a resumptive or NC interpretation for its own negative quantifier and those collected by the Vinf: *sans se plaindre à personne* means 'without complaining to anybody', there is no DN interpretation. An NC interpretation requires that the different negations be interpreted at the same node. In other words, *sans* cannot take as its complement an expression where negations are already scoped (the VPinf complement must be [QUANTS set ([*pos-quant-rel*])], see below). Since negative *ne*, on the other hand, requires that there be negations scoped at that node (36), the properties of *sans* and *ne* are incompatible. *Sans* + VPinf is the one construction where negative adverbs are not interpreted strictly locally.

[22] Other adverbs, such as trop 'too-much' (contrasting with beaucoup in 28b), are incompatible with *ne*:

(i) Il me semble ne jamais trop penser à rien
(He seems ne-never too-much think of nothing)

(ii) ?? Il me semble ne trop penser à rien
(He seems ne-too-much think of nothing).

The feature [NE+] is morphologically realized on a Vfin or on the first word of a VPinf, which is the Vinf, an adverb or a bare quantifier (which is also an adverbial, see Kayne 1975). Its realization as an affix is given by a function $\mathrm{F}_{ne}$ which applies to the inflected form of a word, which may also contain pronominal affixes. If a phrase is [NE+], the feature is shared by the first daughter, and only the first daughter, until it is hosted by a word, and realized as in 30b. The constraint on [NE±] inheritance (30c) says that the first daughter of a [NE+] phrase is itself [NE+], while the others are [NE–], except possibly for a VPinf (whose [NE+] feature is independently semantically motivated, see 31 and 36).[23] Finally, to prevent a VP[NE–] from hosting a non-initial [NE+] word, (* *Voir ne-souvent Paul* (To) see ne-often Paul), we add constraint 30d.

(30) The morpho-syntax of *ne*

a. *sign* ⇒ / [NE–]

b. $$\textit{word}\ [\text{NE}+] \Leftrightarrow \begin{bmatrix} \text{MORPH} & \begin{bmatrix} \text{FORM} & \mathrm{F}_{ne}(\mathrm{F}_{cl}(\boxed{1})) \\ \text{I-FORM} & \boxed{1} \end{bmatrix} \\ \text{CAT}|\text{HEAD} & \text{verb OR adverb} \end{bmatrix}$$

c. $$\textit{phrase}\ [\text{NE}+] \Leftrightarrow \begin{bmatrix} \text{CAT}|\text{HEAD} & \text{VP}_{inf} \vee \text{AdvP} \\ \text{DTRS} & <[\text{NE}+]> \oplus \text{list}\ ([\ \text{NE}-\ ] \vee \text{VP}_{inf}) \end{bmatrix}$$

d. $\textit{phrase}\ [\text{NE}-] \Leftrightarrow [\text{DTRS list}\ ([\text{V}_{fin}] \vee [\text{NE}-])]$

We illustrate the sharing of [NE+] in 31:

(31)

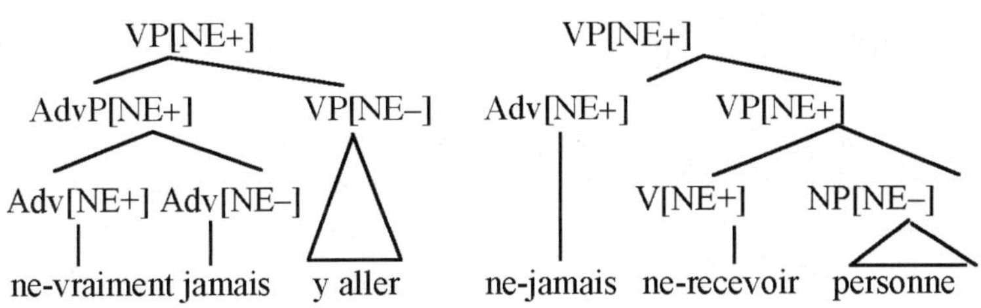


[23] A sign is represented by a partial description (which can reduce to one feature, such as [NE±]); 'list([x])' denotes a list made of signs which have the feature [x]. '⊕' denotes the usual concatenation of lists.

### 3.2.2 The treatment of quantification

Following de Swart and Sag (2002), we treat all negative words as negative quantifiers (see also Corblin et al., chapter 19 this volume, for a presentation of the semantic analysis, in the context of French NC). Although it may not be usual to include the adverbs *pas* and *plus* among quantifiers, this approach allows for a uniform treatment of negations, and deals elegantly with their scope: as we know, sentential negation adverbs have scope over the sentence, and may have scope over a quantifier (see 1 above). The class of quantifiers, whose content is a *quant-relation*, is partitioned between positive and negative quantifiers (with *pos-quant-rel* and *neg-quant-rel*).[24] Their scope is defined by the interaction between two features, Q-STORE (whose value is the set of unscoped quantifiers) and QUANTS (whose value is the list of quantifiers scoped or 'retrieved' at that node). Quantifiers themselves have a Q-STORE value identified with that of their content. Their scope is noted by the transfer of their content from the Q-STORE value to the QUANTS value. Retrieval characterizes expressions associated with a content of type *soa*, notably verbal expressions (V, VP or S).[25] An soa content is partitioned as in 32, where the NUCLEUS value indicates what the quantifiers scope over.

(32)

$$\left[\text{CONT}\ \left[\begin{array}{ll} \multicolumn{2}{l}{\textit{soa}} \\ \text{QUANTS} & \text{list}(\textit{quant-rel}) \\ \text{NUCLEUS} & \textit{relation} \end{array}\right]\right]$$

We show that negative quantifiers require that retrieval be done at two different nodes (for a similar proposal, see Pollard and Yoo 1998): the lexical head when the quantifiers come from arguments, and the phrase when one of the retrieved quantifiers is the content of an adjunct. We assume that the CONT and the Q-STORE values are identical on the head-complements-phrase and its lexical head (following the GHFP); on the other hand, this is not the case for the head-adjunct-phrase and its head daughter: when a quantifier adjoined to a VP is retrieved by the VP, the higher and the lower VPs differ with respect to QUANTS and Q-STORE values (this violates the GHFP).

Following Pollard and Yoo (1998), de Swart and Sag (2002), Ginzburg and Sag (2000:208, 333–36), we adopt a lexicalized treatment of quantifier scoping if the quantifiers are all arguments (33a). The lexical

[24]For a more complex partition, see below (40).

[25]Soa's (originally 'state-of-affairs') denote properties that situations (events, states etc.), which are entities in the world, may have. They are the building blocks of propositions.

predicate collects the Q-STORE values of its arguments (the quantifiers that they contain), and either retrieves (some of) them or passes them up to the mother (see 27 and 33a), which can transmit them to a higher predicate, of which it is an argument. Note that retrieval includes both the ordering of quantifiers (if they have scope over one another) and resumption (if they form a polyadic quantifier, see de Swart and Sag 2002). If there are several negations, ordering corresponds to DN, and resumption to NC; thus, the operation 'retrieve' is indifferent to the distinction between DN and NC. The result of the function 'retrieve($\Sigma 0$)' in 33a is the scoping of the set $\Sigma 0$ of quantifiers interpreted at that node or the formation of a polyadic quantifier. The system of quantifier storage and retrieval allows one to formalize the observation that the different quantifiers have to be scoped in the same domain for NC to be possible (see Corblin 1996, Corblin et al. this volume): this domain can be a unique clause, but can also be non-strictly local, as seen in section 2. Note that constraint 33a is a default; it is violated by quantifiers (33b), which themselves contribute a quantifier (their content is in their Q-STORE); $\Sigma$ is a set.

(33) a. *word* ⇒ /

$$\begin{bmatrix} \text{CAT|ARG-ST} & \langle [\ \text{Q-STORE } \Sigma 1], \ldots, [\text{Q-STORE } \Sigma n\ ] \rangle \\ \text{CONT|QUANTS} & \text{retrieve } (\Sigma 0) \\ \text{Q-STORE} & (\Sigma 1 \cup \ldots \cup \Sigma n) - \Sigma 0 \end{bmatrix}$$

b. quantifiers: $$\begin{bmatrix} \text{CONT} & \left[\ \boxed{1}\ \textit{quant-rel},\ldots\ \right] \\ \text{Q-STORE} & \langle \boxed{1} \rangle \end{bmatrix}$$

The problem is more difficult if the quantifier is (contained in) an adjunct. Since a general analysis of the scoping of quantifiers outside an adjunct exceeds the scope of this work, we restrict ourselves to the data concerning negation. Examples (17c,d) and (34a–c) show that a negative quantifier which is not the head of the adjunct daughter does not escape from the adjunct.

(34) a. * Il ne lit [un journal [contenant aucune photo]].
He ne-reads a newspaper containing no picture

b. Il lit [un journal [ne contenant aucune photo]].
He reads a newspaper ne-containing no picture

c. Il *(ne) lit [aucun journal [*(ne) contenant aucune photo]]. (DN)
He ne-reads no newspaper ne-containing no picture

d. [Jamais [contents de rien]], ces enfants étaient lassants. (NC)
Never happy with nothing (=anything), these children were annoying

Consider the object NP in (34a–c), which contains a participial adjunct. As shown by 34b, scoping within the adjunct VP is perfectly alright; the head of the adjunct (*contenant*) being a finite V (present participle is finite in French), it collects and retrieves its negative quantifier argument, and is realized as a ne-V (see 36a below). If the quantifier could scope outside the adjunct VP in 34a, the V (*lit*) would be able to collect and retrieve it from the NP, and would be a ne-V. Moreover, as shown by 34c, the head of the adjunct (*contenant*) does not collect and retrieve the negative quantifier in the head daughter (*aucun journal*); if it were the case, the matrix V (*lit*) could lack the affix *ne*, and an NC interpretation for the two negations would be available. Similarly, the head N *journal* cannot collect and retrieve the quantifier (*aucune photo*) from the adjunct; otherwise, the V *contenant* would be able to lack *ne*, and there would be an NC interpretation. On the contrary, *ne* is obligatory on both Vs (in the register under consideration), and the interpretation obligatorily contains two logical negations (all the newspapers he reads contain pictures). Thus, in a head-adjunct-phrase, the lexical head of the head-daughter does not collect the quantifier properly contained in the adjunct daughter; nor does the lexical head of the adjunct daughter collect the quantifier contained in the head daughter.

On the other hand, when the negative quantifier is the adjunct, it scopes over the head daughter of the head-adjunct-phrase. In 34d, the adjunct adverb and the negative quantifier argument of the adjective have an NC interpretation, which shows that the two quantifiers are retrieved at the same node. In other words, an adjunct is an island for negations, except if it constitutes the negative quantifier. We propose that the head-adjunct-phrase collects and retrieves the quantifier which is the content of its adjunct daughter. In this system, quantifier scoping is done either lexically (33) or phrasally (35), depending on the grammatical function of the quantifier expression.

The GHFP (27) applies to the head-adjunct-phrase since it applies to headed phrases in general; accordingly, the quantificational features of the phrase (the mother) are, by default, identical to those of the head daughter, so that quantifiers are not allowed to escape from the adjunct daughter in a general way. However, this does not imply that the content, and the quantificational features in particular, should be shared between the phrase and its head daughter. In fact, constraint 35 overrides the default in 27, allowing a negative quantifier adjunct to pass up its own quantifier to the mother phrase.[26]

[26]The quantifier associated with an adverb adjoined to VPinf is retrieved on the mother VPinf, with one notable exception: when the mother VP is the complement

(35) Phrasal retrieval of adjunct quantifiers

$$
\begin{bmatrix} \textit{head-adjunct-phrase} \\ \text{NON-HEAD-DTRS} < \begin{bmatrix} \text{CONT} \ \boxed{2} \ \textit{neg-quant-rel} \\ \text{Q-STORE} \ \{ \ \boxed{2} \ \} \end{bmatrix} > \end{bmatrix}
$$

$$
\Rightarrow \begin{bmatrix} \text{CONT}|\text{QUANTS} & \text{retrieve } (\Sigma 0) \\ \text{Q-STORE} & (\{\boxed{2}\} \cup \Sigma \text{n}) - \Sigma 0 \end{bmatrix}
$$

Accordingly, a negative adverb adjoined to the VPinf, as in 24b, (28a,c), or to the AP as in 34d, can be scoped at the higher VP or AP node (the head-adjunct-phrase); on the other hand, an adjunct is an island for a negative quantifier argument that it contains, as seen in (17c,d) and (34a–c).

### 3.2.3 French negative dependency

We can now formalize the intuition that *ne* is a scope marker for negations. Before going into the intricacies of the data, it is appropriate to say a few words about variation. As already mentioned (see section 1.3), *ne* is often omitted in spoken French. However, it must be stressed that (i) it has not disappeared, even in spoken French, and (ii) intuitions about its use are surprisingly firm and consistent. One reason for the preservation of the form lies probably in its semantic function. In the absence of *ne*, it is impossible to differentiate between local and non-local scoping, with Vs of the 'vouloir-class', see for instance 14a and 14b. The desire to prevent a potential ambiguity may work against the complete disparition of this clitic.

Recall that negative quantifiers cannot scope higher than the ne-V or ne-VP. However, the sign where negative quantifiers are interpreted and the words hosting *ne* are not in a one-to-one relation. First, only verbal categories motivate the feature [NE+], while signs of different categories can do (negative) quantifier retrieval, an AP (see *jamais malades* vs **ne jamais malades* 'never sick') or a PP (see *jamais en charge d'aucun projet* vs ** ne jamais en charge d'aucun projet* 'never in charge of any project') cannot be [NE+]. Second, there is a (possible) discrepancy with VPinf: it is the first word of the VPinf which hosts *ne*, while quantifier retrieval is done on the Vinf or the VPinf. Intuitively, this situation corresponds to a default value for the feature [NE±]: most expressions are [NE–] (see 30a); however, a subset of verbal expressions, the finite (lexical) V and the VPinf, bear the morpho-syntactic feature [NE+], when they are associated with the retrieval of negative quantifiers.

---

of *sans*, see fn 21. Accordingly, we allow but do not force retrieval of this quantifier on the mother (the head-adjunct-phrase) in 35.

We describe French ND as in 36, which expresses the analysis of *ne* as a phrasal affix on the VPinf, and a lexical affix on the Vfin, as well as the fact that *ne* is a scope marker: its presence indicates retrieval of negation, and prevents all negations from taking scope above the V or VP bearing ne.[27]

(36) French negative dependency

a. $\begin{bmatrix} \text{CAT} & \text{V}_{\textit{fin}} \\ \text{CONT}|\text{QUANTS} & \text{retrieve}(\text{neset}([\textit{neg-quant-rel}]) \cup \Sigma) \\ \text{Q-STORE} & \text{set}([\textit{pos-quant-rel}]) \end{bmatrix}$
$\Leftrightarrow \begin{bmatrix} \text{V}\textit{fin} \\ \text{NE+} \end{bmatrix}$

b. $\begin{bmatrix} \text{CAT} & \text{VP}_{\textit{inf}} \\ \text{CONT}|\text{QUANTS} & \text{retrieve}(\text{neset}([\textit{neg-quant-rel}]) \cup \Sigma) \\ \text{Q-STORE} & \text{set}([\textit{pos-quant-rel}]) \end{bmatrix}$
$\Leftrightarrow \begin{bmatrix} \text{VP}\textit{inf} \\ \text{NE+} \end{bmatrix}$

To understand the different cases, another factor must be kept in mind: whether retrieval is lexical (the quantifiers are all arguments) or phrasal (one quantifier is an adjunct). It is immediately clear why we have a V[NE+] every time the retrieval of negative quantifiers is done on the finite verb. On the other hand, because of 30c, the VPfin is always [NE–], although it shares the QUANTS and Q-STORE values with its head. With infinitivals, we must distinguish between two cases. The first case is when the negative quantifier arguments are retrieved at the Vinf node (see 33a). Given that the content and the Q-STORE are shared between V and VP (it is a head-complements-phrase), the VPinf meets 36b and is associated with [NE+]. The Vinf itself is [NE+] if it is the first word of the VP and [NE–] otherwise (30c). For instance, in

[27] Sentence initial negations have been left aside:

(i) Jamais / Jamais plus Paul ne viendra à Paris.
Never / Never more Paul ne-will-come to Paris

(ii) Nulle part Paul n'a trouvé ce qu'il cherchait.
Nowhere Paul ne-has found what he was looking for

The syntax of such sentences is unclear: it is debatable whether the negation is extracted or adjoined to the sentence. The data follow from the proposed analysis in the first case (constraint 33 would apply to the same way with a gap argument). But more needs to be said if adjunction is involved. First, constraint 25b should be amended to allow for adjunction to finite categories. Second, the analysis of ND would be slightly more complex, since the correlation between the feature [NE+] and negation retrieval would be mediated by a head feature, such as [NEG±], in order to account for the occurrence of a finite ne-V which does not retrieve the negative quantifier (it is retrieved by the higher sentence, the head-adjunct-phrase, following 35).

28b, *ne beaucoup parler avec personne*, the V is [NE–]:

$_{\mathrm{VP[NE+]}}[_{\mathrm{V[NE+]}}[\ _{\mathrm{Adv[NE+]}}[$ne-beaucoup$]_{\mathrm{V[NE-]}}[$parler$]]$ avec personne].

Note that a Vinf[NE–] may retrieve negations. On the other hand, a Vinf[NE+] always retrieves negative quantifiers because it is the head of a VPinf[NE+], and their contents are identified.

The second case with infinitivals is when a negative adverb is adjoined to the VPinf. Following 35, it may be (and usually is) retrieved on the higher VPinf (the head-adjunct-phrase) which is then [NE+] following 36b. If so, all other negative quantifiers must be retrieved at the same node (all quantifiers remaining in the Q-STORE are positive). But the lower VPinf (the head daughter of the head-adjunct-phrase) is [NE–] (unless [NE+] is independently motivated as in 38), because the content and Q-STORE of the head-adjunct-phrase and its head daughter are not shared.

We illustrate our analysis with three examples. In the first example, *Personne ne veut recevoir personne* ('Nobody wants to see nobody/anybody', ambiguous between NC and DN), the negative expressions are both arguments, and are retrieved by the same verb *veut*, although one is syntactically an argument of the complement Vinf. The Vinf *recevoir* collects the Q-STORE of its negative argument, does not retrieve it, and shares its Q-STORE value with the VP. The verb *veut* collects and retrieves the Q-STORE values of its subject and of its VP complement. Accordingly, the head Vfin is [NE+] (see 36a), while the VPfin and Sfin are [NE–]. In the second example, *Ne jamais ne recevoir personne* 'Never to receive nobody' (only DN), one negation is an argument, retrieved by the head Vinf, the other one is an adjunct, retrieved by the higher VP. The higher VPinf is [NE+] because it retrieves the negative adjunct; the lower VP is also [NE+], because it shares its content with the head V, and also meets constraint 36b. The lexical Vinf is [NE+], because it is the first word of the VP, cf. 30c. Accordingly, there are two occurrences of *ne*, and the interpretation is obligatorily a double negation: resumption requires that the two negations be retrieved at the same node.

(37)

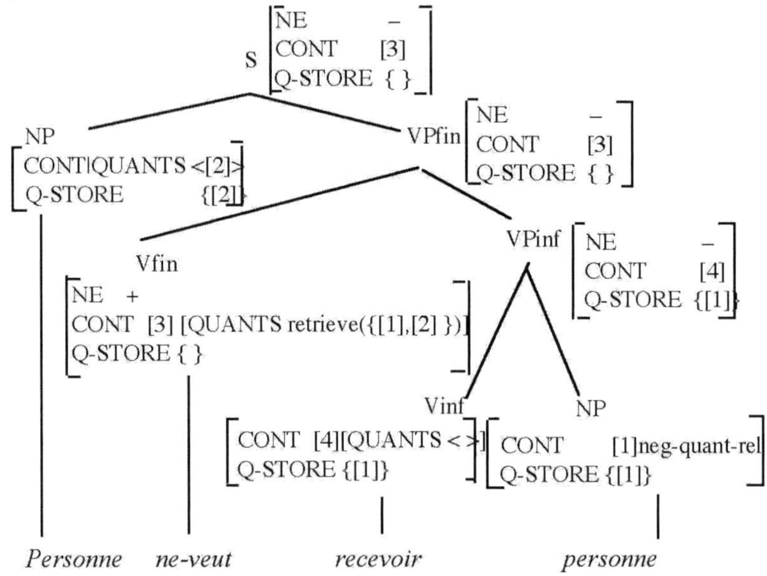


(38)

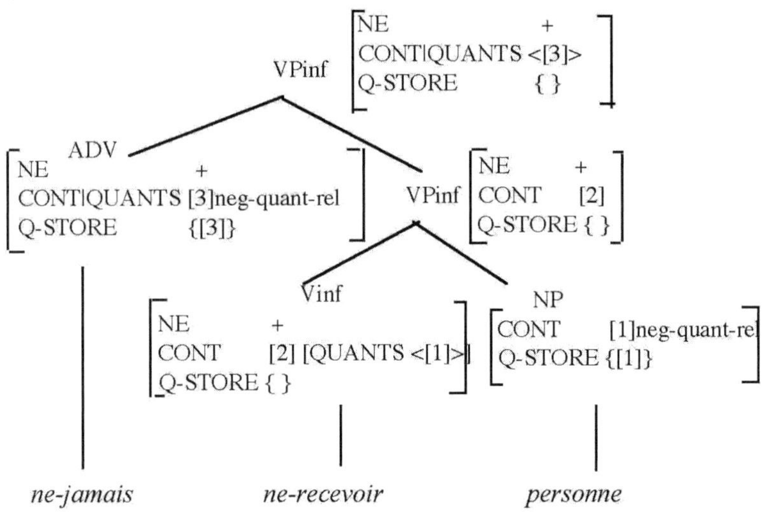


In the last example (39), there are also two negative quantifiers, an adjunct and an argument, but the argument is retrieved on the higher VPinf, at the same time as the adjunct. Accordingly, only the higher VPinf meets the conditions for being [NE+], there is only one *ne*, and the interpretation can be NC or DN.

(39)

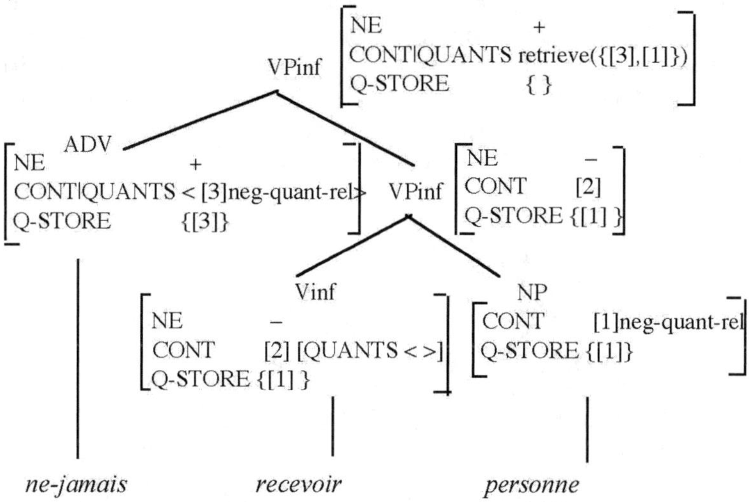


### 3.2.4 Locality constraints

As shown in section 2, ND is not strictly local, but it is bounded. Negative quantifier retrieval is bounded in the same way as universals, in that it never crosses an Sfin, and in most cases cannot go further than a VPinf. However, it is not strictly local: the V inherits it from an NP, an AP or a PP argument (15), and also from a VPinf complement in some cases (for instance, in 14d, 16d, 37). When a lexical head does not retrieve the quantifiers, it collects them in its Q-STORE, according to 33, shares them with the phrase according to the GHFP (27), which passes them to the (higher) V of which it is an argument (33). Since argumental Ns and Ps cannot retrieve quantifiers (we assume that they are not of the right semantic type), nothing more needs to be said. However, Vs have the right soa semantic type for retrieval; so, we must account for non-local dependency involving VPinf.

A general discussion of the constraints on quantifier retrieval is obviously outside the scope of this work (notably, we leave aside definites). Nevertheless, we propose constraints which are more general than we are able to discuss, on the basis of the partition which emerges between indefinites on the one hand, and universals and negations on the other. As noted above (section 2.2), negations pattern with universals with respect to Q-STORE inheritance in French: finite S and argument VPinf are islands in a general way for both types of quantifiers (17a). Exceptions are the VP complement of the 'vouloir-verbs' and raising verbs;

the first allow for non-local ND and raised *tous*, the second retrieve the quantifiers of the raised arguments.[28] Our constraints are based on the Q-STORE feature, whose value is a set of unscoped quantifiers. We partition quantifier-relations along two dimensions, negation and indefiniteness, as in 40. The Q-STORE value *q-store* is then partitioned into two types: the *q-island-store* and the *q-permissive-store*, which we define as in 41a, under the widely accepted assumption that indefinites are not bounded in the same way as universals or negations.[29]

(40)

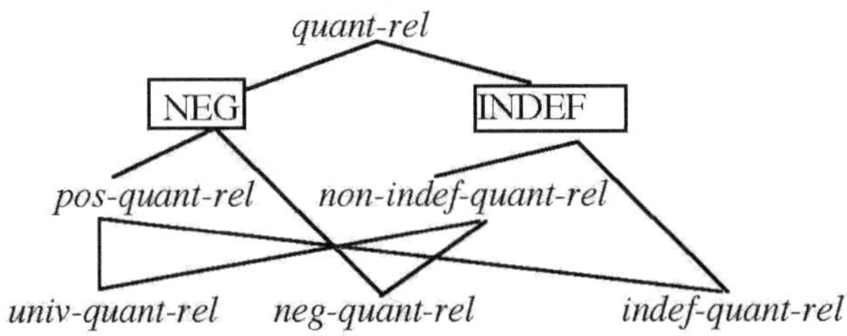


(41) Locality constraints on quantifier retrieval

a. *q-island-store*: [Q-STORE set([*indef-quant-rel*])]
   *q-permissive-store*: [Q-STORE set([*quant-rel*])]

b. S*fin* ⇒ [ Q-STORE *q-island-store* ]

c. VP*inf* ⇒ / [ Q-STORE *q-island-store* ]

d. 'vouloir-verbs':

$$\left[ \text{ARG-ST} < \text{NP}_i, \begin{bmatrix} \text{VP}\textit{inf} \\ \text{SUBJ} <\text{NP}_i> \\ \text{Q-STORE q-permissive-store} \end{bmatrix} > \right]$$

e. storage of raised arguments:
   VPinf[VAL <[Q-STORE Σ1([non-indef-quant-rel])], . . . ,

[28]Object raising verbs behave like subject raising verbs:
(i) * Paul voit personne ne venir (P. sees nobody ne-come)
(ii) Paul ne voit personne venir (P. ne-sees nobody come)

[29]The same conditions seem to apply to universals in a general way. For the speakers who accept sentences such as % *Il faut tous que tu les lises*, lit. It is necessary all that you read them, %*Il faut tout que je fasse ici* lit. It is necessary everything that I do here ([spoken French]), where *tout/tous* seems to be syntactically inherited from a Sfin, see fn 13, 41b should be a default constraint (like 41c), with *falloir* and *vouloir* violating it, even with a finite complement.

[Q-STORE $\Sigma$n([non-indef-quant-rel])]>]
$\Rightarrow$ [Q-STORE $\Sigma 1 \cup \ldots \Sigma n \cup \Sigma 0$]

Given the definitions in 41a, constraint 41b prevents quantifiers other than indefinites from scoping across a Sfin, since only indefinites can still be in store; 41c constrains VPinf in the same way, although by default only: the quantifiers contained in a VPinf, except for indefinites, are generally retrieved within it. Given definitions 41a, 'vouloir-verbs' are defined as subject control or raising verbs (the subject NP is co-indexed with the subject expected by the VP) whose complement VPinf is not an island for quantifiers. The VP complement of such verbs violates the default constraint 41c, being specified as having a quant-permissive-store.

The last constraint 41e addresses the issue of syntactically raised universal and negative quantifiers (non-indefinites, following 40), which obligatorily take scope upstairs. Raised arguments are expected by a predicate, but not realized in the phrase it heads: they are part of the valence of this predicate and also of the phrase (VAL ranges over subject and complements). We analyze the floating quantifier 'tous' as an argument, which can be raised (see Abeillé and Godard 1999). Raising implies the sharing of content and Q-STORE by the raised expression and this expected unrealized argument.[30] Constraint 41e says that, if a non-indefinite quantifier is raised, this quantifier cannot take scope downstairs. Thus, it is amalgamated by the 'vouloir verb' taking such a VP as its complement.

Constraint 41e is worth some more comment. The fact that raised indefinites can take scope either within the VP complement or above (cf. *A unicorn seems to be approaching*) has been widely discussed: not only can it be seen as an argument in favor of 'raising', but it is also an argument in favor of the lexical retrieval of quantifiers (Pollard and Yoo 1998). The scope of indefinites is underdetermined by their syntactic position: they may be interpreted higher or lower than the domain where they occur. On the other hand, negations and universals are largely constrained by the syntactic position where they occur: not only do they seem not to escape from a Sfin (at least in French), but, and this is not usually observed, they cannot be interpreted lower than where they occur.

[30] A controlled subject is also on the valence list, but it is not a quantifier (rather, it is a null pronoun which only shares its index with the controller, cf. Pollard and Sag 1994).

## 3.3 Configurational approaches

We turn to treatments of the French negative dependency in configurational terms, which characterize approaches such as GB or Principles and Parameters. Two features of these frameworks condition the solution. First, there are different levels of structures, related via movement. We are concerned with D-Structure, S-Structure and LF. Second, the set of syntactic categories includes 'functional' categories, as opposed to substantive ones (such as NP, VP etc.). Syntactic categories follow a rigid and possibly universal hierarchical organization. Crucial to our problem are the functional categories NegP, TenseP, and AgrP. A sentence is a ComplementizerP (CP), which dominates AgrP, NegP, TP and VP (e.g. Pollock 1989, Haegeman 1995: 28, who order the functional projections differently).

### 3.3.1 The syntax of negation

We follow Haegeman's account of the syntax of negation (1995), which incorporates an analysis of negation that is widely accepted in these frameworks (see Emonds 1978, Pollock 1989). The hierarchy of functional projections can be seen in 43. negative adverbs are found in the specifier position of NegP, with *ne* as the head.[31] The finite V, base-generated as the head of VP, moves to T, and the 'complex' V+T moves to Agr. As for *ne*, it moves to Agr where it cliticizes on the 'complex' V+T+Agr. Given that NegP is dominated by AgrP, the finite ne-V precedes negative adverbs. As noted by Haegeman (1995: 301), with VPinf, not only does the V not move across NegP, since the adverb *pas* precedes the Vinf, but *ne* does not have to cliticize on V (cf. 24b, 28 above). She suggests that, in French, VPinf is dominated by NegP, and *ne* either cliticizes onto the adverb, or moves to a higher functional projection (left unspecified). However, the difference between the two types of occurrences of *ne* is not accounted for. A distinction similar to that given above in HPSG could be adopted (*ne* could be a lexical affix with Vfin, and a phrasal affix or a post-lexical clitic with a VPinf), but this different behavior casts doubt on the unitary Neg analysis of *ne*: if there is only one element *ne*, how does it know about its environment? And if there are two *ne*'s, how is a unitary Neg analysis justified? We conclude that the syntax of French negation in this framework is incomplete. [32]

---

[31] However, negative adverbs are adjoined to VP in Hirschbühler and Labelle (1993).

[32] It is difficult to see how the fact that modified adverbs can occur postverbally (see 24) can be accommodated in a NegP analysis of adverbs, except by allowing them to have an alternative analysis as complements in the VP, cf. section 3.2.

### 3.3.2 The analysis of ND

Contrasting with the general agreement concerning the syntax of negative adverbs, the account of ND is a matter of debate. We briefly discuss three solutions, two of them relying on the 'NEG criterion' (Haegeman and Zanuttini 1991). For Haegeman (1995, 1997), negative expressions are associated with a semantic feature [NEG], with a syntactic reflex which she formulates as in 42, where a NEG operator is a NEG phrase in a specifier or adjunct position:

(42) NEG criterion (Haegeman 1995:134)

a. A NEG operator must be in a Spec-head configuration with an $X^0$

b. An $X^0$[NEG] must be in Spec-head configuration with a NEG operator

Having motivated the hypothesis that the NEG criterion applies at S-Structure with an analysis of West Flemish, where negative expressions show interesting syntactic constraints, she maintains that it is also adequate for Romance languages, and French in particular. Figure 43 illustrates the case of an object negation.

(43)

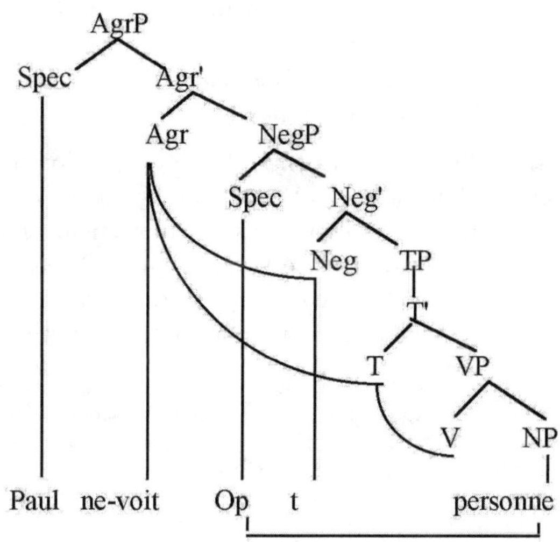


Let us see how this definition of the NEG criterion fares with respect to ND. The ND between *ne* and negative adverbs is relatively straightforward: negative adverbs are in her terms NEG operators, and occur in

the specifier of NegP; since *ne* is moved to AgrP (at least finite *ne*), its trace must count as an X° [NEG]. Nominal negations are more problematic, since they fail to occur in the specifier of NegP. She distinguishes between two cases. If the negation is a subject (*Personne ne voit Paul* 'Nobody sees P.'), the V in Agr is assumed to count as a X° [NEG], by virtue of having amalgamated the head of NegP. Since the subject and Agr are in a Spec-head relation, the NEG criterion is satisfied (p. 211). If the negative word is in the VP, she proposes that the NEG criterion is satisfied by a "representational chain", whose head is a non-overt operator in the Spec of NegP, and whose foot is the negative word (p. 229–230); see 43, where the chain is represented below the words.

The solution is not satisfactory. First, while 'NEG operators' can be seen as negative quantifiers, it is not clear how an X° [NEG] is defined. Second, the Spec-head configuration is satisfied in three different, unconnected ways, which indicates that it is forced onto the data. In particular, the representational chain and the invisible operator are empirically unmotivated. Finally, this version of the NEG criterion completely misses the semantic (scopal) distinction depending on the V which hosts *ne*: as we have seen, the scope of the negation depends on where *ne* occurs; there is a scope distinction between 14a and 14b, repeated below:[33]

(44) a. Paul accepte de ne recevoir personne.
Paul agrees not to see anybody
b. Paul n'accepte de recevoir personne.
Paul does not agree to see anybody

Alternatively, Valois (1997) proposes that the NEG criterion applies at LF: the negative expression moves to the specifier position of NegP at LF (see also Zanuttini 1991). He motivates the movement analysis by pointing out that some constraints are common to ND and an overt movement such as wh-movement (see section 2.2); moreover, as mentioned above, the set of Vs which allow a non local ND is the same as

[33]Haegeman (1995: 29) rejects the idea that *ne* acts as a scope marker, with a surprisingly mistaken argument. Having observed that the scope of *pas* relative to *toujours* depends on their relative positions, she concludes that *ne* does not determine the scope of the negation:

(i) Jean ne se comporte pas toujours bien.
Jean does not always behave well
(ii) Jean ne se comporte toujours pas bien.
Jean still does not behave well

*Ne* determines in which verbal domain the negations are to be interpreted; it has nothing to say regarding the relative scope of different elements within the same domain. On the fact that relative scoping of postverbal adverbs usually follows their order, see Bonami et al., chapter 11, this volume.

that which allow for 'leftward *tous/tout*'. He interprets the partition between Vs in terms of Binding domains (in the antecedent-anaphor or pronoun sense): with 'vouloir verbs' that allow for non-local ND and raised *tous*, the VPinf complement does not constitute a Binding domain, but is merged into the Binding domain of the matrix V. He then proposes that the trace of the negative expression moved at LF to the Spec of NegP (as well as the trace of the bare Q) is an anaphor which must be bound by its antecedent. This is possible if both positions are included in the same Binding domain at LF.

Without going into the account of the constraints on ND (see e.g. Przepiórkowski and Kupść 1999: 217, fn 8) let us point out a number of difficulties with the proposal. First, it is not clear what happens when the negative expression is a subject, since LF movements are not supposed to 'go down'. Second, it is not clear what happens when there are several negative expressions: are there several Specifier positions for NegP? Although not isolated, this hypothesis seems in need of independent justification. Third, and more importantly, this representation does not account for the scope properties of negative expressions *qua* quantifiers. It is usually accepted that quantifier scope is represented at LF (using the rule of Quantifier Raising, which 'covertly' moves the quantifier and adjoins it to IP, in the frameworks under consideration). We could say that negative expressions move 'twice' at LF, first moving to the Spec of NegP, and second adjoining to IP. Valois rightly notes that the second movement undermines the justification for the first. If negative quantifiers are subject to QR, what independent justification is there for the NEG criterion at LF? Yet, the scope of negative expressions cannot be represented adequately by their occurrence in Spec of NegP. Recall, for instance, the ambiguities in 1–2. It is usually assumed that such ambiguities constitute an argument in favor of an LF representation: how are they accounted for in the absence of QR? We conclude that the NEG criterion, which implements the dependency between *ne* and a negative expression as a structural constraint (the two negative elements belong to the same phrase at some level), can only do so at the price of losing the representation of the quantificational properties of negative words. In other words, it is not satisfactory from a semantic point of view.

On the other hand, Déprez (1997) focuses on the quantificational aspect of (standard) French negative expressions. The paper discusses negative concord rather than ND. However, since the two dependencies share the same syntactic and lexical conditions (see section 2.2), the analysis is of interest here. Having contrasted the properties of negative expressions in standard French and Haïtian Creole, Déprez concludes that they are quantifiers in French, although not in Haïtian.[34] Being quantifiers, they get their scope through QR, which adjoins them to some sentential functional projection. In favor of QR, she gives the same evidence used by Valois in favor of LF movement towards the specifier of NegP. This is not surprising, since in both cases we deal with a movement rule. However, as she observes, postulating QR is more attractive for two reasons. First, since the Vs which allow a non local ND also allow bare Q syntactic raising rather than any other kind of argument raising (such as clitic climbing), there is some chance that this property has to do with quantifier scoping. Second, recognizing the role of QR is a step towards understanding NC.

However, the precise syntax-semantics interface remains to be spelled out precisely (it is not sufficient to say that QR is in principle bounded, as she does, to get the conditions enumerated in section 2.1, or to invoke QR to get the grouping of quantifiers which conditions 'pair quantifier formation' in her terms or a polyadic quantifier in de Swart and Sag's terms, in case of NC interpretation). Moreover, regarding the ND problem, we are left without a solution (as observed by Haegeman 1997): what is the relation between the scope as given by QR, and the occurrence of a ne-V? We lack the means to make QR sensitive to the presence of such a V, because QR does not make a distinction between negative expressions and the other quantifiers.

We have examined three solutions in configurational terms to the ND problem. The first, which relies on the NEG criterion at S-Structure, is inadequate. The two others give only partial analyses: one, which appeals to the NEG criterion at LF, is able to state the correlation between a ne-V and the verbal domain where negations are interpreted (although some problems remain), but cannot do justice to their scope properties; the other, which appeals to QR, can in principle deal with the scope properties, but does not account for ND.

## 4 Conclusion

The French negation system appears to spread semantic negation over two elements, the clitic *ne* and negative expressions (*personne, rien* etc.), a phenomenon which we dub 'negative dependency'. We provide criteria that distinguish negative sentences from positive sentences and sentences containing words with a negative flavor, as well as constituent negation; the occurrence of *ne* characterizes sentential negation. We analyze *ne* as an affix, a lexical affix on the finite V, and a phrasal affix

[34]Déprez (1997) proposes that French negations have varying quantificational force, like indefinites. Déprez (2000) concludes that they are quantifiers.

on the VPinf, which does justice both to the commonalities as well as the differences between the two types of occurrences. Furthermore, we adopt the view that words such as *pas, personne* etc. are semantic negations, and more precisely negative quantifiers, while *ne* is a scope marker for negations. Thus, the conditions on negative dependency are analyzed as conditions on the scoping domain of such quantifiers. We examine formal implementations of such conditions in two different approaches, HPSG and GB/Principles and Parameters. The data are amenable to a complete and explicit treatment in HPSG, thanks to its architecture which provides tools for expressing the constraints on the interfaces. On the other hand, transformational approaches distinguish between different levels without always providing the necessary tools for interface problems. The existing analyses aim either at representing the syntax of negative dependency or quantifier scoping, and they do not achieve complete or precise enough representations. It remains to be seen how a new transformational framework, more sensitive to interface problems, can deal with the phenomenon.

## References

Abeillé, Anne, and D. Godard. 1997. The syntax of French negative adverbs. In Forget et al. (1997), pages 1–27.

Abeillé, A. and D. Godard. 1999. A lexical approach to quantifier floating in French. In Webelhuth et al. (1999).

Abeillé, A. and D. Godard. 2000. French word order and lexical weight. In Borsley (2000), pages 325–360.

Abeillé, A. and D. Godard. 2002. The syntax of French auxiliaries. *Language* 78:404–452.

Abeillé, A. and D. Godard. 2003. Les prédicats complexes dans les langues romanes. In Godard (2003).

Amsili, P. 1994. *Calcul de la négation temporelle en français: le cas du terme présuppositionnel ne... plus*. Ph.D. thesis, Université Paul Sabatier.

Attal, P., ed. 1994. *LINX*. Université de Paris X-Nanterre.

Bilger, M., ed. 2000. *Corpus: méthodologie et applications linguistiques*. Paris & Perpignan: H. Champion & Université de Perpignan.

Bok-Bennema, R., B. de Jonge, and B. Kampers-Manhe, eds. 2001. *Adverbial Modification*. Amsterdam: Rodopi.

Borsley, R., ed. 2000. *The nature and function of syntactic categories*, vol. 32 of *Syntax and semantics*. New York: Academic Press.

Borsley, R. and A. Przepiórkowski, eds. 1999. *Slavic in Head-Driven Phrase Structure Grammar*. Stanford: CSLI Publications.

Bouma, G., R. Malouf, and I. A. Sag. 2001. Satisfying constraints on extraction and adjunction. *Natural Language and Linguistic Theory* 19:1–65.

Corblin, F. 1992. Le traitement des complexes négatifs en DRT. In ECCOS (1992), pages 157–175.

Corblin, F. 1994. Sémantique des négatifs multiples. In Attal (1994), pages 278–298.

Corblin, F. 1996. Multiple negation processing in natural language. *Theoria, A Swedish journal of philosophy* pages 214–260.

De Swart, H. 2001. Négation et coordination: la conjonction *ni*. In Bok-Bennema et al. (2001), pages 109–124.

De Swart, H. and I. A. Sag. 2002. Negation and negative concord in Romance. *Linguistics and Philosophy* 25:373–417.

Déprez, V. 1997. A non-unified analysis of negative concord. The syntax of French negative adverbs. In Forget et al. (1997), pages 53–74.

Déprez, V. 2000. Parallel asymmetries and the internal structure of negative expressions. *Natural Language and Linguistic Theory* 18:253–342.

Ducrot, O. 1972. *Dire et ne pas dire*. Paris: Hermann.

ECCOS. 1992. *Actes du colloque ECCOS'92*. Orsay, France.

Emonds, J. 1978. The verbal complex V'-V in French. *Linguistic Inquiry* 9:151–175.

Forget, D., P. Hirschbühler, F. Martineau, and M.-L. Rivero, eds. 1997. *Negation and Polarity*. Amsterdam: John Benjamins.

Gadet, F. 2000. Des corpus pour ne ... pas. In Bilger (2000), pages 156–167.

Giannakidou, A. 1998. *Polarity sensitivity as (non) veridical dependency*. Amsterdam: John Benjamins.

Ginzburg, J. and I. A. Sag. 2000. *Interrogative investigations. The form, meaning and use of English interrogatives*. Stanford: CSLI Publications.

Godard, D., ed. 2003. *Les Langues romanes, problèmes de la phrase simple*. Paris: CNRS Editions).

Haegeman, L. 1995. *The Syntax of negation*. Cambridge: Cambridge University Press.

Haegeman, L. 1997. The syntax of n-words and the Neg criterion. In Forget et al. (1997), pages 115–137.

Haegeman, L. and R. Zanuttini. 1991. Negative heads and the Neg criterion. *The Linguistic Review* 8:233–251.

Haïk, I. 1985. *The syntax of operators*. Ph.D. thesis, MIT.

Hirschbühler, P. and M. Labelle. 1993. Le statut de (ne) pas en français contemporain. *Recherches Linguistiques de Vincennes* 22:31–58.

Horn, L. R. 1989. *A natural history of negation*. Chicago: University of Chicago Press.

Ionescu, E. 1999. A quantification based account of negative concord in Rumanian. In Kruiff and Oehrle (1999), pages 25–27 April.

Jespersen, O. 1924. *The philosophy of grammar*. London: Allen & Unwin.

Kayne, R. 1975. *French Syntax*. Cambridge, MA: MIT Press.

Kayne, R. 1984. *Connectedness and binary branching*. Dordrecht: Foris.

Kim, J. and I. A. Sag. 2002. Negation without head movement. *Natural Language and Linguistic Theory* 20:339–412.

Knüppel, V. 2001. *Die Syntax des Negation im Französischen.* Tübingen: Niemeyer.

Kordoni, V., ed. 1999. *Arbeitspapiere des sonder-forschungsbereichs 340 Bericht Nr 132.* Tübingen Studies in HPSG. Universität Tübingen.

Kruiff, G.-J. and R. Oehrle, eds. 1999. *Proceedings of the Formal Grammar Conference*, Utrecht.

Miller, P. 1992. *Clitics and constituents in Phrase structure grammar.* New York: Garland.

Miller, P. and P. Monachesi. 2003. Les pronoms clitiques dans les langues romanes. In Godard (2003), pages 67–123.

Miller, P. and I. A. Sag. 1997. French clitic movement without clitics or movement. *Natural Language and Linguistic Theory* 15:573–639.

Milner, J.-C. 1979. Le système de la négation en français et l'opacité du sujet. *Langue française 44* pages 80–105.

Milner, J.-C. 1982. *Ordres et raisons de langue.* Paris: Le Seuil.

Muller, C. 1991. *La négation en français.* Genève: Droz.

Pollard, C. and I. Sag. 1994. *Head-driven phrase structure grammar.* Chicago and Stanford: University of Chicago Press and CSLI Publications.

Pollard, C. and E. J. Yoo. 1998. A unified theory of scope for quantifiers and wh-phrases. *Journal of Linguistics* 34:415–445.

Pollock, J.-Y. 1989. Verb movement, UG and the structure of IP. *Linguistic Inquiry* 20:365–424.

Przepiórkowski, A. and A. Kupść. 1999. Eventuality negation and negative concord. In Borsley and Przepiórkowski (1999), pages 211–246.

Recourcé, G. 1996. Une double analyse de la particule *ne*. *Langages* 122:62–78.

Richter, F. and M. Sailer. 1999. A lexicalist collocation analysis of sentential negation and negative concord in French. In Kordoni (1999).

Rizzi, L. 1982. *Issues in Italian syntax.* Dordrecht: Foris Publications.

Valois, D. 1997. Neg-movement and Wh-movement. The syntax of French negative adverbs. In Forget et al. (1997), pages 341–355.

Van der Wouden, T. 1994. *Negative contexts.* Ph.D. thesis, University of Groningen.

Webelhuth, G., J.-P. Koenig, and A. Kathol, eds. 1999. *Lexical and constructional aspects of linguistic explanation.* Stanford: CSLI Publications.

Zanuttini, R. 1991. *Syntactic properties of sentential negation. A comparative study of Romance languages.* Ph.D. thesis, The University of Pennsylvania.

# 18

# Polarity Sensitive Items

LUCIA TOVENA, VIVIANE DÉPREZ, AND JACQUES JAYEZ

## 1 Introduction

The term *polarity sensitive* (PS) items (Baker, 1970) traditionally refers to expressions that need to be licensed by a suitable (positive or negative) trigger within a given domain. Broadly speaking, the context of occurrence of these expressions is modelled by including overt information on polarity along with syntactic and other specifications. For instance, so called Negative Polarity Items (NPI) are felicitous in contexts overtly marked for negation, as shown by the contrast between (1a) and (1b). Note, however, that suitable negative contexts clearly exceed pure manifestations of negation, as shown by the acceptability of (1c).

(1) a. *Elle a dit *quoi que ce soit* d'intéressant.
She said anything interesting
b. Elle n'a pas dit *quoi que ce soit* d'intéressant.
She did not say anything interesting
c. Peu de gens ont dit *quoi que ce soit* d'intéressant
Few people said anything interesting

Approaches to the phenomenon are often cast in terms of licensing, cf. (Baker, 1970; Ladusaw, 1979; Linebarger, 1980; Zwarts, 1981) inter alia, and anti-licensing for positive polarity items (PPIs) (Ladusaw, 1979); yet other views have focused more on the sensitivity of these items to semantic features of the context directly related to properties of their semantic domain (Tovena, 1996b; Giannakidou, 1997). As the bulk of the research has concentrated on the definition of the licensing

*Handbook of French Semantics.*
Francis Corblin and Henriëtte de Swart (eds.).
Copyright © 2004, CSLI Publications.

conditions, the study of the nature of the PS items themselves has often received less attention. Notable exceptions, however, include the work of Fauconnier (1977), Tovena (1996b; 1998), and Israel (1996).

Questions raised by these contextual dependencies can be grouped into three broad categories, depending on whether focus is placed on the PS items themselves, on the dependency or on the context of occurrence of these items.

- What kind of elements can PS items be? Are there lexical, syntactic or semantic limitations on them? What defines/creates their contextual sensitivity?
- What is the nature, the meaning and the form of the relation or dependency into which they seem to enter? Is it local, distant, structural or linear? How does it compare to other relations of similar types in natural language? Should it be captured in syntactic terms, in semantic terms or at the interface of the two components?
- What characterizes the elements or contexts that can be considered as suitable licensers or as meeting the relevant sensitivity requirements of these items? Are they homogeneous or heterogeneous in nature, characterizable in a unified way or not?

All these questions are first and foremost empirical, yet various angles adopted to explore polarity phenomena have often given priority to one of them. Thus, for instance, syntactic accounts have favored a perspective focusing on a licenser-licensee relation, characterizing NPIs as defective elements that need to be licensed by a certain type of licensing element in a particular syntactic relation. They have often emphasized a parallelism between negative dependencies and the ones created by the overt movement of wh–elements. In contrast, semantic accounts have focused more on the nature of semantic factors that PS items are sensitive to, thus showing more interest in the characterization of the items.

In the following sections, we take up the above questions in turn, as we first look at the type of expressions that have been characterized as polarity sensitive in French in section 2, then recall features of the dependency relation in section 3, and finally discuss the types of contexts in which various French PS items can be found in section 4.

## 2 Sensitive items

As in many other languages, polarity sensitive items in French form a motley collection. There seem to be few restrictions on the type of lexical categories PS items can instantiate. As is shown below, these items can be verbs, adjectives, determiners, etc., and even sentential expressions.

At the origin of a classification of a given expression as PS there are various types of linguistic phenomena that are recorded as taking place in contexts of specifically negative or positive polarity. These phenomena are mainly gaps in the distribution and meaning alternations. As noted in Hoeksema (1997), NPIs are often the 'evil negative twin of some innocent nonpolarity item'. In such a case, a classification as NPI aims at capturing the fact that only in negative contexts does the expression acquire an emphatic stereotyped flavor that enhances its information load. For instance, the expression *il n'a pas levé le petit doigt* in its nonpolarity use conveys information on the non actualisation of an action of moving the little finger by a male person. In its polarity use, it also triggers scalar implicatures whereby, the strongest position on the scale being denied, all the other positions on the scale are also denied. Moreover, the action of moving is interpreted as aimed at co-operating in a common goal. So, if he did not do so much as lift a finger, he clearly did not help at all. This operation of stereotyping a rhetorical effect is probably the reason why litotes are often also classified as idiomatic NPIs.

Concerning the range of meanings NPIs can express, some lines of classification seem to emerge. Speakers have intuitions on the domains of the lexicon where NPIs are most likely or most unlikely to occur. For instance, Hoeksema (1994; 1997) argues that expressions of indifference or intolerance are a likely source. However, intuitions seem to be stronger when it comes to ruling out the possibility for a given word to turn into a PS item than when it comes to predict which expressions will indeed turn into polarity sensitive items.

From the data presented below, it will be apparent that the phenomenon of polarity sensitivity in French instantiates both versions described above. Some expressions, that are otherwise quite freely distributed, are seen to take on a particular interpretation or a more salient one in relevant contexts. Other expressions are seen to require such contexts to be interpretable at all, and have as a consequence a rather limited distribution. In this sense, the term PS signals either a change in interpretation, or a distributional restriction linked with licensing contexts. We start our review with NPIs.

## 2.1 Negative polarity

### 2.1.1 Interpretive alternation

In this group we find expressions that can alternate between literal and figurative/idiomatic readings. Only the former is available in non licensing contexts.

- *alternation between literal and idiomatic meaning expressing an understatement*

  (2) Cette procédure n'est pas *très catholique*
  this procedure is not orthodox
  (Fauconnier, 1977)

  (3) ne pas *faire le poids*
  not to compare (not to weigh as much as X)

  - expressions of indifference

    (4) Je n'en ai *rien à cirer, à battre, à faire*
    I don't give a damn

  - intolerance/dislike. Note that the verb *blairer* occurs only in this idiom

    (5) Je ne peux pas *le blairer, l'encadrer, le supporter, l'avaler, le sentir*
    I cannot stand him (I cannot BLAIRER, frame, stand, swallow, smell)

- *modal adjectives* (Fauconnier, 1977)

  (6) C'est une histoire pas *croyable*
  this story is utterly unbelievable

  (7) Il faisait une chaleur pas *tenable*
  it was unbearably hot

- *NP minimizers* (Bolinger, 1972)

  Whenever these expressions occur in non licensing contexts, the possibility of a specific reading of the indefinite NP cannot be ruled out and no scalar inferences are triggered. Schmerling (1971) claims that this type of expression opens up the class of NPIs, making it impossible to characterize in a complete way. However, on the one hand the expression is built on a well–defined pattern, with an indefinite NP designating a minimal unit relevant for the type of action described by the predicate. On the other hand, there is a certain degree of idiomaticity, both in the choice of the N, as shown by the fact that (9b) is perfectly understandable but does not convey the typical scalar inference triggered in (8) and (9a), and in the choice of the verb, as only (11a) triggers the scalar inference, while (11b) doesn't. As noted in Fauconnier (1977), the polarity of these expressions is deduced from their semantic properties rather than being independently marked.

(8) Il n'a pas dit *un mot*
he did not say a word

(9) a. Il n'a pas bu *une goutte*
he did not drink a drop

b. Il n'a pas bu une tasse
he did not drink a cup

(10) ne pas bouger *d'un pouce*, faire *un geste*
not to budge an inch, lift a finger

(11) a. ne pas prendre *une ride*
to remain up–to–date

b. ne pas avoir une ride
not to have a wrinkle

Minimizers are a very important type of expression in French, as they appear to be at the origin of the current system of sentence negation (Schwegler, 1983; Corblin and Tovena, 2001). The negative markers *pas* (not) and *point* (not) and the n-words *personne* (nobody) and *rien* (nothing) are cases of minimizers that have lost the capacity of typing the scale —e.g. *pas* (step) is no longer restricted to scales about quantities of movement— and have acquired the capacity of independently expressing negation. This process of grammaticalisation results also in the loss of gender and number marking.[1]

N-words deserve a special discussion as the type of negative dependencies they illustrate differs quite significantly from that of other NPIs. For instance, in contrast to NPIs, N-words do not require particular contexts to be licensed and induce a logical double negative reading in the presence of the negative *pas*. Yet, their behavior clearly shares certain aspects with that of NPIs when they occur in the scope of other negative elements.[2] For instance, the negative indefinite *rien* differs from *quoi que ce soit*, which is a true NPI, in that it can occur alone in a non-negative contexts as in (12a) and it induces a double negative reading when it cooccurs with *pas* (12c). However, when *rien* cooccurs with another negative indefinite like *personne* its interpretation is then largely equivalent to that of PS *quoi que ce soit*, see (12e), or the other negative indefinite is interpreted as PS item, see (12f).

[1]The appearance of the negative meaning has been claimed to go together with a change of internal syntactic structure by Déprez (1999; 2000).

[2]See Chapter 19 of this book for a more detailed discussion.

(12) a. Qu'as-tu dit? Rien
What did you say? Nothing
b. *J'ai dit quoi que ce soit
c. J'ai pas rien dit (= j'ai dit quelque chose)
I did not say nothing
d. Je n'ai pas dit quoi que ce soit
I didn't say anything
e. Personne n'a rien dit (= n'a dit quoi que ce soit)
Nobody said anything
f. Il n'a rien dit à personne (= n'a rien dit à qui que ce soit)
He did not say anything to anybody

(12e) and (12f) exemplify the so-called negative concord interpretation, whereby the semantic representation is taken to contain a single negation although the corresponding linguistic material seems to include more than one negative expression. This type of negative dependency, mainly restricted to one clausal domain, has given rise to many comparative studies that assimilate them to or distinguish them from other negative polarity dependencies, see Corblin (1994; 1996), Corblin and Derzhanski (1997), Corblin and Tovena (2001), Tovena (1996b; 1996a), Muller (1991), Haegeman (1995), Déprez (1997; 1999; 2000).

- *VP minimizers*

In this group we find expressions that are formed by a negated verb phrase containing a complement that designates a minimal unit. Contrary to the previous case, the complement position need not be instantiated by an indefinite NP. Here the complement NP may well be definite, however it does not have a referential, but rather a quantificational interpretation, in the sense that it identifies the minimal position/quantity on a given scale, see (13)–(14). As shown in (15), it can even be a bare noun.

(13) Il n'a pas *levé le petit doigt*
he did not lift a finger

(14) Daniel ne *se prend* pas *pour la queue de la poire*
Daniel does not think little of himself

(15) Daniel n'a pas *soufflé mot*
Daniel did not say a word

Furthermore, verb and noun do not form default pairs according to standard lexical selectional restrictions, e.g. *say* and *word* in the previous group, therefore they both enter the portion of lexical material that needs to be overtly quoted as constituting the characterized expression. Note also that, although in (13) it is possible to see a metonymy, this is not the case for (14). Thus, the group is in between the case of pure minimizers or sorts of collocations and that of full idioms.

- *degree adverbial expressions*
  These expressions are used to refer to maximal quantities, and the interaction with negation results in the statement being strengthened, as shown in (16)–(18).

(16) Daniel n'a pas *du tout* aimé le concert
Daniel did not like the concert at all

(17) Jamais *de ma vie* je n'aurais cru me trouver dans cette situation
I would never have thought to find myself in such a predicament

(18) *de* + def + time interval
a. Il n'a pas dormi *de la nuit*
he did not sleep at all during the whole night
b. Il n'est pas sorti *de la journée*
he did not go out once in the whole day

On the contrary, *contra* Fauconnier (1977), we would exclude *tout à fait* from the set of NPIs, or at least from the group under discussion, although it might be unacceptable in positive contexts, cf. his contrast in (19a,b). In fact, its interaction with negation results in a slightly weakened rather than enhanced interpretation —in which case a formalisation via a constant function is no longer really suitable— and it can also be used in positive contexts, cf. (19c). Possibly, Fauconnier's characterization can be maintained by restricting it to time expressions containing numbers.[3]

(19) a. Il n'est pas *tout à fait* quatre heures
it is not yet quite four o'clock
b. *Il est tout à fait quatre-heures
c. Il est *tout à fait* sympatique
he is really nice

- *double negative (a case of litote)*
  As for these expressions, the stereotyped rhetorical effect results in a strong assertion of the predicate that is doubly denied, cf. (20).

[3]A search in Frantext returned 7 examples with *tout à fait+jour* all positive, 42 examples with *tout à fait+nuit*, 37 of which are positive, and 5 examples with *tout à fait+n heure* all negative. Thanks to Pascal Amsili for the data.

(20) a. Il *ne se fera pas faute* de lui répondre
not he will not shy from answering him back

b. *Il se fera faute de lui répondre

In the case of (21), the litote is an NPI only when it takes an infinitival S complement. The form with an NP complement is not polarity sensitive, cf. (22).

(21) Daniel *ne* va *pas se priver* de le critiquer.
Daniel will makes no bones about criticising him

(22) a. Daniel ne va pas se priver de dessert.
Daniel will not deprive himself of dessert

b. Daniel va se priver de dessert pendant le Carême.
Daniel will deprive himself of dessert during Lent

### 2.1.2 Restricted distribution

In this group we find expressions that are either strictly parts of idioms, or not interpretable in non licensing contexts.

- *idioms expressing indifference*

(23) a. Daniel n'a pas *bronché*
Daniel did not react

b. *Daniel a bronché

(24) Il n'a pas *moufté*
he did not answer

- *degree expressions*

(25) Daniel n'a pas fait *grand-chose*
Daniel didn't do much

(26) Il n'y avait pas *grand-monde*
there weren't many people

- indefinites
Several different quantifiers or determiners make up this group, for instance *qui/quoi que ce soit* (who/what it may be), cf. (27) adapted from Muller (1991).

(27) a. Daniel n'a pas rencontré *qui que ce soit*
Daniel did not meet anybody

b. *Daniel a rencontré *qui que ce soit*

c. Si *quoi que ce soit* vous dérange, faites-le nous savoir
if anything bothers you, let us know it

Muller also puts in this group the so–called generic use of *tout*[4] (all/every), which can occur in the NP complement of a negative predicate and cannot occur in positive contexts, cf. his examples (28a,b). Note however that, contra the standard case for PS items, this use of *tout* is not available in the scope of an overt negation, cf. (28c). This type of impossibility is a typical feature of free choice items.[5]

(28) a. Luc a perdu *tout* bon sens
Luc lost all his common sense
b. *Luc a recouvré *tout* bon sens
c. *Luc n'a plus *tout* bon sens

- *adverbial* (Gaatone, 1971)

(29) a. Daniel n'a pas protesté *pour autant*
Daniel did not protest, for that matter
b. *Daniel a protesté *pour autant*
c. La question est-elle résolue *pour autant*?
has the issue been settled, for that matter?

The polarity of this expression tends to disappear in spoken French, where *pour autant* is used like *cependant*, cf. the TV quote in (30).

(30) Pour autant le gouvernement a décidé de maintenir son projet.
However, the government decided to keep its project

## 2.2 Positive polarity

The class of PPIs is less well-established in the literature. If accepted, it covers two cases. First, it gathers together cases of restricted distribution of non literal readings, as does its negative polarity counterpart. Second, unlike the negative counterpart, it does not cover cases of holes in the distribution of given items, but rather just those of items exhibiting a strong preference for outscoping negation. As a matter of fact, PPIs do not have licensers, but they seem to be anti-licensed by the very element *not*. Furthermore, instead of being ungrammatical in the scope of negation, PPIs force a reading of negated sentences as contradiction or denial of affirmative propositions, and not as containing negative propositions (Ladusaw, 1979).

---

[4]In this use, *tout* is followed directly by an N′. No determiner can occur in between. See the discussion in (Tovena and Jayez, 1999b) and the proposal they advance in chapter 5 in part I of this volume.

[5]In particular, for an analysis of this use of *tout* in terms of free choiceness, see (Jayez and Tovena, (to appear) and the discussion in chapter 5 in part I of this volume.

### 2.2.1 Restricted readings

- *literal vs. non–literal reading alternation* (Fauconnier, 1977)

(31) a. Gaston *aimerait mieux* se reposer
Gaston would rather have a rest

b. *Gaston n'*aimerait* pas *mieux* se reposer
Gaston wouldn'd rather have a rest

(32) J'en suis *bien aise*
I am delighted

### 2.2.2 Missed complementation

- *adverbs of temporal perspective*

Here negation does not produce the scalar reversal effect we have come to know, altering the focus of the expression, but simply falsifies the sentence, cf. (33) that replicates for French the alternation discussed by Baker (1970) with respect to *already*.

(33) a. Il est *déjà* parti
he has already left

b. ?Il n'est pas déjà parti (il était même en retard)
he has not already left (actually he was late)

- *existential*

Example (34) shows the French analogue of *some* discussed by Baker. If accepted, (34b) is interpreted with the existential outscoping negation.

(34) a. Il a vu *quelqu'un*
he saw someone

b. ?Il n'a pas vu *quelqu'un* (une personne en particulier)
he did not see someone (a particular person)

## 2.3 Free choice

Historically, the discussion of free choice (FC) items is part of the study of PS items, but recently new analyses have been proposed that treat them as an independent class concerned by referential issues rather than structural licensing conditions. Contrary to PS items, FCIs belong only to the syntactic or semantic category of determiners. Jayez and Tovena (2000; (to appear)) show that they originate from existential e.g. *n'importe quel* 'no matter which', as well as universal expressions, e.g. *tout* 'any'. They are fine under modals of possibility (35a), imperatives (35d), generics (36a) and comparative constructions (36c), and out in episodic sentences (35b), negative clauses (35c), leaving aside the double negation interpretation 'it is false he didn't choose a specific card' discussed below with respect to (37), and questions (36b).

(35) a. Il peut prendre *n'importe quelle* carte
he can take any card
b. *Il a pris n'importe quelle carte
c. *Il n'a pas pris n'importe quelle carte
d. Prend n'importe quelle carte
Take any card

(36) a. *Tout* chat chasse les souris
Any cat hunts mice
b. *Est-ce que Marie aime tout chat?
c. Marie a mieux réussi que toute autre élève de la classe
Mary did better than any other pupil in the class

Like FC *any*, French FC items can have an indiscriminative reading (Horn, 2000) in negative contexts, cf. (37).

(37) Je n'ai pas vu *n'importe qui.*
I did not see (just) anybody

Next, a suitable modifier can rescue a FCI in episodic sentences, the phenomenon known as subtrigging, cf. (38).

(38) a. *Tout étudiant a été renvoyé
Any student was dismissed
b. Tout étudiant qui avait triché a été renvoyé
Any student who had cheated was dismissed

Finally, FCIs can be based on scalar implicatures of the type studied by Fauconnier, and more recently by Israel, e.g. *le moindre.* Here the widening effect described by Kadmon and Landman (1993) is the reflection of a scalar concessive value. However, scalarity is not an essential component of free choiceness, as shown by the cases of *n'importe quel* and *tout.*

## 2.4 Polarity sensitive and free choice

French has at least one clear case of an expression which is both polarity sensitive and free choice, namely *le moindre* (the least). It is a synthetic superlative that can denote the endpoint, the strongest position in scales where inferences run in either directions. This case, discussed in Tovena and Jayez (1999a; (to appear), falsifies Fauconnier's (1977, p.9) claim that superlatives that can have a quantificational value of top of a pragmatic scale in positive (negative) sentences, cannot also have the same value of top of the scale in negative (respectively positive) sentences. As shown in (39), *le moindre* points to the top of a positive scale of inferences in (39a), and to the top of a negative scale of inferences in (39b). If we extend to this expression the traditional characterization of *any*, a step that seems supported by the grammaticality of the English glosses, we should consider it both an NPI and a FC expression.

(39) a. Il connaît *le moindre* recoin de la région
he knows any spot in the area around
b. Il n'a pas pris *la moindre* précaution
he did not take any precautions

## 3 On the dependency relation

Examples such as (40) raise the question whether there is a linear dependency between a PS expression and its licenser, that can be expressed in terms of precedence. The issue could also be formulated in terms of a functional dependency, e.g. in terms of a sujet/objet asymmetry, contrast, as in (40) vs. (41a). The lack of contrast in (41), however, goes against this type of description.

(40) a. *Quoi que ce soit d'intéressant ne sera pas révélé à la presse
Anything interesting will not be revealed to the press
b. *La découverte de quoi que ce soit d'intéressant n'a pas été révélée à la presse.
The discovery of anything interesting was not revealed to the press

(41) a. Cet étudiant qui a bien écouté ne croit pas qu'elle va dire quoi que ce soit d'intéressant.
The student who listened well does not believe she will say anything interesting
b. Cet étudiant qui a bien écouté ne croit pas que quoi que ce soit d'intéressant sera dit à cette réunion
The student who listened well does not believe that anything interesting will be said at this meeting

In (41), the negative and the NPI are not clausemates. Negation can occur in the matrix clause and the NPI in the nested one, while the reverse situation leads to unacceptability. However, the presence of a neg-raising verb may be instrumental for cross-clausal boundary licensing, see the marginality of (42) contra (41).

(42) ??Cet étudiant qui a bien écouté ne dit pas que quoi que ce soit d'intéressant sera discuté à cette réunion

In any case, the issue cannot be recast just in terms of a structural/hierarchical dependency, saying that an NPI must be in the scope of a licenser. Indeed, by looking at the sentences in (43) one might draw the conclusion that an NPI is acceptable only if it occurs in the syntactic scope of a negative element, where traditionally the scope relation is defined via c-command. However, exceptions, such as (44) from Linebarger (1980), have been around for a while. They correspond to cases where the indefinite in subject position cannot receive a specific interpretation (Tovena, 1996b, pp.189–193).

(43) a. *Cet étudiant qui n'a pas bien écouté croit qu'elle va dire quoi que ce soit d'intéressant
The student who did not listened believes she will say anything interesting

b. Il n'y a pas d'étudiants qui croient qu'elle va dire quoi que ce soit d'intéressant
There isn't a student who believes that she will say anything interesting

(44) A doctor who knew anything about acupuncture was not available

Reconstruction can be invoked to deal with (44), i.e. the subject of a stage-level predicate may be said to move back to a position inside the VP and thereby to end up inside the scope of negation. Thus, (44) may be rejected as a proper counter–example.

However in recent work, Hoeksema (2000) has put forward a whole set of cases that question precisely a characterization of the relevant scope relation in terms of syntactic c-command, and argues that such a formalization is probably on the wrong track. He argues that the c-command hierarchy seems to work because, in some simple cases, it coincides with semantic scope, i.e. the hierarchy of operators.

### 3.1 Hoeksema's tests

In the following we test whether Hoeksema's observations bear consequences also on the evaluation of the relevance of the c-command condition for French.

1. *Coordination*
   A prediction based on the c-command condition says that NPIs and their triggers cannot be coordinated. This seems to be supported by (45).

   (45) a. *No/Few professor(s) and any student were at the party

   b. *Aucun/Nul ministre et le moindre secrétaire d'état n'était au courant

But there is an asymmetry problem with (46) and (47)[6]. If I meet every professor, (47) becomes true while (46a), (46b) and (46c) are false. This difference in truth conditions tells us that the scope of negation is different in the two examples. In one case it is $\neg(\exists \vee \exists)$ and in the other it is $\neg\exists \vee \forall$. This difference cannot be expressed in terms of c–command.

(46) a. Je n'ai pas rencontré de professeur ou qui que ce soit (d'autre)
I didn't meet a professor or anybody else

b. Je n'ai rencontré aucun professeur ou qui que ce soit d'autre
I met no professor nor anybody else

c. Je n'ai pas rencontré de professeur ou, d'ailleurs, le moindre responsable du département
I didn't meet a professor nor, for that matter, any person in charge of the department

(47) Je ne rencontrerai aucun professeur ou chaque professeur
I will meet no professor or each professor

2. *Topicalization*
The prediction based on the c-command condition is that NPIs cannot be topicalized (at least when they leapfrog negation).

(a) A first case showing the unacceptable result of topicalizing is provided in (48). However, adding some material may improve the sentence, cf. (49) and the pair (50)–(51) for French.

(48) *Any student, I didn't see.

(49) That he cares about any student, I had not expected

(50) a. *Le moindre étudiant, je ne l'ai pas vu

b. *Une question quelconque, je ne l'ai pas posée/ je ne m'y attendais pas

[6]Sentence (46c) is slightly clumsy, a preferred alternative could be *Je n'ai pas rencontré de professeur, ni, d'ailleurs, le moindre responsable du département.*

(51) a. Qu'il s'intéresse au moindre étudiant, ça me surprendrait
That he cares for the least student, it would surprise me

b. Qu'il me pose une question quelconque, j'en serais ravi
That he ask me a question, just any, and I would be delighted

Of course the semantic construal should give something like 'I would be surprised/delighted that ... NPI ...'.

(b) There seems to be no 'equivalent' to the auxiliary-like use of *need* discussed by Hoeksema, which sometimes is qualified as an instance of PS behavior, see the following English and French pairs.

(52) a. You need say no more

b. Il n'est pas besoin d'en dire plus

(53) a. I can stand it no more

b. Je ne peux plus supporter ça

This is not surprising since N–words and negative quantifiers pattern differently in French and English.

(c) Under the header of adverbial NPIs Hoeksema discusses a case exemplified in French by the expression *jusqu'ici*, see the contrast in (54).

(54) a. Jusqu'ici, rien n'a filtré
As yet we haven't heard anything

b. *Jusqu'ici quelque chose a filtré
As yet we have heard something

It is easy to build examples in the same vein with expressions such as *avec la meilleure volonté du monde*, etc.

3. As for the subject–object asymmetry, there are two main problems.

(a) It turns out (Linebarger's observation) that sentences are fine when we can infer a $\neg\exists$ reading. Example (44) is paralleled in French by (55).

(55) Un médecin ayant la moindre connaissance/une connaissance quelconque de l'acupuncture se révéla impossible à trouver.

(b) For the various intervention effects, one must check first that the dominant reading is really a licensing one. For (56a), the reading is 'it is not true that she said anything to each student', *chaque* (each) resists taking wide scope, so we get the representation in (56b).

(56) a. Elle n'a pas dit quoi que ce soit à chaque étudiant
she didn't say anything to each student

b. $\neg\forall x(x \text{ is a student } \Rightarrow \phi)$

Now, $\phi$ is the offending 'she said anything'. It has been observed by Szabolcsi and Zwarts (1993) and Zwarts (1995) that a definite determiner acts as an intervenor. Hoeksema expresses some doubts, but example (57) sounds more robust, (*pace* Hoeksema). However, the NP *the man who has ever V–ed me* is likely to block semantic licensing.

(57) I wouldn't kill the man who has ever helped me

One obtains $\neg\phi(\imath x.\ \psi(x, \ldots \text{NPI} \ldots))$ and, more specifically $\neg\phi(\imath x.\ \exists e(e = x \text{ helped me}))$. Again, we have the offending form $\exists\ldots$ instead of $\neg\exists$. The point is that iota–operators do not combine with negation, thus *no man* gives $\neg\exists$, but there is no way to get '... not ... the man ...' producing such a combination. Variation is possible when *the* is interpreted as a sort of FC ('the man (whoever he is)'), cf. (58).

(58) Je me refuse à nuire à l'homme, quel qu'il soit, qui ait/aurait eu la moindre influence bénéfique sur l'économie du pays.

4. *VP–internal asymmetries*

The idea behind this case is that in some (Dutch) cases the NPI is outside the scope of the negative element. English seems to resist such constructions. If we consider the Dutch example in (59a) and its French counterparts in (59b) and (59c), the question is whether we are going to consider *ne* as really expletive in French, i.e. if or when it does not count as negative.

(59) a. Ik geef de student die *ook maar* één tentamen verzuimt geen enkel kans
I don't give the student who misses as much as one exam a chance

b. (?) Je ne donne à l'étudiant qui manque le moindre examen aucun chance

c. (?) Je ne donne à l'étudiant qui manque ne serait-ce qu'un examen aucune chance

Maybe (60a) is more telling, where negation is expressed by a negative predicate. However, one should keep in mind that *le moindre* in (60a) might be the FC (universal) rather than the

PS one, as suggested by the possible substitution of *tout* for *le moindre*, cf. (60b).[7]

(60) a. Je refuse à l'étudiant qui manque ne serait-ce qu'un examen la moindre chance (supplémentaire)

b. Je refuse toute chance (supplémentaire) à l'étudiant qui manque ne serait-ce qu'un examen

5. *Pseudo-clefts 'break' the c–command relation*

(61) a. What was missing/was not required was any real interest in the problem

b. Ce qui manquait/n'était pas indispensable était un intérêt quelconque pour le problème.

Two remarks are in order. First, it is not clear whether it is possible to have *le moindre* in this type of context. Second, note also that Hoeksema's argument depends crucially on the (standard) assumption that, in pseudo–clefts, the subject appears outside the wh–clause.

In conclusion, French data mainly support Hoeksema's criticisms against the use of c-command for a proper characterisation of the relevant scope relations.

## 4 The nature of licensing elements and environments

### 4.1 Negative polarity

With respect to the issue of how to characterize elements and environments that can license PS items, two main trends of analysis have been developed in the literature. One of them takes negative contexts as the main NPI licensing environment, and works to reduce the other cases to this one. Such a strategy has been exploited mainly in syntactic approaches. The methods used for reducing different cases to the main one vary widely. Baker (1970) proposes a semantically motivated procedure for carving out of the representation of a sentence —containing an acceptable occurrence of an NPI but no negation— a suitable subset that satisfies the principle ruling the main case. His procedure invokes a relation of entailment between propositions. However, the proposal is weakened by the fact that the operation of carving out a subset is not defined because there is no indication of what counts as a legitimate subset. Instead, Linebarger (1980) invokes a negative conversational implicature as indirect licensing mechanism for NPIs. The change from a semantic to a pragmatic account is due to the conviction that the exist-

[7]Recall that *tout* can be treated as FC in its so-called generic usage, but it never qualifies as NPI.

ence of pairs of sentences such as those defined by Baker is not sufficient guarantee for the acceptability of NPIs, rather one must take into consideration the appropriateness of uttering a given sentence. However, her proposal has been shown to be too general. For instance, certain contexts of negative implicature do not act as licensers, e.g. although we have the implicature 'some → not all', *some* does not work as licenser. Similarly, logical double negation may be assumed rather freely, almost any context can be assumed to have a negative implicature and therefore should be a licenser, contrary to fact.

The other trend puts downward monotonicity at the heart of the phenomenon, and treats negation as one of its subcases. This strategy has been exploited mainly in semantic approaches (Fauconnier 1977, Ladusaw 1979, Zwarts 1981, Dowty 1993). The licensing power is not just a feature associated with a morpheme. Monotonicity properties can be asserted separately for each argument of a determiner in a generalized quantifier approach. The pair in (62) shows that *chaque*, being monotone decreasing in its first argument and increasing in its second, licenses only its restrictor, cf. (62a), while *aucun* always licenses NPIs, being decreasing in both arguments, and *quelque* never does, being increasing in both arguments.

(62) a. { *Aucun* / *Chaque* / **Quelques* } étudiant(s) qui avai(en)t quoi que ce soit d'intéressant à dire a (ont) participé à la réunion.

b. { *Aucun* / **Chaque* / **Quelques* } étudiant(s) avai(en)t quoi que ce soit d'intéressant à dire.

Several classical licensing contexts have been analyzed as containing downward monotonic functions.

- predicate negation

  (63) Daniel n'a pas fait *grand-chose*
  Daniel didn't do much

- overt and covert conditionals

  (64) a. Si tu dis *quoi que ce soit*, je t'étripe.
  if you say a word I kill you

  b. Tu dis *quoi que ce soit* (et) je t'étripe.
  Say a single word and I kill you

- downward monotone determiners

  (65) ??Peu de gens ont fait *grand-chose*

few people did much

- n-words

(66) Personne a fait *grand-chose*
nobody did much

- *sans* (without)

(67) Il parle sans dire *grand-chose*
he speaks without saying much

- *avant de* (before)

(68) Il parle avant d'avoir compris *grand-chose*
he speaks before he has understood much

- comparative

(69) Marie a couru plus vite que *qui que ce soit* d'autre dans sa classe
Marie ran faster than anybody else in her class

- *too*-like expressions

(70) Il est bien trop fatigué pour parler à *qui que ce soit*
he is far too tired to talk to anybody

Zwarts (1996) has shown that not all NPIs are satisfied with just downward monotonic functions. Some require a stronger form of negativity. This variation is found in French too, as recorded in table 4.1, overleaf.

However, there are licensing contexts that cannot be easily reduced to downward monotonic functions. Questions are a traditional example.[8]

(71) a. A-t-il lu *le moindre* livre cette année?
did he read any book this year?
b. Est-ce que tu as compris *quoi que ce soit* à ce qu'elle nous a raconté?
Did you understand anything at all in what she told us?

Modals are another problematic context. Only modals of possibility seem to be able to license, whereas modals of necessity cannot, cf. (72). However, Horn (2000) notes that *any* is (unexpectedly) anomalous in sentences like (73). The same difference exists in French, cf. (74).

(72) a. Il peut parler à n'importe qui
he may talk to anybody
b. *Il doit prendre n'importe quelle carte
he must take any card

[8]But see (Gutiérrez-Rexach, 1996) for a different view.

|  | neg | n-wd | qu | cond | ↓ mon | modal | *sans* | *avant* | compar |
|---|---|---|---|---|---|---|---|---|---|
| *grand-chose* | yes | yes | */? | * | ? | * | yes | yes | * |
| *catholique* | yes | yes | * | * | * | * |  |  |  |
| *croyable* | yes | yes | * | * | * | * |  |  |  |
| *un mot* | yes | yes | * | yes | * | * | yes | yes | * |
| *lever le petit doigt* | yes | yes | yes | yes | * | * | yes | yes | * |
| *broncher* | yes | yes | yes | yes | * | * | yes | * | * |
| *du tout* | yes |  | * | * |  |  |  |  |  |
| *de*+def/poss+time int. | yes | ? | * | * | * | * | yes | * |  |
| *encore* | yes | * | * | * | * | * |  |  | * |
| *qui que ce soit* | yes | yes | yes | yes | yes | yes | yes | yes | yes |

TABLE 4.1 Variation in French NPIs

(73) a. It is possible that you meet ??anybody
b. You might meet anybody

(74) a. Il est possible que tu rencontres ??*n'importe qui*
b. Tu pourrais rencontrer *n'importe qui*

## 4.2 Positive polarity

The distribution of PPIs is generally captured via the notion of anti-licensing. For instance, instead of providing a positive rule, Ladusaw (1979) says that they cannot occur in the scope of negation. As it appears from the set of cases presented below, negation seems to be the only consistent anti-licenser.

- negation

  (75) *Daniel n'*aime* pas *mieux* voyager en train
  Daniel would not rather travel by train

- question

  (76) Est-ce que Daniel *aime mieux* voyager en train?
  Would Daniel rather travel by train?

- conditional

  (77) Si Daniel *aime mieux* voyager en train, Luise ne l'accompagnera pas
  If Daniel would rather travel by train, Louise won't go with him

- downward monotone

  (78) Peu d'enfants *aiment mieux* voyager en train
  Few children would rather travel by train

- n-word

  (79) Personne n'*aime mieux* voyager en train
  Nobody would rather travel by train

## 4.3 Free choice

For a certain time, the distribution of free choice items was merely considered not to be subject to specific constraints, see for instance Carlson (1981). But it has recently received considerably more attention. It appears that the notion of intensional quantification or variation play an important role. This notion has been recast in terms of modal force in Eisner (1995), Dayal (1998), or of possible substitution in Tovena and Jayez (1997), Jayez and Tovena (2000), Giannakidou (1997; 2001). Zwarts (1995) proposes that the notion of *non veridicality* is the crucial criterion for characterizing contexts suitable for polarity sensitive and free choice *any*. Giannakidou (1997) generalizes it to all NPIs and all FCIs and proposes abandoning the notion of downward entailment altogether. Non emphatic Greek items like *kanenas* 'nobody/anybody' or *pote* (never/ever) are treated as NPIs licensed by non-veridical contexts. When they bear an emphatic accent, these items must be in the scope of an averidical operator and behave mostly like n-words in a negative concord language. However, Giannakidou's claims do not hold for French.

In French, the situation is more complex. The distribution of items which require non-veridicality is not so uniform. For instance, *un* N *quelconque* is perfect with negative sentences, see (80a) and questions (80b), two contexts she classifies as nonveridical episodic. Another example, containing an idiomatic NPI, is provided in (81).[9]

(80) a. Jean n'a pas lu *un* livre *quelconque* cette année
John didn't read a single book this year
b. Jean a–t–il lu *un* livre *quelconque* cette année?
Did John read any book this year?

(81) a. Il n'a pas *levé le petit doigt*
He didn't lift a finger
b. A–t–il seulement *levé le petit doigt*?
Did he lift a finger?

On the contrary, *un* N *quelconque* is not very natural in generic sentences, cf. (82), which she considers non-episodic, see also (83) with an idiomatic NPI.

(82) ??Un chat quelconque chasse les souris

(83) a. Dans la vie, le plus petit effort est récompensé
In life, the slightest effort is rewarded
b. Dans la vie, ?? lever le petit doigt (pour un ami) est récompensé

Note that the characterization of generic contexts as non-veridical is not uncontroversial (Jayez and Tovena, 2000). It rests more on the choice of the genericity theory adopted than on clear evidence.

## 5 Concluding remarks

In conclusion, French exhibits a large collection of PS items. NPIs belong to several syntactic categories and come in two main types: expressions with gaps in the distribution and expressions that, when occurring in licensing contexts, acquire an emphatic stereotyped flavor

[9]Note however that *seulement* helps to improve interrogative/hypothetical examples where the NPI in isolation might not sound very natural *(?/??) A–t–il levé le petit doigt pour toi?*.

that enhances their informational role. Licensing contexts broadly correspond to the collection of environments standardly identified via the property of downward monotonicity, although this property is insufficient for their fine semantic characterization. The syntactic relation of c-command is equally insufficient for characterizing all suitable configurations.

PPIs are a small collection of expressions that exhibit strong scoping preferences with respect to overt negation, that may lead to unacceptability when violated.

French NPIs and PPIs seem to conform rather closely to the descriptions given for items from other languages. However, French FCIs make up a set that more directly challenges analyses proposed in the literature. They appear to require an approach where variation, intensionality and non-veridicality are facets of a more abstract property of nonindividuation (Jayez and Tovena, (to appear)), and not crucial characterizing features.

## References


Attal, P., ed. 1994. *La négation*. Paris: LINX.

Baker, C. L. 1970. Double negatives. *Linguistic Inquiry* 1:169–186.

Beals, K., ed. 1993. *Twenty-ninth Regional Meeting of the Chicago Linguistics Society*. Chicago.

Bolinger, D. 1972. *Degree Words*. The Hague: Mouton.

Carlson, G. N. 1981. Distribution of Free-Choice *Any*. In Hendrick et al. (1981), pages 8–23.

Corblin, F. 1994. Sémantique des négatifs multiples. In Attal (1994), pages 279–298.

Corblin, F. 1996. Multiple negation processing in Natural Language. *Theoria* 17:214–259.

Corblin, F. and I. Derzhanski. 1997. Multiple negation, optional arguments and the reification of eventualities. In Corblin and Marandin (1997).

Corblin, F. and J.-M. Marandin, eds. 1997. *Empirical issues in Formal Syntax and Semantics*, vol. I. Berne: Peter Lang.

Corblin, F., J.-M. Marandin, and C. D.-Sorin, eds. 1999. *Empirical issues in formal syntax and semantics II*. The Hague: Holland Academic Graphic.

Corblin, F. and L. Tovena. 2001. On the multiple expression of negation in Romance. In D'Hulst et al. (2001), pages 83–115.

Dayal, V. 1998. ANY as inherently modal. *Linguistics and Philosophy* 21:433–476.

DeGraff, M., ed. 1999. *Language creation and language change*. Cambridge: MIT Press.

Déprez, V. 1997. A non unified analysis of negative concord. In Forget et al. (1997), pages 53–74.

Déprez, V. 1999. The roots of negative concord in French and French based creoles. In DeGraff (1999), pages 329–375.

Déprez, V. 2000. Parallel (A)symmetries and the structure of negative expressions. *Natural Language and Linguistic Theory* 18:253–342.

D'Hulst, Y., J. Rooryck, and J. Schroten, eds. 2001. *Going Romance 1999: selected papers*, Amsterdam. John Benjamins.

Dowty, D. R. 1993. Deductive versus semantic accounts of reasoning: the relevance of negative polarity and negative concord marking. In Beals (1993), pages 91–124.

Eisner, J. 1995. '∀'-less in wonderland. In ESCOL (1995), pages 92–103.

ESCOL. 1995. *Proceedings of ESCOL '94*. CLC Publications.

ESCOL. 1996. *Proceedings of ESCOL '96*. CLC Publications.

Fauconnier, G. 1977. Polarité syntaxique et sémantique. *Linguisticæ Investigationes* 1:1–38.

Forget, D., P. Hirshbulher, F. Martineau, and M.-L. Rivero, eds. 1997. *Negation and Polarity*. Amsterdam: John Benjamin.

Gaatone, D. 1971. *Etude descriptive du système de la négation en français contemporain*. Genève: Droz.

Giannakidou, A. 1997. *The Landscape of Polarity Items*. Ph.D. thesis, University of Groningen.

Giannakidou, A. 2001. The meaning of free choice. *Linguistics and Philosophy* 24:659–735.

Gutiérrez-Rexach, J. 1996. Negative polarity licensing and the rhetorical interpretation of questions. In *Proceedings of the Western States Conference on Linguistics*.

Haegeman, L. 1995. *The syntax of negation*. Cambridge: Cambridge University Press.

Hendrick, R., C. Masek, and M. Miller, eds. 1981. *Seventeenth Regional Meeting of the Chicago Linguistics Society*. Chicago: University of Chicago.

Hoeksema, J. 1994. *On the grammaticalization of negative polarity items*. Berkeley: Berkeley Linguistic Society.

Hoeksema, J. 1997. Corpus study of negative polarity items. In *IV-V Jornades de corpus linguistics 1996-1997*. Available from `http://odur.let.rug.nl/~hoeksema/docs/barcelona.html`.

Hoeksema, J. 2000. Negative polarity items: Triggering, scope, and C-command. In Horn and Kato (2000), pages 115–146.

Horn, L. and Y. Kato, eds. 2000. *Negation and Polarity*. Oxford: Oxford University Press.

Horn, L. R. 2000. Pick a theory, not just *any* theory. In Horn and Kato (2000), pages 147–192.

Israel, M. 1996. Polarity sensitivity as lexical semantics. *Linguistics and Philosophy* 19:619–666.

Jayez, J. and L. M. Tovena. 2000. Free–Choiceness as non–locality specification. Talk delivered at *(Preferably) non–lexical semantics*, Paris, available from `http://pweb.ens-lsh.fr/jjayez/`.

Jayez, J. and L. M. Tovena. (to appear). Free–Choiceness and Non Individuation. *Linguistics and Philosophy* .

Kadmon, N. and F. Landman. 1993. *Any*. *Linguistics and Philosophy* 16:353–422.

Ladusaw, W. A. 1979. Polarity sensitivity as inherent scope relations. published by Garland Publishing Inc., 1980, University of Texas at Austin.

Linebarger, M. C. 1980. The grammar of negative polarity. Published by Indiana University Linguistics Club, 1981, Massachusetts Institute of Technology.

Muller, C. 1991. *La négation en français*. Genève: Droz.

Reichler-Béguelin, M.-J., ed. 1999. *Référence temporelle et nominale*. Berne: Peter Lang.

Schmerling, S. F. 1971. A note on negative polarity. *Papers in Linguistics* 4:200–206.

Schwegler, A. 1983. Predicate negation and word-order change: a problem of multiple causation. *Lingua* 61:297–334.

Szabolcsi, A. and F. Zwarts. 1993. Weak islands and an algebraic semantics for scope taking. *Natural language semantics* 1:235–284.

Tovena, L. M. 1996a. Negative concord, events and negative chains. In ESCOL (1996), pages 313–322.

Tovena, L. M. 1996b. *Studies on Polarity Sensitivity*. Ph.D. thesis, University of Edinburgh.

Tovena, L. M. 1998. *The fine structure of Polarity Sensitivity*. New York: Garland.

Tovena, L. M. and J. Jayez. 1997. The modal arbitrariness of *any*. ms Université de Genève and EHESS Paris.

Tovena, L. M. and J. Jayez. 1999a. *Any*: from scalarity to arbitrariness. In Corblin et al. (1999), pages 39–57.

Tovena, L. M. and J. Jayez. 1999b. Déterminants et irréférence. l'exemple de *tout*. In Reichler-Béguelin (1999), pages 235–268.

Wansing, H., ed. 1996. *Negation*. Berlin: Walter de Gruyter.

Zwarts, F. 1981. Negatief polaire uitdrukkingen 1. *Glot* 4:35–132.

Zwarts, F. 1995. Nonveridical contexts. *Linguistic Analysis* 25:286–312.

Zwarts, F. 1996. A hierarchy of negative expressions. In Wansing (1996).

19

# Negative Concord

FRANCIS CORBLIN, VIVIANE DÉPREZ,
HENRIËTTE DE SWART, AND LUCIA TOVENA

## 1 Data: possibilities and impossibilities of negative concord

Negative concord is the general term for cases where multiple occurrences of negative constituents express a single negation. To our knowledge, the term was first introduced by Baker (1970). Labov (1972) also uses it in his work on African American English. Since then, the term has been used for related phenomena in different languages. This chapter starts with an inventory of the expressions that do (*personne* 'no one', *rien* 'nothing', *plus* 'more', *jamais* 'never', *nulle part* 'nowhere', *sans* 'without', ...) and that don't (*pas* 'not') participate in negative concord in standard modern French, and a discussion of their syntactic and combinatory properties (section 1). We continue with a characterization of concord items in relation to negative polarity items (NPIs), and discuss the existence of double negation readings (section 2). In the literature, we find several analyses of negative concord. We introduce the most influential ones, and discuss their strength and weakness as far as their application to French is concerned (section 3).

The phenomenon of negative concord is exemplified in (1):

(1) a. Personne n'a rien vu.
No one NE has nothing seen.
'No one saw anything.'

b. Personne n'a jamais rien pu y faire.

*Handbook of French Semantics.*
Francis Corblin and Henriëtte de Swart (eds.).
Copyright © 2004, CSLI Publications.

No one has ever been able to do anything about it
(Muller 1991: 268)

c. Personne n'a aucune faute à se reprocher.
No one needs to blame himself for anything.
(Muller 1991: 268)

d. Ni Pierre ni Luc n'ont nullement l'intention de démissionner.
Neither Pierre nor Luc have at all the intention to step down.
(Muller 1991: 270)

e. Pierre est parti sans rien dire à personne.
Pierre has left without nothing say to no one.
'Pierre left without saying anything to anyone.'

f. Plus personne n'écoute plus jamais personne.
No one ever listens to anyone anymore.
(Muller 1991: 271)

The expressions involved in negative concord are often called n-words, because in most Romance languages, they start with the letter 'n', as in Italian *nessuno* 'no one', *niente* 'nothing', etc. Others call them (negative) concord items, in opposition to (negative) polarity items. In this chapter, we will use both terms to indicate the group of expressions that are characterized as negative because they license object NPs of the form *de* N, they license negative polarity items like *qui que ce soit* 'anyone', they provide negative answers to questions when used in isolation, etc. (cf. the criteria formulated in chapter 17 above), but when they occur in combination, the sentence has a single negation reading, rather than a double, triple ... multiple negation.

As shown by (1a, c), we find both pronouns (*personne*, *rien*, etc.) and full NPs (*aucune faute*) in negative concord constructions. (1b, d) show that we find concord items not only in argument positions (subject, object, etc.) but also in adjoined, adverbial positions (*plus, aucunement, nullement, jamais*). In (1d, e), we observe that the negative coordination *ni ... ni* and the negative preposition *sans* (cf. Vlachou 2000) also participate in the concord system of French. (1b, e, f) illustrate that the concord chain can contain more than two items. In principle, the number of concord items is unbounded.

These concord items are subject to different syntactic constraints. First of all, there are constraints on position: *rien* most commonly occurs immediately after the inflected verb, unless it is heavily modified or stressed, *personne* occurs after the participle/infinitive verb. *Pas, jamais* and *plus* are adverbials, but they do not apparently occur in the same positions. *Pas* and *jamais* can co-occur, but *pas* and *plus* cannot (Belletti 1994). The syntactic position of n-words has changed throughout the diachrony of French, a change apparently correlated with meaning distinctions (Martineau and Déprez 2003). Prior to the Classical Period (17-18th century), for instance, the distribution of adverbial n-words was relatively free (Martineau 1994). Thus *pas* could commonly occur before *ne* or after an untensed verb form, as in (2a) and (b) respectively:

(2) a. Vray est aussi qui pas ne le mérite.
True is also which does not deserve it.
(Marot, Epîtres, 35, vol I-204, in Martineau 1994)(16th).

b. Car elle (...) commencera à ne le chercher pas.
Because she (...) will start not to look for it.
(Martineau 1994)(CF)

At the same period, adverbial n-words could still occur alone, i.e. without *ne*, in interrogative and other NPI-like contexts, which suggest that they could still have a non-negative reading (Martineau and Déprez, to appear):

(3) a. Car par ainsi pourras eschapper d'en point donner.
And in that way you can avoid giving any.
(Vigneulles, Les Cents Nouvelles Nouvelles, 52, 128, cited in Martineau 1994)(MF)

b. Il est bien difficile de se pas imaginer que...
It is quite difficult to at all imagine/ not to imagine.
(Voiture, I,14, cited in Martineau 1994)(CF)

During the Classical period, however, the syntactic position of adverbial n-words became more restricted (Martineau 1994). At the same time, the discontinuous negation *ne ... pas* became generalized, with *ne* losing its negative force. The position of argumental n-word also underwent changes, both internal i.e. within their nominal structure (Déprez and Martineau, to appear) and external, i.e. relative to their position in the sentence (Moignet 1984).

Contemporary dialectal variations in the position of n-words are also observed. In Geneva French for instance, *personne* can be pre-verbal, just like *rien* (Kayne p.c., 2a). In Québécois French, it can occur sentence finally (Tellier 1987, 4b).

(4) a. Je n'ai personne vu.
I NE have nobody seen.
(Kayne, p.c.)

b. Ils ont pas vu ce film-là, personne.
They have not seen that movie, nobody.

Muller (1991: 269–280) provides a detailed discussion of the pairwise combination of concord items. He observes that negative NPs that occur in argument positions can be freely combined in any order, and can also combine with themselves, compare (1f) above. Adverbial expressions like *jamais, nulle part* do not combine with themselves, presumably because it is generally impossible to provide more than one quantifier over space or time in each sentence. Adverbial expressions like *plus* can occur more than once in a sentence, if they modify different expressions (cf. 2f).

Other restrictions on combinations of concord items are harder to account for. According to Muller, the adverbs *nullement* and *aucunement* are compatible with *ni ... ni*, but not with any other concord item. The distribution of these items might be partly governed by constraints on parallelism (cf. Déprez 1997), partly by collocational properties of the lexical expression in question, rather than by general semantic properties. Similar observations have been made in the area of the distribution of negative polarity items (cf. van der Wouden 1997).

An interesting case is the marker of sentential negation *pas*. In other Romance languages, sentential negation is often crucial to create negative concord. However, that typically involves the preverbal marker of negation that goes back to the Latin negation *non*. But *pas* is outside of the concord system in modern standard continental French. The combination of *pas* with a concord item typically leads to a double negation reading, as in (5a, b):

(5) a. Ce n'est pas rien
It is not nothing (i.e. it is quite something)
(Muller 1991: 259)

b. Il ne va pas nulle part, il va à son travail
He does not go nowhere, he goes to work
(Muller 1991: 259)

As pointed out by Muller (1991: 259), the double negation in (5a) has a special meaning effect, associating the value of 'something important' with it. This is a pragmatic effect due to the litotes context, (cf. Horn 1984, van der Wouden 1996): double negations are semantically equivalent to their affirmative counterpart, but they are clearly marked expressions, as compared to the corresponding simple positive sentence. The marked status of the sentence easily triggers pragmatic meaning effects (cf. Blutner 2004), but the double negation reading can also be more neutral, as shown by examples like (5b), generally used to contradict previous negative utterances.

The fact that *pas* behaves differently from markers of sentential negation in other Romance languages has been attributed to its postverbal position, as opposed to the preverbal negation in languages like Italian and Spanish (Zanuttini 1991), cf. also Corblin and Tovena (2001, 2003) on the importance of 'neg-first' (see section 3 below). It has also been explained by a potentially different grammatical status (i.e. the status of Specifier (or XP = maximal projection), as opposed to that of a head (or $X^0$ = a minimal projection). On this latter view, Italian and Spanish negation head a negative constituent NegP, while French *pas* is its specifier (Moritz and Valois 1994). Déprez (1999), however, provides counterarguments to these views. She observes first, that in Louisiana French Creole, *pa* must always co-occur with n-words, independently of its pre- or post-verbal position.

(6) a. Mo te pa wa person
I did not see anyone
(Déprez 1999:118)

b. Aryen gruj pa
Nothing moves not
(Déprez 1999:118)

Second, some dialects of French such as modern Québécois commonly establish negative concord readings with a postverbal *pas* whose syntactic status (Spec/head) does not differ from that of standard continental French. Third, examples of older French are found in which *pas* seems to be part of the concord system. Martineau and Déprez (to appear) discuss negative constructions in which *pas* co-occurs with an n-word such as *rien, aucun* N, etc. They provide evidence that such constructions occur in diachronic stages or dialects of French where n-words are dependent items whose syntactic and semantic properties resemble those of polarity items, rather than those of negative quantifiers. That is, the n-word can have a positive (existential) reading in such versions of French. For Martineau and Déprez, the participation of negation – and a fortiori of French *pas* – to a negative concord chain is governed by the variable syntactic and semantic status of n-words rather than by the properties of *pas* itself (cf. Déprez 1997, 1999, 2000, 2003, Déprez and Martineau to appear a, b).

Some other possible explanations of why *pas* ended up outside the concord system in standard modern French will be discussed in section 3 below. For now, only the observation that *pas* typically leads to double negation readings in combination with other concord items is relevant. Note that postverbal *pas* is different from pre-determiner or preverbal *pas*, as illustrated in (7):

(7) a. Pas plus au Proche-Orient qu'ailleurs, cependant, la force des

armes n'a jamais suffi à instituer une paix véritable
No more in the Middle-East than elsewhere, though, armed forces have ever managed to create a real peace.
[Muller 1991: 260]

b. Pas un étudiant n'a vu quoi que ce soit.
Not one student has seen anything.

c. Pas un mot à personne! [NC]
Not a word to no one!

d. Pas une personne n'a rien fait [DN]
Not one person has done nothing

Postverbal *pas* is the marker of sentential negation, but preverbal *pas* has narrow scope over the item it modifies. Because *pas un* builds a monotone decreasing NP, it licenses negative polarity items (7b). *Pas un* can be part of a concord construction in elliptical sentences like (7c), but in full sentences, it typically leads to a double negation reading when it is combined with other n-words (7d).

## 2 Concord, polarity and double negation

The diachronic movement that has led to the negative system of current French is known as the 'Jespersen cycle', after Otto Jespersen (1917, 1924), who first described this general development that we find in many languages. Originally, the marker of sentential negation in French was *ne*, derived from Latin *non*. Its behavior is illustrated with the old French examples (8):

(8) Jeo ne di
I not say

Over time, *ne* was used more and more often with postverbal minimizers with adverbial status, e.g. *pas, point, mie, goutte* (cf. Bolinger 1972). Over the centuries, all fell out of use, except for *pas*, and occasionally *point*. The modern French n-words, such as *rien, personne, aucun, nullement*, were originally indefinites indicating minimal amounts. They became negative polarity items when they were used as reinforcement of the negation *ne* and their distribution was narrowed down to those contexts that typically license negative polarity items. At least up to the nineteenth century, items such as *rien, personne, aucun* N, etc. do not only appear in the scope of *ne*, but show up in non-negative, polarity licensing contexts as well, cf. (3) and (9):[1]

[1] The examples in (9) are from *Corinne ou l'Italie* by Madame de Staël, published in 1807.

(9) a. Ai-je jamais fait de mal?
Have I ever done any harm ?

b. Comment vous rien taire dans cette solitude!
How keep anything from you in this solitude!

That *pas* itself could also appear as a negative polarity item up to the 18th century is noted in Hirschbühler and Labelle (1994).

In contemporary French, the use of n-words in contexts like (9) is a relic of a preceding state of the language. It is not productive and has a strong old-fashioned formal taste. However, these items are productively used as negatives. The idea is that, over the centuries, *ne* grew weaker and became incapable of being the sole expression of negation. However, Martineau and Mougeon (2003), Déprez and Martineau (to appear a,b) and Martineau and Déprez (to appear) argue that there is no direct correlation between the weakening negative force of *ne* and the acquired negative value of French n-words. Corpus studies show that the two do not appear to fully coincide in time (Martineau and Mougeon 2003).

In the modern language, sentential negation is expressed in two parts: *ne* ... *pas*. In spoken varieties of French, *ne* is now often dropped, so that *pas* becomes the sole expression of negation. *Pas* is generally recognized as the real expression of sentential negation in modern standard French. The status of the concord items is less clear. As we will see in section 3 below, some linguists associate negative concord with negative polarity, and give concord items a non-negative, existential interpretation. This is supported by the fact that we still find non-negative meanings with a concord item like *jamais*, as in (10a). Other n-words can get non-negative interpretations only if used in combination with *jamais* (10b):

(10) a. Si jamais vous visitez Paris, venez nous voir
If you ever visit Paris, come see us

b. A-t-on jamais rien vu d'aussi beau?
Has one ever seen anything this beautiful?

However, all other uses of concord items are basically restricted to negation and other n-words (i.e. anti-additive contexts, cf. Zwarts 1995, van der Wouden 1997, etc.). Accordingly, other linguists claim that the original indefinites ended up becoming real negatives. One piece of evidence in favor of a real negative meaning of concord items is the existence of double negation readings. As pointed out above, postverbal *pas* always leads to a double negation reading in standard modern French. However, French concord items also allow double negation, as illustrated by the following examples from Corblin (1996):[2]

(11) a. Personne n'aime personne
No one loves anyone [NC]
No one loves no one [DN]
b. Personne n'est le fils de personne
No one is the son of anyone [NC]
No one is the son of no one [DN]

The examples are chosen in such a way that the double negation reading intuitively makes more sense than the negative concord reading. Several factors have an influence on the availability of the double negation readings. Double negation readings can be found between a subject and a direct object (12a), but with an indirect object, it is much harder (12b).

(12) a. Personne n'a rien dit. [DN easy]
No one NE has nothing said.
b. Pierre n'a rien dit à personne [DN difficult]
Pierre NE has nothing said to no one.

Lexical semantics also plays a role, at least in the domain of adverbial n-words. Although a double negation reading is generally excluded for *plus* (13a), it is available for *jamais* (13b, c):

(13) a. Personne ne vient plus. [DN impossible]
No one NE comes no more.
b. Personne ne meurt jamais. [DN easy]
No one NE dies never.
c. Personne n'a jamais menti. [DN easy]
No one NE has never lied.

With pronouns, the concord interpretation is generally preferred over the double negation reading. With full NPs containing *aucun*, the double negation reading is easier to obtain. Sometimes it even becomes the dominant or the only interpretation. Here are some data from Déprez (2000) that illustrate the different possibilities:

(14) a. Personne n'a rien mangé. [NC favored]
No one NE has nothing eaten
b. Aucun enfant n'a rien mangé. [NC/DN]
No child NE has nothing eaten
c. Personne n'a mangé aucun gâteau. [DN favored]
No one NE has eaten no cake.

[2]Compare Zanuttini (1991) and Herburger (2001) for discussion of double negation readings in other Romance languages.

d. Aucun enfant n'a mangé aucun gâteau. [DN only]
No child NE has eaten no cake.

One possible explanation of these data is that negative concord is a form of resumptive quantification (Déprez 1997, 1999, 2000, De Swart and Sag 2002). As suggested by May (1989) there are conditions of parallelism on resumptive quantification, and these conditions could make resumption harder or impossible with full NPs than with pronouns (cf. Déprez 2000 and sections 3.3 and 3.4) below for further discussion). However, it is important to keep in mind that these are tendencies, not hard rules.

The probability of the double negation reading is greatly enhanced by an intonation contour which results in the processing of the sentence being "split in two parts" (cf. Corblin 1996):

(15) a. PERSONNE // ne dit rien à personne.
Nobody NE says nothing to nobody.

b. Personne ne dit rien // à PERSONNE
Nobody NE says nothing to nodoby

Stress on the subject in (15a) or on the indirect object in (15b) makes it easier to obtain the double negation reading. If resumptive quantification is possible only between n-words that occupy the same scope domain (Déprez 1999), then stress may disrupt this condition, favoring a double negative reading. The fact that we find a double negation reading in question/answer pairs like (16), can be explained along the same lines:

(16) Q: Qui n'a rien dit à personne?
A: Personne

The only available interpretation of the answer is the double negation reading 'Nobody said anything to no one', because the two n-words are processed separately.

The fact that in French the sentential marker of negation has grown out of a reinforcement of negation and is not the continuation of the Latin negation *non* could suggest that *pas* is closer in behavior to the other concord items. But as we already pointed out, *pas* is in fact outside the concord system and typically leads to a double negation reading in combination with a concord item. We can use this property to keep negative polarity items and concord items apart: polarity items are licensed by *pas*, but concord items are incompatible with *pas* unless in a double negation context (Haegeman 1995, Corblin 1996, Déprez 1997, 1999, de Swart 2001). (17) provides a series of sentences that illustrates the contrast:

(17) a. Luc n'a pas vu quoi que ce soit [NPI]
Luc has not seen anything
b. Luc n'a rien vu [NC]
Luc has seen nothing
c. Luc n'a pas rien vu [DN]
Luc has not seen nothing

*Pas* licenses the NPI *quoi que ce soit* in (17a). Without *pas*, the sentence would be ungrammatical. The concord item *rien* does not need a licensor to contribute a negation (17b). If we use both the n-word and the negation marker *pas*, we end up with a double negation (17c).

The *pas* criterion allows de Swart (2001) to determine that *ni ... ni* is a concord item, whereas *ni* occurring by itself is a negative polarity item with the meaning 'or':

(18) a. Paul n'a ni bu ni mangé. [NC]
Paul did not either drink or eat.
b. Paul n'a pas bu ni mangé. [NPI]
Paul did not drink or eat.
c. Paul n'a pas ni bu ni mangé. [DN]
Paul did not neither drink nor eat.

(18a) shows that *ni ... ni* does not need a licensor to express negation. The single occurrence of *ni* in (18b) is licensed by the negation marker *pas*. The combination of the concord item *ni ... ni* and the negation marker *pas* in (18c) leads to a double negation reading.

The loss of its negative value changed the status of *ne* considerably. Most linguists take *ne* to be a scope marker in those varieties of the language where it is still found (cf. chapter 17, this volume). Kayne (1981) argues that the contrast between (18a) and (18b) involves the scope of the negation:

(19) a. Je ne demande qu'ils arrêtent personne
I NE ask that they arrest no one
= I don't ask them to arrest anyone
b. Je demande qu'ils n'arrêtent personne
I ask that-they NE-arrest no one
= I ask that they arrest no one

The occurrence of *ne* in the embedded clause indicates the upper limit of the semantic scope of negation. In order to give negation scope over the sentence as a whole, we can insert *ne* in the main clause. Many speakers do not accept the sentences in (19). Note that scope is indeed typically clause-bound, so we can only do this marginally with embedded subjunctive clauses and specific types of infinitive clauses that are well-known to be less strict scope islands (cf. Déprez 1999) such as the example (20b) below:

(20) a. Je peux ne rien faire.
I can NE nothing do = I can do nothing
b. Je ne peux rien faire
I NE can nothing do = I cannot do anything

In main clauses, *pas* and all concord items in any argument or adjunct position obtain sentential scope without the help of preverbal *ne*. This makes *ne* syntactically and semantically redundant in most contexts. French strongly contrasts with other Romance languages in this respect.

## 3 Theories on negative concord

This section presents a number of influential theories on negative concord. The first three theories have been developed for negative concord in general. In section 3.1, we will point out the strength and weaknesses of these theories as far as their application to French is concerned. The last three theories have been developed with particular attention paid to French data. We discuss them in sections 3.2 through 3.4. The theories discussed are:

- Concord items as negative polarity items (Laka 1990, Giannakidou 2000);
- Concord items as self-licensing polarity items (Ladusaw 1992);
- Negative concord as absorption of negation (Zanuttini 1991, Haegemann and Zanuttini 1996);
- Negative concord as optimal variable marking (Corblin 1996, Corblin and Tovena 2001, 2003);
- Negative concord as resumptive numeral quantifiers (Déprez 1997, 1999, 2000);
- Negative concord as polyadic negative quantifiers (de Swart and Sag 2002).

### 3.1 Concord items as polarity items

Theories on negative concord typically start with sentences like (21):

(21) Personne n'a rien vu
No one NE has nothing seen

Although the sentence contains two NPs (*personne, rien*) that count as negative expressions according to the criteria developed in chapter 17 of this volume, the preferred interpretation is a concord reading in which the sentence expresses a single negation. The single negation that the negative concord reading of (21) expresses is conceptually simple, but raises problems for the principle of compositionality of meaning. The principle of compositionality of meaning is a heuristic principle that is at the basis of most semantic theories. It says that the meaning of a complex whole is a function of the meaning of its parts and the way they are put together. If we interpret the negative quantifiers in (21) in terms of first-order logic with negation and universal/existential quantification, we can derive the double negation reading we find for a sentence with two negative NPs, but this leaves the single negation reading (the concord reading) unaccounted for. In order to deal with this problem, different analyses have been proposed in the literature.

One dominant view is to treat negative concord as a variant of negative polarity, and to take the negative concord item to denote an existentially quantified NP, rather than a negative NP (e.g. Laka 1990, Ladusaw 1992, Giannakidou 1997, 2000). This approach preserves strict compositionality, for function application yields the desired single negation interpretation. Different versions of this theory are around in the literature. According to Laka (1990), concord items are licensed by a possibly implicit negation operator. The main problem with this assumption is that it becomes impossible to explain why (22b) is a felicitous answer to the question in (22a), but (22c) cannot be used in this context:

(22) a. Qu'est-ce que tu as vu?
What have you seen?
b. Rien
Nothing
c. *Quoi que ce soit
Anything

Ladusaw (1992) overcomes the problems with Laka's analysis by assuming that negative concord items are negative polarity items that license themselves, because they carry a negation feature. In the absence of a trigger, *rien* licenses itself because it is inherently negative (22b), but *quoi que ce soit* (22c) does not.

An important problem for any treatment of concord items in terms of existential quantification is that the existential interpretation never surfaces. Negative polarity items like *n'importe quel* or *quoi que ce soit* are licensed by contexts other than negation, such as monotone decreasing NPs, verbs with a 'negative' flavor, the antecedent of a conditional, etc. (cf. chapter 18 on negative polarity items, this volume):

(23) a. Il refuse n'importe quel accommodement
He refuses any accommodation

[Muller 1991: 93]

b. Si quoi que ce soit vous dérange, faites-le nous savoir
If anything at all bothers you, tell us

Expressions such as *n'importe quel* or *quoi que ce soit* denote the lowest endpoint of a scale (cf. Fauconnier 1975, 1977, and Tovena, Déprez and Jayez, chapter 18, this volume). In non-negative contexts such as those in (23), the existential interpretation of the polarity item is easily detected. If concord items are negative polarity items, we must treat them as very strict negative polarity items that are only licensed in anti-additive contexts. Anti-additive contexts involve negative quantifiers or sentential negation (cf. Zwarts 1995, Van der Wouden 1997, etc.). The embedding under negation or a negative quantifier explains why the existential interpretation of concord items never surfaces.

Several indirect arguments have been advanced in favor of the existential characterization of concord items. There is diachronic evidence that concord items developed out of indefinites (cf. section 1 above). It is entirely conceivable that n-words have preserved their existential character, but that they became more and more limited in use over time, in accordance with the Jespersen cycle (cf. section 2 above). However, most linguists agree that *pas*, which is originally only a reinforcement of negation, has itself become the bearer of sentential negation in standard modern French (Bréal 1897, Gaatone 1971, Haegeman 1995, Corblin 1996, de Swart and Sag 2002, Godard, chapter 17, this volume). If expressions like *rien, personne* have undergone the same development, it is not inconceivable that they have lost their indefinite nature, and have turned into true negative quantifiers. The other argument that has been advanced in favor of the interpretation of expressions like *rien, personne, jamais* in terms of existential quantification involves modification by *presque* ('almost'). *Presque* is an adverb that has been claimed to combine with universal (24a), but not with existential quantifiers (24b):

(24) a. J'ai invité presque tous les étudiants.
I have invited almost all the students.

b. *J'ai invité presque quelques étudiants.
I have invited almost some students.

Although the highest concord item in a negative chain can be modified by *presque*, embedded concord items cannot, as shown by the contrast between (25a) and (25b), from Van der Wouden and Zwarts (1993):

(25) a. Presque personne n'a rien dit. [ambiguous]
Almost no one NE-has nothing said.
= Almost no one said anything [NC]
= Nearly everyone said something [DN]
b. Personne n'a presque rien dit. [DN only]
No one NE-has almost nothing said.
= No one said almost nothing
= *No one said almost anything

Van der Wouden and Zwarts take the contrast between (25a) and (25b) to indicate that the higher items in a concord chain are inherently negative, but the lower items are to be interpreted in terms of existential quantification.

However, it seems that the data are too weak to support this conclusion. It is well known that items like *presque* can modify other elements besides universal quantifiers, in particular numerals (cf. Horn and Lee 1995, Déprez 1997). Furthermore, Vallduví (1994) points out that the concord reading of the counterpart of (25b) in Catalan is perfectly felicitous, and more than one speaker of French makes the same claim about (25a) and (b). That modification of the lower concord item by *presque* is not always impossible in French is confirmed by attested examples like (25).[3]

(26) a. Un vieil écrivain nous a quittés sur la pointe des pieds sans que presque personne y prête attention.
An old writer has left us quietly without that almost no one paid attention to it.
= hardly without any attention
b. Je n'ai plus trouvé presque rien ridicule
I have no more found almost nothing ridiculous
= There was hardly anything I found ridiculous anymore

According to Muller (1991: 319), *presque* can modify an embedded concord item as long as we interpret the adverb as taking wide scope over the concord chain as a whole. Thus, modification of negative indefinites by *presque* does not provide evidence in favor of an interpretation of the n-word in terms of existential quantification.

Déprez (2000) discusses some more contexts in which n-words seem to be closer to existential quantifiers than to universal quantifiers. They involve the observation that n-words can be modified with a phrase introduced by *de* ('of'), while apparently universal quantifiers cannot:

[3]26a) is from Grévisse *Le bon usage*, section 726. (26b) is from S. de Beauvoir. *Mémoires d'une jeune fille rangée*, Poche p. 355, and is quoted by Muller (1991: 319).

(27) a. Personne d'intelligent ne s'est présenté.
No one of intelligent NE has presented himself.
b. Quelqu'un d'intelligent s'est présenté.
Someone of intelligent has presented himself.
c. *Tout le monde d'intelligent est venu.
Everyone of intelligent has come.

Déprez (2000) further observes that n-words are possible in existential *there* constructions, and impossible in stylistic inversion contexts, just like other existential quantifiers.

Interestingly, we can also provide evidence in favor of a (negative) universal treatment of n-words. Exception phrases constitute such a context, as pointed out by Español-Echevarría (1995). As pointed out by Moltmann (1995), exception phrases can modify a universal, not an existential quantifier. Examples like (28) are thus an argument in favor of the universal nature of n-words:

(28) Personne n'a parlé à personne, sauf Marie à son frère
No one talked to anyone, except Marie to her brother

These observations point to a universal, rather than an existential interpretation of n-words. As pointed out by Giannakidou (2000), we can maintain a view of negative concord as negative polarity if we analyze the concord items as (plain) universal quantifiers that are licensed by negation. Instead of taking narrow (semantic) scope with respect to their licensor, as negative polarity items normally do (cf. de Swart 1998), n-words would take wide scope with respect to negation, according to Giannakidou. This would lead to a sequence of universal quantifiers scoping over a single negation (cf. also Zanuttini 1991), rather than a sequence of existential quantifiers scoping under a single negation, as Ladusaw (1992) and others have proposed. Of course, the truth conditions are the same in each case, but the internal structure of the sentence would be different.

An important problem for any analysis that identifies negative concord with negative polarity is the observation that sentences involving negative quantifiers are actually ambiguous between a double negation reading and a concord reading, but that the polarity approach to concord only derives the single negation reading of examples like (11) above. As pointed out by Corblin (1996), Ladusaw's analysis still suffers from too close an identification of concord items with negative polarity items. The [neg] feature contributed by each n-word is viewed as an agreement phenomenon: it is present multiple times, but only interpreted once. By analogy, this criticism also applies to versions of the negative polarity analysis that treat the concord item in terms of universal quantification, such as Giannakidou (2000). As a result, we only obtain the concord reading. Given that the alternation between negative concord and double negation reading is particularly important for French, Corblin (1996), Déprez (1997, 1999, 2000), and de Swart and Sag (2002) explicitly develop analyses that deal with the ambiguity between concord and double negation readings. Their proposals are discussed in the next three sections.

### 3.2 Negative concord as optimal variable marking

Corblin (1996) develops an analysis of the single negation/double negation readings in the framework of DRT (Discourse Representation Theory, cf. Kamp and Reyle 1993). He proposes a construction rule for negative quantifiers such as *rien, personne, aucun* N, *jamais* that 1) represents the sequence in process as a negative DRS, and 2) interprets the constituent as if it were an indefinite introducing its reference marker in the universe of the negative DRS. If a sentence contains two negative quantifiers within one predicate-argument structure, a rule of parasitism can apply. The intuition underlying parasitism is that the second negative quantifier uses the negative domain made available by a previous expression, instead of creating its own. Formally, parasitism says that if the construction rule for negative quantifiers applies to the output of that rule, only the second half of the rule applies. Parasitism is an optional rule. If it applies to a sentence like (29), we obtain the single negation reading that corresponds with the negative concord interpretation (29a). If it does not apply, we obtain the double negation reading in (30b):

(29) Personne n'aime personne.
No one NE loves no one.

a. $\neg \exists x \exists y$ Love$(x, y)$
No one loves anyone

b. $\neg \exists x \neg \exists y$ Love$(x, y)$
No one loves no one

Corblin (1996) observes that there are important restrictions on the interpretation of sentences with more than two negative quantifiers. Tri-negative readings do not obtain, so parasitism is proposed as a complexity regulator: we have at most one negation nesting, and no more than one binding from outer to inner negation. This is conceived of as a constraint on the on-line processing of negative quantifiers within a clause. As soon as we reach the threshold of complexity, parasitism applies.

The question arises why languages use a sequence of negative quantifiers if not all quantifiers import their own negative domain, but some are parasitic upon a negation introduced by a higher quantifier. Corblin and Tovena (2001, 2003) propose an answer to this question with their hypothesis of optimal variable marking. The intuition underlying the notion of optimal variable marking is that parasitism is the default in natural language. In other words, natural language negation does not behave like negation in a first-order predicate logical language. Corblin and Tovena (2001, 2003) propose an analysis based on three principles:

1. A principle on the lexical marking of argument variables in the scope of a negation.
2. A principle limiting the recursivity of negation within the verb-argument domain.
3. A constraint on the distribution of negative expressions in the clause realization, that is called Neg-first.

Principle (1) says that in most languages, there is a way of unambiguously marking an argument variable as having to be interpreted in the scope of the clause-mate negation. Corblin (1996) contains an algorithm for the generation of all possible interpretations for a sequence of n-words. But not all these interpretations are actually available. This is why we need principle 2. The principle that limits the recursivity of negation within the verb-argument domain has been studied extensively for French in Corblin (1996), and Corblin and Derzhanski (1997) for Bulgarian. As a consequence of this constraint, there is one negation per clause in the default case, and never more than two. Principles (1) and (2) are general principles, valid for most, if not all languages. Neg-first (principle 3) is a constraint that requires the presence of a preverbal negative expression in the surface structure of the clause. It is not a principle specific to Romance languages, but it is not a general principle that applies to all languages either. The main sources for principle (1) are Ladusaw (1992) and Dowty (1993). Principle (2) is inspired by Ladusaw (1992), and previous work by Corblin (1996) and Tovena (1998). The main inspiration for principle (3) comes from Jespersen (1917), Dahl (1979) and Horn (1989).

A language like French exhibits some interesting constraints on lexical marking of argument variables. Lexical items like *quelqu'un* and *quelque chose* can be used for variables interpreted by existential closure (in 30 this is the only available option) and for variables interpreted in the scope of a logical operator, an option available (and preferred) in (31) and (32):

(30) J'ai vu quelqu'un. (existential closure)
I saw someone

(31) Si vous avez vu quelqu'un dites-le. (bound variable/exist. clos.)
If you saw someone/anyone, tell me.

(32) Avez vous vu quelqu'un? (bound variable/exist clos.)
Did you see someone/anyone?

But this is not true for negation. If *quelqu'un* and *quelque chose* occur in the syntactic scope of a negation, which is syntactically correct, they can only be interpreted existentially, as we see in (33):

(33) Je n'ai pas vu quelqu'un (existential closure only)
I did not see someone.

The observations about variable instantiation can be summed up as follows:

1. The lexical instantiation of negated variables of obligatory arguments is sometimes necessary: there are constraints prohibiting covert arguments;
2. the lexical instantiation is always meaningful, for covert arguments in the scope of negation can be interpreted either as negated variables or as anaphoric expressions;
3. some indefinites (called Positive Polarity Items) cannot work as overt negated variables.

It follows that most languages have a way of marking unambiguously that an argument variable must be interpreted in the scope of a clausemate negation. That can be done either by polarity items (which mark a variable depending on a set of operators including negation) or by n-words (which can only mark a variable depending on negation).

In most languages, the lexical marking of negated variables is achieved via n-words, i.e. expressions combining morphologically (or semantically) the expression of sentential negation and some restriction on the variable. The advantage of using n-words is that the dependence of the variable on negation is expressed by the repetition of the negative operator. Thus it would be an optimal strategy if not for the observation that it may give rise to an ambiguity: if we can compute all occurrences of the negative expression as negative, we might end up with an interpretation in terms of double, triple, ... multiple negation, rather than a single negation. The fact that n-words are widely used across languages suggests that the advantage of optimal marking carries more weight than the ambiguity. According to Corblin and Tovena (2001, 2003), this is due to an independently motivated complexity constraint which restricts to a maximum of two (and at an heavy cost) the processing capacity for negation within the boundaries of a clause (the verb-argument domain). This constraint can be illustrated as follows. We know from the discussion in Corblin (1994, 1996) that it is rather difficult to obtain double negation readings for sentences like (34):

(34) Personne ne croit personne
Nobody NE believes nobody
(i) $\neg \exists x \exists y$ Believe$(x, y)$ [NC]
(ii) $\neg\exists x \neg\exists y$ Believe$(x, y)$ [DN]

The preferred interpretation of (34) is the mono-negative reading (i). The truly recursive reading (ii), if not impossible, is restricted to certain contexts, and typically requires a special intonation. Quite generally, Corblin and Tovena argue that it is difficult to obtain a double negation reading for two n-words that are arguments of the same verb. That is, it is difficult to get a translation like $\neg\exists x \neg\exists y V(x, y)$, where $x$ and $y$ are arguments of V. Note that this really seems to be a limitation on the processing of a single verb, since a double negation reading is unambiguously imposed by the use of two different verbs, as in (35):

(35) Il n'y a personne qui ne croit personne
There is nobody who NE believes nobody
(i) $\neg\exists x \exists y$ Believe$(x, y)$ [NC, not available]
(ii) $\neg\exists x \neg\exists y$ Believe$(x, y)$ [DN]

The only interpretation of (35) is the double negation reading spelled out in (35ii). This shows that there is a constraint forbidding the truly recursive interpretation which operates within the boundaries of the clause. Note that this constraint is 'soft', as the double negation reading obtains under certain conditions. Corblin (1996) suggests a constraint about self-embedding complex negation. A self-embedding negation is a negation that has scope over another negation. This self-embedding is simple if negation takes immediate scope over the other negation, and we can eliminate the negation by application of the law of double negation. A self-embedding of negation is complex if there is some variable intervening between the two negations, which creates a structure in which the application of the double negation law is blocked (e.g. 34ii and 35ii). As mentioned in section 2 above, the availability of a double negation reading depends on the expressions involved (pronouns versus full NPs), the syntactic position (direct versus indirect arguments), intonation patterns, and the presence of the negation marker *pas*. If a sentence like (34) is pronounced without any special stress or pause, the preferred interpretation is mono-negative (i.e. 34i).

As pointed out in section 2 above, the double negation reading is always obligatory in the presence of *pas*:

(36) a. Personne n'est pas venu.
Nobody NE has not come

b. Je n'ai pas vu personne.
I NE have not seen no one.

It appears that *pas* introduces a negation in the representation but does not accept variables of negated arguments in its scope. The behavior of this item is exceptional, if we compare it with other n-words in French, and other Romance languages. But note that *pas* appears after the (finite) verb, so it does not satisfy neg-first. The general strategy, captured by the Neg-first constraint, consists of having a negative expression in preverbal position, and computing in its scope all the subsequent variables of negated arguments. The historical development of French, sketched in section 2 above explains how French ended up with a post-verbal marker of negation, rather than a preverbal one. Another tendency of the language is the progressive disappearance of preverbal *ne*. *Ne* gradually lost its status as an autonomous negative marker, because the negative value was associated with *pas*. If we accept that in modern French *ne* is no longer the negative marker, we can say that a change in the role of the elements entering the system of sentential negation has led the language to abandon the constraint of Neg-first. This is the case in spoken French, where simple negative sentences often do not have material lexically associated with negation in preverbal position. The fact that the written, refined French keeps using the semantically empty *ne* can be explained as a survival of a form of Neg-first.

In sum, Corblin and Tovena (2001, 2003) maintain the interpretation of n-words as negative quantifiers, and assume they contain a negation and a variable interpreted in its scope. If the complexity constraint does not apply, n-words are responsible for the introduction of negation with the corresponding argument-variable in its scope. This is the case for instance if the n-word is the only specimen of its class in the sentence. In some languages, for instance in standard English, this is all an n-word can be. The consequence is that their reiteration will be strongly restricted, and will generate one negation per n-word. However, in many languages, two such terms co-occurring in the domain of the same verb will result, by default, in a situation whereby the second is interpreted as a negated variable. This is what we have called parasitism. In this case, n-words are 'negative', but somewhat indirectly: they do not introduce a negation of their own into the representation, they just express a negated argument-variable. Thus, in (37a), the complexity constraint applies, which means that *personne* can be interpreted either as introducing a negation of its own, or as marking a variable in the scope of the negation introduced by the first *personne*. In (37b), the situation is not that different: in standard English, the second occurrence of *nobody* must introduce a negation of its own, in other dialects of English (e.g. African American English), the n-word can be used for marking a variable depending on the negation.

(37) a. Personne n'aime personne

b. Nobody loves nobody

Therefore, in this approach, the use of n-words as expressing variables depending on a clause-mate negation, is bound to properties of negation itself, and is not a consequence of the use of n-words as polarity items. In fact, many authors have observed that many n-words used in negative concord cannot be used in other polarity contexts (antecedent of conditionals, questions, (simple) downward entailing quantifiers, etc.), and that the few examples we find are archaic. We can take the unavailability of the concord reading of n-words in negative sentences like (36) as evidence showing that n-words have lost the ability to be licensed as negative polarity item by negation.

### 3.3 Negative concord as resumptive or cumulative numeral quantification

Déprez (1997, 1999, 2000) offers a detailed comparison and analysis of negative concord in standard French and French-based Creoles (mostly Haitian Creole). Although based on seemingly identical expressions (Creole n-words were inherited from French), concord in these languages manifests striking differences with respect to the four criteria listed below:

1. dependency: the presence of sentential negation or of a non-additive context is required to license n-words
2. resistance to modification: modification by adverbs such as *almost* or *absolutely* is unfelicitous
3. long-distance licensing: a non clause-mate relation is possible between concordant n-words
4. double negation: a double negative reading is possible

Negative concord in Haitian Creole (henceforth HC) manifests the first three of these properties but not the fourth one. Thus, HC n-words require the presence of sentential negation *pa* (38a) or of a non-additive context (38b) to be acceptable. They sometimes resist adverbial modification (38c), can be licensed in non clause-mate contexts (38c), but do not permit a double negation reading (38d).

(38) a. Pèsonn pa janm di pèsonn anyen.
No one ever said anything to anyone.
b. Eske pèsonn rele m?
Did anyone call me?
c. M pa te di Mari (*preske) pèsonn te vini.
I did not say to Mary that almost anyone came.
d. Pèsonn*(pa)di anyen
#No one said nothing

Standard French negative concord in contrast manifests the fourth property but not the first three. Thus French concord is impossible in the presence of sentential negation *pas*, it is unlicensed in non-additive or non clause-mate contexts, and it allows double negative readings under certain conditions. Adverbial modification is felicitous for isolated French n-words and in negative chains, it favors double negative readings (compare section 2 above).

On the basis of these striking differences, Déprez (1997, 1999) Proposes to distinguish two types of negative concord, each representing an extreme pole of cross-linguistic variation. The French-based Creole type is analyzed as a version of negative polarity licensing, essentially à la Ladusaw (1992). HC n-words are indefinite variables that are either existentially closed under the scope of negation or bound by a generic operator outside the scope of negation, as in (39) and (40), respectively:

(39) a. Mwen pa we pesonn
Me not see nobody
b. $\neg\exists x$ (I saw (person $x$))

(40) a. Peson pa vini
Nobody not came
b. [Gen [person $x$][ $\neg\, x$ came]]

Déprez does not specify how the generic operator is introduced in the second case, but a possible suggestion might be that it is introduced by negation (see Giannakidou (1998) for a similar analysis of Greek n-words in the Spec of NegP).

The standard French negative concord type, in contrast, is analyzed as resumptive quantification, following a suggestion by May (1989) for English (cf. also section 3.4 below). Déprez (1997, 1999) argues that French n-words have properties comparable to those of presuppositional indefinites in Diesing's (1992) classification (see figure 1): they have intrinsic quantificational force and are subject to QR.

| | *Generic* | *Existential* | Presuppositional |
|---|---|---|---|
| Q-force? | no | no | yes |
| QR | yes | no | yes |

FIGURE 1 Diesing's Taxonomy of indefinites

In this regard, French n-words parallel numeral expressions like *two*, which in Diesing's model have both strong quantificational and weak cardinal readings. Their negative force comes from a meaning that approximates that of the numeral zero (i.e. a quantification with cardinality zero) and not from the incorporation of morphological negation since French n-words are clearly morphologically positive.

In support of this proposal, Déprez points out that NPs with zero quantifiers as in (41) also permit both a "concord" and a double negative reading:

(41) Zero clients ont mangé zero gâteaux.
Zero clients have eaten zero cakes

Furthermore conditions on the concord reading of zero numerals closely resemble those limiting the concord reading of n-word chains. First, the presence of *pas* forces a double negation reading as in (42a):

(42) Je n'ai pas mangé zero gâteaux. [DN]
I NE have not eaten zero cakes

Second, the concord reading between zero numerals fails to obtain across clausal borders:

(43) Zéro restaurateurs ont avoué que leurs clients avaient mangé zéro gt̂eaux.
Zero restaurant owners have confessed that their customer have eaten zero cakes.

Accordingly, Déprez (1997, 1999) analyzes the concord reading of French n-words as the formation of a polyadic resumptive quantifier that binds multiple variables, adapting a proposal by May's (1989) for English examples like (44):

(44) No one loves no one

On this view, the concord reading for (45a) corresponds to the formation of a single binary resumptive numeral quantifier informally represented as below:

(45) a. Personne n'a rien vu.
Nobody NE has nothing seen
b. NO/ZERO$_{x,y}$ [Person($x$) & Thing ($y$)] ($x$ saw $y$)

Since the formation of a single polyadic quantifier implies the presence of a single negation (or zero numeral-like element), the proposal accounts for the concord reading. Double negative readings obtain whenever polyadic resumptive quantification fails, forcing the semantic computation of each negative quantifier or zero numeral separately. Déprez (1997, 1999) proposes two conditions on resumptive quantification. Only quantifiers that 1) QR in the same scope domain and 2) are sufficiently parallel or similar can form a polyadic resumptive quantifier. Condition 1), which is optimally matched in a single clause domain, has the effect of reducing the clause-mate restriction of French negative concord to the clause-mate restriction on QR. As Déprez (1999) abundantly illustrates, in French, conditions on concord readings between n-words indeed closely match conditions on inverse scope readings between universal and existential quantifiers. Condition 2) on the other hand, builds on May (1989) to explain the double negation reading induced by the presence of *pas*. As noted by May (1989), quantifiers must be sufficiently similar to allow the formation of a resumptive quantifier. Thus, for instance, while resumptive quantification is possible in (46a), it is excluded in (46b), even though the examples arguably share one reading.

(46) a. Few detectives solved few cases.

b. Not many detectives solved few cases.

Déprez (1997, 1999) argues that formation of a polyadic resumptive quantifier between *pas* and any other n-word is prevented by such a lack of parallelism. Being the main marker of negation, *pas* has the semantics of a sentential operator that binds no variable. French n-words, in contrast, are variable binding numeral quantifiers, and are thus clearly distinct in nature. Accordingly, resumptive quantification cannot succeed between *pas* and French n-words. Understood in this way, the proposed parallelism restriction on resumptive quantification has some strong consequences. First, it entails that whenever concord is a form of resumptive quantification, sentential negation cannot take part in it, as it is semantically distinct from n-words. Consequently, languages or constructions in which sentential negation induce a concord reading, like Spanish or Italian, must involve a type of negative concord closer to the Creole type than to the French type, that is, a variable binding operation rather than resumptive quantification. Déprez (2000) provides evidence supporting this conclusion for Italian and other Romance languages. Second, whenever resumptive quantification is involved, the availability of concord readings ought to vary with the nature of the n-words involved. The greater the parallelism between (quantificational) n-words, the stronger the availability of resumptive quantification and concord. The variable availability of concord readings among distinct types of n-words in French is illustrated by paradigms like (47), repeated from Déprez (2000):

(47) a. Personne n'a rien mangé. [NC favored]
No one NE has nothing eaten

b. Aucun enfant n'a rien mangé. [NC/DN]
No child NE has nothing eaten

c. Personne n'a mangé aucun gâteau. [DN favored]
No one NE has eaten no cake.

d. Aucun enfant n'a mangé aucun gâteau. [DN only]
No child NE has eaten no cake.

The key distinction between the two types of negative concord set apart by Déprez (1997, 1999) resides in the differing semantic nature of n-words. HC n-words are variables without quantificational force that must be bound, French n-words are numeral quantifiers with intrinsic quantificational force that can undergo resumptive quantification. Déprez (2000) provides evidence that these differing semantic properties are reflected in the internal syntax of n-words. Cross-linguistic variations in the properties of negative concord seem thus to be determined by the internal structure of n-words rather than by the properties of sentential negation. Nominal negative expressions (*rien/personne*) with intrinsic quantificational force are shown to occupy a position in the higher functional domain of the DP structure and to manifest determiner-like syntactic properties. N-words without intrinsic quantificational force in contrast, occur in the lower domain of the DP structure and manifest syntactic properties close to those of bare nouns: they are dominated by a variable introducing null determiner. The proposed distinction is structurally represented as follows:

(48) a. French N-word type (+ quantificational force)
$[_{DP}$ personne $[_{NP} \ldots]]$

b. Haitian Creole N-word type (- quantificational force)
$[_{DP} \ldots [_{NP}$ pèsonn$]]$

Support for this view comes from an interesting cross-linguistic correlation noted in Déprez (1999, 2000): languages or constructions that manifest negative concord of the variable binding type (i.e. with negation) allow argument bare nouns quite freely. Not so for languages of the resumptive concord type. This correlation suggests that variable-introducing expressions like non-quantificational n-words and bare nouns may be subject to comparable semantic and structural restrictions. In a recent diachronic study of the evolution of French n-words, Déprez and Martineau (to appear a,b) further show that changes in the meaning of n-words correlate with changes in their syntactic properties that are compatible with the distinction in (48).

While the analysis of French concord as resumptive numeral quantification has a number of attractive consequences, it nonetheless leaves one important question unanswered, namely, why, in regular cases, is concord the most salient reading for a simple chain of n-words. Since nothing in the analysis developed by Déprez (1997, 1999) forces resumptive quantification to be the default option, the saliency of concord in French remains unexplained. It could perhaps be argued that double negative readings are always pragmatically costly (cf. the Gricean maxims of Quantity and Manner), thus leaving concord as the better option. Yet a pragmatic account says nothing about the difference between standard French and English. If negative expressions are negative quantifiers in both languages, why should the concord reading be so prominent in standard French and so difficult in standard English?

In an attempt to address this question, Déprez (1998) explores in unpublished work the possibility that the concord reading of French n-words could be likened to the cumulative reading of numeral quantifiers. Like concord, cumulative readings have been argued to require polyadic quantification in Scha (1981) and May (1989). Landman (1995), however, proposes to reduce cumulativity to semantic plurality. Within a neo-Davidsonian framework of event and plurality, he develops a theory of semantic plurality and a theory of scopelessness and shows how cumulative readings fall out of this theory as cases of scopeless plural readings, without having to add any special mechanism of binary/n-ary quantification.

Landman's theory derives (49b) as a representation of the cumulative reading of (49a):

(49) a. Three boys invited four girls

b. $\exists e \in {}^*\text{INVITE}: \exists x \in {}^*\text{BOY}: \mid x \mid = 3 \ \&\ {}^*\text{Ag}(e) = x \ \&\ \exists y \in {}^*\text{GIRL}: \mid y \mid = 4 \ \&\ {}^*\text{Th}(e) = y$

Here *INVITE is the set of all singular inviting events and their plural sums; *BOY and *GIRL are the set of all singular boys and their plural sums and the set of all singular girls and their sums, respectively; *Ag and *Th are the plural agent role and the plural theme role. The essence of Landman's analysis resides in the definition of plural roles:

(50) ${}^*\text{Ag}(e) = \sqcup\{\text{Ag}(e') : e' \in \text{AT}(e)\}$

Given this, (49) means: there is a sum of inviting events with some sum of three boys as plural agent and some sum of four girls as a plural theme and each of these three boys invited at least one of these four girls and each of these four girls was invited by at least one of these three boys. For Landman, cumulative readings are in a sense the most basic readings for sentences like (49), because they involve two plural noun phrases entered into the same scope domain with no scoping operations. What Déprez (1998) suggests is that the concord reading of French n-words may be a special case of cumulative readings conceived in this way, the case where the cardinality of the plural sum is zero. Although further elaboration is needed, this approach promises sufficiently attractive consequences to seem worthy of pursuit. First, the limits of concord readings to mono-clausal or predicative domains are automatically derived as a scopal phenomenon, for the domain of predication in Davidsonian theory is the level where the existential closure takes place over the event argument. Second, only scopeless readings are predicted to lead to concord, since only these readings are cumulative. Any disruption of scopelessness would thus affect the availability of concord. These consequences nicely reflect observed restrictions on French negative concord: as Muller (1991) noted, n-words do not take scope over one another in concord readings, and these readings are limited to mono-clausal or predicative domains (cf. Déprez 1997, 1999, Giannakidou 2000, de Swart and Sag 2002). Third, since cumulative readings are not available for negation, this approach straightforwardly predicts that *pas* cannot participate in concord readings. Finally, the approach suggests a possible distinction between French and English on the basis of the nature of their respective 'negative' expressions. If only French n-words have numeral-like properties, then cumulative readings may be restricted to them. Landman (1998) proposes in fact that truly negative expressions never enter scope domains (cf. his Scope Domain Constraint) with the consequence that English negative noun phrases never allow cumulative readings. Such a constraint may be irrelevant for French if, as suggested by Déprez, n-words are not strictly speaking 'negative' expressions but instead are closer to numeral expressions of cardinality zero.

### 3.4 Concord as resumptive quantification

De Swart and Sag (2002) also maintain the view that n-words are negative quantifiers. Instead of adopting parasitism, they work out a suggestion by May (1989) and Van Benthem (1989) for an analysis of negative concord in terms of a resumptive negative quantifier. The analysis is embedded in the polyadic quantifier approach that has been developed as an extension of the generalized quantifier framework developed by Lindström (1966), Barwise and Cooper (1981), Van Benthem (1986) and others, to sentences involving multiple quantifiers. In the generalized quantifier framework, NPs are analyzed as expressions of type $\langle\langle e, t, \rangle, t\rangle$, and determiners are expressions of type $\langle\langle e, t\rangle, \langle\langle e, t\rangle, t\rangle\rangle$ that denote relations between sets. These type assignments correspond to the Lindström characterization of NPs as quantifiers of type $\langle 1\rangle$ and determiners as quantifiers of type $\langle 1, 1\rangle$. The number 1 indicates that the expression binds one variable of a one-place predicate. This raises the question of how generalized quantifier theory applies to transitive, ditransitive, ... sentences, where we find two-, three- ... $n$-place predicates.

The most straightforward extension of generalized quantifier theory to sentences involving two or more NPs assumes that we combine expressions by function application. Thus we obtain an iteration of quantifiers, corresponding to a scopal order between the NPs. A polyadic quantifier (type $\langle 2\rangle$ or higher) that is reducible to an iteration of monadic quantifiers of type $\langle 1\rangle$ is of the same complexity as the monadic quantifiers. So the question arises whether all polyadic quantifiers can be reduced to an iteration of monadic quantifiers. The general answer to this question is negative, and Keenan (1987), May (1989), Van Benthem (1989), Keenan and Westerståhl (1997) discuss a number of contexts that involve essentially polyadic quantifiers. One example is the multiple *wh*-question in (51):

(51) Qui est censé travailler avec qui?
Who is supposed to work with who?
[WHO, WHO](WORK-WITH)
$?_{x,y}$ WORK-WITH

Higginbotham and May (1981) and May (1989) treat the multiple *wh*-question in (51d) as a case of resumptive quantification. Although the question word occurs twice, it is interpreted only once, as a *wh*-complex that binds two variables. This leads to the so-called pair-list reading (Groenendijk and Stokhof 1984), in which the answer to the question is a set of pairs of individuals who are supposed to work together. May (1989) and Van Benthem (1989) extend the resumptive quantifier approach to the reading of (52) in which the love relation is empty (the 'no love world') (cf. also section 3.3 above):

(52) No one loves no one.
[NO$^{ONE}$, NO$^{ONE}$] (LOVE)
NO$_{x,y}$ LOVE
$= \neg\, \exists x\, \exists y$ Love(x,y)

Although the negative quantifier occurs twice, it is interpreted only once, as a negative quantifier complex that binds two variables. In English, resumptive quantification with negative NPs is the exception, rather than the rule. But de Swart and Sag claim that we can use this approach to account for negative concord in typical concord languages like French. In the polyadic quantifier framework, we thus have more than one mode of composition. Good old function composition leads to iteration, but other ways of interpreting a sequence of quantifiers lead to cumulative and resumptive interpretations. For a sequence of negative quantifiers, two interpretations are particularly relevant. If two negative quantifiers enter a scopal relation as an iteration of monadic quantifiers, we end up with a double negation reading (53a). If two negative quantifiers form a resumptive negative quantifier, we end up with a single negation reading, which corresponds to the concord reading (53b):

(53) a. Personne n'aime personne [DN]
No one is such that they love no one
$[\text{NO}_{\{x\}}^{\{Human(x)\}}, \text{NO}_{\{y\}}^{\{Human(y)\}}]$ (Love$(x, y)$)
$= \neg\exists x \neg\exists y$ Love$(x, y)$

b. Personne n'aime personne [NC]
No one loves anyone
$\text{NO}_{\{x,y\}}^{\{Human(x), Human(y)\}}$ $(Love(x, y))$
$= \neg\exists x\, \exists y$ $Love(x, y)$

Formally, the binary resumption of a type $\langle 1, 1\rangle$ quantifier $Q$ is the resumptive quantifier $Q'$ given by: $Q'^{A,B}_{E}(R) = Q^{A\times B}_{E^2}(R)$, where $A$ and $B$ are subsets of the universe of discourse $E$, and $A \times B$ and $R$ are subsets of $E^2$. Resumption is the preferred strategy in concord languages (French, other Romance languages, etc.), iteration is the default in non-concord languages (English, Germanic languages, etc.).

Resumption is not limited to a sequence of two or three quantifiers. A sequence of three or four monadic quantifiers leads to tryadic or quadratic quantifiers:

(54) a. Personne ne dit rien à personne
No one NE says nothing to no one

b. $\text{NO}_{\{x,y,z\}}^{\{Human(x), Thing(y), Human(z)\}}$ (Say$(x, y, z)$)
$= \neg\exists x\, \exists y \exists z$ Say$(x, y, z)$

(55) a. Personne ne dit jamais rien à personne
No one NE says never nothing to no one

b. $\text{NO}^{\{Human(x), Thing(y), Human(z), Time(e)\}}_{\{x,y,z,e\}}(\text{Say}(x,y,z,e))$
$= \neg\exists x\, \exists y \exists z \exists e\ \text{Say}(x,y,z,e)$

The extension of the definition of binary resumption to $k$-ary resumption of a quantifier $Q$ is a type $\langle 1^k, k\rangle$ quantifier.

In analyses that treat negative concord as a variant of negative polarity, sentential negation is viewed as a licensor, and concord items are either licensed by negation, or are self-licensing. Either way, they are treated as dependent elements. In the polyadic approach, the negative concord reading of a sentence involving two or more negative quantifiers does not involve an asymmetry between licensor and dependent element. The creation of a resumptive negative quantifier as defined so far just requires a sequence of anti-additive quantifiers, and does not imply sentential negation. This raises the question of how the polyadic approach treats negation in concord languages. As far as French is concerned, we have already observed that the combination of *pas* and an n-word usually leads to a double negation reading. In certain varieties and certain constructions, concord readings are available as well, however, and negation certainly plays a role in the concord system of other Romance languages. In order to treat a mixture of negation and negative quantifiers in a polyadic approach, de Swart and Sag (2002) extend the rule for the construction of resumptive negative quantifiers to include non-variable binding operators.

The crucial difference between a quantifier such as *personne* ('no one') and an operator like sentential negation is that the former is a variable-binding expression, whereas the latter is not. In the Lindström characterization, the number of variables bound by the quantifier is reflected in the type assignment: for a type $\langle 1\rangle$ or a type $\langle 1,1\rangle$ quantifier, the number of variables bound is 1. As an extension of the standard view of quantifier types, de Swart and Sag propose to treat a non-variable binding operator such as sentential negation as a quantifier with adicity zero, or a quantifier of type $\langle 0\rangle$. Now recall that a resumptive negative quantifier interprets a sequence of anti-additive quantifiers $Q_1 \ldots Q_k$ of type $\langle 1,1\rangle$ as one complex negative quantifier $\text{Res}_Q$ of type $\langle 1^k, k\rangle$. This means that the resumptive quantifier binds the sum of all the variables of the composing quantifiers. Given that sentential negation does not bind any variables, it does not add any variables to the sum of variables bound. As a consequence, it does not change the type of the resumptive quantifier. The result of combining negation and a sequence of negative quantifiers is then that negation is semantically empty in a concord context.

At first, the semantic emptiness of negation might seem like a somewhat odd result, given the familiar approaches to negative concord in which sentential negation plays an important role as the licensor of the concord item (cf. Laka 1990, Ladusaw 1992, Przepiórkowski and Kupść 1997, Corblin and Tovena 2003). However, as Ladusaw (1992: footnotes 10 and 11) admits, that is in fact an important problem. The participation of sentential negation is subject to considerable cross-linguistic variation, which means that we have to assume that each language has its own set of licensing conditions on n-words. Given that licensing conditions on negative polarity are by and large the same across languages, and that variation only obtains within strict limits, this is not a very attractive result. The polyadic approach provides an explanation of the cross-linguistic variation we find: given that simple negation is semantically empty in concord contexts, languages are free to include or exclude sentential negation from the concord system.

One advantage of the extension of the rule of resumption to include non-variable binding operators is that de Swart and Sag can integrate embedding of concord items under *sans* 'without' in their system. They take *sans* to be a negative preposition that combines with an infinitive to build an intersective modifier. Semantically, it is a type $\langle 0 \rangle$ quantifier:

(56) a. Anne est partie sans dire au revoir
Anne has left without saying goodbye
Leave(anne) & $\neg$ Say(anne, goodbye)

b. Anne est partie sans rien dire
Anne has left without saying anything
Leave(anne) & $\neg \exists x$ Say(anne, $x$)

The assumption that *sans* is a type $\langle 0 \rangle$ quantifier that can build a resumptive negative quantifier with an embedded concord item is sufficient to account for the single negation reading of (56b).

The account in terms of resumptive polyadic quantification developed by de Swart and Sag (2002) takes the situation in French as its point of departure, rather than languages in which a marker of sentential negation is obligatorily present. It allows in fact for the marker of sentential negation to be external to the negative concord system, as is the case for French *pas*. The fact that n-words form the core of the system of negative concord does not exclude the possibility that non variable binding operators such as *sans* 'without' build concord chains with n-words, however. An important question that de Swart and Sag (2002) leave open is the issue of why in certain languages iteration is the default mode of combination, whereas in other languages it is resumption. The beginnings of an answer to this question, in the general spirit of the approach developed by de Swart and Sag (2002) are formulated by de Swart (2004), who proposes an account of the form and meaning of negation in bi-directional Optimality Theory.

## 4 Conclusion

In this chapter, we considered the possibilities and impossibilities of negative concord and double negation in modern standard French, and some of its diachronic and/or dialectal variations. More data have become available through careful empirical research in the last few years, and this has lead to a proliferation of theoretical proposals concerning negative concord in the linguistic literature. The analyses of negative concord developed with special attention to the French case share an emphasis on the possibility of double negation readings, a study of the expression of sentential negation (position of *ne* and *pas*), and an attempt to relate syntactic and semantic characteristics of n-words. Further cross-linguistic research, involving both micro-level and macro-level variation will help to determine the range of possibilities and the limitations on the expression of negation and negative concord in French and other languages.

## References

Ashby, W., ed. 1993. *Linguistic perspectives on the Romance languages*. Amsterdam: John Benjamins.

Attal, P., ed. 1994. *Actes du colloque de Paris X, Nanterre*. numéro spécial de LYNX.

Baker, C. L. 1970. Double negatives. *Linguistic Inquiry* 1:169–186.

Barwise, J. and R. Cooper. 1981. Generalized quantifiers and natural language. *Linguistics and Philosophy* 4:159–219.

Belletti, A. 1994. *Pas* vs. *piu*: a note. In Cinque et al. (1994).

Belletti, A. and L. Rizzi, eds. 1996. *Parameters and functional heads*. Oxford: Oxford University Press.

Blutner, R. 2004. Pragmatics and the lexicon. In Horn and Ward (2004).

Bok-Bennema, R., B. de Jonge, B. Kampers-Manhe, and A. Molendijk, eds. 2001. *Adverbial modification*. Amsterdam: Rodopi.

Bolinger, D. 1972. *Degree words*. The Hague: Mouton.

Borsley, R. and A. Przepiórkowski, eds. 1999. *Slavic in HPSG*. Stanford, CA: CSLI publications.

Bréal, M. 1897. *Essai de sémantique: science des significations*. Paris: Hachette.

Cinque, G., J. Koster, J.-Y. Pollock, L. Rizzi, and R. Zanuttini, eds. 1994. *Paths towards Universal Grammar: Studies in honor of Richard S. Kayne*. Georgetown: Georgetown University Press.

Corblin, F. 1992. Le traitement des complex négatifs en DRT. In *Actes du colloque ECCOS*, pages 157–175. Orsay.

Corblin, F. 1994. Sémantique des négatifs complexes. In Attal (1994), pages 278–298. numéro spécial de LYNX.

Corblin, F. 1996. Multiple negation processing in natural language. *Theoria* 17:214–259.

Corblin, F. and I. Derzhansky. 1997. Multiple negation, optional arguments and the reification of eventualities. In Corblin et al. (1997), pages 219–243.

Corblin, F., D. Godard, and J.-M. Marandin, eds. 1997. *Empirical issues in formal syntax and semantics*. Bern: Peter Lang.

Corblin, F. and L. Tovena. 2001. On the multiple expression of negation in Romance. In D'Hulst et al. (2001).

Corblin, F. and L. Tovena. 2003. L'expression de la négation dans les langues romanes. In Godard (2003).

Dahl, O. 1979. Typology of sentences negation. *Linguistics* 17:79–106.

De Swart, H. 1998. Licensing of negative polarity items under inverse scope. *Lingua* 105:175–200.

De Swart, H. 2001. Négation et coordination: la conjonction *ni*. In Bok-Bennema et al. (2001), pages 109–124.

De Swart, H. 2004. Marking and interpretation of negation: a bi-directional ot approach. ms. Utrecht University.

De Swart, H. and I. Sag. 2002. Negation and negative concord in Romance. *Linguistics and Philosophy* 25:373–417.

DeGraff, M., ed. 1999. *Language creation and language change: creole, diachrony and development*. Cambridge MA: MIT Press.

Déprez, V. 1997. Two types of negative concord. *Probus* 9:103–143.

Déprez, V. 1998. French negative concord. ms. Rutgers University.

Déprez, V. 1999. The roots of negative concord in French lexifier creoles. In DeGraff (1999), pages 375–427.

Déprez, V. 2000. Parallel (a)symmetries and the internal structure of negative expressions. *Natural language and linguistic theory* 18:253–342.

Déprez, V. 2003. Concordance négative, syntaxe des mots-n et variation dialectale. *Cahier de Linguistique Francaise* 25:97 –118.

Déprez, V. and F. Martineau. (to appear)a. Micro-parametric variation and negative concord. In *Proceedings of LSRL*, pages 157–175. J. Benjamins.

Déprez, V. and F. Martineau. (to appear)b. Pour une analyse micro-paramétrique de la concordance négative. In Francis Corblin ((to appear).

D'Hulst, Y., J. Rooryck, and J. Schroten, eds. 2001. *Romance languages and linguistic theories 1999*. Amsterdam: John Benjamins.

Diesing, M. 1992. *Indefinites*. Cambridge: MIT Press.

Dowty, D. 1993. Deductive versus semantic accounts of reasoning: the relevance of negative polarity and negative concord marking. In *Proceedings of CSL*, vol. 29, pages 91–124. Chicago: Chicago University Press.

Espagñol Echevarría, M. 1995. A typology for NPI-licensing. ms. UCLA.

Francis Corblin, L. K., Sylvie Ferrando, ed. (to appear). *Indéfinis et Prédications*. Paris: Presses Universitaires de Paris-Sorbonne.

Gaatone, D. 1971. *Etude descriptive du système de la négation en français*. Genève: Droz.

Gabbay, D. and F. Guenthner, eds. 1989. *Handbook of Philosophical logic*, vol. 4. Dordrecht: Reidel.

Gärdenfors, P., ed. 1987. *Generalized quantifiers*. Dordrecht: Reidel.

Giannakidou, A. 1998. *Polarity sensitivity as (non)veridical dependency*. Amsterdam: John Benjamins.

Giannikadou, A. 2000. Negative ... concord. *Natural language and linguistic theory* 18:457–523.

Godard, D., ed. 2003. *Les langues romanes: problèmes de la phrase simple*. Paris: CNRS Editions.

Grévisse, M. 1993. *Le bon usage*. Paris: Duculot. 13th revised edition.

Groenendijk, J., T. Janssen, and M. Stokhof, eds. 1981. *Formal methods in the study of language*. Amsterdam: Mathematical Centre.

Groenendijk, J. and M. Stokhof. 1984. *Studies in the semantics of questions and the pragmatics of answers*. Ph.D. thesis, University of Amsterdam.

Haegeman, L. 1995. *The syntax of negation*. Cambridge: Cambridge University Press.

Haegeman, L. and R. Zanuttini. 1996. Negative concord in West Flemish. In Belletti and Rizzi (1996), pages 117–179.

Herburger, E. 2001. The negative concord puzzle revisited. *Natural Language Semantics* 9:289–333.

Higginbotham, J. and R. May. 1981. Questions, quantifiers and crossing. *The linguistic review* 1:41–79.

Horn, L. 1989. *The natural history of negation*. Chicago: Chicago University Press.

Horn, L. R. and Y.-S. Lee. 1995. *Any* as an indefinite plus *even*. ms. Yale University.

Horn, L. R. and G. Ward, eds. 2004. *Handbook of Pragmatics*. Oxford: Blackwell.

Jespersen, O. 1917. Negation in English and other languages. reprinted in *Selected writings of Otto Jespersen* (1962), George Allen and Unwin, London, pp. 3–151.

Jespersen, O. 1924. *The philosophy of grammar*. London: Allen and Unwin.

Kamp, H. and U. Reyle. 1993. *From discourse to logic*. Dordrecht: Kluwer Academic Press.

Kanazawa, M., C. Piñón, and H. De Swart, eds. 1996. *Quantifiers, deduction, and context*. Stanford, CA: CSLI publications.

Kayne, R. 1981. Ecp-extensions. *Linguistic Inquiry* 12:349–371.

Keenan, E. 1987. Unreducible $n$-ary quantifiers in natural language. In Gärdenfors (1987), pages 109–150.

Keenan, E. 1992. Beyond the Frege boundary. *Linguistics and Philosophy* 15:199–221.

Keenan, E. and D. Westerståhl. 1997. Generalized quantifiers in linguistics and logic. In Van Benthem and ter Meulen (1997), pages 837–893.

Labov, W. 1972. Negative attraction and negative concord in English grammar. *Language* 48:773–818.

Ladusaw, B. 1992. Expressing negation. In *Proceedings of SALT*, vol. 2, pages 237–259. Columbus Ohio: Ohio State University.

Laka Mugarza, I. 1990. *Negation in syntax*. Ph.D. thesis, MIT.

Laka Mugarza, I. 1993. Negative fronting in Romance. In Ashby (1993), pages 315–333.

Landman, F. 1996. Plurality. In Lappin (1996), pages 425–457.

Landman, F. 1998. Plural and maximalization. In Rothstein (1998), pages 237–271.

Lappin, S., ed. 1996. *Handbook of contemporary semantic theory*. London: Blackwell.

Lindström, P. 1966. First order predicate logic with generalized quantifiers. *Theoria* 35:1–11.

Martineau, F. and V. Déprez. (to appear). *Pas rien/Pas aucun* en français classique. Variation dialectale et historique. *Langue Française.*

Martineau, F. and R. Mougeon. 2003. A sociolinguistic study of the origins of *ne* deletion in European and Quebec French. *Language* 79:118–152.

May, R. 1989. Interpreting logical form. *Linguistics and Philosophy* 12:387–435.

Moignet, G. 1984. *Grammaire de l'ancien français*. Paris: Klincksieck.

Moltmann, F. 1995. Exception sentences and polyadic quantification. *Linguistics and Philosophy* 18:223–280.

Moltmann, F. 1996. Resumptive quantifiers in exception sentences. In Kanazawa et al. (1996), pages 139–170.

Moritz, L. and D. Valois. 1994. Pied-piping and specifier-head agreement. *Linguistic Inquiry* 25:667–707.

Muller, C. 1991. *La négation en français*. Genève: Droz.

Przepiórkowski, A. and A. Kupść. 1999. Eventuality negation and negative concord in polish and italian. In Borsley and Przepiórkowski (1999).

Rothstein, S., ed. 1998. *Event and Grammar*. Dordrecht: Kluwer.

Scha, R. 1981. Distributive, collective and cumulative quantification. In Groenendijk et al. (1981), pages 483–512.

Tellier, C. 1987. Predicate quantifiers. *McGill Working Papers in Linguistics* 4:1–41.

Tovena, L. 1998. *The fine structure of polarity sensitivity*. New York: Garland.

Vallduví, E. 1994. Polarity items, n-words and minimizers in Catalan and Spanish. *Probus* 6:263–294.

Van Benthem, J. 1986. *Essays in logical semantics*. Dordrecht: Reidel.

Van Benthem, J. 1989. Polyadic quantifiers. *Linguistics and Philosophy* 12:437–464.

Van Benthem, J. and A. ter Meulen, eds. 1997. *Handbook of Logic and Language*. Amsterdam: Elzevier.

Van der Wouden, T. 1997. *Negative contexts. Collocation, polarity and multiple negation*. London: Routledge.

Van der Wouden, T. and F. Zwarts. 1993. A semantic analysis of negative concord. In *Proceedings of SALT*, vol. 3. Ithaca (NY): Cornell University.

Vlachou, E. 2000. *Analyse sémantique de sans et de ses équivalents grecs xoris, dhixos, anef*. Master's thesis, University of Paris VII, Jussieu.

Westerståhl, D. 1989. Quantifiers in formal and natural languages. In Gabbay and Guenthner (1989), pages 1–131.

Zanuttini, R. 1991. *Syntactic properties of sentential negation*. Ph.D. thesis, University of Pennsylvania.

# Part V

# Information

20

# Prosodic, Syntactic and Pragmatic Aspects of Information Structure—an Introduction *

CLAIRE BEYSSADE, ELISABETH DELAIS-ROUSSARIE, JENNY DOETJES, JEAN-MARIE MARANDIN, AND ANNIE RIALLAND

## 1 Outline

This part is devoted to the interfaces between Information and Prosody and between Information and Syntax in French Grammar. Our aim is not to propose a particular architecture of Grammar that implements a level of information structure, but to state descriptive generalizations. They are based, on the one hand, on a detailed review of the current literature and, on the other, on our own research. We will show how Focus marking, Discourse Topic marking and the activation state of Discourse Referents are reflected in the prosody and syntax of French.

In this first introductory chapter, we define the categories we use to analyze the different aspects of information that have an impact on Grammar (section 2) and we present the basic features of French prosody (section 3).

The second chapter, chapter 21, is devoted to the prosody of Focus marking (F-marking) and Discourse Topic marking (T-marking). We show that the contrast between broad and narrow focus is marked by

* Jenny Doetjes gratefully acknowledges the support from NWO (grant #355-70-003).

*Handbook of French Semantics.*
Francis Corblin and Henriëtte de Swart (eds.).
Copyright © 2004, CSLI Publications.

placing an illocutionary boundary tone on the right edge of the focal domain and that the reshaping of Discourse Topics (in the sense of Büring 1997) correlates with the presence of a specific accent akin to accent B in English or German (cf. Bolinger 1965).

The last three chapters are devoted to phenomena in French syntax that are often cited in relation to informational categories such as Focus, Ground and the activation state of Discourse Referents. Chapter 22 addresses dislocation. We will consider the syntax and pragmatics of different types of dislocation, which are illustrated in (1)[1]. These sentences present cases of so-called 'hanging topic left dislocation', 'clitic left dislocation' and 'right dislocation', respectively:

(1) a. Cette femme, je n'ai pas confiance en elle.
'This woman, I do not have confidence in her'

b. A la campagne, Paul n'y reste jamais longtemps.
'In the country, Paul never stays a long time'

c. Je ne le connais pas, cet homme.
'I do not know him, this man'

We will discuss the importance of the activation state of discourse referents, as well as some subtle pragmatic and prosodic properties of the different types of dislocated sentences. Dislocation will also be contrasted with topicalization.

Chapter 23 deals with cleft sentences. Cleft sentences are often claimed to constitute a focus-related sentence type. However, we argue that this view is not correct. Focalization does not play a special role in clefts. Different Ground/Focus articulations are possible, and these are reflected by the prosodic structure. Some examples of clefts, which have the form *c'est XP qui/que*, are given in (2):

(2) a. C'est le petit qui est tombé dans l'escalier, pas Marie.
'It is the little one who fell down the stairs, not Marie'

b. C'est avec plaisir que je vous invite à ce séminaire.
'It is with pleasure that I invite you to this seminar'

The material in the relative clause can be either part of the Focus (as in the "atypical", but frequent, cleft in (2b)) or not (as in the "standard" cleft in (2a)). Even though the XP position usually contains at least some focused material, it is shown that this is due to an independent

[1]Throughout this part, we use the following notational conventions for translations, glosses and prosodic structures. Translations into English are put between single quotation marks and they start — unless they do not constitute a full sentence — with a capital. The (more litteral) glosses and the prosodic structures do not start with a capital unless the first word is *I* or a proper name.

factor: the clause introduced by *qui/que* is presuppositional, with the result that clefts will not be used in contexts where only the information in the *que/qui* clause is focalized.

The last chapter, 24, considers subject NP inversion in French. It is commonly accepted that word order variation is related to the Ground/Focus articulation. In Romance languages, subject NPs that are (part of) the focus of the sentence have to or can be placed in sentence final position (see a.o. Costa 1998, Pinto 1997, Zubizarreta 1998). We will consider two types of NP inversion: stylistic inversion in questions and relative clauses (see (3a) and (3b)), unaccusative inversion in subjunctive clauses and in root narrative clauses (see (3c) and (3d)).

(3) a. Où sont allés les enfants?
'Where have the children gone?'
b. Les étudiants qu'entraîne Bernard ont réussi.
'The students that Bernard trained have succeeded'
c. Je veux que vienne Marie.
'I want that Mary comes'
d. Le silence se fit. Alors fusèrent des cris de protestation.
'It became silent. Then shouts of protest burst out'

We show that the main factor in inversion appropriateness is the status of the predicate which constitutes the Ground. For unaccusative inversion there are also conditions on the subject, which have to do with focus, according to some authors, or with the activation state of the discourse referent, according to others.

## 2 Information

It is a well-known fact that there is no consensus among theories and frameworks about the terminology or the concepts that are appropriate for analyzing the status of the informative content of utterances or parts of utterances. Moreover, terms such as *Old/New information, Focus, (Back-)Ground, Topic, Assertion/Presupposition, Contrast, Emphasis* (...) have different meanings in different analyses. Using them or recycling them easily leads to confusion. Therefore, we first define the categories we resort to in order to state sound and cross-theoretical descriptive generalizations.

The framework that we adopt is essentially that of Büring (1997), (1998), to which we add insights or proposals found in Jacobs (1984), Lambrecht (1994) and Lambrecht & Michaelis (1998). It has four main characteristics. First, it relies on propositional definitions of Information, Ground, Focus, Given, Discourse Topic and activation states of Discourse Referents. Second, it is a dynamic approach: utterances are analyzed with respect to the contexts in which they are embedded and the ones they project for pursuing the Discourse. Third, from a methodological point of view, it is an analytical approach. The propositional approach provides a unified framework in which concepts are defined. It also allows the notion of information to be split into three dimensions we consider independent: (i) Ground/Focus articulation in which the potential update of utterances (relative to their contexts) is central, (ii) Discourse strategy in which the partial or total embedding of an utterance in the Discourse Topic is crucial and, finally, (iii) the activation state of Discourse Referents in the current segment of Discourse (active, inactive, accessible). Finally, we take the informational categories as primitives. Given the range and the variety of forms (belonging to morphology, syntax, word order or intonation) which have been recognized as related to the marking of informational distinctions, we choose to ground our definitions in a model of Discourse independently of the grammaticalized forms they receive in the grammar of a given language.

## 2.1 Ground/Focus articulation

The propositional conception of information contrasts with "the segmentational view of information" (Lambrecht, 1994: 49). In this latter view, "the information conveyed by a proposition is factored out and matched with individual sentence constituents" (ibid.). As for the propositional approaches, two types can be distinguished. The first is formulated in informational terms. Ground is defined as the part of the propositional content that is shared or inferable from the context. Focus is the part of the propositional content that is new in the context. In other terms, Focus contributes the informative part of the content.[2] The second type has been proposed by Jacobs (1984). In this view, the Ground-Focus articulation (henceforth GFA) is related to illocutionary semantics. Focus is defined as the part of the content that is specifically affected by the illocutionary operator associated with the sentence: Focus is the "inhaltlich besonders betroffen" content of an utterance in the scope of an illocutionary operator. In both definitions, GFA is conceived of as a partition of the content of utterances. They overlap in the general case since in standard assertions, Focus contributes a proposition that is informative and specifically asserted. However, the illocutionary definition is more general than the informative one since it covers all illocutionary types of utterances. It makes it possible to address the issue of GFA in other utterance types such as questions and commands along

[2]Lambrecht's definition belongs to such a type: "the Focus is the component of a pragmatically structured proposition whereby the assertion differs from the [pragmatic] presupposition" (Lambrecht, 1994: 213; brackets added).

with assertions. In questions, for example, the informative part of the content is not contributed by the focused constituent. In *wh*-questions, *wh*-words are the target of the Question and do not contribute informative content, except for the type of the variable introduced by such words (see Beyssade et al. 2003). Moreover, the illocutionary definition makes it possible to take up a long-standing problem faced by informational definitions: there are assertive utterances in which propositions that are already present in the context or the situation are asserted and marked as broad focus utterances. Examples are the utterance *it's raining* uttered in a situation where both interlocutors do see the raining (see Lambrecht 1994) and an answer such as *Pierre est arrivé* 'Pierre has arrived' to the confirmative question *Pierre est bien arrivé?* 'Pierre has arrived, hasn't he?'.[3]

### 2.1.1 Illocutionary definition

Each utterance is associated with an illocutionary force (Assertion, Question, Command). The illocutionary force is represented by an illocutionary operator (IO) taking the content of the utterance as its argument. The content is partitioned under the IO:

(4) IO $<$Ground, Focus$>$ with IO $\in$ {ASSERT, QUEST, COMMAND}

We distinguish two types of partition: broad focalization and narrow focalization. In the former, the whole content is affected by the operator; in the latter, only part of the content is affected. We give two illustrations of definition (4): answer (5) is an assertion with narrow focalization and (6) an assertion with broad focalization:[4]

(5) (Qui est venu? 'Who came?')
Marie est venue.
'Marie came'

(6) (Qu'est-ce qui se passe? 'What is happening?')
Marie est venue.

The GFA of (5) and (6) is made explicit in (7a) and (7b) respectively:

(7) a. ASSERT $< \lambda x\ \exists e$ (Venu (x,e)), Marie $>$
b. ASSERT $< \lambda P\ P, \exists e$ (Venu (Marie,e)) $>$

---

[3]In both cases, the speaker asserts a presupposed content, pragmatically presupposed in the former, lexically presupposed in the latter (*bien* in this use is a presupposition trigger in French).

[4]Indeed, the answer *Marie est venue* is not the most frequent in ordinary use, but it is the one which makes it possible to generate elliptical answers, such as the most frequent answer *Marie*.

In (7a), the NP *Marie* contributes the focal content, whereas in (7b), the whole sentence *Marie est venue* does. The Ground, being conceived of as an open proposition, is represented as the function $\lambda$P P when it is empty (cf. (7b)). Such a function corresponds to the question *Qu'est-ce qui se passe?*, i.e. the propositions P that are true at the moment of utterance (see section 2.2.3 below).[5]

### 2.1.2 Semantics

Utterances (5) and (6) have the same vericonditional content:

(8) $\exists$e Venu (Marie, e)

However, the two utterances differ in their GFA, as shown in (7). The interpretation of ASSERT is straightforward: Ground is a function applied to Focus. ASSERT <G,F> is reducible to G(F). We distinguish the part of content affected by the illocutionary operator, and by the same token, the part that is specifically asserted in assertions or the part that is specifically questioned in questions. We represent this distinction following Lambrecht (1994) as in (9a) and (9b), corresponding to the assertions in (5) and (6):[6]

(9) a. Assertion: x = Marie
 b. Assertion: P = $\exists$e Venu (Marie, e)

The analysis represented in (9) captures the difference in update value between (5) and (6): the update content is contributed by the NP *Marie* in (9a), whereas it is contributed by the Sentence *Marie est venue* in (9b). In both cases, the update is conceived of as an identity relation between a variable (in the Ground) and a value (contributed by the Focus). By the same token, we can say that a "second layer of meaning" (Büring, 1997: 36) is superimposed on the vericonditional layer.

Formally, we only deal with propositions. Like the frameworks used by Lambrecht (1994) and Büring (1997), our framework is "a purely propositional theory of information structure" (Büring 1997: 40). Ground

[5]The present framework shares some features with Krifka 1992, 1993. Both are of the structured meaning type (Krifka, 1993: 270) and introduce an illocutionary operator into the analysis of the meaning of utterances. In our approach, the illocutionary operator plays a crucial role in the meaning of GFA: the illocutionary operator associated with a given utterance determines the meaning of the partition of the propositional content into focal content and ground content.

[6]We are talking about pragmatic assertions here (cf. Lambrecht 1994). The notion of semantic assertion as opposed to semantic presupposition plays a role in chapter 23, Cleft Sentences, which deals with clefts. The semantic assertion of the sentence is defined as the part of the sentence that is affected by wide scope negation, as opposed to the semantic presupposition, which is not. As we will illustrate in chapter 23 the semantic presupposition can be part of the focus of the sentence, and as such it can be pragmatically asserted.

is a propositional function, on the basis of which we can define the Focus semantic value of the utterance as a set of propositional alternatives. For example, the Focus semantic value of (5) is given in (10):

(10) $[[\text{Marie est venue}]]^{F}$ = {Marie est venue, Pierre est venu, Paul est venu...}

Uttering an assertion implies choosing one propositional alternative in the Focus semantic value of the utterance. Giving a GFA to the assertion comes down to specifying the update content of the utterance. In assertions, the update content can be modeled as a proposition involving an identity predicate. We shall see in chapter 21 (Prosody) that, in French, GFA is transparently marked by illocutionary boundary tones.

### 2.2 Discourse Topic and thematic shifters

In general, the notion of Discourse Topic (henceforth DT) has received two definitions in the literature: (a) the entity the Discourse is about and (b) the issue addressed in the segment of discourse, which is defined as the question under debate (a.o. McNally 1998). Büring's (1997) proposal is an implementation of the latter and explicitly addresses the relations between DT dynamics and GFA. Since the DT is defined as a question, question-answer pairs (henceforth Q-A pairs) provide an empirical domain for observing the effect of broad/narrow focalization and the reflection of discourse topic continuity or discontinuity in utterances. This is so because questions both introduce a piece of information into the context and shape the issue at hand in the discourse or conversation. They intervene in the partition of the content of answers (hence their use as a test to analyze the GFA of a given utterance) and they provide a means to model the notion of Discourse Topic.[7]

#### 2.2.1 Discourse Topic

Büring (1997) draws attention to "deviant answers" in his analysis of Discourse Topics (henceforth DTs). Büring (1998) proposes analyzing deviant answers as a discourse strategy involving several nonexplicit discourse moves (answering, asking a question), whereas direct answers involve only one move (answering) (see also Roberts 1996). An example of a simple strategy is given in (11):

(11) a. Que fumaient les chanteurs de rock?
'What smoked rock singers?'

[7]The idea of modeling the DT as a question is not a new idea. Cf. a.o. Ochs Keenan (1976).

b. (Les chanteurs de rock fumaient) du haschisch.
'Rock singers smoked hashish'

In (12), two questions make up a single turn; the latter presupposes an implicit answer to the former:

(12) a. Are there replacement batteries for this thing? Where can I buy them?
b. Did you kill him? Why did you kill him?
(= ex. 9, Büring 1998)

In (13), Büring proposes that the answer (13b) is linked to an implicit question that is a subordinate question to the initial question (13a) and that we may reconstruct as (13c):

(13) a. Que fumaient les chanteurs de rock?
b. Les chanteurs de rock anglais fumaient du haschisch.
'English rock singers smoked hashish'
c. Que fumaient les chanteurs de rock anglais?
'What did English rock singers smoke?'

The discourse moves in the Q-A pairs (11), (12) or (13) have been made explicit in (14a), (14b) and (14c) respectively, where implicit moves are in brackets:

(14) a. Initial Question – Answer
b. Initial Question – [Answer] – Subordinate Question
c. Initial Question – [Subordinate Question] – Answer

The main idea is that an utterance in discourse may require accommodation of a subordinate answer or question relevant to the initial question. In the case of (13b), the speaker introduces a subordinate question that brings up a sub-issue of the global issue defined by the initial question (a partial topic). Moreover, the answer (13b) opens more sub-issues introducing rock singers of yet other nationalities: American rock singers, French rock singers, etc.

The pair (13a,b) illustrates a Discourse in which the DT is split into different sub-Topics. We will call this a downward complex strategy. The reverse is possible as well: the DT can be enlarged. Consider (15). The answer (15b) to (15a) requires accommodating a larger question such as (15c):

(15) a. Que fumaient les Beatles dans les années soixante?
'What did the Beatles smoke in the sixties?'
b. Les chanteurs pop fumaient du haschisch à cette époque.
'Pop singers smoked hashish at the time'

c. Que fumaient les chanteurs pop dans les années soixante?
'What did pop singers smoke in the sixties?'

We can visualize the discourse move in (15a,b) as in (16). The initial question plays the role of a subordinate question with respect to a superordinate nonexplicit question.

(16) [Superordinate Question] – Initial Question – Answer

In (13), answer (13b) calls for pursuing the Discourse on other subtopics, whereas in (15), answer (15b) calls for the closure of the thematic development.

### 2.2.2 Thematic shifters

Büring observes that answers in a complex strategy present a specific intonation. Take example (17) in German (= ex. (13) in Büring, 1997: 56), which is discursively analogous to (11):

(17) Q: Was hatten die Popstars an?
'What did the pop stars wear?'

A: Die $[\text{WEIBlichen}]_T$ Popstars trugen $[\text{KAFtane}]_F$
'The female pop stars wore caftans'

The accent on *weiblichen* is different from that on *Kaftane*; moreover, it is obligatory. Since it is obligatory, it should be accounted for in the Grammar. Büring calls the constituent bearing the accent related to the reshaping of DTs an *S-Topic*. In order to avoid any confusion with the usual notion of Topic (defined as the particular entity the Discourse is about), we call it a (discourse)-thematic shifter (T-shifter).

### 2.2.3 Modeling the Discourse Topic

In order to model the DT in the way sketched above, we need an analysis of questions. Following Hambling (1973), we will assume that the denotation of a question is a set of propositions. Consider again the question in (11a). We have distinguished two sorts of answers. In (11b), the answer is direct and does not modify the DT. The DT is a set of propositions, the set of relevant propositions that resolve the question:

(18) DT = {rock singers smoked marijuana, rock singers smoked hashish, rock singers smoked Marlboros, ...}

On the other hand, in (13b), the answer is partial: it modifies the DT. The initial question and the subordinate question together make up a set of sets of propositions:

(19) DT = { {English rock singers smoked marijuana, English rock singers smoked hashish, English rock singers smoked Marlboros, ...}, {French rock singers smoked marijuana, French rock singers smoked hashish, French rock singers smoked Marlboros, ...}, {American rock singers ...}, ...}

The main contrast for the issue at stake is that which opposes simple DTs to complex, or "layered", DTs:

(20) DT (simple) = $\{ p^1, p^2, \ldots, p^n \}$
DT (layered) = $\{ \{q^1, q^2, \ldots, q^m\}, \{q'^1, q'^2, \ldots, q'^s\}, \ldots\}$

The definition of Discourse Topic we have just given provides us with the framework we need in order to define the notion of Given content. By Given content, we mean the open proposition that represents the common content of the propositions making up the DT.[8]

In the case of simple DTs, the Given content is equivalent to the content making up the Ground. The Given content in (11b) is represented in (21a). In the case of layered DTs, the Given content is different from the content making up the Ground. The Given content in (13b) is represented in (21b):

(21) a. $\lambda y\ \forall x$ (Chanteur de rock (x) $\rightarrow$ fumer (x, y))

b. $\lambda y\ \lambda Q\ \forall x$ ( (Chanteur de rock (x) & Q (x) ) $\rightarrow$ fumer (x, y))

Crucially, what counts as Given content in plain answers (elaborating a simple DT) and in answers reshaping the DT (hence elaborating a layered DT) is different. We will see in chapter 21 that prosody is sensitive to the constituents that instantiate a variable introduced in the reshaping of the DT (for example, the variable Q in (21b) instantiated by *anglais* in (13b)). In chapter 24, we show that the contrast in content is relevant for the analysis of subject NP inversion.

### 2.2.4 Multiple Foci, contrastive Topic and Focus

Here, we outline how to analyze the descriptive notions of multiple Foci, contrastive Foci and contrastive Topics in our framework.

[8]Büring (1998, p. 40 et sq), following Schwarzschild (1999), defines Givenness in semantic terms, as we do here. Hence, Givenness is not reducible to the fact of being mentioned in the context. Büring's definition is the following: "For NPs, NP will be Given if it has an antecedent in the Discourse, i.e. a coreferring expression. For any other category X, X will be Given if the existential closure of X is implied by the existential closure of some antecedent expression." Our definition does not distinguish between NPs and other categories. On the other hand, we separate treatment of the activation state of DRs associated with NPs (see 2.3 below). In the present framework, a propositional content may be Given, an XP may be Mentioned (in the context) and a DR active (or accessible).

The Q-A pair (22)–(23) is a prototypical example of utterances commonly analyzed as involving multiple foci:

(22) Qui a étudié quoi cette année?
'Who studied what this year?'

(23) Les étudiants de première année ont étudié la syntaxe fonctionnelle et les étudiants de seconde année ont étudié la syntaxe générative.
'The first year students studied functional syntax and the second year students studied generative syntax'

Now consider the Q-A pair (24)–(25):

(24) Qu'ont étudié les étudiants cette année?
'What did the students study this year?'

(25) Les étudiants de première année ont étudié la syntaxe fonctionnelle et les étudiants de seconde année ont étudié la syntaxe générative.

The answer (25) is identical to that in (23). According to our analysis, the answer in (25) requires accommodating subordinate questions like the ones in (26):

(26) a. Qu'ont étudié les étudiants de première année?
'What did the first year students study?'
b. Qu'ont étudié les étudiants de seconde année?
'What did the second year students study?'

We propose analyzing the DTs associated with the answers in (23) and in (25) in a parallel fashion. Question (22) conflates several questions and sets up a layered DT similar to that which is brought up by the answer (25). Such a view predicts that one of the foci in question (22) will be treated as a T-shifter and the other as a Focus in the answer. This is what is observed in the answers (23) and (25) which feature the same intonation: the NPs *les étudiants de première année* and *les étudiants de seconde année* present the intonation that is characteristic of T-shifters (cf. chapter 21, Prosody and Information in French).

The same analysis can be extended to the cases of so-called contrastive topics: they call for a layered DT. The Q-A pair (27) provides us with a case in point:

(27) a. A propos de Marie et Pierre, où sont-ils allés en vacances?
'Speaking of Marie and Pierre, where did they go for holidays?'
b. Marie est allée en Chine et Pierre au Japon.
'Marie went to China and Pierre to Japan'

The DT shaped in question (27a) is split in the answer (27b): the answer treats the coordination distributively. We make explicit the DT shaped by question (27a) in (28a) and the DT reshaped by (27b) in (28b):

(28) a. DT shaped by question (27a):
DT = {Marie et Pierre sont allés en France, Marie et Pierre sont allés en Chine, Marie et Pierre sont allés en Inde ...}
b. DT reshaped by answer (27b):
DT = { { Marie est allée en France, Marie est allée en Chine, Marie est allée en Inde ... }, {Pierre est allé en France, Pierre est allé en Chine, Pierre est allé en Inde ... } }

Finally, we consider contrastive foci whose prototypical instance is illustrated in (29):

(29) (Qui est venu? 'Who came?')
Bernard est venu, pas Marie.
'Bernard came, not Marie'

Our contention is that (29) is another case of a complex strategy involving the shifting from a simple DT to a layered DT. In such a case, it requires the accommodation of two questions: *who came? who did not come?*. Once again, the DT reshaped by the answer is layered as (30) shows:

(30) {{Jean est venu, Marie est venue, Claude est venu ...}, {Jean n'est pas venu, Marie n'est pas venue, Claude n'est pas venu }}

## 2.3 Discourse status of referents of Discourse

Lambrecht (1994) clearly shows that the notion of "new information" (or informative content) should not be confused with that of "new Discourse Referent". "What gives a Focus constituent its flavor as a 'new' element is not the status of its denotatum in the Discourse but its relations to the asserted proposition at the time of utterance. Focus and inactiveness are independent information-structure parameters" (Lambrecht 1994: 261). We take up Lambrecht's distinction between three activation states and briefly indicate how to integrate these in our propositional approach.

Active DRs are inferable from the Given content. The Given content (G) is conceived of as an open proposition (cf. section 2.2.3 above). We note as CL(G) the existential closure of this proposition. A DR x associated with the predicate Q is active if (31) is verified:

(31) $CL(G) \Rightarrow \exists x\ Q(x)$

Accessible DRs are DRs that are introduced in one of the propositions

($P_I$) making up the DT or inferable from the DT. A DR x is accessible if (32) is verified:

(32) $\cap_{i \in DT} P_i \Rightarrow \exists x\ Q(x)$

Inactive DRs are DRs that are not present in the context shared by the interlocutors.

## 3 French prosody: accentuation and intonation

Here, we present the most salient features of French prosody. We introduce its three main components: rhythmic organization, phrasing and intonational patterns.

### 3.1 Rhythmic organization

The rhythmic organization of French has been described with or without such notions as "stress" or "accent". Here we use "accent", and more precisely "metrical accent", as a category referring to the metrical organization. Thus, a metrically accented syllable is a metrically strong syllable that belongs to a metrical structure made of strong and weak syllables.

Metrical accent is not assigned in the lexicon, but at phrasal level in French. Thus, it has no distinctive function as in English (e.g. the contrast *PERmit* vs. *perMIT*). There are two types of metrical accent: the former (primary accent) occurs at the right edge of a phrase that we call Rhythmic Group (RG) and the latter (secondary accent) may optionally be realized at the left edge of a Rhythmic Group (cf. section 3.3). (cf. Di Cristo 1999, Pasdeloup 1990). The main acoustic correlate of metrical accents is lengthening, associated sometimes with a melodic movement. The duration of a syllable bearing a primary accent is at least 20% longer than the duration of its unaccented counterpart.

Primary accent[9] may fall on the last syllable of any lexical item (of category N, V, A), whose nucleus is not a mute *e*. This syllable is often called "accentable" (Mertens 1987, 1993). Several factors determine whether a metrical accent has to be realized: they pertain to syntax or length of the constituents.[10] As primary accent falls on the last syllable, it has a demarcative function: it indicates the right boundary of a Rhythmic Group.

As accentuation is essentially a rhythmic phenomenon, secondary accent can be realized whenever the distance between two primary accented syllables is too important.[11] The secondary accent is realized on

[9]The primary accent is called 'accent interne' by Rossi.

[10]See, among others, Pasdeloup (1990), Delais-Roussarie (1996, 2000).

[11]See Pasdeloup (1990). Secondary accent is called '*ictus mélodique*' by Rossi.

the initial or antepenultimate syllable of a lexical word and is characterized by a "slightly" rising melodic movement. This metrical accent may also have a demarcative function: when realized on the initial syllable of a lexical word, it indicates the left boundary of this word. Such a realization of secondary accent is frequent in some specific speech styles: didactic presentation, news broadcasting, etc.

### 3.2 Phrasing

When one listens to utterances, one clearly recognizes that the acoustic signal is segmented into chunks. These chunks are described as prosodic units or prosodic constituents in many works on sentence prosody or on intonation. However the definition or modeling of the various prosodic units can be apprehended in different ways.

We use prosodic constituents as descriptive units, without addressing a number of theoretical issues that are currently discussed in the literature. We make reference to two distinct types of phrasings: those that reflect the syntactic and metrical organization of the utterance and those that reflect the informational status of the content of the utterance. For the former, two levels of constituency are used: the rhythmic group (RG) and the major phrase (MaP). The informational status of the utterance is reflected by a phrasing in intonational phrases (IntP) (Ground/Focus articulation, Discourse Topic, etc.).

The RG is characterized by the fact that its last syllable is metrically strong (cf. section 2.1).[12] RGs are usually composed of a lexical word and all the grammatical words on its non-recursive side (cf. example (33)).[13]

(33) Les enfants de Jean-François sont allés au cinéma en fin d'après midi.

les enfants)$_{RG}$ de Jean-François)$_{\mathrm{RG}}$ sont allés)$_{\mathrm{RG}}$ au cinéma)$_{\mathrm{RG}}$ en fin)$_{\mathrm{RG}}$ d'après midi)$_{\mathrm{RG}}$

'Jean-François' children went to the movies late in the afternoon'

Any RG can potentially be realized as a MaP, in particular at slow speech rate. The segmentation in MaPs is determined by the syntactic structure and by metrical factors. One of the possible segmentations into MaPs of example (33) is given in (34):

[12] This prosodic unit is roughly equivalent to the phonological phrase (cf. Post 2000, Delais-Roussarie 1996), the prosodic word, etc.

[13] The notation we use is in the spirit of what had been proposed by Chen (1985) and Selkirk (1986) in the "end-based theory of derived domain". In this chapter, it is justified by the fact that right edges play a crucial role in generating the intonation of an utterance since they are anchor points for boundary tones.

(34) Les enfants de Jean-François sont allés au cinéma en fin d'après midi.
les enfants)$_{RG}$ de Jean-François)$_{RG}$}$_{MaP}$ sont allés)$_{RG}$ au cinéma)$_{RG}$ en fin)$_{RG}$ d'après midi)$_{RG}$}$_{MaP}$

As we will show in the next chapter, the segmentation in IntPs is determined by the semantics and pragmatics associated with the utterance, in particular in the marking of the ground/focus articulation. In (35), the position of the first IntP boundary coincides with the end of the focus of the sentence.

(35) a. (Qu'est-ce qui se passe? Jean-François est arrivé.)
'What is happening?' 'Jean-François arrived'
Jean-François)$_{RG}$}$_{MaP}$ est arrivé)$_{RG}$]$_{IntP}$

b. (Qui est arrivé? Jean-François est arrivé.)
'Who arrived?' 'Jean-François arrived'
Jean-François)$_{RG}$]$_{IntP}$ est arrivé)$_{RG}$ ]$_{IntP}$

### 3.3 Intonational patterns

Different approaches may be used to describe the intonational patterns of a language.[14] Here, we adopt a framework that is inspired by the metrical and autosegmental framework developed by Bruce (1982) and Pierrehumbert (1980), among others; we also take up proposals made by Rossi (1985), (1993), (1999) and Mertens (1987 and *seq.*). We resort to tones as minimal units in our descriptions and analyses.

It is currently admitted that tones are divided into "boundary tones" (associated to prosodic boundaries) and "pitch accents" (associated to accented syllables). The intonational contours associated with an utterance result from an interpolation of these two types of tonal units. They are implemented in registers (compressed or expanded), which also belong to the phonology of intonation.

In French, the tonal elements that play a role in generating the intonational patterns associated with an utterance are: boundary tones, pitch accents (pragmatic and modality accents) and registers.

[14]Models differ along two dimensions: (a) the minimal units they postulate (e.g. among models devoted to French: slopes on prosodic constituents or on accented syllables (Caelen-Haumont 1981, Martin 1981); "*contours*" (Delattre 1966, Vaissière 1975, Aubergé 1991); "slopes and pitch levels" (Morel & Danon-Boileau 1998); "pitch movement" (Rossi et al. 1981); "*intonèmes*" (Rossi 1985, 1999) ; tones (Dell 1984, Mertens 1987 and seq., Post 2000), and (b) the domain of these units and their anchoring mode: the *contours* or the slopes most often cover a whole prosodic constituent while the *intonèmes* or tones are anchored on stressed syllables. We refer the reader to Lacheret-Dujour et al. (1999) for an overview of the models proposed for French.

### 3.3.1 Boundary tones

Boundary tones occur at prosodic constituent boundaries. In the model we use for our description of French, we make a distinction between two types of boundary tones: demarcative tones and illocutionary boundary tones (IBTs).

Demarcative tones occur at the right edge of prosodic phrases (RGs and MaPs), and as such their distribution is determined by syntactic and metrical factors. The demarcative tone does not carry any specific meaning and can be seen as a "default" tone. We will mainly consider the $H^{cont}$ demarcative tone, which is inserted at the end of a MaP.

Illocutionary boundary tones are realized at the right edge of IntPs. The form of the illocutionary boundary tones is related to the illocutionary force of the utterance. Their localization is determined by the semantics and pragmatics of the utterance, in particular, the ground-focus articulation (see chapter 21, Prosody). There are several IBTs that are distinguished by their F0 curve and the meaning they convey. Some of those that will appear in our examples in our survey, are listed in the table below.

| | *Melodic Movement* | *Prototypical use in final Intonational Phrase* |
|---|---|---|
| H% | Rising pitch movement | In questions : Est-ce que "tu viendras? H%$]_{IntP}$" |
| L% | Falling pitch movement | In assertions and commands : "Jean est venu L%$]_{IntP}$", "Viens tout de suite L%$]_{IntP}$" |
| HL% | Rising-falling movement | In confirmation requests: "C'est bien pour Chirac HL%$]_{IntP}$ que Mathilde a voté HL%$]_{IntP}$". |

At the left edge of prosodic and intonational phrases, demarcative boundary tones are optional. If they are realized, they are found on one of the first three syllables of the phrase. At the right edge, boundary tones are realized on primary accentable syllables. Note that illocutionary boundary tones are different from ordinary demarcative tones since they convey meaning.

The examples in (36) illustrate the use of the $H^{cont}$ demarcative tone and the L% illocutionary tone:

(36) a. Le frère de Pierre est arrive hier.
'Pierre's brother arrived yesterday'
le frère$)_{RG}$ de Pierre$)_{RG}$ $H^{cont}\}_{MaP}$ est arrivé$)_{RG}$ hier$)_{RG}$L%$]_{IntP}$

b. Le frère de Pierre est arrivé hier en fin d'après-midi.
'Pierre's brother arrived yesterday late in the afternoon'
le frère)$_{RG}$ de Pierre)$_{RG}$ $H^{cont}\}_{MaP}$ est arrivé)$_{RG}$ hier)$_{RG}$ $H^{cont}\}_{MaP}$ en fin)$_{RG}$ d'après-midi)$_{RG}$ $L\%]_{IntP}$

### 3.3.2 Pitch accents: pragmatic and modality accents

Pitch accents constitute a different layer in the intonational organization.[15] Among these accents, we distinguish pragmatic and modality accents. Modality accents are anchored on primary or secondary stressed syllables. They express the speaker's attitude. Moreover, they may combine with boundary tones to form *'melodic clichés'*. Though these accents are necessary to account for the intonation of French (e.g. expression of doubt, surprise, etc.), their description goes beyond the scope of this book. Pragmatic accents have the following characteristics. They are located at the beginning of rhythmic groups (one of the first three syllables, even if metrically weak). They are anchored on a syllable, with a lengthened initial consonant. They involve an H tone. The high tone associated with an accent will be noted H*.

In chapter 21 (Prosody and Information in French), we isolate one of these pragmatic accents that we call C accent.[16] It is crucially involved in the marking of complex Discourse strategies (see section 2.2.1 above). It is realized as an H tone (henceforth $H^{*C}$).

### 3.3.3 Registers

The phonetic implementation of boundary tones and pitch accents is in part determined by the pitch register: the target of an H tone is not the same in the case of expansion or compression of the pitch range. We show in the next chapter that the setting of the pitch register plays a crucial role in the expression of Ground/Focus articulation.

## 4 Conclusions

The main results of our survey in the next four chapters concern the mapping of prosody and the ground-focus articulation, the syntactic and prosodic correlates of discourse topic marking (in the sense of Büring 1997, 1998) as opposed to focus marking, and the interfaces with syntax.

The partition that corresponds to the ground-focus articulation and

[15] For a similar conception of the role of these accents in the intonational organization, see Rossi (1999).

[16] Why such a label? This accent bears a pragmatic resemblance to English B accents and German T accents (see Bolinger 1965 and Büring 1997, 1998), but we do not want to imply that their fine-grained prosodic and pragmatic features are identical.

that we analyze as a partition of content under the illocutionary operator associated with the utterance is marked by phrasing in French in two ways: (i) the focused XP, i.e. the XP that is specifically asserted or questioned, is realized as an autonomous phrase bearing on its right edge a tone related to the illocutionary force of the utterance; and (ii) a narrow focus XP occurring sentence internally is put forth by the very fact that there is a difference in register setting affecting the post-focus domain: it is realized in a more compressed register, which results in highlighting the part of the utterance that precedes.

As claimed by Büring (1997, 1998), F(ocus)-marking and T(opic)-marking should be distinguished. We will provide further support for such a claim: T-marking in French resorts to accentuation, which is clearly distinct from phrasing that is characteristic of French F-marking. An accent, that we label C accent descriptively, occurs in utterances that reshape the Discourse topic that we model, following Büring, as a question. French T-marking has its own features that are distinct from those of the equivalent in German (as described by Büring): (i) it may be realized anywhere in the utterance (in particular, it may appear on focused XPs and may be realized to the right of focused XPs) and (ii) in reshaping utterances, it is compulsory on the leftmost XP that signals the perspective taken to reshape the question, and in other instances may be realized optionally on other XPs, in particular on the focalized XPs.

More generally, the modeling of the structure of the current Discourse Topic as a hierarchy of questions enables one to define a contrast between "the utterances that reshape the DT" and "the utterances that further elaborate the DT". As we have just seen, it is relevant for the occurrence of C accents: C accents are compulsory in the former. It is also relevant for syntax as well, as it provides a way to define the contextual appropriateness of several syntactic constructions: (i) subject inversion is never appropriate in utterances that reshape the DT, (ii) in a similar way, left dislocation is never appropriate in such utterances, whereas (iii) topicalisation typically occurs in such utterances.

Such a generalization that cuts across formal dimensions (prosody, word order and syntactic constructions) is crucial, since it requires that we postulate, next to the Ground/Focus articulation identified in our approach to a level of illocutionary semantics, another dimension related to Discourse Topic dynamics.

As for the role of syntax, we do not think that focus is important in the syntax of French. For cleft sentences, for instance, we argue that focus is not marked in the syntactic structure. Our data give strong evidence against an approach in which the XP of the *c'est XP que/qui...*

occupies a specific focus position in syntax (contra É. Kiss 1997). In most types of inversion focus does not play a role either; the status of focus in unaccusative inversion is currently a matter of debate. We can conclude that the role of focus in the syntax in French is — at most — a small one. On the other hand, syntax does "mark" elements as not being part of the focus. An example is dislocation. Right dislocation can be seen as a means to syntactically indicate that the dislocated constituent is not part of the focus of the sentence, which is reflected by the prosody of this sentence type. As for left dislocation and topicalization, the question whether the syntactic, pragmatic and prosodic differences that we have observed should be partly accounted for by or correlated with different syntactic positions at the left periphery is an issue for further research.

## References

Aubergé, V. 1991. *La synthèse de la parole: des règles au lexique*. Ph.D. thesis, Université de Grenoble.

Beyssade, C., J. Marandin, and A. A. Rialland. 2003. Ground/focus revisited. A perspective from French. In Núñez-Cedeño et al. (2003), pages 83–98.

Blanche-Benveniste, C., M. Bilger, C. Rouget, and K. v. d. Eynde, eds. 1990. *Le français parlé: Etudes grammaticales*. Paris: Editions du CNRS.

Bolinger, D. 1965. *Forms of English: Accent, Morpheme, Order*. Cambridge (MA): Harvard University Press. Abe, I. and T. Kenekiyo, eds.

Brüce, G. 1982. Developing the Swedish intonation model. *Working Papers* 22:51–116. Dept. of Linguistics and Phonetics, University of Lund.

Büring, D. 1998. Focus and topic in a complex model of discourse. Ms. Bürings website.

Caelen-Haumont, G. 1981. Structures prosodiques de la phrase énonciative simple et étendue. In *Hamburger Phonetische Beiträge*, vol. 34. Hamburg Buske.

Chen, M. 1985. The syntax of phonology: Xiamen tone sandhi. Ms University of California. San Diego.

Costa, J. 1998. *Word order variation*. The Hague: Holland Academic Graphics.

Delais-Roussarie, E. 1996. Phonological phrasing and accentuation in French. In Nespor and Smith (1996), pages 1–38.

Delais-Roussarie, E. 2000. Vers une nouvelle approche de la structure prosodique. In Laks (2000).

Delattre, P. 1966. Les dix intonations de base du français. *The French Review* 40:1–14.

Dell, F. 1984. L'accentuation dans les phrases en français. In Dell et al. (1984), pages 65–122.

Dell, F., D. Hirst, and J. Vergnaud, eds. 1984. *Forme sonore du langage: structure des représentation en phonologie*. Paris: Hermann.

Di Cristo, A. 1999. Le cadre accentuel du français contemporain. Première partie. *Langues* 3(2):184–205. Deuxième partie. *Langues* 4(2): 258-267.

É. Kiss, K. 1997. Identificational focus versus information focus. *Language* 74:245–273.

Fant, G., K. Hirose, and S. Kiritani, eds. 1993. *Fujisaki's Festschrift. Speech Communication*, vol. 13. Amsterdam, The Netherlands: Elsevier Science.

Féry, C. 2001. The phonology of focus in French. In Féry and Sternefeld (2001), pages 153–181.

Féry, C. and W. Sternefeld, eds. 2001. *Audiatur Vox Sapientiae. A Festschrift for Arnim von Stechow*. Berlin: Akademie-Verlag.

Ginzburg, J., Z. Khasidashvili, C. Vogel, J.-J. Lévy, and E. Vallduví, eds. 1998. *The Tbilisi symposium on logic, language, and computation*. CSLI Publications.

Hamblin, C. 1973. Questions in Montague grammar. *Foundations of Language* 10:41–53.

Jacobs, J. 1984. Funktionale satzperspektive und illokutionssemantik. *Linguistische Berichte* 91:25–58.

Jacobs, J., ed. 1992. *Information Struktur und Grammatik*. Verlag.

Krifka, M. 1992. A compositional semantics for multiple focus constructions. In Jacobs (1992), pages 17–53.

Krifka, M. 1993. Focus and presupposition in dynamic interpretation. *Journal of Semantics* 10:269–300.

Lacheret-Dujour, A. and F. Beaugendre. 1999. *La prosodie du français*. CNRS Langage. Paris: CNRS Editions.

Laks, B., ed. 2000. *Langue Française*, vol. 126. Larousse.

Lambrecht, K. 1994. *Information structure and sentence form: Topic, focus and the mental representations of discourse referents*. Cambridge: Cambridge University Press.

Lambrecht, K. and L. A. Michaelis. 1998. Sentence accent in information questions: Default and projection. *Linguistics and Philosophy* 21:477–544.

Li, C., ed. 1976. *Subject and Topic*. New York: Academic Press.

McNally, L. 1998. On recent formal analyses of 'topic'. In Ginzburg et al. (1998), pages 147–160.

Mertens, P. 1987. *L'intonation du français: de la description linguistique à la reconnaissance automatique*. Ph.D. thesis, Leuven University.

Mertens, P. 1990. Chapter IV. L'intonation. In Blanche-Benveniste et al. (1990).

Mertens, P. 1993. Accentuation, intonation et morphosyntaxe. *Travaux de Linguistique* 26(93):21–69.

Mertens, P. 1997. De la chaîne linéaire à la séquence de tons. *Traitement automatique des langues* 38:27–51.

Morel, M.-A. and D.-B. L. 1998. *Grammaire de lintonation: le cas du français*. Ophrys.

Nespor, M. and N. Smith, eds. 1996. *Dam Phonology: HIL Phonology Paper II*. La Haye: Holland Academic Graphics.

Núñez-Cedeño, R., L. López, and R. Cameron, eds. 2003. *Selected papers of LSRL 2001*. John Benjamins.

Ochs Keenan, E. and S. B. 1976. Topic as a discourse notion in the conversations of children and adults. In Li (1976).

Pasdeloup, V. 1990. *Modèles de règles du français appliqué à la synthèse de la parole*. Ph.D. thesis, Université de Provence.

Pierrehumbert, J. 1980. *The phonology and phonetics of English Intonation*. Ph.D. thesis, M.I.T.

Pinto, M. 1997. *Licensing and interpretation of inverted subjects in Italian*. Ph.D. thesis, Utrecht University. LEd, Utrecht.

Post, B. 2000. *Tonal and Phrasal structures in French Intonation*. Ph.D. thesis, Nijmegen. Thesus Publisher. Den Haag.

Roberts, C. 1996. Information structure in discourse: towards an integrated formal theory of pragmatics. In Yvon and Kathol (1996).

Rossi, M. 1985. L'intonation et l'organization de l'énoncé. *Phonetica* 42(2-3):135–153.

Rossi, M. 1993. A model for predicting the prosody of spontaneous speech. In Fant et al. (1993), pages 87–107.

Rossi, M. 1999. *L'Intonation, le système du français: description et modélisation*. Paris: Ophrys.

Rossi, M., A. D. Cristo, D. Hirst, P. Martin, and Y. Nishinuma, eds. 1981. *L'intonation. De l'acoustique à la sémantique*. Paris: Klincksieck.

Schwartzchild, R. 1999. Givenness, AvoidF and other constraints on the placement of accent. *Natural Language Semantics* 7:141–177.

Selkirk, E. 1986. On derived domains in sentence phonology. *Phonology Yearbook* 3:371–405.

Vaissière, J. 1975. La structuration acoustique de la phrase française. In *Annali Della Scuola Normale Superiore Di Pisa*, pages 530–560. Pisa: Tipografia Pacini-Mariotti.

Yvon, J. H. and A. Kathol, eds. 1996. *OSU Working Papers in Linguistics*, vol. 49. Ohio State University.

Zubizarreta, M. L. 1998. *Prosody, Focus and Word Order*. Cambridge MA: MIT Press.

21

# Prosody and Information in French *

CLAIRE BEYSSADE, ELISABETH DELAIS-ROUSSARIE, JENNY DOETJES, JEAN-MARIE MARANDIN, AND ANNIE RIALLAND

## 1 Introduction

It is a well-established fact that in many languages of the world the prosodic realization of utterances is partly determined by the informational dimension, in particular by the Ground/Focus articulation (GFA). In section 2, we show that Focus marking resorts to illocutionary boundary tones in French. In section 3, we present the prosodic realization of post-focus sequencess. In section 4, we deal with pitch accents. In particular, we make explicit the rules for one of them, that we call a C accent.

## 2 Prosody of the Ground/Focus articulation

### 2.1 Focus Marking

In chapter 20 (Introduction), the focus constituent was defined as the constituent (Sentence, XP or sub-constituent of XP) affected by the illocutionary operator associated with the utterance. French provides direct support for such an approach: Focus is not marked by a specific tone or accent associated with the focalized constituent, but by a boundary tone that varies with the illocutionary force associated with

*We would like to thank G. Rebuschi who contributed to the analytical work which motivated this study. Jenny Doetjes gratefully acknowledges the support from NWO (grant #355-70-003).

*Handbook of French Semantics.*
Francis Corblin and Henriëtte de Swart (eds.).
Copyright © 2004, CSLI Publications.

the utterance (illocutionary boundary tone).[1] Consider the assertive utterances and figures 1 to 3 below. The focus is contributed by the subject NP in (1), the whole sentence in (2) and a sub-constituent in (3):

(1) Qui a acheté une mandoline?
 'Who bought a mandolin?'
 Mallarmé a acheté une mandoline.
 Mallarmé)$_{\text{RG}}$ L%]$_{\text{IntP}}$ a acheté)$_{\text{RG}}$ une mandoline)$_{\text{RG}}$ L%]$_{\text{IntP}}$
 'Mallarmé bought a mandolin.'

FIGURE 1 F0 curve of example (1), *Mallarmé a acheté une mandoline.* (Speaker GJT, man)

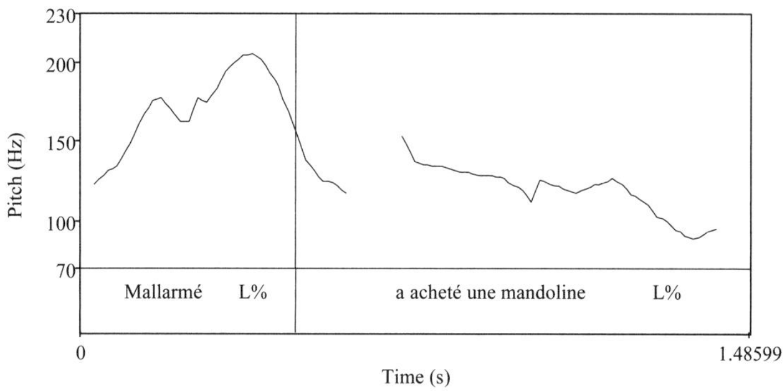


(2) Qu'est-ce qui se passe?
 'What's happening?'
 Jean-Pierre est arrivé.
 Jean-Pierre)$_{\text{RG}}$ est arrivé)$_{\text{RG}}$ L% ]$_{\text{IntP}}$
 'Jean-Pierre has arrived.'

(3) Il a écrit combien de romans policiers?
 'How many detective novels did he write?'
 Il a écrit dix-sept romans policiers.
 Il a écrit)$_{\text{RG}}$ dix-sept)$_{\text{RG}}$ L%]$_{\text{IntP}}$ romans)$_{\text{RG}}$ policiers)$_{\text{RG}}$ L%]$_{\text{IntP}}$
 'He wrote seventeen detective novels.'

These examples clearly show that focused constituents are marked by a boundary tone on their right edge: the L% that is characteristic of assertion in (1)–(3). Moreover, the same tone is realized at the end of the sentence.

[1]Note that the use of specific construction types (cleft sentences, *il y a* construction, etc.) is not necessary to express focus in French. See also chapter 23 (Cleft sentences).

FIGURE 2 F0 curve of example (2), *Jean-Pierre est arrivé.* (Speaker FER, woman)

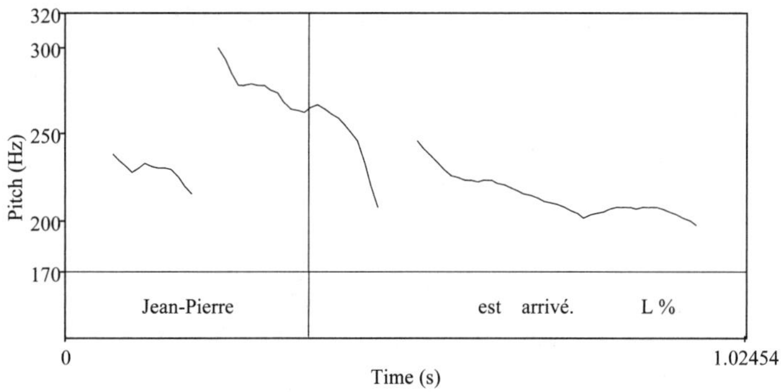


FIGURE 3 F0 curve of example (3), *Il a écrit dix-sept romans policiers.* (Speaker FER)

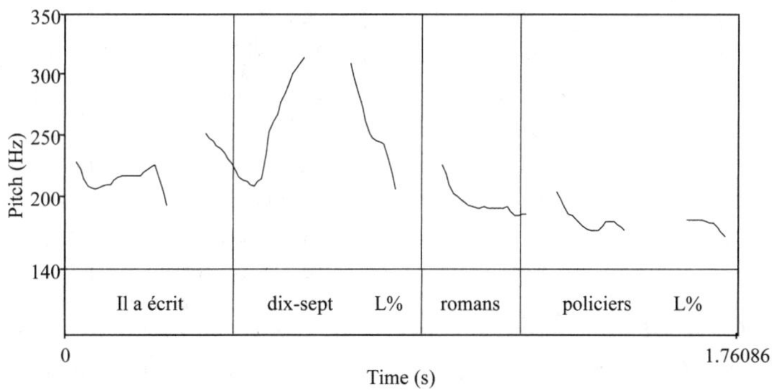


Consider now what happens in declarative questions such as (4) and (5): the XP that is specifically questioned is marked by an H% in (4) and an HL% in (5) (see figure 4). H% and HL% are the two tones that are used in declarative questions, HL% being characteristic of "requests for confirmation".

(4) Tu pars dans la voiture de Jean-Bernard dimanche prochain?
H% H%
'Are you leaving in Jean-Bernard's car next Sunday?'

(5) Jean-Bernard est venu hier?
'Jean-Bernard came yesterday, didn't he?'
Jean-Bernard$)_{RG}$ HL%$]_{IntP}$ est venu$)_{RG}$ hier$)_{RG}$ HL%$]_{IntP}$

FIGURE 4 F0 curve of example (5), *Jean-Bernard est venu hier?* (Speaker FER)

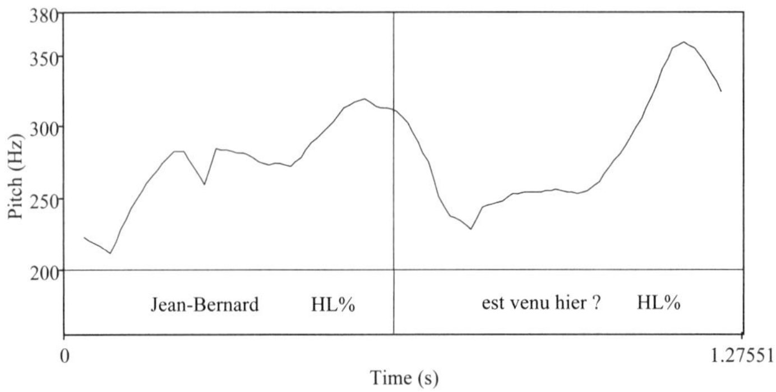


Thus, the generalization is the following: a boundary tone that is determined by the illocutionary force of the utterance is realized on the last syllable of the focal domain and at least one copy of this tone is realized at the end of the utterance. In addition to the realization of a boundary tone determined by the illocutionary force of the utterance at the end of the focus constituent, a melodic rise may occur at the beginning of the focal domain. This H tone must be distinguished from the pitch accent that will be presented in section 4. The initial rise has more in common with the sentence initial accent that has been described in the literature (cf. among others, Pasdeloup 1990).

## 2.2 Discussion

McNally (1998) makes the sweeping claim that "focus [rheme in her terminology] is never marked in any interesting ways". Indeed, the claim is twofold:

(a) The first claim is that Focus marking is not specific to Focus or GFA (in the sense in which part of verb inflection is specific to tense distinctions, for example).[2]

(b) The latter is that focus or GFA has no "interesting" features (for us: has no relevant effect in the grammar).

According to our analysis, claim (a) is true in French: the tones used at the right boundary of focal domains in French are essentially

[2]"Focus/rheme constituents are unmarked: they all appear in their canonical position in the sentence, and do not bear any special morphology or intonation other than the default intonational contour associated with the sentence" (ibid.: 178). McNally adds: "with the apparent exception of English".

related to illocutionary semantics (which explains their variation in realization). Claim (b) is quite controversial: the actual placement of illocutionary tones in sentences is meaningful. Nothing except the distinction "broad vs. narrow focus" can explain the contrast between (6) and (7):

(6) Qui est venu? Bernard est venu.
'Who came?' 'Bernard came.'
Bernard$)_{RG}$ L%$]_{IntP}$ est venu$)_{RG}$ L%$]_{IntP}$

(7) Que s'est-il passé? Bernard est venu.
'What happened?' 'Bernard came.'
Bernard$)_{RG}$ est venu$)_{RG}$ L%$]_{IntP}$

Indeed, the marking in (6) and (7) is "interesting" since it may result in inappropriateness that a grammar should account for, as illustrated in (8):

(8) a. Que s'est-il passé?
#Bernard$)_{RG}$ L%$]_{RG}$ est venu$)_{RG}$ L%$]_{IntP}$
b. Qui est venu?
#Bernard$)_{RG}$ est venu$)_{RG}$ L%$]_{IntP}$

Moreover, French's uninteresting way of Focus marking (in the sense of claim (a)) is interesting from a theoretical point of view. McNally observes that no conception of GFA can predict the generalization that "all sentences have a focal segment". She claims that only a dynamic conception of sentence meaning can do so: "since all sentences have some update potential, they all have a focal segment" (Vallduví & Engdahl 1995: 9). In McNally's parlance: "if all languages have sentences or constituent types of the same semantic type as sentences in English, it will follow that Add information (understood as the basic interpretive rule for the assertion) will be manifest in all languages" (ibid.: 175). By the same token, all sentences in all languages do present a GFA marked in a non-predictable way.[3] The claim is certainly true for assertive utterances. But, what about other illocutionary types? As we have just seen, utterances with Question force present the same pattern of illocutionary tone placement as assertive utterances (cf. (4) and (5) above). Moreover, the placement of these tones plays a crucial role in the semantics of the questions since it determines what is questioned

[3] McNally's approach is constructional in essence: "in treating information packaging instruction as the semantic interpretations for linguistic markings, we are immediately confronted with the realization that, just as we cannot take it for granted that Catalan has a word whose sense is identical to that of the English word *thundershower*, neither can we take it for granted that English encodes exactly the same information packaging instruction as Catalan left detachment" (ibid.: 175).

(Beyssade et al. 2003). This observation leads us to the claim that the interpretation of the contrast "broad focus vs. narrow focus" depends on the illocutionary force associated with the utterance. When Assertion is involved, the propositional content of the focus contributes the update: it may be the whole proposition (in utterances with broad focus) or a part of it (in utterances with narrow focus) (cf. section 2.1.2 of chapter 20, Introduction). When Question is involved, the focus contributes the type of information the speaker is questioning: it may correspond to the whole content (in utterances with broad focus) or a part of it (in utterances with narrow focus).

The illocutionary conception of Ground/Focus articulation does predict that "all sentences have a focal segment". All sentences have a focal segment because all sentences (i.e. matrix sentences) are associated with a given illocutionary force. Moreover, it predicts that the content of all sentences, whether assertive or not, can be partitioned into Ground and Focus and that the interpretation of such a partition varies with the illocutionary force of the utterance.

## 2.3 Focus as a pivot: the case of narrow focus sentences

The focus constituent can be analyzed as a pivot in the sense used in different syntactic formalisms. In these frameworks, a position or a term is a pivot insofar as it determines two domains for a specific dimension. In French, the focus constituent can serve as the basis to determine two "domains": (a) the pre-focus domain and (b) the post-focus domain (see also Le Gac 2001).

These domains display specific prosodic characteristics that are best described by analyzing the prosody of narrow focus sentences. Consider example (9):

(9) Qu'est-ce que Jean-Pierre a offert à ton fils?
'What did Jean-Pierre give to your son?'
Jean-Pierre a offert un train électrique à mon fils.
Jean-Pierre)$_{\text{RG}}$ H$^{\text{cont}}$}$_{\text{MaP}}$ a offert)$_{\text{RG}}$ un train électrique)$_{\text{RG}}$ L%] à mon fils)$_{\text{RG}}$ L%]$_{\text{IntP}}$
'Jean-Pierre gave an electric train to my son.'

In the pre-focus domain, the phrasing does not include the focus constituent. The verb constitutes a rhythmic group (RG) on its own. The intonation associated with the pre-focus domain is characterized by a non-compressed pitch register. In the post-focus domain, on the other hand, the intonation is usually characterized by the compression of the pitch register. A complete analysis of the prosody associated with this domain is proposed in section 3.

FIGURE 5 F0 curve of example (9), *Jean-Pierre a offert un train électrique à mon fils.* (Speaker FER)

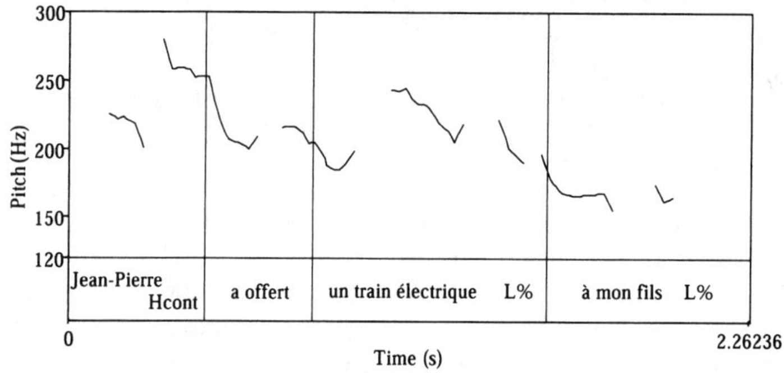


To conclude, the focus constituent can be considered as a pivot as the prosody associated with pre- and post-focus domains are completely different. These differences rely mostly on differences in pitch register. While the register is not compressed in the pre-focus domain, it is in the post-focus one.[4]

## 3 Realizations of post-focus sequences

As mentioned in section 2.3, the prosody associated with the post-focus domain displays specific characteristics. In our data, we found three different realizations. Our observations diverge from what is commonly assumed in the literature: post-focus sequences are described as steadily flat in pitch (see, among others, Di Cristo (1998), Rossi (1999) and Touati (1987)) and also dephrased. We observed, however, that post-focus sequences are far from being "dephrased": rhythmic groups keep their duration cues (cf. also Di Cristo et al. (1999), Jun & Fougeron (2000)) and Major phrases keep not only their duration cues but also the property of ending with a boundary tone.

### 3.1 Realization as a low 'plateau'

In the first case, the post-focus sequence is realized as a low plateau (see fig. 6): a fall is realized at the end of the focus constituent and the rest of the utterance is realized with a compression of both the F0 register and the intensity. This realization of post-focus sequences has been described in different works on focus in French (see, among others, Di Cristo (1998), Rossi (1999) and Touati (1987)). This type of intonational pattern has also been observed in other languages (Japanese,

[4]Phrasing usually reflects the division into domains (see Féry 2001).

English, etc.).

The main features of this type of realization are as follows. First, the post-focus sequences are composed of at most two rhythmic groups that are phrased in a single Major Phrase. Thus, these sequences are relatively short in length. Secondly, the constituents in the sequence are associated with active Discourse Referents. Finally, the sequence does not serve to modify the discourse topic and to elaborate a complex strategy (see section 4). This is illustrated in (10):

(10) Qu'est-ce que Jean-Bernard a lu pendant ses vacances?
'What did Jean-Bernard read during his holiday?'
Jean-Bernard a lu trois romans policiers pendant ses vacances.
Jean-Bernard$)_{RG}$ $H^{cont}\}_{MaP}$ a lu$)_{RG}$ trois romans$)_{RG}$ policiers$)_{RG}$ $L\%]_{IntP}$ pendant ses vacances$)_{RG}$ $L\%\ ]_{IntP}$
'Jean-Bernard read three detective novels during his holiday.'

FIGURE 6 F0 curve of example (10), *Jean-Bernard a lu trois romans policiers pendant ses vacances.* (Speaker GLR, man)

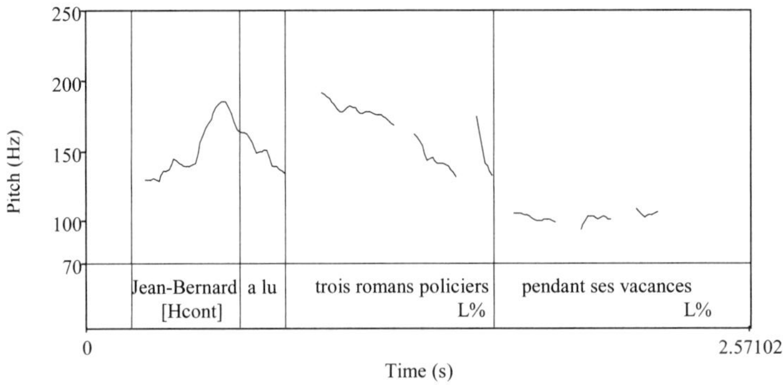


In (10), the post-focus sequence *"pendant ses vacances"* is composed of a single rhythmic group and does not bring any new information or modification to the Discourse Topic. Thus, it is realized as a low plateau.

### 3.2 Realization with a succession of downsteps and a copy of the boundary tone

In the second case, the post-focus sequence is realized as a succession of Major Phrases whose boundary tones are a copy of the illocutionary Boundary tone realized at the end of the focus constituent. Thus, in this context, there is no H "default tone" on the right edge of MaPs. Actually, the tonal copy is the second way of providing a boundary tone to Major Phrases.

The flat contour associated with each IntP is lowered, compared to the preceding one (see figure 7). This realization has been observed in cleft sentences in Clech-Darbon et al. (1999), but it is not restricted to clefts. Consider for instance example (11).

(11) Qu'est-ce que tu as donné aux étudiants de Licence pour le concours blanc ?
'What did you give the third year students for the practice exam?'
J'ai donné trois exercices de syntaxe aux étudiants de Licence pour le concours blanc.
j'ai donné$)_{RG}$ trois exercices$)_{RG}$ de syntaxe$)_{RG}$ L%$]_{IntP}$ aux étudiants$)_{RG}$ de licence$)_{RG}$ L%$_{copy}\}_{MaP}$ pour le concours blanc$)_{RG}$ L%$]_{IntP}$
'I gave three syntax exercises to the third year students for the practice exam'

FIGURE 7 F0 curve of example (11), *J'ai donné trois exercices de syntaxe aux étudiants de Licence pour le concours blanc.* (Speaker GJT)

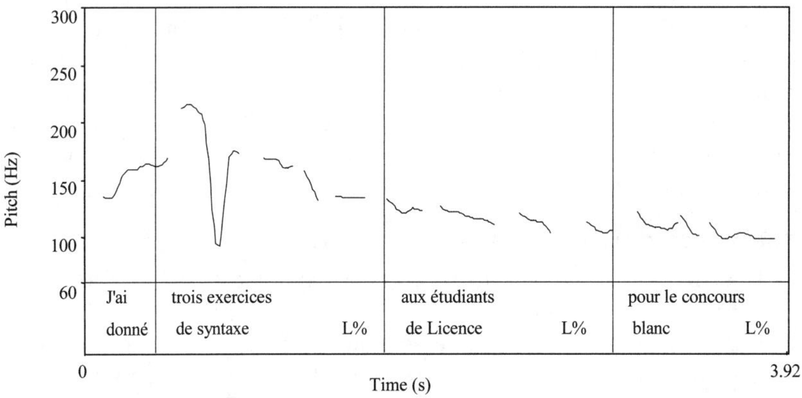


An assertive L% boundary tone is realized at the end of the focus constituent *trois exercices de syntaxe*, at the end of the utterance, and a copy of it at the end of the MaP *étudiants de licence.* In addition to the copy of the L% boundary tone, the successive tones are downstepped and the pitch register is more and more compressed.

When the post-focus sequence is realized as a succession of downsteps, the realization of the various MaPs is apparently determined by the discourse characteristics of the constituents. Whenever the discourse referent associated with the element expressed by the MaP is active, or the meaning expressed by the MaP does not modify the discourse topic, each MaP is realized as a low plateau ending with an L illocutionary tone. Example (11) above illustrates such a case.

On the other hand, a Major Phrase in the post-focus domain ends with an $H^{cont}$ whenever the discourse referent associated with the element expressed by the MaP is not active, or the meaning expressed by the MaP modifies the discourse topic. Example (12) represents such a realization (see also figure 8):

(12) Qu'est ce que tu as donné pour le concours blanc ?
'What did you give for the practice exam?'
J'ai donné trois exercices de syntaxe aux étudiants de Licence pour le concours blanc.
j'ai donné$)_{RG}$ trois exercices$)_{RG}$ de syntaxe$)_{RG}$ L%$]_{IntP}$ aux étudiants$)_{RG}$ de Licence$)_{RG}$ $H^{cont}\}_{MaP}$ pour le concours blanc$)_{RG}$ L%!$]_{IntP}$
'I gave three syntax exercises to the third year students for the practice exam.'

The MaP *aux étudiants de Licence* is realized as a plateau at the low level reached at the end of the focus constituent. The boundary tone is not a copy of L%, but Hcont. From the semantic point of view, the constituent *aux étudiants de Licence* brings some new information and modifies the discourse topic. On the contrary, the constituent *pour le concours blanc*, which is given in the question, is realized with an L% boundary tone. The intensity curve follows the compression associated with the downstep triggered by the first L%.

### 3.3 Realization with a continuous fall

In the third case, the post-focus sequence is not realized as a low plateau. Even if an L% boundary tone is realized at the end of the focus constituent (as in any assertive sentence), the L% does not reach its target (i.e. the baseline of the speaker). It is only at the end of the utterance that the Low target is reached, F0 falling gradually in the post-focus sequence (see figure 9). In this case, the compression of the pitch range and the intensity after the focus constituent is not as clear as it is in the previous examples. An example of this type of realization is given in (13):

(13) Qu'est-ce qu'il fume?
'What does he smoke?'
Il fume des cigarettes le dimanche.
il fume$)_{RG}$ des cigarettes$)_{RG}$ L%$]_{IntP}$ le DImanche$)_{RG}$ L%$]_{IntP}$
$H^{*c}$

FIGURE 8 F0 curve of example (12), *J'ai donné trois exercices de syntaxe aux étudiants de Licence pour le concours blanc.* (Speaker GJT)

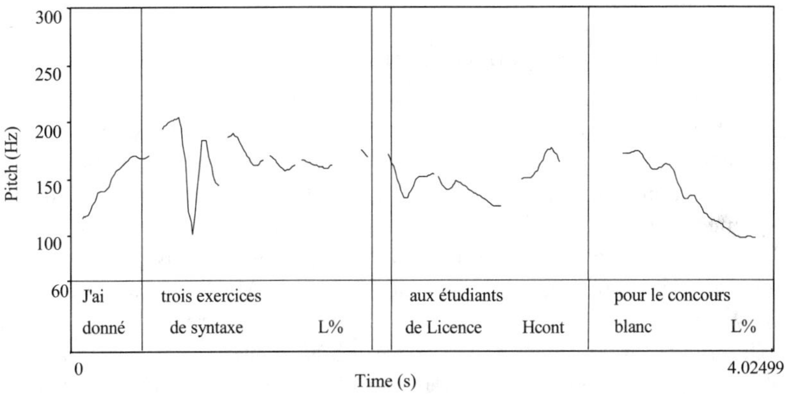


'He smokes cigarettes on Sundays.'

FIGURE 9 F0 curve of example (13), *Il fume des cigarettes le DImanche.* (Speaker FER)

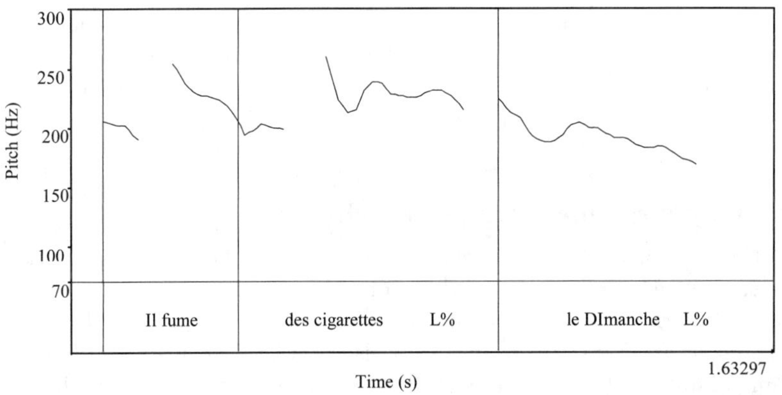


In this sentence, an L% boundary tone is realized at the end of the focus constituent *des cigarettes* since the utterance is an assertion. But the L target is not reached at the end of the focus constituent, but only at the end of the post-focus sequence. Since the element *le dimanche* modifies the discourse topic (the answer is a partial answer), a C accent is realized on the syllable 'DI'. The presence of the pragmatic accent $H^{*c}$ may explain why the post-focus sequence is realized as a continuous fall. Such a realization occurs when (a) the post-focus sequence is composed of at most two RGs that are phrased in a single MaP, (b) the elements expressed in the post-focus sequence are not active discourse referents and (c) the post-focus sequence contains elements that modify the discourse topic.

### 3.4 Summary and generalizations

The three realizations we observe for post-focus sequences apparently are not in free variation, but determined along two dimensions: (a) the metrical organization of the sequence and (b) the informational status of the element contained in the sequence. On the one hand, when the sequence is relatively short in length and can be phrased in a single MaP, it is realized as a continuous fall or as a low plateau. By contrast, long sequences are realized as a succession of MaPs whose boundary tones are a copy of the illocutionary boundary tone realized at the end of the focus domain and utterance, or a high continuation tone in some cases. On the other hand, when the elements have active Discourse Referents, the post-focus sequences tend to be realized flat with compression of the pitch register. On the contrary, if the sequence contains elements that modify the discourse topic and that are realized with a C accent, the L% boundary tone of the preceding MaP does not reach its target and compression of the pitch register does not occur. This might result from the presence of the $H^{*c}$ tone. More observations are necessary to confirm these results. However it is important to note that the observations made so far are compatible with what has been observed in the realization of right dislocated constituents (see chapter 22, Dislocation).

## 4 Discourse marking in French

In the previous sections, we have shown how the Ground/Focus articulation is reflected in the prosody of the utterance. We mostly dealt with F-marking and the realization of post-focus sequences. However the discourse thematic organization also plays a crucial role in determining the prosody associated with an utterance. In German and English, a specific category of pitch accent plays a role in marking discourse moves (B accents as described by Bolinger 1965). In this section, we present how discourse moves and discourse organization — Büring's (1998) T-marking — are prosodically marked in French.

### 4.1 Evidence for T-marking in French

Büring (1998) makes a distinction between two types of discourse strategy (see section 2.2 of chapter 20, Introduction): (a) simple discourse strategies in which questions in Q-A pairs are resolved by a direct answer and (b) complex discourse strategies in which questions in Q-A pairs are partially resolved by the answer. The answer introduces an implicit question it resolves and thus changes the current discourse topic.

Moreover, he argues that the item which signals the recourse to a complex (downwards) strategy has to be accented in German and English. In German, a rising pitch movement (a pitch accent) is realized on the first syllable of the item (see Büring 1997 and 1998).

We observe that a complex strategy is signaled in French as well. Taking up an analog of Büring's example, we observe that an accent is realized on *anglais*, or on the head of the NP *chanteurs* or on both (see section 4.3). Moreover, one of these accentuations is compulsory (see (14a/a'/a") vs. (14b)):[5]

(14) Que fumaient les chanteurs de rock?
'What did rock singers smoke?'

a. Les chanteurs de rock ANglais fumaient des cigarettes.

a'. Les CHANteurs de rock anglais fumaient des cigarettes.

a". Les CHANteurs ANglais fumaient des cigarettes.

b. #Les chanteurs de rock anglais fumaient des cigarettes.
'English rock singers smoked cigarettes.'

FIGURE 10 F0 curve of example (14a), *Les chanteurs anglais fumaient de la marijuana.* (Speaker GRL, man)

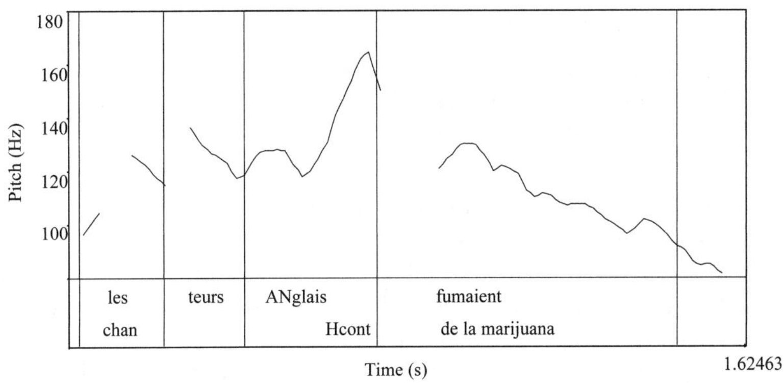


Note that the Ground/Focus articulation of example (14) can be analyzed as (15). As the analysis in (15) shows, the accent on *anglais* cannot be related to GFA:

[5]Capital letters indicate C accents.

FIGURE 11 F0 curve of example (14a") ('prosodic arc'), *Les chanteurs anglais fumaient...* (Speaker FER)

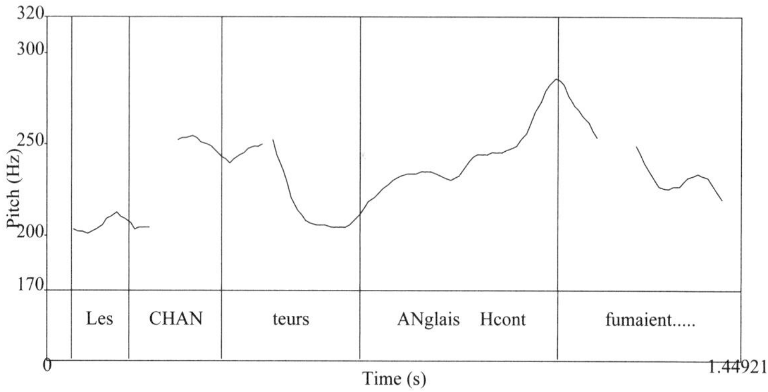


(15) ASSERT <λy ∃e ∀x ((chanteur-de-rock(x) & anglais(x)) → fumer (e,x,y)), cigarettes>

As a first approximation, the accent on *anglais* is a high tone on the first syllable (see § 4.3.1 below). We call this accent a C accent.

We turn now to the distribution of C accents in utterances with respect to GFA. Accepting a descriptive partition of utterances into three domains (pre-focus, focus, post-focus), we observe that C accents may occur in all of the three domains. Example (14) above illustrates C accent in the pre-focus domain, (16) does so in the post-focus and, crucially, (17) in the focus:

(16) Que fume Bernard?
'What does Bernard smoke?'
Bernard fume des cigarettes le DImanche.
'Bernard smokes cigarettes on Sunday.'

(17) Qu'ont fait les étudiants cette année?
'What did the students study this year?'
Les (Z)étudiants (or éTUdiants) de première année ont fait de la syntaxe Générative, les (Z)Étudiants (or éTUdiants) de deuxième année ont fait de la syntaxe FONctionnelle.
'First year students studied generative syntax and second year students studied functional syntax.'

Note that the analysis we have presented above applies to (14), (16) and (17). The answer in (16) changes the "Bernard-smoking material" issue into "Bernard-smoking material-date" issues (*Bernard fume des cigarettes le dimanche, et des gauloises le reste de la semaine*). The answer in (17) changes the "students-subject matter" issue into "groups of students-subject matters" issues. Moreover, (17) shows that C accents may occur on focalized XPs (*de la syntaxe générative, de la syntaxe fonctionnelle*).

Summarizing the distribution of C accents, the generalization is the following:

(18) a. C accents occur in utterances performing a complex discourse strategy.
b. C accents may occur on XPs contributing content to the Ground or to the Focus.

Question-Answer Pairs in (19) and (20) give further support to (18). They are prototypical illustrations of contexts analyzed as involving contrastive topics (19) and contrastive foci (20): C accents may occur on the so-called contrastive XPs regardless of their role in Ground/Focus Articulation:

(19) A propos de Marie-Pauline et Bernard, où sont-ils allés en vacances?
'As for Marie-Pauline and Bernard, where did they spend their holiday?'
MArie-Pauline est allée en Chine et BERnard au Japon.
'Marie-Pauline went to China and Bernard to Japan.'

(20) Qui est venu?
'Who came?'
BERnard est venu (, pas Marie)
'Bernard came, not Marie.'

As for C accents on focalized XPs, C accent is compulsory on *Bernard* in (20) if a contrastive move is intended, whereas they are not in (17) (on *de la syntaxe générative* and *de la syntaxe fonctionnelle*).[6]

## 4.2 Discourse rules for T-marking in French

In this section, we have to characterize the relation between the bearing of a C accent and the reshaping of the question (and the DT), i.e. the relation between C accentuation and Discourse strategy. First, we characterize the localization of C accents and then explain how it is used to express discourse moves.

[6]Here we leave aside the occurrence of C accents in questions: as our preliminary survey shows, they do appear in questions. Nothing in the analysis we adopt prevents them from doing so: they appear in explicit sub-questions (in the discourse perspective). Surprisingly, Büring reports that T accents do not occur in questions in German. We do not know whether this limitation is due to a feature of German or to a limitation of Büring's analysis.

### 4.2.1 Localization of C accents

As (18) suggests, not all C-exponents are T-shifters. The two generalizations (given in (21)) account for the distribution of C accents in French:[7]

(21) Localization:

a. C accents occur in the presence of a complex downwards strategy.

b. C accents are borne by XPs instantiating some variable in the question.

We must now define the notion of instantiation in (21b). Consider again (14) and (15) in a more precise way. It is common practice to analyze a question as an open proposition, i.e. a set of propositions in which an element is a variable. Formally, the analysis of (14), repeated in (22) may be made explicit as (22b) or (22c): (22b) is given in an intensional notation (an open proposition) and (22c) in an extensional one (a set of propositions):

(22) a. Que fumaient les chanteurs de rock?

b. $\lambda$y $\exists$e $\forall$x (chanteur-de-rock(x) $\rightarrow$ Fumer (e,x,y))

c. {$\exists$e $\forall$x (chanteur-de-rock(x) $\rightarrow$ Fumer (e,x,marijuana)), $\exists$e $\forall$x (chanteur-de-rock(x) $\rightarrow$ Fumer (e,x,gitanes)), $\exists$e $\forall$x (chanteur-de-rock(x) $\rightarrow$ Fumer (e,x,haschisch))...}

In (22b) and (22c), the variable *y* corresponds to what will be the focus in the answer, in others words, what is smoked.

In the case of a complex strategy, two distinct variables are instantiated in the partial answer: a variable which is responsible so-to-speak for the partition of the DT and a variable which corresponds to the piece of information the speaker is searching for. We call the former thematic instantiation and the latter focal instantiation.

Take the partial answer (23) to the question (22a):

(23) Les chanteurs de rock ANglais fumaient des cigarettes
'English rock singers smoked cigarettes.'

The answer (23) may be analyzed as introducing the implicit question (24a), which is a sub-question of the more general question (24b):

(24) a. Que fumaient les chanteurs de rock anglais?
'What did English rock singers smoke?'

[7]Büring proposes the following generalization for T accents in German: "[accent] T is chosen in the presence of a [complex] strategy, but it will be obligatory only if it serves to mark non-Given elements at the same time" (1998: 51).

b. Que fumaient les chanteurs de rock de chaque nationalité?
   'What did rock singers of each nationality smoke?'

Questions (24a) and (24b) receive the analysis (25a) and (25b):

(25) a. $\lambda$y $\exists$e $\forall$x ((chanteur-de-rock(x) & anglais(x)) $\rightarrow$ Fumer (e,x,y))

b. $\lambda$y $\lambda$P $\exists$e $\forall$x ((chanteur-de-rock(x) & nationalité(P) & P(x)) $\rightarrow$ Fumer (e,x,y))

In such a case, there are two elements which vary: the nationality of the singers and what is smoked. *Anglais* is the instantiation of the predicate variable P in *de nationalité P* (the thematic instantiation) and *des cigarettes* is the focal instantiation. Thus, in a downward complex discourse strategy, DTs are partitioned via the introduction of a new variable and answers present pairs (thematic instantiations and focal instantiations). This is especially clear with a pair-list answers:

(26) a. Que fumaient les chanteurs de rock?
   'What did rock singers smoke?'

b. Les ANglais de la marijuana, et les FRANçais des gitanes.
   'The English ones marijuana and the French ones gitanes.'

### 4.2.2 Realization of C accents

Generalization (21a) says that C accents may occur on focal or thematic instantiations. Now, we are in a position to characterize the realization of C accents in French (see (27)). Intuitively, a complex strategy should be signaled. In French, it must be signaled once on a thematic instantiation. Once it is, the marking of other instantiations (either thematic or focal) is a matter of choice for the speaker:[8]

(27) Realization:

a. A C accent is compulsory on the first thematic instantiation, i.e. the thematic shifter (TS).

b. C accents are optional on other XPs instantiating variables in the question.

Generalization (27a) captures the fact that a compulsory C accent may fall on a focal XP. This is the case in (20): *Bernard* is at the same time a focal instantiation and the thematic shifter. The answer sets up a double issue: *who came and who did not come?*. Generalizations (27a) and (27b) together capture the fact that in (16), repeated in (28), *le dimanche* (which is the TS) must be accented and *des cigarettes*

[8] We are not yet in the position to specify the parameters of this choice. It requires an extended observation of actual discourses.

is optionally accented; this holds whether *le dimanche* is in situ or preposed (see (28b/b')):

(28) Que fume Bernard?
'What did Bernard smoke?'

a. Bernard fume des cigarettes le DImanche (, le reste de la semaine, il fume la pipe).

a'. Bernard fume des CIgarettes le DImanche (, le reste de la semaine, il fume la pipe).

b. Le DImanche, Bernard fume des cigarettes (, le reste de la semaine, il fume la pipe).

b'. Le DImanche, Bernard fume des CIgarettes (, le reste de la semaine, il fume la pipe).
'Bernard smokes cigarettes on Sunday (, the rest of the week he smokes his pipe).'

Generalization (27) also accounts for the fact that in (17), *les étudiants de première année* must bear a C accent and that the other thematic instantiations (*les étudiants de deuxième année*) and focal instantiations (*de la syntaxe générative, de la syntaxe fonctionnelle*) may or may not bear a C accent. Note that C accents are generally never realized on the last element of a complex answer (see (29)):

(29) Que sont devenus leurs enfants?
'What became of their children?'
Les enfants de BERnadette sont à la faculté et les garçons de Jean-Bernard sont partis à l'étranger.
'The children of Bernadette go to university and the boys of Jean-Bernard went abroad.'

As we will show in the chapters on dislocation and inversion, the distribution of obligatory and non-obligatory C accents correlates with conditions on the use of left dislocation and subject NP inversion. In those contexts where the C accent is compulsory, dislocation and inversion are excluded.

### 4.2.3 C accent realization and Discourse move

We are currently investigating the hypothesis (30):

(30) The XP bearing the obligatory C accent signals what move the speaker is performing in his/her utterance.

We illustrate (30) with the three answers in (32) to question (31):

(31) Qui a préparé la tarte?
'Who prepared the pie?'

(32) a. Bernard a éPLUché les pommes, Marinette a fait la pâte.
b. BERnard a épluché les pommes, Marinette a fait la pâte.
c. BERnard a éPLUché les pommes, Marinette a fait la pâte.
'Bernard peeled the apples, Marinette made the crust.

Consider (32a): the past participle *épluché* is the sole constituent marked with a C accent in the utterance. The DT is split according to the sub-parts of the process of preparing the pie (peeling apples, making the crust, putting the crust in the pie plate, etc.). This is made explicit in (33):

(33) Initial Question: who prepared the pie?
[Subordinate question 1: who peeled the apples?]
Answer: Bernard peeled the apples.
[Sub-question 2: who made the crust?]
......

Consider (32b): the NP *Bernard* is the constituent marked by a C-exponent in the utterance. The TD is split according to the persons involved in preparing the pie. This is made explicit in (34):

| (34) | | |
|---|---|---|
| | Initial Question: | who prepared the pie? |
| | [Subordinate question1.1: | who peeled the apples?] |
| | [Sub-question1.2: | who didn't peel the apples? |
| | Answer: | Bernard peeled the apples. |
| | [Subordinate question 2: | who made the crust?] |

According to (34), answer (32b) signals a two-step move: such a move is more complex than the one in answer (32a). This might explain why, according to our intuition, answer (32b) is much less natural than answer (32a).

Consider now (32c): there are two constituents marked by a C accent in the utterance: *épluché* and *Bernard.* One is the thematic shifter, and the other one an instantiation of a variable in the DT. The marking results in "ambiguity": it may signal either move described above. Nevertheless it seems that there is a preference for the move described in (33); this corroborates the claim that a complex move requires more than C-marking. This justifies an in-depth investigation of natural occurrences of C-accents.

## 4.3 Prosodic characterization of C accents

### 4.3.1 C accents and other pitch prominences

C accents are usually realized on the first syllable of the lexical item that corresponds to the thematic shifter, or on the head of the XP including it (see (14) and figure 10). In some cases, they are realized on both elements of the XP (see figure 11): a prosodic "arc" is thus realized over the whole XP (see Rossi (1999)). C accents have the following acoustic features: (a) a sharp rise of F0, (b) a lengthening of the onset of the accented syllable and (c) a rise of intensity.

As other melodic movements may be realized on the initial syllable of rhythmic groups in French, it is important to distinguish them from C accents. In French, an initial rise can be realized at the beginning of an utterance or an Intonational Phrase (see Di Cristo (1998) and Rossi (1999) among others). This rise has features that are different from those of C accents. The High target may be reached on the second syllable in case of an initial rise, while it is usually reached at the end of the nucleus for C accents. The initial rise is characterized by a melodic movement, but intensity and duration usually remain unchanged. By contrast, C accents are realized with a lengthening of the syllable onset and a relatively important rise in intensity. The initial rise is optional and can be realized on a function word, which is apparently impossible for C accents. Moreover, C accents differ from secondary stress realized on the initial syllable of a lexical word: the melodic movement is more important in case of C accents. C accents are also different from so-called *accents d'insistance* or emphatic accents: the lengthening of the syllable onset is usually more important in the case of emphatic accents.

### 4.3.2 Realizations of C accents

Intonation differs in pre-focus, focus, and post-focus domains: in post-focus sequences, for instance, the pitch range is more compressed. Thus, we expect C accents to be realized differently depending on their location in the utterance.

In the pre-focus part of the utterance, C accents are realized by an important melodic movement, as the H tone reaches the top of the speaker's range. When the word bearing a C accent has two syllables and when an Hcont demarcative tone (continuation rise) has to be realized for syntactic reasons on the second syllable, the realization of the continuation is lowered: pitch drops or remains level. (35) is an example of such a realization that has also been mentioned by Rossi (1999) (see figure 12):

(35) Qu'est-ce que fumaient les chanteurs de rock dans les concerts des années 70?
'What did the rock singers smoke in the concerts in the 70's?'
Les anglais de la marijuana et les français
'The English smoked marijuana and the French ...
les ANglais)$_{\mathrm{RG}}$ H$^{\mathrm{cont}}$}$_{\mathrm{MaP}}$ de la marijuana)$_{\mathrm{RG}}$ H$^{\mathrm{cont}}$}$_{\mathrm{MaP}}$ ...
H$^{*c}$

FIGURE 12 F0 curve of example (35), *Les anglais de la marijuana et les français...* (Speaker FDG, woman)

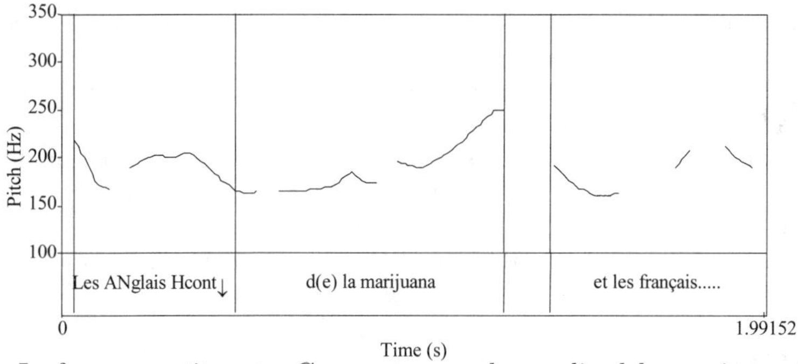


In focus constituents, C accents are also realized by an important pitch rise on the first syllable of the lexical word (or of the head) of the XP instantiating the variables in the question. Duration of the onset is usually lengthened and intensity augmented.

The realization of C accents in post-focus domains is different from the typical realization of accents. As pitch range is usually compressed after focus (see among others Di Cristo (1998), Jun & Fougeron (2000)), C accents cannot be realized with an important pitch rise. In this case, C accents are characterized by a rise of intensity or a lengthening of the onset. The presence of the rising melodic movement (H* tone) can be observed in the realization of the post-focus sequence: the post-focus sequence is not realized by a low plateau (indicating the presence of an L target just after the focus constituent), but by a continuous fall (cf. example (36) and figure 9):

(36) Qu'est-ce qu'il fume ?
'What does he smoke?'
Il fume des cigarettes le dimanche.
il fume)$_{RG}$ des cigarettes)$_{RG}$ L%]$_{IntP}$ le DImanche)$_{RG}$ L%]$_{IntP}$
H*$^{c}$

## 5 Conclusion

In French, Ground/Focus articulation and discourse articulation play a role in the determination of the prosody associated with an utterance. F-marking does not resort to a specific tone or accent, but to illocutionary boundary tones. Moreover Ground/Focus articulation influences phrasing: the focus constituent is realized as an Intonational Phrase on its own.

While Ground/Focus articulation is essentially marked by intonation and phrasing, Discourse organization is marked by the use of a pragmatic accent called *accent C*. This accent is observed in the presence of a complex strategy. It signals the enlargement, the narrowing down or the shifting of the current Discourse Topic. T-marking in French makes use of the same discourse trigger as German or English T-marking, even though the fine-grained rules for its realization may be different across those languages.

The crucial theoretical import of T-marking is that accentuation may be sensitive to discourse moves and not to the informative contribution of the utterances to the context. By the same token, the analysis of intonational marking should not be restricted to the Ground/Focus articulation.

## References


Beckman, J., ed. 1996. *Proceedings of the North East Linguistic Society*. U. of Pennsylvania.

Beyssade, C., J. Marandin, and A. A. Rialland. 2003. Ground/focus revisited. A perspective from French. In Núñez-Cedeño et al. (2003), pages 83–98.

Bolinger, D. 1965. *Forms of English: Accent, Morpheme, Order*. Cambridge (MA): Harvard University Press. Abe, I. and T. Kenekiyo, eds.

Botinis, A., ed. 2000. *Intonation: Analysis, Modelling and Technology*. Dordrecht: Kluwer Academic Publishers.

Büring, D. 1998. Focus and topic in a complex model of discourse. Ms. Bürings website.

Clech-Darbon, A., G. Rebuschi, and A. Rialland. 1999. Are there cleft sentences in French? In Rebuschi and Tuller (1999), pages 83–118.

Di Cristo, A. 1998. Intonation in French. In Hirst and Cristo (1998), pages 195–218.

Di Cristo, A. 1999. Le cadre accentuel du français contemporain. Première partie. *Langues* 3(2):184–205. Deuxième partie. *Langues* 4(2): 258-267.

Féry, C. 2001. The phonology of focus in french. In Féry and Sternefeld (2001), pages 153–181.

Féry, C. and W. Sternefeld, eds. 2001. *Audiatur Vox Sapientiae. A Festschrift for Arnim von Stechow*. Berlin: Akademie Verlag.

Ginzburg, J., Z. Khasidashvili, C. Vogel, J.-J. Lévy, and E. Vallduví, eds. 1998. *The Tbilisi symposium on logic, language, and computation*. CSLI Publications.

Hirst, D. and A. D. Cristo, eds. 1998. *Intonation Systems. A Survey of Twenty Languages*. Cambridge University Press.

Jun, S.-A. and C. Fougeron. 2000. A phonological model of French intonation. In Botinis (2000), pages 209–242.

Le Gac, D. 2001. *Structure prosodique de la focalisation: le cas du somali et du français*. Ph.D. thesis, Univ. Paris VII.

McNally, L. 1998. On recent formal analyses of 'topic'. In Ginzburg et al. (1998), pages 147–160.

Núñez-Cedeño, R., L. López, and R. Cameron, eds. 2003. *Selected papers of LSRL 2001*. John Benjamins.

Pasdeloup, V. 1990. *Modèles de règles du français appliqué à la synthèse de la parole*. Ph.D. thesis, Université de Provence.

Rebuschi, G. and L. Tuller, eds. 1999. *The Grammar of Focus*. Amsterdam: Benjamins.

Rossi, M. 1999. *L'Intonation, le système du français: description et modélisation*. Paris: Ophrys.

Touati, P. 1987. *Structures prosodiques du suédois et du français*. Ph.D. thesis, Lund University. Published as *Travaux de l'institut de linguistique de Lund*, 21.

Vallduví, E. and E. Elisabet. 1996. Information packaging and grammar architecture. In Beckman (1996), pages 519–533.

# 22

# Dislocation *

ELISABETH DELAIS-ROUSSARIE, JENNY DOETJES, AND PETRA SLEEMAN

## 1 Introduction

Dislocation involves various constructions in which a constituent is separated from the rest of the clause by a pause and/or is pronounced at a different intonational level than the adjacent segments. Moreover, when this constituent is left out, what remains is a correct sentence, both from a syntactic and from a prosodic point of view (cf. Fradin 1990). We will focus in this chapter on cases where the associated sentence contains a pronoun or another placeholder for the prosodically detached constituent.[1]

The dislocated material is usually found at the left periphery (left dislocation) or at the right periphery (right dislocation) of a proposition:

(1) a. Cet homme, je ne le connais pas.
this man, I don't know him

b. Je ne le connais pas, cet homme.

Section 2 discusses different types of left dislocation and compares

*We wish to thank the members of the PICS project group on Information and in particular Jean-Marie Marandin for comments and discussion. Jenny Doetjes gratefully acknowledges the support from NWO (grant #355-70-003).

[1]This means that we will not consider cases in which an adverbial phrase is prosodically detached from a sentence, as in (i):

(i) Ce soir, je ne peux pas venir. / Je ne peux pas venir, ce soir.
this evening, I NE can not come / I NE can not come, this evening
'I cannot come this evening'

*Handbook of French Semantics.*
Francis Corblin and Henriëtte de Swart (eds.).
Copyright © 2004, CSLI Publications.

left dislocation with topicalization, another construction in which the left periphery is involved. Section 3 investigates right dislocation as well as some cases where the dislocated element occupies a non-peripheral position. In both sections syntactic, semantic and prosodic factors will be discussed.

## 2 Left dislocation

Left dislocation involves the prosodic detachment of a constituent at the left edge of the clause. The dislocated constituent is picked up further on in the clause by a placeholder (resumptive element). It is a construction that is essentially used in the spoken language, just like right dislocation. Various kinds of left dislocation have been distinguished in the literature, depending on the categorial status of the left dislocated constituent, the nature of the resumptive element and the syntactic relation between these two. These various kinds of left dislocation constructions have also been associated with different pragmatic properties. In this section we examine the syntactic (2.1) and pragmatic properties (2.2) of left dislocation in French. Furthermore, we investigate whether left dislocation constructions always have the same prosodic properties (2.3).

### 2.1 Syntactic properties of left dislocation

The left detached constituent can be an NP, a PP, an AP, an infinitival clause or a tensed clause. It can also be a pronoun or a proper name.

(2) a. Cette femme, je n'ai pas confiance en elle.
this woman, I do not have confidence in her

b. A la campagne, Paul n'y reste jamais longtemps.
in the country, Paul never stays there a long time

c. Heureuse, elle ne l'a jamais été.
happy, she has never been it

d. Partir, c'est mourir un peu.
to leave, that is to die a bit

e. Qu'il se soit trompé, c'est évident.
that he has made a mistake, that is clear

f. Moi, personne ne veut m'aider.
me, nobody wants to help me

g. Pierre, je n'aime pas cet idiot.
Pierre, I do not like that idiot

The resumptive element can be a clitic (2b,c,f), a strong pronoun (2a), a demonstrative pronoun (2d,e) or an epithet such as *cet idiot* 'that idiot' (2g).[2]

Since Hirschbühler (1974, 1975) and Cinque (1977), it is commonly assumed that there are at least two types of left dislocation. For Italian, Cinque (1983) distinguishes between Clitic Left Dislocation (ClLD) and Hanging Topic Left Dislocation (HTLD) on the basis of the properties in table 1.

TABLE 1 Syntactic properties of HTLD and ClLD in Italian (Cinque 1983)

| HTLD | ClLD |
|---|---|
| (a) The lefthand phrase can be of category NP only | (a) The lefthand phrase can be of category NP, PP, AP, CP (essentially any XP) |
| (b) The 'resumptive element' can be an epithet or an ordinary pronoun, either tonic or clitic. | (b) The 'resumptive element' can be a clitic pronoun only. |
| (c) There is no Case matching between the lefthand phrase and the resumptive element. | (c) There is obligatory Case matching between the lefthand phrase and the resumptive element. |
| (d) The relation between the lefthand phrase and the resumptive element is not sensitive to island constraints. | (d) The relation between the lefthand phrase and the resumptive element is sensitive to island constraints. |
| (e) There may be at most one lefthand phrase. | (e) There is no (theoretical) limit to the number of lefthand phrases. |
| (f) The lefthand phrase occurs typically to the left of a 'root' sentence. | (f) The lefthand phrase can occur to the left of 'root' and 'non-root' sentences. |

[2]With verbs such as *aimer*, 'to love' or *connaître* 'to know', the accusative clitic can be left out (see, e.g. Fónagy 1985 and Zribi-Hertz 1996):

(i) Le bon yogourt, il aime.
the good yoghurt, he likes

Note that the sentence is equally good when the left dislocated constituent is left out: the absence of the pronoun (or rather the presence of a non-overt pronominal category) is independent of the presence or absence of *le bon yogourt.* In this respect cases such as (i) differ from topicalization, another construction with a constituent in the left periphery of the clause which will be considered below. In topicalization there is no resumptive element and dropping the topicalized constituent normally leads to ungrammaticality.

Furthermore, a dislocated constituent can be loosely related to the clause, without its relation to the clause being explicitly expressed by a pronoun or an epithet (see, among others, Barnes 1985):

(ii) Le métro, avec la carte orange on va n'importe où.
the subway, with a ticket orange you go anywhere

According to criterion (a), sentences (2b-e) are ClLDs, since the left dislocated phrase is a category other than NP. Criterion (b) distinguishes (2a) and (2g) as HTLDs. Sentence (2f) is ambiguous between HTLD and ClLD, just like (3):

(3) Pierre, je ne l'aime pas.
    Pierre, I do not like him

Unlike Italian, French has no case marking on strong pronouns, which have a unique form (*moi, toi* etc.). However, the third criterion (c), can be used to distinguish HTLD and ClLD when the placeholder is a dative clitic (*me, te, lui, nous, vous, leur*), *y* (locative, dative) or *en* (genitive). In the case of ClLD these require the presence of a preposition (*de* 'of' or *à* 'to, in' or other locative prepositions such as *sur* 'on', *en* 'in' or *dans* 'in'). An example is (2b). The use of the PP distinguishes the sentence as a case of ClLD. If, in (2b), the PP is replaced by an NP, as in (4), we are dealing with a HTLD (see also Blasco 1999):

(4) La campagne, Paul n'y reste jamais longtemps.
    the country, Paul never stays there a long time

As for the fourth criterion (d), French is parallel to Italian. The clitic left dislocated constituent is sensitive to island constraints whereas a hanging topic is not (see also Hirschbühler 1975 and Cinque 1977).[3] This is illustrated in (5). In this respect, ClLD (5a) resembles topicalization (6), in which a constituent is moved to a sentence-initial position without leaving a copy *lui* 'to her':

(5) a. *A Marie, je connais le flic qui lui a retiré son permis.
       to Marie, I know the cop who has taken her her license
    b. Marie, je connais le flic qui lui a retiré son permis.
       Marie, I know the cop who has taken her her license

---

[3]According to De Cat (2002), ClLD is not sensitive to islands. She claims that sentences such as (5a) are marginal because the presence of the preposition *à* is dispreferred in root contexts. This means that, in her view, the left dislocated constituent in (5a) would have the same status as the one in (2b). This sentence is much better without the preposition, even though the presence of the prepostion is preferred in non-root contexts (see the discussion of the last criterion (f) below). De Cat's claim can easily be tested on the basis of ClLD in non-root contexts. The minimal pair in (i) suggests that ClLD in French is sensitive to island constraints and that there is a difference in grammaticality between (5a) and (2b):

(i) a.*Je crois qu'à Marie, je connais le flic qui lui a retiré son permis
      I think that to Marie, I know the cop who has taken her her license
    b.Je crois qu'à Marie, le flic lui a retiré son permis.
      I think that to Marie, the cop has taken her her license

We can conclude that there is a correlation between island sensitivity and the presence of the preposition.

(6) *A Marie je connais le flic qui a retiré son permis.
to Marie I know the cop who has taken her license

Thus the fourth criterion allows us to distinguish (7) as a case of HTLD:

(7) Marie, je connais le garçon qui l'aime.
Marie, I know the boy who loves her

With respect to the criteria (e-f), there are clear differences between Italian and French. It seems that in French there is no theoretical restriction on the number of left dislocated constituents, either in HTLD (8) or in ClLD (9):

(8) a. Pierre, sa voiture, cet idiot ne s'occupe pas d'elle
Pierre, his car, this idiot does not treat it
correctement.
properly

b. Marie, ce crime, je crois que je ne lui en parlerai pas.
Marie, this crime, I think that I will not tell her about it

(9) A Marie, de ce crime, je crois que je ne lui en parlerai pas.
to Marie, of this crime, I think I will not speak to her about it

A combination of the two types of dislocated constituents is also possible, but, interestingly, only with the hanging topic first:

(10) a. Marie, de ce crime, je crois que je ne lui en parlerai jamais.
b. *A Marie, ce crime, je crois que je ne lui en parlerai jamais.
c. Ce crime, à Marie, je crois que je ne lui en parlerai jamais.
d. *De ce crime, Marie, je crois que ne lui en parlerai jamais.

As a last difference between ClLD and HTLD, Cinque mentions the type of clause the dislocated constituent may be detached from (criterion f). Whereas a hanging topic typically occurs to the left of a 'root' sentence, a clitic left dislocated constituent can occur to the left of 'root' and 'non-root' sentences. Larsson (1979: 76-78) notes however that in French ClLD seems to be very rare (impossible for some speakers) in 'root' contexts (11a), but possible to various degrees in embedded contexts (11b). In 'root' contexts, their place is taken by HTLD structures (12a). In 'non-root' contexts, a hanging topic is less natural but not impossible. Some speakers only accept it after expressions such as *je crois, je pense* 'I think', *il est possible* 'it is possible', *il semble* 'it seems' (12b):

(11) a. A ce confort, on s'y habitue très vite.
to this comfort, one gets accustomed very fast

b. Je crois qu'à ce confort, on s'y habitue très vite.
I think that to this comfort one gets accustomed very fast

(12) a. Ce confort, on s'y habitue très vite.
b. Je crois que, ce confort, on s'y habitue très vite.

The conclusion of this section is that the distinction between ClLD and HTLD is less prominent in French than in Italian (see also Larsson 1979 and Fradin 1990). For many cases of LD, we cannot distinguish between the two types. Moreover, in most cases where we can, only one criterion applies. As a result we cannot decide on the basis of these cases whether there is a distinction between two types of LD or whether there is just one type of LD which is more permissive than both ClLD and HTLD in Italian. However, there are some cases that show that there is at least some syntactic distinction between two types of left dislocation in French. As shown in (5), there is a correlation between the presence of a preposition in the left dislocated constituent and sensitivity to islands. Moreover, as shown in (10), the order of two LD constituents is restricted by the presence vs. absence of the preposition. It will become clear in the next two sections, that the distinction between ClLD and HTLD in French does not seem to affect either pragmatics or prosody.

### 2.2 Pragmatic/semantic properties of left dislocation

Left dislocation is essentially used in oral speech, at least in French. Since it is even more used than the simple SVO order in spoken French, Lambrecht (1981) distinguishes the syntax of spoken French from the syntax of the written style. He claims that a dislocated constituent is always a topic. He concludes that spoken French is topic-oriented, whereas written French is subject-oriented.

The notion of 'topic' is often associated with 'givenness' in the sense that the referent of a topic must be assumed by the speaker to be present in the addressee's consciousness (Chafe 1976). Lambrecht (1981) shows that different classes of left dislocated constituents can be distinguished on the basis of the properties of the discourse referent (DR) they denote. We will take the definition of a given DR in in the introduction to this part (chapter 20, section 2.3) as point of departure for the classification. Given (or active) DRs are inferable from the Given content G, the existential closure of which is noted as CL(G):

(13) $CL(G) \Rightarrow \exists x\ Q(x)$

This definition creates a set of DRs in the preceding discourse, which all define proper referents for a dislocated constituent. In what follows we will use the terminology of Prince (1979) and Lambrecht (1981). Lambrecht shows that a distinction should be made between "strictly given" DRs, that can be referred to by non-accented pronouns, and "non-strictly given" referents. This latter class will be called "textually evoked". Dislocation also allows for a referent that is present in the extra-linguistic context or situation. In this case the DR is "situationally evoked". The last type of DR is "inferable" from the context. Basically, DRs that can be inferred from (strictly) given or evoked DRs are possible DRs for a dislocated constituent as well. Discourse new DRs are not allowed. Before going over some examples illustrating these different cases, we can conclude that the conditions on dislocation are very similar to the conditions on the use of definite descriptions (cf. for instance Hawkins 1978). In general, a DR is a possible referent for a definite description in a non-dislocated position, this definite description can be dislocated as well. As we will see below, there is one interesting exception to this generalization: the use of a dislocation construction is incompatible with a complex discourse strategy (see chapter 20, Introduction).

Quite generally, we have not found clear pragmatic differences between ClLD and HTLD.[4] The presence/absence of a preposition in oblique dislocated consituents seems to be a purely syntactic issue. In what follows, we will talk about left dislocation (LD) in general.

Let us first consider a case where the dislocated expression is strictly given, that is, where there is a choice between the use of a pronoun and the use of left dislocation. Lambrecht argues that "strict givenness" is not a sufficient condition for the use of left dislocated constituents. In the answer in (14) the speaker uses a dislocated construction instead of a simple pronoun that would suffice to express the topic status of the subject:

(14) Q: Comment va ton frère?
'How is your brother?'
A: Mon frère, il va bien.
my brother, he is fine

In Lambrecht's view, this suggests that the function of the left dislocation is the establishment of some sort of communicative agreement between the speech participants. The left dislocation strategy marks the referent as important for the conversation.

In all other cases of left dislocation, the dislocated expression cannot simply be replaced by a pronoun. Lambrecht argues that in these cases the communicative function of the left dislocation construction is to mark a shift with respect to the previously established topic, or, when no previous topic was established, to create a new topic. The DR is

[4]In this respect French seems to differ from Italian; see Cinque (1983), who argues that the pragmatic conditions for ClLD and HTLD are not the same in that language.

not strictly given but **textually** (15) or **situationally evoked** (16) or **inferred** (17), as defined above:

(15) Le bout de papier provient de l'étiquette d'une boîte de conserve, et la boîte dont il a été arraché, je l'ai eue en main un peu avant de vous rencontrer. (Hergé)
'The piece of paper comes from the label of a can, and the can from which it has been torn off, I had it in my hands just before I met you.'

(16) After having paid and having received a lot of coins:

Mon portemonnaie, il est devenu lourd.
my purse, it has become heavy

(17) L'air de la ville n'est pas plus mauvais qu'un autre. Et entre nous, la mer, qu'est-ce que c'est? (Reiser)
'The air in town is not worse than other air. And between us, the sea, what is it?'

In all of the cases mentioned above, the left dislocated constituent is not used contrastively. But this is also a possibility, as noted by Lambrecht (1981):

(18) Q: Qu'est-ce que tu vas donner à Pierre et à Marie?
'What are you going to give to Pierre and to Marie?'
A: (A) Pierre, je lui donnerai un livre, (à) Marie,
to Pierre, I will give him a book, to Marie,
je lui offrirai des fleurs.
I will offer her flowers

The use of sentences such as the answer in (18) turns out to be restricted in an interesting way. Kerleroux & Marandin (2002) show that certain contexts which allow for contrastive topicalization exclude LD:

(19) Marie a réuni les élèves. Aux filles, elle a donné des exercices d'algèbre. Aux garçons, elle a dicté un problème de géométrie.
'Marie brought together the pupils. To the girls, she gave algebra exercises. To the boys, she dictated a geometry problem.'

(20) # Marie a réuni les élèves. Aux/Les filles, elle leur a donné des exercices d'algèbre. Aux/Les garçons, elle leur a dicté un problème de géométrie.
'Marie brought together the pupils. (To) the girls, she gave them algebra exercises. (To) the boys, she dictated them a geometry problem.'

The example in (19), a case of topicalization, reshapes the discourse topic: instead of talking about the children in general, as in the previous sentence, the second sentence distinguishes between boys and girls.[5] Thus, there is a shift from a simple discourse strategy simple discourse strategy to a complex strategy, whereby the constituent *aux filles* 'to the girls' functions as a thematic shifter (see chapter 20, Introduction). The inappropriateness of (20) suggests that left dislocation does not allow shifting from a simple to a layered discourse topic. The appropriateness of (18) can be understood as follows. In this example, the question can be interpreted as a double question ('what will you give to Pierre and what will you give to Marie?'). As a result, the answer does not imply a change of discourse strategy. The layered discourse topic is shaped by the question. Interestingly, some speakers note a contrast between the examples in (21b,c), as answers to (21a). Note that an answer with two topicalizations is always preferred, even for those speakers who find (21c) more or less appropriate in this context:

(21) a. Qu'a-t-elle dit aux étudiants?
'What did she say to the students?'

b. #(A) Durand, elle lui a dit qu'elle ferait cours,
(to) Durand, she said to him that she would teach,
(à) Dupond, elle lui a avoué qu'elle envisageait de
(to) Dupond, she confessed him that she thought about
tout arrêter.
quitting everything

c. ?A Durand, elle a dit qu'elle ferait cours, (à) Dupond,
to Durand, she said that she would teach, (to) Dupond,
elle lui a avoué qu'elle envisageait de tout arrêter.
she confessed him that she thought about quitting everything

The contrast between (21b) and (21c) shows that the left dislocated constituent cannot be a thematic shifter, but for some speakers it can be used once the shift has been made in an elaboration of the discourse topic. This observation is particularly interesting with respect to two

---

[5]Topicalization (i) has to be distinguished from focus preposing (ii) (see also note 9 below):

(i) A: Tu as pensé à mon frère?
'Have you thought of my brother?'
B: Non, à ton frère, je n'avais pas encore pensé.
'No, of your brother, I have not thought yet.'

(ii) A: A qui as-tu téléphoné?
'Whom did you call?'
B: A mon père j'ai téléphoné.
'To my father I made a call.'

other generalizations in French. First, as we will see in chapter 24 (Subject NP Inversion), several types of inversion are subject to a similar constraint. In these cases, the verbal predicate cannot be a thematic shifter, but it can be used in a sentence elaborating a layered discourse topic. Second, as we have seen in chapter 21 (Prosody and Information in French), a C accent is obligatorily realized in utterances that reshape the discourse topic, while it is optional in utterances that elaborate the discourse topic. These otherwise unrelated phenomena show that the distinction between reshaping and elaborating a DT is encoded in the grammar of French.

Lambrecht (1981:61) notices that from the fact that left dislocated constituents are always topics, it follows that they must be (referentially) definite. They can only be introduced by indefinite articles in the generic reading. In such cases, the resumptive element is usually *ça* 'that' (see a.o. Muller 1987, Maillard 1987):

(22) a. Un garçon, ça attend pas devant la porte.
a boy, that does not wait outside the door

b. Des chats, ça miaule.
cats, that miaows

It turns out however, that an indefinite left dislocated constituent is not always generic. In these cases the resumptive element is usually *en*. In (23a) the left dislocated constituent is introduced by the indefinite article *des* and denotes a set whose defining property is strictly given, textually/situationally evoked or inferred. Some (but certainly not all) speakers also accept (23b). In this example the dislocated constituent is introduced by *de* (Barbaud 1976, Larsson 1979). The *de NP* corresponds to a property which is strictly given, textually/situationally evoked or inferred. This type of example preferably contains a negation.

(23) a. Des bonbons, Jean en avait même donné à sa fille.
candies, Jean of-them had even given to his daughter

b. ?De médecin, je n'en ai vu aucun.
of doctor, I of-them have seen none

Having discussed the semantic and pragmatic properties of left dislocation and topicalization, we now turn to their prosodic properties.

## 2.3 Prosodic properties of left dislocation

It is a well-established fact that in French and in many other languages the prosodic realization of an utterance is sensitive to syntactic and pragmatic information. In this section we will compare the prosodic properties of left dislocation and compare them with topicalization.

A left dislocated or topicalized constituent constitutes an independent prosodic phrase (Major Phrase (MaP) or Intonational Phrase (IntP), see chapter 20, Introduction). The boundary of this phrase is marked by either a $H^{cont}$ demarcative tone, or an illocutionary tone H(L)% (see also Rossi 1999).

The $H^{cont}$ demarcative tone signals the boundary of a MaP. It is characterized by a F0 rise and an important lengthening of the final syllable. The H target is usually reached at the end of the syllable. This tone can be compared to Rossi's CTr '*intonème*'. H(L)% is an illocutionary boundary tone and is equivalent to the one realized at the end of an echo question or a confirmation request. It is characterized by an important F0 rise on the last syllable, the H target being reached at the end of the nucleus and a slight fall being sometimes realized on the syllable coda.[6] This tone can be compared to Rossi's CTi '*intonème*'. In case the illocutionary tone is selected, an Intonational Phrase (IntP) boundary is inserted.[7]

We have compared and analysed a number of sentences with HTLD, ClLD and topicalization. It turns out that the distribution of the two tones is not free but determined by both syntactic and pragmatic factors. In ClLD and HTLD we find either of the two tones, depending on pragmatic factors. In topicalization, only the $H^{cont}$ demarcative tone can be used.

Let us consider first ClLD and HTLD. The choice between the two possible tones is determined by pragmatic factors, and seems to be independent of the distinction between ClLD and HTLD. This confirms the conclusions of the previous section, in which we have seen that there are no clear pragmatic differences between the two types of LD.[8] What crucially determines the tone that is realized at the right boundary of the left detached constituent is the speaker's attitude towards the other participants. A $H^{cont}$ demarcative tone is chosen if the speaker assumes that an agreement is established between the different participants with

---

[6]This boundary tone has a variant (a L% illocutionary boundary tone or a fall) that is obligatorily used on left dislocated constituents in questions:

(i) Marie, est-ce que c'est sûr qu'elle va partir?
'Marie, is it certain that she will leave?'

This variant can be optionally realized in assertions.

[7]See also Introduction. In general, MaP boundaries are determined by syntactic and metrical factors, while IntPs, which are characterized by illocutionary boundary tones, are subject to pragmatic conditions.

[8]According to Cinque (1983: footnote 4) HTLD may differ intonationally from ClLD in Italian: a HTLD constituent may have a rising intonation. This correlates with the clear syntactic and pragmatic differences between HTLD and ClLD in Italian.

respect to the choice of the topic. This intonation is illustrated in (24) and in figure 1. Note that the same intonation is possible when the preposition *à* is left out.

(24) à mon prof)$_{RG}$ de linguistique)$_{RG}$ H$^{cont}$ }$_{MaP}$ je
to my linguistics professor, I
lui ai donné)$_{RG}$ un livre)$_{RG}$ L% ]$_{IntP}$
gave him a book

FIGURE 1 F0 curve of example (24), *À mon prof de linguistique, je lui ai donné un livre.* (Speaker FER, woman)

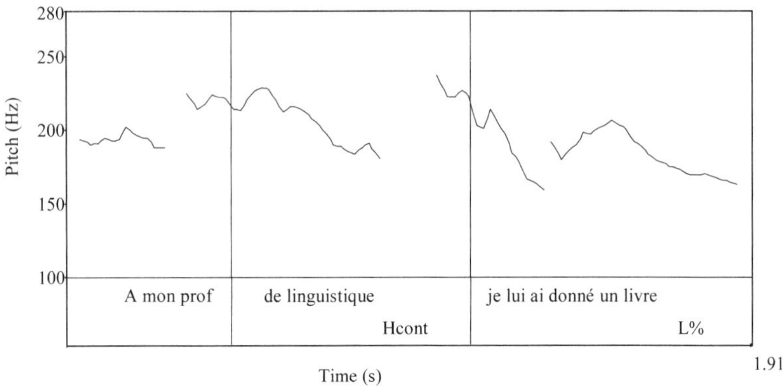


This utterance is typically used in contexts where the discourse referent of *mon prof* is strictly given, as strictly given DRs usually define non-controversial topics. Similarly, H$^{cont}$ is selected in (25b), where the DR of *Jean-Marie* is strictly given:

(25) a. Qu'est-ce qu'il a offert à Jean-Marie?
'What did he give to Jean-Marie?'

b. à Jean-Marie)$_{RG}$ H$^{cont}$}$_{MaP}$ il lui a offert)$_{RG}$ un compact disque)$_{RG}$ L%]$_{IntP}$
to Jean-Marie, he gave him a CD

When the speaker does not assume that an agreement on the choice of the topic is established between the participants, he tentatively proposes one. In this case, the illocutionary boundary tone H(L) % that is found in confirmation requests and echo questions is realized at the end of the IntP. Examples (26) and (27) show that the H(L) % illocutionary boundary tone may be realized in both constructions HTLD and ClLD (see also figures 2 and 3):

(26) à Jean-Marie)$_{RG}$ H(L)% ]$_{IntP}$ il lui a offert)$_{RG}$ un compact-disque)$_{RG}$ L% ]$_{IntP}$
to Jean-Marie, he gave him a CD

FIGURE 2 F0 curve of example (26), *À Jean-Marie, il lui a offert un compact disque.* (Speaker FER)

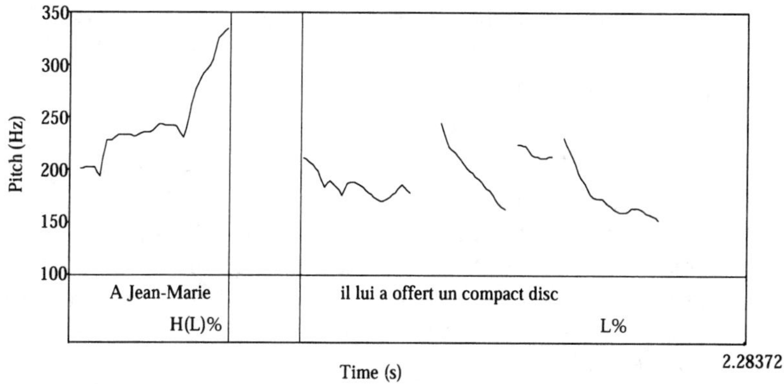


(27) Marie)$_{RG}$ H(L)% ]$_{IntP}$ c'est clair)$_{RG}$ $H^{cont}$}$_{MaP}$ qu'elle sera fâchée)$_{RG}$ contre son frère)$_{RG}$ L% ]$_{IntP}$
'Marie, it's clear that she will get angry with her brother.'

FIGURE 3 F0 curve of example (27), *Marie, c'est clair qu'elle sera fâchée contre son frère.* (Speaker FAD, woman)

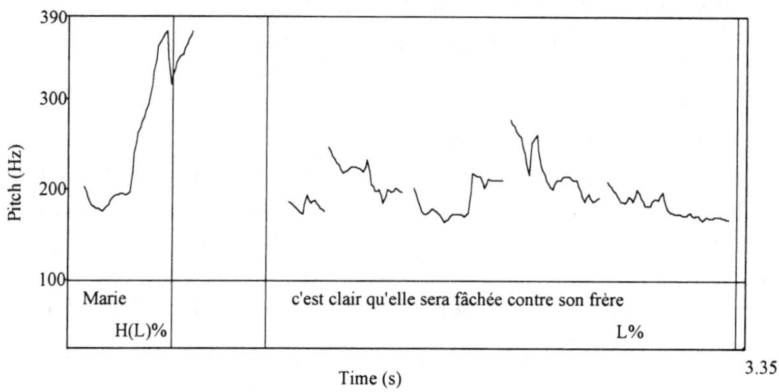


Normally, these sentences are used in contexts in which the discourse referent is not strictly given, and therefore they are more easily subject to a potential disagreement about the choice of the referent for the topic of the utterance. However, even in a context where the discourse referent of the dislocated constituent is strictly given, this tone may be used. Consider again (26). This utterance can be the answer to the question in (28) below. By using the name *Jean-Marie*, instead of repeating *mon fils*, the speaker indicates that there might be a disagreement about the choice of *Jean-Marie* as the topic of the utterance. This is why the H(L)% boundary tone has to be used rather than $H^{cont}$.

(28) Qu'est-ce qu'il a offert à ton fils?
'What did he give to your son?'

The two tones ($H^{cont}$ and H(L)%) are also used in sequences of left dislocated constituents. In this case, the selection and the distribution of the tones depends partly on the pragmatics. In addition, some constraints apply on the use of these tones (cf. among others, Rossi 1999). The successive tones may be either identical or different. In case they are identical, a succession of two H(L)% or two $H^{cont}$ may be observed. In case they are different, the first boundary tone has to be H(L)% and the second one $H^{cont}$. The sequence $H^{cont}$ H(L)% is thus forbidden.

Let us now turn to topicalization.[9] Topicalization resembles HTLD and ClLD insofar as the left peripheral constituent is phrased as an independent MaP. However, there is no choice between the two boundary tones: the right edge of the topicalized constituent has to coincide with a $H^{cont}$ demarcative tone (relatively important F0 rise and important lengthening). The prosodic realization of (19) is given in (29) and in figure 4:

(29) aux filles$)_{RG}$ $H^{cont}\}_{MaP}$ elle a donné$)_{RG}$ des exercices d'algèbre$)_{RG}$ $H^{cont}\}_{MaP}$ et aux garçons$)_{RG}$ $H^{cont}\}_{MaP}$ elle a dicté$)_{RG}$ des problèmes$)_{RG}$ de géométrie$)_{RG}$ L%$]_{IntP}$
'To the girls she gave algebra exercises and to the boys she dictated geometry problems.'

The difference between topicalization (H(L)% excluded) and LD (H(L)% possible) shows that syntax influences the choice of the boundary tone. The relation between syntax and the choice of the boundary tone might be either direct or mediated by pragmatics. In case of a direct relation, the syntax of topicalization would not allow for insertion of the H(L)%

[9] In focus preposing (see note 5 above), the peripheral constituent is a narrow focus. The end of this constituent is marked by an illocutionary boundary tone associated with focus (L% in assertions). The rest of the sentence is a post-focus sequence. Hence the intonation is in accordance with our findings in chapter 2 (Prosody).

FIGURE 4 F0 curve of example (29), *Aux filles elle a donné des exercices d'algèbre ...* (Speaker FER)

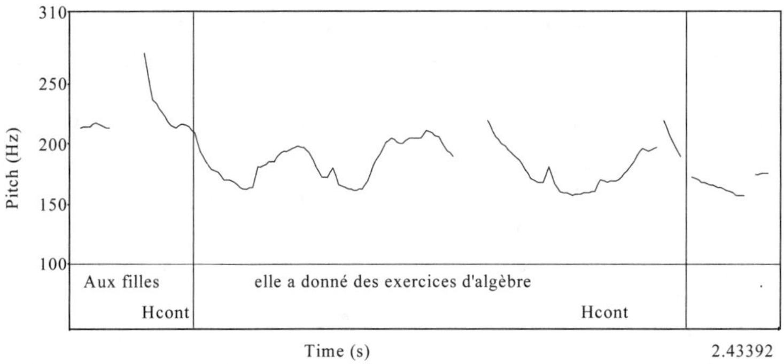


tone at the right edge of the topicalized constituent. Alternatively, the syntax of topicalization might be incompatible with the pragmatics that are required for insertion of the H(L)% tone, in which case there would be an indirect relation between syntax and the choice of the H(L)% tone. We will leave this issue for further research.

To summarize, it appears that two dimensions come into play in the prosodic realization of left peripheral constituents. The syntactic dimension allows us to distinguish left dislocation from topicalization. The pragmatic dimension comes into play whenever an agreement concerning the choice of the topic is not fully established between the speech participants. In that case, the H(L)% illocutionary boundary tone is realized at the right edge of the IntP. Otherwise, we find the $H^{cont}$ demarcative tone.

## 3 Right dislocation

Right dislocation (RD) is at first sight more closely related to clitic left dislocation than to the hanging topic construction. As in ClLD, RD involves case agreement on the dislocated element, as in (30).[10]

(30) Je lui ai donné un livre, *(à) Marie
I to-her have given a book to Marie

[10] A loose aboutness relation (cf. note 2) is excluded, as shown in (i):

(i) *Elle$_i$ s'est complètement cassée, mon frère, sa voiture$_i$
she is completely broken, my brother, his car
'My brothers car is ruined'
(cf. *Mon frère, elle$_i$ s'est complètement cassée, sa voiture$_i$*)

Furthermore, the antecedent of the RD element is usually a clitic pronoun. However, in what follows we will show that the resemblance between ClLD and RD is quite superficial. For instance, the presence of a clitic is not always required, as it is in the case of ClLD. The fact that we have a clitic in most RD sentences can be shown to be due to independent factors.

French also allows for dislocation in a string medial position (examples will be treated below). Following Ronat (1979), Larsson (1979) and Fradin (1988, 1990), we consider middle dislocation (MD) as a special case of RD. In this we diverge from, for instance, Lambrecht (1981, 2001), who claims that the right dislocated element is always located at the right edge of a clause.

In this section we will discuss the properties of RD from a syntactic (3.1), a pragmatic/semantic (3.2) and a prosodic (3.3) point of view.

### 3.1 Syntactic properties of right dislocation

From a syntactic point of view, right dislocation initially seems to have much in common with clitic left dislocation. As the example in (30) shows, there is case matching between the RD constituent and the pronoun it is associated with.[11] As in the case of ClLD, the RD expression is not necessarily a DP. It can also be a pronoun (31a), an NP preceded by the element de 'of' (31b), a PP (usually with *de* 'of', *à* 'to', but less frequently also with some other locative prepositions such as *sur* 'on' (31c)), an AP (31d), a finite clause (31e) or an infinitival clause (31f) (see for instance Fradin 1988, Larsson 1979). There can be several RD constituents, the order of which is not fixed (32) (cf. Lambrecht 1981):

(31) a. Je l'ai vu, moi
I saw him, me/I

b. Il en a mis trois sur la table, de livres
he put three of them on the table, of books

c. Paul y grimpe en un clin d'oeil, sur le toit
Paul climbs on it in a wink, on the roof

d. Ils savaient bien qu'elle l'était, lourde à porter,
they knew well that-it was it, heavy to carry,
la valise
the suitcase
'They knew that the suitcase was heavy to carry.'

[11] Pronouns do not need to show case matching. A RD pronoun can be used in oblique contexts in the absence of a preposition (cf. Lambrecht 1981, Ronat 1979, Fradin 1988, Ashby 1988, 1994). *Il m'a parlé, moi* is fine, while **Il lui a parlé, Pierre* is excluded.

e. Je ne le savais pas, que c'était interdit
I did not know it, that it was forbidden

f. Elle le fera toute sa vie, danser
she will do it all her life, to dance

(32) a. Je le lui donne, moi, le livre, à ton frère
I will give it to him, me/I, the book, to your brother

b. Je le lui donne, le livre, à ton frère, moi

c. Je le lui donne, à ton frère, moi, le livre

However, there are also a number of differences between RD and ClLD. These differences clearly indicate that RD is not simply the mirror image of left dislocation. In the first place, RD and ClLD obey different locality conditions. In the second place, the placeholder for a right dislocated constituent is not necessarily a clitic.

Let us consider the locality conditions on RD and ClLD first. Whereas ClLD is subject to subjacency, a right dislocated constituent has to occur directly to the right of the proposition containing the coindexed pronoun (cf. Ross' 1967 *Right Roof Constraint*, Larsson 1979, Lambrecht 1981, 2001, Fradin 1988, Kayne 1984, Cecchetto 1999):

(33) a. *Qu'elle sera fachée contre son frère, c'est clair, Marie
that she will be mad with her brother, that's clear, Marie

b. Qu'elle sera fachée contre son frère, Marie, c'est clair
that she will be mad with her brother, Marie, that's clear

Interestingly, Larsson shows that the locality restrictions on RD go even further. She discusses a number of examples in which the RD element cannot be clause-final, as it has to remain in either a DP or a PP. This phenomenon can be illustrated by dislocation of a *de NP* in the context of a determiner without a noun. Under certain conditions, the *de NP* is preferably, and for some speakers, necessarily adjacent to the DP containing an empty pronoun. An example is given in (34):

(34) a. ??Le sien avait toujours été propre, d'uniforme officiel
his one had always been clean, of official uniform

b. Le sien, d'uniforme officiel, avait toujours été propre
the his, of official uniform, had always been clean

'HIS official uniform had always been clean'

These data suggest that dislocated *de NPs* are not always placed at the right periphery of the clause. The exact conditions for the adjacency requirement need further investigation. The presence of the Q adverb *toujours* seems to play a role. As noted already by Larsson, adjacency is not always required (cf. *La nôtre est faite, d'opinion* lit.: 'ours is made, of opinion').

For PPs, Larsson also shows that there is an adjacency requirement. It is not possible to have a RD element in sentence-final position if it is associated with a PP, as in (35a). However, there are cases in which a constituent that behaves otherwise like an RD expression is found at the right edge of a PP containing a pronoun, as in the sentence (35b):

(35) a. *C'était le moment d'essayer sur elles une solution corrosive, (sur) les punaises (Céline)

b. C'était le moment d'essayer sur elles, les punaises,
it was the moment to try on them, the pins,
une solution corrosive
a corrosive solution

We might tentatively formulate a locality condition that captures all cases in (33) through (35): RD elements usually remain inside the minimal XP that contains the pronominal expression with which they are associated. Obviously further research is necessary in order to develop this idea.

Cases such as (35b) - if we are right in considering them to be cases of right dislocation — also illustrate a second difference between RD and ClLD: the pronoun which is coreferent with the dislocated constituent does not need to be a clitic. Turning back to the 'standard' cases of RD, where the RD constituent comes at the end of the clause, we can also find cases in which a non-cliticized pronoun is used. An example, again due to Larsson (1979), is given in (36):[12]

(36) Je trouve ça écoeurant, la dénigration systématique
I find that disgusting, denigration systematic

This is only possible in cases where the pronoun is not prosodically marked as part of the focus, which excludes most cases of non-clitic pronouns. For instance, if a PP is in sentence-final position, right dislocation with respect to a full pronoun in the PP is difficult (cf. (35b), which is fine). The sentence *??Je parle souvent avec lui, Jean-Pierre* 'I often speak with him, Jean-Pierre' is not very good, even though judgments vary. The restriction follows from the assumption that RD is not available if the placeholder is part of the focus. As we will see below in

[12]Note also that right dislocated epithets such as *cet imbécile* 'the idiot' can be coreferential with a full DP. We will not elaborate on this type of sentences.

(i)Pierre a cassé la cafetière, cet imbécile
'Pierre broke the coffee pot, the idiot'

section 3.2, this assumption is in accordance with the pragmatic properties of RD, which typically backgrounds the dislocated constituent.

The examples in (34b) and (35b) present cases in which the dislocated element is not at the right edge of the sentence, but at the right edge of a DP or a PP, which contain the placeholder. There are also cases of dislocation in which the dislocated element is not located at the right edge of the sentence even though the placeholder is an argument of the verb. This phenomenon is illustrated in (37):

(37) a. Il$_i$ est passé de Harris, notre prof de linguistique$_i$,
he is gone from Harris, our prof of linguistics,
à la grammaire générative
to generative grammar

b. Il est venu, son ami d'enfance, de Paris à Marseille
he came, his old friend, from P. to M.
en voiture
by car

This construction, which we will call middle dislocation or MD is uniformly treated in the literature as a special case of RD (see Larsson 1979, Ronat 1979, Fradin 1988). However, in part of the literature on RD, MD is either ignored or its possibility is, contrary to fact, denied.[13] As we will see below, the prosodic properties of MD and RD confirm the hypothesis that we are dealing with one and the same phenomenon. From a pragmatic point of view, there does not seem to be a difference between MD and RD either.

## 3.2 Pragmatic and semantic properties of right dislocation

RD is said to foreground the new information in the sentence and to place the theme or topic at the background (cf. Larsson 1978, 1979). It is not the case, as a naïve analysis of right dislocation might suppose, that a right dislocated expression is necessarily completely predictable from the context. Both Larsson (1979) and Lambrecht (1981) show that RD is possible in contexts in which a pronoun alone would be unintelligible. This is illustrated by (38), cited in Larsson (1979) from

[13]Lambrecht claims that the RD element cannot precede the main intonation peak of the sentence, as in (i) (judgment as in Lambrecht 1981):

(i)*Il a envoyé une lettre, Jean, à PIERRE
'He sent a letter, Jean, to Pierre'

However, the analogous example in (37a), adapted from Ronat (1979), is grammatical. According to Larsson (1979), the acceptability of MD depends, among others, on rhythmic properties of the sentence. The part of the sentence following the dislocated expression should not be too short, for instance. MD also exists in other languages that allow for RD, such as Dutch.

a novel by Michel Butor:

(38) [. . . ] comme dans le fond de leur coeur, avec quelle sincérité ils se jurent d'être fidèles l'un à l'autre! Combien de temps vont-elles durer ces illusions?
'As from the bottom of their hearts, with great sincerity they promised each other to be faithful to one another! How much time are they going to last, these illusions?'

If we want to interpret the pronoun *elles*, the presence of *ces illusions* is necessary. This clearly shows that the RD element is not added after having finished the sentence in order to make sure that the addressee knows the reference of the pronoun. When using the pronoun, the speaker already has the intention to make a dislocated sentence, in order to foreground the new information.

As in the case of left dislocation, we can distinguish different types of RD constituents (see Lambrecht 1981). In the first place, RD constituents can have a strictly given or discourse old DR. This class includes, for instance, the rather frequent pronominal cases such as (39a) (cf. Ashby 1988, who reports 70% of pronominal RDs in his corpus). RD of a pronoun is excluded in English, which is in accordance with the observation that English prohibits RD of a constituent with a strictly given discourse referent (cf. Ziv 1994). The class also includes cases where the RD constituent is an epithet, as in (39b):

(39) a. Je ne sais pas, moi
I don't know, me
b. J'ai vu mon frère hier. $Il_i$ a voté pour Giscard, cet $imbecile_i$
'I have seen my brother yesterday. He has voted for G., that idiot'

In the second place, RD constituents have a DR which is textually or situationally evoked or inferred. An example of a RD constituent with a textually evoked DR, taken from Ashby (1988), is given in (40):

(40) Overall discourse topic: the charm of Touraine
A: La Loire est belle. Vous avez visité la Vallée de la Loire?
'The Loire is beautiful. Did you visit the Loire valley?'
B: Oui, pas mal
'Yes, quite a bit'
A: Elle est belle, la Loire, hein?
she is beautiful the Loire eh

The pronoun *elle* would refer to *la Vallée de la Loire* if the dislocated constituent had been left out.

In (41), the RD constituent has a situationally evoked DR:

(41) Situation: guest looking at book on host's bookshelf and shouting to host who is working in the kitchen:
Tu l' as lu, le dernier roman de Grass?
'Did you read it, the last novel of Grass?'

In (42), the DR of the RD constituent *le Portugal* is inferentially accessible (cited in Lambrecht 1981 from a novel by Reiser):

(42) Situation: Paris; racist Frenchman watching a Portuguese worker doing road work: Ça en fait du bruit, un Portugais. C'est sale. C'est dangereux. [...] Ça ne doit pas être un beau pays, le Portugal (Reiser)
'They are noisy, those Portuguese. They are dirty. They are dangerous. [...] It can impossibly be a pretty country, Portugal.'

In the contexts discussed so far, the pragmatic conditions on LD and RD are similar. However, whereas RD foregrounds the new information in the sentence and places the topic in the background, LD foregrounds the topic. This implies that they are not always used in the same contexts. In the first place, Ashby (1988) notes that LD can be used to mark turn taking, while RD cannot. RD, on the other hand, can be used to signal turn closing. A further difference between RD and LD is their use in contrastive contexts (cf. Larsson 1979, Lambrecht 1981, Barnes 1985 and De Cat 2002). While LD can be used in an answer to a double question, RD is excluded in this context (cf. (18) above):

(43) Question: what are you going to give to Pierre and to Marie?
#Je lui donnerai un livre, à Pierre, et je lui offrirai des fleurs, à Marie
I will give him a book, to Pierre, and I will give her flowers, to Marie

We can conclude that RD can never be used to mark an opposition.[14] This implies that it cannot be used as a thematic shifter either.

As in the case of LD, the fact that the RD constituent is part of the ground has consequences for its interpretation. This is particularly clear in the case of dislocated indefinites (for an overview, see Larsson 1979). They are often used as generics. When indefinites are interpreted generically, the resumptive element is usually *ça*:

[14]Vallduví (1994) uses this observation as evidence for his analysis in which LD constituents are 'links' and RD constituents are 'tails': whereas links point to a specific file card for the entry of the focus, the tail further specifies how the information provided by the focus fits on a given file card. As such, the tail is expected not to be contrastive.

(44) a. Ça peut se tromper, un médecin.
that can be mistaken, a doctor

b. Ça existe, des voitures très récentes
that exists, very recent cars
à des prix promotionnels
on special offer

In some cases the indefinite RD constituent is not generic and introduces a set or a mass, the defining property of which is strictly given, textually/situationally evoked or inferred. This is possible in contexts that allow for existential *en* (see also chapter 3, 'Towards a uniform characterization of Noun Phrases with *des* or *du*'):[15]

(45) a. T'en veux, de la soupe?
you want some, soup

b. Jean en avait même donné à sa fille, des bonbons.
Jean had even given some to his daughter, candies

RD of a *de NP* is similar to left dislocation with a *de NP*, although less restricted. The *de NP* indicates a property which is strictly given, textually/situationally evoked or inferred. An example is given in (31b), repeated here in (46):

(46) Il en a mis trois sur la table, de livres.
he put three of them on the table, of books

The conditions on right dislocation and left dislocation of indefinites are rather similar, even though dislocation of *de NPs* yields a much better result in the case of RD. We will leave this issue for further research, and continue with prosodic properties of right dislocation.

### 3.3 Prosodic properties of right dislocation

It is usually assumed that in a sentence with a RD element, the prosody of the main clause is equivalent to the prosody that the clause will have without the dislocated constituent. Consider for instance the prosody associated with (39b) (see figure 5):

(47) il a voté$)_{RG}$ pour Giscard$)_{RG}$ L% $]_{IntP}$, cet imbécile$)_{RG}$ L% $]_{IntP}$

An L% boundary tone is realized on the last syllable of *Giscard*, and copied at the end of the RD element *cet imbécile*. The clause *Il a voté pour Giscard* has the same intonation as when it is uttered on its own.

In the literature, the prosody associated with RD elements is analyzed as a low parenthesis, the boundary tone being a copy of the L%

[15] Existential *en* is usually excluded in the absence of a DP without a noun: *Il en a oublié #(deux)* 'he of-them forgot #(two)'. The sentences in (45) allow existential *en*, for reasons that are not fully understood.

FIGURE 5 F0 curve of example (39b) and (47), *Il a vote pour Giscard, cet imbecile.* (Speaker FER)

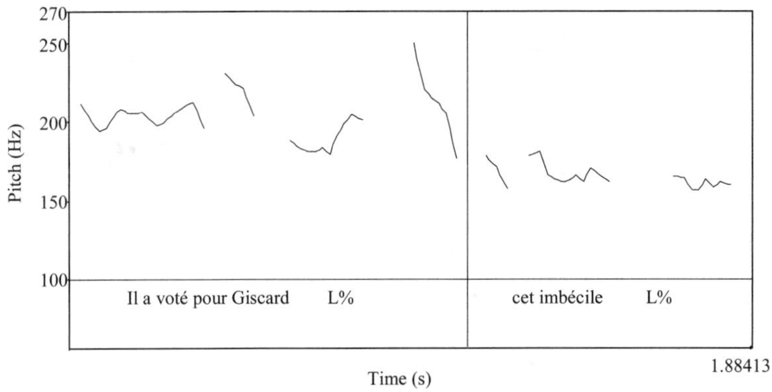


boundary tone (see, among others, Rossi 1981, 1985, 1999, Delattre 1966)[16]. The IntP that includes the RD element is also considered to be deaccented and dephrased in the majority of the work. The deaccentuation can be explained by the fact that RD elements cannot be used to modify discourse topics (cf. section 3.2). Concerning dephrasing, it might result from the short length of the RD elements studied. Thus, the prosody of RD elements can be compared to the one found in post-focus sequences (see chapter 2, Prosody).

In interrogative utterances, the intonation associated with RD elements is usually described as a high parenthesis (cf. Delattre 1966): the boundary tone H% that characterizes interrogation is copied at the end of the right dislocated constituent (cf. figure 6 and (41)):

(48) tu l'as lu)$_{RG}$ H%]$_{IntP}$ le dernier roman)$_{RG}$ de Günther Grass?)$_{RG}$ H%]$_{IntP}$

To summarize, RD constituents are realized as a plateau (low or high), a copy of the boundary tone found at the end of the clause being realized at the end of the RD element. In 3.2, it has been shown that RD elements may be strictly given (39), textually or situationally evoked ((40) and (41)), or inferred (42). These pragmatic differences do not

[16]According to Wunderli (1983), an H% boundary tone (continuation rise) might be realized at the end of the main clause in an assertion, the RD element being realized as a high parenthesis right bounded by an L% :

(i) il est venu)$_{RG}$ de Paris à Marseille)$_{RG}$ en voiture)$_{RG}$ H%] son ami d'enfance)$_{RG}$ L%]

In our data, this realization was very rare.

FIGURE 6 F0 curve of example (41) and (48), *Tu l'as lu, le dernier roman de Günther Grass?* (Speaker FER)

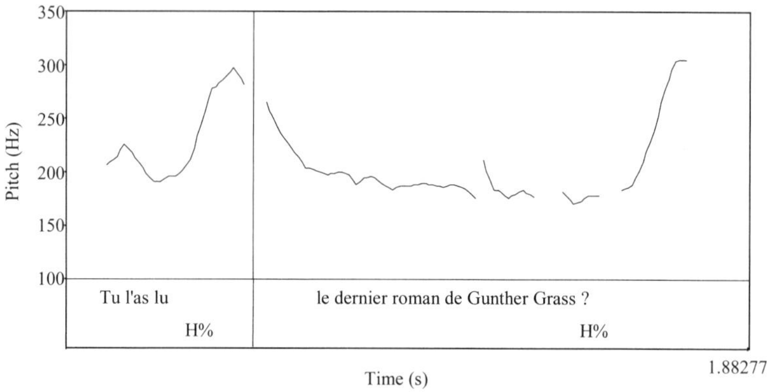


have any influence on the prosodic realization of RD elements (see also Ashby 1994).

The prosodic realization of a non-sentence-final RD is equivalent to the realization of incidental clauses, appositions, descriptive relative clauses. In these cases, the constituent in the middle of the sentence is realized with a flat contour and a compression of both pitch register and intensity (cf., among others, Rossi 1999). The boundary tone realized at the end of the element is a copy of the preceding boundary tone (usually a demarcative $H^{cont}$ tone). Consider (49) (see figures 7 and 8):

(49) a. la femme)$_{RG}$ qui lui a parlé)$_{RG}$ $H^{cont}\}_{MaP}$
the woman who talked to her,
à Marie-Antoinette)$_{RG}$ $H^{cont}!\}_{MaP}$ m'agace)$_{RG}$ L%]$_{IntP}$
(to) Marie-Antoinette, annoys me

b. il est venu)$_{RG}$ $H^{cont}$ $\}_{MaP}$
he came,
son ami)$_{RG}$ d'enfance)$_{RG}$ $H^{cont}\}_{MaP}$
his old friend,
de Paris)$_{RG}$ à Marseille)$_{RG}$ en voiture)$_{RG}$ L%]$_{IntP}$
from Paris to Marseille by car

The $H^{cont}$ demarcative tone at the end of the dislocated constituent in sentence middle position is a copy of the preceding demarcative tone. This is so in cases where we traditionally speak of RD (49a), and in cases of middle dislocation (49b). Thus the realization of MD is identical

FIGURE 7 F0 curve of example (49a), *La femme qui lui a parlé, à Marie-Antoinette, m'agace.* (Speaker GLR, man)

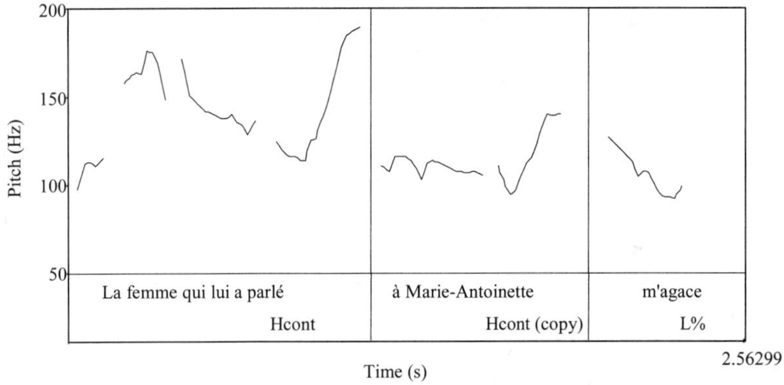


FIGURE 8 F0 curve of example (49b), *Il est venu, son ami d'enfance, de Paris à Marseille en voiture.* (Speaker GLR)

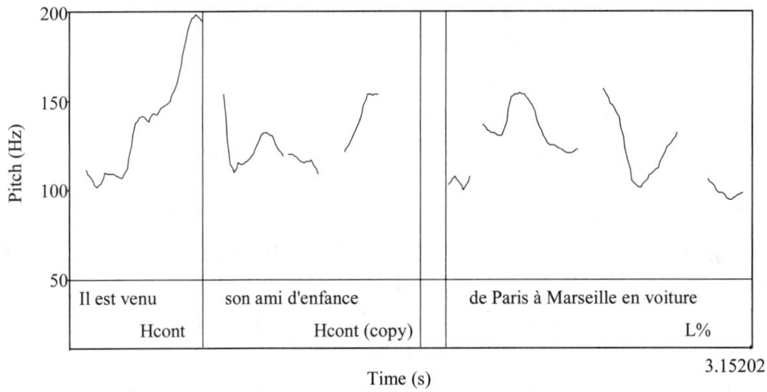


to the one found in non-sentence-final RD, which is in accordance with the idea that MD is a special case of RD.

## 4 Conclusion

The different types of dislocation studied in this chapter contrast in interesting ways. At the left periphery, HTLD, ClLD and topicalization differ from each other not only syntactically, but also from a pragmatic and prosodic point of view. All three function as topic constructions, excluding discourse new discourse referents, but unlike topicalized constituents, left dislocated constituents cannot function as thematic shifters. The prosody of the left peripheral topic constructions turns out to be both sensitive to syntax and to pragmatics.

Comparing the phenomena at the left periphery and right dislocation we found a striking asymmetry between the left and the right periphery. LD should in fact be seen as a phenomenon that plays at the left periphery of clauses. RD constituents are not necessarily located at the right periphery of a clause (*contra* Lambrecht 2001). Sentence internal cases of RD include the so-called middle dislocation and dislocation from DPs and PPs. The claim that MD should be seen as a subcase of RD is confirmed by the prosodic analysis of the two sentence types.

From a pragmatic point of view, LD and RD are similar, but since RD backgrounds the topic, it does not allow for a contrastive reading. In both cases the dislocated constituent cannot correspond to a discourse new DR. The discourse referent is strictly given, textually or situationally evoked or inferred.

From a prosodic point of view, LD and RD are very different. This observation is in accordance with the observations in chapter 2 (Prosody) and the position of the LD and the RD constituent with respect to the focus. The end of an LD constituent is marked by an $H^{cont}$ demarcative tone or an H(L)% boundary tone, depending on whether the speaker assumes that the speech participants agree on the choice of the topic. RD constituents typically have the prosodic features that characterize post-focus and incidental sequences in general.

## References


Ashby, W. 1988. The syntax, pragmatics and sociolinguistics of left and right dislocation in French. *Lingua* 75:204–226.

Ashby, W. 1994. An acoustic profile of right-dislocations in French. *Journal of French Language Studies* 4:127–145. Cambridge University Press.

Barbaud, P. 1976. Constructions superlatives et structures apparentées. *Linguistic Analysis* 2(2):125–74.

Barnes, B. 1985. *Left Dislocation in Spoken French*. Amsterdam: Benjamins.

Blasco, M. 1999. *Les dislocations en français contemporain. Etude syntaxique*. Paris: Champion.

Cecchetto, C. 1999. A comparative analysis of left and right dislocation in romance. *Studia Linguistica* 53(1):40–67.

Chafe, W. 1976. Givenness, contrastiveness, definiteness, subjects, topics and points of view. In Li (1976), pages 25–55.

Cinque, G. 1977. The movement nature of left dislocation. *Linguistic Inquiry* 8:397–411.

Cinque, G. 1983. Topic constructions in some European languages and connectedness. In Ehlich and Van Riemsdijk (1983), pages 7–41. [Reprinted in: E. Anagnostopoulou, H. van Riemsdijk and F. Zwarts (eds.) 1997. *Materials on Left Dislocation.* 93–118, Amsterdam, Netherlands: Benjamins].

De Cat, C. 2002. *French Dislocation.* Ph.D. thesis, University of York.

Delattre, P. 1966. Les dix intonations de base du français. *The French Review* 40:1–14.

Ehlich, K. and H. Van Riemsdijk, eds. 1983. *Connectedness in Sentence, Discourse and Text*, vol. 4 of *Tilburg Studies in Language and Literature.* Hogeschool Tilburg.

Fónagy, I. 1985. Jaime _ je connais _. verbes transitifs à objet latent. *Revue Romane* 20:3–35.

Fradin, B. 1988. Approche des constructions à détachement: la reprise interne. *Langue française* 88:26–56.

Fradin, B. 1990. Approches des constructions à détachement: inventaire. *Revue Romane* 25(1):3–34.

Haspelmath, M., E. König, W. Oesterreicher, and W. Raible, eds. 2001. *Language typology and language universals: an international handbook.* Berlin: Mouton de Gruyter.

Hawkins, A. 1978. *Definiteness and Indefiniteness.* London: Croorn Helm.

Hirschbühler, P. 1974. La dislocation à gauche comme construction basique en français. In Rohrer and Ruwet (1974), pages 155–165.

Kayne, R. 1984. *Connectedness and Binary Branching.* Dordrecht: Foris Publications.

Kerleroux, F. and J. Marandin. 2001. L'ordre des mots. In Marandin (2001), pages 277–302.

Kleiber, G., ed. 1987. *Rencontre(s) avec la généricité.* Metz: Klincksieck.

Lambrecht, K. 1981. *Topic, Antitopic and Verb Agreement in Non-standard French.* Amsterdam: Benjamins.

Lambrecht, K. 2001. Dislocation. In Haspelmath et al. (2001).

Larsson, E. 1978. *Effet communicatif de la dislocation dun NP en français*, vol. 16 of *Working Papers Lund University*, pages 87–104. (WPLU).

Larsson, E. 1979. *La dislocation en français. Etude de syntaxe générative.* Lund: Gleerup.

Li, C., ed. 1976. *Subject and Topic.* New York: Academic Press.

Maillard, M. 1987. Un zizi, ça sert à faire pipi debout. Les références génériques de *ça* en grammaire de phrase. In Kleiber (1987), pages 157–206.

Marandin, J.-M., ed. 2001. *Cahier Jean-Claude Milner.* Paris: Verdier.

Muller, C. 1987. A propos de l'indéfini générique. In Kleiber (1987), pages 207–233.

Prince, E. 1979. On the Given/New distinction. In *Chicago Linguistic Society Papers*, vol. 15, pages 267–278.

Rohrer, C. and N. Ruwet, eds. 1974. *Actes du Colloque Franco-Allemande de Grammaire Transformationnelle*, Tübingen. Max Niemeyer Verlag.

Ronat, M. 1979. Pronoms topiques et pronoms distinctifs. *Langue française* 44:106–128.

Rossi, M. 1981. Intonation, enonciation, syntaxe. In Rossi et al. (1981), pages 184–233.

Rossi, M. 1985. L'intonation et l'organization de l'énoncé. *Phonetica* 42(2-3):135–153.

Rossi, M. 1999. *L'Intonation, le système du français: description et modélisation*. Paris: Ophrys.

Rossi, M., A. D. Cristo, D. Hirst, P. Martin, and Y. Nishinuma, eds. 1981. *L'intonation. De l'acoustique à la sémantique*. Paris: Klincksieck.

Vallduví, E. 1994. Detachment in Catalan and information packaging. *Journal of pragmatics* 22:573–601.

Wunderli, P. 1983. L'intonation des complexes de parenthèses. *Revue Romane* 18(2):183–215.

Ziv, Y. 1994. Left and right dislocations: Discourse functions and anaphora. *Journal of pragmatics* 22:629–645.

Zribi-Hertz, A. 1996. *L'anaphore et les pronoms*. Villeneuve d'Ascq: Presses universitaires du Septentrion.

# 23

# Cleft Sentences *

JENNY DOETJES, GEORGES REBUSCHI, AND
ANNIE RIALLAND

## 1 *C'est XP que/qui...* in French: the definition of clefts

In this chapter we will discuss the distribution, the semantics and the prosody of cleft sentences in French. Cleft sentences have the form *c'est XP que/qui...* 'it/that is XP who':

(1) Moi, c'est la linguistique que je préfère.
me it/that-is the linguistics that I prefer
'It's linguistics that I prefer.'

As we will show below, cleft sentences typically allow for XPs of different categories in the *c'est XP que/qui*-frame, a property which distinguishes them from a number of related sentence types. The *que/qui...* clause, which we will call the CODA, is neither a restrictive, nor a non-restrictive, relative clause — insofar as its relation with the preceding XP (when X=N) is concerned.

In our approach and analysis, we will take Clech, Rebuschi and Rialland (1999) (henceforth CR&R) as our starting point. However, we will take into account a much wider array of data, and show that the typical clefts in which the focus corresponds to the XP and the rest of the sentence is given are but one possible type of cleft sentence. In fact, the wider array of data gives further motivation for their basic insight.

*We wish to thank the members of the PICS project group on Information and in particular Jean-Marie Marandin for comments and discussion. Jenny Doetjes gratefully acknowledges the support from NWO (grant #355-70-003).

*Handbook of French Semantics.*
Francis Corblin and Henriëtte de Swart (eds.).
Copyright © 2004, CSLI Publications.

CR&R argue in favour of a maximally simple analysis of clefts, which is not based on construction specific rules. Given the existence of relative clauses, the semantics of *ce* and basic combinatorial rules of syntax, the properties of clefts presented in this paper can be obtained: this approach is maximally consonant with the Principles and Parameters Program, according to which constructions are descriptive artefacts.

An important conclusion of this chapter, which was not reached in CR&R, is that clefts are not a focusing construction: the XP position is not a special syntactic focus position, and the coda can be included in the focus domain. However, we will show that the coda in clefts is always semantically presuppositional. As a result, what all clefts have in common is to lay emphasis on the XP to the left of the coda.

The structure of this chapter is as follows. Section 2 discusses the basic syntactic properties of clefts that allow us to distinguish them from other, related sentence types. Section 3 addresses semantic and pragmatic properties of clefts. In this section we show that there are two basic types of clefts: "focus-ground" clefts and "broad focus" clefts. We show that in both types of clefts the coda is presuppositional, which interacts with the discourse properties of clefts. Section 4 presents an analysis of clefts, which hinges on the existence of so-called "truncated clefts". Truncated clefts also play a role in our account of so-called explicative *c'est XP qui/que* sentences. Section 5 focuses on the prosodic realization of clefts: our analysis will be shown to receive strong support from prosody. In all cases, an illocutionary boundary tone is realized on the last syllable of the focused constituent. What follows has the prosodic characteristics of post-focus sequences (see chapter 21, Prosody and Information in French).

## 2 Syntactic properties of clefts

The most striking syntactic property of cleft sentences is the categorial freedom of the XP, and the variety of functions the XP can have with respect to the coda (subject in (2a), indirect object in (2b), locative in (2c) etc.).

(2) *Clefts*

a. C'est [le petit]$_{DP}$ qui est tombé dans l'escalier, pas la grand-mère.
'It's the young one that fell down the stairs, not the grand-mother.'

b. C'est [à Marie]$_{PP}$ que je dois ma réussite.
'It's to Marie that I owe my success.'

c. C'est [dans la/cette maison]$_{\text{PP}}$ que j'ai dormi.[1]
'It's in the/this house that I slept.'

d. C'est [verdâtre]$_{\text{AP}}$ qu'elle était(, l'eau,) pas limpide du tout!
'It is greenish that the water was, not transparent at all!'

e. C'est [manger des frites]$_{\text{infinitival clause}}$ qu'il préfère.
'It's eating french fries that he prefers.'

f. C'est [quand elle partira]$_{\text{finite clause}}$ que je serai content.
'It's when she leaves that I will be happy.'

This can best be illustrated by contrasting clefts with a number of related sentence types, in all of which the XP *must* be a DP. Consider first the explicative *c'est XP qui...* sentence, illustrated in (3):

(3) *Explicative* c'est ... qui...
C'est le petit qui est tombé dans l'escalier.
≈ C'est que le petit est tombé dans l'escalier
'(It's because) the little one fell down the stairs.'

Such structures, which have a distinctive intonational pattern to which we will come back below, are labeled 'explicative' because they are typically uttered as an answer to a question such as *Qu'est-ce qu'il y a?* 'What's wrong?'. Interestingly, (2b–f) do not have an explicative counterpart. The example in (2c), for instance, does not have the same meaning as *C'est que j'ai dormi dans la maison* 'It's because I slept in the house'. The XP in explicative *c'est XP que/qui* sentences must be a DP and therefore it can only correspond to the subject or the object of the relative clause. We will return to explicative *c'est ... qui...* sentences in relation to clefts in section 4.2 below.

Presentational *avoir* sentences have the form *il y a XP qui...*[2] In these constructions the XP must be a DP as well. Moreover, it must correspond to the **subject** of the relative clause.

(4) *Presentational* avoir *sentences*

a. Il y a ma voiture qui est en panne.
it there has my car that is broken
'My car broke down.'

---

[1]Cf. the relativization of PPs in restrictive and non-restrictive clauses, where the preposition always appears within the relative clause: *C'est la maison où j'ai dormi* 'That's the house where I slept'; see CR&R.

[2]Presentational *avoir* sentences are discussed at length in Lambrecht (1981), (1994). Next to the *il y a*-cases, there is a variant containing a possesive pronoun as in *J'ai ma voiture qui est en panne* 'I have my car that is broken'. It must be noted that, at least in colloquial French, *J'ai que ma voiture est en panne* is just as felicitous as a reply to *Qu'est-ce qu'il y a?* as the former sentence.

b. *Il y a dans cette voiture que je suis venu.
it there has in this car that I am come
'I came in this car.'

c. *Il y a ma bicyclette qu'on a cassée.
it there has my bike that one has broken
'Someone broke my bike.'

We can conclude that cleft sentences have the following properties that distinguish them from the other sentence types discussed here: (i) the XP can be of different categories (DP, PP, AP, IP/VP, CP) and (ii) the function corresponding to the XP in the relative clause is relatively free.

It is not the case however, that just any (sub-)constituent can be clefted. The possibility of so-called subextraction of part of a DP is severely constrained. As shown in (5a) for instance, it is not possible to cleft the adjective *grande*. In order to obtain the desired interpretation ('big' as opposed to 'small'), the whole DP has to be clefted, as in (5b):

(5) a. *C'est grande qu'elle a acheté la table, pas (la) petite.
it/that-is big that-she has bought the table not the small

b. C'est la grande table qu'elle a achetée, pas la petite.
'It's the big table that she bought, not the small one.'

Subextraction of a constituent corresponding to a quantity is not as easy as we might expect on the basis of the possibility of subextraction of *combien* in questions, as in (6a).

(6) a. Combien a-t-il lu de romans policiers?
how-many has-he read of novels detective
'How many detective novels did he read?'

b. *?C'est beaucoup qu'il a lu de romans policiers, pas un ou deux.
it/that-is a lot that-he has read of novel detective, not one or two

c. *C'est dix-sept qu'il a lu de romans policiers, pas un ou deux.
it/that-is seventeen that-he has read of novels detective, not one or two

d. C'est beaucoup/dix-sept qu'il en a lu, de romans policiers.
it/that-is a lot/seventeen that-he of-them has read of novels detective

e. C'est beaucoup de/dix-sept romans policiers qu'il
it/that-is a lot of/seventeen detective novels that he
a lus, pas deux.
has read, not two.

The impossibility of (6b,c) shows that subextraction of *beaucoup* and *dix-sept* is not possible. It is only possible to cleft *beaucoup* or *dix-sept* in contexts where their NP is cliticized as *en* as in (6d) or to cleft the whole DP as in (6e). Only part of the XP in (6e) is focalized, which becomes clear when we look at the semantics and the prosody of the sentence. The same obtains for (5b). We will return to this in the next two sections.

## 3 Semantic and pragmatic properties of clefts

### 3.1 Introduction

CR&R only consider clefts in which the XP is focused and the coda is part of the ground. It turns out that the syntactic structure that we have identified with the cleft can have different informational properties as well. The French data offer evidence for a distinction between two types of clefts: "focus-ground" clefts, in which all focused material is located in the XP position, and "broad focus" clefts, in which both the XP position and the coda are included in the focus (this second type of cleft has also been described in the literature on English, cf. a.o. Declerck 1984, 1988, Delin 1989, 1992 and Hedberg 1990, 2000). The data we will discuss provide strong evidence against an analysis of clefts in terms of movement of the clefted XP into the specifier of a focus projection, as has been recently proposed by É. Kiss (1997).

In "broad focus" clefts, even though the coda is part of the focus of the sentence, there is still some sort of a *mise en relief* of the XP, which we call an effect of "zooming". We will argue that this effect is due to the presuppositional properties of clefts.

### 3.2 "Focus-ground" clefts

The "focus-ground" cleft corresponds to the type of cleft that is most commonly considered in the literature. An example is given in (7):[3]

(7) C'est le petit qui est tombé dans l'escalier, pas ma fille.
'It's the young one who fell down the stairs, not my daughter.'

In this example, *le petit* corresponds to the focus. Given the definition of focus in chapter 20 (Introduction), focus is defined with respect to an

[3] For reasons of space we restrict ourselves to corrective contexts, which constitute one of the context types in which "focus-ground" clefts occur.

illocutionary operator. In the example in (7), the focus corresponds to the part of the clause that makes sure that the clause as a whole adds new information to the Common Ground, which is the normal case for assertive sentences (but see the discussion in chapter 20, section 2.1). The example also illustrates that a focused constituent (in this case the definite *le petit*) may have a discourse referent which is already present in the preceding discourse (see chapter 20, Introduction and Lambrecht 1994).

Sentences such as (5b) and (6e) above should be seen as a subtype of the first type of cleft. The XP contains not only the focus but also part of the ground:

(8) C'est dix-sept romans policiers qu'il a écrits, pas deux.
'It's seventeen detective novels that he has written, not two.'

In (8), the numeral *dix-sept* is the focus of the sentence, *romans policiers* and *qu'il a écrits* constitute the ground.

In this first type of cleft, the coda as a whole is simply part of the ground. As in the case of the discourse referents of dislocated constituents, the information provided by the coda does not need to be strictly given in the preceding discourse. It can also be situationally/contextually evoked (cf. Prince 1979). Consider for instance the example in (9), taken from the internet, where the coda *qu'il faut cliquer* is situationally evoked:

(9) Hé, c'est pas sur cette trace qu'il faut cliquer! C'est sur celles qui sont à côté des photos!
'Hey, it's not on this trace that you should click! It's on the ones that are next to the pictures!'

The second sentence also illustrates that a coda can be left out when it can be predicted or recovered from the context, resulting in what is usually called a 'truncated cleft' (see for instance Hedberg 2000). Truncated clefts will be discussed in section 4.3 below.

### 3.3 "Broad focus" clefts

In the second type of cleft, the information in the coda is part of the focus. An example is given in (10):[4]

[4]As pointed out to us by Jean-Marie Marandin, the difference between the two types of clefts correlates with the (im)possibility of inversion in the coda. Inversion is possible only in "focus-ground" clefts (cf. Chapter 24, Subject NP inversion):

| (i) | Où | déjeune | Paul? | C'est | dans | la | cafétéria | que | déjeune | Paul. |
|---|---|---|---|---|---|---|---|---|---|---|
| | where | has-lunch | Paul | it's | in | the | cafeteria | that | has-lunch | Paul |

| (ii) | #C'est | avec | plaisir | que | vous | accueillera | mon | fils |
|---|---|---|---|---|---|---|---|---|
| | it's | with | pleasure | that | you | will-receive | my | son |

(10) C'est avec plaisir que je vous invite à participer à ce séminaire.
'It is with pleasure that I invite you to this seminar'

In addition to the fact that cleft sentences can be "broad focus" sentences, this example clearly shows that a clefted XP is not necessarily exhaustive. According to É. Kiss (1997), English clefts always have an exhaustive interpretation. This is, according to her, related to their syntax, in which the clefted constituent occupies a derived position, which she identifies as the specifier position of a focus projection. She claims that this position triggers the exhaustive reading of the focused XP. Her claim is not in accordance with the possibility of (10). The XP in (10) is not exhaustive, as can be illustrated by the fact that we can add *et par ailleurs aussi avec fierté* 'and besides with pride too' as a parenthesis between the XP and the coda. In section 4.1, where we develop our analysis of clefts, the necessity of an exhaustive interpretation in cases such as (7) as opposed to the absence of such an interpretation in (10) will be accounted for.

Some more examples of "broad focus" clefts are given in (11):[5]

(11) a. Le Cécom est le distributeur de cette vidéo. C'est à lui qu'il faut s'adresser pour se la procurer.
'Cécom is the distributor of this video. It's to them that one has to go to get it.'

b. C'est pour cette raison que Marie n'y est plus jamais revenue.
'It's for that reason that Marie never went back there.'

Both sentences are felicitous in contexts where the contents of the coda provide new information.

The distinction between "focus-ground" clefts and "broad focus" clefts is confirmed by clear prosodic differences between the two: in the latter case, the illocutionary boundary tone that signals the end of the focus is located inside the coda, whereas in a "focus-ground" cleft the illocutionary boundary tone associated with the focused XP (or part of the XP) is located on that (part of the) XP: see section 5 below.

### 3.4 The presuppositional nature of clefts

Even though there is no difference in terms of focus and ground between the XP and the coda in "broad focus" clefts, the sentences still emphasize in some sense the contents of the XP rather than the contents of the coda. Consider the example in (12):

[5] According to Katz (2000), sentences such as (11b) form a separate type which she calls the causal *c'est* cleft. We do not think there are adequate grounds for setting this type of sentences apart from the other "broad focus" clefts.

(12) C'est à Nicolas Ruwet et à Maurice Gross que je dois l'essentiel de ma formation dans cette discipline.
'It's to Nicolas Ruwet and to Maurice Gross that I owe the essential part of my training in this discipline.'

This sentence comes from the introduction of a dissertation. In the preceding context, the author discusses her theoretical framework. The fact that she owes the essential part of her linguistic training to one person or another has not been mentioned in the preceding discourse. However, it is clear that this information is more predictable than the information provided by the rest of the sentence.

It turns out that it is not by accident that the more easily predictable information is located inside the coda. Quite generally, the information provided by the XP — whether we are dealing with a "focus-ground" cleft or with a "broad focus" cleft — is foregrounded with respect to the information in the coda. In what follows we will try to make specific where this effect of "zooming" comes from. An important question that we have not addressed so far is what makes clefts different from non-cleft sentences. The answer is that despite not being a specific focusing construction, the cleft is a presuppositional construction. This is not only true for clefts of the "focus-ground" type, but also for the other type of clefts (cf. Prince 1978 and Delin 1989, 1992 for English). The material in the coda is always (semantically) presupposed, as we can show on the basis of the interpretation of negation.[6] A property of presuppositions is that they are not affected by a negation that has scope over the whole sentence. In the following examples, the negation test is applied to two clefts (13a,b) and to their non-cleft counterparts (13a',b') ((13a) is (11b)):

(13) a. #On dit que c'est pour cette raison qu'elle n'y est plus jamais revenue, mais ce n'est pas vrai: elle y est revenue plusieurs fois.
'They say that it's for that reason that she never went back, but that's not true: she went back several times.'

a'. On dit que pour cette raison elle n'y est plus jamais revenue, mais ce n'est pas vrai: elle y est revenue plusieurs fois.
'They say that for that reason she never went back etc.'

b. #Pierre dit que c'est en pratiquant tous les jours qu'on peut s'améliorer. Ce n'est pas vrai: on ne peut pas s'améliorer.

[6]In "broad focus" clefts the coda is typically not "pragmatically presupposed", see Introduction, note 5. We assume that "pragmatic" presuppositions are always presupposed in the more general sense, but not vice versa (cf. Jackendoff 1972; Geurts & Van der Sandt 1992 on the relation between presuppositions and ground).

'Pierre says that it's by training every day that one can get better. That's not true: one cannot get better.'

b'. Pierre dit qu'en pratiquant tous les jours, on peut s'améliorer. Ce n'est pas vrai: on ne peut pas s'améliorer.
'Pierre says that by training every day, one can get better etc.'

The contrast between (13a,b) and (13a',b') shows that clefts introduce a presupposition, while their non-clefted counterparts do not. The example in (13a) is preferably pronounced with a "broad focus" intonation ($H^{cont}$ demarcative tone on the right boundary of the XP and L% illocutionary tone at the end of the utterance, see section 5.2 below). This intonation is also possible in the case of (13b). This shows that presuppositional properties do not depend on whether the coda is included in the focus or not.

We can conclude that even though the coda can contain focused material, it is always given as presuppositional. In (11b) the speaker gives information about the existence of a causal relation between the antecedent of *cette raison* and the event described by the coda in the first place. This event itself is presupposed, even though it can be part of the new information provided by the utterance in those cases where the coda is included in the focus of the sentence (see also Prince 1978 and Delin 1992 for discussion).

This property of clefts should be related to their embedded syntax; embedded clauses or CPs are often presupposition triggers. According to Rooryck (1992), only a specific class of predicates (*believe* type verbs) selects a CP which is transparent for negation. In all other contexts, C blocks negation: a negation outside of the CP cannot be interpreted inside of the CP. The non-transparency of the CP can be seen as the source of the presuppositional nature of the coda in clefts.

The presuppositional nature of the coda can explain the effect discussed in relation to (12) above: superficially, the effect of clefting is to foreground the material in the XP as opposed to the presupposed information contained in the coda, whether it is part of the focus of the sentence or not. The opposition between presupposed and non-presupposed material introduces an additional means of organizing information, next to the focus-ground articulation. "Broad focus" clefts make use of this possibility and foreground part of the focus.

A further consequence of the presuppositional nature of the coda is that we do not expect there to be a third type of cleft, in which all focused material would be located inside the coda. As the information in the coda is presuppositional, the cleft sentence will not be used to provide the information in the coda exclusively, as this would result in a fully presupposed sentence (see also note 6 above).

# 4 The role of *ce* and truncated clefts

## 4.1 The semantics of *ce* and the analysis of clefts

We will mainly follow CR&R, who propose that clefts result from the semantics of the *ce*. *Ce* relates two predicates, one of which corresponds to the XP (Q) and the other is (provided by) the coda (P) (see Kroch & Heycock (1999) for a similar approach to pseudo-clefts).[7]

(14) $[_{\text{D}}\ \text{ce}] \Rightarrow \lambda \text{Q}[\text{Q}(\ \iota x(\text{P}(x)))]$

From a syntactic point of view, the coda is base-generated in a position right-adjoined to the Tense Phrase (TP):[8]

(15) $[_{\text{TP}}\ [_{\text{TP}}\ \text{C'est XP}]\ [_{\text{CP}}\ \text{OP}_i\ [_{\text{C'}}\ \textit{que}\ [_{\text{TP}}\ \ldots t_i \ldots]]]]$

A strong argument for this type of approach is that it allows us to generalize over so-called "truncated clefts", in which the coda has been left out (see example (9)). Truncation is usually possible in contexts where "focus-ground" clefts can be used; in contexts where a "broad focus" cleft is used, truncation is always excluded (cf. also Hedberg 2000 on truncated clefts in English). The semantics and syntax of clefts proposed in (14) and (15) predict that the coda can be left out, as long as its contents are recoverable from the context, which is typically the case in contexts where "focus-ground" clefts are used. From a syntactic point of view, the adjoined relative clause can be left out, leaving a syntactically complete TP. From a semantic point of view, *ce* introduces a definite description $\iota x(\text{P}(x))$, which contains a predicate P that has to be identified by the context. This can be done in one of three ways: (i) in a (non-truncated) cleft sentence, the coda identifies the predicate: owing to the ordinary semantics of relative pronouns and (abstract) relative operators, the compositional interpretation of the coda yields a property. This possibility allows for two types of codas: codas that are already given or evoked by the context and codas that contain part of the focus of the sentence; (ii) in truncated clefts, the predicate P is identified by the preceding context;[9] (iii) in deictic *c'est* XP sentences,

[7] For reasons of space, details of their analysis are not repeated here. Note that we slightly diverge from their analysis in order to include clefts that are not of the "focus-ground" type.

[8] For an extensive overview of different syntactic approaches to clefts, see CR&R and Hedberg (2000).

[9] One could assume that this is a purely pragmatic process, or, alternatively, that the truncated cleft contains a silent relative clause. We will not address this issue here.

P is directly identified by deixis. The three possibilities are illustrated in (16):

(16) a. (Qui va se marier?) C'est Jean qui va se marier.
'(Who will get married?) It's Jean who will get married.'

b. (idem) C'est Jean.

c. (pointing) Ça, c'est Jean.
that, that's Jean

This approach predicts that it is not possible to have a combination of a deictic *ce* and a coda. The predicate P is already deictically identified in (16c), $\iota x(\mathrm{P}(x))$ corresponding to 'the individual x over there'. As a result the coda cannot be interpreted (or, alternatively, *ça* could not be). This turns out to be right: clefts are not appropriate when *ce* is doubled by a dislocated deictic pronoun, as illustrated by the fact that (16a), which has an intonation that is typical of cleft sentences with an L% boundary tone on the XP and a copy of this boundary tone on the coda, cannot be preceded in any context by a dislocated *ça*.

## 4.2 Exhaustive listing

The analysis allows us to account for the contrast between cases which have an exhaustive reading and the ones that do not (see also Declerck 1984). The "focus-ground" cleft in (16a) above has an exhaustive reading. This is expected on the basis of the semantics of *ce*. P is identified by the relative clause, so that $\iota x(\mathrm{P}(x))$ corresponds to 'the x who will get married'. This definite description is identified by *est Jean*, containing equational *be* and the referential expression *Jean*. This yields an exhaustive reading: if *the x who will get married* is Jean, it cannot be someone else at the same time. Let us now return to the example in (10), repeated in (17) below, which presents a non-exhaustive reading:

(17) C'est avec plaisir que je vous invite à participer à ce séminaire.

$\iota x(\mathrm{P}(x))$ corresponds in this case to the event that consists in my inviting my guest to this seminar. This event is predicated over by *avec plaisir*. As *avec plaisir* is not a referential expression (unlike *Jean*), the verb *est* is not equational and the predicate does not uniquely identify the subject. As a result the sentence can be completed by a sequence such as *et par ailleurs aussi avec fierté* 'and besides with pride too'. We predict that exhaustive readings are found in those cases where *ce* is uniquely identified by a predicate containing equational *be* and a referential expression. This is the case in (16a), but not in (17).

We can conclude that, given that *ce* introduces a definite description, we can assign different properties to this definite description, but we can identify it only once.[10]

### 4.3 Explicative *c'est XP que/qui* sentences as truncated clefts

As we said in section 2, explicative *c'est XP qui...* sentences differ syntactically from clefts by the fact that they are restricted to DPs. This DP usually corresponds to the subject of the relative clause, but it can also be related to the object position. PPs can never be in the XP position. Moreover, these sentences are all-focus sentences and have an explicative interpretation.

(18) (Why are you so worried?)
C'est le petit qui est tombé dans l'escalier.
'It's because the little one fell down the stairs.'

Given the possibility of truncated clefts, it is possible to assume that (18) is an example of a cleft sentence in which the visible *qui*-clause does *not* constitute the coda of the cleft. In our view, the sentence in (18) should be considered the truncated variant of (19):

(19) C'est le petit qui est tombé dans l'escalier qui me tracasse.
'It's the little one who fell down the stairs that bothers me.'

The explicative nature of the sentence can be traced back to the predicate identifying the reference of *ce*. The sentence is typically uttered as an answer to 'Why are you so worried?'. As an answer to this question we can also use a "focus-ground" cleft with the coda *qui me tracasse* 'that worries me'. (18) can be seen as the truncated variant of this cleft. As a result of this analysis, the first *qui*-phrase in this example is not a coda, but should be viewed as a non-restrictive or pseudo-relative clause (Guasti 1988, Rafel 2000) as in *J'ai rencontré le petit/Jean qui est tombé dans l'escalier* 'I met the little one/Jean who fell down the stairs'.[11]

Our analysis is corroborated by the following observation about the exhaustivity property of these clefts: the sentence in (19) is, given the semantics we assign to it, an identificational sentence. Therefore we expect that both (18) and (19) have an exhaustive reading, and this turns out to be correct, as is illustrated by opposing (18) to the corresponding presentational *avoir*-sentence, which is *not* exhaustive. Continuing after (18) by saying: *et puis, papa est en retard* 'and besides, father

[10] Cf. Declerck (1984), who argues cleft sentences are exhaustive iff they are instances of identificational sentences.

[11] The analysis could be extended to cases such as *C'est que le petit est tombé dans l'escalier* 'It's because the little one fell down the stairs' — see Delahunty (1984). CR&R suggest relating this sentence and the one in (19) transformationally.

is late' is not felicitous. However, such a continuation is possible in a presentational *avoir* sentence:

(20) Il y a le petit qui est tombé dans l'escalier et puis, (il y a) papa (qui) est en retard.
'The little one fell down the stairs, and besides, Father is late.'

The exhaustive reading of sentences such as (18) provides evidence both for our approach to exhaustivity and for a parallel semantics for clefts and truncated clefts.

## 5 The prosody of cleft sentences

In the preceding sections we have discussed three types of *c'est XP que/qui* sentences: "focus-ground" clefts, "broad focus" clefts and presentational or explicative *c'est XP que/qui* sentences, which we have analysed as truncated clefts.

In what follows we will study their prosody within a framework of informational organization involving two axes or dimensions: the ground/focus dimension (topic, focus, post-focus), and the DT (Discourse Topic) dimension in Büring's (1997) terminology (see also chapter 20, Introduction).

### 5.1 Focus-ground cleft sentences

The prosody of "focus-ground" clefts has been studied in various publications. Based on this literature and on our own recordings[12], we will present their main characteristics, introducing new proposals (in the analysis of the post-focus sequence, for example) at certain points.

Let us begin with the ground/focus axis, involving the focus/post-focus structure in which the focus corresponds to all or part of the XP and the post-focus to the relative clause. The prosody of "focus-ground" clefts can be characterized as follows. At the end of the focus, we find an illocutionary boundary tone selected according to the illocutionary force of the utterance (assertion, question...); see also chapter 12, Prosody and Information in French, CR&R, Rossi (1999), Di Cristo (1998), Le Gac (2001). The coda is realized as a post-focus sequence. There is intonational agreement involving a copy of the "illocutionary tone" and we find a reduced register (same references as above). Finally, the end of the XP has to coincide with a Major Phrase boundary. In case the end of the XP coincides with the end of the focus, this boundary is

[12]Two types of recordings were made : 1) 15 cleft sentences in Question/answer contexts by two male speakers (MR, AV) and two female speakers (EF,RV), 2) one cleft sentence recorded with various attitudes and emotions by five speakers. The acoustic analysis was performed with PRAAT.

also an Intonational Phrase boundary. In case the end of the XP does not coincide with the end of the focus, an additional Major Phrase boundary is inserted, which is realized as a copy of the illocutionary boundary tone which marks the focus.

The illocutionary tone, expressing the illocutionary force (assertion, interrogation, etc., see CR&R and chapter 21, Prosody and Information in French), is the same as the one which occurs at the end of an utterance, that is, at the end of a "broad focus": it also marks the end of the narrow focus part of sentences without clefting, for example the end of *Brutus* in *Qui a tué César?* 'Who killed Ceasar?' *Brutus a tué César* 'Brutus killed Ceasar' (Rossi 1999). Thus, it signals the end of any focus domain, whether "narrow" or "broad", and it marks focus along the ground/focus dimension. This analysis is basically the same as that of Rossi (1999), despite the difference in terminology ("focus" instead of Rossi's "rheme").

FIGURE 1 F0 curve of example (21), *C'est pour Jospin que Mathilde a voté?* (Speaker MR, man)

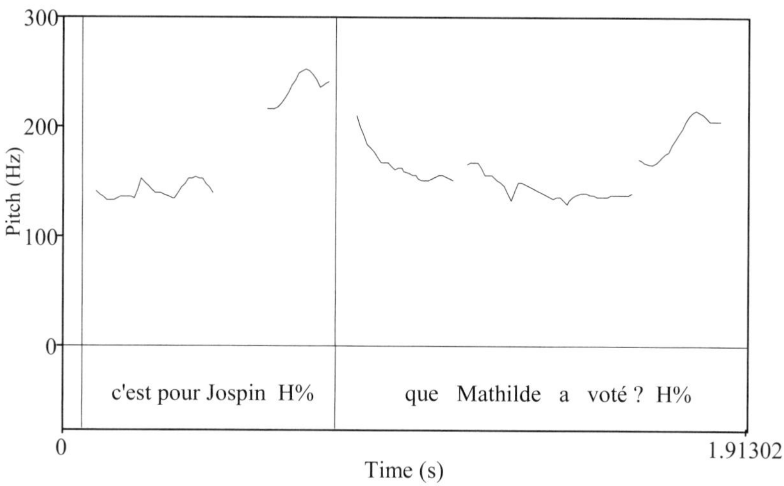


Intonational agreement only concerns the post-focus part. It consists in the repetition of the illocutionary tone occurring at the end of the focus. Intonational agreement is particularly obvious in questions as illustrated by the sentence in (21) and Figure 1 (F0 curve of (21)), which has an interrogative H% boundary tone at the end of the focused

XP (*Jospin*) and another at the end of the utterance (*voté*).[13]

(21) c'est pour Jospin)$_{RG}$H% ] $_{IntP}$ que Mathilde a voté)$_{RG}$ H%]$_{IntP}$?
'Is it for Jospin that Mathilde voted?'

Though less obvious, the repetition of the assertive boundary tone L% is also present in statements, as in example (22) and Figure 2 (F0 curve of (22)):

(22) c'est pour Tournier)$_{RG}$ L%]$_{IntP}$ qu'elle va voter)$_{RG}$ L%]$_{IntP}$
'It's for Tournier that she is going to vote.'
(as an answer to: Pour qui Mathilde va-t-elle voter?
'For whom is Mathilde going to vote ?')

FIGURE 2 F0 curve of example (22). *C'est pour Tournier qu'elle va voter.* (Speaker AV, man)

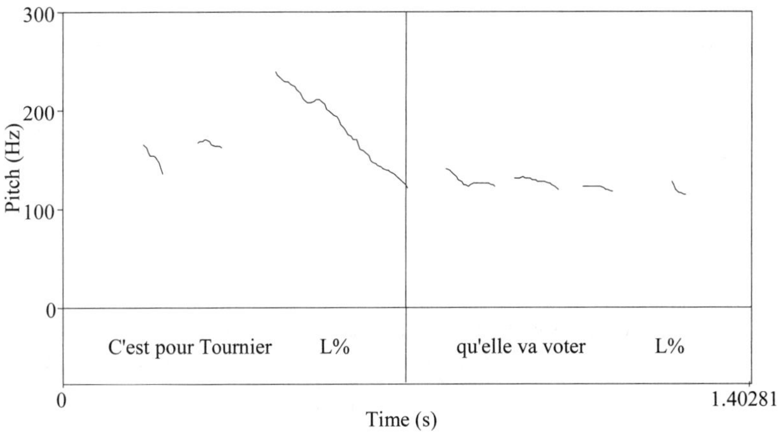


The first L% is responsible for the falling contour of the focus part and can also be posited at the end of the post-focus, as there is a low plateau going from the first L% to the end of the utterance. The presence of the low boundary tone has been shown to be the main perceptual cue to the division between the focused and post-focus parts of clefts (Rossi 1999, 1974).

Turning to the post-focus coda, we note that it may consist of several Major Phrases, each of which ends with a terminal boundary tone. Statements of this type are realized with a sequence of downstepping L

[13]For the notational conventions, see chapters 20 and 21 (Introduction and Prosody and Information in French).

tones as in example (23) and Figure 3 (F0 curve of (23)) (see chapter 21, Prosody and Information in French, section 3.2, for a similar realization of a non-clefted sentence):

(23) c'est dix-sept)$_{RG}$ L%]$_{IntP}$ romans policiers)$_{RG}$ L}$_{MaP}$ qu'il a écrits)$_{RG}$ L%]$_{IntP}$
'It's seventeen detective novels that he wrote.'
(as an answer to: *C'est combien de romans policiers qu'il a écrits?*
'It's how many detective novels that he wrote?')

FIGURE 3 F0 curve of example (23). *C'est dix-sept romans policiers qu'il a écrits.* (Speaker MR, man)

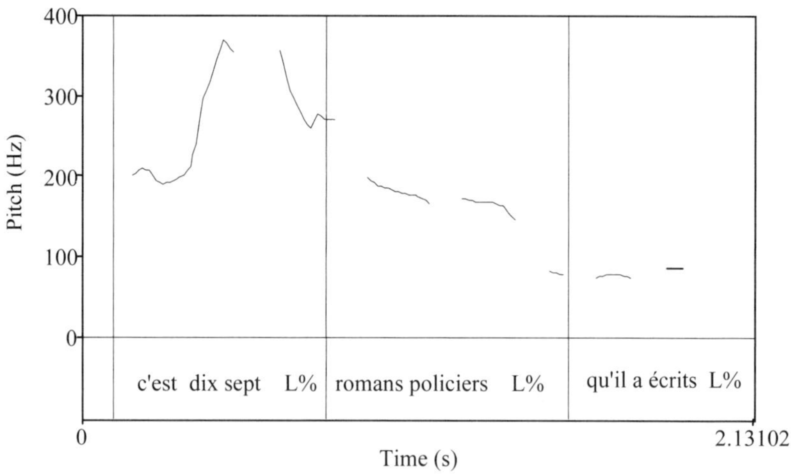


The focus is on *dix-sept*, that is, on the first part of the XP, which ends with a L%. The post-focus part is divided into two intonational phrases, [*romans policiers*] and [*qu'il a écrits*], each of which ends with a L%. Each L% triggers downstep on a following one, creating a lowering of the pitch range associated with a reduction in intensity. This type of downstepping realization has been studied previously by a few scholars (Di Cristo and Jankowski, 1999) but without being related to the presence of the L% and to the copy mechanism occurring in the post-focus sequence. The obligatory presence of a boundary at the end of the XP can be linked to the syntax of clefts. The end of the XP coincides with a TP boundary, which always coincides with either a Major Phrase or an Intonational Phrase boundary.

Intonational agreement can be regarded as the main prosodic feature of the post-focus sequence, showing its dependence on the focus part, the other important and well-known characteristic of the post-focus sequence being the reduction of the overall register (compression of the pitch range), of varying magnitude.

Let us now consider a second axis of informational organization which we tentatively call 'discourse articulation' (which corresponds partly to DT in Buring's terminology), and analyze the role of C accents in clefts.

First consider a so-called "prosodic arch" (*arc prosodique*), which is a variant of the C accent (see chapter 20, Introduction and chapter 21, Prosody and Information in French). Its realization involves (at least) two prominences (H*) occurring on stressed syllables, located at the end or the beginning of rhythmic groups. They are stronger than weak prominences which may occur on the same points in sentences without prosodic arch. This can be illustrated by example (24) and Figure 4 (F0 curve of (24)).

FIGURE 4 F0 curve of example (24), *C'est celui de vingt et heures que j'ai pris.* (Speaker AV, man)

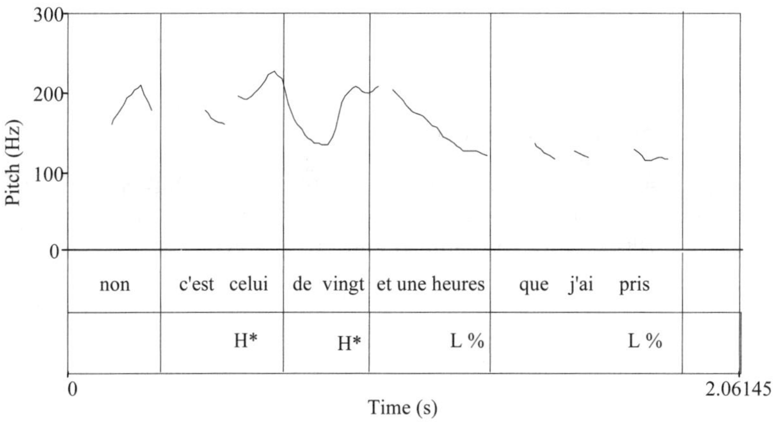


(24) ...c'est celui)$_{\mathrm{RG}}$ de vingt)$_{\mathrm{RG}}$ et une heures)$_{\mathrm{RG}}$ L%]$_{\mathrm{IntP}}$ que
H* H*
j'ai pris)$_{\mathrm{RG}}$ L%]$_{\mathrm{IntP}}$
'It's the 9 PM train that I took.'
(as an answer to the question: *Tu as pris le train de dix-neuf heures?* 'Did you take the 7 PM train?')

This contour signals reference to a context set (in (24) this set contains *le train de dix-neuf heures* and its contextual alternates) and forces a partition of the Discourse Topic (in Büring's terms). However, this type of intonation does not characterize cleft sentences or even the focus parts of the utterance. The prosodic arch may occur in any part of the ground/focus line (topic, focus or post-focus in which it will appear with a reduced pitch register). This dimension is orthogonal to focus/post-focus organization, in its realization and its informational role, and it is not related to the clefting.

### 5.2 "Broad focus" clefts

The second type of cleft sentences is not used to answer questions: see the examples (12) and (17) above. In order to study this type we recorded short dialogs, the reading aloud of an article published in *Le Monde*[14], and we extracted "broad focus" clefts from a conversation between two students recorded in a phonetics laboratory (the 'Basset corpus').

They have two main intonational characteristics. In the first place, the XP ends with an $H^{cont}$ demarcative tone, and not with an illocutionary tone. In the second place, the coda is not realized as a post-focus sequence: there is no intonational agreement or register compression. Again, the obligatory presence of a Major Phrase boundary, at the end of the XP, can be seen as a reflexion of the TP boundary in the syntactic structure.

An example of the intonational characteristics of "broad focus" clefts is given in (25) and Figure 5 (F0 curve of (25)).

(25) ce sont les visiteurs$)_{RG}$ $H^{cont}\}_{MaP}$ qui les déposent$)_{RG}$ $H^{cont}\}_{MaP}$ le plus simplement du monde$)_{RG}$ $H^{cont}\}_{MaP}$ ...
'It's the visitors that simply put them down.'

[14]"Un détenu témoigne du prosélytisme islamiste dans les prisons françaises", *Le Monde*, 31/10/2001

FIGURE 5 F0 curve of example (25). *Ce sont les visiteurs qui les déposent le plus simplement du monde.* (Speaker AV, man)

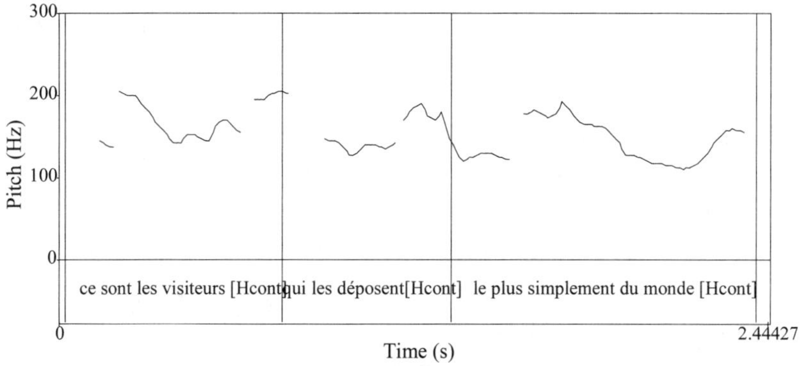


This utterance, which is included in a longer text (and, thus, ends with a continuation rise), is divided into Major Phrases (MaP), each of which ends with a $H^{cont}$ demarcative tone or continuation rise. The XP *les visiteurs* ends a MaP, which can be analyzed as part of a broad focus. The following relative does not correspond to any given information and is not realized as part of the ground. Examples (26) [= (17) of 4.2], with Figure 6 (F0 curve of (26)) and (27) below have exactly the same properties:

(26) c'est avec plaisir$)_{RG}$ $H^{cont}$}MaP que je vous reçois$)_{RG}$ L%$]^{IntP}$
'It's with pleasure that I receive you.'

(27) c'est il y a quelques mois$)_{RG}$ seulement$)_{RG}$ $H^{cont}\}_{MaP}$ que les galibis$)_{RG}$ ont adopté un alphabet...
'It's only some months ago that the Galibis adopted an alphabet.'

FIGURE 6 F0 curve of example (25), *C'est avec plaisir que je vous reçois.* (Speaker AV, man)

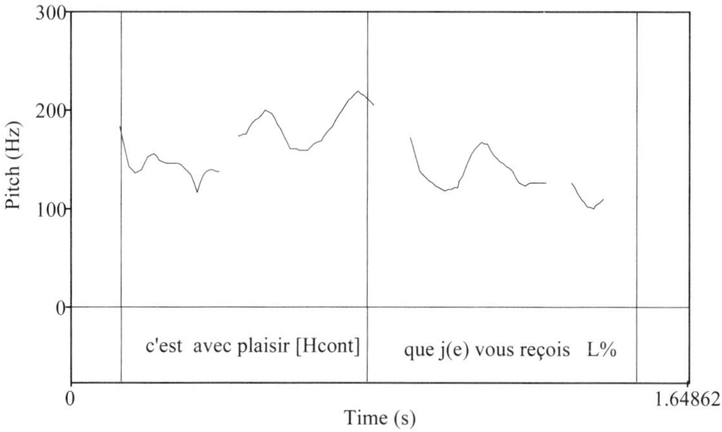


This utterance has been extracted from a recorded conversation between two students (cf. Basset corpus).

## 5.3 Explicative *c'est XP que/qui* sentences

The prosody of explicative *c'est XP que/qui* sentences has been studied by Boulakia (1978). They have two main intonational characteristics. In the first place, there is only one illocutionary tone, located at the end of the utterance: this terminal intoneme may be of any nature, marking statements, questions or requests for confirmation. In the second place, the end of the XP is not characterized by either an illocutionary boundary tone or an $\mathrm{H}^{\mathrm{cont}}$ demarcative tone. We find a small lengthening and a minor rise (h) at the end of the XP, which signals the end of a rhythmic group, but not the end of a Major Phrase: the utterance corresponds to one unique Major Phrase and is not obligatorily divided into two Major Phrases.

This type of intonation can be illustrated by example (28) and Figure 7 (F0 curve of (28)):

(28) c'est le petit (h))$_{\mathrm{RG}}$ qu' est tombé dans l'escalier)$_{\mathrm{RG}}$ L%]$_{\mathrm{IntP}}$
'It's because the young one fell down the stairs.'

FIGURE 7 F0 curve of example (28), *C'est l(e) petit qu'est tombé dans l'escalier.* (Speaker RV)

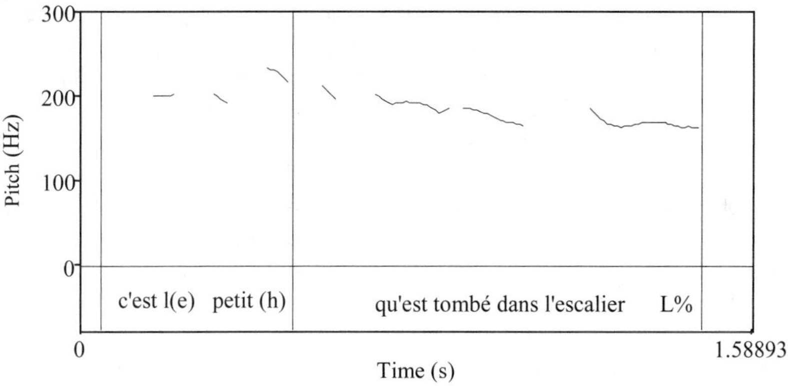


As was argued above (section 4.3), we consider such sentences as truncated clefts: the clause *qui est tombé dans l'escalier* is not the coda which has been left out.

## 6 Conclusions

Cleft sentences are not instances of a special, focus-related construction type. There are no construction specific rules needed in order to account for the properties of these sentences. Following CR&R, we assign clefts a maximally simple syntax, in which the relative clause is adjoined to a TP, and identifies a predicative gap in the semantics of ce, the subject of this TP. As we have shown, the basic approach in CR&R can be extended to account for a much wider array of data. We have distinguished two basic types of clefts: "focus-ground" clefts and "broad focus" clefts. In addition, we have shown that the coda is always presuppositional, independently of whether it contains focalized material or not. As we argued, this can be directly derived from the embedded status of the coda, whose presuppositional nature accounts for the effect of "zooming".

The intonational properties of the two types of clefts can be predicted on the basis of the pragmatic properties of the clefts and their syntactic structure. At the end of the focus we find the illocutionary boundary tone.

In "focus-ground" clefts, this tone is located within the XP or at the end of the XP. The rest of the sentence is a post-focus sequence, which is marked by a copy of the boundary tone. In case the end of the focus is not the end of the XP, we need an additional major phonological boundary at the end of the XP, which is marked by a copy of the illocutionary boundary tone as well. The presence of this MaP boundary can be related to the presence of a TP boundary in the syntactic structure.

In "broad focus" clefts, the end of the TP must be marked by a continuative rise ($H^{cont}$), as the end of the interpretative unit containing focus has not been reached. This is in accordance with the observation that in a sequence of assertive utterances that constitute an interpretive unit, all utterances are marked by $H^{cont}$ demarcative tones, except for the last one, which bears an illocutionary boundary tone (assertive L% or interrogative H% ...). Because the coda of the "broad focus" cleft contains part of the focus, the first occurrence of the illocutionary tone, which marks the end of the focus, cannot precede the coda. Unless the utterance is part of a larger interpretive unit, the illocutionary boundary tone is located within the coda, where it is possibly followed by a post-focus sequence.

We have argued that explicative *c'est XP que/qui* sentences are instances of truncated clefts. This is in accordance with the observation that these sentences do not contain an $H^{cont}$ boundary at the end of the XP. Unlike the clefted *que/qui* clause, the *que/qui* clause in explicative *c'est XP que/qui* sentences acts as a relative clause, and forms a constituent with the XP, which has to be a DP. This approach directly accounts for the presence versus absence of a major phonological boundary at the end of the XP: the boundary is present at the end of a clefted XP, as the end of the XP coincides with a TP boundary, but it is absent in the explicative sentences, because they do not contain a TP boundary between the XP and the *que/qui* clause.

## References


Boulakia, G. 1978. *Phonosyntaxe: Etudes psycho-acoustiques et linguistiques sur l'intonation et ses rapports avec la syntaxe, notamment l'ordre des mots, en français*. Ph.D. thesis, Univ. Paris VII.

Büring, D. 1997. *The Meaning of Topic and Focus: The 59th Street Bridge Accent*. London: Routledge.

Clech-Darbon, A., G. Rebuschi, and A. Rialland. 1999. Are there cleft sentences in French? In Rebuschi and Tuller (1999), pages 83–118.

Decker, P. and M. Stokhof, eds. 1992. *Proceedings of the Eleventh Amsterdam Colloquium*.

Declerck, R. 1984. The pragmatics of *it*-cleft and *wh*-clefts. *Lingua 64* pages 251–289.

Declerck, R. 1988. *Studies on copular sentences, clefts and pseudo-clefts*. Dordrecht: Foris.

Delahunty, G. 1984. The analysis of English cleft sentences. *Linguistic Analysis* 13:63–113.

Delin, J. 1989. *Cleft constructions in discourse*. Ph.D. thesis, University of Edinburgh.

Delin, J. 1992. Properties of it-cleft presuppositions. *Journal of Semantics* 9:289–306.

Di Cristo, A. 1998. Intonation in French. In Hirst and Cristo (1998), pages 195–218.

Di Cristo, A. and L. Jankowski. 1999. Prosodic organisation and phrasing after focus in French. In ICPS-14 (1999), pages 1565–1568.

É. Kiss, K. 1997. Identificational focus versus information focus. *Language* 74:245–273.

Geurts, B. and R. van der Sandt. 1992. Presuppositions and backgrounds. In Decker and Stokhof (1992), pages 37–42.

Guasti, M. 1988. La pseudo-relative et les phénomènes d'accord. *Rivista di Grammatica Generativa* 13:35–58.

Hedberg, N. 1990. *The Discourse Function of Cleft Sentences in English*. Ph.D. thesis, Universitiy of Minnesota.

Hedberg, N. 2000. The referential status of clefts. *Language 76:4* pages 891–920.

Heycock, C. and A. Kroch. 1999. Pseudocleft connectedness: Implications for the lf interface level. *LI* 30(3):365–397.

Hirst, D. and A. D. Cristo, eds. 1998. *Intonation Systems. A Survey of Twenty Languages*. Cambridge University Press.

ICPS-14. 1999. *Proceedings of the XIVth International Congress of Phonetic Sciences*, San Francisco CA. University of California.

Jackendoff, R. 1972. *Semantic interpretation in Generative Grammar*. Cambridge (Ma.): MIT Press.

Katz, S. 2000. Categories of *c'est*-cleft constructions. *Revue Canadienne de Linguistique* 45(3/4):1001–1021.

Lambrecht, K. 1981. *Topic, Antitopic and Verb Agreement in Non-standard French*. Amsterdam: Benjamins.

Lambrecht, K. 1994. *Information structure and sentence form: Topic, focus and the mental representations of discourse referents*. Cambridge: Cambridge University Press.

Le Gac, D. 2001. *Structure prosodique de la focalisation: le cas du somali et du français*. Ph.D. thesis, Univ. Paris VII.

Prince, E. 1978. A comparison of Wh-clefts and It-clefts in discourse. *Language* 54:883–906.

Rafel, J. 2000. From C to P: Evidence from Romance. *Probus* 12:139–163.

Rebuschi, G. and L. Tuller, eds. 1999. *The Grammar of Focus*. Amsterdam: Benjamins.

Rooryck, J. 1992. Negative and factive islands revisited. *Journal of Linguistics* 28(2):343–373.

Rossi, M. 1974. L'intonation prédicative dans les phrases transformées par permutation. *Linguistics* 103:64–84.

Rossi, M. 1999. *L'Intonation, le système du français: description et modélisation*. Paris: Ophrys.

24

# Subject NP Inversion*

Brigitte Kampers-Manhe, Jean-Marie Marandin, Frank Drijkoningen, Jenny Doetjes, and Aafke Hulk

## 1 Introduction

It is commonly assumed that word order variations result from the interplay of structural and informational constraints. As for informational constraints, the most common hypothesis is that word order variations reflect or mark the partition of the content of utterances into Focus and Ground. French is reputed to be a fixed order language. Nevertheless, French does have word order variation and in particular, it has subject inversion: subjects may be postverbal. Moreover, even the most naïve survey of French texts should acknowledge the fact that subject inversion is far from being a rare phenomenon in French discourses. We will not study the syntactic licensing of inversion in any detail here, but will attempt to sort out which dimension is involved in inversion appropriateness among those we have posited in the introduction to this part: Ground/Focus articulation, Discourse Topic or the activation state of the Discourse Referents. We briefly introduce the main types of inversion in French in section 2. Then, in sections 3 and 4, we discuss recent analyses of a few contrasts that have resorted to some informational constraint to explain inversion appropriateness. Due to space limitation, we mainly restrict our study to Stylistic inversion in questions

*We wish to thank the members of the PICS project group on Information and in particular Jean-Marie Marandin for comments and discussion. Jenny Doetjes gratefully acknowledges the support from NWO (grant #355-70-003).

*Handbook of French Semantics.*
Francis Corblin and Henriëtte de Swart (eds.).
Copyright © 2004, CSLI Publications.

and relative clauses and to Unaccusative inversion in subjunctive and root narrative clauses.

## 2 Types of inversion

The descriptive category 'Subject inversion', borrowed from the grammatical tradition, is misleading. Since Kayne's seminal study (1972, 1983), it has been generally acknowledged that two types should be distinguished: subject clitic inversion and subject NP inversion.

Both types have different licensing conditions. Subject clitic inversion is licensed in root sentences only and can be found in three types of sentence: questions (non *wh*- and *wh*-questions) (1),[1] declaratives with fronted adverbials of a certain class (2)[2] and asymmetric coordination of root clauses (3):

(1) a. Où sont-ils allés?
'Where have they gone?'

a'. Est-il parti?
'Has he left?'

b. *Je me demande où sont-ils allés.
'I wonder where they went.'

b'. *Je me demande si est-il parti.
'I wonder whether he left.'

(2) a. Peut-être viendra-t-elle.
'Maybe will she come.'

b. *Je pense que peut-être viendra-t-elle
'I think that maybe she will come.'

(3) a. Viendrait-elle, (que) je ne changerais pas d'avis.
'Should she come, I would not change my mind.'

a'. *Il pensait que, viendrait-elle, (qu')il ne changerait pas d'avis.
'He thought that, should she come, he would not change his mind'

---

[1] It is also appropriate in exclamatives with interrogative syntax:

(i) a. Est-elle idiote!
'Is she dumb!'

b. Quelle concession ne ferait-elle pas!
'What concession wouldn't she make!'

[2] Adverbs that are compatible with subject clitic inversion are the following: *peut-être* 'maybe', *ainsi* 'so', *aussi* 'thus', among others. *Toujours* (= *en tout cas*) 'anyway' and *tout au plus* 'at the very most' are some of the adverbs that require subject clitic inversion in main clauses.

b. A peine était-il entré, (que) les cris se mirent à fuser.
'As soon as he entered, shouts began to burst out.'

b'. *On lui a raconté qu'à peine était-il entré, (que) Marie s'est mise à crier.
'They told him that as soon as he entered Marie began to shout'

Subject clitic inversion allows for the presence of a preverbal Subject NP in each context (called complex inversion in Kayne 1972, 1983): [3]

(4) a. Où les enfants sont-ils allés?
'Where did the children go?'

b. Peut-être Marie viendra-t-elle.
'Maybe Marie will come.'

c. Marie viendrait-elle, (que) je ne changerais pas d'avis.
'Should Marie come, I would not change my mind.'

d. A peine Pierre était-il entré, (que) les cris se mirent à fuser.
'As soon as Pierre entered, shouts began to burst out.'

Subject NP inversion is usually called Stylistic inversion. However, recent analyses have shown that Stylistic inversion is too gross a category from a syntactic point of view. One should distinguish at least three types of inversion with different licensing conditions and syntactic composition: inversion in extraction contexts, unaccusative inversion and elaborative inversion.

We will briefly consider the properties of each of the three types.

## 2.1 Inversion in extraction contexts

Inversion in extraction contexts has received much attention in the Generative framework, both in the transformational approach (see Kayne & Pollock 1978 and, for a recent synthesis, Hulk & Pollock 2001) and in the syntagmatic approach (Bonami et al. 1999). Its licensing condition is complement or adjunct extraction by *wh*-movement (in questions, relative clauses and clefts).[4] It is considered optional (from a syntactic

---

[3] Subject clitic inversion in parentheticals do not share this feature:

(i) a. Pierre, dit-elle, est arrivé.
'Pierre, she says, has arrived.'

b. *Pierre, Marie dit-elle, est arrivé.
'Pierre, Marie says, has arrived.'

[4] French also has a kind of locative inversion akin to locative inversion in English or Italian (i). Its analysis is still disputed. It is either treated as an instance of PP topicalization (Bonami et al. 1999) or as a case of unaccusative inversion (Kampers-Manhe 1998):

(i) a. Sur la place se dresse la cathédrale Saint Paul
'On the square stands St Paul's Cathedral.'

point of view) and it is independent of the root/non-root contrast:[5]

(5) a. Root *wh*-question:
Où est allé Pierre? Où travaille Pierre?
'Where has Pierre gone? Where does Pierre work?'

b. Embedded *wh*-question:
Je me demande où est allé Pierre/où dort Pierre.
'I wonder where Pierre has gone to/where Pierre sleeps.'

c. Relative clause:
La rue où va Pierre, la pièce où dort Pierre
'The street where Pierres goes, the room where Pierre sleeps.'

d. Codas of clefts:[6]
C'est dans la cafétéria que déjeune Paul.
'It's in the cafeteria that Paul has lunch.'

## 2.2 Unaccusative inversion

The second type of inversion that we consider here, can be characterized by the restrictions on the (embedded) verb: only ergative and passive

---

b. Dans le chateau dormait un régiment de soldats
'In the castle slept a regiment of soldiers.'

In some cases of PP extraction with intransitive verbs (topicalization) inversion is obligatory:

(ii) a. A Pierre est revenu le premier prix.
b. *A Pierre le premier prix est revenu.
'The first prize went to Pierre.'

Topicalization of an NP or Adverb (which belongs to non-standard French) does not license stylistic inversion:

(iii) a. Trente francs, Pierre l'a payé.
b. ??Trente francs, l'a payé Pierre.
'Thirty francs, Pierre paid for it.'

We will not discuss these types of inversion further.

[5]There is another constraint on stylistic inversion that involves the relation of the extracted constituent and the canonical constituents in the clause (Korzen 1983). The precise analysis of this constraint is still disputed (see Korzen 1983, Kayne 1986, de Wind 1995). It is illustrated below:

(i) a. le cadeau qu'a envoyé Jean à Marie
'the present that John sent to Marie'
b. *le jour où a écrit Jean à Marie
'the day when John wrote to Marie'

(ii) a. la fille de qui s'est plaint Jean à Marie
'the girl about whom John has complained to Marie'
b. *la fille à qui s'est plaint Jean de Marie
'the girl to whom John has complained about Marie'

[6]Cleft sentences do not always allow for inversion. In cases where the phrase introduced by *que/qui* is part of the focus of the sentence, inversion is disallowed (see also chapter 23, Cleft sentences).

verbs (see (6)) are generally accepted by most native speakers:

(6) Je voudrais que soient distribués ces prospectus.
    I would-like that be distributed those leaflets

This leads Kampers-Manhe (1998) and Marandin (2001) to consider this type of inversion as an unaccusative construction in which the embedded inverted subject is in complement position.[7]

Some speakers also allow unergative intransitive activity verbs like *travailler* or *dormir* (cf. (7a,b)) in this construction. Examples such as (7a,b) have been attested by one of the authors, but are not acceptable for all speakers:

(7) a. ?J'aimerais que travaille Marie.
       I would-like that works Marie
    b. ?Je voudrais tant que dorment les enfants.
       I would-like so-much that sleep the children

We distinguish two cases of unaccusative inversion in French: (i) in subjunctive clauses and (ii) in root clauses introduced by temporal adverbs like *alors* or complement clauses of perception verbs like *entendre* 'to hear'. Subject inversion is possible in subjunctive complement clauses in noncolloquial French; it is fully optional.[8]

(8) a. J'aimerais que vienne quelqu'un/une femme.
       'I would like that came someone/a woman.'
    b. J'aimerais que quelqu'un/une femme vienne.
       'I would like that someone/a woman came.'

Since inversion is not legitimate in complement clauses in the indicative mood, as illustrated in (9), it has been assumed that the subjunctive is the licenser in that context. That would explain the grammaticality of (10) in an unmarked adverbial clause:[9]

(9) a. *Je dis que viendra quelqu'un/une femme
       'I say that will-come someone/a woman.'
    b. Je dis que quelqu'un/une femme viendra.
       'I say that someone/a woman will come.'

(10) Vienne la nuit, sonne l'heure
     Les jours s'en vont, je demeure

[7]However, the analyses proposed by those two authors for this construction are completely different. We will not discuss them here.

[8]Not all subjunctive clauses accept subject inversion. For an overview of the restrictions, see Kampers-Manhe (1998).

[9]The example in (10) is an excerpt of a poem by Apollinaire 'Le Pont Mirabeau' (in *Alcools*).

'Come the night, ring the hour,
Days go by, I stay.'

Nevertheless, unaccusative inversion occurs in a variety of other utterances in the indicative (Marandin 2001): root clauses in narratives usually featuring anaphoric temporal adverbs such as *alors* 'then', *soudain* 'suddenly' and *auparavant* 'beforehand',[10] complement clauses of perception verbs like *entendre* 'to hear' or *voir* 'to see' and temporal adverbial clauses (see also Lahousse 2003a,b):

(11) Alors entrèrent trois soldats.
'Then came in three soldiers.'

(12) Il vit que sortaient deux individus masqués
'He saw that came out two men with masks on.'

(13) a. Quand passent les cigognes.
when pass by the storks

b. tandis qu'aboyaient les chiens
while barked the dogs

Marandin (2001, 2003) and Cornish (2001) report that some unergative verbs are allowed, but they have to denote usual properties of the subject; for example *sonner* in combination with *les cloches*:[11]

(14) a. Alors sonnèrent les cloches.
'Then rang the bells.'

b. Il entendit que sonnaient les cloches.
he heard that rang the bells

### 2.3 Elaborative inversion

The third type of inversion we distinguish here is called Elaborative inversion. It requires the NP to be on the right edge of the sentence[12]

[10]Note that the presence of a fronted adverbial is not compulsory. This is also observed in stage directions:

(i) Entre Perdican
'Enters Perdican.'

[11]Sentences like (11) or (13) have been analyzed as cases of Locative inversion (a.o. Cornish, 2001). As the class of verbs is more restricted that the one used in Locative inversion, they should be distinguished.

[12]The subject is not emarginated from a prosodic point of view. The typical intonation of utterances with elaborative inversion is the following: continuation boundary tone on the right edge of the VP, illocutionary BT on the head of the Subject NP (in particular when it is an enumeration) and/or at the end of the whole NP. For example:

(i) passeront devant le conseil de discipline $H^{cont}\}_{MaP}$ les élèves suivants: $L\%]_{IntP}$ Pierre Dupond, $H^{cont}\}_{MaP}$ Marie Dubois $H^{cont}\}_{MaP}$ et Paul and it is akin to heavy NP shift, even though not all heavy NPs do license it. In (15a), the heavy *l'élève de troisième C (...) hier soir* is not felicitous, whereas the NPs in (15b–d) are. Some sort of semantic plurality is involved in the licensing of this type of inversion. Elaborative inversion is insensitive to the root/non-root contrast.[13]

(15) a. #Passera devant le conseil de discipline
will come before the disciplinary committee
l'élève de troisième C qui a été surpris
the pupil of 3$^{rd}$ grade who has been caught
en train de fumer un joint dans les toilettes de la cour
smoking pot in the toilets
hier soir.
yesterday evening

b. Passeront devant le discipline
will come before the disciplinary committee
les élèves suivants:
the following pupils:
Pierre Dupond, Marie Dubois et Paul Personne.
...

c. Passeront devant le conseil de discipline
will come before the disciplinary committee
tous les élèves qui ont été surpris en train de fumer un joint
all the pupils who ...
dans les toilettes de la cour.
...

d. Passera devant le conseil de discipline
will come before the disciplinary committee
tout élève de l'établissement au comportement incivil.
every pupil of the school with inappropriate behavior

---

Personne L%]$_{\text{IntP}}$
will come before the disciplinary committee the following students: Pierre Dupond, Marie Dubois and Paul Personne

[13]It is not subject to the "contrainte de redondance fonctionnelle", i.e. the ban on two canonical NPs in inverted clauses that is observed in stylistic inversion, as illustrated in (i) below:

(i) a. *le professeur à qui rendront un devoir supplémentaire
the teacher to whom will hand in an extra assignment
tous les élèves qui ont échoué
all the pupils that failed

b. Rendront un devoir supplémentaire tous les élèves qui ont échoué.
will hand in an extra assignment all the pupils that failed

In the next sections, we will concentrate on the informational properties of the two first inversion types, without discussing elaborative inversion in further detail. As for inversion in extraction contexts, we will focus on *wh*-questions and relative clauses.

## 3 Subject inversion in *wh*-clauses

In this section we will present data discussed in the literature on inversion in *wh*-questions and on inversion in certain types of relative clauses. We will see that properties of the subject and/or the predicate interact with the informational properties of the utterance.

### 3.1 Properties of the (inverted) subject in *wh*-questions

From the beginning of generative work on inversion in French, it has been noticed that subject inversion in *wh*-contexts is incompatible with indefinite subjects (Cornulier 1974, Kupferman 1983, Kayne & Pollock 2001) on the basis of the contrast in questions like (16):[14]

(16) a. Quel gâteau a mangé Jean?
which cake has eaten Jean?

b. *Quel gâteau a mangé quelqu'un?
which cake has eaten someone?

The contrast carries over to embedded questions (17a, b) and may involve other types of indefinite NPs (17c,d):

(17) a. *Elle a demandé quel gâteau a mangé quelqu'un.
'She asked which cake someone has eaten.'

b. *Je te dirai quand sera venu la voir un ami quelconque. (Kupferman, 1983)
'I'll tell you when some friend of hers has come and seen her'

c. *Quel livre lit un étudiant?
'Which book does a student read?'

d. *Où dorment trois chats?
'Where do three cats sleep?'

The observation has been made more precise. First, not all indefinites are banned from the context, as shown in Drijkoningen & Kampers-

[14]The effect has been termed the 'counter-indefiniteness effect'; the term suggests a link with the independent 'definiteness effect' found in the impersonal construction (see the contrast in (i)). On the theoretical level there has been no generalized explanation for these two effects.

(i) a. *Il est arrivé Jean.
it is arrived John

b. Il est arrivé quelqu'un.
there is arrived someone

Manhe (2001): NPs of the type *aucun* N, 'no N', make fully grammatical inverted subjects as (18) shows:

(18) Quel livre n'a compris aucun étudiant?
'Which book didn't any student understand?'

Moreover, indefinite NPs are fully acceptable when some sort of genericity is involved in the question:

(19) a. Quels romans doit avoir lu un étudiant de français
which novels must have read a student of French
pour être accepté dans le programme?
to be admitted in the program?

b. Où va une femme quand elle se querelle
where goes a woman when she has an argument
avec son mari?
with her husband?

In discussing this so-called 'counter-indefiniteness effect', Kayne & Pollock (2001) make a similar observation. They insist on the fact that the effect obtains only with what they call 'real indefinites'. Their analysis of these cases of Stylistic inversion involves movement of the subject to a (topic) position in the left periphery of the sentence, followed by 'remnant movement' of the rest of the clause to the left of the moved subject. 'Real indefinite' subjects cannot be topicalized: they cannot be moved to such a (topical) position in the left periphery and therefore inversion cannot be derived.

Drijkoningen & Kampers-Manhe (2001) restate the 'counter-indefiniteness effect' in terms of the following restriction: "do not pose questions about entities that you introduce in the discourse while posing the question". In doing so, they deal with the interesting observation that the same distributional pattern obtains when the indefinite Subject NP is preverbal, as shown in (20):[15]

(20) a. *Quel livre quelqu'un a-t-il lu?
'Which book did someone read?'

b. *Où trois chats dorment-ils?
'Where do three cats sleep?'

c. Quel livre aucun étudiant n'a-t-il compris?
'Which book did no student understand?'

d. Quels romans un étudiant de français doit-il avoir lu pour être accepté dans le programme?

[15]Note that questions in (20) are appropriate as reprise questions in dialogues, e.g. when the speaker did not hear or understand a previous turn 'someone has read a X book'.

'Which novels does a student of French need to have read in order to be accepted in the program?'

In other words indefinite NPs introducing a new (non-identified) entity in the discourse are banned from *wh*-questions.[16] In the activation state terminology, adopted in chapter 20 (Introduction), such NPs correspond to NPs associated with inactive Discourse Referents: *wh*-questions disallow subjects which correspond to inactive DRs.

Hence, we may conclude that the activation state of the DR associated with the postverbal NP is a relevant factor for the analysis of *wh*-questions as such, but not for the analysis of stylistic inversion in general.

### 3.2 Properties of the predicate (and its relation to the inverted subject) in relative clauses

Recently some intriguing data have been introduced in the literature (Beyssade, Marandin and Rialland 2003 and Marandin 2003; henceforth we refer to these two articles as BMR/M), involving informational properties of the predicate in relative clauses with inversion. Consider first the question in (21):

(21) Que sont devenus les étudiants dont Bernard s'est occupé?
'What happened to the students Bernard took care of?'

This question can be answered in different ways, depending on whether we are dealing with a complete or a partial answer. BMR/M include a study of possible answers to this question. They show that there is a correlation between the appropriateness versus non-appropriateness of inversion in the relative clause and the type of answer the utterance provides.

---

[16]Such a ban does not hold in other types of questions as (i) and (ii) show:

(i) Quelqu'un/un étudiant est-il venu me voir?
someone/a student has he come to see me?

(ii) Trois chats dorment-ils là-bas?
three cats do they sleep over there?

It does not hold for other types of inversion either, as shown by the following examples:

(iii) a. Je voudrais que vienne un médecin
'I would like that a doctor comes.'

b. Alors sont entrés cent soldats armés.
'Then a hundred armed soldiers came in.'

c. Ont rendu leurs armes une dizaine de talibans de Kaboul et deux régiments de Peshawar.
'A dozen Talibans from Kabul and two regiments from Peshawar have surrendered their arms.'

A first set of possible answers is given in (22) and (23). The answers differ in the choice of the embedded verb (*s'occuper* in (22) and *soigner* in (23)):

(22) a. Les étudiants dont s'est **occupé** Bernard ont tous brillamment réussi.

b. Les étudiants dont Bernard s'est **occupé** ont tous brillamment réussi.
'All the students Bernard took care of have been successful.'

(23) a. #Les étudiants qu'a **soigné** Bernard ont intégré l'équipe de France.[17]

b. Les étudiants que Bernard a **soignés** ont intégré l'équipe de France.
'The students Bernard treated joined the French team.'

We observe that when the verb in the answer is identical to the one in the question, as in (22), both relative clauses with and without inversion are possible. Moreover, there is no semantic contrast between (22a) and (22b).

However, when the verb in the answer differs from the one in the question, inversion in the relative clause is not appropriate, as shown in (23a). In the appropriate example in (23b), we are dealing with a partial answer: it concerns a subgroup of the students Bernard took care of and calls for a context in which the speaker distinguishes at least two of those subgroups.

BMR/M claim that inversion in this type of answer is appropriate only if the predicate is 'given'. 'Given' is a notion which expresses an informational property of (part of) the 'Ground'. In the introduction to this part (chapter 20), 'Given content' has been defined as the common content of the Discourse Topic (henceforth DT); it is modeled as an open proposition.[18] The DT is viewed as a question, i.e. a set of propositions in the case of a simple DT or a set of sets of propositions in the case of a layered DT.

The question in (21) sets up the following DT:

(24) {les étudiants dont Bernard s'est occupé ont réussi, les étudiants dont Bernard s'est occupé ont échoué, ...}

---

[17]In the examples with inversion, we leave the past participles without agreement, following the 17$^{\text{th}}$ century grammarian Vaugelas, among others (cf. *la faute que Paul a faite* 'the mistake that Paul made+FEM' vs *la faute qu'a fait/??faite* Paul 'the mistake that made/made+FEM Paul').

[18]In other words, the open proposition that represents Given content expresses the common denominator of the DT (Prüst 1973).

In both answers (22), the property denoted by the RC belongs to the Given content as formalized in (25):

(25) Given: ∃x ((étudiants (x) & S'occuper (x, Bernard) → P (x))

Following the analysis of BMR/M, this makes inversion appropriate in (22a). The answer (23) however, modifies the DT in the following way:

(26) Discourse Topic (modified by the answer): { {les étudiants dont Bernard s'est occupé ont réussi, les étudiants dont Bernard s'est occupé ont échoué, ...}, {les étudiants que Bernard a soignés ont réussi, les étudiants que Bernard a soignés ont échoué,...} }

As a result, the Given content should now be formalized as in (27):

(27) Given: ∃x ((étudiants (x) & Q (Bernard,x) → P (x))

This means that the property denoted by the Relative Clause does not belong to the Given content, and thus BMR/M correctly predict inversion to be ruled out.

A further set of answers to (21) discussed by Marandin (2003) is given in (28):

(28) a. Les étudiants qu'a **entraîné** Bernard ont tous réussi aux Olympiades universitaires.
b. Les étudiants que Bernard a **entraînés** ont tous réussi aux Olympiades universitaires.
'The students that Bernard trained have been successful at the University Olympics.'

Here both answers are appropriate, but speakers report a difference of meaning between the two of them: (28a) is a complete answer: the students that Bernard took care of are those that he trained and they have succeeded. (28a) is interpreted as (22) above. (28b) is an incomplete answer: the students that Bernard trained make up a subgroup of those that he took care of and that subgroup has succeeded. (28b) is interpreted as (23b).[19]

Marandin's analysis runs as follows. In the former case (28a), *entraîner* and *s'occuper de* are taken as equivalent (in a context where taking care of students is training them): the property denoted by both Relative Clauses *dont Bernard s'est occupé* and *que Bernard a entraînés* are equivalent. Therefore the predicate contributes to the Given content as formalized in (29b) and inversion is appropriate:

[19]Moreover, answer (28b) crucially presents a C accent (on *Bernard* or *entraîner*) in the intended reading.

(29) a. Discourse Topic: {les étudiants dont Bernard s'est occupé ont réussi, les étudiants dont Bernard s'est occupé ont échoué, ...}

b. Given: [s'occuper de ≡ entraîner] ∃x ((étudiants (x) & Entraîner (Bernard,x) → P (x))

As expected, in a context in which *entraîner* describes a specific manner of looking after students (i.e. is not equivalent to *s'occuper*) and where the speaker wants to distinguish several groups of students, inversion is no longer an option.

Now, consider yet another pair of possible answers to the question in (21):

(30) a. Les étudiants que Bernard a **entraînés** ont tous réussi aux Olympiades universitaires, ceux qu'a **entraîné** Jean-Marie ont repris un cursus normal.
'The students that Bernard trained have been successful at the University Olympics, those that Jean-Marie trained returned to their studies.'

b. Les étudiants que Bernard a **entraînés** ont tous réussi aux Olympiades universitaires, ceux qu'a **pris en charge** Jean-Marie ont repris un cursus normal.
'The students that Bernard trained have been successful at the University Olympics, those that Jean-Marie took charge of returned to their studies.'

Inversion is not appropriate in the first relative clause (since the predicate is not given), but it is in the second relative clause. This is not unexpected in (30a), since the predicate in the second Relative Clause is identical to that in the first relative clause, but (30b) is problematic since *entraîner* and *prendre en charge* are different.

This could be explained by taking into account the role played by the utterances in the development of the Discourse Topic in the following way: inversion is not appropriate in utterances that initiate the reshaping of the Discourse Topic, but it is appropriate in those that further elaborate the Discourse Topic. As for the answers in (30b), the different predicates enable the speaker to distinguish several groups of students.[20]

[20]Here, we may draw an interesting parallel with C accents. As stated in the introduction (Chapter 20), C accent is compulsory in the utterance reshaping the current DT whereas it is optional in the utterances that further elaborate the DT. As for inversion, it is not appropriate in the utterance reshaping the current DT whereas it is in utterances that further elaborate it. For some speakers, similar effects are found for left dislocation (see chapter 22, Dislocation).

Another observation is relevant here: the predicates in the utterances that further elaborate the current DT must ensure a coherent splitting of the current DT. This is the case in (30b), whereas it is not in (31b) below where inversion in the Relative Clause is no longer appropriate in the second clause:

(31) a. Les étudiants que Bernard a **entraînés** ont tous réussi aux Olympiades universitaires, ceux que Jean-Marie a **interviewés** étaient montés sur le podium.

b. # Les étudiants que Bernard a **entraînés** ont tous réussi aux Olympiades universitaires, ceux qu'a **interviewé** Jean-Marie étaient montés sur le podium.
'The students that Bernard trained have been successful at the University Olympics, those that Jean-Marie interviewed won a medal.'

Inversion in the Relative Clause is no longer appropriate in the second clause as (31b) shows; the second clause in (31a) can only be interpreted as a comment on the answer provided by the first clause.

In the spirit of BMR/M, who argue that inversion abides by the constraint that states that the predicate should be given, we could explain the data in (30)–(31) by assuming that inversion is never appropriate in utterances that reshape the DT. The choice of the predicate in the second clause is severely restricted by this constraint. In order to have inversion in the second clause, the predicate must be interpretable within the elaboration of the DT initiated by the reshaping of the Discourse Topic in the first clause. Thus, the predicate is not individually given, nonetheless the type and the content of the predicate is severely restricted. In (30b), it must denote a property that defines a subgroup of students in a way that is coherent with the one used in the first clause and both clauses should provide a coherent splitting of the group of students under debate in the initial question. The verb *prendre en charge* is permitted since it describes, like *entraîner*, a specific manner of looking after students. The verb *interviewer* in (31b) is not sufficiently similar to *entraîner* in order to make a coherent splitting of the group of students. As a result, the second clause can only be interpreted if it reshapes the DT. Since inversion is never appropriate in utterances reshaping the DT, it cannot be appropriate in the second clause of (31b).[21]

[21]The verb *interviewer* in (31) does not allow for inversion, although it would in another context as in (i):

(i) a. Les étudiants que Paul a interrogés disent qu'ils ont trouvé un bon travail grâce à son enseignement, ceux que Jean-Marie a interviewés

Next to givenness and the ban on inversion in utterances reshaping the DT, Marandin (2003) states yet another factor that may intervene in inversion appropriateness: the relation between the property denoted by the predicate and the referent of the subject in the knowledge shared by the interlocutors. It is best observed in identifying RCs in 'out of the blue' utterances.[22] Consider the Relative Clauses in (32) and (33): in (32), inversion in the relative clause is fully appropriate, whereas it is not in (33):[23]

(32) a. La liste des livres qu'a lu (acheté, écrit) Proust à l'automne 1917 ne nous est pas parvenue.

b. La liste des livres que Proust a lus (achetés, écrits) à l'automne 1917 ne nous est pas parvenue.
'The list of books that Proust read (bought, wrote) in the fall of 1917 is unknown to us.'

(33) a. ?# La liste des livres qu'a brûlé Proust à l'automne 1917 ne nous est pas parvenue.

b. La liste des livres que Proust a brûlés à l'automne 1917 ne nous est pas parvenue.
'The list of books that Proust burnt in the fall of 1917 is unknown to us.'

More precisely, (33a) would be much more appropriate in a context in which the burning of books by Proust somehow has been introduced

---

sont plus réservés.

b. Les étudiants que Paul a interrogés disent qu'ils ont trouvé un bon travail grâce à son enseignement, ceux qu'a interviewé Jean-Marie sont plus réservés.
'The students that Paul questionned say they have got a good job thanks to his teaching, those that Jean-Marie interviewed are less affirmative.'

[22] Identifying RCs are anchoring RCs: they provide a property that identifies the DR associated with the NP.

[23] Note that inversion would not be appropriate if the RC in (31) occurs in an answer splitting the DT:

(i) Connaît-on la liste des livres que Proust et Mallarmé ont achetés à l'automne 1917?
'Do we know the list of books that Proust and Mallarmé bought in the fall of 1917?'

a. Les livres que Proust a lus nous sont connus grâce au fichier de la bibliothèque Doucet, ceux qu'il a achetés ...

b. # Les livres qu'a lu Proust nous sont connus grâce au fichier de la bibliothèque Doucet, ceux qu'il a achetés ...
'The books Proust read are known thanks to the catalog of the Bibliothèque Doucet, those he bought...'

in the context, as in (34):[24]

(34) Proust et Mallarmé étaient très déprimés par leurs échecs, ils détruisaient manuscrits sur manuscrits. On ne connaîtra jamais la liste des livres qu'a brûlé Proust à l'automne 1917.
'Proust and Malarmé were quite depressed by their failures, they were destroying their manuscripts. We will never know the list of books Proust burnt in the fall of 1917.'

Marandin introduces the notion of disposition to explain the contrast between (32) and (33): the predicate denotes a property that the speaker assumes to be specific of the referent of the subject, either because it is stereotypical or shared in the current context. Given Proust (a writer) and the sort of eventualities typically involving books, to identify a set of books with "Buy (Proust, books)" does not require much specific knowledge. On the contrary, to identify a set of books with "Burn (Proust, books)" requires the knowledge of a particular eventuality the hearer may not have, except if it has been activated in the current context of discourse as in (34).[25]

### 3.3 To sum up

In section 3.1, we have seen that subjects in *wh*-questions — whether inverted or not — cannot be 'real indefinites'. This 'counter-indefiniteness effect' has mainly been studied in generative syntax and has recently been related to the discourse informational status of the subject (Kayne & Pollock 2001, Drijkoningen & Kampers-Manhe 2001). In the framework adopted here, this property can be phrased as follows: in *wh*-questions the subject cannot refer to an inactive discourse referent. Even though the phenomenon is typically discussed in the literature on inversion, this property seems to be related to pragmatic properties of questions. In section 3.2, we have considered a number of properties of the predicate in a specific type of Relative Clauses and we have

[24]Discourse (34) is pure fiction ...

[25]French grammatical tradition has noticed the fact. It proposes a kind of rule of thumb for the felicity of inversion in RCs. Inversion is appropriate whenever the relative clause can be replaced by a "*de* NP" phrase. As Corblin (2001) observes, the preposition *de* in the phrase $[\text{N } de \text{ NP}]_{\text{NP}}$ is interpretable as denoting any relation easily recoverable in context between the discourse referent associated with the matrix NP and the NP complement of *de*. In other words, *de* denotes an underspecified relation between two discourse referents. The rule of thumb essentially captures the condition we are pointing at. Utterance (i) may be interpreted (in context) like (32), but certainly not like (33):

(i) La liste des livres de Proust à l'automne 1917 ne nous est pas parvenue
the list of books DE ('of') Proust in the fall of 1917 is unknown to us

seen that inversion is possible when the predicate in the RC is identical or equivalent to the one in the question it constitutes an answer to. Beyssade et al. (2003), Marandin (2003) have analysed this property in terms of 'givenness': inversion is appropriate when the predicate contributes to the Given content. Moreover, we have seen that in yet another type of RC, used in 'out of the blue' contexts, the notion of 'shared knowledge' plays a role in licensing inversion.

## 4 Unaccusative inversion

In section 2.2 we have defined unaccusative inversion on the basis of the properties of the main verb (ergative or passive) in the inverted clause. We have distinguished between two cases of unaccusative inversion: inversion in subjunctive clauses and inversion in indicative clauses (root narrative clauses, complement clauses of perception verbs or temporal adverbial clauses). The next two sections are devoted to the pragmatic properties of unaccusative inversion and the way these are accounted for in the literature. It turns out that the literature on unaccusative inversion either concentrates on properties of the subject and crucially resorts to the notion of focus (see Kampers-Manhe 1998) or concentrates on the predicate and tends to unify the analysis of unaccusative inversion with that of inversion in RCs (Marandin 2003). In the following two subsections we will discuss both types of approaches in detail. Even though the authors concentrate on either subjunctive inversion or unaccusative inversion in non-subjunctive contexts, it turns out that the two uses of unaccusative inversion behave uniformly with respect to the criteria discussed in the literature.

### 4.1 Unaccusative inversion and the status of the subject

Kampers-Manhe (1998) discusses subjunctive inversion focusing on the discourse status of the subject. Quite generally, she observes that the subject is either part of a broad focus including the predicate or the subject is the only focus of the sentence. The predicate cannot be a narrow focus, which, in her view is due to a constraint on the subject: in subjunctive inversion, the subject should be (part of the) focus of the sentence. These generalizations are illustrated in (35) to (39).

Consider first the broad focus reading. The sentence in (35a), with an inverted subject, is an appropriate answer to both questions (36a) and (36b), just like (35b) with a preverbal subject:

(35) a. Je veux que vienne Bernadette.

b. Je veux que Bernadette vienne
'I want that Bernadette comes'

(36) a. Que veux-tu?
'What do you want?'

b. Qu'as-tu?
'What is the matter with you?'

As for the narrow focus reading on the subject, we can have either an inverted subject or a non-inverted subject. Both sentences in (35) are suitable answers to question (37):

(37) Qui veux-tu qui vienne?
'Who do you want to come?'

Note that the narrow subject reading affects the prosody of the sentence with the non-inverted subject. When used as an answer to one of the questions in (36), both (35a) and (35b) are characterized by an L% boundary tone at the end of the sentence, which coincides with the end of the focus. As expected on the basis of the prosodic properties of focus in French (see chapter 21, Prosody and Information and French), the L% boundary tone that marks the right edge of the focal domain necessarily falls on the rightmost syllable of the subject and not on the predicate if (35b) is an answer to (37). The predicate forms a post-focus sequence the end of which is marked by a copy of the boundary tone.[26]

(38) Je veux que Bernadette L% vienne L%

When only the verb is focused (narrow focus), inversion is excluded. (35a) is not a suitable answer to (39), independently of the prosody, while (35b) is:

(39) Que veux-tu que Bernadette fasse?
'What do you want that Bernadette does?'

Consider now the contrast between (40) and (41). In (40), inversion is not allowed, while it is in (41):

(40) [Marie]$_i$ avait été annoncée. #Aussitôt, il ordonna qu'entre [la jeune fille]$_i$.
'Marie had been announced. At once he ordered that the young woman should enter.'

(41) Marie$_i$ était heureuse de s'être débarrassée du roi. Lui était désespéré. Il songeait à se venger. Alors, il ordonna que soit exécutée la jeune fille$_i$
'Marie was glad to have got rid of the king. He was desparate.

[26]Note that the prosodic analysis of those sentences is not based on experiments: it is based on intuitions and follows the analysis presented in chapter 21 of this volume.

He thought about vengeance. Then he ordered that the young woman be executed.'

In (40) the discourse referent of the inverted subject is given in the preceding sentence. In (41) it is separated from its antecedent by a number of other sentences. These data can be accounted for in accordance with Kampers-Manhe's idea that the subject has to be (part of) the focus in the following way. In (40), the discourse referent is active, as it has been introduced in the previous sentence. This seems to block a reading of the second sentence in which *la jeune fille* is part of the focus of the sentence. In (41), *Marie* is introduced much earlier in the text, and can be considered to be deactivated. As a result *la jeune fille* can be part of the focus of the sentence.

Kampers-Manhe concentrates on subjunctive contexts, but unaccusative inversion in the context of perception verbs and the adverb *alors* behaves in a parallel way. Consider for instance the data in (42) and (43), which are parallel to the ones in (40) and (41):

(42) Il attendit longtemps en observant la porte. Elle s'ouvrit soudain. Il vit que sortait la reine.
'He waited for a long time, looking at the door. The door flew open. He saw that the queen went out.'

(43) Il observa les moindres gestes de Marie-Antoinette. #A minuit il vit que sortait la reine.
'He observed every move of Marie-Antoinette. At midnight he saw that the queen went out.'

The condition on the subject is, according to Kampers-Manhe, due to the focus properties of the inverted subject position. In the inverted sentence, the subject is the most embedded constituent of the sentence. Following Zubizarreta (1994, 1998), the most embedded position of the clause is the one where primary stress is assigned so that it is the nuclear focus position. We will pursue this idea here while adapting it to the prosodic analysis of French focus presented in the first two chapters of this part, in which the Nuclear Stress Rule does not apply.

It has been shown in chapter 21 (Prosody) that focus is signaled by the presence of an L% boundary tone associated with the IntP boundary at the end of the focus domain. The boundary tones can be rather freely realized, as shown by the possibility of focalising a subject by placing the L% boundary tone on the subject as in (38) (see also Introduction). However, at the end of an utterance, the presence of a boundary tone is obligatory: in case the last constituent of the utterance is (part of) the focus, we find a final boundary tone which marks focus and in case this constituent is not part of the focus, the end of the utterance bears a copy of the boundary tone that marks the end of the focus. In this view, we might hypothesize that a structure with a sentence-final focus is the default case. The cost of a non-final focus is the obligatory insertion of an extra IntP boundary, and hence of extra prosodic structure.[27] This would allow us to identify a default focus position in French without assuming that the nuclear stress rule applies. Obviously, the framework does not necessarily imply the presence of a neutral focus position; however, given the assumption that insertion of an extra boundary would make a derivation more costly, the framework is compatible with an approach which uses the neutral focus position.

Consider now the contrast between (44) and (45):

(44) a. *Je veux que parte Paul immédiatement/aux Etats-Unis
'I want that Paul leaves immediately/for the United States'

b. *J'aimerais que soient distribués ces prospectus par les enfants/avant mon départ
'I would like that those leaflets would be distributed by the children/before I leave'

(45) a. Je veux que partent trois étudiants immédiatement/aux Etats-Unis.
'I want that three students leave immediately/for the United States'

b. J'aimerais que soient distribués cent prospectus par les enfants/avant mon départ.
'I would like that a hundred leaflets would be distributed by the children/before I leave'

No constituent may follow the inverted definite subject, while this restriction does not seem to hold for indefinite ones. (45a) can be an answer to (46a,b), but not to (47), which is in accordance with the idea that the subject should be (part of) the focus of the sentence: a narrow focus reading on the sentence-final PP is excluded. As expected, when (45a) is used as an answer to (46a), the right edge of the subject must be marked by an L% boundary tone and a copy of that tone must mark the sentence-final position:

(46) a. Qui veux-tu qui parte immédiatement/aux Etats-Unis?
'Who do you want to leave immediately/for the United States?'

[27] A similar approach is found in Szendrői (2001), who argues that Italian IntP boundaries are preferably inserted at the end of the sentence.

b. Que veux-tu?
'What do you want?'

(47) #Quand/Où veux-tu que partent trois étudiants?
'When/Where do you want three students to go?'

The only appropriate answer to (47) would be (48), without inversion.

(48) Je veux que trois étudiants partent immédiatement/aux Etats-Unis.

The question is why definite NPs are excluded in (44). The answer is not easy. Kampers-Manhe argues that it lies in the nature of definite NPs, which are less naturally focused than indefinites. Indefinites usually correspond to discourse new referents: as such they naturally form part of the new information conveyed by the sentence. Definites correspond rather to given or accessible discourse referents, which can be either focus or ground. In the inverted sentence, the definite subject occupies the default focus position. This ensures a focus interpretation of the definite. Kampers-Manhe argues that, whenever they are followed by further material, they have to be interpreted as part of the ground. As this is not permitted for an inverted subject, the sentence is ill-formed. As for indefinite NPs, they are not easily considered as ground (cf. chapter 22, Dislocation) and can be interpreted as (part of the) focus, even though they do not occupy the last position of the sentence. Within Kampers-Manhe's approach, the discourse status of a referent is not completely independent of the focus-ground partition. Rather, definites are preferably part of the ground and indefinites preferably part of the focus because of the status of their discourse referents.

An intriguing question with respect to (44) is why these examples cannot be made grammatical by an L% boundary tone after the inverted subject even though a narrow focus domain can always be marked by an L% boundary tone on its right edge in assertive clauses as we have seen above. One could give the following tentative explanation. If a definite subject is a narrow focus, it can be marked as such by a boundary tone L% as in (38), or it can be placed in sentence-final position, where the L% tone comes for free. In order to have a narrow focus interpretation of the subject in (44), we would have to add an extra L% boundary tone in addition to the special position of the subject; as such the non-inverted counterpart is more economical: it only involves insertion of an extra L% boundary. As a result, the non-inverted sentence is the only available sentence here.

Notice that the sentences in (49) are judged to be grammatical, even though judgments vary.

(49) a. Je veux que soit convoqué le tribunal avant demain
I want that is convoked the tribunal before tomorrow

b. Je regrette qu'ait été impliquée la classe politique dans cette affaire
I regret that has been implicated the political class in this case

This indicates that it is only strong definite subject NPs that cannot be inverted when not in sentence-final position, the default focus position. The NPs *le tribunal* or *la classe politique* refer to entities that are identified cross-contextually (they are weak definites), and therefore they might be expected more easily to be part of the focus of the sentence.

Even though Kampers-Manhe bases her analysis on subjunctive inversion, it can be shown that non-subjunctive unaccusative inversion behaves similarly. As in the case of subjunctive inversion, narrow focus on the predicate is excluded, and a definite inverted subject needs to be sentence-final. The latter generalization is illustrated in (50):

(50) a. On ferma les portes. Aussitôt entrèrent dix policiers avant même qu'on les ait annoncés.
'The doors were closed. Immediately ten policemen came in even before they had been announced.'

b. *Ce jour-là fut assassiné César sans pitié.
'That day Ceasar was assassinated without pity.'

The analysis proposed by Kampers-Manhe crucially relies on the assumption that the sentence-final position is a default focus position in French as well as on the assumption that the status of a discourse referent of a constituent makes it more or less appropriate for being part of the focus of the sentence. These assumptions allow her to derive the distribution of unaccusative inversion on the basis of a condition on subject focus. As long as the subject is part of the focus of the sentence, unaccusative inversion is allowed. This correctly excludes a narrow focus reading on the verb.

## 4.2 Unaccusative inversion and discourse properties of the predicate

Marandin (2003) analyzes unaccusative inversion in terms of conditions on the predicate in the inverted sentence rather than in terms of the focus-ground repartition in relation to the subject. He considers mostly non-subjunctive contexts, but again, it seems to be the case that the conditions for the two types of unaccusative inversion are similar. Moreover, it applies to elaborative inversion as well. Marandin argues that differences in syntactic construal of inversion do not correlate with differences related to the informational status of the predicate or the subject.

Let us first look at the constraint on givenness and more generally, at the ban on inversion in utterances reshaping the DT in the context of subjunctive clauses. Inversion is appropriate if the predicate is given, as in (51a), and not in answers which reshape the DT by introducing a different predicate, as in (51b). This explanation extends to (52b).

(51) Qui veux-tu qui vienne?
'Who do you want to come?'

a. Je veux que vienne Paul.
'I want that Paul comes'

b. #Je veux que parte Paul
'I want that Paul leaves'

(52) Que veux-tu que Pierre fasse?
'What do you want that Pierre does?'

a. Je veux que Pierre vienne

b. #Je veux que vienne Pierre
'I want that Pierre comes'

The same is observed for elaborative inversion as (53) shows:

(53) Qui est reçu?
'Who passed?'

a. Sont reçus Pierre, Paul et Bernadette.
have passed Pierre, Paul and Bernadette

b. #Ont échoué les deux élèves que présentait Paul.
have failed the two students presented by Paul

Moreover, unaccusative inversion, as well as elaborative inversion, shows the sensitivity to the discourse role of the utterance we have described for inversion in RC in section 3.2. The examples (54) and (55) are parallel to (31) above:

(54) Qui veux-tu qui vienne?
'Who do you want to come?'

a. Je voudrais que vienne Marie et que parte Paul
I would like that comes Marie and that leaves Paul

b. Je voudrais que Paul parte et que vienne Marie.
'I would like that Paul leaves and that comes Marie.'

(55) Qui est reçu?
'Who passed?'

a. Sont reçus tous les élèves de Marie, ont échoué
passed all the students of Marie, failed
les deux élèves que présentait Paul.
the two students presented by Paul

b. Tous les élèves de Marie ont échoué, sont reçus
all the students of Marie failed, passed
les deux élèves que présentait Paul.
the two students presented by Paul

The analysis cannot be tested for root narrative clauses since they are never appropriate as answers for some reason that we leave unresolved here:

(56) Et puis, qu'est-ce qui s'est passé?/Qui est arrivé à ce moment-là?
'And then, what happened?/Who arrived at that moment?'
#Alors est arrivée Marie
then is arrived Marie

Marandin (2003) argues that unaccusative inversions in all focus utterances, and in particular in root narrative clauses, abide by a constraint according to which the predicate has to be 'dispositional', and that is related to the presentational nature of unaccusative inversion. He distinguishes two cases: the predicate is known to be stereotypical of the referent of the subject (57a,b) or the predicate belongs to a conventional way of introducing a character in a narrative (58).

(57) a. Le silence se fit. Alors se leva une tempête d'applaudissements
'It became silent. Then came up a thunderous applause.'

b. Le silence se fit. #Alors se leva Marie.
'It became silent. Then Marie got up.'

(58) Le silence se fit. Alors entra Napoléon.
'It became silent. Then Napoleon entered.'

To summarize, the constraints on the use of inversion in relative clauses, as discussed in BMR/M can account for a number of properties of unaccusative inversion as well. In all focus utterances, we find constraints on the predicate that can be related to specific properties of unaccusative inversion, which are typically presentational sentences. It would be interesting to see whether the properties of definite subjects (see (45) above) as discussed by Kampers-Manhe (1998) and the data in (40)–(43) could be accounted for without making reference to focus. As the status of the DR seems to play a role in the examples that she argues are cases of subject focus, it might be possible to formulate the restriction in relation to the activation state of the DR only, without making reference to focus. On the other hand, it might be possible to relate the conditions on the predicate (partly) to the focus properties of the subject. We leave these issues for further research.

## 5 Conclusion

Three dimensions have been distinguished to characterize the aspects of information that Grammar is sensitive to: Ground/Focus articulation, Discourse Topic and the activation state of the Discourse Referents. As for the first factor, it has been shown that it does not play a role in inversion in relative clauses nor in inversion in *wh*-questions. Its role in unaccusative inversion is disputed and remains an issue for further research. The givenness of the verb or the VP in the Discourse Topic or shared knowledge are decisive for inversion in RC; it is a factor in unaccusative inversion, but depending on the role attributed to focus, authors give a different status to this factor: it is either seen as a consequence of the focus condition or as an independent factor that generalizes over different types of inversion. The third factor, the activation state of the Discourse Referent, plays a role in several types of inversion: in *wh*-questions, NPs associated with inactive discourse referents are excluded as postverbal subjects (full NPs or clitics associated with full NPs), whereas NPs whose referent is part of the DT are excluded in unaccusative inversion. It does not seem to play a role in RC. In unaccusative inversion, the activation state of the discourse referent seems to play a role, even though the exact role remains an issue for further research. As far as the data discussed in this survey are concerned, two questions remain open concerning the contextual appropriateness of Subject NP inversion in French. The first question is whether inversion is a unified phenomenon from the point of view of information structure, although it is not from a syntactic point of view (cf. the differences in syntactic construal or licensing between inversion in questions, inversion in relative clauses, unaccusative inversion and elaborative inversion). The second question is which analysis is to be given to the fact that inverted subjects associated with active DR are excluded from *wh*-questions and sentences featuring unaccusative inversion (while they are not in relative clauses). More specifically, we want to know whether this is due to a general condition on inversion or to the semantic/pragmatic properties that are associated with *wh*-questions and unaccusative inversion respectively.

## References

Beyssade, C., J. Marandin, and A. A. Rialland. 2003. Ground/focus revisited. A perspective from French. In Núñez-Cedeño et al. (2003), pages 83–98.

Bolinger, D. 1965. *Forms of English: Accent, Morpheme, Order*. Cambridge (MA): Harvard University Press. Abe, I. and T. Kenekiyo, eds.

Bonami, O., D. Godard, and J.-M. Marandin. 1999. Constituency and word order in French subject inversion. In Bouma et al. (1999).

Bouma, G., E. Hinrichs, G.-J. Kruijff, and R. Oeherle, eds. 1999. *Constraints and Resources in Natural Language syntax and semantics*. Stanford: CSLI.

Casagrande, J. and B. Saciuk, eds. 1972. *Generative Studies in Romance Languages*. Rowley, Mass.: Newbury House.

Cinque, G., J. Koster, J.-Y. Pollock, L. Rizzi, and R. Zanuttini, eds. 1994. *Paths Towards Universal Grammar. Studies in Honor of Richard S. Kayne*. Washington, DC: Georgetown University Press.

Corblin, F. 2001. Défini et génitif: le cas des définis défectifs. In Marandin (2001a).

Cornish, F. 2001. L'inversion sujet-verbe en français, italien et anglais: quelques propriétés syntaxiques, sémantiques et discursives. Unpublished paper presented at the Journées de syntaxe, Université Montaigne de Bordeaux.

Cornulier, B. d. 1974. Pourquoi et l'inversion du sujet non clitique. In Rohrer and Ruwet (1974), pages 139–163.

De Wind, M. 1995. *Inversion in French*. Ph.D. thesis, University of Groningen, Groningen.

d'Hulst, Y., J. Rooryck, and J. Schroten, eds. 2001. *Romance Languages and Linguistic Theory*. Amsterdam: John Benjamins.

Drijkoningen, F. and B. Kampers-Manhe. 2001. *On the Interpretation of Postverbal Subject Positions*, vol. 21. Utrecht Studies in Romance Linguistics.

Godard, D., ed. 2003. *Langues romanes. Problèmes de la phrase simple*. Paris: Editions du CNRS.

Herslund, M., O. Mørdrup, and F. Sørensen, eds. 1983. *Analyses grammaticales du français*, vol. 24 of *Revue romane, numéro spécial*. Copenhagen: Akademisk Forlag.

Hulk, A. and J.-Y. Pollock, eds. 2001a. *Subject Inversion in Romance and the Theory of Universal Grammar*. Oxford: Oxford University Press.

Hulk, A. and J.-Y. Pollock. 2001b. Subject positions in Romance & the theory of Universal Grammar. In Hulk and Pollock (2001a), pages 107–162.

Kampers-Manhe, B. 1998. 'je veux que parte Paul': a neglected construction. In Schwegler et al. (1998), pages 131–141.

Kayne, R. 1972. Subject inversion in French interrogatives. In Casagrande and Saciuk (1972), pages 70–126.

Kayne, R. 1983. Chains, categories esternal to s and French complex inversion. *Natural Language and Linguistic Theory* 107:1–39.

Kayne, R. 1984. *Connectedness and Binary Branching*. Dordrecht: Foris Publications.

Kayne, R. 1986. Connexité et inversion du sujet. In Ronat and Couquaux (1986), pages 127–147.

Kayne, R. and J.-Y. Pollock. 1978. Stylistic inversion, successive cyclicity and Move NP in French. *Linguistic Inquiry* 9:109–137.

Kayne, R. and J.-Y. Pollock. 2001. New thoughts on stylistic inversion. In Hulk and Pollock (2001a), pages 595–621.

Korzen, H. 1983. Réflexions sur l'inversion dans les propositions interrogatives en français. In Herslund et al. (1983), pages 50–85.

Kupferman, L. 1983. Syntaxe et conditions pragmatiques. *Lingvisticae Investigationes* 7:385–400.

Lahousse, K. 2003a. *The distribution of postverbal nominal subjects in French. A syntactic, semantic and pragmatic analysis*. Ph.D. thesis, KU Leuven and Université de Paris 8.

Lahousse, K. 2003b. On the non-unitariness of NP subject inversion. a comparison of French NP subject inversion in interrogatives and temporal subordinates. In Quer et al. (2003).

Marandin, J.-M., ed. 2001a. *Cahier Jean-Claude Milner*. Paris: Verdier.

Marandin, J.-M. 2001b. Unaccusative inversion in French. In d'Hulst et al. (2001), pages 195–222.

Marandin, J.-M. 2001c. Unaccusative inversion in French. Unaccusative inversion in French. In *Selected papers of Going Romance 1999*, pages 195–222.

Marandin, J.-M. 2003. Inversion du sujet et structure de l'information dans les langues romanes. In Godard (2003).

Núñez-Cedeño, R., L. López, and R. Cameron, eds. 2003. *Selected papers of LSRL 2001*. John Benjamins.

Prüst, H. 1992. *On Discourse Structuring, VP Anaphora and Gapping*. Ph.D. thesis, University of Amsterdam.

Quer, J., J. Schroten, M. Scoretti, P. Sleeman, and E. Verheugd, eds. 2003. *Romance Languages and Linguistic Theory, 2001, Selected Papers from 'Going Romance'*. Amsterdam/ Philadelphia: John Benjamins Publishing Company.

Rohrer, C. and N. Ruwet, eds. 1974. *Actes du Colloque Franco-Allemande de Grammaire Transformationnelle*, Tübingen. Max Niemeyer Verlag.

Ronat, M. and D. Couquaux, eds. 1986. *Grammaire modulaire*. Paris: Minuit.

Schwegler, A., B. Tranel, and M. Uribe-Etxebarria, eds. 1998. *Romance Linguistics: Theoretical Perspectives*. Amsterdam/ Philadelphia: John Benjamins.

Szendrői, K. 2001. *Focus and the Syntax-Phonology Interface*. Ph.D. thesis, University College London.

Zubizaretta, M. L. 1994. Some prosodically motivated syntactic operations. In Cinque et al. (1994), pages 473–485.

Zubizarreta, M. L. 1998. *Prosody, Focus and Word Order*. Cambridge MA: MIT Press.

# Index